The Elusive Quest of the Spiritual Malcontent

The Elusive Quest of the Spiritual Malcontent

Some Early Nineteenth-Century Ecclesiastical Mavericks

Timothy C. F. Stunt

WIPF & STOCK · Eugene, Oregon

THE ELUSIVE QUEST OF THE SPIRITUAL MALCONTENT
Some Early Nineteenth Century Ecclesiastical Mavericks

Copyright © 2015 Timothy C.F. Stunt. All rights reserved. Except for brief quotations in critical publications or reviews, no part of this book may be reproduced in any manner without prior written permission from the publisher. Write: Permissions. Wipf and Stock Publishers, 199 W. 8th Ave., Suite 3, Eugene, OR 97401.

Wipf & Stock
An Imprint of Wipf and Stock Publishers
199 W. 8th Ave., Suite 3
Eugene, OR 97401

www.wipfandstock.com

ISBN 13: 978-1-4982-0931-1

Manufactured in the U.S.A.   08/27/2015

In Memoriam

Christopher . . . *vita frater amabilior*

Contents

Preface | ix
Acknowledgments | xi
Abbreviations | xiii
Introduction | 1

Quakers

1. The Changing Face of Early Nineteenth-Century Quaker Life | 7
2. Early Brethren and the Society of Friends | 32
3. John Jewell Penstone, Quaker and Plymouth Brother | 59

Irvingites

4. "Trying the Spirits": The Case of the Gloucestershire Clergyman | 69
5. "Trying the Spirits": Irvingite Signs and the Test of Doctrine | 80

Brethren

6. J. H. Newman and Proto-Plymouth Brethren at Oxford | 91
7. Anthony Norris Groves: A Radical Pioneer of Missions | 102
8. Influences in the Early Development of John Nelson Darby | 119
9. John Synge and the Early Brethren | 143
10. The Soltau Family of London and Plymouth | 166
11. From Wandsworth to British Guiana: The Strong Family Saga | 175
12. Elitist Leadership and Congregational Participation among Early Plymouth Brethren | 196
13. Radical Evangelicals and Brethren Origins in Hereford | 204
14. Plymouth Brethren and the Armed Services | 218

Freelance Independents

15 Robert Mackenzie Beverley: A Study in Dissatisfaction | 241
16 Arthur Augustus Rees: The Sailor Who Became the "Pope of the North" | 265
17 George Henry Stoddart: An Ecclesiastical "Rolling Stone" | 275
18 The Soltau Family and Christian Missions | 283

Bibliography | 293
Archives Consulted | 327
Unpublished Theses, Dissertations | 332
Index | 333

Preface

THE ESSAYS IN THIS collection were written over a period of some fifty years, and although they have a common author, his attitudes to ecclesiastical history have developed in the course of that half century and therefore the final result is fairly variegated. Some of the pieces were originally published in the *Journal of Ecclesiastical History* or, having been delivered at one of the conferences of the Ecclesiastical History Society, appeared in the society's series of *Studies in Church History* and I am grateful to both the journal and the society in question, who hold the copyright, for their permission to reissue these essays though inevitably some errors have had to be corrected. Similar adjustments were necessary when reprinting two essays, which appeared in books of essays issued by Paternoster Press, and again I am grateful for the publishers' cooperation in this venture.

Other pieces were more specialist in their focus and appeared in a journal, which, under a series of different names, has catered for a readership whose common denominator is an interest in the Plymouth Brethren. The organization which originated in the 1960s as the Christian Brethren Research Fellowship, produced a Journal (*CBRFJ*), which in due course came to be known as the *Christian Brethren Review* (*CBR*). This was reborn in 1997 as the *Brethren Archivists and Historians Network Review* (*BAHNR*), a title that contracted ten years later to the very much more manageable *Brethren Historical Review* (*BHR*). Six of the essays here reprinted appeared in one of this series of journals.

When such a collection is drawn from so many independent pieces, the task of eliminating repetition is challenging, and for the occasions where I have been less than successful, I crave the indulgence of my readers. On the other hand there are several more recent essays in this volume, which have not previously seen the light of published day. It is my hope that while expanding on some of my earlier lines of enquiry, these will raise fresh questions and open up new perspectives.

Acknowledgments

When my esteemed octogenarian friend, Dr. Andrew Walls, with typical generosity, referred to me some years ago in public as "one of the last gentleman-scholars," I was, needless to say, flattered, but I was also confronted with one of the realities of my existence, the implications of which I had not hitherto formulated. The freelance writer plows a lone furrow and rarely has a fellow scholar close at hand to provide constructive criticism. There have consequently been many occasions when I have yearned for a colleague off whom I could bounce an idea or a theory. The isolation of not having such a companion—someone who knows what one is talking about—can be paralyzing.

All the more special therefore are those friends with whom one has corresponded, but whom one meets on rare but very special occasions. Sometimes they have generously read and commented on early (and often-inchoate) drafts of essays, but more importantly they have been able to share in the quest which most of the time seems to be the writer's solitary obsession. They understand what I am writing about and why I feel it is worth writing about. There are many moments in the pages of this book where I have gratefully acknowledged specific help wherever it has been given to me, and I have to admit there are numerous other individuals who have worked in many different archives and libraries, professionals whose names I have never known, but who, over a period of many years, have made me the beneficiary of their knowledge and skills. To all of these I would express my heartfelt gratitude.

But here I would specifically like to acknowledge the kind and patient encouragement that I have received from a wide range of friends who have shared and enriched my enquiries. The list could doubtless be larger and I fear that I shall omit some worthy names. If you feel that yours is one of those names I beg your forgiveness and trust that you know that the omission is not deliberate. With immense gratitude I pay tribute to Derek Beales, David Bebbington, Neil Dickson, Crawford Gribben, Philip McNair, Massimo Rubboli, Neil Summerton, Andrew Walls, John Walsh, and Stefano Woods, who "at sundry times and in divers manners," have shared and encouraged me in these enquiries. In a rather different category I would also acknowledge the love and patience of the members of my family who, over the years have refrained from

Acknowledgments

groaning at the mention of names like Newton and Darby. Finally, I wish to honor and thank my wife, Nancy, who, in addition to being married to a maverick, has shared with longsuffering patience and lightness of heart the burden of this book, along with so many other trials.

Timothy Stunt

Newtown, Connecticut
The Feast of the Holy Innocents, 28 December 2014

Abbreviations

Al. Cantab.	*Alumni Cantabrigienses*
Al. Dub.	*Alumni Dublinenses*
Al. Oxon.	*Alumni Oxonienses*
ANB	American Dictionary of National Biography
BAHNR	Brethren Archivists and Historian Network Review
BFBS	British and Foreign Bible Society
BDEB	Blackwell's Dictionary of Evangelical Biography
BHR	Brethren Historical Review
BL	British Library
BU	Birmingham University
CBA	Christian Brethren Archive (in the JRULM)
CBRFJ	*Journal of the Christian Brethren Research Fellowship*
CBR	Christian Brethren Review
CIM	China Inland Mission
CMS	Church Missionary Society
CW	*Collected Writings*
DNB	Dictionary of National Biography
DNZB	Dictionary of New Zealand Biography
EIC	East India Company
EM	*Evangelical Magazine*
FIBIS	Families in British India Society (www.search.fibis.org)
HWS	Henry William Soltau
IGI	International Genealogical Index
JEH	*Journal of Ecclesiastical History*
JJP	John Jewell Penstone

Abbreviations

JRULM	John Rylands University Library of Manchester
LMS	London Missionary Society
LSPCJ	London Society for Promoting Christianity amongst the Jews
MW	*Morning Watch*
ODNB	*Oxford Dictionary of National Biography*
RTS	Religious Tract Society
SCH	*Studies in Church History* of the Ecclesiastical History Society
SPG	Society for the Propagation of the Gospel

Introduction

> But ye are a chosen generation, a royal priesthood,
> an holy nation, a peculiar people.
>
> 1 PETER 2:9

Growing up, as a boy, among Plymouth Brethren, who used the King James Version and quite often referred to themselves as "a peculiar people," I was challenged more than once to try and establish what it was about us, that was peculiar. There was of course a further, and much more complex question: were we Brethren because we were peculiar or were we peculiar because we were Brethren? Readers may well be relieved to learn that I shall not begin even to attempt to answer those questions in the following pages, but such questions led me to a broader enquiry into my ecclesiastical origins and to examine the "rock from which I was hewn" (Isa 51:1).

This may help to explain the fact that so many of the "peculiar" folk who are discussed in the following essays, were in one way or another associated with the Brethren. Not surprisingly therefore, the third and largest group of essays investigates people in this category. Some readers may consider this section to be a sequel to my earlier work *From Awakening to Secession*, though perhaps it is better described as a supplement rather than a sequel. Certainly all the characters, who are considered in this section, experienced an "awakening" which eventually led them to feel so different or *peculiar* that they had to consider the possibility of "secession."

In the early nineteenth century, many aspects of Christianity seemed to be very much engrained in the life and culture of moderately well-educated people in Britain, and although a thinking person didn't have to scratch very far beneath the surface to discover the pagan and materialistic reality of everyday life, it was fairly reasonable in those days for the average person to assume that he was a Christian living in a "Christian" society. Even today in our very much more secular world, there are some occasional churchgoers who are surprised (and liable to feel insulted) when an earnest believer refers to them as "nominal" (rather than "committed") Christians. This was very much more the case, two hundred years ago, and for such ordinary, respectable, church-attending folk, those other people who stressed the distinction between being a "mere" churchgoer and being a "true" believer, were definitely "peculiar."

The word *peculiar* is derived from the Latin word for a herd or flock (*pecus*), and certainly the "peculiar" Christians, who have been the focus of my inquiries for more than fifty years, regarded themselves as part of a special flock, membership of which rendered them different from others. Whether it was easy to be different from your next-door neighbor was liable to depend on your temperament. If you were a naturally reclusive person, the retreat into a smaller community might be an easier substitute for social obligations, which you found disagreeable, but by the same token, a naturally sociable person could find the restraints of "peculiarity" a burden—particularly if he or she had been born into such a community. For such people, the attendant costs of "peculiarity" could be great.

This was particularly true of the dissatisfied Quakers who are the subject of my first group of essays. We need to bear in mind that they were part of a community whose clothing had made them, for many years, *visually* distinctive. There was no hiding the fact that one was a Quaker and there were probably a good number who secretly yearned to be rid of this badge of peculiarity. If the family bonds of Quakerdom had not been so strong, one suspects that many more of the younger and less committed Quakers would have shed the costume and slipped away to attend a less distinctive expression of Christianity, like Anglicanism. When to these social peculiarities were added ecclesiastical issues of principle, the *malaise* could become acute. Whether they could find a satisfactory alternative became a serious question for dissatisfied Quakers in the early nineteenth century.

My second section deals with a special problem faced by the followers of Edward Irving. There was no question that in 1830 *glossolalia*, or speaking in tongues, was "peculiar," but was it sometimes a bit *too* peculiar, even for its advocates? Was it genuine or was it a façade? Was it "of God"? Or might it be diabolic? To his credit, this was a question that Irving dared to ask, and the way he did so has seemed to me to be worthy of investigation.

More than one reader of my work has commented on my passion for the "micro-biographical" and the way my footnotes often provide what may seem to be superfluous biographical material of apparently insignificant people. For this I am unrepentant. The Christian community has been made up of a great multitude, which few can name and no man can number, and too often our church historians only chronicle the "famous" outgoing extroverts who "made their mark," and they find no place for those less demonstrative (but very much more numerous) folk, faithful laborers in the vineyard, whose quiet lives have often been unsung but cumulatively significant. Something that they said or their presence on a certain occasion may bring their name to our attention and we need to find a context for them, albeit often not much more than a family background. They may not be included in biographical

INTRODUCTION

dictionaries, but there will always be a place for them in my footnotes! My declaration in this matter is all the more necessary as the essays in this book focus on men who were *not* self-effacing and very rarely remained in the shadows.

Throughout the history of Christianity there have been independent thinkers who, one might say, were born for peculiarity and almost reveled in it. Some of them, like the Apostle Paul or Martin Luther have helped to shape the faith; others, like the Capuchin Vicar-General Bernardino Ochino (1487–1564) or the Jesuit Jean de Labadie (1610–74), found themselves in ever-contracting circles of like-minded thinkers; others like Michael Servetus (1509–1553) and Nicolas Antoine (1602–32) were eventually burnt for their stubborn independence of thought.

It is with people of this ilk that many of these essays (particularly in the last section) are concerned, though in the nineteenth century the consequences of being such a lone figure were rather less dire. These were people who were ready to go where their conscience and reason led them, people for whom "peculiarity" was almost a welcome reassurance that they were being true to their calling. These were folk for whom some sort of persecution came with the territory that they occupied. In referring to some of them as mavericks, I am reverting to the imagery of the herd or flock (*pecus*), because often there was no flock that could contain these strangely independent thinkers and in consequence they may usefully be likened to the unbranded cattle of Samuel A. Maverick (1803–70). They were difficult to label because in many ways they were truly *sui generis*.

Some critics of my earlier book expressed disappointment that I took the story no further than 1835 and consequently said very little about later developments in the Irvingite community and the Plymouth Brethren. The fact is that I have to admit that I am much more interested in the dynamic process of spiritual and intellectual development, and less concerned with the more static situation when people's beliefs and convictions become more settled. The folk who travel hopefully tend to be more interesting than those who reckon that they have arrived, and I am always thankful for the ones who, having arrived, still consider themselves to be seekers.

A similar criticism may perhaps be leveled at this collection of essays and some will suggest that in focusing on the frequently tempestuous and unpredictable careers of these individualists, I have neglected the serener virtues of the communities with which the malcontents so often found fault. In my defense perhaps I may make a simple point. I am not suggesting that my subjects are heroes whose faith we should follow, though some of them, like Norris Groves, I trust, surely come into that category. Rather do I hold these "difficult" people in high esteem for their courage and honest sincerity, while I still feel free sometimes to question the wisdom of their way of doing things. It is occasionally said that historians tell us as much about themselves as about their subjects. To what extent that may be true of this book is not for me to say, but clearly it would be foolish to deny the possibility. The church must surely have a place for the maverick, but I have not yet found it!

Quakers

1

The Changing Face of Early Nineteenth-Century Quaker Life

Quaker Piety: William Allen and Luke Howard

When William Allen (1770–1843), a seventeen-year-old Quaker, resolved in 1789, "through divine assistance, to persevere in the disuse of [sugar] until the Slave Trade shall be abolished,"[1] his decision was no fleeting gesture of the moment. It was only in 1833 when the slaves in the British colonies were finally emancipated that Allen felt free to resume this particular self-indulgence. In the intervening forty-four years his energies—unfortified with sugar—were tirelessly devoted to an astonishing stream of activities undertaken for the betterment of the world.

The son of a Spitalfields silk manufacturer, Allen, as a young man, went into partnership at first with an older Quaker apothecary, John Gurney Bevan, and later for some ten years with his friend Luke Howard in a successful pharmaceutical business at Plough Court (off Lombard Street, in the city of London) with a laboratory and manufacturing premises at Plaistow in Essex.[2]

In a short while Allen established his name as a respected man of science.

His researches, carried out in cooperation with men like Humphrey Davy, embraced astronomy, botany, human biology, physics and chemistry and put him at the forefront of scientific enquiry. At the same time, Allen fervently believed that it was the task of the Christian to change society. In 1789, on hearing of the fall of the Bastille in Paris he had recalled Cowper's earlier thought that

> There's not an English heart that would not leap
> To hear that ye were fallen . . .[3]

and when, in 1807, the slave trade was made illegal, many of the optimistic assumptions of the eighteenth-century enlightenment can be found in Allen's prayer of thanks "to the Almighty Parent of the universe, that he may be pleased to regard this kingdom

---

1. Allen, *Life of Allen*, 1:7.
2. Cripps, *Plough Court*, 25–51.
3. Allen, *Life of Allen*, 1:4.

for good and direct its future councils to such further acts of justice and mercy, as may promote his glory, in the harmony of his rational creation."[4]

In fact, the Quaker world into which Allen was born had abandoned many of the revolutionary aspirations of the earliest followers of George Fox in the seventeenth century, but their testimony was still a potentially radical one and could lead to their falling foul of the Establishment. Their steadfast refusal to compromise over tithe payment and military service could easily result in imprisonment and the seizure of their property. Likewise misunderstandings were liable to arise when they refused to remove their hats because of their belief that in doing so they were according to men an honor that was due to God. On the other hand like many other English observers, Allen had soon become disillusioned with French revolutionary developments. His Quaker abhorrence of war meant that the failure of the Peace of Amiens, in 1803, troubled him deeply and from time to time his journal has laconic references to the long drawn-out conflict with France, which only came to an end in 1815. Allen certainly had no brief for Napoleon, but he was hardly enthusiastic about the return of the Bourbons to the French throne on account of "the system of priestcraft which Louis [XVIII] will bring in his train."[5]

This usefully illustrates the ambivalent position in which Quakers like Allen found themselves in their relations with the Establishment. Commercial success and prosperity could effectively place them in the ranks of the influential but, nevertheless, they had a radical agenda for the improvement of society and their religious principles questioned many evils that the authorities seemed to accept. In addition to his objections to warfare and slavery, Allen was a tireless opponent of capital punishment, poverty, ignorance and cruelty of any sort.[6] While his business at Plough Court prospered and his experiments and lectures secured his election as a Fellow of the Royal Society, his journal reveals a ceaseless record of philanthropic concern. In 1812 he noted that he needed to

> take double care not to overload myself with engagements . . . The following great objects are enough for one man, and I must resist all attempts to engage me in more, viz:—the Overseership of Gracechurch Street Monthly [Quaker] Meeting; [Joseph] Lancaster's [School] concern; Spitalfields Local Association

---

4. Ibid., 1:86. Cf. "In all the great powers of nature, we observe such marks of contrivance, such adaptation of cause to effect and the whole executed by means so sublimely simple, that we cannot avoid concluding with Archdeacon Paley, such designs must have had a designer, and that designer must be God," 1:72–73. Characteristic, too, in these earlier years of his life are Allen's references to God as "the Most High," "the Supreme Being," "the Almighty Power," "the Deity," "the Great Master" (1:92, 119, 123, 164, 195).

5. Ibid., 1:235.

6. That his compassion was not confined to humanity is apparent from his comment in February 1790. "There appears to me such a meanness and lowness of disposition, in those who are cruel to animals, that I think I could not put confidence in them, even in the common concerns of life." Ibid., 1:11.

for the Poor; Spitalfields School; Philanthropist [a magazine]; Lectures; General Association for the Poor; Bible Society.[7]

In fact these were but a part of the story. His other concerns included relentless campaigning against capital punishment, slavery and the slave trade and his efforts for the welfare of the settlers in Sierra Leone. He was prepared to cooperate with Robert Owen for the success of the New Lanark Mills project (in spite of Owen's avowed rejection of Christian faith).[8] Such activities together with frequent prison visiting (with other Quakers like Elizabeth Fry) all reflect a deep rejection of social injustice and a sense of obligation to do something about it. Similarly radical was the implicit egalitarianism of the Quaker insistence that all people should be addressed with the familiar "thee" and "thou" instead of the more respectful "you," as well as the Quakers' refusal to remove their hats even when addressing royalty.

From an ecclesiastical point of view, the Quaker spirituality with which Allen was imbued was scarcely less radical. The members of the Society of Friends sought to take the injunctions of the Savior at their face value. When he forbad retaliation this was taken to mean that violence of any sort was unacceptable. If he said that a Christian's "yea" was to be "yea" and his "nay" "nay," then oaths were not to be countenanced—even when enjoined in the courts of the land. On the other hand, in the Quaker way of thinking, such obedience to the letter did not extend to some of the sacramental instructions of the New Testament, which they chose to interpret in a spiritual sense. Quakers sat lightly to the Lord's Supper and water baptism, which they regarded as outward forms of little importance whereas divine nourishment and cleansing were integral aspects of the ongoing spiritual struggle, which was such a transparently sincere feature of Allen's journal. In contrast to the objective details of his daily activities, meticulously described in all their variety, is the record of his state of mind that swings wildly from fearful feelings of inadequacy to a sublime enjoyment of spiritual encouragement.[9] Such fluctuations are apparent when we consider his confidence in the possibility of achieving social reforms, as when discussing such matters as the slave trade and religious persecution with the Russian emperor at Verona in 1822. In contrast only five days later he declares that

7. Ibid., 1:153.

8. The readiness of Quakers to cooperate and indeed mix socially with skeptics and unbelievers is striking. The association of Samuel Galton with the freethinking Dr. Erasmus Darwin will be mentioned shortly. For what she later regarded as Erasmus Darwin's "baleful" influence on her own thinking see the observations of Samuel Galton's daughter in Hankin, *Life of SchimmelPenninck*, 201–2.

9. Typical entries in the course of a year read: "Very low on many accounts, but received some comfort at meeting on first-day morning" (24 Sep 1810). "I was under some depression of mind, and the darts of the enemy were almost too powerful for my shield of faith, when, blessed be the name of my God . . . my faith was renewed, in some degree . . . Thus in this world of sorrow and trial, stepping stones are graciously placed at intervals" ([1] Oct 1810). "Prayer in the night, followed by secret comfort. Lord, I believe, help thou mine unbelief" (25 Feb 1811); "Though the tide of consolation has not risen very high, I have had a few seasons of refreshment" (25 May 1811); Allen, *Life of Allen*, 1:125, 131–32.

> my mind has been deeply impressed, with consideration of the transitory nature of all things here below, and the approach of the final close, and earnestly have I desired to seek after a still deeper interest in the Saviour.[10]

In a communion in which formal statements of doctrine were often discounted and in which the role of the Holy Spirit as instructor and director was emphasized, it was understandable that there would be some variations in Quaker emphases. From the earliest days of the movement, many Quakers had often been chary of theological formulations and their quietist preference for spontaneous rather than rational, prepared ministry had produced a reluctance to engage in systematic study of the Bible. The "Inner Light" shed by the Holy Spirit on the submissive heart of the believer was to be valued above the "notional" religion of the Scriptures. On the other hand the movement had inevitably been influenced by the rationalism of the Enlightenment and in the more successful Quaker families, where wealth and education went hand in hand, there was a growing appreciation of scriptural study, which is well exemplified by the evangelical piety of a notable contemporary and associate of William Allen.

Luke Howard (1772–1864) is best remembered as a pioneer of meteorology and cloud nomenclature,[11] but when his partnership with William Allen was amicably dissolved in 1806, he retained control of the chemical factory at Plaistow as a very successful business, working in partnership with another remarkable Quaker, Joseph Jewell.[12] Howard had eloquently (though anonymously) defended the Society of Friends against the scorn of Francis Jeffrey in the *Edinburgh Review*, where they had been described as "a tolerably honest, painstaking and inoffensive set of Christians. Very stupid, dull and obstinate . . . in conversation; and tolerably lumpish and fatiguing in domestic society."[13] Coming from a cultivated world of progressive scientific achievement, Howard effectively challenged such a judgment, citing the French revolutionary J. P. Brissot who had found in Quaker homes in America, "momens de gaieté, d'épanchement, de conversation affectueuse et agréable."[14]

For the first fifty years of his life, Howard's loyalty to the Quakers never seems to have been in question. On the other hand his careful study of the Bible and his friendship with evangelical Christians outside the Quaker movement led him to challenge what he thought to be unorthodox opinions of Quakers whose ministry he otherwise valued. Thus when some speculative ideas of an American Quaker, Job Scott (1751–93), were posthumously published in 1824, Howard published a lengthy repudiation of them as unbiblical speculation. His pamphlet, addressed to his fellow Quakers, is of particular interest because at the very end he clarifies the nature of his loyalty

---

10. Ibid., 2:289 (4 Nov 1822).

11. For Howard's original proposal of the categories, cumulus, stratus and cirrus, see Luke Howard, *On the Modifications*. For Luke Howard, see *ODNB*; Scott, *Luke Howard*.

12. For Jewell see below, ch. 3n3.

13. [Jeffrey], 102; [L. Howard], *Brief Apology*.

14. Brissot, *Nouveau voyage*, 2:179; Brissot was guillotined in 1793.

to the Society. Vigorously rejecting the idea that only the Society of Friends is "the true church" and the suggestion that other professors are "ignorant" and "aliens," he frankly recognizes the recent spread of religious knowledge and sanctification outside "the pale of our own society" and the evident "piety... in many whom I know of other denominations." Noting that the labors of these non-Quakers have been blessed, he observes also that in these activities "*we* (as a body) have taken hitherto so little part" and that this gives him cause to tremble for the Society's reputation. He continues:

> We are, it may be said, a peculiar people, and have peculiar Testimonies, in some respects, to bear to the simplicity, peaceableness and purity of Christ's kingdom. Granted—no one believes this, I trust, more firmly than I do: not many, perhaps, more sincerely desire that we may be faithful to our duty in these respects. The day will come, however, soon or late, when *we* must merge (if we remain so long a society) into the great assembly of the visible church.[15]

It is clear that Luke Howard, like William Allen, could value the distinctive testimony of Friends without rejecting the common ground he shared with fellow evangelicals in the other denominations.[16]

Quaker Affluence

The Society of Friends had been founded in the seventeenth century when the production of wool and cloth had been central to the English economy. Not surprisingly many of the early Quakers had been yeoman-farmers, who produced wool and whose cottage industries (particularly in the Westmorland and Yorkshire fells, but also in East Anglia) included weaving and dying. One historian of Quaker industry has suggested that there may have been a generic link between the pastoral life with its "nights and days of solitude on the hills and in all weathers" and "the thinker-prophet cast of mind"[17] that figures so prominently among the Society of Friends. Indeed George Fox himself exemplifies both the herdsman and the prophet. However, if the frugal lifestyle of the homes of these ruggedly independent Quakers was to be productive they needed a reliable outlet for their produce, and in Norfolk this had been provided by one of Fox's earliest followers.

John Gurney of Norwich successfully established himself in the wool business and even survived three years imprisonment in the 1680s for refusing to take the oath

---

15. Luke Howard, *Letter*, 19–20. An indignant American Quaker replied that Friends would only "merge in the great assembly of the visible church" if they abandoned their distinctive testimony, as a result of which "the great husbandman will visit our vineyard... take away the hedge... break down the wall... and will lay it waste." Anon., *Letter from a Friend*, 53.

16. It is worthy of note that Howard's evangelical sympathies were often liberal rather than radical as can be seen in his refusal to support the anti-Apocryphal party in the Bible Society controversy.

17. Raistrick, *Quakers in science and industry*, 72.

of allegiance. In the hands of his sons[18] and grandsons the family business continued to prosper, not only buying wool from farmers and putting it out to spinners and weavers, but also lending them money on reasonable terms. By the late eighteenth century the family had established Gurney's Bank and their prosperity was reflected in John and Catherine Gurney's move to a splendid new home, Earlham House, outside Norwich. But with affluence the family's Quaker identity had begun to waver. The family's lifestyle was a far cry from the earlier Quaker frugality, and no Gurney could now claim, with the prophet Amos, to have been "an herdman and a gatherer of sycomore fruit."[19]

Although Catherine Gurney was a great granddaughter of the early Quaker apologist Robert Barclay, she and her husband John mixed freely with non-Quakers and their children were exposed to a degree of education and artistic culture that had been not typical of the early movement. Old fashioned Quaker visitors were liable to be shocked at the Gurneys' colorful clothing, their love of music and their attendance of dances, but when Catherine died in 1792, her widowed husband reverted to a somewhat stricter form of Quaker observance and his children found themselves torn in their loyalties. Some of them like Hannah and Richenda Gurney became Anglicans while Joseph John Gurney (1788–1847) and his sister Elizabeth Fry (1780–1845) continued as members of the Society of Friends but with a decidedly evangelical orientation. Joseph John Gurney's case is of particular interest for us because a key element in his development and involvement with evangelical Christians outside the Quaker fold, was the part played by the unusual tutor, under whom he was sent to study at Oxford from 1803 to 1805.

Almost the only information we have about his tutor, John Rogers, is based on Gurney's account of him.[20] He appears to have been previously the vicar of Durweston in Dorset from 1788 but resigned this living in 1792 to be associated for a time with the Society of Friends, though by the time he was tutoring Gurney he is said to have resumed his position as a clergyman. He was tutoring at least one other Quaker and sometimes took Gurney to a "desultory" meeting of Friends and sometimes to Anglican worship. In fact their ecclesiastical associations seem to have been quite varied. One Sunday afternoon at Oxford Gurney was taken with his fellow students to the home of Samuel Collingwood (1762–1841) where the daughters of the household "entertained us with music and singing . . . as bad as any I ever heard."[21]

---

18. One of his sons, John Gurney, was known as "the weaver's advocate" having successfully made the case for the woolen manufacturers of Norfolk in the House of Lords in 1720. For the early history of the family see Hare, *Gurneys of Earlham*, 1:8–16.

19. Amos 7:14.

20. See Braithwaite, *Memoirs of Gurney*, 1:18–26.

21. Quoted in Swift, *Joseph John Gurney*, 34. The name is given as Colingwood (with only one 'l') but as, twenty-eight years later when visiting Oxford, Gurney refers to Samuel Collingwood as "my old friend" the identification seems justified. Braithwaite, *Memoirs of Gurney*, 1:438.

Significantly, Samuel Collingwood's ecclesiastical identity is as hard to define as that of Rogers. Born into a Kentish family of Independents, Collingwood had trained as a printer and in 1792 had been appointed as the superintendent of the Clarendon Press at the University of Oxford. Although G. V. Cox in his *Recollections* claimed that "it was a proof of the liberality of the University, that its chief printer was known to be a zealous Dissenter,"[22] it is very probable that Collingwood's loyalties were less evident at an earlier stage. Subsequent to his arrival in Oxford, his second marriage in 1797, the baptisms (and in several cases the early burials) of his children, the burial of his first wife, as well as the marriage of his daughter Frances in 1813, were all performed in the parish Church of St. Mary Magdalen. Indeed as *Preli Clarendoniani Procurator* he had matriculated *privilegiatus* at Oxford in 1796,[23] and in that process he would have had to take an oath of loyalty to the university and subscribe to the Thirty-nine Articles.[24] But in reality Collingwood's ecclesiastical loyalties seem to have been remarkably fluid. When a Baptist Church in Eynsham, outside Oxford, was "formally established with fifteen members, many of them 'dismissed' from the New Road Baptist Chapel in Oxford," Samuel Collingwood was one of the twelve trustees appointed in 1816.[25] The relations between the several Baptist churches in Oxford is confusingly complicated[26] but in 1830 Collingwood is again named as a paedobaptist associated with "a breakaway group of twelve New Road [Baptist Church] members," who met for a time in his house before the Congregational Chapel in George Street was opened in 1832.[27] With such a complex story, Collingwood, the university printer, may well be considered something of an ecclesiastical maverick and his earlier friendship with John Rogers (who was also a Greek proofreader for the Clarendon Press) suggests that they were both part of an ill-defined evangelical, trans-denominational "hinterland,"[28] which may have shared some common ground with the outlook of uncertain or dissatisfied Quakers.

Joseph John Gurney had an immense respect for Rogers, as did he and his brother for another Anglican clergyman, Edward Edwards, the rector of Lynn. These men certainly had an important role in the process by which Gurney found his way back to a more serious and vital piety. Rogers's somewhat imprecise ecclesiastical attachments may also have contributed to Gurney's ultimate rejection of the Anglican alternative,

22. Cox, *Recollections*, 317.

23. Al. Oxon., 1:278.

24. For details of the "privileged tradesmen" of the university (often barbers or tonsores), see Crossley and Elrington, *History of the County of Oxford*, 4:161–65. http://www.british-history.ac.uk/report.aspx?compid=22804.

25. Wenger, "Baptist Church in Eynsham," 9, 12.

26. See Grass, "Restoration," 283–84.

27. Crossley and Elrington, *History of the County of Oxford*, 421.

28. Collingwood's daughter Frances married another Kentish Collingwood and her son William Collingwood (1819–1903) continued the radical evangelical tradition as an Open Plymouth Brother; see Pickering, *Chief Men*, 96–98.

taken by some of his sisters, and his adoption in 1812 of the position of a "decided" Quaker—a commitment which meant keeping his hat on when entering the home of the local Squire Southwell or the bishop of Norwich.[29]

To the end of his life Joseph John Gurney's evangelical Quakerism was something of a hybrid that upset Quakers and evangelicals alike. His wealth, the extent of his education and his emphasis on the importance of biblical instruction in the Friends' school at Ackworth, made him the object of pointed criticism from "primitive" Quakers like his cousin John Barclay and the elderly Thomas Shillitoe whose "straightened circumstances" and "Spartan way of life" put them in a different league.[30] With a certain logic, Gurney's quietist critics, like John Wilbur in America, realized that if Gurney's evangelical position were adopted, with its emphasis on a conversion experience rather than a gradual growth in holiness, then the distinctive Quaker lifestyle, of which Gurney seemed to approve, would become superfluous.[31] At the same time, although Gurney enjoyed the respect of many an evangelical Anglican like his brothers-in-law, Francis Cunningham[32] and the MP, Thomas Fowell Buxton,[33] his highly visible Quaker identity and defense of their "peculiarities"[34] put him somewhat at odds with the larger Evangelical community.

A somewhat exceptional example of the impact of Gurney's readiness to embrace the distinctive peculiarities of Quaker life, was interestingly to be found in the decision of a notable Norwich lady to abandon her earlier connections and instead be associated with the Society of Friends. Amelia Opie (1769–1863) was the daughter of Dr. Alderson of Norwich and had married a successful portrait painter, John Opie (1761–1807), in 1798. Brought up in a world of Presbyterian Unitarianism, she had been something of a political radical, mixing with such freethinkers as Francis Godwin and Mary Wollstonecroft,[35] and her novels and poetry were well received. These intellectual gifts were recognized in a fashionable literary circle in London, which she continued to frequent even after moving back to Norwich on the death of her husband in 1807. Amelia Opie, who was a sparkling conversationalist, caused some surprise therefore when, having abandoned what Gurney (in a letter to her in 1814) had called

---

29. For these crucial years in his development see Braithwaite, *Memoirs of Gurney*, 1:18–81.

30. Swift, *Joseph John Gurney*, 165–66, cf. 59–60.

31. Hamm, *Transformation of American Quakerism*, 30.

32. Francis Cunningham (1785–1863), rector of Pakefield and Vicar of Lowestoft, married Richenda Gurney. He was the younger brother of John Cunningham, Vicar of Harrow, famously caricatured by Mrs. Trollope in *The Vicar of Wrexhill*, see Rosman, *Evangelicals and Culture*, 81–84.

33. Thomas Fowell Buxton (1786–1845), whose mother (née Anna Hanbury) was of Quaker origins married his cousin Hannah Gurney and was a brewer, philanthropist and MP, see Buxton, *Memoirs*.

34. See Gurney, *Observations on Friends' peculiarities*. This was a work with which William Allen was "much pleased," Allen, *Life of Allen*, 2:357.

35. Brightwell, *Memorials of Amelia Opie*, 59–62.

the "gay whirlpool of London,"[36] she adopted, in 1824 after some personal conflict, the Quaker manner of dress and plain speech, and the following year was admitted to membership of the Society. The influence of Gurney was tantamount.

Quakers and Freethinkers

We would be mistaken, however, if we were to imagine that evangelical Friends like William Allen and Joseph John Gurney were typical Quakers. Although their wing of the movement was becoming quite as vocal as the more traditional elements, it was far from being the Quaker norm. Quite as typical was the world in which Mary Anne Galton (later Mrs. SchimmelPenninck) grew up. Her father Samuel Galton (1753–1832), had been disowned by the Quakers for his activities as an arms manufacturer but continued to attend Quaker worship. His wife Lucy was a great granddaughter of the Quaker expositor, Robert Barclay, but as a member of the Birmingham Lunar Society, Galton regularly associated with a variety of learned men like the Unitarian chemist and minister Joseph Priestley and the freethinking Dr. Erasmus Darwin, whom he often entertained in his home. There was a worldly and enlightened tone to the lifestyle of such Quakers and yet they still appreciated vital piety rather than orthodoxy. Mary Ann Galton, whose later convictions were decidedly evangelical, insisted that an "estimable Unitarian" like the heterodox Priestley at least "resembled a living man with the loss of some important limb," in contrast to "many orthodox professors who, like a corpse or a mummy, exhibited all the form and lineaments of truth, but were destitute of one vital spark."[37]

On the other hand there can be no doubt that much Quaker thinking had elements that were decidedly nearer to deistical philosophy than has often been recognized. When Tom Paine (1737–1809), the revolutionary pamphleteer and freethinking deist, disputed that there were any grounds for believing in Christian dogma beyond a simple theism, he argued that religion was a private matter between the individual and God. He rejected any idea of priesthood and insisted that religion should be without show or noise, and instead rather, be concerned with helping the poor, and the education of children. Making these claims in his famous letter to the French revolutionary politician Camille Jourdan, on the subject of church bells, he observed:

> The only people who, as a professional sect of Christians provide for the poor of their society, are the people known by the name of Quakers. Those men have no priests. They assemble quietly in their places of meeting and do not disturb their neighbours with shows and noise of bells.[38] Religion does not unite itself to show and noise. True religion is without either.

---

36. Ibid., 171.
37. Hankin, *Life of SchimmelPenninck*, 32.
38. The Quaker aversion to church bells is well illustrated from the recollections of Alfred Newton Harris (1838–?) of Plymouth, whose mother had been a Quaker before she joined the Brethren. "A

His statement was apposite and based on personal knowledge. Reverting to the subject he explained:

> I have already spoken of the Quakers—that they have no priests, no bells—and that they are remarkable for their care of the poor of their society. They are equally as remarkable for the education of their children. I am a descendant of a family of that profession; my father was a Quaker; and I presume I may be admitted an [sc. in] evidence of what I assert. The seeds of good principles, and the literary means of advancement in the world, are laid in early life. Instead, therefore, of consuming the substance of the nation upon priests, whose life at best is a life of idleness, let us think of providing for the education of the children of those who have not the means of doing it themselves. One good schoolmaster is of more use than a hundred priests.[39]

This kinship of rational Deism with the simplicity of Quaker piety is highly significant and helps us to identify some of the aspects of traditional Quaker thinking which evangelicals, like Allen and Gurney, with their emphasis on the importance of Scripture, were calling into question.

Quaker Malcontents in Ireland

Mainstream Quaker thinking was more concerned with a living piety than doctrinal verities but in their efforts to maintain their identity, these folk were also inclined to be unduly concerned with procedural formalities and status. Inevitably, in a community, which encouraged participation, questions arose over what was the final authority within the Society and over administrative and disciplinary procedures. In Ireland, particularly, tensions of this sort among Quakers had come to a head around the turn of the eighteenth and nineteenth century.

In a country where the majority of the population was Roman Catholic and the ruling Establishment was widely perceived as an occupying power, Irish Quakers had

---

Quaker relative of my mother gave to church bells the name of 'useless' . . . She [Harris's mother] has often heard him say to his wife [on Sunday mornings] 'Get ready for meeting, Mary, the useless are ringing.'" Harris, "Plymouth Brethren, Reminiscences," 90. For the identity of A. N. Harris, a "licensed victualler," see Stunt, "Plymouth Family."

39. Paine, "Worship and Church Bells," 4:250, 252. Paine's deist sense of kinship with the Quakers is even more apparent when he claims in *The Age of Reason* that "the religion that approaches the nearest of all others to true Deism, in the moral and benign part thereof, is that professed by the Quakers," but he adds that while respecting their philanthropy, he is thankful that their tastes were not "consulted at the creation" which would have been singularly "silent and drab colored . . . Not a flower would have blossomed its gaieties, nor a bird been permitted to sing." Ibid., 4:65–66. Later, in the second part of *The Age of Reason* he is even more explicit about their affinities when he writes: "The only sect that has not persecuted are the Quakers and the only reason that can be given for it is, that they are rather Deists than Christians. They do not believe much about Jesus Christ and they call the scriptures a dead letter." Ibid., 4:185–86. Paine's father was a Quaker but his mother was an Anglican; see Vickers, *Paine and the American Revolution*, 63–66.

often been given a favorable reception and their standing was often enhanced by their refusal to take part in the ongoing conflicts that plagued Ireland in the seventeenth and eighteenth centuries. The knowledge that Friends would not have firearms in their homes meant that they were often spared some of the intrusive searches that characterized Irish life particularly at the time of the 1798 rising. Internally however their problems were greater.[40]

A Narrative of Events that have lately taken place in Ireland among the Society called Quakers[41] was published in 1804 and while it makes no mention of the political upheavals of the time, it tells of the divisions and arguments that had surfaced within the Quaker community in the preceding years. A particular source of disagreement was the role of the Holy Spirit. Some free spirits complained that the public reading of the *Christian and Brotherly Advices given forth from time to time by the Yearly Meetings in London* interfered with the role of the Holy Spirit. One of these critics was an elder, Abraham Shackleton of Ballitore,[42] who also objected to describing the Bible as the "Sacred" Scriptures, whose reliability he questioned when "the extirpation of the Canaanites ... was [said to have been] undertaken by the express command of God."[43] In due course Shackleton was disowned by the Society but he was not alone in expressing such critical opinions.

Others found a cause for protest in the complicated procedures and the required public declarations, with which Friends proposing to marry had to comply. Matters came to a head in Lisburn, co. Antrim, when a couple decided to bypass "the useless forms of a society grievously entangled in a wilderness of customs and opinions received by tradition, and adopted without examining the nature, tendency or necessity thereof."[44] Having made their protest, John Rogers and Elizabeth Doyle were married in the schoolhouse, where Doyle was a teacher and in due course they (and many others who attended the ceremony) were disowned by the Society.[45]

Another highly vocal Irish critic of the Quaker Establishment at this time was the linen manufacturer and philanthropist John Hancock II (1762–1823), a respected Quaker member of the Lisburn community.[46] He published three carefully reasoned statements explaining his withdrawal from the Society and the nature of his

---

40. For a fuller discussion of the Irish dimensions of Quaker life at this time, see Newhouse, "Irish Separation," and [Grubb], "Friends in Ireland."

41. See [Rathbone], *Narrative of Events*.

42. [Rathbone], *Narrative*, 39–41; see also Grubb, "Abraham Shackleton." This Abraham should not be confused with his grandfather of the same name, one of whose pupils was Edmund Burke, see Leadbeater, *Memoirs and Letters*, 3.

43. [Rathbone], *Narrative*, 50–52.

44. Ibid., 126.

45. Ibid., 127–29. There is no reason to think that this John Rogers had any connection with J. J. Gurney's tutor of the same name.

46. For Hancock, see Newhouse, "John Hancock," 41–52.

disagreements with them.⁴⁷ Like most of the other so-called Separatists he does not appear to have joined any other religious group and many disowned Friends seem to have continued to frequent Quaker meetings but somewhat "under a cloud." Less vocal than Hancock was the case of another Irish Quaker, Charles Stokes Dudley (1780–1862), whose mother, Mary Dudley, had been for many years a widely itinerant minister among Friends. Although he had established his own business as a provision merchant, the tragic death of his wife and baby, as well as his increasing involvement in the work of the Bible Society, resulted in his leaving the management of the business (in which he was effectively only a sleeping partner) to his brother George. When in 1818 George Dudley suspended payments and was declared bankrupt, both the brothers were disowned by the Quakers, but in all probability Charles had been in any case increasingly attracted to the Church of England, which he soon joined.⁴⁸

A few years later, however, another Irish Quaker decisively abandoned the Society though his secession was not publicized at the time. Joseph Baylee (1807–83) was the son of a Quaker schoolmaster in Limerick but when he entered Trinity College Dublin in 1828 his ecclesiastical loyalties seem to have been uncertain. He was older than his fellow undergraduates and prior to his arrival he is described in the college records as "self-educated." Some years later he was ordained and for many years was the Anglican principal of St. Aidan's training college in Birkenhead. But from his own account, it is clear that he spent some of his earlier years of uncertainty in Dublin sharing his doubts with a number of other dissatisfied people from a variety of denominations. His description of the circle in which he found himself in 1829 is worthy of quotation at length and, before we go any further, we may observe that although Baylee mentions no names, we can be fairly sure that the minister around whom the story revolves was the respected (but highly sensitive) Richard Pope,⁴⁹ who had detached himself from the Established Church in the mid-1820s and for a time was associated with a little group of separatists who met in the old Lutheran church in Poolbeg Street.⁵⁰ Baylee's account is as follows:

> A truly pious and eminent minister of the Church of England became unsettled upon some matters of ministerial conformity. Many parties were eager to claim him as their own; and his mind was soon filled with the doubts and cavils of others. The issue was, an effort on his part to found a church free from all imperfections and entirely conformable to the scriptural model. An

---

47. These were combined in one volume; see Hancock, *Reasons for withdrawing*.

48. The best account of C. S. Dudley, a stalwart champion of the Bible Society's Women's auxiliaries, is by Edward H. Milligan in the *ODNB*; see also Edwards, "Charles Stokes Dudley."

49. Richard Thomas Pembroke Pope (1799–1859) was described as "a victim to over-refinement in spiritual things, and to morbid sensitiveness, he deserted our Church to seek one more pure, which he failed to find, and so came back again—alas! With broken health, but with a spirit, if it were possible, more subdued and Christlike than ever." Brooke, *Recollections*, 23. Cf. Stunt, *From Awakening*, 174.

50. For the variety of folk who, in the early nineteenth century, used this place of worship, commonly referred to as the "Dutch Church," see Smyrl, *Dictionary of Dublin Dissent*, 184–85.

> old foreign church in the city of Dublin was rented for their meetings. A railing was drawn across the centre of the building: the members were admitted within the railing; all others were to sit outside. The author [sc. Joseph Baylee] was present at their first meetings in the year 1829. For a few weeks all seemed to promise well; but the scene speedily changed. Every one having equal authority (or, rather, no authority) dissension and division soon reared their heads. One was for an adult baptist, another a pædo-baptist; one was for close communion, another for open communion; all had an equal right to deliver public addresses. The minister confessed to a brother minister, that many effusions were "agonizing rather than edifying" to him, from the crude and erroneous views of the speakers. The most forward and the least qualified were the foremost to speak; the humblest and best instructed shrunk from a field already preoccupied.
>
> The minister himself was one day induced to receive the communion from the hands of a pious Presbyterian minister. On his return to Dublin he communicated this to the church. The members immediately quitted the room and separated from him, leaving him to his own bitter reflections upon the folly of building Utopian schemes.
>
> But this was not all. After his separation from them they had meetings for the admission of members; these were usually held in the evenings, and, it is not too much to say, [they] became coteries of scandal; Instead of the broad Scriptural rule of admitting all who "call on the name of Jesus Christ the Lord," the character of each applicant was minutely scrutinized—the shape of a bonnet, or the amount of ribbons upon it, became sometimes a deciding point; and a miserable spirit of judging and seeking for faults increased rapidly amongst the members.
>
> Some ladies came to the conclusion, that adult baptism was the only scriptural one. They formed a party, and accompanied by a gentleman (a member of the church), proceeded to a public bath, where they were dipped into the water by him. They returned home, and found themselves as unsettled as ever.[51]

We have to bear in mind that this account was written by someone who, at the time of writing, had finally decided that the Establishment was where he wanted to be and therefore we may conclude that it is a disillusioned if not jaundiced narrative. However the final part of his account of Richard Pope suggests that this was part of a more familiar story.

> The minister alluded to, who was eminently qualified to profit the church of God, is now in retirement, and (as far as we can learn) laid aside from all usefulness. The church separated into different societies—one party joined Mr.

---

51. Baylee, *Institutions*, 174–76.

[Thomas] Kelly's church—another was (we believe) the origin of the Aungier-street or Plymouth [Brethren] church.[52]

The fissiparous tendencies of these separatists were unlikely to have much appeal for a Quaker, already disillusioned with the divisions in his home communion, but it is a familiar story. The fluid ecclesiastical associations in Dublin in the late 1820s from which the early Brethren emerged (before they were associated with Plymouth) have been analyzed at length and it is not our intention to cover this familiar ground, but the circle described by Baylee would seem to tally with John Bellett's account of Anthony Norris Groves's visit to Dublin in late 1828 when he "preached in Poolbeg Street at the request of dear Dr. Egan, then in connection with the little company formed there, of whom Richard Pope, well known in Ireland at the time, was one."[53] It was perhaps a little ironic that Baylee in his quest for something other than the Society of Friends should have found himself on the edge of what another of the early Brethren, Edward Cronin, described as "a small company of Evangelical malcontents."[54] It seems to have convinced him that the Established Church was where he wanted to be and in January 1831 he was baptized in Saint John's Church, Limerick.

It is not clear which aspect of his Quaker upbringing caused Baylee to turn against them, but the harsh way in which different sorts of Quakers could be treated by the Society was liable to exacerbate the doubts of second- and third-generation Friends. The varying treatment given to convinced members, birthright members, or disowned members, was not just a problem connected with marriage procedures, and several experiences of Quakers in the South West of England illustrate the disappointments and tensions that could arise, and consequently produce a grey area of ecclesiastical uncertainty.

Quaker Uncertainty in Devon

Another Irishman, John Byrth (1757–1813), was born and brought up as a Quaker in Kilkenny, Co. Meath, but in 1786, at Plymouth Dock (later known as Devonport), he married Mary Hobling, a Wesleyan Methodist member of an old Cornish family living in that neighborhood. Their first child was baptized in Morice Street Wesleyan chapel, Devonport, in 1789, but after that there is no further indication of membership.[55] John was described as a Plymouth dock grocer in 1791[56] and two years later his son Thomas was born, but there is no ecclesiastical record of the event. Although John

---

52. Ibid., 176. In a footnote to his account, Baylee notes that the group's connection with the Brethren is "denied by Mr. [Charles] Hargrove" (one of the earliest Irish Brethren) but Baylee insisted that he still thought "the statement is correct."

53. Bellett, *Interesting Reminiscences*, 5.

54. Ibid., 10.

55. These details are all taken from the IGI.

56. [Barfoot], *Universal Directory*, 4:273.

had "married out" he was still a Quaker and his name is included in a list of Devon Friends for 1809.[57] That the family's religious allegiances were flexible is indicated by the variety of schools to which Thomas was sent. These included a brief attendance at the parish school at Callington, eight years in a private school "kept by two brothers, Unitarian ministers, whose unhappy incompetence as teachers was mitigated by their zealous good intentions," and finally a year at a school in Launceston run by the congregational minister, Richard Cope (1776–1850).[58] This final attendance was cut short by a downturn in John Byrth's circumstances as a result of which Thomas was apprenticed to a Plymouth company of chemists and druggists founded by William Cookworthy (1705–80), the Quaker pioneer of English porcelain manufacture.

Although his education had been somewhat deficient, Thomas Byrth was an avid reader and scholar and this brought him into contact with his almost exact contemporary, the talented young bookseller, Samuel Rowe (1795–1853), "soon to be his close friend and fellow-spirit."[59] Byrth was largely self taught and valued Rowe's superior education. "We used to meet whenever we could, for the purpose of reading Greek together."[60] In 1814 they launched a *Plymouth Literary Magazine*, embarked on an antiquarian tour of Cornwall, and then established in Plympton, a boarding school whose existence, like that of their magazine, was short lived. Byrth, who in 1815 began to take pupils in the home of his widowed mother, was still associated with the Quakers in Plymouth, though "after much spiritual questing among the various denominations" he "found his way to evangelical doctrines through slow intellectual conviction."[61]

The early religious orientation of Samuel Rowe is less evident. His family were farmers but his intellectual bent suggested a different career. Interestingly, we are told that from an early age he was religiously inclined and, as he had "ever an insuperable distaste for agricultural pursuits," at one stage "it was proposed to send him to Oxford, with a view to his taking Holy Orders" but this plan was abandoned and instead he was apprenticed to a bookseller at Kingsbridge before setting up his own bookshop in Plymouth.[62] There certainly were dissenters in Devon named Rowe and Samuel's family may have been less than staunch Anglicans. Reading between the lines we may reasonably wonder whether in those early years he had been unsure of his loyalty to the Establishment, and perhaps he too had been "questing among the denominations."[63]

57. Selleck, *Plymouth Friends*, 2:247, where the name is misprinted as Byrsh.

58. The early biography (Moncreiff, *Remains of Byrth*) has fewer details of Byrth's early career than the article written in 1958, Anon., "Nineteenth Century Apprentice," 270–71.

59. Ibid., 271.

60. Rowe, "Samuel Rowe," 397.

61. Anon., "Nineteenth Century Apprentice," 272.

62. See the memoir of Rowe in Samuel Rowe, *Perambulation*, 345.

63. Rowe certainly had the opportunity for an encounter with Quakers when he was apprenticed to the Kingsbridge bookseller Richard Southwood, whose premises were described as "a few doors above the Quaker Meeting House," [Hawkins], *Kingsbridge and Salcombe*, 49.

His piety was never in question, but by the early 1820s he was a churchwarden at St. Andrew's in Plymouth where the minister was the evangelical John Hatchard. In 1822 he matriculated from Jesus College, Cambridge, and in 1824, he was ordained to be a curate under John Hatchard at St. Andrew's.

In the intervening years Rowe and Byrth had been active in the early life of the Plymouth Institution (or Athenaeum) of which Rowe became a member in 1817 and the secretary in 1821.[64] Described as "the centre of all literary, scientific and artistic life in South Devon," this circle of learning had an ambience comparable to that of the Lunar Society in Birmingham. The founder, Henry Woollcombe, was a respected Plymouth lawyer, alderman and philanthropist. He was one of the seven *literati*, members of the institution, who published a letter, in 1823, to raise sufficient money for John Kitto, a deaf (but highly literate) pauper in the poorhouse, to be employed as a sub-librarian in the Plymouth Public Library.[65] Another member of the Athenaeum in its early days was the young Anthony Norris Groves, before he moved to Exeter, and it was through his connections with this association of scholarship that he learnt of Kitto with the result that a year later the deaf scholar became part of Groves's household.[66] In this circle of lively intellectual enquiry, Byrth was not the only Quaker. John Prideaux (1785–1859), whose family was a pillar of the West Country Quaker community, was a respected chemist, who contributed to the Institution's *Transactions* and had also befriended Kitto as a young man.[67] The advice that he gave to Kitto (together with a large number of books) was later recalled by the recipient and it again reminds us of the way in which eighteenth-century rationalism had influenced Quaker thinking:

> His grand point was this, "That it was the duty of every rational creature to devote whatever talents God had given him to useful purposes—to aim at the largest usefulness, of which he might be capable—and that so far as I did this—and abstained from rendering the good gifts of God ministrant to the idle vanities of life, so far might I expect His blessing upon the studious pursuits to which I seemed inclined, and which had hitherto done me much honor."[68]

However, Byrth's connection with the Quakers was less secure than Prideaux's, and when in 1819 he applied for formal membership of the Society of Friends *on the grounds of birthright* it was refused, though he later wondered whether his application might have succeeded *on the grounds of conviction*. The rebuff may be seen as a

---

64. The institution was founded in 1812 and the *Athenaeum* properly refers to the building (built in 1819) in which they met.

65. Ryland, *Memoirs of Kitto*, 77n1; cf. Eadie, *Life of Kitto*, 72–74.

66. [H. B. Groves], *Memoir*, 3; Ryland, *Memoirs*, 142, see below, ch. 7. For an excellent account of Kitto and his subsequent career with Groves in Bagdad, and later, see Dann, *Father of Faith Missions*, 33–41, 99–104, 120, 125, 173–74, 198–99, 307–15.

67. Ryland, *Memoirs*, 84n1.

68. Kitto, *Lost Senses*, 79.

decisive factor in Byrth's separation from the Quakers, because in October 1819 he was baptized as an Anglican in St. Andrew's,[69] but in fact the process of his detachment was more complicated. Late in the previous year he had entered his name, as a mature student, on the books of Magdalen Hall, Oxford[70] where a course leading to a degree, could only be embarked on by an Anglican, and yet as late as August 1819 he had attended a Quaker wedding in Plymouth, signing his name as a witness.[71] It seems clear however that his object was ordination, because even before he received his degree from Oxford in 1826, he was ordained to the curacy of Diptford, near Totnes in April 1823 by the bishop of Bristol.[72]

We noted earlier that Byrth had taken pupils in his mother's home, and in fact this had been a successful venture, with his having at one point as many as sixty students. It is not clear how he kept the school going during his studies at Oxford but it was only when he was ordained that he finally closed the school in Plymouth. As a curate in Diptford, he took some pupils, one of whom he had been teaching for some years. This was Benjamin Newton whose widowed mother had a long standing Quaker connection and whose family further illustrates some of the uncertainties within the Society at this time.

Newton's maternal grandfather, Roger Treffry[73] (1746–1818), was a generation older than William Allen and Joseph Gurney, and unlike them was not born into Quakerdom. He came from an old and respected Cornish family and had been baptized in the parish church of St. Budeaux, on the outskirts of Plymouth. As a boy he had moved with his parents, a few miles further north, to Bere Barton,[74] where, at the age of fifteen he lost his father. He had trained as a maltster and became an enlightened and progressive farmer, whose careful observations, during extensive travels in England, were incorporated into a publication concerned with wheat disease.[75] As a young man however he was attracted to the Society of Friends and at the age of twenty-five he had married Mary Veale, a member of a large and active family of Quakers from St. Austell in Cornwall. For some ten years he lived and farmed outside Falmouth, but in 1780 he moved back to the home of his childhood at Bere Barton. It

---

69. Moncreiff, *Remains of Byrth*, 64–71.

70. *Al. Oxon.*, 1:207.

71. Marriage certificate of George Fox and Rachel Collier Hingston, at Plymouth Quaker Meeting House, 4 Aug 1819, Plymouth and West Devon Record Office, MS 105/109.

72. The ceremony took place in Christ College Chapel, Cambridge because throughout his time as bishop of Bristol (and indeed during his first years as bishop of Lincoln), John Kaye was also the Master of Christ's College (CCEd Record ID: 157012; Bristol Record Office, EP/A/1/13 (Act book 1810–36).

73. This Cornish name is pronounced similarly to "decry." For most of the following paragraphs I have used Rideout, *Treffry Family*, 46; [Penney], "Treffry," 37–41.

74. Bere Barton is now Beer Ferrers on the peninsula bounded by the Rivers Tavy and Tamar some five miles north of Plymouth.

75. Treffry, *Dissertation*.

would be a mistake to think that Treffry's involvement with the Quakers was a casual arrangement of convenience arising out of his marriage. In fact his commitment appears to have been total. According to one of his grandsons, he turned his back on the lifestyle of his family and "studiously kept all knowledge of the heraldry of the family from his sons. He destroyed every coat of arms and everything of that sort. He thought it was worldly."[76] Back in his old home at Bere Barton, he became an active Quaker in the region. He was a trustee of the Plymouth Meeting House, took part in meetings for action against the slave trade and was appointed to attend the Friends' yearly meeting in London in 1785. He even started holding Quaker meetings in his own home because of the distance of Bere Barton from Plymouth. In the 1780s and '90s he was repeatedly in difficulty with the authorities because of his refusal to pay tithe or church rates.[77]

In the early 1800s he moved to Lostwithiel but many of his children remained in the Plymouth area and several remained with the Quakers. His first two sons, Joseph (1771–1851), a flour merchant, and Robert (1772–1832), a wine merchant, were listed in 1809 as Friends in Plymouth as was his daughter Sarah (1776–1853), who married a Plymouth grocer, Benjamin Fox (1776–1856).[78] Another son, Samuel, moved away but was a minister among Friends, while yet another son, Richard, entered the Wesleyan ministry.[79] His daughter Anna appears to have "married out" of the Society when she married Benjamin Wills Newton in March 1807.[80] Newton had been a draper in Liskeard and now had a shop in Plymouth Dock.[81] Before the year was out however she was a widow with a son who never knew his father. On the younger Benjamin Newton's Quaker birth certificate, Anna Newton was listed as "n[on] m[ember],"[82] but in her early widowhood, she continued to meet with Friends and this explains why from 1815 onward her son was enrolled in Thomas Byrth's school.

The flexibility of Quaker attitudes in doctrinal matters and their associations with less orthodox varieties of belief are well illustrated by the experience of another member of the Treffry family. When Roger's sister Jane married Joseph Honeychurch,

76. Recollections of B. W. Newton in 1893, recorded in Wyatt MS, 2:91 (now missing) and copied into the "Fry MS" (JRULM, CBA 7049, 17).

77. Rideout, *Treffry Family*, 135–36.

78. They are all included in the 1809 list of "Friends of the Western Monthly Meeting of Friends in the County of Devon," in Sellek, *Plymouth Friends*, 2:246–47.

79. Richard Treffry was president of the Methodist Conference in Manchester in 1833. He died in 1842.

80. Although her husband's parents were married in an Anglican Church (St. Philip and St. Jacob, Bristol, 17 Nov 1770), he was christened in an Independent Chapel, Broadway Somerset (12 Aug 1777). For the Trinitarian Independents at Ilminster who broke away to found the "Broadway Meeting" in the 18th century, see Weaver and Mayo, *Notes and Queries*, 5:202–4.

81. *Exeter Flying Post*, 13 Dec 1804; 6 Feb 1806; 17 Dec 1807.

82. F. W. Wyatt who consulted the Quaker birth records after B. W. Newton's death conjectured that Anna's non-membership was because her father had been disowned. It is more likely that it was because of her marriage to Benjamin Newton, whose family appears to have had no Quaker connection.

a cooper of Falmouth, she too became part of a respected Quaker family. Falmouth had an important Quaker community in which the families of Fox, Tregelles and others maintained a notable tradition of learning and enlightenment. Of Jane Honychurch's two daughters, born in Falmouth, the younger, Mary, married Samuel Lloyd of Birmingham and in due course became a respected Quaker minister. The elder daughter's brief pilgrimage was less tranquil.

By her union with John Butler Toulmin (1788–1860), Amy Honeychurch (1789–1823) was marrying into the world of Unitarianism. Her husband was a son of Joshua Toulmin[83] (1740–1815), the Unitarian Baptist minister who served first in Taunton[84] and later in Birmingham with Joseph Priestley. Their first child, Amy Jane, was born in Birmingham in 1814, shortly after which, Amy (the mother), wrote to her cousin, Anna (Benjamin Newton's mother), inviting her to visit her in Birmingham. From her letter it is clear that the friendship was a close one, but in 1817, John and Amy Toulmin emigrated to Alabama. There in 1825 Amy died giving birth to another child. Before her death she arranged with her husband to take the older child, Amy Jane, back to England where she became part of Anna Newton's family.[85] The reasons for this are not entirely clear. The widowed John Toulmin seems to have realized that he couldn't at that stage provide a home for his nine-year-old daughter, but whether, as was later claimed in Newton's household, the dying Amy had regrets about her marriage to a Unitarian and wanted her child reared in a more orthodox milieu, is less certain.[86]

A Single-Minded Critic

Hardly surprisingly, the early life of the younger Benjamin Wills Newton was unsettled. His mother had been born in the Treffry household at Bere Barton but around the turn of the century her parents had moved away and in her early widowhood Anna Newton seems to have abandoned the home in Plymouth, where she had briefly lived with her husband, and took Benjamin with her, to live with her parents in Lostwithiel where Benjamin attended the grammar school.[87] People living on or near the south coast of England during the Napoleonic Wars could hardly have been unaware of the

83. For details of the Toulmin family, see *ODNB* and http://www.toulmin.family.btinternet.co.uk/DescendentsAbrahamChard.htm.

84. It was in 1798, in the Unitarian chapel at Taunton, that Samuel Taylor Coleridge had "performed the divine services" for Toulmin when the latter was grieving for his drowned daughter Jane. Writing to another Unitarian, Dr. J. P. Estlin, Coleridge observed, "The good Dr. Toulmin bears it like the true practical Christian,—there is indeed a tear in his eye, but that eye is lifted up to the Heavenly Father." Coleridge, *Letters of S. T. Coleridge*, 1:247.

85. The original plan was that her sister would bring up Amy, but as Mary was only newly married to Samuel Lloyd of Birmingham, little Amy Jane Toulmin became a member of the Newton family and was thus, effectively, a younger sister of Benjamin Newton.

86. Some Toulmin letters and memoranda relating to this episode on the subject are transcribed in the Fry MS (JRULM, CBA 7049) 18–24.

87. Ibid., 47.

hostilities. Lostwithiel was not on the coast but Newton later could remember having breakfast in October 1813 (when he was not yet six) when a neighbor arrived with the news that Captain John Norway of the post office packet service had been cut in two by chain shot during a skirmish with an American vessel.[88] He also recalled returning from school, in February 1815, to find his mother, having learnt of Napoleon's escape from Elba, wringing her hands in despair and exclaiming, "Now torrents of blood will be shed."[89] For Quakers, whose religious tenets forbad any involvement in violence, the war economy was liable to create special problems, and the family's uncertainties must have been exacerbated by the absence of a father.[90]

In 1815, with the end of the war, Newton's mother returned to Plymouth bringing her parents with her. The boy now went to Thomas Byrth's school in Park Street and later, in 1823, he lived at Diptford with Byrth for further tutoring when the latter was ordained. It is clear from Newton's letters that he did not like Byrth, but he certainly received a good classical grounding, which was the basis for his later success at Exeter College, Oxford. By matriculating at Oxford, in 1824, two days before his seventeenth birthday, Newton was following Byrth's example and decisively turning his back on Quakerdom, but at this stage his reasons were ones of ambition rather than doctrine. In an account written some four years later, after his evangelical conversion, Newton claimed that going to Diptford to study with Byrth had been

> the turning point of my life and this occurrence first roused me from my [spiritual] slumber. For the separation from Friends alarmed me. I had always been taught to believe that Spiritual Religion was confined to them, and I did believe it, for though I found not comfort in their meetings, yet nevertheless I found less at Church and when I analyzed my motives for joining it I trembled to acknowledge that they were chiefly for the gratification of worldly pride and the thirst for worldly honor.

On the other hand his time with Byrth seems to have brought a doctrinal dimension to his thinking, which had been lacking in his experiences among Quakers. Making allowances for his dislike of his tutor and for his later doctrinal certainty, we may still give his account of these next years some credence:

> Mr Byrth was a powerful preacher of the Law; his mind was writhing under its terrors: he saw that he was guilty and condemned, and knew not where to fly; and his preaching was of course the expression of such feelings as would naturally arise from such a state of anguish. This had a most powerful effect on me so much so that I began entirely to despair of salvation and for three

---

88. Ibid., 49. The Norways were a Lostwithiel family and ancestors of the novelist Nevil Shute. For Captain Norway's death, see Norway, *History*, 256–59. Newton also refers to his mother's experiences in Falmouth when many fled the town fearing a French raid, but this was in 1803 before she was married and when she was nursing her dying aunt; Fry MS (JRULM, CBA 7049) 47.

89. Ibid., 48.

90. For other details of Newton's boyhood, see below, ch. 14n3.

years from that time never entertained the hope ... My only method of relief was the fixing my mind intensely on my reading in order that it might so engross my thoughts as to leave me no room for reflexion: and with dread did I contemplate the time when my University Reading would close and my mind be left comparatively unemployed ... Humanly speaking had I not made this change in my Religious profession, I should never perhaps have been brought to explore the sink of my own heart, but have gone on to the end of life, satisfied with a Life of strict Morality and fancied excellence.[91]

How Newton's time at Oxford would affect him spiritually was something that neither he, nor any of the Quaker circle in which he had grown up, could have foreseen. His life continued to be as studious as ever. As a child he had been encouraged in such ways,[92] and his years at school had been demanding when he had been set by Byrth to read what Newton later claimed were the "most difficult books: Logic, Greek poets and plays with no notes, badly edited."[93] His financial means were limited so there was little chance, at Oxford, of his wasting his substance in riotous living—indeed, his letters to his mother, both before and after his evangelical conversion, reflect the single-minded efforts of a young man bent on obtaining the highest honors in the university. His efforts were initially rewarded in June 1826, when, as only an eighteen-year-old undergraduate, he was awarded a fellowship at Exeter College, but in consequence Newton now came into contact with another Exeter Fellow from Plymouth, the cheerful extrovert Henry Bellenden Bulteel, who himself had experienced an evangelical conversion some months earlier.[94] In Plymouth late in December 1826, Bulteel persuaded Newton to attend a service at Charles Church where the celebrated Calvinist minister Robert Hawker was preaching one of his last sermons.[95] In his account (from which we quoted earlier) written to his mother, almost exactly a year after the event, Newton explains that he was in despair from reading "a book written by an American on the principles of Friends in which there is a chapter on Justification and Sanctification, full of the most horrid error." In the midst of this despair he came to the realization that "he that believeth is saved already. O what a change my feelings then experienced ... all my doubts and fears vanished as the morning dew: in a word, I felt that I was saved."[96]

91. BWN to mother, 30 Dec 1827, JRULM CBA 7179 (5).

92. As a boy he had read the poetry of Milton and Cowper with his mother; Fry MS (CBA 7049) 51.

93. Quoted Rowdon, *Origins*, 60.

94. For a discussion of the conflicting evidence concerning Bulteel's conversion, see Stunt, *From Awakening*, 315–17.

95. For more details of Newton's conversion, see Stunt, *From Awakening*, 195–96. Although Robert Hawker was sick early in January 1827, he did preach on the last Sunday of 1826 and this must have been the occasion when Newton was in the congregation, see Williams, *Works of Hawker*, 1:247.

96. BWN to his mother, 30 Dec 1827, CBA 7179 (5). It is of interest to note that the American book had been lent to him by Hannah Abbott, whom Newton would marry six years later.

Certainly in this account of his conversion Newton was making clear that an integral part of the experience was a final turning away from what he regarded as the errors of Quakerdom and in consequence he was now permanently at variance with the faith of his upbringing. From this point on therefore, his letters give expression to anxieties other than those concerning his exams and the hoped-for first-class degree. There is a new and urgent concern arising from his family's continuing connection with Quakers. This was a new situation for West Country Friends among whom there was a tradition of tolerance and mutual forbearance and where disagreement (especially on matters of doctrine) was not a cause for separation. Unlike men like William Allen and Joseph John Gurney, who wanted to testify evangelically within the Quaker movement, Newton, who had already left the Society, was advocating separation because he felt that the movement was incurably wedded to teachings of which he disapproved. In fact his mother, his grandmother and his aunts were now subject to a barrage of evangelical pressure from one of their family who would only be satisfied if they too quit the Society. To appreciate the fervor with which he pursued the matter, some quotation from his letters is needed.

In April 1827 while thanking his mother for sending the Plymouth newspapers' account of the death of Dr. Hawker, he exclaims, "What a revolution there has been in my views and feelings," and observes that he is "more than apprehensive that the majority of [F]riends are strangers to 'the excellency of the knowledge of Christ Jesus their Lord.'"[97] It is true that, at times, especially in the earlier letters, his own position seems a little tentative and incomplete as when, after some doctrinal exposition, he begs his mother to rest "assured that I wish to attach myself to no party, nor blindly to follow any human example." He is cautious too, about the possible consequences of his evangelical position: "The time is not yet come for me to declare my sentiments openly to the world—therefore be pleased to be silent." He also sometimes seeks to be conciliatory, so that, after giving his full approval to the seventeenth article of the Church of England concerning the "sweet, pleasant and unspeakable comfort" afforded by a consideration of predestination, he adds: "Don't think I would press the belief in election as necessary, on any one."[98] But such ambiguities are few and when it comes to his opinion of the Quakers his disapproval is emphatic.

In October 1827 he promises to write a letter to his aunt, in which he will "give an explicit statement of my feeling with respect to [F]riends. Individuals among them I love more and more and I don't think anyone more than John Wadge . . . He and many others I verily believe to be truly regenerated Children of God, but I am sure that an awful torpor in religion hath deadened the souls of a large proportion of those whom it hath been my lot to know."[99] At the end of December he is expressing his pleasure

---

97. BWN to his mother, 23 Apr 1827, CBA 7179 (1).
98. BWN to his mother, 3 Sep 1827 CBA 7179 (3), [Wyatt 2:15v–16v].
99. BWN to his mother, Oct 1827, transcribed in Fry MS (CBA 7049) 117–18. John Wadge, a Quaker grocer of Liskeard, was a witness at the wedding of Newton's uncle Joseph Treffry in 1800, see

to hear that Amy [Toulmin] and you have been to the Church upon the hill. Would that you had entirely left the Quaker's meeting and went *there* always, or at least somewhere where the Gospel is preached. God, it is very true, may influence the heart by the preaching of his Spirit in a silent meeting or by our own fireside, but it is not his ordinary way of conveying the knowledge of his Son . . . Be not deceived, my dear Mother, Friends, as a Society, have *not* the knowledge of God. Never have I heard the Gospel either in their meetings or in their conversation in private; but often do I remember to have been present when its peculiar characteristic doctrines have been controverted.[100]

As if this were not enough, two weeks later he returns to the charge with a further battery directed again at his mother:

You are not aware of the immense interval between Friends' Principles and mine. Far be it from me to doubt that there are many Spiritual hearted people among them—on the contrary, I well know many who, I am sure, feel their need of their Saviour and love him with a saving love—but there is Spiritual knowledge as well as Spiritual love.

Giving notice of a future confrontation and his readiness to take issue with the Quaker Establishment, he then asks her to obtain for him "by hook or by crook, Penn's 'Sandy Foundation shaken' and also let me have the most Spiritual diary or work of any kind that was ever written by a Friend." A page later he announces (with all the self-confidence of a twenty-year-old), "It is my earnest wish that you and several other of my friends should sit under my Ministry. I can tell without reading your heart that you do find no peace from your present principles."[101]

Very probably it was his uncle Joseph Treffry who was the relative "who gave me £50 to spend on a holiday," to celebrate his first-class degree. It was therefore to this uncle, his mother's oldest brother, that Newton wrote a lengthy letter in August 1828 from near Caithness during his holiday in Scotland, to fulfill "the promise I made of giving you a written statement of my religious sentiments—at least those which are considered peculiar." In the letter that follows, the young Oxford Fellow presents to his Quaker uncle (and the senior member of the Treffry family) an uncompromisingly Calvinist account of salvation and conversion, bolstered with an appropriate quotation from John Newton's *Omicron Letters*. In conclusion, he hopes that his account has been given "with becoming humility and yet with a firmness proportioned to the strength of the conviction I feel as to their being the truths of God."[102] We have no record of how Joseph Treffry reacted to his nephew's letter at that point, but eight years later, at the time of the Beaconite controversy, when Newton published his *Re-*

Rideout, *Treffry Family*, 139.

   100. BWN to his mother, 30 Dec 1827, CBA 7179 (5).

   101. BWN to his mother, 13 Jan 1828, transcribed in Fry MS (CBA 7049) 143–44.

   102. The letter is transcribed (from a copy of the original) in Fry MS (CBA 7049) 148–51.

monstrance to the Society of Friends, his uncle published a reply defending the Society against Newton's criticisms.[103]

Although Benjamin Newton would be a leading figure in the early development of the Plymouth Brethren in the 1830s and '40s, we have to bear in mind that in the late 1820s no such ecclesiastical identity yet existed. Newton himself might bewail that "the light of Christianity is almost quenched in this Island," feeling that Bulteel and he were somewhat solitary witnesses, in Oxford, in an Establishment whose articles were sound but in which Evangelicalism was under attack. On the other hand, Plymouth in the 1820s was not without an evangelical witness. From 1824, the vicar of St. Andrew's, John Hatchard, could be said to have inherited the mantle (albeit without its colorful Calvinistic lining) of Robert Hawker, and there were other younger curates like Septimus Courtney and Benjamin Vallack who were sympathetic to evangelicalism. As an Anglican who was contemplating ordination, Newton was cautious about getting on too well with Dissenters, but if his mother went to Trinity Chapel, "a High Calvinist place of worship" built for Arthur Triggs, a former member of Hawker's congregation, this would, in Newton's eyes, be better for her than staying with the Quakers.

Unlike many dissatisfied Friends who might occasionally worship in other churches but still regularly attended Quaker worship, Newton shunned the Society's meetings but went out of his way to maintain contact with Quakers both in his family and outside it. In 1830 when visiting his mother's cousin Mary Lloyd (née Honeychurch) in Birmingham, he was delighted to find that Samuel Lloyd was "not only a friend but a Christian friend—indeed I have seldom met with any with whom I could more cordially exchange the hand of fellowship."[104] In the same letter he comments on some of the problems of the heirs of the recently deceased John Thomas (1752–1827), a highly respected Bristol Quaker, pioneer and advocate of the canal link between Bristol and London.[105] Newton is insistent that he would have "willingly, if it had been necessary, given my share towards setting up poor Thomas of Prior Park. Let him take any of my books he chooses." Similarly he adds that he was "very well pleased with the opportunity of seeing a Plymouth Friend in the person of Rob. Adair."[106] But one gets the impression that while nurturing such contacts, he was always hoping to wean them from the Society.

This makes his own development in the next few years all the more ironic. Between 1830 and 1833, Newton (together with John Darby, Percy Hall, and George Wigram) was to become a leading figure in a Plymouth group of evangelical Christians who arranged lectures and meetings at Providence chapel and in due course came to be known as the Plymouth Brethren. The irony lies in the fact that whether

---

103. Treffry, *Strictures*.

104. For further details and the sequel to this visit, see below, ch. 2n34.

105. For details of this remarkable man, see Anon., "John Thomas." Prior House, his Palladian home on the outskirts of Bath, is now a Roman Catholic college.

106. BWN to his mother, 22 Apr 1830, transcribed in Fry MS (CBA 7049) 191–92.

he realized it or not, Newton's new ecclesiastical identity owed a great deal to the spirituality and lifestyle of the Quakers. Sarah Crewdson (née Fox) of Kendal had grown up in the same (Quaker) home (in Plymouth) as Hannah Abbott, who married Newton in 1832, and when revisiting Plymouth she wrote several letters describing the new community, referring to it at first as a "party" and then as a "congregation," but in several ways she gives the impression that it had Quaker roots.[107] As we shall see in the next chapter many of the early Brethren in Plymouth and the surrounding area had unmistakably Quaker origins.

Part of the fascination of Quaker life during the 1820s may lie in the strange mixture of enthusiasm and uncertainty to be found among the younger generation—a mixture that possibly reflects both the relief that accompanied the ending of the Napoleonic Wars, but also the challenges posed by the post-war economy. The enthusiasm of evangelical certainty could sometimes be supremely optimistic (especially among the somewhat older generation) about spreading the gospel and changing the world, but it could also be shot through with a pessimism that found the prospects of humanity and more particularly Christian civilization far from reassuring. The evangelically inclined Quaker, like William Allen, would soldier on, swinging to and fro between enlightened confidence in the "Great Master" of the universe and an awareness of the nearness of the end. Similarly Luke Howard, for a time at least, was looking forward to the day when Quakers would be reunited with their evangelical brethren in other denominations. On the other hand J. J. Gurney and others, having tasted for a while the delights of the wider world, could retreat into the shelter of an evangelical version of Quakerdom. Many Friends retained their loyalty to a radical non-dogmatic community in which they were able to pursue a wide variety of intellectual inquiries, but others hovered uncertainly on the fringes of the movement, denied full membership but attracted by the Society's personal involvement in their lives. Occasionally a single-minded man of conviction, like Benjamin Newton, could wean a significant number from the Society, but interestingly, such folk would often be attracted to a new community rather than to an existing denomination. A few years later, the struggle for the soul of Quakerdom would become more intense and the voice of controversy would soon become more strident.

---

107. For a fuller account of the earliest beginnings of the Brethren at Plymouth including some extracts of Sarah Crewdson's letters on the subject, see Stunt, *From Awakening*, 290–95.

2

Early Brethren and the Society of Friends[1]

A COMMENT THAT IS often heard upon the lips of those who have just made their first acquaintance with the ecclesiastical outlook of Brethren is something to the effect that some of their practices seem very similar to those of Quakers. Brethren usually disclaim any direct association with the Society of Friends, and some will probably go further and say that in fact the majority of the early Brethren were drawn from the Established Church. This latter statement is, broadly speaking, true if we make the exception of certain leading figures like Craik (Presbyterian), Chapman (Baptist), Dorman (Congregational), and Trotter (Methodist). In one respect however, the statement is seriously at variance with the facts, and this relates to the Society of Friends.

It is the object of this paper to consider the links between Quakers and Brethren between 1830 and 1840. We shall consider first the state of affairs in the Society of Friends at the time, and the family structure of Quaker society, and then we shall look at some of the Friends who became Brethren, inquiring how this happened. Lastly we shall examine some of the effects, which may have been felt by the Brethren movement as a result of the new Quaker influence.

The Quaker Dilemma

The tensions within the Society of Friends, which we considered in the previous chapter, began to become more pronounced in the late 1820s. Where the older movement's mystical tendencies had given it a distinctively tolerant character, together with a retiring quietism, which had often cut its members off from other Christian denominations, the growing involvement of Quakers in public affairs and philanthropic activities (with a particular interest in the campaign against slavery and in prison reform), was fostering a more outward-looking attitude—an outlook which, as we have noted, often went hand in hand with a new evangelical emphasis. Quaker

---

1. This chapter was written in the 1960s and was published in 1970 as an "Occasional Paper" of the Christian Brethren Research Fellowship. In its present form, I have corrected some errors, expanded some footnotes, and eliminated some youthful infelicities in the text. Other changes are designed to avoid reduplication of material in the previous chapter, but it is substantially the same paper as it was fifty years ago!

evangelists like William Allen and his occasional coworker, Stephen Grellet, were widely respected names among the Friends of this period.[2]

On the other hand, with this emergence from their earlier isolation, some of the Friends' writings were becoming far more dogmatic in tone. The earlier tolerance is replaced by more definitive attitudes, and one discerns a growing division during the 1820s over the direction that Quaker dogma should take. On one side was the teaching of men like the American, Elias Hicks,[3] whose emphasis upon the Inner Light as the spiritual source of authority had led him into a Christological position which was all but Unitarian. On the other side there were "Evangelical" Friends like another American, Elisha Bates,[4] and the English John Wilkinson,[5] whose sympathies were with the more evangelical John Joseph Gurney,[6] who, as we noted earlier, was calling for a recognition of Scripture as the true source of authority rather than the more subjective idea of the Inner Light.

It was Hicks's unorthodox teaching in America, which caused the controversy to assume serious proportions, as a large number of Friends were very critical of his Unitarian thinking. The result was the "Great Separation" in America (1827–1828), which divided numerous families and Quaker communities. In England, however, the dispute was not so much concerned with Hicks's heresy but more with the issue that gave rise to it—namely, the question as to where was authority for the Quaker. Thus, in the words of a recent historian of the Society of Friends:

> Gradually two bodies of Friends were beginning to grow up: one convinced that the evangelical preaching of Stephen Grellet and others contained the true message of Quakerism for the world of their day; the other deeply aware that the increasing emphasis on the efficacy of sound doctrine was undermining the mystical basis of Quakerism, with its dependence upon the Inner Light in the soul of man.[7]

The difficulty for the Evangelical Friends was that Hicks and his followers were standing in the more historic Quaker position as far as their teaching on the Inner Light was concerned. George Fox's famous protest at Nottingham had been: "Oh no! It is not the Scriptures: it is the Holy Spirit."[8] In their quest for a *spiritual* religion the

---

2. For William Allen, see above, ch. 1, [x-ref]. Grellet was an American Quaker (of French birth) with whom Allen cooperated in two extended European mission tours in 1818–19 and 1832–33, see Seebohm, *Memoirs of Grellet*, 1:356–2:38; 2:245–334.

3. For Elias Hicks (1748–1830) of New York, see Hicks, *Journal*, and Wilbur, *Life of Hicks*.

4. For Elisha Bates (1781–1861), see Good, "Elisha Bates and Social Reform."

5. John Wilkinson (1783–1846) was the son of an Anglican clergyman and his widow who raised him among Friends in Wycombe, Bucks; see Summers, *Memories of Jordans*, 265. See also *BDEB*.

6. For John Joseph Gurney, see above, ch. 1, [x-ref].

7. Vipont, *Story of Quakerism*, 179–80.

8. Armistead, *Journal of George Fox*, 1:76.

early Quakers had rejected both the sacraments of Baptism and the Lord's Supper. The Quaker pioneers, William Penn and Robert Barclay had taken strongly non-predestinarian views of salvation, which, together with the abandonment of the sacraments, was another source of questioning among the Evangelical Friends. There were similarly other problems disturbing those who wished to make the Scriptures their sole authority, as for example, the Quaker practice of allowing women to be ministers.

In England matters came to a head in 1835 when Isaac Crewdson, of Kendal and Manchester, published a pamphlet entitled *A Beacon to the Society of Friends*,[9] in which he outlined the main discrepancies between the Scriptures and historic Quaker teaching, laying great emphasis upon the long-neglected doctrine of justification by faith. There were, of course, some immediate replies, the most well known being Thomas Hancock's *A Defence of the doctrines of Immediate Revelation*,[10] and *A Letter to the Author of "The Beacon"* by Thomas Thompson of Liverpool.[11] To these there were rejoinders from evangelical Quakers like Richard Ball of Taunton who published in the same year (1835) *Holy Scripture, the test of Truth: An appeal to its paramount authority against certain passages in Dr. Hancock's "Defence" and in the writings of Barclay and Penn*,[12] with others following suit.[13]

The result was almost inevitable, as the so-called Beaconite controversy extended throughout the Society. For a short time, it was thought that the evangelicals might be contained within the society, as, largely owing to the influence of J. J. Gurney, the epistle of the yearly meeting in 1836 contained a passage upholding the verbal inspiration of the Bible. It was only a temporary accommodation however, and soon large numbers seceded, finding their way to a variety of different spiritual homes. Some like Thomas Geldart and his future wife Hannah Martin of Norwich joined the Baptist communion;[14] others like Robert Braithwaite became Anglicans;[15] it is hardly a matter for surprise that many were attracted to another group of evangelicals who had recently withdrawn from various denominations in the quest for a biblical and yet unsectarian fellowship. The common anti-clerical ground between Quakers and Brethren is self-evident. However, before we consider those who did become as-

---

9. Crewdson, *Beacon*.

10. Hancock, *Defence*.

11. Thompson, *Letter*.

12. Ball, *Holy Scripture*.

13. For the ensuing controversy see Ash, "Beacon Controversy"; Thomas, "Beaconite Controversy"; Good, "Elisha Bates and the Beaconite Controversy." For an excellent recent account of the wider context of the controversy, see Kennedy, "Condition of Friends."

14. [Penney], "Notes on Emma Marshall," 117.

15. Robert Braithwaite (1816–82) was a son of Isaac and Anna Braithwaite of Kendal (see below). He became the Vicar of Chipping Camden, Gloucs (1873–82) and edited *The Life and Letters of William Pennefather*. His son Robert became a Roman Catholic in 1864, and corresponded on religious matters for many years with Francis Newman. The letters have recently been published online, by Tod E. Jones, *Letters of F. W. Newman*.

sociated with Brethren, we must examine the family structure within the Society of Friends, as it is clearly a significant factor in the process with which we are dealing.

Quaker Families and Intermarriage

The striking feature of the Quaker genealogies is the constant intermarriage within their own community, with the result that almost any Quaker could call any other Quaker his cousin. We shall not go into great detail as the families were very large, but we shall outline the links between some of the main families, which concern us more particularly.

In the Kendal Quaker community, which "was one of the largest in the North of England"[16] two of the most important families were closely related to each other by marriage. These were the Braithwaites and the Crewdsons. W. D. Crewdson (senior) was married to Deborah Braithwaite. At the same time, two of her brothers, Isaac and George Braithwaite, and one of her sisters, Rachel, had married members of a distinguished Quaker family of Birmingham, the Lloyds of banking fame.[17]

On the other hand, both the Crewdsons of Kendal and the Lloyds of Birmingham were related to Quaker families in the West Country. No fewer than five of W. D. Crewdson's children married members of the large Fox family, which had branches in Plymouth, Wellington, and Exeter. At the same time, as we noted in the previous chapter, Samuel Lloyd of Birmingham had married Mary Honeychurch, whose mother was a Treffry, an important Cornish Quaker family, while his sister Sarah had married Alfred Fox of Falmouth.[18]

To complete this network of families, we must mention their links with the Howard family of Tottenham, on the outskirts of London, and Acworth in Yorkshire. W. D. Crewdson's daughter Maria married John Eliot Howard, while Samuel Lloyd's sister, Rachel, married Robert Howard, John Eliot's brother.[19] The links could be extended at enormous length, but it is to be hoped that we have given some idea of the family networks that linked Quakers in the North with others in the South-East and South-West. The significance of these connections will shortly become apparent.

---

16. Braithwaite, *Memoirs of Anna Braithwaite*, 41. For an excellent and comprehensive account of Quaker developments in Kendal, reference should be made to pages 169–230 of the recent work of Dr. Rosemary Mingins, whose *Beacon Controversy . . . in Manchester and Kendal* appeared more than thirty years after this essay was first published but was the first work to make effective use of my researches.

17. For the various genealogical networks from which, in this and the following paragraph, we have made only a minute selection, see: [Foster], *Pedigree of Forsters*; [Foster], *Pedigree of Wilson*; Boase and Courtney, *Bibliotheca Cornubiensis*, 1:97; [Thomas], *J. Bevan Braithwaite*; Lloyd, *Lloyds of Birmingham*; and [Lloyd], *Descendants of Samuel Lloyd*.

18. For the enormous Fox family and Quaker pedigrees of the West Country, see, *inter alia*, Foster, *Revised genealogical*; [S. M. Fox], *Two Homes*; H. C. Fox, *Quaker Homespun*, appendix B.

19. Details of the Howard pedigree can be found in various of the works cited in n17.

Some Quakers Who Became Brethren

One of the earliest names associated with the Brethren was B. W. Newton of Plymouth, and in the previous chapter we considered his Quaker upbringing and the uncertainties of some of the Friends in his circle together with the impact on his family of his evangelical conversion in 1827.[20] Convinced that his new-found faith was incompatible with Quaker principles Newton soon emerged as one of the leading figures in the group of Brethren who began to meet at Plymouth, and among whom there would be a significant number of former Quakers. We mentioned earlier the daughter of his mother's cousin, Amy Toulmin, who became a devoted follower of Newton for the rest of her life,[21] but Quakers from other families also followed him.

Of these West Country Quakers associated with the early Brethren, the best known must be Newton's cousin by marriage, Samuel Prideaux Tregelles, the textual scholar, who came from an old Quaker family in Falmouth,[22] where, as a boy, he attended the Classical School. In 1828, on the death of his father who had recently lost a fortune in speculation, Tregelles moved with his mother and sister to Neath Abbey in South Wales where he worked for a while in the iron works established by Peter Price (1739–1821) whose wife Anna was a sister of Tregelles's grandfather. This work was uncongenial to the young man whose enthusiasm was for the study of ancient languages. Of a somewhat skeptical turn of mind, typical of the free-thinking Quakers to whom we referred earlier, Tregelles returned in 1834 to Falmouth where he took students for a while, but he met Newton in Plymouth around the time that Newton was married to Hannah Abbott, whose mother was a cousin of Tregelles's grandfather. Impressed by Newton's scholarship and doctrinal certainty, he became interested in his ideas on prophecy. According to Newton's reminiscences, Tregelles had been "on the very borders of scepticism and almost had decided for infidelity." He read some of Newton's writings and came to one of his sermons, and it proved to be the means of his evangelical conversion. He "cast in his lot, as a believer, with the Brethren, which when his relatives heard, they cut him completely and would do nothing for him."[23]

---

20. See above, ch. 1.

21. Amy Toulmin was responsible for the preservation of much of the material in the Fry Collection. For her family background, see above, ch. 1.

22. For S. P. Tregelles (1813–75), see *ODNB*, *BDEB*, and Stunt, "Some Unpublished Letters." His great-great-great grandfather, John Tregelles (1637–1706), a tailor of Falmouth had been one of the earliest Friends in Cornwall; Coate, *Cornwall*, 348.

23. Fry MS (JRULM, CBA 7049) 29. Here the date of Tregelles's conversion is given as "around 1832." G. H. Fromow (*Teachers*, 4) gives the date as 1835, but later (p. 27) implies an earlier date. I prefer a date nearer 1834 for the following reasons. Tregelles was working at Neath Abbey, Glamorgan, until 1834 and his meeting with Newton would (prima facie) be more likely to have occurred after his return to Falmouth. Tregelles did not join the Brethren at Plymouth until early 1835 (Tregelles, *Three Letters*, 4). Lastly, two of Tregelles's letters addressed to Aneurin Owen Pughe in July and September 1833 exhibit all the style of Quaker usage (eg., "thee" and "thy," for "you" and "your," "7 mo" for "July," etc.), while there is no indication of interest in spiritual matters. (Aberystwyth, N.L.W. Ms. 13232 [Mysevin MS 12.])

When, in 1839, Tregelles married Sarah Anna Prideaux, he was marrying into another Quaker family several of whom had become Brethren. Sarah Anna's father Walter, and her mother Sarah Elizabeth Ball (née Hingston) Prideaux moved in 1812 from Kingsbridge to Plymouth,[24] and one of her brothers was Frederick Prideaux (1817–91), who in his teens was a pupil of Benjamin Newton. Sixty years later in 1891 his widow, Fanny Prideaux (née Ball), wrote to her nephews and nieces, about the family of her recently deceased husband, whom she had married in 1853, and observed that she had known the second wife of Frederick's maternal grandfather, Catherine Phillips Hingston (née Tregelles), who was "always called Grandmama Hingston by her step grandchildren . . . I remember her as a vigorous and decided old lady of the Quaker type though she had left the Society of Friends some years before and like many members of your Uncle's family and of mine was associated with the Plymouth Brethren."[25]

However, not all the Hingstons became Brethren. Charles Hingston (1805–1872), the heroic Plymouth physician, famed for his work during the cholera epidemic of 1832, remained a Quaker but his wife Louisa Jane (1816–1885+), daughter of Admiral Sir William Parker (1781–1866), met with the Brethren.[26] It was another member of this family whose loft in Kingsbridge was used as a meeting place by a group of Christians to whom the Brethren writer J. L. Harris addressed a letter in 1847.[27]

Other Quakers who are described as having "been amongst the earliest to join the Plymouth Brethren when that sect made its appearance at Plymouth in 1830" were John and Joseph Cookworthy, great nephews of William Cookworthy, the pioneer of English porcelain manufacture. Another, rather less well known family of Quakers were the Balkwills of Kingsbridge and Galmpton, where Richard and John Balkwill took a leading part in the Brethren assembly.[28] It is also worthy of note that some

24. H. Prideaux, "'Tis sixty years since," typescript c. 1870 (Devon Record Office, Acc.61). It was in Plymouth that Walter Prideaux established the banking company of Hingston and Prideaux.

25. F.A.P[rideaux], *In Memoriam F.P.*, 14–15. Frederick Prideaux later had a distinguished legal career as a result of which he is immortalized in the memory of lawyers as the author of the Handbook of Precedents in Conveyancing (1856) [a.k.a. *Prideaux's Precedents*] 25th ed. (1959).

26. In the Hingston household, "the theatre and music were prohibited as 'worldly,' no alcoholic drinks were permitted in the house, and all extravagances in dress were discouraged. But Louisa was a very lively person, even when she was over 70. Her speech was vigorous and direct and she did not suffer fools gladly. Children . . . were in awe of her. It was incredible to them that once, when newly married, she had in a moment of exasperation thrown a hot potato at her husband across the table." See "Descendants of Andrew Hingston" at http://www-civ.eng.cam.ac.uk/cjb/hingston/hd.htm.

27. Harris, *Letter to the Christians*.

28. C. W. H. Rawlins, "Recollections of a Nonagenarian," 138. Shortly before Dr. Joseph Cookworthy's appointment as mayor of Plymouth (1839–41), B. W. Newton wrote to remonstrate with him about his "political associations" (Newton to Cookworthy, Jun 1837, CBA Box 23 [10]). On the other hand Cookworthy was one of the four brethren nominated by Newton to represent him in the dispute of 1845, Burnham, *Story of Conflict*, 177n184. For William Cookworthy, the porcelain manufacturer, see *ODNB*. For the Balkwills, see Stunt, *From Awakening*, 299n78. For another episode involving the Brethren and the Cookworthy family, see below, ch. 14nn14–20.

Quakers played a part in the early spiritual development of the pioneer Brethren missionary Anthony Norris Groves. Members of the Dymond and the Paget families were Quakers who were part of the earliest circle of Christians in Exeter with whom Groves was associated as a very young man in the 1820s, and although we know little of her family, Bessie Paget, whom Groves regarded as his "mother, in the things of God," was also brought up among Friends.[29]

The case of another person of Quaker origin who (as a teenager) was attracted for a time to the Brethren is instructive. This was the hymn writer Frederick W. Whitfield (1827–1904), whose biography (written by his daughter) provides us with no information about his early years, but by whose own account was associated with Brethren for "nearly twelve years."[30] We may supplement this scrap of information with the recollection of Samuel Tregelles, who in a characteristically plainspoken letter written in 1863, recalled Whitfield with whom he had been acquainted in the early 1840s:

> He had then I think left "Friends" but without much light of any kind; he was at Cambridge (at St. John's College, I believe), for a time. His education had been next to nothing: he wanted to remedy its defects, and to become a clergyman on very high Church grounds. On getting into intercourse with Brethrenites, he took up views in an opposite extreme: at once left Cambridge, and was a very earnest and not very wise exponent of the views he had adopted.
>
> It is I should think more than twenty years since I saw him; so that he has had time to become much wiser: (he could hardly be *less* so in any subject than he was): some years ago he sent about a letter (printed) giving publicity to his having left "Brethren": he then went, I believe to Trinity College Dublin; he was ordained in the Church of England I should think five or six years ago.[31]

Whitfield's connection with the Brethren was a very youthful one and didn't last very long.[32] In fact Tregelles's comment seems to have been occasioned by a pamphlet[33] (no longer extant) written by Whitfield criticizing William Kelly, the Brethren expositor. Although Tregelles's account of Whitfield is very opinionated, it usefully illustrates how dissatisfied Friends were liable to turn to a variety of alternative ecclesiologies—High Church Anglican, Brethren, and finally evangelical Anglican.

Developments in the North of England

In the North of England, where Isaac Crewdson was a widely respected figure, Evangelical Quakers were more numerous than in the West Country. Nevertheless, as we

---

29. [H. B. Groves], *Memoir*, 40; Stunt, *From Awakening*, 121.

30. Quoted in Reid, *Plymouth Brethrenism*, 42–43.

31. S. P. Tregelles to B. W. Newton, 16 Feb 1863 (JRULM, CBA 7181 [47]).

32. The twelve years would appear to have been between 1842 and 1854. He was at Trinity College, Dublin from 1856–59 and after ordination in 1859 served as a curate in Otley, Yorkshire (1859–61).

33. Frederick Whitfield, *Plymouth Brethren*. For fuller details see Stunt, "Trinity College," 64.

observed earlier, there were strong family ties among Quakers throughout the country, and as Newton and his wife, Hannah Abbott, whom he married in 1832, were related to many other Quaker families their links with the North were natural enough. When Hannah Abbott was only three years old, her mother died and soon after, her father, John Abbott, a flour merchant, married Sarah, a daughter of the Kendal Quaker, Isaac Wilson. In business, Abbott was closely associated with another highly regarded Plymouth Quaker, the chemist Francis Fox.[34] When Fox and Abbott died in 1812 and 1813, it seems that the two widows established a home together, with the result that Hannah appears to have treated Sarah Fox, who was three years her junior, as her sister.[35] The link with North Country Quakers was further strengthened in 1825 when Sarah Fox married the younger W. D. Crewdson and moved to Kendal. When, in 1832, she visited her native Plymouth, her letters to her sister-in-law in Kendal provide a fascinating glimpse of the early life of the Plymouth Brethren assembly in which her "sister" Hannah and Benjamin Newton were playing an important part.[36]

An aunt of Newton's mother was Jane Treffry, who had married Joseph Honeychurch. Of their two daughters, one married John Butler Toulmin and was the mother of Amy Toulmin whom we have already mentioned, while the other, Mary Honeychurch, married Samuel Lloyd of Wood Green, Birmingham.[37] In one of his letters to his mother, dated 22 April 1830, Newton describes his visit to Wood Green.[38] He stayed with them for a long week-end, and found Mary Lloyd "so taken up with her children that she has little room in her head or heart for anything else besides." On the other hand he found plenty in common with her husband:

> S.Ll[oyd]. is exceedingly engaged in business, but I saw rather more of him than of Mary. I found him not only a friend,[39] but a Christian friend,—indeed I have seldom met with any with whom I could more cordially exchange the hand of fellowship. His Society gave me more pleasure and satisfaction than anything else I met with on my journey.

In the course of the visit he also dined at "Farm," the home of Samuel Lloyd Sr. and this is of significance because, ten years later, Samuel Lloyd Sr. would sever his connection with the Quakers in 1840. The process was gradual, but in the end it

---

34. Anon., "Francis Fox of Plymouth," 46.

35. There is a list of the members of the Western Monthly Meeting of Friends in 1809 in Selleck, *Plymouth Friends*, 246–48. Both Hannah Abbott and Sarah Fox are to be found in the Plymouth list with their parents, but B. W. Newton's mother is not included, as she had "married out" to a non-Quaker. The Kingsbury and Modbury meeting includes the names of several members of the Hingston and Prideaux families, including Sarah Anna Prideaux, who would later marry Samuel Tregelles.

36. For some extracts from these letters, see Stunt, *From Awakening*, 291–95.

37. Most of the details of Newton's Quaker relatives are found in the Fry MS (JRULM, CBA 7049) 24–26.

38. Ibid., 190–91.

39. In several places it is not clear whether Newton means a friend in the normal sense or with a denominational significance. Similarly the word "society" is vague as his use of capital letters is erratic.

was complete. The Beaconite controversy obviously added to questions that Newton's earlier conversation had raised. With Lloyd's changing position, Brethren and future Brethren became regular visitors at "Farm." Robert Mackenzie Beverley, whom we shall consider more fully in a later chapter, noted in his Diary:

> April 7th 1835. Dined at Farm, at Mr. Lloyd's the Quaker and banker, where I dined once before: an agreeable day: the conversation not trifling. I had much conversation with Mr. Lloyd, apart from the rest. I find his views of the Gospel not in the slightest degree tinged with mysticism. He is of the Evangelical, the modern school of Quakerism . . . The more I converse with this good old man the more I respect and love him.[40]

Lloyd's interest in the Brethren became still stronger when Robert Howard, who in 1825 had married his daughter Rachel, joined the Brethren together with his brother, John Eliot Howard. Slowly old Samuel Lloyd made up his mind. In November of 1838 he was baptized in Manchester by Isaac Crewdson,[41] and the final step came on 12 February 1840 when after much conversation with his son-in-law and other Brethren, he sent in his resignation to the Society of Friends. "The step was irrevocable, and my grandfather joined the Brethren."[42] Only a part of his family took the same step. "He and his son, Sampson Lloyd, attended and chiefly sustained a meeting of 'Brethren' held in a room in Waterloo Street, Birmingham."[43]

In characteristic fashion, the Crewdson family of Kendal was related to both the Lloyds of Birmingham and other Quaker families, but it was not always clear how the Crewdsons and other Kendal families first encountered Brethren ideas. In the opening paragraph of his chapter on Westmorland in *Brethren: The Story of a Great Recovery*, David Beattie mused on the bad conditions of roads between Plymouth and Kendal, and upon the "incredible" fact that "in a comparatively short time from the start in Plymouth" an assembly was founded at Kendal. "While it is generally assumed," he wrote, "that the assembly came into being as a result of personal intercourse with early Brethren at the very commencement of the spiritual Movement in the South, yet there appears to be no documentary evidence to support this."[44] Beattie then went on to consider the possibility that it might have been solely under the guidance of the Holy Spirit that these developments took place.

Today, we have rather more evidence than Beattie had on this question, and we naturally turn in the first place to any account given to us by the Crewdsons themselves. William Dillworth Crewdson was the eldest son of the Kendal banker W. D.

---

40. Lowe, *Farm and its Inhabitants*, 65. Beverley had left the Anglican Church and was a congregational pastor. For fuller details, see below, ch. 15.
41. *Inquirer* 1 (Nov 1838) 351.
42. Lloyd, *Lloyds of Birmingham*, 185.
43. Lowe, *Farm and its Inhabitants*, 73.
44. Beattie, *Brethren*, 186.

Crewdson. In 1825 as we noted earlier, he married Sarah Fox of Plymouth, but for some years they remained Quakers as they had been brought up.[45] But, in Sarah Crewdson's words:

> Towards the end of that [first] decade of our [married] pilgrimage, the things of the kingdom of God came more earnestly under our consideration. Christian people from my beloved Plymouth came to us and to other dear friends, whose minds were also in an awakening process as to the great verities of the Christian religion.[46]

Thus it is clear that by 1835, the Crewdsons were in touch with Brethren and their ideas. This is confirmed by some other interesting evidence, which sheds light on one of the leading figures of the Brethren movement.

Six miles south of Kendal is the village of Levens. It was here, in 1832, in the parsonage of the Rev. William Stephens, that a sixteen-year old Irish boy came to study with the rector preparatory to his entering Trinity College, Dublin. His name was William Pennefather, and in the following year he was introduced to William and Sarah Crewdson, who soon after moved to Sizergh Hall, which is only two miles from Levens. The result was that they were frequently in touch with the boy, and a strong and lasting friendship grew up.[47] The fact that they were Quakers and he was an Anglican does not seem to have troubled them. When Pennefather left England in the summer of 1834, he kept in touch by correspondence until he returned a year later for a prolonged period of convalescence after a severe illness.[48] In the course of this correspondence there is an interesting letter, which we shall quote at some length for reasons that will soon become apparent. The extracts are reproduced here exactly as they stand in *The Life and Letters of William Pennefather*.

The first letter was written by William's sister. It is dated 14 March 1835 and was written from Merrion Square, Dublin. A part of it reads as follows:

> Papa is on circuit, and we are leading a very quiet life here. Mr. ——— is in Dublin, and we have the enjoyment of seeing him sometimes. He calls here occasionally and seems to communicate the joy in heavenly things, which he feels. He presses *rejoicing* on believers very much, because he says, "Christ not only died, but is risen, and has purchased everything for us, and believers are children and heirs." This joy in believing, he thinks is the surest way of bringing about deadness to the world. I believe that you know his views about the Church of England: he wishes to draw believers out of it, although he admits there is salvation in it. On this subject he has not spoken to any of

---

45. That the Crewdsons were evangelical Quakers, is clear from their support of the Religious Tract Society. They were the main financial supporters of the Society's Auxiliary at Manchester and Salford; see Religious Tract Society, *31st Annual Report*.
46. [S. Crewdson], *Short Memorial*, 2.
47. R. Braithwaite, *Life of Pennefather*, 14.
48. Ibid., 21–22.

us. Surely we may be living as risen with Christ, whether connected with the Church of England or not. Many real Christians on this ground do not like to associate with Mr. ——— ; but this I cannot enter into when there are so many delightful spots of common meeting. He appears to be engaged from morning till night preaching, expounding, visiting, etc.: he now seems ready to go anywhere either to dine or call, always premising, "If you will allow me to preach;" and he never goes anywhere unless about his Master's business. He says he feels his office principally lies in urging believers to walk worthy of their high and holy calling.[49]

These remarks are followed by a description of a weekly meeting at Powerscourt at which Mr. ——— "read 1 John 1, and spoke beautifully on the Christian's hopes and present comforts," and a brief reference to the "many wild and unsatisfactory opinions" that were voiced at the "prophecy meeting" at Powerscourt in 1834.

In a letter from Pennefather himself to Mrs. Crewdson, he observes:

> My sister has told you that Mr. ——— is now in Dublin: he has kindly called on me several times, and his visits I have greatly enjoyed. He, happily, has never touched on those points on which I cannot agree with him, and which would only disturb us both: I know no-one more calculated to deal with sincere but desponding Christians. The privileges of believers and the enjoyments of heaven are placed by him before the mind with the vividness of reality. He was speaking a good deal one evening on seeing Christ in the Psalms, and what he said was very beautiful: if we view Christ as the speaker in the Psalms, we shall find an additional reason for enjoying the reading of them, . . . [there follows a fairly lengthy outline of this subject], . . . I know not whether I have made myself intelligible. What are your views on the Psalms? I know Mr. I. holds the same opinions as Mr. ———.[50]

Anyone acquainted with the early life and writings of John Nelson Darby will have guessed that he was the person with whom these extracts were concerned. Add to the suspicions, which arise from the account of his teaching, the fact that Darby's sister was married to William Pennefather's uncle,[51] together with the other remarks about the Powerscourt Conferences, and the suspicions become a virtual certainty. Quite apart from the light shed upon Darby's own early attitudes, the implications of this letter are significant. Pennefather speaks of Darby as a name with which Sarah Crewdson will be quite familiar. Only his sister offers any information about Darby, and this is introduced with the words "I believe that you know." Evidently, at the time

---

49. Ibid.

50. Ibid., 25–27. "Mr. I." was possibly Henry Irwin who was the minister at Sandford Chapel, Dublin.

51. It was in the home of William Pennefather's uncle, who in 1841 became Lord Chief Justice of Ireland, that Darby, in 1827–28, had met Francis W. Newman who was tutor to William's cousins; see Stunt, *From Awakening*, 205–6.

of the Quaker crisis in 1835 the Crewdsons were well aware of the Brethren and their opinions. In addition to their familiarity with the Brethren whom they had earlier visited in Plymouth, they were hearing from Pennefather about the part played by Darby and other Brethren in Dublin.[52] So although Mrs. Crewdson said that it was "people from my beloved Plymouth" who caused them to leave the Quakers, evidently she had rather more precise information about the movement than most other inquirers into the beliefs of the Brethren would have had.

Kendal and *The People from Plymouth*

Before we discuss the identity of the "people from . . . Plymouth," we ought to look more closely at the state of affairs in the Quaker community itself. In the same year as Pennefather's letter to Mrs Crewdson (1835), the *Beacon* was published, and by 1836 the division among the Quakers, between evangelicals and the believers in the Inner Light, was rapidly coming to a head. Originally the argument had been about justification by faith and the deity of Christ, but as the evangelicals began to form Scripture study groups and examined their Bibles more closely, they found themselves facing a number of other problems, especially over the question of the sacraments. In the autumn of 1836 "the work of the Yearly Meeting's Committee in Manchester Meeting ended in the resignation of fifty prominent members and heads of families including the author of the *Beacon* and his wife, and other near relatives of the Braithwaites."[53] The secession at Kendal was less definite and matters were more uncertain, but those who left were no less numerous. Naturally the influence of the author of the *Beacon* was important as he was the uncle of William Dillworth Crewdson and was related to many other Kendal Quakers.

In the midst of the sort of uncertainty that faces any people who leave their former communion and do not know where to turn, there were other influences at work. The Crewdsons certainly knew more than most about the Brethren but now "the people from Plymouth" seem to have become rather more insistent. Their number included the young B. W. Newton, whose crusading zeal was as strong as ever. Being related by marriage to Sarah Crewdson, Newton had visited them at Kendal sometime before 1833.[54] Taking advantage of the unrest among Friends during the Beaconite controversy, he published in 1835, a tract entitled *A Remonstrance to the Society of*

---

52. Darby himself was shortly to address the Quakers in print. A number of denominational writers had sought to advise the Friends in their uncertainty. In 1836, Dr. Ralph Wardlaw, an independent minister from Glasgow and formerly a fellow worker of Robert Haldane, published *Friendly Letters to the Society of Friends* to which Darby replied with "Remarks on Light and Conscience" (in the *Christian Witness*, Oct 1836, reprinted in Kelly, *Writings of Darby*, 3:57–72. In this work, significantly, he eschewed ecclesiastical questions as such, but went deeper, deprecating the unsatisfactory teaching of other Christians on the subject of the Holy Spirit.

53. [Thomas], *J. Bevan Braithwaite*, 72–73.

54. See below, 46.

Friends.[55] Two years later he went with his wife to Kendal and continued his mission among the wavering seceders. We are fortunate to have a letter that was written partly by Newton and partly by his wife, from the home of the Crewdsons at Sizergh, near Kendal, when he was there at this time.[56]

Hannah Newton begins the letter with remarks about her husband's health, and then continues:

> His engagements are not very laborious just now—altho' the Friends at Kendal are too kindly disposed to allow him much leisure, & he has also been busy with Edward Wakefield in visiting those who are in communion with us. We have had visitors at our lodgings very soon after breakfast and almost the whole day in succession, & invitations more numerous than we well know how to manage in the uncertainty of our tarriance here; so that the door seems wide open, and as there seems no reserve in the consideration of any scriptural subject amongst the Friends here, as is the case in other places, I can hardly think it would be right to leave the field immediately, unless the want at Plymouth should be very urgent; and if Mr. Darby should come they will be enriched at once.

She then regrets the news they have received that Sir Alexander Campbell has a sore throat, and therefore is unable to do any teaching, and says that if Darby cannot get to Plymouth, her husband

> would feel it his place to return home as quickly as possible; but otherwise I think he would much desire, after having staid here a week or ten days longer, to see a little of the friends at Liverpool & Manchester—the former of whom are just ready to faint and give up a little meeting they have hitherto held on Sunday mornings—& the latter in danger of settling into a sectarian society again, which Benjamin would wish at least to have an opportunity of testifying against, before it is done and E. Wakefield has offered to accompany him to Manchester with this view.

Evidently Newton's primary object was to encourage the seceding Quakers to form what he regarded as independent and nonsectarian churches. This is confirmed in Newton's own part of the letter, when he writes:

---

55. Newton, *Remonstrance*. When Newton's uncle Joseph Treffry replied anonymously ([Treffry], *Strictures*), Newton published a further pamphlet (Newton, *Vindication*).

56. Tantalizingly, the date of the letter is given as April, and the last figure of the postmark has made no contact with the paper, so only "183" shows. From internal evidence however, the date must be 1837. There is mention of the meeting of ex-Quakers at Manchester, which only began in autumn 1836; also the letter mentions the possibility of Darby arriving in Plymouth, which was impossible in 1838 as he was in Switzerland. By 1839, the friendliness of Anna Braithwaite would have been out of the question. April 1837 must be the date, and the letter is transcribed in the Fry MS (JRULM, CBA 7049) 296–99.

There is a great opening of preaching here. I have had the opportunity of preaching three times to large congregations and I do think [Captain Percy] Hall when he comes will find an open door. Tonight we are to have a reading meeting at the room where we meet to break bread. The Friends are kind and courteous: there were several present at the meeting last evening for preaching: but if anything is done among them it must be, I believe, by striving gradually to soften their prejudices which are at present very great and we are very feeble. Tomorrow I hope if the Lord will, to go to Hawkshead to see Mr. [Samuel] Lloyd who is a friend of Hall's and Darby's and very likeminded with us.

We may gather from these extracts some useful information. First, although many Friends were in doubt about their position as Friends, relatively few in April 1837 were committed to a Brethren position. The group at Manchester, who are described as being "in danger of falling back into a sectarian society again" evidently wanted to remain Friends, and therefore in Newton's eyes would remain sectarian. They seem to have retained this position, in spite of Newton's testimony against it, as in April 1838 they are referred to in the *Inquirer* as a "chapel of evangelical Friends,"[57] though in the previous month the same journal refers to them as an "infant congregation, now assuming the character of a Christian Church," to whom "many eyes and many hearts must be turning, with keen observation and affectionate sympathy."[58]

A second point from Newton's letter is that it confirms that there was already an assembly of Brethren in Kendal, by 1837, but with only a few Friends in it.[59] One of these as we shall see was William Crewdson himself. There was, however, opposition from certain other Friends. One of the leading Kendal Quakers, who had considerable doubts about the young man from Plymouth, was Anna Braithwaite, a sister-in-law of Crewdson's mother. With a matriarchal position of authority she was to remain for the rest of her life both evangelical and Quaker. One is hardly surprised to find that Hannah Newton was a little apprehensive of her. "Anna Braithwaite has been very courteous towards us, and we are to spend an evening with them next week, but I do not know how dearest Benjn. will get on with her. She is exceedingly pained by their little meeting, but what her hopes or desires are I do not know."

In fact Anna Braithwaite was trying very hard to heal the differences in her own Society. Years before, she had been to America to try and reconcile opponents in the Hicksite controversy. At the time of the troubles in Kendal she was suffering from illness and therefore was less able to keep in touch than she would have wished. In

---

57. *Inquirer* 1 (Apr 1838) 124; cf. Pierson, *James Wright*, 158.
58. *Inquirer* 1 (Mar 1838) 84.
59. "The Christian Brethren . . . originally met for worship in the Whitehall lecture room, in 1836," Anon., *Guide to Kendal*, 14. Cf. "The Christian Brethren . . . emanated chiefly from the Society of Friends in Kendal. They first assembled in regular congregation about 1837 in one of the public room of the Whitehall . . . buildings," Nicholson, *Annals*, 167.

her Memoranda at the beginning of 1838, she wrote: "I have longed to go to meeting, my heart is full of love and sympathy for my friends. I think I do comprehend their varied views and conflicts, and gladly would I break down the partition wall, which exists, but I believe the language applies to these things, 'this kind goeth not out but by prayer and fasting.'"[60]

It can thus be seen that Newton's mission was rather less simple than it might have seemed at first sight. But in spite of the opposition, some Friends had supported him. Hannah Newton explained at some length:

> We are very agreeably surprised in the state of Wm & S Crewdson, at present finding them in cordial union with our views of Christian fellowship, in practice as well as theory, and altogether more humble loving & spiritually minded than I have ever known them before. Sarah still clings a little to the idea of the Church of England but it is very faintly & with the confession that it is the repugnance of her heart to the self-denial she sees involved in the principles of the Plymouth brethren, that hinders her desire entirely to embrace them: whilst on the other hand she has received so many testimonies to the blessing which has already attended Wm in the position he has taken, as convince her that it is at least the right one for him and I am sure she will not be happy where he is not . . . Their union is wonderfully cemented since I was last their guest at Kendal, so that indeed I do feel that the Lord has done great things for them whereof I am glad.

We may observe at this point that Sarah Crewdson's liking for the Church of England may well have been due to the influence of the saintly character of the young William Pennefather, who evidently made a great impression on the family and remained their lifelong friend.[61] The previous time Hannah Newton was their guest at Kendal must have been before 1833 as it was in that year that they moved to Sizergh Hall,[62] which she now goes on to describe:

> It is indeed more splendid or rather *poetically grand* than even I had imagined—tho' dear Amy James's description had prepared me for a great deal. I can only say with regard to it that they seem to me to have too much of the mind of Christ & of desire for conformity to him, long to remain encumbered with so much that is certainly not of the Father but of the world, tho' what will be their way of deliverance I do not see & certainly it will not be easy. Sarah's mind is evidently uneasy, her understanding being more opened than William's to the nature of Christ's kingdom as altogether heavenly & taking his followers into practical conformity with his humiliation *now* just in proportion as they are faithful.

60. Braithwaite, *Memoirs of Anna Braithwaite*, 154.

61. According to Dr. Mingins, William and Sarah Crewdson did later leave the Brethren to join an Anglican congregation, Mingins, *Beacon Controversy*, 220.

62. R. Braithwaite, *Life and Letters*, 12.

This ascetic attitude was linked to their ecclesiastical position. In Newton's mind renunciation of luxury came into the same category as separation from denominations and sectarian groups. Thus his wife writes a little later of another Friend, Edward Wakefield, whose family had been associated with the Crewdsons in business for many years,[63] as one who is "altogether in heart & understanding like one of our own brethren, I believe quite loathing the elegancies by which he is surrounded, wishing to be free tho' scarcely knowing how."[64]

In fact there is recurring evidence that, in spite of the emphasis on an unsectarian communion, Brethren had already come to stand for separation from other denominations rather than communion with all Christians. The references to "our views" and "our own brethren" give Newton's mission a decidedly proselytic flavor, with a principle aim of "getting *them* to join *us*." In addition to this Hannah Newton seems to expect a nonsectarian assembly to show all the characteristics of other Brethren assemblies. We may conclude these extracts with a passage, which, to many readers, may well seem as sectarian as any:

> Wm [Crewdson] does not clearly see the different dispensations to the Jews & to the Ch. nor is he yet much interested in prophecy. But the Lord giveth more grace unto the humble and I do think he is of that number & now having cast in his lot with brethren to whom so much light has been given, he will not I trust be able to close his eyes howsoever the flesh might desire it.

Newton's labors at Kendal were not without results, and the Brethren assembly prospered there.[65] David Beattie tells us that the names of Crewdson and Wakefield were well represented among its members.[66] We can accept this, but we must reject his speculations about how the movement at Kendal began, as the evidence for direct contact is undeniable. In fact this episode seems to be the occasion of part of the following criticism leveled at the Brethren a few years later in the *Congregational Magazine*:

---

63. The Kendal Bank was established in 1788 and was the firm of Messrs. Wakefield, Crewdson and Co. See Anon., *Guide to Kendal*, 15.

64. Edward William Wakefield (1799–1858) was a son of John Wakefield, whom the Quakers had disowned on account of his gunpowder production (Punshon, *Portrait in Grey*, 115). I am informed by Mr. J. W. Marshall of Kendall (letter 2 Feb 1971) that the earliest brethren meeting was prior to 1837, when some 10 or 12 friends met at Wakefield's home, Birklands, on the outskirts of Kendal, for the breaking of bread. "The ornamental pond in the grounds was often used for baptisms." The importance of Edward and Susannah (née Birkbeck) Wakefield in the establishment of the Brethren in Kendal is confirmed in an e-mail (7 Jun 2006) from Mr. John Cartmell whose dissertation (Glasgow, 1999) was entitled "Friends and Brethren in Kendal: A Critical Analysis of the Brethren Church in Kendal from the Quaker Meeting between 1835 and 1858." An early product of Wakefield's move from Quaker to Brethren was his pamphlet *Brief Remarks on . . . water baptism* published in 1836.

65. The chapel, which the Brethren built in 1857, near Stramongate Bridge, could accommodate upwards of three hundred, Anon. *Guide to Kendal*, 13.

66. Beattie, *Brethren*, 187.

They seek individuals who are wealthy with singular devotedness. Journeys from Plymouth to Taunton, and from Devonshire to Westmoreland have been multiplied, to secure a person whose coffers are well-filled, or whose names would be likely to aid their cause.[67]

The journeys from Plymouth to Taunton refer to Richard Ball's association with the movement, to which we shall refer shortly.

Developments in the South of England, and the Howard Family

We have dealt at some length with the events and personalities at Kendal and in the North, as we have been fortunate in having fairly extensive material for reconstructing these events. When however, we turn to other links between Quakers and Brethren, the material is less forthcoming. One source however, is particularly useful. At the beginning of 1838, certain evangelical Friends (including John Eliot Howard) began to publish a monthly journal entitled the *Inquirer* from which we have quoted already.[68] The Prospectus of this journal explained that it "originated with that portion of this [Quaker] Society which has received the doctrine of justification by faith."[69] Although the emphasis of the editor changed in 1839 when he became more concerned to establish the true doctrine of the Church of God, the first year of publication (1838) shows great interest in the affairs of seceding Quakers, and their problems. Each month a column of "intelligence" was published which proves invaluable for our purposes, and which is particularly informative about baptisms. These frequently took place at Baptist Churches though the newly baptized often became Brethren and not Baptists.

In June 1837, Grace Spence was baptized in the Wellington Baptist Church by John Dyer[70] and in August Charles and Sarah Fox of Wellington were baptized by Mr. Davis the Baptist minister of Tottenham.[71] It is not clear where the latter two were baptized, though it was probably in a Baptist church at Tottenham, where as yet there was no Brethren assembly. Sarah Fox was a sister of William Crewdson, and her family would take a leading part in the Wellington assembly.[72] It was her son, Dillworth

---

67. Anon, "Plymouth Brethren," 704.

68. The *Inquirer* was probably edited by J. E. Howard. Almost the only signed article in the magazine is the first one on "Sacrifice" over the initials IEH; *Inquirer* 1 (1838) 3–13.

69. *Inquirer* 1 (Jan 1838) 2.

70. Ibid., 1 (Feb 1838) 64. Thanks to the researches of her Australian descendant, Ms. Julia Crawley, it is clear that Grace Spence was a member of a Quaker family from Birstwith in Yorkshire and that a few years later she became the second wife of the Brethren teacher, Sir Alexander Cockburn-Campbell.

71. Ibid., 1 (Feb 1838) 64.

72. The Wellington assembly may have been established before 1837. Sir Edward Denny the Brethren hymn writer, whose sister Elizabeth married John Bellett's brother George, lived at Werescot. John Bellett's cousin Richard was living nearby at Sampford-Arundel. William Jarratt, who moved to Plymouth in 1832 to join the Brethren, was a son of the vicar of Wellington; Stunt, *From Awakening* 287n17 (where the reference to John Hill's Diary should read 14b and not 146), 294.

Crewdson Fox, who edited the *Wellington Hymn Book*, which is but a variation of other Brethren collections of hymns.[73]

Also in August, Richard Ball, a leading evangelical Quaker from Taunton, who had published several books and who had taken part in the Beaconite Controversy in 1835, was baptized by B. W. Newton, at the Baptist chapel in Exeter.[74] His change of allegiance was probably the occasion of the *Congregational Magazine*'s allusion to the Brethren's proselytizing journeys to Taunton.[75] Evidently Ball had links with Bristol as he had moved there by 1850.[76] Two months after his own baptism, his wife Mary followed his example, though she was baptized "at Bethesda Chapel, Great George Street, Bristol, by its pastor, H. Craik."[77] Richard Ball became an important figure among Brethren, and a significant voice in the current Quaker discussions, as he published a small book,[78] in which he recommended evangelical Friends to a careful perusal of Charles Hargrove's *Reasons for retiring from the Established Church*.[79] Later, Ball was associated with the Brethren in London who promoted interest in missionary work in China, through the work of the Chinese Evangelization Society and later the China Inland Mission. Hudson Taylor's first biographers, referring to Ball's work in the production of *The Gleaner in the Missionary Field*, describe him as a "man of literary gift as well as spiritual insight."[80] He also published a powerful indictment of exclusive practices among Brethren, in 1851, entitled *Principles and their Results*.[81]

Another Quaker to be baptized in Bristol, at Bethesda, was James Ireland Wright.[82] This was the father of the James Wright who was George Muller's son-in-law and successor at the Ashley Down Orphanage. The latter was only eleven years old in 1837 when his father was baptized together with his two daughters, Mary and Rachel. James Wright (Jr.) was baptized two years later.[83]

Most influential of all the Quakers who became Brethren were Robert and John Eliot Howard, sons of the famous meteorologist, Luke Howard with whom they were partners in the pharmaceutical company of Luke Howard and Co. at Plaistow.[84] Both

---

73. [Fox], *Wellington Hymn Book*. This collection is omitted in both Julian, *Dictionary of Hymnology*, and Andrews, "Brethren Hymnology."

74. *Inquirer* 1 (Feb 1838) 64.

75. See above, n67.

76. See Ball, *Principles*, which was written from Portland House, Bristol, in Dec 1850.

77. *Inquirer* 1 (Feb 1838) 64.

78. Ball, *Dissuasive Considerations*.

79. Hargrove, *Reasons for retiring*. Hargrove had been one of the earliest Brethren in Ireland.

80. Taylor, *Hudson Taylor in Early Years*, 90n.

81. See above, n76.

82. *Inquirer* 1 (Feb 1838) 64.

83. Pierson, *James Wright*, 3. James Wright (junior) was baptized at Brook Street Chapel, Tottenham in 1839 (p. 9), though he only finally resigned his membership of the Society of Friends in 1845 (pp. 28–29). This again shows just how fluid allegiances were in many cases.

84. For Luke Howard's earlier career, see above, ch. 10–11.

of them were brought up as Quakers and married into Quaker families. Robert's wife, whom he married in 1825, was Samuel Lloyd's daughter Rachel (1803–92),[85] while John married William Crewdson's sister, Maria. We do not know when Robert left the Society of Friends,[86] but John Howard and his wife were baptized in August 1836,[87] after coming to an understanding of the doctrine of justification by faith, a year previously, and in October they resigned from the Society of Friends.[88] For a year or two he was associated with the Baptist Chapel at Tottenham where he was engaged in a good deal of local evangelism until he founded a Brethren assembly there in 1838.[89] In fact it is possible that Howard had previously been associated with Brethren in other localities, as his friend J. J. Penstone recalled being introduced to the Brethren and becoming acquainted with Howard in 1836.[90] Before he left the Quakers, Howard edited a newspaper, called the *Patriot*, in which the controversies among Friends were discussed.[91] Almost certainly he was also the editor of the *Inquirer*, and wrote numerous articles in it. With some reason therefore did his biographer write that "J.E.H. was actively engaged in the controversy amongst Friends."[92] In 1838 his father, Luke Howard, who had been a leading figure among Friends, and who can be seen in a contemporary picture of the Friends' yearly meeting, was disowned by the Society and in reply published a protest.[93] He spent his last years at the home of his son Robert, at Bruce Grove, Tottenham.

Both Robert and John Eliot Howard played some part in the controversies among Brethren in the late 1840s. Neatby suggests that Robert Howard was more kindly disposed to Darby's position, in the earlier stages.[94] However both brothers eventually came out strongly in favor of the independence of the local church and sided with Müller and Craik over the Bethesda Question.[95]

85. H. Lloyd, *Quaker Lloyds*, 287.

86. There is no indication in Anon., *Brief Record of . . . Robert Howard*.

87. The date is given as 28 July 1836 in Pickering, *Chief Men*, 59, but in the journal of Howard's sister, the date is 26 Aug 1836 or shortly before: see L.H[oward], *Memoranda*, 233. Rachel Howard's own uncertainty and anguish at her brother's action is characteristic of many Quakers at the time. Very shortly before she died she was baptized as well.

88. Fifty years later, the widowed Maria Howard recalled: "On the 6th October 1836 we resigned our connection with the Society of Friends, and a few days afterwards we renounced the Quaker garb, a step far more painful and formidable than can at this distance in time be understood." H. Lloyd, *Quaker Lloyds*, 265.

89. Before Brook St. Chapel was opened in 1839 they met in a house in Stoneleigh South; see Anon., *Brook St. Chapel*.

90. Penstone, *Caution*, 3. For a fuller account of Penstone, see below, ch. 3.

91. The writer has been unable to trace any copies of this newspaper. There are references to it in [A. B. Thomas], *J. Bevan Braithwaite*, 72.

92. Pickering, *Chief Men*, 59.

93. L. Howard, *Appeal to the Christian Public*. See also below, ch. 15n102.

94. Neatby, *History*, 178.

95. Ibid., 178–80; cf. R. Howard, *Church Principles*. J. E Howard, *Caution*, which went through

The Howards were not the only Friends at Tottenham who threw in their lot with the Brethren. The husband of Robert Howard's sister-in-law, Deborah Lloyd, remained a Quaker, but his sister, Mary Stacey, followed the example of the Howards. When John Bevan Braithwaite, who also remained a Quaker, visited London in 1838, he wrote to his cousin in October:

> We greatly enjoyed thy Aunt [Mary] Stacey's company, although we should have had a greater degree of enjoyment and mutual instruction could we have seen eye to eye on some important points (with respect to what are technically called the Plymouth views), yet their visit was less alloyed by our differences than might have been expected; and we look back upon it with no small pleasure. The conversations, which I had with thy Aunt Mary did not by any means remove the conviction I previously had that the views just alluded to are not likely to promote the growth of true religion.[96]

Mary Stacey's "Plymouth views" also remained unchanged, and she was a significant member of the Tottenham assembly, which developed important missionary interests. Elizabeth Wilson, a member of another Quaker family at Kendal (many of whom also became Brethren), and in later years a CIM missionary, recalled meeting Hudson Taylor at Mary Stacey's home.

> He came for one of the little rests he so much needed and that Miss Stacey rejoiced to give him, leaving him the run of the garden and library and protecting him from much company and conversation. He was then a medical student and living I think on very little . . . No doubt the excellent dinners now and then did him good, as well as the ministry of the Tottenham meeting.[97]

Before we turn to consider the effects this influx of Friends may have had upon Brethren life and practice, we should perhaps note in conclusion the continuing solidarity these former Friends retained. Without going again into the intricacies of family trees, which are perhaps best left alone as they come down to present times, we should just observe the following. Of Robert Howard's children, his three sons' marriages are significant. Theodore, who was later to be a home director of the China Inland Mission married into the old Quaker family of Jowitts. Samuel Lloyd Howard married Caroline who was the daughter of Richard Ball of Taunton and Bristol. Their brother, Robert Luke Howard, married Henrietta Maria Fox who was a daughter of Henry and Rachel (née Crewdson) Fox. Henrietta Maria's sister, Rachel Crewdson Fox married John Edward, one of the sons of Edward Wakefield whom we observed accompanying B. W. Newton on his visits to Kendal. Similarly John Eliot Howard's daughter Sarah Maria married Thomas Fox, a cousin of the two Fox sisters whom we

---

many editions and was an expansion of the introduction that he wrote for Ball, *Principles*.

96. [Thomas], *J. Bevan Braithwaite*, 81.
97. Taylor, *Hudson Taylor in Early Years*, 171n.

have just mentioned.[98] It is not always clear whether these families were Quakers or Brethren, but evidently the old family solidarity was maintained.

Quaker Cultural Influences on Brethren

As we come to consider in conclusion the importance of the influence that Friends may have exercised on early brethren, we must guard against the dangers of false generalization. Clearly Quakers were of greater significance in Kendal and Tottenham than in Plymouth and Wellington as, in the former places, they formed the mainstay of the assemblies. We should also bear in mind that sometimes in such ecclesiastical development, the Brethren identity was not yet fully defined and the final ecclesiastical destinations of several notable brethren like B. W. Newton and S. P. Tregelles, as well as less prominent figures like Frederick Whitfield would be elsewhere.

One way in which the Quaker influence may have been important is in the question of the implications of separation. Many Friends were part of a Society, which appreciated the importance of culture and learning, and was seriously engaged in scientific enquiry and pursuing literary interests. The Kendal Friends were well acquainted with the romantic poets of the Lake District, and there is little to suggest in Pennefather's later correspondence with the Crewdsons that they abandoned these interests, though in itself this is only negative evidence. One recalls, however, that Newton and his wife were very anxious that the Crewdsons should give up their splendid mansion at Sizergh. To Pennefather's grief they did move to another house in 1846 but we do not know anything about its size or nature.[99] There seems to be no strong reason for assuming that Friends who became Brethren greatly changed their way of living, other than in the very visible abandonment of the "Quaker garb."

Hudson Taylor's biographers refer to his first impression of the Quakers. "Passing Devonshire House in the city, he was struck by the calm and gracious bearing of both men and women as they passed out from 'Yearly Meeting,' in their old time Quaker dress . . . Later on he found that the Howards of Tottenham had been brought up as Friends, and learnt from their beautiful lives the value of much that is distinctively 'Friendly' in thought and spirit."[100] Along with this positive assessment, however, we must bear in mind the testimony of a Quaker granddaughter of Robert Howard who recently portrayed her grandfather's household as a very strict and austere one, and suggested that this was the reason for her father's becoming an Anglican.[101] Obviously much more extensive research would be required to establish any reliable evidence one way or the other, but it is true to say that many Brethren who trace their historical spiritual ancestry to the Tottenham community, have often been less rigidly "sepa-

---

98. These further genealogical observations are based on the sources listed in n17 and n18.
99. R. Braithwaite, *Life of Pennefather*, 187–88, 191.
100. Taylor, *Hudson Taylor in Early Years*, 117–18.
101. E. F. Howard, *Downstream*, 14.

rate" from other denominations and cultural interests, than many other Brethren. We should observe perhaps that Mary Stacey felt free to attend all of the first twenty Barnet and Mildmay Conferences sponsored by the Rev. William Pennefather.[102] Similarly we should remember that T. P. Rossetti, whose spiritual home in England was the Tottenham assembly, retained for the rest of his life his literary and historical interests[103] just as John Eliot Howard maintained his scientific ones.[104]

The Ecclesiastical Dimension

Changing Attitudes to Ministry

Another and perhaps more important question is how far the Quakers carried over their ecclesiastical and theological ideas into their new surroundings. Admittedly those, who were seceding, were also rethinking their attitudes, but it would have been perfectly natural if they retained some of their earlier preconceptions. The following suggestion is of necessity somewhat conjectural, but it seems worthy of consideration. The traditional Quaker doctrine was that of the "Inner Light." This gave rise to a mystical understanding of the work of the Holy Spirit. The evangelical Friends were very anxious to insist that this "Inner Light" could never supersede Scripture, but frequently would not go further than this in modifying the mystical emphasis of the Quakers. The natural tendency would be a belief in "impulsive" guidance of the Holy Spirit both in ministry and church government. Of course some former Quakers like Newton and Tregelles came out strongly *against* impulsive ministry and worship, and were strongly in favor of recognized teachers and elders, but this need not have been a general change among seceding Quakers. Bearing this in mind, the considerable influx of Quakers into Brethren circles is perhaps more significant than has been generally realized.

In the earliest days of the Brethren movement, it is clear that the ministry and government of the assembly were far from impulsive or democratic. Teachers were recognized by their gift, elders were acknowledged, and there was full communion with Bethesda chapel at Bristol, where George Müller and Henry Craik were two recognized "pastors." At Plymouth in the early days of the movement, Benjamin Newton

---

102. R. Braithwaite, *Life of Pennefather*, 306.

103. In Pietrocola-Rossetti, *Religione di Stato*, 73, he castigates contemporary art and literature. "Le arti belle son cadute,—si sporcano tele, ma non si fanno disegni corretti. La scultura cerca di ritemprarsi su'modelli greci, e imitando è mediocre, creando è ridicola e volgare, La lirica ha dato gli ultimi suoi gemiti . . . e poi è morta in mezzo a un'arcadia di parole patriotiche e di concettini sguaiati." But this is an assessment of the contemporary arts not a judgment of the arts in general. He happily quotes Dante and Ariosto and even translated Christina Rossetti's *Goblin Market* and Lewis Carroll's *Alice in Wonderland* for Italian readers.

104. For J. E. Howard's scientific interests see the article in *ODNB*, which, while mentioning his founding of the Brook Street Chapel, avoids making any reference to his involvement with the Brethren.

and James Harris were elders with sufficient authority to interrupt ministry when they thought it was unprofitable and there was no shibboleth against the preparation of a sermon in advance, before its delivery. However, by the time of the controversies of the late 1840s much of this had changed. With the notable exception of Plymouth, any recognized government in the local assembly was frequently nonexistent and was often replaced by a meeting of all male members of the church. Similarly, by 1840 one of the publicly defined principles of the Brethren was their "willingness to allow all whom they so acknowledge as Christians to speak, if they can speak to the profit of those assembled"[105] and this liberty of ministry often came to mean "any-man-ministry." Similarly, the advance preparation of sermons came to be regarded as so improper that T. P. Haffner of the Plymouth assembly maintained in writing that when Newton did this, he "did thus *practically* deny the *present* leadings and guidance of the Spirit of God."[106]

The Development of Darby's Views

The question we must ask ourselves then, is how this transformation took place in less than twenty years. One immediate answer may lie in the development of J. N. Darby's thinking during these years—a development, the slow stages of which one can certainly discern in his pamphlets and letters. The first important step is his beginning to teach the doctrine of the "Ruin of the Church." It is possible that his thought in this matter may have been influenced by Irvingite ideas that were prevalent in the church where he was working in Geneva between 1837 and 1840.[107] It was from Geneva in October 1840 that he wrote in a letter, as if in answer to an inquiry about a new opinion, "As to the ruin of the Church, the theory came for me after the consciousness of it, and even now, the theory is but a small thing to my mind."[108]

A paper attributed to Darby, entitled *The Apostasy of the Successive Dispensations* had appeared in the Plymouth periodical the *Christian Witness* in October 1836, and had been preceded in the two previous years by papers written by different authors, tending in the same direction. A very definite statement of Darby's thinking in this respect appears in the course of his lectures at Geneva in 1840, on the subject of *The*

---

105. Report in the *Limerick Chronicle*, 17 Sep 1840, quoted in the *Courier* (Hobart, Tasmania), 2 Mar 1841.

106. T. P. Haffner's *Confession*, 5–6, quoted in Tregelles *Three Letters*, 30–31. The somewhat elusive Thomas Pittman Haffner (c. 1819–1901) lived in Plymouth for only a few years. He was admitted to Lincoln's Inn, Nov 1838; married, at Heavitree, Devon, Charlotte Whittle (daughter of Lieutenant Whittle), 10 Dec 1839; was living with his wife and four servants in Honiton, Devon in 1841; his daughter was born in Plymouth 1847 but the family later moved to Moretonhampstead where he died. (IGI and census records).

107. Stunt, *From Awakening*, 307–8.

108. Darby, *Letters*, 1:42.

hopes of the Church of God, which dealt mainly with prophetic subjects and may have occasioned his comment (quoted above) in October. Here we find Darby asking:

> Has the Church kept itself in this goodness of God? Truly Christendom has become completely corrupted; the dispensation of the Gentiles has been found unfaithful: can it be restored? No: impossible. As the Jewish dispensation was cut off, the Christian dispensation will be also.[109]

Once Darby had come to accept the idea of the "Fallen Condition of the present dispensation," then the idea that there could be a "local church" based on the example of the early church was strongly undermined. This latter view is expressed at some length in his pamphlet *On the Formation of Churches*, which was published in Switzerland in about 1840, and which, when translated into English, was significantly entitled *Reflections on the Ruined Condition of the Church; and on the efforts made by Churchmen and Dissenters to Restore it to its Primitive Order*. In this tract, Darby came to the conclusion that there was no longer any possibility of founding a local church. He prefaced his pamphlet however, with the observation that he was "bound by the strongest ties of affection of love in Christ to many who belong to bodies assuming the title of *Church of God*" and that he had "studiously avoided all collusion [collision] of judgment with his brethren on this subject, although he has often conversed with them concerning it."[110]

Once his mind was made up, Darby's attitudes began to harden so that by the time he was back in London in August 1843 he had published his *Remarks on the State of the Church*, which had been completed in October 1842, and where he had suggested with regard to the Lord's Supper: "Never make any regulations; the Holy Spirit will guide you if you rest on Him, and if you rely on God who is ever faithful."[111]

Clearly, however, Darby still did not go as far as some wanted him to go in the matter of the role of the Spirit. Tregelles recalled (and we should remember that the accuracy of his memory was well established) that "once (in the end of 1843) he [Darby] said, in allusion to the manner in which some Brethren spoke of the Spirit in connection with the assembly, that 'if they talked in such a way, it might be truly said of them that they met in the name of the Holy Spirit and not in the name of Christ.'"[112] Evidently Darby's time in England for several months until he returned to France in March 1844, resulted in considerable dissension on this very question of the Spirit's role especially in ministry, and it was this unrest in London that according to Tregelles gave rise to Wigram's tract *On Ministry in the Word*, in 1844. Here Wigram took a far

---

109. Kelly, *CW of Darby*, 2:320–21.
110. Ibid., 1:138.
111. Ibid., 1:274.
112. Tregelles, *Three Letters*, 11.

from "impulsive" view of ministry as his pamphlet was in line with earlier Brethren's views which supported a "stated but not exclusive ministry."[113]

The final and logical step of the course Darby had taken was the abandonment of the office of elder in the local church, which according to Darby could no longer exist. God might raise up elders and if he did, believers should recognize and submit to them, but this was a charismatic gift rather than an office—a suggestion to which Darby gave fullest expression in his *Scriptural views on the subject of elders* in 1849.[114]

So we find that what had been "but a small thing in my mind" had become the basis of a complete change in Darby's thinking and indeed in the thinking of the numerous Brethren who accepted his exclusive discipline in the Bethesda affair. However, we need to ask the question whether we can account for the idea's wide acceptance among Brethren, solely in terms of the persuasiveness or forcefulness of Darby's character? To this writer it seems highly probable that the influx of evangelical Friends among the Brethren was of crucial importance in the process.

Receptive Former Quakers

Two months after Darby's return to England in 1843, he wrote from Kendal in November as follows: "We had a blessed meeting at Liverpool; I think that the brethren enjoyed themselves more than at preceding ones; perhaps less of fresh knowledge, but more solid and more serious, and new souls that found there precious links with the brethren, several localities being newly opened."[115] Reading between the lines, may we not perhaps conclude that Darby was finding the meetings in the North where there were numerous former Friends, highly congenial to his own attitudes? It is possible that we are reading too much into the evidence, but we should observe that in his discussion of the nature of the Church in 1849, Darby is very emphatic when dealing with the ministry of the word that "liberty has existed and still exists among the Quakers," though not among other denominations.[116]

The really significant evidence that encourages us to conclude that it was Quaker influence that led to such a wide acceptance of Darby's novel ideas, is the fact that they were accepted by many "open" brethren who did not accept Darby's other pronouncements.[117] Both in the matter of "open" ministry and the government of the local as-

---

113. Ibid., 12–13. I have expanded on this below in ch. 12nn24–28 (Stunt, "Elitist Leadership," 333–34).

114. Kelly, *CW of Darby*, 4:181–227.

115. Darby, *Letters*, 1:66.

116. Kelly, *CW of Darby*, 4:138.

117. Another example of Quaker influence among "open" brethren can be found in the person of Henry Bewley of Willow Park, Booterstown, Co. Dublin. He was an important figure in the early history of Merrion Hall, but at first had sided with Darby (see Neatby, *History*, 150n2). He was a member of a respected Quaker family whose coffee shops were for many years the delight of polite society in Dublin.

sembly the newer position was widespread outside exclusive circles. Whereas the early Brethren had recognized official elders and even pastors, many who rejected Darby's "Bethesda discipline," nevertheless came to accept the idea of the "Ruin of the Church" and as a result rejected the office of elder. The Howards' assembly at Tottenham is an interesting case in point. One suspects that they had seen too much of Quaker yearly meetings for them to support Darby in his opposition to the independence of the local church, but the Tottenham assembly had (and still has) an "open" oversight meeting to which any man in the assembly, who believes that he is an elder, may come.

This is a charismatic view of eldership rather than one of office, and therefore very near to Darby's own rather hesitant attitude as we find it in his *Scriptural views upon the subject of elders*. Here he writes:

> I have then in the word of God very clear authorities for recognizing those who are in the position in question . . . [but] To demand the establishment of elders is at once to plunge oneself into all sorts of questions on the subject of their establishment, . . . Who will choose them? Who will establish them? Who will lay on hands? If everyone is not agreed, there is a new sect. . . . Meanwhile, I obey the word in recognizing those who have the rule over us . . . Although they have not been named, I can recognize those who do a good work, and I would even recognize them in their work although they had entered thereon irregularly, and although the pretension of reconstituting the Church places them in a position which we cannot recognize as belonging to them.[118]

Conclusion

In these latter paragraphs we have spent some time establishing that the development of Darby's belief in the ruin of the church led to a serious change in his views on ministry and authority in the assembly between 1839–49. This development was ignored by Neatby and others, who have been inclined to treat Darby's thinking as a static body of thought. The question that we may now be able to answer is why the development of Darby's thought became very largely the pattern for Brethren development generally. The suggestion of this paper is that, thanks to the Beaconite controversy and other causes of dissatisfaction, there had been a significant influx of former Quakers into the ranks of the Brethren in the 1830s. This meant that there was a growing number of Brethren between 1836 and 1846 whose formative years had had been spent among Friends. Coming from a background of impulsive ministerial attitudes these former Quakers found it easy to accept Darby's ideas. Indeed this positive reception of his ideas may have encouraged Darby's own thinking.

One further piece of significant evidence for this thesis is to be found in a tract whose author is not given, though he (or possibly she) is described as an "ex-member

---

118. Kelly, *CW of Darby*, 4:225–27.

of the Society of Friends." The basic theme of the pamphlet is that Open communion and liberty of ministry can be the only basis for Christians gathering together. The fourth edition was published in 1840 and evidently these ideas had been circulating for a while beforehand and the tract notes that earlier editions had met with not a little approval.[119] This does indeed lend further weight to the suggestion that it was the influence of former Friends that altered the original emphasis of early brethren teaching. Where in the earliest period the cry had been that "the blood of the Lamb" was to be the basis for the union of saints, there was now a decisive shift to make the *mode of gathering*, with especial emphasis on an impulsive "Liberty of Ministry," the basis for union. Perhaps Darby's success was more dependent on the fallow ground of Quaker experience, than anyone realized.

---

119. Anon., *Open Communion with Liberty of Ministry*. A previous edition reached A. N. Groves in India early in 1838, see [H. B. Groves], *Memoir*, 382.

3

John Jewell Penstone, Quaker and Plymouth Brother[1]

Origins and Early Brethren

AT LEAST SEVEN GENERATIONS of Penstone ancestors were born and had lived in Stanford in the Vale, Berkshire, before John Jewell Penstone (1817–1902, hereafter sometimes abbreviated to "JJP") was born in Clerkenwell, London, in 1817. His father, John Penstone (1792–1840) was the eldest of a large family and although the parish register entry of his marriage hasn't survived, we have a sworn statement, made in June 1816, of his intention to marry Ann Jewell of the parish of Saint James, Clerkenwell, Middlesex—a statement, which accompanied his request for a marriage license.[2] JJP's mother was a daughter of Joseph Jewell who also came from Stanford in the Vale and who had been attracted to the Quaker communion when he came to London.[3] It was through this maternal grandfather, whom he described as "a beloved and aged servant

---

1. In 1972 the *Journal of the Christian Brethren Research Fellowship* published a note by Mr. R. Howard concerning the portrait of J. N. Darby by E[dward] P[enstone] which he had recently inherited and which is now in the National Portrait Gallery, London (JCBRF broadsheet [Apr 1972] 4–5). The painting had been bought some forty years previously from "a lady living in Stamford Hill, London," who, Mr. Howard believed, was a Miss Penstone who had "kept some of her father's paintings." In an editorial footnote, Mr. Roy Coad mentioned that Edward Penstone had exhibited 25 pictures at the Suffolk Street Gallery and one at the Royal Academy between 1871 and 1889, and speculated that he was "a relative of John Jewell Penstone" associated with the early Brethren. That was when my investigations into the Penstone family began and continued spasmodically for the next thirty-five years. The text of this paper is very much as it appeared in *BHR* 5.1 (2008) 25–39.

2. A copy of this document has been given to me by Ms. Barbara Williamson to whom I am deeply indebted for many of these genealogical details. Ms. Barbara Williamson is descended from JJP's grandfather. Some but by no means all of the details can be corroborated in the International Genealogical Index [IGI.] Where I have given no source it can be assumed that Ms. Williamson provided the information.

3. Joseph Jewell, whose mother died when he was ten years old, was the son of a horse dealer and began life as a farm drudge and a bricklayer. Successively an ostler, drayman, and glazier, he became a porter in the Old Plough Court Pharmacy, in Lombard Street, founded by the Quaker Silvanus Bevan in 1715. There, under the direction of William Allen and Luke Howard, Jewell became head of the laboratory and a highly successful manufacturer of chemicals, overseeing the company's move to Plaistow and later Stratford in Essex. For details of his extraordinary career, see Slater, "Memoir of Jewell," 113–78. Cf. Chapman-Huston and Cripps, *Through a City Archway*, 32.

of Christ" that John Jewell Penstone, when he was about nineteen years old [c. 1836] "first heard of the meetings of the Brethren and became acquainted with Mr John Eliot Howard."[4] However we should perhaps note that the only published account of Penstone in Pickering's *Chief Men among the Brethren* is somewhat misleading as its references to his early friendship with the Howards of Tottenham suggest that this association continued to the end of his life.[5] In fact, when controversy swept through the Brethren movement, unlike the Howard brothers, Penstone supported Darby after 1846 even to the point of engaging in printed controversy with his former friends. The recollection of his first meeting with Brethren, cited above, is taken from his published answer to a pamphlet by John Eliot Howard,[6] the very man to whom he had been introduced by his grandfather.

Marriage and Family

In 1845 John Jewell Penstone married his first wife, Matilda Harman Gould (1813–78), who was born in Grosvenor Square, London, and she was the mother of at least seven children—Mary (b. 1845, died young), Persis Mary (1846–1904), William (1847–1880), Edward (1849–1916), Fanny (1850–1910), Charles (born c. 1853), and Sarah (born c. 1856). The family was living in Chelsea until 1850 when they moved to Stanford in the Vale where JJP's father and both his [JJP's] grandfathers had been born, but by 1861 they were living on Commercial Road, in Oxford next door to what at that time was still known as Bulteel's Chapel. We know nothing more of Matilda Gould but three years after her death in 1878, JJP married a second time and his second wife was Elizabeth Messer Wright (1815–1892). She was from a Bristol Quaker family and was a cousin of James Wright (1826–1905), George Müller's son-in-law and successor in the Ashley Down Orphan Homes.[7]

Scholar and Artist

In describing JJP as a "Bible scholar and Christian poet" the writer in *Chief Men among the Brethren* was diminishing somewhat the scope of his subject's talents. Penstone was evidently well read in secular history and his interests were certainly not confined

---

4. Penstone, *Caution to the readers*, 3. The event was recalled in autumn 1866 as "thirty years since."

5. Pickering, *Chief Men*, 82–83.

6. Howard, *Caution against the Darbyites*. For some useful recent work on J. E. Howard, see Kirkwood and Lloyd, *John Eliot Howard*.

7. For details of Elizabeth Messer Wright and her cousin James see the IGI; Foster, *Pedigree of Wilson*, 103–4; Pierson, *James Wright of Bristol*, 3. I am beholden to Mr. David Napier for saving me from a false conjecture in the matter of the date of her death. At present we are ignorant of the identity of the deceased person remembered in Penstone, *Dustless tomb*, but the date indicates that it was not his wife.

to sacred studies. In the late 1850s he raised questions and responded to other people's questions in the monthly journal, *Notes and Queries*, on literary, artistic and historical subjects.[8] The chances of Penstone, who was then living in Stanford in the Vale, reading such a journal as *Notes and Queries* would appear to be slim unless he was a subscriber.[9] However he seems to have been something of an antiquarian and evidently was friendly with the prolific amateur Alfred John Dunkin (1812–79) to whose *Monumenta Anglicana* he contributed "A visit to the village church of Stanford in the vale, whilst undergoing restoration."[10] This was not the only help JJP gave to Dunkin who acknowledged in one of his reports for the British Archaeological Association in 1848 that JJP had provided him with not only etchings of Sudeley Castle but also with information about the opening of King John's tomb in Worcester Cathedral in 1797.[11]

If such scholarly interests conflict with an anti-intellectual, philistine stereotype popularly associated with the early Brethren, other activities of our subject give us further reasons for abandoning it. In the census of 1851 JJP described himself as an "artist and Proprietor of houses" while ten years later he gave his occupation as "Historical and Portrait Painter" and although the work of his son, Edward, is better known, JJP's artistic work was not insignificant. As early as 1838 he exhibited *The Saxon Bride* at the Royal Academy where some of his paintings were shown in the 1840s and also as late as 1895.[12] Inevitably his religious interests combined with his style for him to be classified as a Pre-Raphaelite.[13]

In his day he was probably best known for his work as an engraver. The entry for Edward Pusey's older brother Philip (1799–1855) in the *Dictionary of National Biography* discusses his iconography and explains that "the engraving of 1851 was by a local artist J. Fewell [sic] Penstone, Stanford, Berkshire."[14] This is doubly misleading because Penstone cannot be dismissed as a local artist as his engravings can be located further afield. The National Portrait Gallery has his stipple engraving of Rosina Bulwer-Lytton, Lady Lytton (1802–82), based on a portrait by Alfred Edward Chalon

---

8. Penstone, "Was Addison a plagiarist?," 49; "Pictures of Raffaelle in England," 130; "Forged Assignats," 134–35.

9. There are other contributions to *Notes and Queries*, in later years, that are signed "JJP" and which show a familiarity with jurisprudence but we cannot be sure that they are the work of our subject.

10. Dunkin, *Monumenta Anglicana*. For a less than flattering account of Dunkin, see *DNB*.

11. Dunkin, *Report of the proceedings*; JJP also provided the engraving of Dunkin's portrait. He had earlier produced an engraving of Dunkin's father, the topographer, for the frontispiece in J. Dunkin, *History and Antiquities of Dartford*.

12. Graves, *Royal Academy of Arts*, 6:104.

13. One of Penstone's characteristically Pre-Raphaelite works is *Love Is Strong as Death* (1894) a title taken from Scripture (Song 8:6), which he presented to Edith Churchill, possibly on the occasion of her marriage, when he was living at Stamford Hill in London. It was sold by Peter Nahum at the Leicester Galleries, Ryder Street, London, and can be viewed at http://www.leicestergalleries.com/metadot/index.pl?isa=Metadot::SystemApp::AntiqueSearch;op=detail;id=13522.

14. The spelling error has been perpetuated in the *ODNB*.

(1780–1860), as well as his stipple engraving (1852) of the daughter of Sir Robert Peel, Julia, Countess of Jersey (1821–93).[15] Indeed, in an article seeking more information about JJP's work as an engraver, W. H. Quarrell observed in *Notes and Queries* (1944) that the old British Museum catalogue described Penstone as "Painter and Engraver for Julia, Countess of Jersey."[16] Another engraving, *Enamoured Days*, was based on a work by his contemporary Edward Corbauld (1815–1906) and appeared in the 1848 edition of *Fisher's Drawing Room Scrap Book*, being one of the works singled out in the *Eclectic Review* as having "afforded us much gratification."[17] JJP's gifts in this field would explain why the Brethren hymn writer Sir Edward Denny (1796–1889) valued his help in the preparation of the charts in which he outlined his views of prophecy.[18]

Both of JJP's sons seem to have followed in their father's artistic footsteps. His older son William was the architect who supervised the building of Stanford in the Vale Primary School,[19] and the younger son, Edward, is described in the 1881 census as an unmarried painter living in London. Edward like his father exhibited at the Royal Academy in 1877, 1894, and 1896,[20] and he himself presented a copy of his "etching and aquatint" of John Nelson Darby to the National Portrait Gallery in 1903. The gallery's more recent acquisition (1972) formerly owned by Mr. Howard, is listed as a "watercolour over photograph after Edward Penstone."[21]

Persistent Quaker Identity

Although, like many evangelical Friends, JJP came to be associated with the Brethren, his Quaker connections are a recurrent element in his life from his maternal grandfather's experience, through his early friendship with the Howard family and later in his second marriage. There is in the Newport Museum and Art Gallery, a watercolor by JJP of "Swarthmore Hall," in Cumbria, the home of Margaret Fell, whom George Fox, the founder of the Quakers, married in 1669.[22] Swarthmoor Hall (as it is more commonly spelt) was for many years an important center of Quaker activity and we may

---

15. National Portrait Gallery [NPG] D14533; NPG D7536. See http://www.npg.org.uk/collections/search/person/mp11122/john-jewell-penstone?role=art and http://www.npg.org.uk/collections/search/person/mp53762/john-penstone?role=art. The engraving of Lady Lytton is reproduced in *ODNB*.

16. Quarrell, "Penstone" 58.

17. Anon., "Notice of Fisher's Drawing Room Scrap Book," 766. For a colored reproduction of this very romantic Victorian item, see http://www.antique-prints.de/shop/catalog.php?list=KAT74.

18. Cornwall, *Songs of Pilgrimage*, 26.

19. See Cuff and Brooks, "Outline History of Stanford in the Vale," at http://www.stanford-in-the-vale.co.uk/history_schoollib.shtml.

20. Graves, *Royal Academy of Arts*, 6:104.

21. NPG D11119, NPG 4870, see http://www.npg.org.uk/collections/search/person/mp07415/edward-penstone?role=art.

22. The picture can be viewed (and bought as a print) from http://www.art-prints-on-demand.com/a/penstone-john-jewell/swarthmore-hall.html.

safely assume that the two principal figures in the group of Friends in the foreground of his painting are Margaret Fell and George Fox. We have no date for this work but clearly JJP was in sympathy with much of the Quaker ethos.

In the late 1830s, his friend John Eliot Howard edited a magazine, the *Inquirer*, which was primarily addressed to uncertain members of the Society of Friends encouraging them to leave the Quakers and to observe the sacraments of baptism and the Lord's Supper in the manner of the Brethren.[23] An interesting allusion to JJP's ecclesiastical experiences can be found written in the copy that John Howard gave to Elizabeth Wright forty years before her marriage to JJP.[24] In the front of this copy there are two inscriptions. First: "Elizth Wright, with J. E. Howard's kind Christian love March 1841." Second, in J. J. Penstone's hand: "Afterwards it passed to me. I value these volumes much—but their perusal now awakens many a recollection of sorrowful regret that a movement which was undoubtedly of God should have been taken hold of by men for their own purposes and selfish ends—hence the 'Brethrens' [*sic*] decay. John Jewell Penstone." It seems reasonable to assume that these words were written after the death of JJP's second wife in 1892. For many years previously he had taken part, albeit with a subdued disappointment,[25] in Brethren controversies but the note of disillusion in this later inscription is palpable. Being that little bit younger than the very first Brethren and having sided with Darby in the earliest division he lived to see what he felt was the disintegration of the movement.

Poet

Apart from a little pamphlet *Village teachings concerning the Lord Jesus*,[26] JJP's non-controversial religious writing was his poetry and with that aspect of the artist we shall conclude this paper. The writer in *Chief Men among the Brethren*, who described JJP as a "Christian poet," believed that his poem "The Servant's Path in a Day of Rejection" had been "of spiritual help to believers in all parts of the world." There are two published editions of this poem, but they are only to be found in the Christian Brethren Archive, in Manchester. With such a dearth of surviving copies one might be inclined to wonder how a poem of this sort can have circulated. It is a very personal poem, two (random) verses of which will be sufficient to explain why it was unlikely to find its way into any congregational hymnal—let alone one used by Brethren:

---

23. See above, ch. 2, [x-ref].

24. *Inquirer* 2 (1839). This copy was originally in the library of the late Mr. W. R. Lewis, a former editor of *Echoes of Service*. It is now in Manchester (JRULM CBA, periodicals, KR3637).

25. The following items are all (uniquely, I believe) in the CBA, Manchester: 1, *Occasional reflections*, [CBA 5608 (9)]; 2, *Notes on passing events* [CBA 6102 (23)]; 3, *Inductive theories of baptism*, [CBA 1308]; 4, *To brethren in Christ* [CBA 230.]

26. Penstone, *Village teachings*. This is one of the only two pamphlets by Penstone to be found in the British Library.

SERVANT of Christ, stand fast amid the scorn
Of men who little know or love thy Lord;
Turn not aside from toil: cease not to warn,
Comfort and teach, trust Him for thy reward;
A few more moments' suffering, and then
Cometh sweet rest from all thy heart's deep pain.

Cleave to the poor, Christ's image in them is.
Count it great honor if they love thee well;
Nought can repay thee after losing this,
Tho' with the wise and wealthy thou shouldst dwell.
Thy Master oftentimes would pass thy door
To hold communion with His much-loved poor.[27]

Even before the advent of photocopying machines, this genre of poem appeared in numerous journals and magazines and probably was repeatedly copied into commonplace books and personal anthologies. Ironically the fullest version to be found on the internet is on a website associated with the Bible Students' Association, which originated in the work of Charles Taze Russell, many of whose followers are known as Jehovah's Witnesses.[28]

The most important book of poems written and illustrated by John Jewell Penstone is his *Songs of Salvation and Records of Christian Life*.[29] It is of interest to readers of a journal connected with the Brethren for more than one reason. One item is a little poem entitled "Neutrality" describing the last interview between George Müller and J. N. Darby in which the former said that he was not prepared to discuss Darby's point of view because of the bad behavior of those taking an exclusive position. Penstone's poem appears to be in line with the tradition that Darby accepted Müller's criticism as valid.

Of rather greater interest is the fact that one of the author's etchings (opposite p. 40) is a picture entitled "Reading the word of God A.D. 1838." In the picture it has sometimes been assumed that one could identify J. N. Darby, S. P. Tregelles, Lady Powerscourt, as well as some others, and that this was one of the Powerscourt conferences, but the owners of Powerscourt House in the late 1960s (before Powerscourt was gutted by fire in 1974) assured me that there was no window in the house like the one in the etching.[30] The fact that the picture is dated 1838 and the fact that Penstone's earliest association with Brethren dated from 1836 (the year of Lady Powerscourt's

27. [Penstone], *Servant's path*, 1–2.
28. See http://www.agsconsulting.com/volumes/htdb0192.htm, 148–49. Five of the nine verses are available at the website of the Free Church Defence Association, http://myweb.tiscali.co.uk/theword/foundations/foundations7.html.
29. Penstone, *Songs of Salvation*.
30. My reference is to the late Mrs. Gwen Slazenger, who showed me round Powerscourt in the summer of 1968.

death), makes her pictorial identification very much less probable. If this picture can be associated with the tradition of conferences associated with Powerscourt, the date would suggest the series of meetings in the Gloucester Hotel at Clifton in June 1838.[31] However, the fact that it is the work of John Jewell Penstone gives an added piquancy to the fact that his son produced the only portrait known to us of John Nelson Darby.

---

31. See Stunt, "Early Account of the Brethren in 1838," 6.

Irvingites

4

"Trying the Spirits"

The Case of the Gloucestershire Clergyman[1]

THE POLITICAL TURMOIL, WHICH characterized the decade from 1825 to 1835, is interestingly reflected in altered religious perceptions, by which the established church and traditional nonconformity alike were found by many critics to be spiritually wanting. Millenarian and charismatic movements are often, in part, an expression of social uncertainty, and the early nineteenth century is no exception.[2] Any analysis of the origins of such movements as the Plymouth Brethren or the self-styled "Catholic Apostolic Church" must take into account their social milieu which, at that time, included political agitation—for causes like Roman Catholic Emancipation, parliamentary reform, currency reform and nascent socialism—as well as anxiety arising from the outbreak of cholera and social unrest, together with several European revolutions in the background. It may not be entirely fortuitous that, when Edward Irving was expelled from his church in Regent Square in 1832, his congregation (not without some misgivings) met for a while in Robert Owen's lecture hall in the Gray's Inn Road.[3]

Old and New Sources

Although the structures and order of service became severely institutionalized in the later development of the Catholic Apostolic Church, the charismatic element was decisive during its formative years in the calling of the apostles. Irving and his followers had, for years, been praying for an outpouring of the Holy Spirit and they were hardly likely to question closely the authenticity of the healings and glossolalia of the early

---

1. Originally published in *JEH* 39 (Jan 1988) 95–105.

2. The classic exposition of this thesis is in Cohn, *Pursuit of the Millennium*; for its application to the early nineteenth century, see Harrison, *Second Coming*, 218–25.

3. Oliphant, *Life of Irving*, 2:301–4; not the Rotunda, which is in Blackfriars, see Stunt, *From Awakening*, 265n96. Some recent analysts have been inclined to dismiss the importance of what they often refer to as "deprivational theory" in the development of millennial attitudes, but I have argued elsewhere that the balance in this matter needs to be redressed, Stunt, "Trinity College," 73–74.

1830s. Irving claimed that he examined the phenomena carefully for several months before permitting charismatic utterances in the formal worship of his church, but, as his biographer shrewdly noted, "his investigations were necessary only to satisfy his conscience and not to convince his heart."[4] The episode which seems most to have reassured Irving that he was able to "test the spirits of prophecy" and distinguish between them, is known as "the case of the Gloucestershire clergyman," two of whose children "prophesied" so convincingly that their parents believed them and, for a time, followed their instructions faithfully. Eventually, when the children's directions became extreme to the point of folly, it was decided to "try the spirit"—though one of the children "prophesied" against this suggestion, declaring, "Ye may try the spirits in men, but ye may not try them in babes and sucklings." When, at last, the spirit possessing the child refused to confess that "Jesus Christ is come in the flesh," the children were released and the spirit never returned.

Such is the barest summary of the story, which is to be found in three printed accounts, all written within a decade of the events. The earliest is Irving's own description, which appeared in the Irvingite magazine, the *Morning Watch*, in March 1832.[5] In the following year, Robert Baxter, disillusioned with his own experience of prophesying and of the Irvingite movement in general, described the events in Gloucestershire in an account which is apparently independent of Irving's but is, nevertheless, strikingly corroborative except in minutiae.[6] Perhaps on account of Baxter's hostility to the movement, one of its earliest apostles, Henry Drummond, took the trouble to stress that Baxter's account of the events was "imperfect as to the facts" and based on "idle, hearsay reports."[7] The third account was given to Caroline Fox in 1839 when she was visiting her aunt, Mrs. Sarah Fox, at Trebah. She describes it as "an interesting and consecutive account," though she gives no indication of who gave it to her. It was included when her *Journals* were published some forty years later. Her Quaker origins prevented her from decrying the idea of possession by spirits, though she had little sympathy with the folly of the parents.[8]

In all three accounts, the names of the people involved are either omitted or only indicated by the first letter of the surname; their identity has been lost until now, and further details of the story have been unattainable. Two manuscript sources, however, have now made the identification of the family possible, and we are able to establish the story more accurately. The first new source is a letter in Trinity College, Dublin, from a widowed mother, Mrs. L. S. La Touche Truell, written from "Spa Gloster"

---

4. Oliphant, *Life of Irving*, 2:190.

5. *Morning Watch* 5 (1832), 152–54. The account in Norton, *Restoration of the Apostles*, 74–75, derives from Irving's account and is, in turn, the basis for the description in Miller, *History . . . of Irvingism*, 1:100–102.

6. Baxter, *Narrative*, 97–98.

7. [H. Drummond], *Spirit in Mr. Baxter*, 38.

8. Pym, *Journals . . . of Caroline Fox*, 1:76–78.

[*sic*] on 27 October 1831 to John Synge. Mrs. Truell was well acquainted with the Gloucestershire clergyman's family and, while away in Wales, had received letters from someone called "Fanny" who was living with the family. Mrs. Truell may have been the mother of Robert Holt Truell of Clonmannon, County Wicklow, and was almost certainly, like her correspondent, John Synge, an evangelical member of the Church of Ireland. Her information is valuable as it describes matters preceding the decision to "try the spirits."[9]

The Gloucestershire family in question was that of Edmund Probyn (1788–1837), second son of John Probyn, archdeacon (and later dean) of Llandaff.[10] The Probyns had been lords of the manor of Longhope, Gloucestershire, for many years and, although Edmund Probyn had married Juliana Webb in 1821, and they were living at Fairsted in Essex in 1826, he returned to his home territory, in the following year, to be vicar of Longhope and rector of Abinghall in succession to his father. Clearly the family was of some standing in the locality, which may explain why their religious extravagances were tolerated for so long. Their association with what may be described as the more radical and experimental wing of evangelicalism, and their contact with Irving, went back at least to 1826 when the archdeacon, Probyn's father, attended the first conference on unfulfilled prophecy at Albury Park.[11] Also present at this conference was another character in the story. This was the Hon. John James Strutt (1796–1873), later (on the death of his mother in 1836) the second Baron Rayleigh of Terling Place, near Chelmsford, Essex, who had become an active evangelical in 1822 but whose religious sentiments were not shared by his father with whom he had a rather stormy relationship.[12] In his religious isolation at home, the younger Strutt made a point of associating with local evangelicals. It may have been after his meeting Archdeacon Probyn at Albury that, in November 1826, he "became very friendly with" Edmund Probyn and his wife Juliana who was some years younger than her husband.[13]

Strutt's relationship with Mrs. Probyn was an equivocal one and has given rise to conjecture, in view of his later marital infidelities, as to whether she was his mistress. Certainly, when the Probyns moved back to Longhope, Strutt was a frequent visitor, staying with them sometimes for months at a time; and, when he was in Essex, he maintained a prolific correspondence with Juliana. His letters were addressed to Edmund Probyn, but they were written to Mrs. Probyn in most affectionate terms.

---

9. Mrs. L. S. La Touche Truell to John Synge, 27 Oct 1831 (Trinity College, Dublin, MS 6189, env. 1). For John Synge's career see Stunt, "John Synge," 39–62, below ch. 9.

10. See Phillipps. "Supplement to the Pedigree of Probyn and Spicer," 196. This must be supplemented by reference to *Al. Oxon.*, and the inscriptions in Longhope Parish Church.

11. Boase, *Supplementary Narrative*, 745; Miller, *History of Irvingism*, 1:141. For the growing dichotomy within evangelicalism see Newsome, *Parting of Friends*, 10–12; and Stunt, *From Awakening*, 95.

12. Strutt, *Strutt Family*, 72–76.

13. Juliana Probyn (1799–1840), daughter of Philip Webb, Esq., of Milford House, near Godalming, Surrey (Inscription in Longhope Parish Church).

As if to "fantasize" their relationship and thereby, perhaps, to make it more "spiritual" (or at least acceptable to Edmund), Strutt and Mrs. Probyn used invented names in their correspondence. He calls her "my dearest Mary" and signs himself "your most attached Pauly," and throughout, her husband is referred to as "Tim." Certainly their friendship gave rise to speculation. It is the correspondence between Strutt and Mrs. Probyn, which furnishes us with a second source of information for the episode of the "Gloucestershire clergyman." Although Strutt appears to have been with the Probyns until shortly after the exorcism of the children, the correspondence, which followed his departure from Longhope on 11 November, is full of valuable information.[14]

Prophets: Young and Old

It was in the course of October 1831 that Edmund Probyn and his wife visited London for a fortnight with their seven-year-old son, Julian. They were attending meetings at Irving's church during the very weeks when prophetic utterances were first heard during the formal services of the church, rather than at private house meetings or weeknight prayer meetings.[15] While they were away, Julian's twin sister, Juliana, was left in the care of their governess, Miss Banks, whose predilection for the more enthusiastic varieties of spirituality seems to have been considerable. Mrs. Truell's letter describes her violent admonitions and denunciation of the Church of England and how "in prayer she threw herself on the floor in violent contortions." This struck a sympathetic chord in other women in the household whose consequent "shrieking and hysteria" were hardly calculated to maintain an orderly atmosphere. In her parents' absence, the twin sister "spoke in the Spirit," and Mrs. Truell (who apparently had some influence in the family and considered Miss Banks's influence to be harmful) took the girl into her own care until Mr. and Mrs. Probyn returned. In fact, the parents learned of their daughter's utterances while they were in London.[16] They had been expected to stay the night at Oxford with the vice-principal of St. Edmund Hall, Dr. John Hill, but instead, they hurried on home and disappointed Mrs. Truell, on their arrival, by giving their approval to the hysteria.[17]

---

14. Both sides of the correspondence have survived in the Strutt family archives at Terling, Essex, as are some letters written by Edward Irving and his wife, and by Henry Drummond, which were received by either the Probyns or by J. J. Strutt. They are quoted by kind permission of Lord Rayleigh. I am greatly indebted to the Hon. Guy Strutt for his most obliging assistance with my enquiries.

15. See Davenport, *Albury Apostles*, 48; Miller, *History of Irvingism*, 1:67–70.

16. Oliphant, *Life of Irving*, 2:152–53.

17. For their non-arrival at Oxford, see B. W. Newton's recollection: "Mr. Hill wished me to meet him, and I came at the appointed time, but unaccountably he [Probyn] didn't turn up" (Manchester, JRULM, CBA 7057, Wyatt MS, 1:353). There is no mention of the incident in Hill's diary, but it does confirms that the Probyns had visited him previously (Oxford, Bodleian Library, St. Edmund Hall MS 67/7, 67/8, Diary of John Hill, 29 Oct 1829; 25 Oct 1830).

Although the Probyns accepted the manifestations in their daughter at their face value and were delighted when her twin brother also began to prophesy, Mrs. Truell was sure that the phenomenon was only one of excitement noting that another child, Emily—perhaps her own daughter—"while she was here . . . was constantly in play affecting to have it [the gift of prophecy] and imitating this Miss Banks." The only writer to have discussed this particular episode in the light of child psychology recognized the possibility of imitation,[18] but the interesting fact that twins do sometimes develop their own "secret" or "autonomous" language has never been mentioned in this context. It is just possible that, in her brother's absence, Juliana used such a language to impress the readily suggestible Miss Banks.[19] Most of the children's "utterances," on the other hand, were evidently in plain English because the parents understood, and were apparently impressed by their "recital of Scripture and such power of argument and exhortation . . . certainly quite out of the compass of children of their age and understanding."[20]

It is easy to exaggerate the role of the children in the debacle, which followed. Irving and Baxter make no reference to the disastrous consequences for the parents who took their children so seriously but Caroline Fox's account is harrowing:

> These little beings gave tongue most awfully, declaimed against Babylon and things appertaining. Their parents placed themselves entirely under the direction of these chits, who trotted about the house, and everything they touched was immediately to be destroyed or given away as Babylonish! Thus the poor deluded man's house was dismantled, his valuable library dissipated, and himself and family thoroughly befooled. At last the younglings pointed out Jerusalem as the proper place for immediate family emigration and everything was packed up and off they set.[21]

However, this version is partially at variance with another earlier source, which cannot be ignored. The local Monmouthshire newspaper, the *Merlin*, gives what Mrs. Probyn described as "really a very true account in most things,"[22] describing the story at some length but with scant sympathy. In certain important respects it differs from Caroline Fox's presentation. Although the prophesying of the children, and the parents' desire to obey them, is mentioned, there is no suggestion that their commands

---

18. Drummond, *Edward Irving*, 202.

19. For the "autonomous" speech of twins (cryptophasia), see Savić, *How Twins Learn to Talk*, 140–41. Cf. Zentner, *Twins*, 101.

20. Baxter, *Narrative of the Facts*, 97.

21. Pym, *Journals of Caroline Fox*, 1:76. Cf. B. W. Newton's recollection: "The parents obeyed the children wonderfully but when at last they were commanded to sell all their goods and go to Jerusalem to meet the Lord Jesus who was coming, the old Curate took upon himself to exorcise these children," Wyatt MS, 1:353.

22. Mrs. J. Probyn to J. J. Strutt, 12–15 Nov 1831, Terling, Essex, Strutt Archives; *Monmouthshire Merlin*, 12 Nov 1831.

were concerned with more than trivial or momentary affairs. The children would give instructions when questions arose in a particular situation, but not apparently when matters were of more basic importance. Thus, "the teachers and the children were ordered to stay from church, on pain of incurring a most grievous sin if they went." Similarly, during a house meeting in the village "one of the children cried out, 'Send the multitude away.'" In contrast, it is Probyn's curate, Mr. Wolfe, who is said to have announced on Sunday 30 October that Christ would be returning before the end of the week and that it was necessary to prepare themselves. Similarly, the newspaper is significantly specific about the origin of the proposal to leave the house and to emigrate. "In passing through Gloucester some of Mr. Probyn's Millenarian friends had told them they must give up all they had, and go forth as hermits or pilgrims. They accordingly spent the whole of last week in fasting and praying and getting ready for departure." Once that decision had been taken, presumably the children were consulted when deciding what should and should not be taken. The *Merlin* continues:

> Mr. Probyn's library of books were all distributed amongst the teachers and scholars by prediction. They were given according to the prophesyings of the little Probyns . . . on the 7th inst. people were giving away the prints, flannels, calicoes and the remaining part of Mr. Probyn's books to everyone they met. The residue of the blankets, books and other things not given away by prophecy, were burnt by the word of the Lord.

If the idea that the children were the chief instigators of the hysteria is abandoned and if, instead, they are assigned an ancillary role, the story becomes far more credible. Children of all ages are usually amazingly adaptable and sensitive to what is expected of them. The parents may have been subject to their whims, but the initiative had come from their elders. If, after the denouement, the adults were inclined, by way of self-exculpation, to apportion to the children more blame than was justified, in humiliation there is a need for scapegoats. After the exorcism, there was evidently no shortage of "judicious discipline" and "flogging" meted out.[23]

Restraint and Exorcism

Throughout the story there hovers in the background the restraining figure of Archdeacon Probyn, the twins' seventy-year-old grandfather, who evidently lived nearby[24] and who was, according to Caroline Fox, "infinitely distressed at all these goings-on and goings-off, and with a pretty strong power intercepted his son at the commencement

---

23. The first phrase is Caroline Fox's. The references to flogging occur in Mrs. Probyn's letters to Strutt.

24. Mrs. Probyn to Strutt, 12–15 Nov 1831: "The poor dear A[rch]D[eacon] has just walked up in the snow."

of his pilgrimage and confined him to the house."²⁵ According to the *Merlin*, this was on Monday night (7 Nov), after a frenzied weekend of public warnings and farewells given by Probyn to his parishioners. Constables were employed to watch the house and to put a stop to the pilgrimage if it was attempted.

In fact, this was the evening before the exorcism of the children, which, according to Caroline Fox, was carried out in accordance with a formula sent by Edward Irving. He had met Miss Banks and learned of the failure of many of her prophecies and decided that the children's spirit had to be tested. According to Irving's account, the family "then remembered that they had 'believed the spirit' without 'trying the spirit' . . . and accordingly determined to do this forthwith."²⁶ The only surviving letter of Irving to Probyn is dated 10 November and was written after the news of the exorcism had reached him.

Throughout Mrs. Probyn's letters, it is apparent that she looked to the curate for direction, and, significantly, his was the key decision at the height of the crisis. On Monday evening, Julian rejected the idea of the test, threatening the adults if they went ahead with it. The next morning, when the father was again too weak to withstand his son, it was the curate Mr. Wolfe who adjured the spirit to confess that Christ was come in the flesh and who bade it depart. There can be little doubt that the clergyman in question was Robert Cope Wolfe, formerly curate to the rector of Albury. With his father, the rector of Crawley, Robert Barbour Wolfe, he had attended the Albury conference in 1826 (the year after he came down from Cambridge). Mrs. Probyn's letters in subsequent weeks expressed her fears that the bishop would withdraw Wolfe's license to preach. But the young clergyman weathered the storm and put the scandal behind him; after a brief curacy in Montgomeryshire he served as vicar of Braithwell, in Yorkshire, for the rest of his life.²⁷ Probyn's subsequent career was less fortunate. The *Merlin* described the vicar as having "the appearance of a man in the most desperate state of insanity,"²⁸ and Probyn's own father expressed the opinion that he should "yet live to see him put in a mad house."²⁹ The old man was right: by the end of May 1835, Mrs. Probyn had had "to abandon him to strangers," because he had become "more like an animal than a human being."³⁰

The Millenarian Context of 1831

It would be too easy to dismiss the "case of the Gloucestershire clergyman" as an example of mindless religious enthusiasm coupled with incipient madness. Although

25. Pym, *Journals of Caroline Fox*, 1:76.
26. *Morning Watch* 5 (1832) 153.
27. *Al. Cant.*; Boase, *Supplementary Narrative*, 746.
28. *Merlin*, 5 Nov 1831.
29. Mrs. Probyn to Strutt, 12–15 Nov 1831.
30. Mrs. Probyn to Strutt, 30 May 1835.

Probyn displayed clear signs of mental instability, a diagnosis of insanity sidesteps the real question.[31] To have submitted meekly to the commands of his seven-year-old twins does appear extraordinary. If it was believed that Christ's return was imminent and that the family should leave their home so as to be ready for the Second Coming, then the affair goes deeper than the "prophesyings" of the children and Probyn's mental disorder.

Of all the times for such an extravaganza, the end of October 1831 was probably the most appropriate. Just a year earlier, the southern counties had witnessed the "largest outbreak of rural rioting in modern British history,"[32] in the "laborers' revolt." October 1831 also marked the arrival of cholera in England from the Continent, "hanging over the country as a curse" as the Irvingite apostle, Spencer Perceval, later claimed in the House of Commons.[33] Worst of all, the Reform Bill had been read before the House of Lords, and, of the thirty bishops in the House, seven abstained and only two supported the measure. If the twenty-one "mitred Iscariots," as the *Times* referred to them, had voted the other way the bill would have been passed by a majority of one. In London, a mitered effigy was burned on Guy Fawkes Day, and a clerical hatter in the Strand sold off his shovel hats for thirty shillings a dozen.[34]

Nearer to Longhope were the notorious Bristol riots of 29–30 October, when two sides of Queen's Square, the Custom House and Excise Office, several jails and toll houses, together with the bishop's palace were pillaged and burned.[35] The elderly William Wilberforce and his friends anxiously watched from Blaise Castle outside the city: "The redness of the sky from the conflagration was quite a dreadful sight to us in the distance . . . I cannot but fear for the Church in these days."[36] Irving was unmistakably identified with the disdain for reform which characterized the High Tories, as he and his sympathizers had been united in their opposition to Catholic Emancipation three years earlier and to other forms of change. The fervent Irvingite preacher, Nicholas Armstrong, who had been preaching throughout October in Cheltenham and Gloucester, not only described the Church of England as "a cage of *unclean birds*," but also condemned uncompromisingly anything faintly democratic: "*Vox populi, vox Dei* is the shout of a maddened world; *vox populi, vox diaboli* were a truer speech, until the people all be sanctified."[37]

---

31. See Harrison, *Second Coming*, 209–17. Cf. Scull, *Mad-houses*.
32. Gash, *Aristocracy and People*, 146.
33. Quoted by Briggs, *Age of Improvement*, 254n.
34. Halevy, *Triumph of Reform*, 42; Brock, *Great Reform Act*, 248.
35. Ibid., 252.
36. Furneaux, *William Wilberforce*, 446.
37. See Mrs. L. Truell to John Synge, 27 Oct 1831; Armstrong, Cain, *Balaam and Core*, 13. Armstrong who was all but six-and-a-half feet tall, made a tremendous impact in his preaching. He was forbidden to preach in the open air by the bishop of London and was called as the fifth Irvingite apostle in 1834.

The Probyns as landowners and churchmen associated with the opponents of reform had every reason to be fearful. A pilgrimage to Jerusalem (if that *were* the original destination) or at least away from the vicarage would serve to demonstrate to the world at large that their treasure was in heaven, a kingdom not of this world. The distribution of property also could be interpreted as a gesture of solidarity with the less fortunate. Such reasoning was probably not consciously formulated, but fears and anxiety were high. Even a fortnight after the riots (and a week after the exorcism), Mrs. Probyn mentioned in her letter to Strutt that "Mr. Wolfe came about 9 o'clock with no particular news of Bristol but that all was quiet."[38] Social anxiety had combined with religious exhilaration fuelled by the millenarian preaching of men like Irving and Armstrong to provide the Probyn twins with a marvelously receptive audience and fruitful ground, albeit for only a few weeks.[39]

A Charismatic Moment

In London, Irving was greatly encouraged to find that the "spirit" in the children had refused to confess that Christ had come in the flesh. So this *was*, he concluded, a reliable test, and he at once tried the spirits of the prophets in his own church by asking them the same question. Not only did they reply in the affirmative, but they cried "vehemently for about the space of half an hour, 'The Lord of glory was the Virgin's child, the babe in the manger was Jehovah's fellow, the King on the throne of Heaven was compassed in sinful flesh, He who died on the cross shall come to reign over this earth for ever,' &c &c with a great deal more to the same effect."[40] The particular reference to "sinful" flesh must have encouraged him especially: it was this aspect of his Christology that had brought him under attack from the authorities of the Church of Scotland.

With some reason, however, the Irvings were anxious lest the experience of the Probyns "deter you from seeking the Lord for His own Spirit" and cast doubt on the authenticity of the movement.[41] "The work of the Lord," Irving had earlier assured Probyn, "will proceed and cannot be let";[42] but at Longhope, at any rate, recent experiences had rendered them more cautious as to what was "the work of the Lord." Contrary to Mrs. Truell's expectations, the Probyns did not leave the Church of England. Soon, Robert Wolfe was explaining the process of exorcism to Mrs. Probyn in terms

---

38. Mrs. Probyn to Strutt, 12–15 Nov 1831.

39. We have no information concerning their later lives, except that Juliana married John William Good Spicer of Esher Place, Surrey, whose sister, Mary, apparently married the twins' elder brother Edmund. Julian, the other twin, died unmarried (Phillipps, *Genealogia*).

40. Henry Drummond to J. J. Strutt, 10 Nov 1831, Strutt Archives; see below, ch. 5, for a fuller treatment of this part of the story.

41. Mrs. Isabella Irving to Mr. and Mrs. Probyn, 25 Nov 1831 (Strutt Archives).

42. Edward Irving to Edmund Probyn, 10 Nov 1831.

of "animal magnetism."⁴³ In the course of a few weeks, perspectives had changed: the children had submitted, the spirits had been tried and—perhaps most important of all—the specter of revolution had begun to recede.

The Probyns' short-lived enthusiasm for charismatic experiences is by no means unique. There are many instances of conventional Christians who, at this time, expected, and gave credence to, some sort of miraculous intervention but later reverted to non-charismatic, traditional piety. A few examples must suffice. Joseph Wolff, the celebrated convert from Judaism and supremely extrovert missionary to his own people, hovered on the fringes of Irvingism in the early 1830s before settling down as a conservative and slightly Tractarian Anglican.⁴⁴ A. N. Groves, the pioneering missionary of the Brethren, set out for Persia in 1829, expecting at first to see miracles "arise among missionaries to the heathen," but by 1834, he decided that the miraculous gifts were plainly "not needed."⁴⁵ Thomas Erskine of Linlathen, a Scottish Episcopalian, took the 1830 manifestations of glossalalia and healing in Western Scotland very seriously, but concluded, a few years later, that the utterances of Mary Campbell of Row were not comparable to those recorded in the Acts of the Apostles.⁴⁶ Finally, although Thomas Arnold of Rugby was a very different sort of churchman from Edmund Probyn and his friends, even he was prepared in the fateful month of October 1831 to give some credence to the manifestations in Irving's London congregation.⁴⁷

The subsequent history of the so-called Catholic Apostolic Church follows a similar pattern. The charismatic era of the movement was at its height in the first half of the 1830s, when the "apostles" were called by prophecy; once the "apostolate" was complete, enthusiasm for such utterances began to wane. The prophets had served as "a catalyst in the search for legitimacy, providing the 'break' from tradition, but once they had instituted new authorities they [the prophets] became otiose or even dangerous."⁴⁸ Inspired utterances had fulfilled their purpose by 1835 and were no longer necessary. It hardly needs pointing out that the political turbulence at the turn of the decade had also subsided, and the Whig reformers were proving less radical than many had expected.

Irving has often been scorned as a "blinded eagle," carried away by his own enthusiasm and eloquence, perhaps even an opportunist. In fact his unpublished correspondence in the archives of the Duke of Northumberland at Alnwick reveals a

---

43. Mrs. Probyn to J. J. Strutt, 8 Dec 1831. The Probyns were not entirely without support in the area as can be seen by the reaction of Robert Strong, the rector of Brampton Abbotts, see below, ch. 11, "Strongs of Wandsworth," n37.

44. Wolff, *Travels and Adventures*, 485; cf. Pym, *Journals of Caroline Fox*, 1:4; Stunt, *From Awakening*, 97–98, 139.

45. [A. J. Scott], *Journal of Mr. Anthony N. Groves*, 99–100; [H. B. Groves], *Memoir*, 313.

46. Drummond and Bulloch, *Scottish Church*, 199.

47. Stanley, *Life of Thomas Arnold*, 1:273.

48. Robert Lee Lively Jr., "Catholic Apostolic Church and the Church of Latter-Day Saints," unpublished DPhil diss., Oxford, 1977, 101.

realistic and consistent person, a man of principle struggling to find a place for the manifestations within the life of the Church and, at the same time, acutely aware of the need for pastoral discernment and restraint. The tensions of the last two years of Irving's life, before his death in 1834,[49] and his efforts to avoid charismatic anarchy, have not yet been described fully. Growing opposition to him came from the prophet Edward Taplin, who had nominated most of the apostles, and from certain of the apostles themselves, such as J. B. Cardale, Henry Drummond, and Francis Woodhouse. The intensity of their opposition is an indication of Irving's awareness of the potential for misuse of charismatic utterance and his perception that, in time of crisis it might not truly serve the needs of the Church. Undoubtedly, Irving stands out as the one who made the most serious attempt to "try the spirits": there can be little doubt that his experience in the case of Edmund Probyn led him to think that it was both necessary and possible.

---

49. For the last years of Irving's life, see Oliphant, *Life of Irving*, 2:329–406; Davenport, *Albury Apostles*, 88–91. However, neither of these works does justice to the ecclesiastical dimension of his situation. Even Dr. Lively, who consulted the unpublished correspondence in Alnwick for his dissertation, did not draw attention, for example, to Irving's stern rebukes on several occasions in his last years directed at unbridled and unspiritual charismatic activity, letters from Edward Irving to Henry Drummond, 14 Sep 1832–11 Nov 1834 (Alnwick, Northumberland Archives, Drummond Papers C/9/8-44).

5

"Trying the Spirits"

Irvingite Signs and the
Test of Doctrine[1]

The Challenge from Coleridge

WHEN SAMUEL TAYLOR COLERIDGE read Edward Irving's sermon in 1825 on the apostolical missionary ideal, he was disappointed that Irving had not met at the outset what would be the main objection of his more cautious antagonists. Irving was chiding modern missionaries for their worldly and prudent caution, and bidding them to throw such restraints aside in the apostolic spirit of dependence on God.[2] Coleridge found this unrealistic, as the absence in modern times of the *miraculous* gifts of the apostolic missionaries was a problem that hung

> like a dead weight around the neck of his [Irving's] Reasoning. They [Irving's antagonists] say to themselves ["]To whom Christ commended a supernatural independence of human means and aids, to them in the same commission he delegated superhuman powers conferred for their performances.["] This argument Mr. Irving should have met at the outset: for the Removal of this obstacle is as the foundation of all he would build up; inasmuch as not being removed it prevents the foundation from being laid.[3]

It was fair criticism and for five years, Irving waited for the miraculous seal of divine approbation. When heavenly approval appeared to have been granted in "gifts," it was somewhat ironic that the world scorned the miracles as well as Irving's missionary ideal.

---

1. This paper was delivered at the University of Exeter at a conference of the Ecclesiastical History Society in 2003. It was later published in Cooper and Gregory, *Signs, Wonders, Miracles*, 400–409, SCH 41 (2005).

2. Irving, *For Missionaries*; for the context of this sermon, see Stunt, *From Awakening*, 98–101; cf. Gilley, "Edward Irving," 98–99.

3. The copy of the sermon, given to Coleridge, was endorsed by Irving "to his dear friend and kind instructor" (London, British Library, C.61. c.8; the MS comments are on pp. 131–32).

The "Manifestations"

The origins of the Catholic Apostolic Church emerging from Irving's congregation in the 1830s were from the start associated in the popular mind with "miraculous" signs. These manifestations began in Fernicarry, Clydeside, on 30 March 1830 when the consumptive Mary Campbell spoke in an unknown tongue. During the previous year south of the river, in Port Glasgow, another invalid, Margaret Macdonald had experienced spiritual ecstasies though apparently without glossolalia. Two weeks after Mary Campbell's experience, Margaret was bidden by her brother James to "arise and stand upright" and on doing so was restored to bodily health. That day, James Macdonald wrote a similar command in a letter to Mary Campbell, who, on receiving the letter, rose from her bed and declared herself healed. In the following months Mary Campbell, Margaret Macdonald and her brothers frequently spoke in tongues and prophesied, attracting great interest and many visitors.

Inevitably there was debate over their previous medical condition and whether the healings and utterances were of divine origin, but the circle around Irving in London felt that these events were an answer to criticisms like those made earlier by Coleridge. In August 1830 they sent a deputation, led by John Cardale, whose favorable report was the earliest written account of the events.[4] Other contemporary descriptions by sympathizers were also written with access to precise details. Irving himself was well informed, and Robert Norton, who visited Clydeside, later married Margaret Macdonald. His two accounts were written after her death but *before* his involvement with the Catholic Apostolic Church.[5]

Satisfied that the manifestations were genuine, several members of Irving's congregation gathered in Cardale's home to pray for a similar outpouring. On 17 October 1830 the rector of Albury, Hugh McNeile, proclaimed from a London pulpit that such gifts could be expected, and within a week Eliza, the crippled daughter of the Rev. Thomas Fancourt, was reported to have been miraculously cured.[6] Christian journals discussed the cure, but there were no further manifestations until the following April when Cardale's wife (who had *not* accompanied him to Port Glasgow) spoke in an unknown tongue. Shortly before this, Mary Campbell (now Mrs. William

---

4. Cardale, "On the Extraordinary Manifestations," 869–72.

5. Irving, "Facts Connected"; Norton, *Memoirs*; Norton, *Neglected and controverted Scripture Truths*; and Norton, *Restoration*. R. H. Story gave a more critical account in his memoir of his father, who had been a close associate of the participants. See also A. L. Drummond, *Edward Irving*, 136–51; Strachan, *Pentecostal Theology*, 62–75; and Stunt, *From Awakening*, 228–36. Other sources relating to subsequent developments in Port Glasgow are given in Grass, "Taming of the Prophets," 58–70.

6. Henry Drummond, later an apostle in the Irvingite Church, urged Thomas Chalmers to read Eliza Fancourt's account as Chalmers had recently opined that "there was too much of seriousness about the accounts from Port Glasgow [for them] to be treated in the loose offhand manner that they had been by some," Stunt, *From Awakening*, 248–49.

Caird) had arrived in London from Clydeside and she too prophesied in the Cardale household.[7]

With this gathering charismatic momentum, further healings were reported—most notably in July 1831, that of Maria Hughes a member of the congregation of Park Chapel, Chelsea. This followed a sermon in which the Rev. Henry Owen had expressed his delight that his parishioners were willing to pray for divine healing. So far none of these events was *formally* associated with Edward Irving's congregation though some members of his church had been holding prayer meetings since May in his Church in Regent Square—albeit unofficially. When, in August 1831, Edward Oliver Taplin, a schoolmaster, spoke in an unknown tongue at one of these meetings, the identification was stronger—the more so in mid-October when there were similar occurrences during the church's formal services. In the week prior to these public utterances the enthusiastic Henry Bulteel, a recent seceder from the established Church at Oxford, returned from London fully satisfied that the manifestations were genuine. During the next ten days he was responsible for two healings (including that of his sister-in-law) in Oxford.

The Debate: Miracles and Sound Doctrine

The arguments following these rather sensational episodes were predictable. Although some commentators reserved judgment, scoffers often mocked the credulous, while believers rebuked the skeptics. The *Morning Watch* described the scornful *Edinburgh Review* as "the leader of the infidel party in Great Britain," and warned evangelicals that to reject the miracles as spurious was to ally themselves with Socinians, Neologists, and blasphemers.[8] When the *Christian Observer* maintained that it was "dangerous and unscriptural" to think that the age of miracles was revived, Eliza Fancourt's father trounced the magazine for not rescuing his daughter's healing "from the sneer of the profane scoffer."[9] Similar recriminations characterized the pamphlet controversy between Bulteel and his critics in early 1832.[10] Meanwhile a correspondent of the *Evangelical Magazine* protested that "the pretended gifts, and prophecyings [sic], and solemn babblings" of the "unhappy visionaries" are "among the most profane symptoms of the age in which we live," and enjoined readers "never to give the extravagancies [sic] now going forward" their occasional sanction by setting foot in Irving's church even out of mere curiosity.[11]

---

7. For fuller details of this and the following paragraph, see Stunt, *From Awakening*, 260–62, 268–69.

8. Ibid., 250n41.

9. *Morning Watch* 3 (Mar 1831) 156–57.

10. Carter, *Anglican Evangelicals*, 276–78; Grass, "Restoration of a Congregation," 286–87.

11. *EM*, n.s., 9 (Dec 1831) 522.

Lurking behind these polemics however, there was a theological dimension to the debate. The manifestations in both Scotland and London had occurred in the context of pastoral ministries that had provoked charges of heterodoxy. McLeod Campbell of Row had won the hearts of his parishioners but had earned the disfavor of the ecclesiastical authorities by stepping away from the Westminster Confession, rejecting a limited atonement, and insisting that Christ had died for all mankind. This issue was taken up by the Rev. Baptist Noel, minister of St. John's Chapel, Bedford Row, who had numbered among his parishioners John Cardale. Aware that, since his visit to Clydeside, Cardale was now all but a member of Irving's congregation, Noel was far from scornful of those claiming the gifts, but unhesitatingly he advanced the theological issue as a cause for apprehension:

> God has never yet set the seal of miracles to error: else, where is the value of them as the seal of truth? But, unless I am misinormed [sic] and misunderstand their writings, these pious persons have embraced the unscriptural notion that all men, even though they believe not in Christ, are so pardoned that sin is *no more imputed to them than to the believer*; that their guilt is done away through Christ, *just in the same sense that his* [the believer's] *is*; and that the only difference between them and him is that he [the believer] has become through faith really righteous, while they remain through unbelief essentially depraved.[12]

In his emphasis on Christ's compassion for mankind, McLeod Campbell had stressed the identification of Jesus with those whom he came to save. Irving in London had gone further and was already under investigation in 1830 for his insistence that although Christ had been completely without sin, he had shared "the fallen nature" of mankind. Such had been the Lord's humanity, Irving argued, that he had been *capable* of sinning (*peccable*). This Christological aspect was more crucial than even the extent of the atonement and had a direct bearing on the issue of the miraculous. Both Irving and his assistant Alexander Scott had claimed that if Christ with a fallen human nature could perform miracles, then a redeemed humanity could expect to do likewise. Indeed their reasoning was said to have prepared Mary Campbell and the Macdonald brothers for the possibility of the miraculous.[13]

Late in 1831, the editor of the *Record* who had no time for the manifestations took up the theological issue, being convinced

> that the appearances [sc. manifestations] which have their centre and home in Mr. Irving's church in Regent Square, are delusive and visionary. Breaking out in Scotland in support of the evil figment of *universal pardon* they now exert themselves in Regent-square church as an adornment of that far deeper

---

12. Noel, *Remarks on the Revival*, 28–29.
13. Stunt, *From Awakening*, 233–34.

heresy which has issued from that sanctuary, which declares the *sinfulness* of the flesh of Christ.[14]

The *Morning Watch* retaliated that Irving had always emphasized Christ's sinlessness,[15] but such was the anxiety felt by many about Irving's Christology that writers, sympathetic to the manifestations, nevertheless often felt obliged to dissociate themselves from Irving's heterodoxy. Thomas Boys, the editor of the *Jewish Expositor*, was a rigorist, with no time for the Apocrypha or continental neology, and had argued in a series of articles that miracles were a part of the Christian dispensation. Republishing the articles with a sympathetic account of Miss Fancourt's case, Boys maintained that "where the doctrine of a Church or religious community is unsound, it does not follow that the community can have no miraculous manifestations."[16]

Significantly, Boys nevertheless felt the need to reject Irving's teaching on Christ's humanity though he found extenuating circumstances. Claiming that the controversy had unmasked docetic[17] tendencies among Irving's critics, he suggested that Irving's errors were only the product of circumstance and that, given time, the great preacher might abandon the language of peccability. In the meanwhile he felt that the religious world could be thankful that covert forms of Arian and Sabellian heresy had come to the surface and been recognized for the errors that they were. Clinging to straws of this sort, he was evidently troubled by the accusation that "those who exercise [the gifts] testify expressly to that view [Irving's] of Christ's humanity," but he was not sufficiently troubled to question their validity or to conclude that "the gifts and the heresy must stand or fall together." Nevertheless these anxieties were further exacerbated by critics who said that the manifestations could be the work of an evil spirit.

Confessional Authenticity

In the days of primitive Christianity, faced with rival pagan oracles such as the utterances of the Pythoness at Delphi, the Apostle John had made clear that ecstatic utterances could be demonic and had instructed believers to "try the spirits whether they be of God" (1 John 4:1). While St. Paul insisted that the speaker must be able to confess that "Jesus is the Lord" (1 Cor 12:3), the Johannine seal of divine authenticity was that the inspired speaker would be able to confess that "Jesus Christ is come in the flesh" (1 John 4:2). The second of these confessions had an understandable appeal to those emphasizing Christ's humanity. Norton, in his earliest account of the Clydeside utterances, tells us that because of such apostolic injunctions "a meeting was held for this purpose, when, after prayer that utterance might be given, a confession of Christ

---

14. *Record*, 21 Nov 1831.
15. *Morning Watch* 5 (Dec 1831) 182–83.
16. Boys, *Christian Dispensation Miraculous*, 104.
17. The docetic heresy emphasized Christ's deity at the expense of his humanity.

was made by each one of the gifted persons present." Norton's transcription of the Macdonald brothers' confession includes repeated, explicit allusions to Christ's human nature: "Jesus, son of the Virgin's womb . . . Jesus in our nature . . . Glory to the word made flesh! Glory to the incarnate God . . . Glory to the Unity with our flesh . . . Glory to the risen Man! To God in our nature."[18]

The question of confessional authentication was an issue that evidently troubled Irving, particularly when he learned of the case of the Gloucestershire clergyman Edmund Probyn, in whose household several prophetic manifestations had occurred with the active participation of his young twin children.[19] Irving had been somewhat reassured to learn that Probyn and his curate had "tried the spirits." The curate had called upon the spirit in one of the twins to "confess that Jesus Christ is come in the flesh" but was met with a loud refusal and shortly afterwards the boy was delivered and the spirit left him.[20]

However, it is clear from his letter written to Probyn on 10 November 1831 that Irving had doubts about such a simple confessional test[21] and wanted further authentication of the prophets in his own church. Gathering the "gifted" and some of the "most judicious" brethren[22] he read them Probyn's letters:

> Before the second letter was half read, one of them [Miss E. Cardale] was made to speak in great power calling to try the Spirits, whereupon I rose in the middle of her utterance and put the question, "Oh Spirit, believest thou that Christ is come in the flesh?" She continued to prophesy in the most glorious and powerful manner, confessing and adoring and lauding the humiliation of Christ and his glory. One joined and another, but they all, as it were in a divine chorus, went on testifying to the whole truth. Then singly one and another took up the burden of their Redeemer's work, and did so magnify and celebrate the Lord as that I never heard the like. So that we were all lost in admiration of the unity of the Spirit, and the superabundant evidence which he gave us of his being the Holy Ghost . . .
>
> [They then sang a psalm.] The Spirit having thus entirely satisfied us of his oneness with Jesus Christ, we proceeded after a second prayer to deliberate concerning you [Probyn] and your dear children. I had just opened my mouth intending to shew my mind, which was that you must not be content

---

18. Norton, *Neglected Truths*, 396–97.
19. For a fuller discussion of this episode, see above, ch. 4.
20. *Morning Watch* 5 (Mar 1832) 152–54.
21. E. Irving to E. Probyn, 10 Nov 1831 (Terling, Essex; Strutt Archives). Henry Drummond's letter to J. J. Strutt of the same date is in the same collection. In places it provides specific details [which I have sometimes added in square brackets] but in general, Irving's account is slightly more dispassionate.
22. Drummond's letter indicates that those present (other than Irving and himself) were John Cardale, his wife and sister, William and Mary [née Campbell] Caird, Miss Hall, Edward Taplin, John Tudor and Nicholas Armstrong [two of the future apostles], Dr. J. Thompson, David Brown [Irving's assistant minister], and a Mr. Barclay.

> with categorical answers but observe whether it be the habit and delight of the Spirit to testify unto the personal work of Jesus in the flesh and his present work and glory in the spirit, when Mr. Taplin was made to speak with great power these words first in a tongue and then in our own language, "Tell him to hear no Spirit that testifies of himself, but that testifies of Jesus, that he was crucified in the flesh, in our flesh, in our fallen flesh, and that he reigneth in the heavens, and that he will be glorified in his members who shall reign with him on the earth for ever and ever!"[23]

Further "prophesyings" by Miss E. Cardale and others proclaimed, "that there was no safety or protection against the evil spirits but by abiding in Jesus and watching our most secret thoughts."[24]

> We then proceeded to deliberate and were all of one mind, that the spirit [in the Probyn twins] was an evil spirit, and that it answering yes or no to the test was no proof, and that this is not the thing intended by confessing but a thorough impenetration of their utterances with the spirit of that truth, and that you must seek to be filled with the spirit in order to discern this. It was observed by one [Cardale] that Hermas in his Shepherd gives it as a test of the evil spirits that they desired to be consulted like the oracles, but the Holy Ghost speaks full of his own will.[25]

An Eclectic Approach to Trying the Spirits

We have quoted from this letter at some length partly because it is not easily available for consultation but also because it provides several useful pointers to Irving's thinking on the authentication of prophecy. One striking aspect of his response is its eclectic use of both objective and subjective tests. Although at first he sought to comply with the Johannine test, he soon fell back on very much more temperamental and subjective modes of reassurance. "Abiding in Jesus and watching our most secret thoughts" is probably the least precise mechanism for validation as it is entirely concerned with the condition of the observer as opposed to the conduct of the prophet. It is thus on a par with Irving's later advice to Probyn that he "must seek to be filled with the [Holy S]pirit" if he is to discern the mind of the spirit speaking in his children. On the other hand, when he seeks objectively to consider the spirit's utterances, Irving adopts the suggestion that a true "confession" on the part of the spirit should be found

---

23. E. Irving to E. Probyn, 10 Nov 1831 (Terling, Essex; Strutt Archives).

24. Ibid.

25. *The Shepherd of Hermas*, book 2, *Mandates*, 11:1–7, 11–16, which identifies a false prophet as one who likes to be consulted as a soothsayer; see Lake, *Apostolic Fathers*, 2:119–23, but Cardale would only have been familiar with the text in Wake, *Genuine Epistles*, 342–44, based on Latin manuscripts. For a detailed analysis of this passage, see Reiling, *Hermas*.

in the overall "impenetration" of the utterances rather than in a single "categorical" answer of "yes" or "no."

Recalling, too, that Irving had long been an opponent of any use of the Apocrypha, one is surprised to find him basing his position on a noncanonical Scripture, like *The Shepherd of Hermas*. It is also significant that when Taplin, the leading prophet in Irving's congregation, testified to the humanity of Christ he adopted the specific language for which Irving had been accused of heresy, referring to Christ "crucified ... in our fallen flesh."[26] In this respect he was far from being alone, as is apparent from Drummond's account of the same occasion where we learn that Miss Cardale

> and all the gifted persons present broke out in one simultaneous crash like the voice of many waters, & continued crying vehemently for about the space of half an hour[:] "The Lord of glory was the virgin's Child, the babe in the manger was Jehovah's fellow, The King on the throne of Heaven was compassed with sinful flesh, He who died on the Cross shall come to reign over this earth for ever," &c &c with a great deal more to the same effect.[27]

Doubtless the prophetic adoption of his Christology was reassuring for Irving, but for others it was liable to be a stumbling block. However sympathetic they may have been to the piety and spirituality of those involved, both Noel and Boys found the doctrinal issue a cause for incredulity or at least anxiety. In some cases believers were so impressed by the signs of divine intervention that they were able temporarily to shelve these doctrinal concerns. When Henry Bulteel, an uncompromising Calvinist, became "satisfied of the genuineness of the miracles of healing and tongues" his friend John Hill was pained to find that he had become "convinced moreover of their doctrine of general redemption." Significantly he reverted to his former Calvinism when he later concluded that the signs were of demonic origin, details of which he confided to another disillusioned prophet, Robert Baxter.[28]

In 1832 Robert Baxter published an extended critique of the early Irvingite prophesyings, which he now considered to have been spurious and (by implication) demonic. The exposure was all the more devastating because he had been a participant in the manifestations for several months. He now agreed with Irving that the "categorical" confession had been insufficient, but he also argued that, in November 1831, Irving had been disqualified from trying the spirits because of his "own erroneous views concerning Christ's flesh."[29] It seems that eventually Baxter's doctrinal orthodoxy had caught up with him, leading him to abandon a stance, which he had adopted

---

26. E. Irving to E. Probyn, 10 Nov 1831 (Terling, Essex; Strutt Archives).

27. Partly quoted in Stunt, "Gloucestershire Clergyman," 103.

28. For an extract of Bulteel's disillusioned letter to Baxter, see Carter, *Anglican Evangelicals*, 279–80; cf. Stunt, *From Awakening*, 269, 271.

29. Baxter, *Narrative of the Facts*, 131–32. Drummond claimed that Baxter's information "was imperfect as to the facts" but did not take up the question of Irving's "erroneous" Christology, [Drummond], *Spirit in Mr. Baxter*, 38.

for emotional or "temperamental" reasons. Another who lost his earlier enthusiasm for the phenomena was Hugh McNeile. By December 1831 he was maintaining that the prophets did not comply with St. Paul's instructions to the Corinthians about interpretation, but he also had more pragmatic objections. Those exercising the gifts tended to be self-complacent and to set themselves apart as superior to other Christians. "A feeling is inculcated and cherished amongst them of their being martyrs . . . making a cross of this, glorying in suffering for conscience sake."[30] In short, the gifts seemed to minister to pride.

Whether Irving's Christology was heterodox or not is a question with which we are not concerned. Although doctrinal factors were adduced in opposition to (and sometimes in support of) the validity of the phenomena, they appear usually to have been of secondary significance. With the exception of Noel who avowed that he felt "more sympathy with an honest though hurtful enthusiasm, than I can with a sour and supercilious orthodoxy,"[31] more often than not, critics only used the doctrinal issue to confirm positions, which they had previously adopted for other reasons. Although Coleridge had correctly identified the criticism that Irving's readers might raise, perhaps he had not realized the emotional reservations that fueled them.

30. McNeile, "Nature and Design of Miracles," 244–45.
31. Noel, Remarks, 29.

Brethren

6

J. H. Newman and Proto-Plymouth Brethren at Oxford[1]

Was Newman's Disagreement with the Evangelicals Just a Myth?

IN THE NUMEROUS STUDIES of the life of Cardinal Newman, too much attention has often been paid to his own personal development while the circles in which he moved have often been ignored. This is particularly true of some of his early associations at Oxford. Newman's celebrated disagreement with the Evangelicals over his co-secretaryship of the Oxford Auxiliary of the Church Missionary Society [CMS] became something of a legend in his own lifetime. So much was this the case that in 1879, a friend sought to "demythologize" it with some help from the cardinal. In an article on Newman in the *Fortnightly Review*, W. S. Lilly wrote as follows:

> Among the many legends which have grown up about him is one attributing his final separation from them [the evangelicals] to the rejection in 1826 of 250 amendments said to have been moved by him to the draft of the annual report of the Oxford Bible Society of which body, according to the story, he was the "third secretary": amendments directed to the purgation of that document from the strange verbiage which was the outward and visible sign of the Low Church spirituality. Unfortunately a word from Cardinal Newman has dispelled this amusing myth. "I never was any kind of secretary to the Bible Society" he tells me, "and I never moved any amendments at all."[2]

Newman, of course, knew perfectly well that in Lilly's "myth" the Bible Society had been confused with the Church Missionary Society, though apparently he preferred at the time to refrain from saying more than he did. His younger brother, however, sprang with characteristic alacrity to rebut the implication that there had

---

1. This paper was originally published in 1970 as "John Henry Newman and the Evangelicals," in *JEH* 21 (1970) 65–74. I have made a few minor corrections and expansions, as well as having changed the title.

2. Lilly, "Cardinal Newman," 6. William Samuel Lilly (1840–1919) was a lawyer and essayist who converted to Roman Catholicism in the 1870s. See his obituary in the *Times*, 1 Sep 1919.

been no such incident. In a letter to the editor of the *Fortnightly Review*, dated 13 July 1879, he outlined his own recollections. Mr. Lilly

> says that Cardinal Newman denies that he was ever a secretary to the Bible Society. The denial must have been barely *that he was Secy in the year 1826*, the year named by Mr. Lilly. I think the affair was late in 1829 and early in 1830. I was myself one of the committee. Rev. B. P. Symons, tutor of Wadham College, *Co-Secy* with Mr. Hill of Edmund Hall [sic], proposed my brother's name as third Sec, *without consulting him as I believe*. The appointment was notified to him and undoubtedly not rejected; for ere long, when Mr. Hill presented his report (in 1830?) the Rev. J. H. Newman moved 254 amendments of it. Meanwhile he had written a most hostile tract and sent it to every clergyman in Oxford, exhorting the soundminded (i.e. High Churchmen) to afford 10/- each to make themselves voting members and by their votes take the management of the Society out of the (silly) hands, which had raised and administered it. Mr. Hill had done the work in Oxford for years past. His report was in the usual Evangelical style, which he had always used and had never been objected to. Thus to snub an excellent, laborious man, a senior man also, seemed to me highly improper. (To my memory the number of emendations was 254: Mr. Lilly says 250. They were designed to transform the evangelical style into one, which perhaps was better; but that is not here of importance). The members who met in committee were
>
> Chairman: Dr. Macbride, Professor of Arabic.
> Rev. Mr. Hill of Edmund Hall
> Rev. Mr. Dornford, Rev. Mr. J. H. Newman, Fellows of Oriel College
> Rev. Mr. Bulteel, Minister of St. Aldate's Church
> F. W. Newman, myself, Fellow of Balliol College.
>
> The amendments proposed by Rev. J. H. Newman found only Mr. Dornford to support them: thus they dropped through.
>
> The annual meeting soon followed; at which my friend Mr. Benjamin Newton, Fellow of Exeter College, proposed "that the Rev. J. H. Newman be no longer secretary." This was carried at once, and I believe, *nemine contradicente*: but I stayed away from that meeting on purpose, not wishing to vote against my brother needlessly.
>
> Mr. Lilly will probably, on reading this, see that he had no reason to explode the story told to him as an amusing fiction.[3]

The letter was not published, but some correspondence passed between Frank Newman and Lilly, and Frank admitted that he might have confused the Bible Society with the Church Missionary Society, saying, "The two societies were worked by the same energies and almost by the same individuals." In fact, Frank had merely assumed certain inaccuracies in Lilly's account to be true, as he was really contesting the

---

3. Frank Newman's letters to the *Fortnightly Review* are in the Birmingham Oratory (F. W. Newman file 2) and are quoted by permission.

suggestion that the whole story was a legend. Thus he also accepted Lilly's use of the word "amendment," later using "emendation." It will be observed that some of this account reappeared in Frank's bitter memoir of his brother in 1891, where he reverted to his original mistake, suggested by Lilly, of confusing the CMS with the Bible Society.[4]

John Henry's account of the episode is to be found in the 1885 edition of the *Via Media* where the original tract relating to the CMS was reprinted.[5] Explaining that his object in writing the tract had been to put forward the view that the CMS should be under the control and direction of the bishops, he maintained that he thought this could have been effected, by encouraging the Anglican hierarchy to become involved in the Society. "My letter however, gave great offence to the leading members of its Oxford Branch, to which I belonged; and at the next annual meeting consisting mainly of junior members of the University, Dr. Symons of Wadham in the chair, they unanimously voted another, I forget who [sic], into the office I held."[6]

The Background to the Episode

So much for the notorious tract, which according to Frank's final account was described by Samuel Rickards as "unworthy of him [J.H.N.] and really mean."[7] However this was but the finale of earlier developments. In December 1829, Newman had written to Dr. Hill, the vice-principal of St. Edmund Hall, and Newman's co-secretary, inquiring whether the sermons by Henry Bulteel[8] and R. W. Sibthorp,[9] preached at St. Ebbe's in aid of the CMS collections, could be disowned by the Society as not necessarily representative of its views. Hill replied that he would oppose any such action as he approved warmly of the ministry of both men.[10] The matter came up at the committee meeting and Hill's comments in his diary are informative:

> Mon. Dec. 14. Committee of Ch. Miss. Soc. Newman introduced a proposal to add in the next report a paragraph stating that the Congregational collections were not held at the request of the Committee, though they thankfully received them. This insidious proposal was introduced as Newman had previously told me, to act as a sort of disclaimer on the doctrines of the sermons preached on Sunday the 6th. This being the case I strenuously opposed it (as I forewarned Newman I should), Sibthorp supported me as far as delicacy would allow, he

---

4. Newman, *Contributions*, 28–30.
5. [Newman], "Suggestions respectfully offered," 2:3–10.
6. Ibid., 2:4.
7. Newman, *Contributions*, 29–30.
8. Minister of St. Ebbe's and not of St. Aldate's as Frank Newman had incorrectly recalled. For Bulteel, see *ODNB*, and for fuller details of these years at Oxford, see Stunt, *From Awakening*, 195–97, 254–56.
9. For Richard Waldo Sibthorp at Oxford, see Trott, *Life of Sibthorp*, 68–73.
10. For the full text of this exchange, see Ker and Gornall, *Letters and Diaries of Newman*, 2:178.

having been one of the preachers alluded to. Of the rest Ball,[11] Moberly[12] of Balliol, D.[sic] Martin[13] of Exeter Coll. opposed me, Wilberforce[14] and F. Newman were silent—and Dr. Mcbride [sic][15] moderated between the two. Nothing was decided.[16]

The matter came up again, however, on 10 February 1830, when Newman's proposal was rejected. Hill's Diary recounts:

> Committee of Ch. Missy Socy. Adjourned meeting to consider best way of increasing the influence and receipts of our association. See Dec. 14. Newman brot [sic] forward a proposal much altered from his former proposal, including also a note of thanks to the individuals in question. It was happily thrown out. The Committee amounted to 21 persons, Tyndale,[17] Philpott [sic],[18] Langley[19] came in for the purpose.[20]

In a letter sent to the Rev. Josiah Pratt, general secretary of the CMS, Hill enlarged on this:

> At our Committee (of which my friend Wigram wrote to you) the offensive paragraph which was to have headed the list of Congregational Collections stating that they were not made at the request of the Committee, was not proposed, but instead of it, it was proposed that into our next report should be introduced an expression of "thanks to those who had preached for the society especially as they had done so without having received any application from the Committee." This however harmless and true in itself, was felt to be aimed as a [?] sting on our dear friends Bulteel and Sibthorp and was happily thrown out.[21]

Clearly, Newman's doubts about the position of the CMS originated in his feeling that it was too much associated in a sectarian way with the Calvinist "party" identified with Bulteel and Sibthorp. It was the language of this party that he was contesting in

11. John Ball of St. John's College.
12. George Moberly (1803–85), later bishop of Winchester.
13. Richard Martin (1802–88), later Canon of Truro.
14. Robert Wilberforce [?] (1802–57).
15. John David Macbride (1778–1868), principal of Magdalen Hall.
16. Diary of John Hill (Oxford, Bodleian Library, St. Edmund Hall MS 67, 7:73b–74a).
17. Thomas George Tyndale (1785–1865), of Trinity College, rector of Holton, Oxon.
18. For Joseph Charles Philpot (1802–69), of Worcester College, see below.
19. William Hawkes Langley (c. 1796–1874+), of Christ Church, Perpetual Curate of Wheatley, Oxon (1824–49) is elusive. He was suspended from his office for some months in 1842 under the newly passed Church Discipline Act (1840) because of his aggressive conduct during public worship towards his "Puseyite" critics. See the case of Burder v Langley in Thornton, *Notes of Cases*, 1:542–52.
20. Hill's Diary, 7:80a.
21. Birmingham University, CMS Archives G/Ac/3, Hill to Pratt, 20 Feb 1830.

the other CMS skirmish outlined by his brother Frank in his letter to the *Fortnightly Review*.

In the cardinal's account of this incident he points out that Frank uses both "amendment" and "emendation" (ignoring the fact that Frank was merely correcting Lilly's language) and then observes that this

> seems to explain the difficulty of the wonderful number to which they run. Not one "amendment" did I "move" as far as I remember or believe; but it is very likely from what he says, that at a preliminary meeting the intended Annual Report was read to the Committee, of whom I was one; and though I recollect nothing about it now, perhaps or probably I objected to the conventional Evangelical phraseology in which it was drawn up, and the friends of its author on counting up my proposed "emendations" of style, found 254 words affected by my criticism. I am sure there was no moving, voting, and dividing upon them. If this explanation will not hold, I can give no other; anyhow in the received meaning of the word, the notion of 254 amendments is absurd.[22]

The cardinal's explanation seems quite feasible, even though he had no recollection of the events, but his certainty that there was no voting on the issue cannot be checked. Frank's general recollection of the incident is confirmed by Hill's "Diary" for 2 March 1830:

> Committee of Church Missionary Socy to read the report to which Newman my co-secretary objected having marked upward of 50 passages with which he was dissatisfied:—mostly passages referring to Xt or his Spirit or alluding to Scripture.[23]

It will be seen, therefore, that there was more disagreement than merely the clash over Newman's tract. Although the composition of the auxiliary's committee varied and although many members in outlying Oxfordshire parishes did not always attend meetings, Hill could call in support when he needed it, as he did in February 1830. It could be that Hill regarded the earlier conduct of Newman as worse than the contents of his tract, for curiously, he makes no allusion in his diary to the annual meeting when Newman was thrown out. It is also interesting to note that Bloxam of Magdalen recalled that Newman had said once that of all his opponents "Sibthorp was the only one who behaved like a gentleman."[24]

---

22. Newman, *Via Media*, 2:6–7.
23. Hill's Diary, 7:81b.
24. "Cardinal Newman," in Magdalen College Library, cited by Middleton, *Newman at Oxford*, 34.

Radical Allies Who Become Opponents

In outlining in some detail the course of events in Newman's clash with the CMS, the object has been to establish the precise nature of the opposition he encountered. It is no longer sufficient to say that his opponents were Evangelicals, as Evangelicalism was deeply divided at this time. It is possibly the failure to recognize this that has led some writers completely to ignore the episode.[25] Just because Newman retained some contact with Evangelicals for some time longer, it does not render this incident any less decisive. Recent work has indicated the extent of the disagreement between what we shall here refer to as traditional and radical Evangelicals.[26] The rift was partly one of temperament. The language and behavior of men like Edward Irving and Nicholas Armstrong were a far cry from the respectable sobriety of Charles Simeon and Daniel Wilson. Although both parties were interested in the study of prophecy, the radicals made it a matter of far greater urgency. At the same time, the traditional school was suspicious of the radicals' High Calvinism, which often seemed to smack of antinomianism.

The radical position, however, went still further. It stemmed from a preoccupation with ecclesiology—a subject much neglected by the older evangelical tradition. This interest found expression in a strongly anti-Erastian voice and in a search for some visible manifestation of the body of Christ, free from division. Some of the traditionalists, like William Marsh and Hugh McNeile, were attracted for a time to this emphasis but with the growth of extravagant behavior and teaching they drew back.

The Evangelicals at Oxford were not untouched by this division. The late John Reynolds emphasized the "Ultra-Calvinism" that separated Dr. John Hill and St. Edmund Hall from Oxford Evangelicalism as a whole,[27] but there was more to the division than that. Hill was really the most conservative man in the group around him, and many of his friends were much more radical, dissatisfied with the Erastianism of the Establishment, as well as looking for a fuller ecclesiology. The growth of this radical group requires full-length treatment since its history is, as yet, [in 1970] unchronicled, but here we must be content with sketching the development of its hardcore, most of whom eventually seceded from the Established Church.

Very early in 1827,[28] B. W. Newton of Exeter College was converted as a result of contact with Henry Bellenden Bulteel of the same college, who had become curate

25. E.g., Trevor, *Pillar of the Cloud*; and Robbins, *Newman Brothers*.

26. Newsome, *Parting of Friends*, 10–15. The author refers to the unpublished Hulsean prize essay by H. Willmer, entitled "Evangelicalism 1785–1835."

27. Reynolds, *Evangelicals at Oxford*, 84, quoting Gladstone's assessment in "Evangelical Movement," Gleanings, 7:211–12: "A school of ultra-Calvinism which lay far in advance of the ordinary evangelical tenets."

28. The bulk of the sources for the following paragraphs is in MS form, and includes John Hill's "Diary" (Oxford, Bodleian); "Letters" of F. W. Newman (Birmingham Oratory); "Letters and Recollections" of B. W. Newton (formerly in the possession of C. E. Fry, but now in Manchester, John Rylands University Library, Christian Brethren Archive). Printed sources include: Newman, *Phases of Faith*;

of St. Ebbe's in October 1826.[29] By April 1827 Newton had made the acquaintance of Frank Newman, who had obtained a double first in the previous year. At Worcester College, Frank had met Joseph Philpot, who came back from Ireland in 1827 where he had been tutor to the sons of Lord Chief Justice Pennefather. While in Ireland, Philpot had experienced an Evangelical conversion, possibly through contact with John Nelson Darby, Pennefather's brother-in-law. On returning to Oxford, late in 1827 Philpot was introduced to Dr. John Hill, and Frank Newman went to take Philpot's place in Ireland, where he, too, was profoundly influenced by Darby, later bringing him to Oxford in 1830. Other significant members of the circle around Hill included George V. Wigram and William Jarratt of Queen's, Charles Brenton of Oriel, W. G. Lambert of Corpus and William Tiptaft, vicar of Sutton Courtney.

That these men were enthusiasts is undeniable, and their later careers demonstrate that their radicalism was not just a momentary flash of youthful fervor. Bulteel's manner of preaching offended both his churchwardens and certain university officials, so that the vice-chancellor tried to prevent undergraduates from attending.[30] Philpot together with another Worcester Fellow, Henry Bisse, who was a former curate of St. Ebbe's, got into trouble with their college authorities for "having exposition and prayer in the Common Room at a party of friends," in November 1828.[31] Tom Mozley's description of the dean of Oriel's disgust at the "hideous device, by which a great weight is released at the appointed hour and drags off your bed clothes," which Brenton used at five every morning, in preparation for his devotions, is known well enough.[32] These are but a few examples of the fervor and energy displayed by the group.

In February and March 1829, Hill and his friends were tirelessly campaigning to have Sir Robert Inglis elected in place of Sir Robert Peel, whose Erastian record over Catholic Emancipation was regarded by the radical Evangelicals as a great betrayal.[33] The same group was continuously engaged in organizing auxiliaries for the Bible Society, the CMS, the Society for promoting Christianity among the Jews, and the Reformation Society. They were evidently in close touch with William Marsh,[34] Hugh

---

Philpot, *Seceders*; the *Gladstone Diaries*, and numerous tracts, see below, nn43 and 44. Fuller details of all the radical evangelicals mentioned in this paragraph can be found in Stunt, *From Awakening*.

29. For the negotiations relating to the appointment, see Hill's "Diary," 6:37b–42a. Cf. Stunt, *From Awakening*, 196–97.

30. See Ward, *Victorian Oxford*, 76, based on Hill's "Diary," 6:115b–117b.

31. Hill's "Diary," 7:20b.

32. Mozley, *Reminiscences*, 2:116. However, Frank Newman later wrote to his brother: "His [Mozley's] account of my friend Charles Brenton quite astounded me . . . It would be quite a literary curiosity if I had been asked to give my Reminiscences of Charles Brenton, to compare it with T.M's" (Birmingham Oratory, F. W. Newman file 2). For Brenton, see Stunt, *From Awakening*, 296–98.

33. Herein lay another difference between the Radicals and some traditional Evangelicals. Their dissatisfaction with the latter is reflected in Brenton's disparaging remarks about the Record. He recalled how it "vacillated . . . and what an uncertain answer was returned to the question Ought the Roman Catholics to be admitted into Parliament or not." Brenton, *Sermon on Revelation*, 2nd ed., 46.

34. "Such was his enthusiasm for the study of prophecy that he became known as 'Millennial

McNeil, J. Haldane Stewart, and Joseph Wolff, who had all attended the conferences on prophecy at Albury associated with Edward Irving and Henry Drummond. From few of the lives of John Henry Newman would one ever imagine that he had much contact with this brand of Evangelicalism at Oxford, except in a rather distant and distasteful relationship with his brother Frank and the family of Walter Mayers at Worton.

Nevertheless, in July 1825 Newman was attending a "meeting of clergymen etc at Mr Hill's about the expediency of establishing a Church Missionary Association in Oxford," and a few months later accompanying Hill to Deddington for another such meeting.[35] In March 1828 we find him dining with the newly converted Joseph Philpot who had recently returned from Ireland.[36] Although Hill was "deeply disappointed"[37] when he heard Newman preach at St. Mary's on Psalm 145:10, in November 1828, both he and Newman had been campaigning against Peel earlier in the year. The fact that as late as March 1829 Newman could be elected co-secretary to the CMS auxiliary, which was so peculiarly Hill's domain, is an indication that relations were, as yet, not too strained.[38] It is similarly noteworthy that B. W. Newton, who was a regular member of the group around Hill, had been able to write to his mother in December 1827 referring to Newman as "the best Examiner we have at present in the Schools and is thought by many to be one of the most clear-headed, deep-thinking men in Oxford."[39] After all, if John Henry could allow his dangerously enthusiastic brother to help him in his parish work at Littlemore as late as 1830,[40] then for all his differences with the Calvinist enthusiasts, his relations with them must have remained cordial for some time.

The Division Hardens

The CMS crisis in 1829–30 must be taken in this context. Newman had not only been an Evangelical, but he had been respected by the radical Evangelicals and indeed, he had probably been attracted by some of their emphases. A few years later, the Tractarian movement would also be courageously anti-Erastian, and Newman's own search for a nonsectarian expression of the Church is reflected in the very tract, which in 1830 caused all the commotion.

Marsh,'" Russell, *Short History*, 78.

35. Ker and Gornall, *Letters and Diaries*, 1:246, 257; Hill's "Diary," 5:48a–b, 71a. Deddington was the parish of another radical evangelical, Richard Greaves, see Stunt, *From Awakening*, 189–90.

36. Ker and Gornall, *Letters and Diaries*, 2:63.

37. Hill's "Diary," 7:20a.

38. Ibid., 7:38b.

39. B. W. Newton to his mother 23 Dec 1827 transcribed in the Fry MS (Manchester, JRULM, CBA 7049) 121.

40. Robbins, *Newman Brothers*, 32–33. It is shown there that Maisie Ward's conjecture that Frank's parish visiting was done in 1826 is incorrect.

By 1829, however, he was beginning to feel out of place. Unlike his brother Frank, who, when in Ireland in 1827–28 had visited a Kellyite dissenting chapel,[41] and was rapidly discarding both infant baptism[42] and, indeed, any sacramental system, John's formalized concept of the Church was hardening in a totally different way. At the same time his understanding of the role of the Established Church was becoming incompatible with that of the radical Evangelicals. For John Newman, the Establishment was acceptable so long as it was not controlled or dismembered by "Godless Whigs." The year 1830–31, on the other hand, saw Bulteel, Brenton, Lambert, Tiptaft and Wigram all condemning the idea of Establishment as apostasy,[43] while Frank Newman, B. W. Newton and Joseph Philpot more reluctantly were beginning to distance themselves from it, regarding it as an unclean adjunct of a worldly age.[44] Possibly mesmerized by the impetuous but compelling personality of John Nelson Darby, who visited Oxford in May and December 1830,[45] radical Evangelicals were now feeling the need to abandon the Establishment. The criticisms of Bulteel's teaching with which Daniel Wilson had greatly pained John Hill,[46] proved themselves only too well warranted, when Bulteel became an Irvingite and later a Plymouth Brother.

Of course, not all the radical group abandoned the Establishment. Walter John Trower,[47] later bishop of Glasgow and Galloway, Richard Sibthorp, the uncertain convert to Rome, John Bramston, later dean of Winchester, and other evangelicals went with John Henry Newman for a time at least. But radical Evangelicalism within the Church of England was dead. Thus Hill, in a cry of despair notes in his "Diary" at the opening of 1832, "I have scarcely a friend left in Oxford who is altogether likeminded,"[48] but Newman himself continued to co-exist peacefully with the more traditional evangelicals up till the late 1830s.[49] It had been with the radicals that he had parted company in 1830 when the clash occurred in the CMS.

---

41. Newman, *Contributions*, 62.

42. Newman, *Phases of Faith*, 6.

43. See Bulteel, *Sermon on I Corinthians 2:12*; Brenton, *Sermon on Revelation*, 9; Lambert, *Call to the Converted*; Philpot, *Memoir of Tiptaft*; Wigram, *Protest against the National Establishment* (as yet unlocated).

44. See Newman, *Phases of Faith*, and Newton, *Answers to questions*. Philpot's secessionary letter is in Philpot, *Seceders*, 1:276–88.

45. See Hill's "Diary," 8:7a–8a, 29b. In December "Darby preached in St Ebbe's from Romans 11:22, on the rejectn [sic] of the Gentile Church."

46. See the "subjoined notes" in Wilson, *Character of the Good man*; Hill's "Diary," 8:53b.

47. For W. J. Trower (c. 1805–77), Fellow of Oriel, see Stunt, *From Awakening*, 203–4.

48. Hill's "Diary," 9:3b. Inaccurately but more fully quoted by Ward, *Victorian Oxford*, 77, where "not" is mistakenly inserted before "altogether likeminded."

49. See Newsome, "Justification and Sanctification," 36.

The Showdown

When we come to inquire what happened at the annual meeting of the CMS subscribers, Hill's "Diary" tells us nothing because he was not there, but he did give some account to Josiah Pratt in his correspondence with him. In a letter of 20 February before the annual meeting he wrote: "The pamphlet Wigram sent you has occasioned much disgust in the minds of many. The author has called in all the copies remaining."[50] Newman's repentance however, came too late. In a further letter, in March, Hill wrote of the annual meeting "(amongst other business) it was determined that the Revd. Mr. Philpott [*sic*], M.A., Fellow of Worcester College should be associated with me in the office of secretary in the place of Mr. Bisse who has left Oxford and of Mr. Newman of Oriel."[51]

From this summary we find that both Lilly's account of the "legend" and Frank Newman's memory were accurate when they referred to John Henry Newman as the "third secretary." The career of the second secretary, who left Oxford in 1829, only serves to show how much the CMS was characterized by radical Evangelicalism. Henry Bisse (sometimes written as Biss) matriculated in 1810 from Worcester College[52] of which he later became a fellow. It was he who with Philpot had upset the college authorities by having a prayer meeting in the common room in November 1828. This incident had made him *persona non grata* and as a result he was excluded from the bursarship of his college[53] and the provost refused to give testimonials to the bishop of Salisbury for his taking the living of Kennington.[54] In August 1829 he left for Southampton where he had been appointed to the chapel of the penitentiary.[55] Such was the ecclesiastical coloring of Newman's other co-secretary.

Hill's account of the annual meeting does not do justice, however, to the occasion, which was undoubtedly a lively one. Tom Mozley's reference to Newman's being "ousted by an immense majority, Bulteel and his satellites and half of Edmund Hall being in attendance,"[56] tells us more but remains somewhat enigmatic. Frank Newman's recollection was that "my friend Mr. Benjamin Newton . . . proposed 'that the Rev. J. H. Newman be no longer Secretary.' This was carried at once, and I believe, *nemine contradicente*: but I stayed away from that meeting not wishing to vote against my brother needlessly." Though this is still not a complete account, it is substantially accurate; but the lie to Frank's display of fraternal piety is found in B. W. Newton's own recollection of the episode, according to which Frank was the instigator of the whole attack.

---

50. Birmingham, CMS Archives G/Ac/3, 20 Feb 1830.
51. Ibid., 11 Mar 1830.
52. Foster, *Al. Oxon.*
53. Hill's "Diary," 7:25b.
54. Ibid., 7:21a.
55. Ibid., 7:56a.
56. Ker and Gornall, *Letters and Diaries of Newman*, 2:199.

His brother Frank came to me telling me that his brother John was the author of an anonymous pamphlet in the Tractarian interest [this was recalled long after in the 1890s—hence the anachronistic use of the word Tractarian] that had created much excitement while no-one could imagine who had written it. Frank Newman said it was too bad, and John ought not to continue his secretaryship. Would I propose that he should be suspended? I replied that I was too young for that, but I would willingly second a resolution. So at the meeting Bulteel proposed it, but made such a muddle of it that actually the chairman said "The question is that Mr. Philpot be appointed colleague and thus that two secretaries be etc. etc." I could not second that and I had to rise and propose an amendment to it, which was that Mr. Newman's name must be omitted and Philpot's name stand alone. Newman was sitting very near me and was very angry. The amendment was carried by a large majority.[57]

How far Newton's memory served him reliably and whether he embroidered his recollections in his old age is open to debate, but if his account can be trusted it is of crucial interest. It tallies with the fact that there had been three secretaries, as the fact that one was retiring in any case while another was being displaced would account for the confusion after Bulteel's speech. The account explains why Frank was at such pains to put the record straight in his old age and clarifies exactly what Mozley meant by "Bulteel and his satellites." Lastly it demonstrates precisely who were Newman's real opponents. In addition to G. V. Wigram who, as we have seen, had complained to the central authorities of the CMS about Newman's tract, the opposition was centered on the activities of Bulteel, Newton, Frank Newman, and Philpot. All of these seceded from the Establishment in the course of the next five years. All, except for Philpot, were associated at some time or other with Plymouth Brethren; Wigram's association with them was permanent while Newton's lasted for about fifteen years. Bulteel spent nearly two years with the Irvingites while Frank Newman soon found himself at issue with the Plymouth Brethren and eventually became a Unitarian.[58] Philpot became a Strict Baptist in 1835. Once it is accepted that Newman's separation was from a particular segment of evangelicalism, the "legend" that Lilly was at such pains to dispel, becomes not only plausible but must be regarded as a significant episode in the ecclesiastical development of the early nineteenth century.

---

57. Recollections of B. W. Newton in the Fry MS (JRULM, CBA 7049) 195.

58. Prof. Owen Chadwick refers to Brenton, Bulteel, and F. W. Newman as being "on the fringe of a Strict Baptist group," *Victorian Church*, 1:416. However, of the Radical Evangelicals whom we have mentioned only Philpot and Tiptaft can be labeled as Strict Baptists. Brenton, Bulteel, and Frank Newman were all for a time associated with the Plymouth Brethren, although that name only became current around 1835.

7

Anthony Norris Groves

A Radical Pioneer of Missions[1]

Introduction

IT WAS TO A packed audience in the Tabernacle in Tottenham Court Road that Edward Irving preached one of his most eloquent sermons to the London Missionary Society in 1825. As he warmed to his romantic ideal of the Christian missionary, he poured scorn on what he called "the principle of expediency, and . . . the rules of prudence," which, he claimed, characterized the missionary societies.[2] It was not the sermon that his listeners were expecting, as it seemed to belittle all their efforts of the previous decades. On the other hand their discomfort was probably mild when compared with the reactions of churchmen who read the sermon when it was published later in the year. Irving's manifest excitement was giving substance to some of the worst fears that respectable men and women of the Establishment had felt for some time about the swelling voice of the missionary movement.

Quite as alarming as the perceived possibility that missionary work might disturb colonial business, was the widespread feeling that although this sort of enthusiastic activity might be expected of Dissenters, it was inappropriate for a churchman or gentleman. These attitudes had been reflected in the early dearth of missionary volunteers suffered by the Church Missionary Society (CMS) and in its heavy dependence during the first quarter of the nineteenth century on German and Swiss recruits—a situation which calls to mind the usefulness of Hessian mercenary troops in the establishment of the earlier British Empire. Indeed, Jon Miller has argued that the CMS Committee preferred "tough" peasant recruits, with an "appropriately modest" background, from places like Wurtemburg, to staff the Society's expanding program, and

---

1. This paper has been delivered a number of times (in Princeton [1997], Cambridge [1998], and Gloucester [2003]) and has benefitted from the several constructive reactions of my hearers. It was finally published in Dickson and Grass, *Growth of the Brethren*, as "Anthony Norris Groves in an International Context: A Re-assessment of His Early Development." Much of the paper was written before the publication of *From Awakening to Secession*, which sometimes gives fuller details.

2. Irving, *For Missionaries*, xiv.

considered middle-class recruits in England to be "a less than desirable solution."[3] In consequence, during the early part of the nineteenth century there was a well-worn path, taken by missionary volunteers coming from Germany and Switzerland, by way of the Basel Mission Institute, to London. Here the recruits experienced some months of linguistic, social and even theological adaptation (which after 1825 took place in the CMS College in Islington) before they set sail for what would usually be an English-speaking mission field. The ordination of these continental recruits was normally Lutheran, and this was a potential source of embarrassment, liable to reinforce the perception that missionary activity was not really an occupation for Anglicans, but there was no particular need to publicize the continental connection and for a while it was largely ignored. It had been quite an unusual event in 1822 when Dr. Blumhardt, the Director of the Basel Institute, addressed the annual meeting of the CMS, because foreigners rarely spoke on such occasions.[4] In fact, a year earlier, when members of the CMS were given some details of the Basel Mission Institute, a somewhat better informed Anglican evangelical wrote that it seemed "like a new discovery, so little is it [the Institute] known in England."[5] Nevertheless an important link had been forged in the chain of co-operation with the continent—albeit a link deriving from opportunist expediency rather than ecumenical principle and it is in this context that we need to look more closely at the neglected career of the missionary strategist Anthony Norris Groves.

Biographical Summary

Any attempt to reevaluate Groves's career is fraught with difficulties, not the least of which is the aura of sanctity which has gathered around the memory of a man who had decidedly ascetic tendencies and yet seems to have been consistently generous and winsome toward his fellows. The basic outline of his life is not in dispute.[6] Born on 1 February 1795 in Newton Valence, Hampshire,[7] he grew up in London where he

---

3. Miller, *Social Control of Religious Zeal*, 42. Before 1814 (when the prohibition on missionary work in India was lifted) fourteen out of seventeen CMS missionaries were foreigners, and even in the next five years barely two-thirds were English. Only two out of the forty-four English missionaries enrolled prior to 1824 were university graduates. [Barry], *CMS Register*, 1–11.

4. Stock, *History of the CMS*, 1:263.

5. Basel, Mission Archives, Gemischte Briefe, Q-3-4, Francis Cunningham to C. G. Blumhardt, May 1821. I am indebted to Mr. Paul Jenkins, archivist of the Basel Mission, for his unfailing help over a period of many years. For C. G. Blumhardt, see Lewis, *BDEB*, 1:110.

6. See F. R. Coad, in *BDEB*, 1:485–86, and the less accurate article by G. C. Boase in *DNB* 7:742–43. The basic sources for all existing accounts of Groves are his published journals [see below, n23] and [H. B. Groves], *Memoir*. Sensitive reworkings of this account are to be found in Rowdon, *Origins*, 38–40, 188–200; and Coad, *History*, 15–24. More recently Rob Dann has given us what will surely be the definitive account of Groves, see R. B. Dann, *Father of Faith Missions*.

7. Details of Groves's youth and family are elusive. Mr. Dann (whose eagle eye has saved me from several errors in this paper) has established from records in the Hampshire County Record Office,

studied chemistry, had some experience of walking the wards of a London hospital and trained as a dentist with his uncle James Thompson. In 1814 he established a successful practice in Plymouth but after marrying his cousin Mary Bethia Thompson, he moved to Exeter in 1818.[8] His first Christian (and indeed missionary) commitment occurred during his time in Plymouth when he was more of a churchman than an evangelical—the latter identification dating from the early 1820s when he was influenced by the poet and curate of Broad Clyst, near Exeter, John Marriott,[9] and by a dissenting lady Elizabeth [Bessie] Paget. Enrolling with the CMS in 1825, Groves prepared for ordination as a non-resident student at Trinity College, Dublin, where he attended for examinations and where he came into contact with several radical evangelical Christians like John Bellett and John Darby who would later be known as Plymouth Brethren.[10] Abandoning his plans for ordination, he withdrew from the CMS and in June 1829 set out as a freelance missionary, travelling with his family to St. Petersburg and then overland to Baghdad. In the course of the journey, at Shushee, they met Karl Gottlieb Pfander with whom Groves discovered an immediate rapport. Pfander joined the party and worked with Groves in Baghdad for over a year.[11] During 1830 a school was established and some apparently useful contacts were made through Groves's medical work, but in March 1831 everything began to change for the worse. Groves now had to endure an epidemic of plague (which eventually carried off his wife and baby daughter), disastrous flooding and finally the paralysis of civil war. By the spring of 1833 Groves, deeply depressed, was recognizing an apparently negative response to his self-sacrificial efforts to bring Christ to the inhabitants of Baghdad.

In June, Groves set out for India with Sir Arthur Cotton, leaving his two sons in the care of John Parnell (later Lord Congleton) and Edward Cronin, fellow missionaries who had arrived from Britain in June 1832.[12] In India Groves embarked on a lengthy tour of mission stations where he was impressed and thrilled by the work and success of the German missionary Rhenius. However, the decision by the CMS

Winchester, that the Newton mentioned in [H. B. Groves], *Memoir*, 1, was Newton Valence where Groves was privately baptized (5 Feb). His parents were Anthony and Lydia Groves of Lymington (Dann, *Father of Faith Missions*, 17).

8. The marriage took place in Fulham Parish Church on 22 Oct 1816 (*Exeter Flying Post*, 7 Nov 1816). The removal to Exeter is given in [H. B. Groves], *Memoir*, 3, as "soon after" his marriage, but 1818 is the date given by a writer possessed of good Plymouth sources (Ryland, *Memoirs of Kitto*, 142).

9. For the evangelical rather than High Church position of Marriott ("one of the most polished and accomplished gentlemen of his time"), see the life of Marriott in Burgon, *Lives*, 1:299.

10. Cf. Stunt, "Evangelical Cross-Currents," 220–21.

11. For Pfander, see Powell, *Muslims and Missionaries*, 131–57. Cf. her article in *BDEB*, 2:879–80.

12. His readiness to leave his sons was undoubtedly facilitated by the loyal care for them given by the Chaldean nurse Hanie (also Hannai, Harnie) Thomas whose conversion and devotion to the Groves family was one of the few lasting blessings dating from his time in Baghdad. See H. Groves, *Faithful Hanie*, 37–38. "Hannah Thomas" was the first named beneficiary in Groves's will, which has recently been located in the archives of the Müller Homes in Bristol.

to require all their missionaries to submit to Anglican ordination had given rise to a dispute over the validity of Rhenius's Lutheran credentials—a controversy in which Groves became involved. In 1833 Groves traveled and worked for several months with a Lebanese Christian, Mokayel Trad, who had earlier been associated with other European missionaries like Joseph Wolff and Samuel Gobat.[13] In 1834 Groves sailed for England where he married a second time and gathered another missionary party with whom he returned to India in 1836. Reunited (after more than three years) with his sons, the rest of his life was devoted to independent missionary work, principally at Chittoor not far from Madras. In this he was supported by his German brother-in-law George Müller of Bristol and other Brethren. His health began to fail in 1852 and the last eight months of his life were spent in England where he died in 1853.

Problems of Historiography

Otherworldliness and self-denial meant that Groves wrote very little about himself as a subject that could be considered of interest in its own right. If events in his earlier life had some bearing on, for example, the discovery of biblical truth or the furtherance of the preaching of the gospel, then there was reason for him to mention them, but his own account of his earlier life is singularly devoid of personal detail.[14] During the 1820s Groves came to the conclusion (forthrightly expressed in his booklet *Christian Devotedness* [1825]) that the accumulation of any wealth, beyond the immediate needs of the day, was in conflict with the teaching of Christ. This conviction, together with the need for minimal encumbrances when travelling, seems to have led to the disposal of much of his substance and with it, presumably, the sort of mementos and memorabilia which would have been useful for a biographer.

Another problem is posed by the personal involvement (and prejudices) of the editor of Groves's *Memoir*, namely his second wife, Harriet,[15] the second daughter

---

13. For Mokayel Trad's earlier career, see Railton, *Transnational Evangelicalism*, 147n50.

14. For instance, there is no mention of the birth of his sons Henry and Frank who were christened in St. David's, Exeter, respectively on 18 Jun 1819 and 17 Mar 1820 (IGI). Henry is said to have been born in November 1818 (Pickering, *Chief Men*, 98).

15. [H. B. Groves], *Memoir*, 35. After the death of his first wife, Groves proposed to Harriet Baynes by post from Baghdad sometime in 1832—a proposal that was initially refused. Two years later (c. 1834), "hearing that she had been grievously injured and disfigured by a wagon which crushed her face in a narrow Devonshire lane, he renewed his proposal and was accepted," Meyer, *Author of the Peep of Day*, 65–66. For the postal proposition of marriage from Baghdad, see H. Groves, *Memoir of Lord Congleton*, 43. The marriage was celebrated in the Priory Church of St. Mary, Great Malvern, on 25 Apr 1835 (IGI). For other details of Harriet Baynes and her family, see E. K. Groves, *George Müller*, 36, 60–61. This curiously polemical autobiography, by her son, has been regularly ignored by Brethren writers for a number of reasons. The author's adoption of a belief in conditional immortality was unacceptable to many Brethren, as was the fact that he dared to question the infallibility of Müller's judgment. His frank admission that he had suffered mental disturbance was also probably a factor in their disapproval.

of Major-General Edward Baynes of Sidmouth.[16] Her personal acquaintance with Groves dated from 1829 when his spiritual development and his independent convictions were fairly well established, so the early part of the *Memoir* is marred by vagueness, inconsistencies and hindsight. For example, the date of Groves's evangelical enlightenment is far from clear and though there are occasional references to his earlier Arminianism, it is only from a very careful scrutiny of the *Memoir* that we begin to realize how comparatively late was his adoption of Calvinist evangelical views and the disintegration of his earlier "exact" churchmanship.[17] His widow plays down the resilience of Groves's earlier Christian commitment with its involvement in local social welfare and not just missionary dedication. She mentions her husband's adoption of the deaf pauper, John Kitto, in 1824, but makes no reference to the part played in the arrangement by Groves's early "Christian friend," Robert Lampen, who was a noted opponent of the Calvinist clergy in Plymouth.[18] There is similarly no allusion in the *Memoir* to his participation at the meeting for the establishment of an Exeter Mendicity Society in 1825[19] for aiding the indigent, nor of the part he played in the work of the local anti-slavery society of which he was the secretary as late as 1827.[20] There are references to his friendship with the Exeter schoolmaster, William Hake, whose question about the lawfulness of war led Groves to question the Thirty-Nine Articles of the Church of England, but one suspects that Hake only earned a mention because of his later association with the Brethren. Harriet Groves makes no mention of the fact that both Bessie Paget (whom Groves regarded as his "mother, in the things of God"[21])

16. For Edward Baynes (1771–1829), see Borthwick, *History and biographical Gazeteer*, 255–56. He had been Adjutant-General to the forces in British North America, where Harriet lived as a child though (according to the Census records) she was born in Jersey in 1807. For the Jamaican origins of Harriet's mother, Ann Frances Cator, see D. A. Livesay, "Children of Uncertain Fortune: Mixed Race Migration from the West Indies to Britain, 1750–1820," (PhD diss., University of Michigan, 2010). Harriet's younger brother, William Craig Baynes (1809–87), returned to Canada in 1843 where he became secretary of McGill University (Collard, *Oldest McGill*, 69–74) and was a leading figure among the Plymouth Brethren. For some details of an initiative by Harriet Baynes to promote evangelism at Colaton Raleigh near Sidmouth just after Groves's departure for Baghdad, see Stunt, "Some Very Early Plymouth Brethren," 103–4, which made use of some genealogical research by Mr. Gordon Faulkner available online at http://www.faulkner-history.fsnet.co.uk/Passmore_Files.

17. As late as November 1825, Groves was suggesting to his children's tutor, Robert Nesbit, that "the high Calvinistic tenets of the Scottish Church were unfavourable to the missionary spirit." Mitchell, *Memoir of Nesbit*, 28.

18. [H. B. Groves], *Memoir*, 3; at the time, Groves's sister "resided in the Rev. Mr. Lampen's family," Ryland, *Memoirs of Kitto*, 142; for Lampen's opposition to Calvinism, see Exeter, Cathedral Archives, ED 11/85, 2:23–24, "Bishop Phillpott's Visitation Journal."

19. *Exeter Flying Post*, 30 Jun 1825. The Mendicity Society's well intentioned attempts to distinguish between paupers in need and "professional" vagrants was a cause in which several Quakers like William Allen (see above, ch. 1) also took an active part, see M. J. D Roberts, "Reshaping the Gift," 201–31.

20. *Exeter Flying Post*, 2 Mar 1826; *Exeter Pocket Journal* (1827).

21. [H. B. Groves], *Memoir*, 40.

and Hake had connections with the Society of Friends.[22] These circumstances, taken with the fact that Groves's fellow secretary in the anti-slavery society was another Quaker, George Dymond,[23] suggest not only that Groves's thinking in these years may have benefited from a rather greater input from the Society of Friends than his widow wanted to admit, but that his spiritual development as an evangelical was interestingly unconventional.

Similarly Mrs. Groves's personal attitudes influenced her account of his later career and also her selective use of the *Journals*, which Groves kept when travelling to Persia and during his first year in Baghdad—*Journals* which were published in London in 1831 and 1832. A comparison of the original publications with the extracts reproduced in the *Memoir* suggests that Harriet Groves felt free to "improve" them not only grammatically.[24]

The problem is further compounded by Groves's connection with the early Plymouth Brethren. When the great rift developed in the 1840s between the Exclusive Brethren (gathered under the unofficial leadership of J. N. Darby) and the Open Brethren (one of whose most respected figures was Groves's brother-in-law, George Müller) there was naturally much argument about what had been the original principles of the "Brethren." Almost inevitably, Groves was hailed by Open Brethren as the "prototype" of their less exclusive ideals, while Exclusive Brethren dismissed him as having been only "on the fringes" of the movement.[25] There is some truth in both statements, but Brethren writers have tended to hijack the story of Groves's development to tally with their own particular ecclesiastical preferences. Although his early influence on the Brethren was diminished by geographical distance, the importance of his early role in the movement cannot be disputed and clearly he kept in close touch with Brethren in later years. On the other hand, a later generation of Open Brethren whose ecclesiastical identity was more clearly defined, played down some important aspects of Groves's career, fearing, perhaps, that his easygoing involvement

---

22. E. K. Groves, *George Müller*, 370; Hake's fellow secretary of the Exeter auxiliary of the Society for the Promotion of Permanent and Universal Peace was the Quaker, Jonathan Dymond, *Exeter Pocket Journal* (1827). Cf. Brock, "Peace Testimony," 32.

23. *Exeter Pocket Journal* (1827). The Quaker connection is further underlined by Groves's contacts with Sarah Kilham in St. Petersburg, A. N. Groves, *Journal . . . during a Journey*, 27, 29–30, 32; A. N. Groves, *Journal of a Residence*, 36; cf. Ryland, *Memoirs of Kitto*, 303–4, 443–44.

24. E.g., although she included some of Groves's comments on the possible dangers of education, Mrs. Groves evidently felt, in the aftermath of the Crimean War, that it was wiser to omit a paragraph where her husband had observed, "I would certainly much rather have to do with a Russian peasant than an English one, and with any one rather than those who are the self-designated learned among the English operatives [referring to an earlier comment on 'the spirit from which emanates Mechanic Institutes and such like;]" A. N. Groves, *Journal . . . during a Journey*, 45; [H. B. Groves], *Memoir*, 59.

25. The two tendencies are well exemplified respectively in Lang, *Anthony Norris Groves*, which contains a sustained critique of some attitudes of the Exclusive Brethren among whom Lang had grown up, and in Weremchuk, *John Nelson Darby*, 66–69.

with Christians outside the Brethren orbit was liable to tarnish his credentials among the less liberal of the Open Brethren.

Another aspect of the historiographical problem is that even by the time Harriet Baynes was married to Groves, and certainly by the time she was preparing his *Memoir*, the name of Edward Irving was inextricably associated with the charismatic manifestations of the early 1830s and with the Catholic Apostolic Church of the Irvingites—an ecclesiastical cul-de-sac despised and reviled by most Brethren. There has, therefore, been a reluctance to identify Groves with Irving. Temperamentally, of course, they were very different, but in the later 1820s Groves must have been aware of the similarity of his missionary ideal to that of Irving. The fact that the second and third editions of his pamphlet *Christian Devotedness* were published by James Nisbet, a member of Irving's congregation, and that Groves's *Journals* (also published by Nisbet) were edited by Irving's fellow worker, Sandy Scott, cannot be ignored. Groves continued to regard the possible revival of the pentecostal gifts as an open question for some time after his departure for Baghdad in 1829.

The Church Missionary Society Connection

Groves's first personal contact with the CMS authorities was early in 1825 when the possibility arose of his protégé, John Kitto, working as a printer's apprentice in the missionary College at Islington. This led to Groves's explanation to Edward Bickersteth, the Society's secretary, of his own long-standing wish to engage in missionary service.[26] So in August, the secretary was able to report to the committee that an unnamed individual "in a respectable situation in life" had offered his services to the Society but that circumstances [the expected opposition of Mary's family] "prevent him coming forward at present to avow his intentions." The secretary added that "both from his conversation with the individual . . . and from the unanimous testimony of the friends of the Society in the neighbourhood where he lives" it was "peculiarly eligible [sic] to engage his services." The Society's minutes record that Groves was acquainted with Latin, Greek, Hebrew, French, and Italian and that he wanted "to know in what quarter it is probable that he may be employed, if eventually accepted." Although Groves later recalled that the CMS "accepted my offer, and begged me to change from India to Persia,"[27] the minutes make clear that when the committee accepted his offer "with satisfaction" they indicated that Groves might "be most advantageously employed in the Mediterranean Mission" recommending him "more particularly to study Italian, Modern Greek and Arabic and to acquire as much medical knowledge as practicable."[28] It was only in February 1827 when the inimitable Joseph Wolff, self-

---

26. Birmingham, University Library, CMS Archive, G/C/1, A. N. Groves to E. H. Bickersteth (25 Mar 1825), transcribed in CMS Minutes (20 May 1825), 7:517; [H. B. Groves], *Memoir*, 11–12.

27. [H. B. Groves], *Memoir*, 23.

28. CMS Minutes (9 Aug 1825), 8:9–10.

appointed missionary to Jews worldwide, gave an account to the CMS Committee of his travels and observations in Persia, that its members were immediately reminded of "the qualifications of Mr. A. N. Groves . . . for entering on such a sphere of labour" and recommended that his "course of study and preparation be directed with a view to his being employed in a mission to Persia in prosecution of the Society's objects."[29]

Great must have been the rejoicing among the members of the CMS Committee at Bickersteth's discovery of a respected Christian, competent in more than one language, who was willing to serve with the Society—especially when he proved (to begin with at any rate) very ready to comply with the committee's recommendations and seemed to be blessed with no mean powers of endurance. In his later years, Groves was inclined to hold worldly learning in low esteem, and some of his admirers have been inclined to belittle the importance of study as a preparation for missionary service. Some of his early letters are all the more revealing, therefore, as they indicate just how seriously Groves originally considered the matter of preparation. In the Mediterranean Mission to which he was originally assigned, Groves would have been working with William Jowett whose *Christian Researches*[30] he now read with care. In consequence he gave first priority to his Greek and Arabic studies, "by way of preparing me for future service." With the help of the former rabbi, Michael Alexander (later bishop of Jerusalem), in whose conversion to Christianity he had played a significant part, Groves also aimed to improve his Hebrew, though on his own admission his progress was impeded by professional responsibilities. It is sometimes supposed that a university degree was required for Anglican ordination, but in fact men could be ordained without such a qualification. It appears to have been Groves's decision, with Bickersteth's approval, to work for a degree and in March 1826, and nine months after his original commitment we learn of his plans to attend regularly at Dublin and possibly to take his degree at Oxford. In the meanwhile, apart from the Bible, his reading was almost totally devoted to Latin and Greek.

> I trust that in the end I may not disappoint your hopes, yet at times when I contemplate the necessary requisites even of a natural kind in the station to which you have thought it best to direct my thoughts, I am almost overcome with the sense of their magnitude.[31]

Remembering that Groves would soon part company with the CMS because he found its requirements too restrictive, the submissive tone of these early letters is noteworthy. And yet Groves was in a very different category from many of the CMS

---

29. CMS Minutes (20 Feb 1827), 9:29–30; this explains Groves's suggestion in a letter as late as 2 April 1827 that his reader might not "know our destination is finally fixed for Persia," [H. B. Groves], *Memoir*, 19.

30. Jowett, *Christian Researches*. Groves found himself in agreement with much of what Jowett had written and felt it would be a good basis for "successful co-operation." Groves to Bickersteth, 15 Sep 1825 (CMS Archive, G/Ac3/Sept 1825).

31. CMS Archive, G/Ac3/March 1826, Groves to Bickersteth, 14 Mar [1826].

recruits. He was well educated and if not yet a graduate, he soon would be; he was older, in his thirties (barely ten years younger than Bickersteth), with almost a dozen years of professional experience; his income was far from negligible; and he was English [!]. Would such considerations affect the way the CMS authorities would view him, if he were to disagree with them? The authoritarian paternalism with which they were inclined to treat their recruits could easily be offensive and more than one of the young continentals who spent time in London has left a record of how insensitive he found the CMS authorities.[32] Tantalizingly, the CMS archives appear to make no reference to Groves's decision to break with the Society and become an independent missionary. In consequence, the only available details are taken from his later recollections.[33]

There were, in fact, several elements that contributed to his abandoning the plans for ordination and his subsequent withdrawal from the CMS. First, there were the doubts raised in Groves's mind by Henry Townley, a retired LMS missionary, about the usefulness of studying for a degree.[34] Then, in October 1827, there was the "providential" theft of Groves's travel money preventing him from going to Dublin.[35] Shortly afterwards when questioned on the subject by Hake, Groves realized that he could not subscribe to the thirty-seventh article of the Church of England in its approval of armed warfare "at the command of the Magistrate." Of the CMS reaction to his decision Groves merely tells us that he "was still so far attached to the Church of England that I went to London to arrange my going out as a layman for the Church Missionary Society; but as they would not allow me to celebrate the Lord's Supper, when no other minister was near, it came to nothing."[36] Such a suggestion was clearly quite beyond the mind-set of the CMS authorities and one can imagine their sigh of relief when they realized that they would be no longer responsible for a candidate who was turning out to be of a suspiciously radical turn of thought.

Brethren writers, with their anti-clerical perspectives, have understandably seen Groves's break with the CMS as part of a wider ecclesiastical emancipation from restrictive institutional restraints, and certainly it coincided chronologically with his abandonment in 1827–28 of his previously strict churchmanship. But it can also be argued that both developments were logical outworkings of the much more fundamental

---

32. Cf. Stunt, "Leonard Strong," 102; First and Scott, *Olive Schreiner*, 31. The problem would become more acute with the retirement of Bickersteth in 1830 and his replacement by the zealous but narrow Dandeson Coates.

33. [H. B. Groves], *Memoir*, 41–42.

34. "Mr. T., of Calcutta," [H. B. Groves], *Memoir*, 41. Townley was doing deputation work in Devon in the summer of 1827, *EM* 5 (1827) 498.

35. The account of the burglary in the local newspaper confirms Groves's recollection that the robbery was on a Sunday morning and that other money "put aside for a particular use" [taxes] escaped the attention of the thieves. More than a year later a tailor, Thomas Salter, was charged with theft committed on Groves who "declared he would not proceed against a fellow creature in such distress and instantly tendered him pecuniary aid." *Exeter Flying Post*, 24 Oct 1827, 4; 19 Mar 1829, 3.

36. [H. B. Groves], *Memoir*, 42. I can find no reference to this suggestion in the CMS Minutes, though Groves continues to be mentioned in connection with Kitto; see below, n42.

asceticism and otherworldliness which were central to the case which Groves had argued in his earlier pamphlet *Christian Devotedness*. In passing we should perhaps note that the "powerful appeals" of this work had contributed to the missionary convictions of Robert Nesbit who, as a tutor, had joined Groves's household in November 1825 but who, less than three months later, was preparing to offer himself for service with the Scottish Missionary Society.[37]

It is evident from a cursory reading of *Christian Devotedness* that Groves's profound fear of anything which might be categorized as treasure laid up on earth or, in his colorful phrase, "poisonous heaps of gold,"[38] was leading him to be increasingly wary of exercising "worldly" influence of any sort, whether it was financial, educational, social or religious, all of which he treated as aspects of "the silken age into which we are fallen."[39] That these implications of his pamphlet had continued to occupy him is apparent from the third edition, published in 1829, in which he refers to the subject of another pamphlet (as yet unwritten[40]):

> I shall endeavour to show, that a grain of the pure gold of Christian influence, which is the exhibition, in truth, of the mind of Christ, springing from the love of Christ in the soul, is no wise increased in value by being beaten out into plates as thin as imagination can conceive, and employed to gild the brassy admixture of earthly influence, the titles, honours, rank, wealth, learning and secular power of this world. It looks indeed like a mighty globe of gold . . . but the least scratch proves its brassy character. If this simple principle had been perceived, how differently would many public religious bodies have been constituted for the purpose of extending the influence of Christ's kingdom.[41]

---

37. Piggin and Roxborough, *St. Andrews Seven*, 98. Cf. Edinburgh, New College Archives, CHA 4.60.5, 7, R. Nesbit to T. Chalmers, 17 Feb and 13 Mar 1826, where he commends the pamphlet to the serious attention of his fellow students. Characteristically Groves's testimonial for Nesbit in 1826 emphasized his "simple sincerity of purpose . . . religious consistency and single devotedness of heart," Mitchell, *Memoir of Nesbit*, 34. One of Nesbit's fellow students, Alexander Duff, later wrote to Groves from Calcutta "of his first glow of devotedness, as having arisen" from reading Groves's pamphlet, [H. B. Groves], *Memoir*, 295. Duff's biographer makes no mention of this early influence on his subject though he pays tribute to Groves's tireless care of the dysentery-stricken Duff in 1834. Duff's son was named Alexander Groves Duff, Smith, *Life of Alexander Duff*, 121–22.

38. A. N. Groves, *Christian Devotedness* (London, 2nd ed. 1826), 1–2.

39. Ibid., 33–34. Cf. the reference in his journal (Aug 1830) to "sentimental Christianity" as 'a thing to talk about, on silken sofas with all the refinements of this pampered and luxurious age," [H. B. Groves], *Memoir*, 57–58.

40. A. N. Groves, *On the Nature of Christian Influence* (Bombay, 1833).

41. A. N. Groves, *Christian Devotedness* (3rd ed., 1829), preface. An important indication of how Groves's thinking on prophetic matters had recently developed is apparent in this third edition. Here he adopted a premillennial position and excised an earlier suggestion that if Christians were to take the New Testament precepts seriously "the day would indeed be dawning when 'the knowledge of the Lord shall cover the earth, as the waters cover the sea,'" (2nd ed. 1826, 51). Although there were three English editions of Christian Devotedness there are apparently no extant copies of the first (1825). The online catalogue (www.copac.ac.uk) lists an edition in New College Library, Edinburgh, which is dated 1828 "re-printed at the Church Mission Press, Madras." If the date is truly 1828 there is a

In shunning the pedestals of influence provided by clerical and institutional hierarchies, Groves was finding himself at odds with the condescending and arrogant tendencies of his own class towards those whom they regarded as socially inferior—attitudes which often characterized the behavior of the CMS towards its volunteers, and more specifically their rather high-handed treatment of Groves's intelligent but awkward pauper protégé, John Kitto. In 1826 Kitto had somewhat hastily tendered to the CMS his resignation and then, thinking better of it, asked for readmission. The CMS refused and it was only Groves's eloquent pleadings on Kitto's behalf that caused them to change their minds.[42] Kitto was now sent to Malta where he worked in the CMS printing house for more than a year (1827–29) but again he came into conflict with his superiors—this time over a matrimonial proposal—and resigned a second time.[43] On his return to England in February 1829 he was once more *persona non grata* with both the CMS and his former patrons in Plymouth. It was typical of Groves that his concern transcended considerations of class and although he was preparing for his own imminent departure for Baghdad he was again ready to help Kitto find employment with his friend John Synge of Teignmouth, although ultimately Kitto accepted Groves's invitation for him to join his party and come to Baghdad as a tutor for his boys.[44]

The Basel Connection

Some twenty years later Kitto recalled the time he had spent with the CMS at Islington and, in a glowing testimonial, described the continental recruits (to whom he always referred as "Germans" even though some of them, like Samuel Gobat and Paul Pacifique Schaffter, were French-speaking Swiss):

> [There] were ten Germans from the excellent Missionary Institution at Basle who . . . were regarded with peculiar interest, and with some curiosity as the first foreigners most of [the students] had ever known . . . While the German brethren secured respect by their parts, their learning and deep experience in

---

delicious irony in the pamphlet having been issued by the CMS in India in 1828 before Groves left for Baghdad (and presumably even before he broke off his enrolment with them). It would have been this edition that Daniel Poor passed on to Sir Arthur Cotton, [H. B. Groves], *Memoir*, 273; cf. 259.

42. CMS Minutes 9 (6 Feb, 20 Feb, 20 Mar 1827), 17, 30, 55; Birmingham UL, CMS G/Ac3/March 1827, Groves to Bickersteth, 10 Mar 1827. In a letter to Robert Lampen, Kitto paid a heartfelt tribute to the patient care and concern of Groves whom he described as his "guardian angel," see Ryland, *Memoirs of Kitto*, 231.

43. CMS Minutes 10 (3, 17 Jun 1828), 563, 579. Kitto's biographer makes no mention of the matrimonial issue.

44. Ryland, *Memoirs of Kitto*, 289–93. The CMS Minutes (9 Aug 1825) indicate that from the outset Groves's younger sister, Lydia, had wished to accompany Groves "to undertake the children's education." In fact she had to return home on account of poor health when the party reached St. Petersburg.

the things of God, they won universal regard by the affectionate tenderness of their demeanour and the Christian simplicity of their character.[45]

It was very probably through Kitto that Groves made his earliest, firsthand acquaintance with the Basel missionaries with whom he felt a natural affinity.[46] That this appreciation was mutual is suggested by the fact that when George Müller came to the Seminary from Germany in early 1829, he soon heard favorable reports of Groves who was on the point of leaving the country.[47] It is against this background that we may better understand Groves's intense delight at meeting, on his way to Baghdad, Karl Gottlieb Pfander and his German coworkers at Shushee. In contrast to the Moravian colony at Sarepta which he considered "as a little church gathered together in the wilderness, but not at all as a missionary station, or as having missionary objectives,"[48] the Basel missionaries at Shushee shared Groves's concern for identification with the people around them:

> That perfect unity of sentiment which subsists between us as to the importance of laying aside every thing of this world's greatness, and descending to the level of the people, is most grateful [sc. gratifying] to me; and this is not the sentiment of one of these dear brethren but of all.[49]

It was this emphasis that led Groves into a sort of self-contradiction when he was in India. Much has been made by his admirers of his readiness to nurture native leadership and with some reason he has been hailed as a pioneer of "indigenization." What is sometimes forgotten is that in his enthusiastic support for Rhenius Groves was siding with a nineteenth-century rejection of an earlier pietist missionary tradition in India that had been far readier to countenance Indian leadership and this put Groves into a position of some ambiguity. The Tamil pastors, to whom the earlier German missionaries Ziegenbalg and Pluetschau had given responsibility, had been happy to work within some social and cultural traditions that later Rhenius (and Groves with him) would challenge.[50] In this respect, although Groves strove for identification he seems to have brought to India his own quite radical social agenda, which placed

---

45. Schlienz, *Pilgrim Missionary Institution*, xxii. Christoph Schlienz, for whom Kitto wrote this introduction, was a year older than Kitto, whom he had known in Malta where he worked with the CMS from 1827 to 1842 before being appointed as principal of the St. Chrischona Institution in Basel.

46. There is a further parallel here between Groves and Edward Irving who was also enthusiastic about the "German" missionaries, Oliphant, *Life of Irving*, 1:308–9, 352–54.

47. Müller, *Narrative*, 1:44. The CMS College seems to have been shared by the students training with the London Society for Promoting Christianity among the Jews. Cf. Stock, *CMS History*, 1:153–54. It was only later that Müller married Groves's sister, Mary, and only in 1834 that he met Groves himself.

48. A. N. Groves, *Journal . . . during a Journey*, 47.

49. Ibid., 80–81.

50. See Singh, *First Protestant Missionary to India*; Hudson, *Protestant Origins in India*, 30–51; Peterson, "Bethlehem Kuravañci," 16–17; H. Liebau, "Country Priests," 70–92.

him in opposition to some social *mores* in India, which earlier missionaries had accepted as "a part of the territory." This opposition was apparent on his first arrival in Tinnevelly when he wrote, "As I desire to break down caste among the Hindoos, to pave the way for the reception of the truth, so do I desire to break down caste in the Christian church to prepare the way for publishing it [sc. proclaiming the truth]."[51]

Although Groves prized most highly his Christian liberty and although his withdrawal from the CMS reflects his deep fear of the institutional shackles, which so often accompanied worldly "influence," we must resist the suggestion that he would have nothing to do with Christians whose opinions on such matters differed from his. Before his departure from England he arranged a meeting with Henry Drummond with a view to obtaining the latest information Joseph Wolff could provide about Persia.[52] At his request the LSPCJ provided him with books for use in Persia[53] and he was similarly glad to make use of the administrative infrastructure of the British and Foreign Bible Society with whose committee and secretaries he was regularly in contact from 1829–32.[54] Regular reports of his work appeared in the *Missionary Register* where his explanation of the case for developing a trade route to India by way of the Tigris and Euphrates was surprisingly cognizant of the practical realities of commerce for a man with such otherworldly perspectives.[55] It is similarly refreshing to find that, in spite of the earlier disagreements, Groves had an arrangement with the CMS for forwarding mail to him and was earnestly encouraging the Committee of the Society (in a letter of October 1832) to send someone to Ispahan to whom "we would be delighted to give . . . a brotherly help by the way in the language or one of us would go with him till he got a little accustomed to his work."[56] Of all the missionary societies, however, for Groves the Basel Mission Institute was in a special category of its own and increasingly he began to look in the direction of Switzerland for reinforcements who would

---

51. [H. B. Groves], *Memoir*, 242; cf. 268, 274, 282.

52. Alnwick, Northumberland Archives, C/1/200, 201, A. N. Groves to H. Drummond, two undated letters [c. Feb–Jun 1829].

53. Oxford, Bodleian Library, Dep CMJ, Minutes of the General Committee of the London Society for Promoting Christianity among the Jews, 13 (1829) 289.

54. Five letters from Groves (5 Jun 1829, 28 Aug 1830, 18 Sep 1831, 2 May and 20 Oct 1832) are in Cambridge University Library, BFBS Archives. Cf. Bible Society, Twenty-eighth Report (1832) lviii–lix.

55. *Missionary Register* (1831) 376. Shortly before leaving India in 1834, Joseph Clulow, an administrator in Madras had forwarded to Lord William Bentinck, the governor-general of Bengal and India, a copy of Groves's proposal for using the Tigris and the Persian Gulf as the best route from the Mediterranean to India; (Nottingham University, Dept of MSS and Special Collections, Bentinck Papers. Pw Jf 791–92, Correspondence of J. Clulow, 1834). For Clulow, see below, ch. 10n41. The extent to which Groves became involved with government officials in Baghdad is not quite clear. On at least one occasion during the plague epidemic (29 Mar 1831) he accompanied Dr. Montefiore, the medical officer to the Residency, on a visit to the "Arab infected quarter" (London, India Office Records, R. Taylor's Dispatch, 17 Jun 1831, L/PS/9 [Persia 1831], 46:497).

56. [H. B. Groves], *Memoir*, 53; Birmingham UL, CMS G/Ac3/October 1832, A. N. Groves to T. Woodroffe, 25 Oct 1832.

share his own concern for a simple lifestyle and his disregard for social status. After his meeting with Pfander we find Groves writing to Admiral Pearson of the need to establish an Armenian female school:

> I wish Mr. [Joseph] Greaves and [his wife] your daughter could come here from Basle . . . or at all events stir up the Basle Committee to send them some one or two faithful men to encourage and strengthen them.[57]

In fact, this was but the start of an important relationship with the continental evangelical movement. Extracts from Groves's *Journal* were published in French in Neuchâtel in 1834,[58] and, in the same year, details of Groves's work in Baghdad with Pfander were reported in the *Journal des Missions Évangéliques*.[59] Groves himself was corresponding with Dr. Blumhardt and others at Basel[60] both before and after his visit to Switzerland in 1835 when he gathered new recruits for the Indian mission field. These included the redoubtable German, Hermann Gundert[61] (a grandfather of the novelist, Hermann Hesse), Rodolphe de Rodt[62] from Geneva and Ferdinand Gros from Lausanne, as well as two Swiss women from Rolle,[63] one of whom, Julie Dubois, would later become (in spite of the hostility of the second Mrs. Groves) the wife of Dr. Gundert.[64]

Indeed, for a while at least, Groves's thinking in missionary matters had a discernable impact on the policies of the Basel Mission. In his account of the missionary Samuel Hebich, Gundert indicates that it was Groves's plea for a simpler lifestyle that led to Blumhardt's proposal that the Basel missionaries "should receive no stated income, but simply draw what was necessary for their subsistence from the society, it

---

57. Basel, BMA, GB/Q-3-4, 2 MS copies of A. N. Groves to Admiral Pearson, 14 Oct 1829. An inaccurate extract from this letter is reproduced in Ehret, "Der Rückzug der Basler Mission aus Russland," 164–65. For Greaves, see Stunt, "Greaves Family," 406.

58. [A. N. Groves], *Extraits du Journal* [copy in Zürich Zentralbibliothek].

59. *Journal des Missions Évangéliques* (1834) 209–12.

60. By April 1834 Groves is mentioning "Mr Blumhardt's letters" and his own plans to visit Basel, [H. B. Groves], *Memoir*, 285. Other surviving letters from Groves to Basel include: Basel, BMA. GB/Q-3-4; Personalfaszikell series Q-13 BV235 [Gundert], Groves to Blumhardt, 22 Jun 1834; Groves to W. Büchelen, 30 Nov 1835 and 22 Mar 1836; Basel Staats-Archiv, Pr. Arch. 653.v.11, Groves to C. F. Spittler, 7 Apr 1835; Dec 1835. The earlier letter to Spittler is inaccurately cited in Staehlin, *Die Christentumsgesellschaft*, 2:506–7.

61. See Brecht, "Relationship between Established . . . and Free Church," 137.

62. Bouterwek, *Leben und Wirken Rudolf's von Rodt*, 6. Cf. Anon., "Memoir of R. de Rodt," 561–84; and Rodolphe de Rodt, "Letters."

63. The earliest issues (1836 and 1837) of the *Feuille de la Commission des Églises Associées pour l'Évangélisation*, contained regular details of the Swiss recruits. It also contains a letter from Groves (20 Mar 1836) written before embarking at Milford Haven, *Feuille* 1 (1836) 5:120–22, and others of his letters from Madras. For specific details of those travelling with Groves in 1836 (evidently based on unspecified MS material), see Bromley, *They were men sent from God*, 14–16.

64. For Harriet Groves's opposition, see Gundert, *Tagebuch aus Malabar*, 34. Gundert's journals and letters edited by Albrecht Frenz are a useful independent source for Groves and his work in India after 1835 (Gundert, *Schriften und Berichte*; and Gundert, *Calwe Tagebuch*).

being understood that their mode of life was to be as simple as possible, conforming, whenever they could do it, to the habits of the natives of the country."[65] In his correspondence with the Basel authorities and other societies, Groves's fundamental concern was to mobilize manpower for the gospel and he was not primarily concerned with labels and affiliations. His enthusiastic participation, on his way to Baghdad, in the chapel activities of Richard Knill, the LMS worker in St. Petersburg, and his appreciation of the financial help given to him by the members of Knill's congregation are at variance with any sectarian evaluation of Groves.[66]

It is true that on a regular basis, Groves was not always the easiest man to work with, as may be seen from the departure of John Kitto from Baghdad in 1833 and the later problems of Hermann Gundert in India.[67] However, on the wider front there is very little evidence to suggest that Groves would only cooperate with those who shared his own ecclesiastical ideals. His involvement in the rupture between Rhenius and the CMS was clearly motivated by Groves's concern that the German missionary's work should not be put at risk. The disagreement was over the validity of Lutheran ordination on the mission field—an issue to which Groves sat very lightly—and he was certainly not inveigling Rhenius to "join the Brethren."[68] Even if, in personal practice, he found the principle difficult to implement, Groves believed that missionaries should be free from human restrictions and answerable only to God. His position was clearly expressed in a letter to Blumhardt:

---

65. Gundert, *Life of Samuel Hebich*, 55–56. In another account, Gundert makes clear that a little later, the Basel Mission's leaders were less enthusiastic about Groves's proposals for fully autonomous missionaries (Gundert, *Herrmann Moegling*, 75, 77).

66. [H. B. Groves], *Memoir*, 54–55; *EM* (1829) 551–52; cf. London, School of Oriental and African Studies, Council for World Mission Archives A2 [14] 1:3 "Journal of Richard Knill" 1 (23 Jun–4 Jul 1829) 252–55.

67. Rowdon, *Origins*, 193–94; Brecht, "Relationship," 139–40.

68. The best account of Groves's involvement with Rhenius is Rowdon, *Origins*, 196–97, though he appears not to have used Rhenius's biography. Such was the bad odor in which Brethren were held at the time, that Groves's part in the episode is minimized in accounts favorable to Rhenius, e.g., Rhenius, *Memoir of C. T. E. Rhenius*. The CMS historian Eugene Stock (*CMS History*, 1:283, 320) casts Groves as the villain of the story, but in this respect he cannot be taken too seriously as, in the same paragraph, he claims that Groves was responsible for the society's loss of Kitto, which is a ludicrous suggestion. For CMS anxieties about Groves at the time, see Basel, BMA, CMS correspondence series QK-3, 1D, Coates to C. G. Blumhardt, 12 Mar 1835. A postscript marked "strictly confidential," in Dandeson Coates's own hand, warns the Basel authorities against any co-operation with Groves. For Groves's affectionate account of his "holy parting moment" with John Tucker, the authoritarian Madras secretary of the CMS, see [H. B. Groves], *Memoir*, 332. John Henry Newman (who, through his brother Frank, knew about Groves) was enthusiastic about Tucker's "most sensible account of the state of India" (in which Groves was mentioned) and felt that his [Newman's] differences with Tucker "would in India almost be a matter of a few words." (Ker and Gornall, *Letters and Diaries of J. H. Newman*, 4:338, 361–62. For fuller details see my review of Callahan, *Primitivist Piety* in BAHNR 1.2 [1998] 120–21). For further light on the Rhenius affair, see Frykenberg, "Impact of Conversion," 187–243. For a disappointingly partisan approach to Groves, see Neill, *History of Christianity in India*, 220, 349, 408, 455. We await with anticipation Dr. Frykenberg's forthcoming edition of the Rhenius memoir.

I wish them [missionaries who might be sent out by the Basel Mission] to look on themselves as only Christ's servants and responsible to him as we are also[.] relative to marrying or not marrying, schools or anything else[,] all we can say is this[:] that as private individuals we might be open to be consulted or applied to for help, yet any expenses arising out of these circumstances shall never in any measure be allowed to be considered expenses connected with which we have anything to do otherwise than as private brothers. In fact our whole desire is not to get dependent servants of ours but free servants of Christ whom our desire is to help. I will not however deny that I do feel the generally expensive plan of missionary establishments in these countries as not only not helping on the cause in proportion to their expense, but in nearly that proportion unfitting them for coming at [sic] the natives in that simple way which I desire. I never shall forget the dear brethren at Shoushee[:] their simplicity edified me and their devotion stimulated me.[69]

Conclusion

In the early decades of the Brethren movement there was a significant element, particularly in Plymouth and the West Country, where the "missionary imperative" appears to have been lost sight of in a preoccupation with the eschatological details of the Savior's imminent return. It is, therefore, a little ironic that although Groves has come to be honored as a founding father of the movement, his lively missiology was at first appreciated by so few of the British Brethren. After a visit to Plymouth in 1840, John Bowes, a former Primitive Methodist preacher, was critical of the Brethren's dogmatism on such subjects as the premillennial advent of Christ and also observed that "many of them will not support this good man [Groves] because his spirit is too catholic."[70] There was undoubtedly, a "universality" in Groves's approach to humanity.

On one occasion at the beginning of his travels, Groves described his feelings on hearing the British National Anthem being played—"a circumstance which gave that sort of national pleasure, which will steal through the heart [even] of one who wishes to become a citizen of the world, as far as national attachment goes."[71] It was an honest admission from one who strove, for some thirty years, to be first and foremost a citizen of heaven and not of the world, let alone of Britain. Although Groves was an individualist, he knew that his Christian mission was in this world (albeit not of it), and he constantly delighted in the wide fellowship that he enjoyed with all the children of God wherever he found them. Nevertheless from the evidence adduced in the

---

69. Basel, BMA, GB series Q-3-4, Groves to Blumhardt, Calcutta, 22 Jun 1834.

70. Bowes, *Autobiography*, 236. I am grateful to Dr. Tim Grass for drawing my attention to this important source of independent evidence for the criticism and diminishing support from English Brethren alluded to in [H. B. Groves], *Memoir*, chs. 15 and 16. I have discussed the matter a little more fully below in ch. 10, [x-ref].

71. A. N. Groves, *Journal . . . during a Journey*, 16.

foregoing paper, Groves seems to have concluded that in his efforts to detach himself from the exercise of worldly influence and to be truly unsectarian in his Christian mission, he was more likely to find like-minded fellow workers in the world of Swiss and German piety than in the wealthier circles of English evangelicalism.

8

Influences in the Early Development of John Nelson Darby[1]

To consider the early career and teaching of John Nelson Darby is to walk into a minefield of current controversy. For many evangelical Christians today the millennial timetable is a burning issue of huge importance and it is unlikely that their interest in "the last days" was reduced by the quasi-apocalyptic events of September 2001. The importance of Darby's influence in such eschatological thinking (and more particularly in the development of the dispensationalist hermeneutic) is widely acknowledged, but the controversy, which occupies so many evangelical web sites, is concerned with whether his influence has been the bane or the benison of the evangelical world.[2] The following study is not a contribution to that debate. We shall be concerned with Darby's early intellectual and spiritual development, and some of the influences that contributed to his eschatological thinking. But we must first, by way of introduction, consider a significant shift in the eschatological outlook of the evangelical world, which was occurring in the 1820s at a crucial stage in Darby's development.

Background: An Eschatological Shift

Although the early evangelicals had frequently found themselves in conflict with the values and assumptions of the world of the Enlightenment, there was a significant element of eighteenth-century optimism in their worldview. Soon after the cataclysmic developments in France of the 1790s, a violent massacre of Europeans in Southern India had confirmed many people like Sydney Smith, writing in the *Edinburgh Review*, in their opinion of the "complete hopelessness" of Christian missions in India.[3]

---

1. This article appeared originally in 2004 in Gribben and Stunt, *Prisoners of Hope*, 44–68. I have revised several parts and have added an important section relating to Darby's time at Trinity College.

2. It is an indication of the extent of his influence that Darby's portrait appeared in *Time*'s cover feature, 1 Jul 2002, "Bible and the Apocalypse: Why More Americans Are Reading and Talking about the End of the World."

3. *Edinburgh Review* 12 (Apr 1808) 169.

In striking contrast were the optimistic expectations of William Carey and his fellow missionaries in Serampore:

> He who raised the sottish and brutalised Britons to sit in heavenly places in Christ Jesus, can raise these [Indian] slaves of superstition. The promises . . . make us anticipate that not very distant period when He will famish all the gods of India, and cause these idolaters to cast their idols to the moles and bats, and renounce for ever the work of their own hands.[4]

In this older perspective the millennium was to be ushered in by the faithful diligence of believers and would conclude with Christ's return, the "restoration of all things," and the last judgment. In a somewhat self-congratulatory but not untypical letter to the *Evangelical Magazine* it was claimed in 1820 that instead of "calculating prophetic dates" for the commencement of the millennium, the Bible, Missionary and Tract Societies "are introducing it."[5] Such a millennium might be more literal than Augustine's symbolic thousand years but Christ's return was clearly envisaged as postmillennial and for many years only a marginal minority took seriously the suggestion of Joseph Mede that Christ's return could be expected before the millennium. These "millennialists" were easily dismissed by the established evangelical journals as a product of the fanatic fringe and labeled as chiliasts or antinomians, reminiscent of the Diggers, the Fifth Monarchists and other wild men of the seventeenth-century interregnum. Indeed, in the 1820s, Edward Irving's histrionic tendencies and his eccentricities of language contributed further to the image of a premillennialism

> whose poverty and puerility in theological science, and whose lamentable deficiency in the very rudiments of biblical learning . . . are united with a startling wildness of imagination, [whose] thoughts [are] governed by no law of logic, and exhibiting a strange caricature of genius, a mode of writing which is the very panorama of affectation, and a haughtiness of dogmatism which is no symptom of the calm perception of evidence and the firmness of conviction.[6]

The first two decades of the nineteenth century had seen a proliferation of strange writing on prophetic subjects and even though there were sober and thoughtful men among those invited to Albury, the home of Henry Drummond, for the purpose of prophetic study, enthusiasts like J. H. Frere and Lewis Way, who founded the Society for the Investigation of Prophecy in 1826, were widely regarded as eccentric

---

4. In the original text of this article, I cited this quotation as it was given in Murray, *Puritan Hope*, 153, using the word Scottish instead of sottish. I now find, thanks to the learned diligence of Professor Brian Stanley, who had access to the "Serampore Form of Agreement" (1806), that the original text used sottish as found in George Smith, *Life of Carey*, 442.

5. Sheva, "Reflections," 280. See also the following passage from Bogue's *Discourses* quoted with approval seven years later in the same magazine: "By the preaching of the Gospel, the reading of the Bible, and the zeal of Christians in every station . . . will the glory of the latter days be brought about." *EM*, n.s., 5 (1827) 68.

6. *EM*, n.s., 6 (1828) 348.

or peculiar.[7] Nevertheless, with some reluctance, the *Evangelical Magazine* had to recognize in 1828 that not all premillennialists could be reduced to this caricature. In a lengthy review of Gerard Noel's *Brief Inquiry into the Prospects of the Church of Christ in connexion with the Second Advent*, a contributor systematically rejected "the radical [premillennial] errors running through his whole system" but was constrained to recognize that Noel's *Inquiry* was the work "of a holy and devout Christian and it manifests a constant anxiety to promote the interests of practical godliness." That the reviewer was somewhat disconcerted by the unexpected phenomenon of responsible and reasonable premillennialism is apparent in his references to "the incongruities in reasoning, and the great misunderstanding of Scripture passages, which we lament to find in any writing, from such an excellent man, and valuable servant of Christ, as Mr. Gerard Noel." While emphasizing his "alarm and apprehension of the *baneful practical effect* of the revived millennary doctrine," the reviewer was nonetheless relieved that "Mr. Noel's better feelings and holy benevolence have prevented him from being quite carried away by the narrow and absorbing influence of the system in which he is entangled" and concluded with an extract "which breathes the amiable, holy and conciliatory spirit of its author."[8]

This changing attitude has to be born in mind when we examine the early spiritual development of John Nelson Darby.[9] His conversion, as we shall see, dated from several years earlier but it was to his experience of spiritual renewal, late in 1827, that he looked back repeatedly in subsequent years as a time of deliverance and assurance.[10] This experience, which effectively served to identify him as an evangelical, came, therefore, at a time when a little of the stigma that had previously attached to premillennialism was beginning to diminish. Admittedly this eschatological perspective was particularly associated with the colorful preaching of Edward Irving, but even the uncompromising rigorists for whom Irving was something of a standard bearer were still considered as an integral element in the evangelical movement.[11] After all, Irving's followers were as yet untainted with charges of Christological heresy, and although the possibility of Pentecostal manifestations had been mooted there had not yet been any tongue speaking or miraculous healings. So, for a churchman to be identified with the evangelical movement did not preclude his showing public sympathy for millennialism. However we must be careful not to confuse Darby's experience of 1827 with his conversion,

---

7. The phenomenal outpouring of prophetic interpretation in the wake of the French Revolution is well illustrated in Froom, *Prophetic Faith*, 3:263–65. But Froom is far from exhaustive as he omits any reference to the more extreme characters like Richard Brothers or Joanna Southcote, or even to the less celebrated interpreters of Napoleon's place in the prophetic scheme like Lewis Mayer whose works went through several editions between 1803 and 1809.

8. *EM*, n.s., 6 (1828) 351, 348, 390–91.

9. For basic outlines of Darby's career see *ODNB*, *BDEB*; and Larson, *Biographical Dictionary*.

10. Although some have insisted that this experience occurred in 1826, the evidence for late 1827 is overwhelming; see below, nn59 and 63.

11. For the rigorist wing of evangelicalism, see Stunt, *From Awakening*, 95–102, 114.

which had occurred "six or seven years" before, in 1820 or 1821.[12] These previous years require closer attention for reasons that will become apparent later.

Early Uncertainties and an Impressive Family

There was one specific moment in Darby's early years that seems to have recurred in his thoughts repeatedly for the rest of his life. Whether it occurred when he was at Westminster School or at Trinity College, we cannot say. He was reading a passage in Cicero's *De Officiis* (*On Duty*), which referred to truth as being "the material under the control" ("*materia . . . subiecta*") of the philosopher.[13] In his early thirties Darby recalled that this was before his conversion "when I was a poor dark creature," but that even then he had been struck by the realization that such an idea implied the impossibility of any rational knowledge of God, as this would deny divine supremacy.[14] Such a recollection tallies with other statements, which suggest that in his youth Darby was of a serious-minded inclination. He had been "brought up to know the Scriptures" and "believed that there was a Christ as much as I do now."[15] He also tells us that his "sense of beauty" had awakened him to the possibility of a relationship with God beyond that of merely a creature.[16] To make sense of that awakening and the conversion that followed we need to digress somewhat into the family environment that nurtured him prior to going to Trinity.

Darby was descended from gentry who had profited from commerce. On his father's side his ancestors had settled in Ireland and owned Leap Castle in County Offaly, but his father as a younger son had pursued a mercantile career. Resident in London,[17]

---

12. For repeated references to "six or seven years," see Darby, *CW*, 1:36; Darby, *Notes and Jottings*, 304; Darby, *Letters*, 2:310, 433; 3:298. Max Weremchuk has published a transcription of some autobiographical marginal notes in Darby's Greek New Testament, which is now in the JRULM, CBA, Darby Sibthorp Collection, Box 157. The text is carelessly written with hardly any punctuation but includes the extraordinarily imprecise statement, "[I] loved Christ, I have no doubt sincerely and growingly since June or July 1820 or 21, I forget which," Weremchuk, *John Nelson Darby*, 204.

13. "Quo circa huic, quasi materia quam tractet et in qua versetur subiecta est veritas"; Cicero, *De Officiis*, 1:16. Curiously in Walter Miller's Loeb Classical Library translation, the weight that Darby gave to the word *subiecta* is lost: "So, then, it is truth that is, as it were, the stuff with which this virtue has to deal and on which it employs itself."

14. Darby, *Letters*, 1:20 (Aug 1833). His later accounts of this episode are in Darby, *CW*, 6:27–28 (1853); 32:339 (c. 1870?); and he cites the same Latin phrase from Cicero in Darby, *Notes and Comments*, 1:293; 2:174 (c. 1872). Although Darby was very familiar with the patristic writings he makes no reference, as far as I know, to the not dissimilar reservations (about knowing God rationally) entertained by Ambrose in his *De Officiis Ministrorum*, 1:26—a work which was consciously modeled on Cicero's work.

15. Darby, *Notes and Jottings*, 379; Darby, *CW*, 27:368. Compare this with his remark in 1853, "I always regarded with indignant contempt Mr. Hume's argument against miracles," Darby, *CW*, 6:47.

16. Darby, *Notes and Comments*, 2:174.

17. His business was in Milk Street, Cheapside, but his home was first in Hackney and later in Westminster where John Nelson Darby was born. Weremchuk, *John Nelson Darby*, 21.

John Darby Sr. profited from the Napoleonic Wars by securing lucrative government contracts.[18] Earlier, when he was a young man, it was probably through business that he came into contact with Samuel Vaughan (1720–1801), a wealthy businessman with sugar-plantations in Jamaica. Vaughan owned large estates in Maine at Hallowell, a settlement which he founded with a Boston merchant, Benjamin Hallowell, whose daughter he had married in 1747. Naturally Vaughan's sympathies were with the colonists in the War of Independence and as the war drew to a close he went, with his family, to live in Philadelphia. When John Darby Sr. wed Samuel Vaughan's daughter, Ann, in 1784, he was marrying into a family widely respected for its learning and philanthropy, "lovers of science, humanity and America."[19] We do not know much about John Nelson Darby's father other than his commercial activity, but the background of his wife, Ann, gives us a good idea of the world into which our subject was born.

John Nelson Darby's mother was half American and as a young woman in her mid-twenties, before she married, had lived with her parents in Philadelphia where her father, a respected naturalist, was entrusted with the landscaping of Independence Square.[20] George Washington had visited their home and for some years corresponded with her father.[21] Forgotten two hundred years later, the members of Ann Darby's family represented in their day a galaxy of late eighteenth-century achievement. Like their father, her brothers were active in a wide range of fields outside their own business life. William Vaughan (1752–1850), a London merchant and Fellow of the Royal Society, was an advocate of canal construction, a pioneer in the development of the London docks and the establishment of the first savings bank in 1815.[22] Samuel Vaughan Jr. (1762–1802) watched with interest (and reported on) the earliest stages in the development of the American constitution,[23] proposed an ambitious plan of mineral exploration to support the coinage of the recently established US Mint,[24] and later provided details of breadfruit cultivation for Sir Joseph Banks.[25] Another broth-

---

18. According to the recollections of B. W. Newton, the contracts (to supply victuals to the navy) were obtained through Lord Nelson, presumably with Darby's naval brother Henry as an intermediary; JRULM, CBA 7060, Wyatt MS, 6:38.

19. *ANB*, 22:294. Mr. Max Weremchuk has very kindly informed me that the marriage was solemnized in Trinity Church Parish, New York on 21 Jul 1784. (Letter, 15 Dec 2003).

20. Darlington, *Memorials of John Bartram*, 556–57.

21. One of the earliest plans of Washington's home at Mount Vernon was prepared by Samuel Vaughan; see the letter from Washington to Vaughan, 12 Nov 1787; Fitzpatrick, *Writings of George Washington*, 29. The text is available at the Electronic Text Center of the library of the University of Virginia, http://etext.lib.virginia.edu/washington/fitzpatrick.

22. *DNB*, 58:187–88.

23. For his interest in the Constitutional Congress see his letter to James Bowdoin, 30 Nov 1787, in Jensen, *Documentary History*, 2:262–63.

24. J. J. Lloyd, "Link That Failed."

25. William Vaughan to J. Banks, 16 Jul 1794, with extract from letter by Samuel Vaughan; State Library of New South Wales, Sir Joseph Banks Archive, Series 72.191 (www.sl.nsw.gov.au). In 1790 William and Samuel had provided Thomas Jefferson with seeds of mountain rice; see Jefferson to S.

er, John Vaughan (1756–1841), a wine merchant, served the American Philosophical Society as treasurer and librarian for some forty years.[26] The most distinguished of the brothers was the eldest, Benjamin Vaughan (1751–1835), whose friendship with Lord Shelburne and with Benjamin Franklin resulted in his giving significant assistance in the negotiation of the peace at the end of the War of Independence in 1782–83.[27]

For John Nelson Darby, to have grown up in the shadow of such activity may well have been intimidating, but the significance of this influence becomes clearer when we bear in mind that the members of the Vaughan family were Unitarians. Par excellence, they were a product of the eighteenth-century Enlightenment. Their circle included radical thinkers like Benjamin Franklin, Jeremy Bentham and Joseph Priestley, whose Warrington Academy the older Vaughan brothers had attended. Priestley's Unitarianism was very much a product of the deist rationalism of the day and although John Darby's family were Anglicans we may reasonably surmise that a man who married into the Vaughan family shared some of their rationalist self-confidence and optimistic faith in humanity. John Nelson Darby's subsequent conversion may therefore be seen as a possibly (but not necessarily) unconscious rejection of this aspect of his family's tradition. The attraction of "vital" and spiritual Christianity may have outweighed the self-confident and manifestly "human" good works of his family. It is in this context therefore that we should consider the academic and religious world that he encountered at Trinity College in Dublin.

Education and Trinity College

We don't know why John Darby, at the tender age of fourteen, just a fortnight after the Battle of Waterloo, left Westminster School, located conveniently near his home in London, to attend Trinity College in Dublin,[28] though the close proximity of his sister Susannah who had married, a few years earlier, a Dublin lawyer, Edward Pennefather, may have been a contributing factor. Many of his contemporaries would certainly have continued at Westminster for several more years, as had his older brother Christopher.[29] Sixty years before, to enroll at fourteen had been normal at Trinity, but by 1815 the earlier "atmosphere of a boarding-school, with the tutors discharging the quasi-paternal functions of house masters"[30] had changed somewhat as there had been a significant increase in the number and also the age of undergraduates. This

---

Vaughan, 27 Nov 1790, in *Letters of Thomas Jefferson*, available online at www.ai.mit.edu/people/hqm/writings/jefferson.

26. *ANB*, 22:294–96.
27. See *DNB*, 58:158–59; *Dictionary of American Biography*, 19:233–34; *ANB*, 22: 289–90.
28. *Al. Dub.*, 210.
29. Barker and Stenning, *Record of Old Westminsters*, 1:245.
30. McDowell and Webb, "Trinity College in 1830," 75:4.

meant that, although Darby lived in College,[31] and his tutor would still have been very much *in loco parentis* for the fourteen-year-old boy, far more of his fellow students were living out in lodgings, and the "school community" atmosphere would have been less prevalent.

In his early fifties Darby observed, "I think I am intellectual enough, and my mind—though my education was in my judgment not well *directed*, save by God—cultivated enough to enjoy cultivated society."[32] We can only speculate whether Darby's later reservations were concerned with the predominantly classical system of his day or with the way it was applied at Westminster School and Trinity. Whatever the perceived shortcomings of his teachers, his later publications and correspondence suggest that they did nothing to quench his spirit of almost universal enquiry—a spirit that was fascinated by a wealth of ideas ranging from such subjects as language or philosophy to geology or politics.[33]

With hindsight, knowing Darby's later career, more than one writer[34] has wondered, not unreasonably, what part the teaching faculty of Trinity College Dublin may have played in the spread of premillennialist thinking among Irish evangelicals, but such an enquiry can shed only minimal light on Darby's early development. His studies at Trinity (1815–19) were classical as opposed to theological, and they were finished some time before his conversion. The eschatology of lecturers at Trinity may help to explain how Darby's ideas were later received, but to look for the roots of his own prophetic thinking in the theological publications of his classical teachers is of limited value.[35] It is quite possible that in his last years at Trinity Darby had a growing focus on theology, but hardly upon the study of prophecy. With such limitations in mind, it would be a more useful line of enquiry to consider the wider orientation of the Fellows at Trinity, with a view to identifying the wider intellectual climate that prevailed in the college.

Although Trinity College "was routinely criticized . . . for being wealthy, exclusive, indolent and outmoded,"[36] it was more than just a bastion of staunch churchmanship as it enshrined a well-established tradition of Protestant piety. When John Wesley had attended Sunday chapel in 1756 he famously noted in his journal:

---

31. Information from Bernard Meehan, acting keeper of MSS, Trinity College in a letter (24 May 1982) to Max Weremchuk, to whom I am indebted for much help in these matters.

32. Darby, *Letters*, 1:205.

33. Some examples of this range will be found in my "John Nelson Darby," 70–74.

34. E.g., Sandeen, *Roots of Fundamentalism*, 90.

35. This was Gary Nebeker's elusive objective in "John Nelson Darby," 87–108. Such a line of enquiry may perhaps be likened to looking for the origins of Luther's teaching on justification in the Nominalism in which he was reared and which pervades much of his thinking. It's a start but not much more than that.

36. Stephen Farrell, "Dublin University," online at http://www.historyofparliamentonline.org/volume/1820-1832/constituencies/dublin-university.

Dr [James] K[night] preached a plain, practical sermon after which the sacrament was administered. I never saw so much decency at any chapel in Oxford, no not even at Lincoln College. Scarce any person stirred, or coughed, or spit from the beginning to the end of the service.[37]

Although Trinity undoubtedly evolved in the following sixty years, there is no reason to think that this heritage was lost. Protestant piety could take different forms but we can identify certain elements to which we may usefully refer as a "Trinity piety" though we must shun the temptation to project the evangelicalism of the 1830s onto the earlier era.

More often than not we are dealing with what is liable to be called a high-church piety but what is perhaps better (and less exclusively) referred to as one of exact churchmanship. It was a way of thinking, which valued the Anglican liturgy and the sacraments of the episcopal order and was hostile to anything simplistic or emotional, into which category most dissenting religion would fall. It was theologically Arminian with a tendency to dismiss Calvinism as antinomian. It was more concerned with sanctification than justification, and emphasized indwelling grace as opposed to imputed righteousness. It took issue with Roman Catholicism not so much over points of doctrine as on historical grounds, asserting the superiority of the Irish Church's successional continuity with the primitive church of St. Patrick. This opposition to the Roman Church was declared but not intolerant as such. Catholics had been allowed to matriculate and receive degrees at Trinity since 1793 and it is perhaps of interest that no fewer than three of the Fellows in Darby's day came originally from Roman Catholic families.

In the early nineteenth century such attitudes characterized the provost Thomas Elrington (1760–1835) and his successor Samuel Kyle (1772–1848), and other influential Fellows like William Magee (1766–1831), all of whom eventually found their way to the Episcopal bench.[38] Theirs was what might be called a sacramental rationalism. They would have vehemently rejected any suggestion that they were disciples of Voltaire, but within the context of the Irish Protestant tradition, they were unquestionably products of the Enlightenment of John Locke (1632–1704) and Bishop Berkeley (1685–1753). The same could be said for the less sacramental and more evangelical piety of Fellows like Richard Graves,[39] Whitley Stokes,[40] Joseph Stopford,[41] and John Walker.[42] Their rational and unemotional approach to sacred

---

37. Ward and Heitzenrater, *Wesley's Journals and Diaries*, 4:48.

38. Elrington was bishop of Limerick (1820) and of Leighlin and Ferns (1822); Kyle was bishop of Cork (1831); Magee was bishop of Raphoe (1819) and archbishop of Dublin (1822).

39. (1763–1829) Fellow of Trinity (1786); Professor of Divinity (1814).

40. (1763–1833) Fellow of Trinity (1788); resigned his fellowship to join the Walkerites (1816), see Stunt, "Trinity College," 51.

41. (C.1765–1833) Fellow of Trinity (1790).

42. (1768–1833) Fellow of Trinity (1791); seceded to found the Walkerites (1804).

matters was also, unmistakably, a product of the "Age of Reason." In the four volumes of Richard Graves's *Works* no fewer that 223 pages are devoted to establishing that the apostles and evangelists were not enthusiasts and cannot be charged with fanaticism because their conduct was rational.⁴³ The essay is in effect a Protestant reply to the skepticism of Gibbon's account in *The Decline and Fall of the Roman Empire*, where the early church is portrayed as a community of regrettably enthusiastic fanatics. We need not be surprised that the works of John Locke took pride of place in the second year of the undergraduates' reading list nor indeed that Burlamaqui's *Natural Law* was paired with Conybeare's *Natural Religion* in the final year's reading.⁴⁴ On both the sacramental and evangelical wings, the piety of Trinity College was part of an eighteenth-century culture of reason.

But there was a younger generation of Fellows whose formative years had been overshadowed by the turbulence of the French Revolution and the uncertainties of the Napoleonic Wars, not to mention rebellions at home. Historians are rightly cautious in making generalizations about the so-called Romantic Movement but this was a generation that was more at home in the expression of emotion and feeling. Younger evangelicals, like Robert Daly,⁴⁵ who graduated from Trinity in 1803, developed an oratorical style that an earlier generation would have shunned. In this category could be included Henry Maturin (a Fellow from 1792 to 1797), described as "a fluent extempore preacher, and inclining to Calvinistic views; he had words softer than the droppings of oil from a cruet, and singular conversational powers."⁴⁶ Such men were significantly fewer among the Fellows of Trinity, but their number was growing.

On his arrival at Trinity, Darby's choice of tutor had immediately introduced him to this other more assertive evangelical piety. Of all the tutors at Trinity, the youthful Joseph Henderson Singer (1786–1866)⁴⁷ would soon be recognized as one of the most outspoken and uncompromising Evangelicals in the college. It is quite possible that the fourteen-year-old Darby was originally unaware of his tutor's ecclesiastical position and it may well be that his choice reflected rather his preference for one of the youngest tutors who had been a gold medalist when he graduated.

We have an interesting description of Singer, made by another student who chose him for his tutor a few years later:

---

43. Graves, "Essay on the character of the Apostles," 4:ccxvii–ccxxxvi, 1–223.

44. For the Trinity curriculum, see Anon., "University of Dublin," 6:215.

45. Robert Daly (1783–1872); rector of Powerscourt (1814); bishop of Cashel (1843). As early as 1820 the archbishop of Canterbury refused to give Daly a bishopric on the grounds that he was a "fanatic," see Nockles, "Church or Protestant Sect," 465n49.

46. Brooke, *Recollections*, 58–59.

47. J. H. Singer, admitted as a fellow 1810; BD and DD 1825; Professor of Modern History 1840; bishop of Meath 1852. "Mr. Singer" is named as Darby's tutor in the Trinity Admissions Register for July 3, 1815. (Dublin, TCD MUN/V/23/4 page 234).

> My tutor was Dr. Joseph Henderson Singer, afterwards Bishop of Meath. He had obtained his fellowship at the early age of 23, and was a man of universal and accurate information, possessing very polished manners and a kind and winning address. He was a prodigious reader, not even despising the lighter literature of the day,[48] which he swallowed, but probably did not care to digest; a steady preacher of Evangelical truth and a bold upholder of Scriptural education . . .
>
> His pet name among the college alumni was "Cantor."[49] We liked to see him ascending the chapel pulpit. His sermons were neither original, profound, nor dogmatic, but they were gentle, sound and moderate, and thoroughly fluent. He had, if anything, too much of the *copia fandi*.[50]

With Singer as his tutor for four years, we may reasonably assume that Darby became equally familiar with the parameters of the newer evangelicalism, as with the sacramental rationalism and exact churchmanship of the other older fellows. Indeed, bearing in mind that Darby's conversion occurred a year or two after he graduated, and that in those first years of Christian commitment, he was a High Churchman, it is not unreasonable to conclude that his later years at Trinity were ones of spiritual enquiry in which he was well aware of such an alternative.

Curiously this awareness would have been further augmented by Darby's contacts with the Bellett brothers. John Bellett who was six years older (and who some years later would be numbered among the Plymouth Brethren) had been admitted to Trinity a few weeks before Darby, but his younger brother George, who was only three years older than Darby, was admitted on the same day as Darby, and this must have given rise to the brothers' friendship with the significantly younger Darby. In their later time at Trinity the brothers came under the influence of the new incumbent of their home parish at Kilgobbin, Henry Kearney, who had graduated from Trinity in 1802. It is fascinating to find that Kearney's exact churchmanship affected the brothers so differently, George developing into an exact Churchman with a preference for Arminian theology while John rapidly became a fully committed Calvinist evangelical. This can only have added to Darby's uncertainty.

Most of these paragraphs dealing with Darby's time at Trinity have of necessity consisted of circumstantial conjecture. One specific piece of hard evidence is to be found in a dilapidated eighteenth-century volume (in the author's possession) entitled *The Character of a Primitive Bishop in a letter to a non-juror*, by a Presbyter of the

---

48. "The lighter literature of the day" is almost certainly an allusion to Scott's "romantic" novels.

49. The Latin for "singer."

50. Brooke, *Recollections*, 8–9. A later anecdote in Brooke's account describes an older Fellow addressing Singer as "Dulcissime Doctor," and using the words of the poet Horace, to warn him to "take care lest you stumble." The implication is that in his older colleague's estimation, Singer may have been perhaps a little too popular with the students. The phrase *copia fandi* suggests that words came to him a little too easily. For the anxieties that Singer's evangelicalism could produce in a High Churchman, like James Henthorn Todd, some twenty years later, see Stunt, *From Awakening*, 158n17.

Church of England (1709)—a work usually attributed to the non-juror John Pitts. The fact that inside the front cover there is the MS endorsement "J.N.Darby 1819" suggests that in his last year at Trinity, our subject was exercised about Episcopal succession and the authenticity of Anglican orders. Within a couple of years he experienced a conversion which was probably a moment of commitment rather than one of theological clarity—an experience in which submission to God and a decision to follow the Savior were the principal elements.

Years of Uncertainty

It was soon after his conversion that Darby was called to the bar in January 1822 and many writers say that he never practiced.

> I was a lawyer; but feeling that, if the Son of God gave Himself for me I owed myself entirely to Him, and that the so-called christian world was characterised by deep ingratitude towards Him, I longed for complete devotedness to the work of the Lord, my chief thought was to get round amongst the poor Catholics of Ireland. I was induced to be ordained. I did not feel drawn to take up a regular post, but being young in the faith and not yet knowing deliverance, I was governed by the feeling of duty towards Christ, rather than by the consciousness that *He* had done *all* and that I was redeemed and saved; consequently it was easy to follow the advice of those who were more advanced than myself in the christian world.
>
> As soon as I was ordained [in August 1825], I went amongst the poor Irish mountaineers, in a wild and uncultivated district, where I remained two years and three months, working as best I could.[51]

If Darby never practiced as a barrister there are some three years to be accounted for between the completion of his legal studies at Lincoln's Inn in 1822 and ordination in 1825. In view of his remarkable familiarity in later years with the patristic writings (not to mention numerous other works of divinity) we may reasonably conclude that a significant part of this time was spent in theological reading. Such studies had had no place in his earlier classical curriculum and therefore would previously have been a subsidiary line of study.

On various occasions in later life he drew attention to his far from evangelical outlook at this time and how near he was to becoming a Roman Catholic.[52] Compar-

---

51. Darby, *Letters*, 3:297, to Professor F. A. G. Tholuck of Halle University, c. 1855.

52. Writing to a French Catholic journalist in 1878, "Rome, at the beginning of my conversion, had not failed to attract me. But the tenth chapter of the Epistle to the Hebrews had made that impossible for me," Darby, *Letters*, 2:434. He likens "the hopeless effort of Romans 7" to "an honest monks' [sic] labour, which I have tried," Darby, *Letters*, 3:90. Darby's account written in his Greek New Testament includes the following: "my mind had passed, after its own repentance, under the dark cloud of the popish system . . . I used to hold up Christ to my brother as availing against the claim of men on their points yet it prevailed so far as to prevent my mind from finding comfort in the truths I honestly

ing the perspective of John Henry Newman's *Apologia pro Vita Sua* (1866) with his own earlier lack of assurance he recalled:

> I too, governed by a morbid imagination, thought much of Rome, and its professed sanctity, and catholicity, and antiquity . . . Protestantism met none of these feelings, and I was rather a bore to my clergyman by acting on the rubrics. I looked out for something more like reverend antiquity . . .
>
> [Y]ears before Dr Newman . . . I fasted in Lent so as to be weak in body at the end of it; ate no meat on week days—nothing till evening on Wednesdays, Fridays, and Saturdays, then a little bread or nothing; observed strictly the weekly fasts, too. I went to my clergyman always if I wished to take the sacrament that he might judge of the matter. I held apostolic succession fully, and the channels of grace to be there only. I held thus Luther and Calvin and their followers to be outside. I was not their judge, but I left them to the uncovenanted mercies of God. I searched with earnest diligence into the evidences of apostolic succession in England, and just saved their validity for myself and my conscience.[53]

It is important to bear in mind that though Darby's devotions may have been unusually meticulous they were an extension of the Trinity College tradition of piety, with which Darby was familiar, and were indeed part of a well-established tradition of exact churchmanship in Ireland to which the confident sense of assurance that characterized the evangelicals was alien. Henry Woodward, the rector of Fethard, who was married to one of Darby's cousins, observed that there had developed in the diocese, in which he found himself, "a disposition to preserve a cautious distance from, what had begun for some time to be called the Evangelical clergy," though in due course he began to cooperate with them.[54]

When Darby was ordained in 1825 he was sent to work in what was not yet the separate parish of Calary not far from the Delgany home of his brother-in-law Edward Pennefather and Robert Daly's parish of Powerscourt. It is clear that like Henry Woodward he began to work with his evangelical fellow clergy but by his own account

---

urged on him which I had found in what poor reading of Scripture I had," cited by Weremchuk, *John Nelson Darby*, 205. For Darby's older brother, William Henry (at one time a Roman Catholic, later associating with the Brethren), see B. W. Newton's recollections in JRULM, CBA 7061, 131; CBA 7064, 25. W. H. Darby's fifth son (born 1864) was named John Nelson Darby.

53. Darby, *CW*, 18:146, 156. This may be compared with another account (1878): "I gave way to it at the beginning of my conversion. I said to myself, If I fast two days, three would be better, seven better still. Then that would not do to go on, but I pursued the system long enough. It led to nothing, except the discovery of one's own powerlessness," Darby, *Letters*, 2:429. See also Darby, *CW*, 17:91, where he notes the parallels with the Gnostic teaching that "matter was an evil thing."

54. Woodward, *Essays*, 451. I have expanded on this tradition of exact churchmanship in Stunt, *From Awakening*, 151–55.

the next two and half years were still part of the eight years during which "universal sorrow and sin pressed upon my spirit."[55]

> I was troubled in the same way when [I was] a clergyman . . . going from cabin to cabin to speak of Christ, and with souls, these thoughts sprang up, and if I sought to quote a text to myself it seemed a shadow and not real. I ought never to have been there, but do not think that this was the cause, but simply that I was not set free according to Romans viii.[56]

Commenting in 1863 on how often converted Christians "are as if outside God's house and circle, and desiring, hoping, praying that it may be well with them, and that they may be found within,"[57] he is far from scornful, adding, "I was a good while so myself . . . The only safe state, so to speak then, is rigid legality and devotedness on that ground—a kind of Thomas à Kempis life."[58] Only in December 1827, after a serious riding accident, when Darby underwent a time of enforced convalescence on crutches in the home of his sister, Susannah Pennefather, did the assurance of his being "risen with Christ" bring him experimentally (i.e., in terms of spiritual experience) into the evangelical ranks.[59]

However we must resist the temptation of making the episode in 1827–28 so decisive that we ignore the continuities, which extended from the earlier period into his later life. For example the rigorous anti-Erastian note that characterized his *Considerations addressed to the Archbishop of Dublin* (written in 1827 *before his accident*) was to remain a characteristic emphasis in his approach to ecclesiastical issues.[60] Even more significant for our purposes is the fact that his interest in eschatology had clearly begun in the earlier period. Years later he observed:

> A man may not know much about the rapture of the church, and yet be waiting for someone to come and take him out of this scene. Before ever I knew about the Lord's coming, I think I loved His appearing. I knew nothing about the doctrine, but the principle of loving His appearing was in my mind, though I could not define it. I do not talk now of the rapture, though it is most

---

55. Darby, *Letters*, 1:345.

56. Ibid., 3: 453–54.

57. Ibid., 1:354; cf. "I remember when I was converted all the Christians I met, were like people outside, and trusting they would be right when they got in, instead of being already inside," Darby, *Notes and Jottings*, 219.

58. It was this sort of austerity that gave rise to Frank Newman's much-quoted references to Darby's "severe deprivation" and his eating "food unpalatable and often indigestible . . . his whole frame might have vied in emaciation with a monk of La Trappe," F. W. Newman, *Phases of Faith*, 17–18.

59. See Stunt, *From Awakening*, 171n86, where I have summarized the reasons for believing that Bellett miswrote the year in his letter, which should have been dated 31 January 1828 and not 1827. His statement in January that Darby had been "laid up for nearly two months from a hurt in his knee" enables us to place the date of the accident fairly precisely.

60. Darby, *CW*, 1:1–19.

blessed to get that, too. What I delight in, is Christ's coming and setting aside the whole thing I am in.⁶¹

In 1874 when his Swiss friend, Charles Eynard referred to the need for tranquility in a time of political agitation, Darby replied:

> Nearly fifty years ago [c. 1825 or 1826] I remarked that, when speaking of shaking the heavens and the earth (Heb. 12:26), Paul says, "he [God] hath promised [saying, Yet once more I shake not the earth only but also heaven.]" I, a conservative by birth, by education and by mind; a Protestant in Ireland into the bargain; I had been moved to the very depths of my soul on seeing that everything was going to be shaken. The testimony of God made me see and feel that all should be shaken, but . . . that we have a kingdom that cannot be shaken.⁶²

There can be little doubt that this apocalyptic realization that the earth was destined for destruction also predates his experience of deliverance. Indeed it probably goes back to the growing confrontation between Catholics and Protestants that gave rise to Archbishop Magee's Charge of 1826 and the Petition to the House of Commons for Protection in February 1827. Frank Newman arrived in the Pennefather household in September 1827, some two months before Darby's accident, and yet one of his first letters (8 October 1827) is an indication of the impact Darby's apocalyptic thinking had already made on him.

> I think I now fully feel that this world is not only horribly disordered but that God proposes no remedy for its disorder . . . but he proposes to gather to himself out of the world a peculiar people to suffer with Christ here, that they may reign with him hereafter.⁶³

The realization that Darby's eschatology had already taken a millennial direction *before* his experience of assurance and deliverance—i.e., before he could be identified as an evangelical—is of considerable importance. An enquirer after truth who, on his own admission, had regarded "Luther and Calvin and their followers to be outside" the covenanted mercies of God, would have been studying patristic and catholic theology in those early formative years. What these works were is hard to establish from his early writings where he makes no reference to them. It is nevertheless apparent

---

61. Darby, *Notes and Jottings*, 99–100.
62. Darby, *Letters*, 2:254.
63. The letter is quoted more fully in Stunt, *From Awakening*, 207–8. I dissent from Weremchuk's claim that Newman's first encounter with Darby was after Darby's accident. His account was written more than twenty years later. The reference to Darby "on crutches in a drawing-room" need not have been his first impression. If Darby was already incapacitated on Newman's arrival, when would the latter have seen the devoted austerities that so impressed his parishioners?

from some of his later works of controversy that, at an earlier stage, he had made himself familiar with the Fathers and with many Roman Catholic writers.[64]

Looking in Darby's publications for the sources of his ideas is, on the whole, a fruitless task. In the vast bulk of his writing, he tended only to quote from the works of other writers when he was disagreeing with them in controversy or when he was giving a source of information rather than an opinion.[65] In his very earliest works the names of a few older churchmen like Archbishop John Tillotson (1630–94),[66] Dean Humphrey Prideaux (1648–1724), and William Lowth (1660–1732) are occasionally cited with approval but these are exceptions.[67] There is no doubt however that at some stage in 1827 or 1828 he read Irving's translation of *La Venida del Mesias en gloria y magestad*, the celebrated work of the Jesuit Manuel Lacunza.[68]

The extraordinary influence of this work on other writers was meticulously outlined by Alfred-Félix Vaucher in 1941, and his wry comment that "if the Plymouth Brethren had been in the habit of citing their sources, Lacunza's name would have frequently recurred in their writings," is perhaps justified.[69] However in Darby's first published work on prophecy he specifically referred to Irving's translation and went so far as to say that, although he disagreed with the translator on many things, he considered some of Irving's work as "profitable and timely."[70] In the same article he mentions Thomas Erskine's *Freedom of the Gospel*, observing that he found the work "in many respects useful and that *extensively*."[71] These positive references are striking because by 1829 both Irving and Erskine were beginning to be regarded as *enfants terribles* in the religious world and their doctrinal credentials were being questioned by some evangelicals. It is therefore all the more remarkable that Darby, a man who so rarely cited other writers with approval, felt free to commend them. However, these

64. See Stunt, "John Nelson Darby: The Scholarly Enigma," 71–72.

65. E.g., in his autobiographical marginal notes, Darby says, "Scott's essays gave a strong determination to my thought at one time," Weremchuk, *John Nelson Darby*, 204. I have not observed a single quotation from Scott in Darby's writing.

66. Referred to by Darby as Dean Tillotson as he was Dean of St. Paul's at the time of his protest against Erastianism; Darby, *CW*, 1:11.

67. We must distinguish between William Lowth (1660–1732) and his son Robert Lowth, bishop of London (1710–87). William's Commentary on the Prophets led Darby in 1829 to call him "the calm and judicious Lowth," Darby, *CW*, 2:26. This Lowth was later cited by Darby against B. W. Newton (c. 1848) when arguing that "chief prince" in Ezekiel 38 should be translated "prince of Rosh"; Darby, *CW*, 1:295–96. In contrast he allows (1834) that Robert Lowth may have been a useful grammarian and scholar but insists that he cannot be trusted for interpretation; Darby, *CW*, 13:9. Later he dismissed the bishop's work on Isaiah as "never to be trusted," Darby, *Notes and Comments*, 4:31.

68. Lacunza, *Coming of Messiah*.

69. Vaucher, *Célébrité oubliée*, 97.

70. "Reflections upon the Prophetic Inquiry," in Darby, *CW*, 2:7. In one of his tiresome polemics accusing Darby of deceitfulness, MacPherson draws attention at tedious length to the similarities in Darby's language to that of Lacunza and Irving; MacPherson, *Rapture Plot*, 90–99. The significance of the fact that many of the phrases cited are also biblical seems to be lost on him.

71. Darby, *CW*, 2:20.

are exceptions and his writings give very little indication of what he was reading or what books he may have possessed in this early period.[72]

A further point needs to be made about Darby's experience in 1827–28. Some of his later accounts of it are immediately followed with other realizations, which came to him soon after and, which indeed were logical consequences arising from his experience. We may nevertheless identify three original elements that Darby stresses as the essence of his experience of deliverance.[73] First was the total faith that he was now able to place in the authority of the Scriptures. A second emphasis was the assurance that he (together with all Christians as opposed to Christendom) was risen and spiritually united with Christ in heaven. The third element, which he consistently related to his reading of Isaiah 32, was the converse of the second. As the Christian hope was a heavenly one, the earthly promises of the prophets must relate to the restoration of the Jews. Darby recognized in retrospect, "I was not able to put these things in their respective places or arrange them in order,"[74] and in the following confused account, his reference to forty years suggests that he may at this stage have been thinking in terms of some intervening events before Christ's return:

> Isaiah xxxii. it was that taught me about the new dispensation. I saw there would be a David reign, and did not know whether the church might not be removed before forty years' time. At that time I was ill with my knee. It gave me peace to see what the church was. I saw that I, poor, wretched, and sinful J.N.D., knowing too much yet not enough about myself, was left behind, and let go, but I was united to Christ in heaven.[75]

---

72. According to Frank Newman, Darby explained that his reading of 2 Tim 4:13 "saved me from selling my little library," F. W. Newman, *Phases of Faith*, 19. That library should not be confused with the substantial collection of his later years, the more important items of which were sold by auction after his death; (Catalogue of the Library of the Late J. N. Darby, Esq.). That the catalogue gives little indication of Darby's earlier reading is apparent for several reasons. It is not a comprehensive list—unnamed books are included in some lots. It includes nothing by Scott, Tillotson or Prideaux (with whose works we know Darby was familiar) and scarcely one of the volumes of which Darby published reviews or refutations. For example there are no works by Edward Irving, S. R. Maitland or William Burgh, with all of whom he entered into published controversy; Darby, *CW*, 2:6–10, 32–42, 33:1–12. Most of the books listed were published after 1830 or before 1800.

73. All three elements are to be found in the following accounts—the year of writing is shown in brackets: Darby, *Letters* [185?], 3:298–99; *Letters* [1863], 1:344; Darby, *CW* [c. 1865], 1:38, 36; Darby, *Letters* [1878], 2:433.

74. Darby, *Letters* [185?], 3:299.

75. *Bible Treasury*, 12:353. I am grateful to Mr. Andrew Poots for this reference, which is not in the *CW*. Darby's realization in 1827–28 that earthly Jewish promises should not be appropriated by the Christian church, is circumstantially corroborated in Frank Newman's letter to B. W. Newton (17 Apr 1828), written after Darby's deliverance experience, where he makes a similar distinction between the promises made to Israel and those made to the Church: "But where it is merely a prediction under the form of a promise . . . we are not justified in saying that 'Israel' means anything other than the nation of the [sic] Israel," transcribed in Wyatt MS, 2:120 and recopied in Fry MS, 63 (Manchester, JRULM, CBA 7049).

Evangelical Involvement

In fact for some years after his experience of deliverance there was something decidedly ambivalent about some of the positions adopted by Darby. Eschatologically, his two pamphlets in 1829 and 1830 indicate that he was sympathetic but by no means irretrievably committed to a futurist premillennialism.[76] Ecclesiastically he was by no means fully detached from the Establishment. After his time of convalescence he does not appear to have returned to Calary but for a year or two worked in a variety of parishes as a freelance missioner. A threatening letter from "Captain Rock" (a variant on the more notorious "Captain Moonlight") telling Darby to keep his "Bible business" out of Corofin (2 Feb 1829) suggests that he was working with the somewhat maverick Protestant landlord Edward Synge in County Clare.[77] It would also have been during this time that he worked in Cloughjordan with Frederick Trench to whom we shall refer shortly. At some point between 1830 and 1834 Darby was invited to be an assistant chaplain at the Magdalen Asylum in Leeson Street, Dublin. The suggestion was presumably made by the principal chaplain, Joseph Henderson Singer, who having been Darby's tutor at Trinity, knew him well, and who as a leading evangelical would have been anxious to keep Darby from secession and therefore may have hoped to provide him with a position where there would be few restraints on him.[78] In fact, Darby's decision to leave Ireland in 1830 may have been prompted by the uncertainty of his position.[79]

Much has been written of the impact of his visit to Oxford in 1830, but Darby also recalled that earlier in the year he had visited Cambridge where he had been

---

76. Darby, *CW*, 2:1–42. In these pamphlets he asks almost as many questions as he answers and some important prophetic topics are almost ignored. For example there is scarcely a single reference to Antichrist. In contrast his critique, in the *Christian Herald*, of William Burgh's Lectures on the Second Advent and the Apocalypse Unfulfilled (1832) is rather less tentative. He basically approves of Burgh's interpretation with regard to the Jewish prophecies but takes issue with his analysis of Revelation and the nature of the Gentile apostasy. He decidedly rejects Burgh's idea of a future personal antichrist, insisting that "The time and principles of Antichrist I believe to be daily developing themselves," Darby, *CW*, 33:2.

77. Captain Rock to J. N. Darby, 2 Feb 1829 (JRULM, CBA, JND/5/2; see Enright, "Edward Synge," 8. Edward's father, George Synge (1757–1837), was an uncle of John Synge of Glanmore Castle. Darby's association with Edward Synge is confirmed in Newton's recollections; Fry MS, 239 (JRULM, CBA 7049).

78. Bellett, whose chronology is unreliable, says that in 1834 Darby decided against the appointment and began to worship regularly with the Brethren in Aungier Street. From internal evidence in Bellett's account, 1832 is a more probable date; see Bellett, *Interesting Reminiscences*, 8. The Diocesan records confirm that there was a hiatus in the assistant chaplaincy between 1828 and 1836; see Leslie and Wallace, *Clergy of Dublin and Glendalough*, 135. For Darby's association with Singer in 1831, see Stunt, *From Awakening*, 258n65.

79. For his ecclesiastical undecidedness in London, Oxford, and Plymouth (1830–31) and Limerick (1832), see Stunt, *From Awakening*, 253, 258, 291–92, 276–77. Hitherto it has been assumed that Darby's first visit to Plymouth was in December 1830. However as early as 20 October 1830, the *Falmouth Packet and Cornish Herald* reported that "the Rev. J. N. Darby" had recently addressed the annual meeting of the Plymouth auxiliary of the LSPCJ.

given a less sympathetic hearing.[80] His experience there has been ignored by most Brethren historians, but it effectively indicates how ill at ease Darby was beginning to find himself with some aspects of traditional evangelicalism. Frederick FitzWilliam Trench, a friend in whose parish of Cloughjordan Darby had assisted with mission work, had been converted as a student at Peterhouse, Cambridge, sometime between 1818 and 1822.[81] In 1830 Trench took Darby to meet Charles Simeon, who had been the instrument of his conversion. We must bear in mind that Darby wrote his account of the episode more than thirty years after the event, in the context of an ongoing controversy with Trench. Whatever the exact details of the interview may have been, it is clear that the enthusiastic Darby felt that he had been rebuffed by the doyen of the evangelical movement whose eschatology was decidedly postmillennialist.[82] It is only conjecture, but the experience may have contributed—perhaps more than he realized—to the hardening of Darby's premillennialism.

A French Dimension

There are two accounts of Darby's activities in 1830, which indicate that even before he went to Cambridge and Oxford, the undecided Irish separatist had visited Paris. One of these was published in the *Schaff-Herzog Encyclopedia* and was written by Edward Elihu Whitfield, who as an Oxford undergraduate had corresponded with Darby in 1870 but who later seems to have moved to a less exclusive Brethren position.[83] The other account contains the brief statement, by a more recent Brethren writer, Theodore William Carron, that Darby "visited the Continent for the first time in 1830 when he supported the labors of F. P. Monod in France."[84] We should note that two of Darby's former neighbors in Ireland were also visiting Paris in the spring of 1830. Robert Daly, with whom Darby was possibly beginning to be ecclesiastically estranged, was there from 21 March to 4 April, while among the letters of Lady Powerscourt (later associated with the Plymouth Brethren), one dated 6 April and two others from May and

---

80. Darby, *Letters*, 3:301, to Tholuck, 1855.

81. Frederick FitzWilliam Trench (1799–1869), the perpetual curate of Cloughjordan (1823–54), was a cousin of Richard Chenevix Trench, later archbishop of Dublin. He must not be confused with another cousin, Frederick FitzJohn Trench, who was the father of John Alfred Trench (a personal friend of Darby) and of George Frederick Trench who is included in Pickering, *Chief Men*, 133. For details of Fitzwilliam Trench, see *Al. Cantab.*, pt. 2, 6:226; J. B. Leslie, ed., "Biographical Succession Lists," Dublin, Representative Church Body Library; and Brooke, *Recollections*, 46–49.

82. Darby, *CW*, [1863] 10:133–34.

83. In Jackson, *New Schaff-Herzog Encyclopedia*, 3:357, Whitfield is described as a "Retired Public Schoolmaster, London." He was a graduate of Oriel College, Oxford (Shadwell, *Registrum Orielense*, 2:558). Darby wrote a letter to Whitfield in 1870; (Darby, *Letters*, 3:410–12). Still later Whitfield contributed an article on Darby to the Open Brethren publication Pickering, *Chief Men*, 11–15.

84. Carron, *Christian Testimony*, 346. I am indebted to Mr. Andrew Poots of Belfast for this reference.

June were written in Paris.[85] We cannot say whether these friends were in touch with Darby, but it is quite possible.

For Daly's visit to Paris, his journal is informative. Besides deploring the apparent godlessness of the Parisians, he visits the Louvre and the secondhand bookshops. He also attends services in the English Church and the *Oratoire* as well as a Protestant mission house in the Faubourg de Mt. Parnasse, meeting a variety of English residents and French-speaking Protestants like François Olivier ("Mr. Oliviet") and Fréderick Monod ("Mr. M.").[86] In addition to these fairly predictable responses to the life of the French capital, Daly recorded what he was told about the "descendants of the Jansenists" in Paris "who knew the truth, and, though they held many Roman Catholic errors, rejoiced in hearing the doctrines of grace." He also learned of another group of former Roman Catholics (with Jansenist origins), "*La Petite Église*," who, in protest against the desecration of the Church by the French revolutionaries and the concordat signed between the pope and Napoleon, had broken away from the pope and from the French clergy.[87] It is surely not unreasonable to suppose that if these developments interested a long-standing Protestant like Daly, they would have been of even greater interest to Darby whose formative period had been dominated by Catholic thinking. The ideals of Jansenism could only arouse his sympathetic approval and for reasons, which will shortly become apparent, we must glance briefly at some aspects of that movement.

The Jansenists had been meticulously devout in their practices and had shunned the worldliness of the Roman Catholic Church.[88] With the suppression of the Jesuits in 1773, they seemed to have lost their *raison d'être* but the rampant atheism of the French Revolution gave them a late burst of energy. They were appalled at the desecration of the churches and the Erastianism of the new régime as much as by the concessions made by the Church in the face of such interference. Witnessing at close quarters the cataclysmic events of the 1790s, they believed, perhaps with more cause than anyone, that they were living in the last times. They had long been preoccupied

---

85. Madden, *Memoir of Daly*, 168–75; Daly, *Letters of Viscountess Powerscourt*, 84, 108, 111. Lady Powerscourt was probably the unnamed lady to whom Daly spoke disapprovingly on 23 March (*Memoir*, 169) "about her conduct at Brussels." Lady Powerscourt had been in Brussels earlier in the month (*Letters*, 107) and had attracted the interest of certain newspapers. The *Sentinel and Star in the West* reported: "The young beautiful fascinating Irish widow Viscountess Powerscourt is preaching and expounding the scriptures at public assemblies at Brussels, with an eloquence and fervour that would do honor to Rowland Hill or orator Irving. She opens her services with a hymn of which after touching a piano-forte she gives out the melody and first stanza" (Cincinnati, May 29 1830, p. 272). This appears to be an abbreviated version of a longer piece in *Freeman's Journal* (24 Feb 1830) where the meetings are said to have taken place in the home of Lady Powerscourt's sister, Mrs. Steele. For this latter reference I am beholden to Dr. Samuel McBride.

86. For further details, see Stunt, *From Awakening*, 163.

87. Madden, *Memoir of Daly*, 172, 173–74.

88. For Jansenism in the eighteenth century, see the magisterial work by J. McManners, *Church and Society*, 2, chs. 39 and 48. For later Jansenist developments and the origins of La Petite Église in Lyon, see Chantin, *Les Amis de l'Oeuvre de la Vérité*.

with the question of the return of the Jews to Palestine and more than ever they turned to the study of prophecy.[89]

One of the foremost among them was the Dominican Bernard Lambert (1738–1813), who had formerly been the protégé of Malvin de Montazet, the Jansenist-sympathizing archbishop of Lyon. From 1776 Lambert, an energetic writer and controversialist, was a member of the Dominican community in the Rue du Bac, in Paris.[90] He vigorously protested on behalf of the Dominicans (ominously known as Jacobins in France until the revolutionary party took over their name as well as their convent), fearlessly denounced the "blasphemies and calumnies of the church's enemies" and rebuked the Church for its readiness to compromise. In 1793 he published a pamphlet explaining that the apostasy of the church suggested that the return of the Jews was imminent, and increasingly from that point he appears to have been preoccupied with the implications of living in the last times.[91] It is possible that he knew of Lacunza's work, which was circulating in MS after 1790, but some time before *La Venida del Mesias en gloria y magestad* was in print Lambert published his own *Expositions des prédictions et des promesses faites à l'Église pour les derniers temps de la gentilité* in 1806.[92]

A younger Jansenist writer, the Parisian lawyer and judge Pierre-Jean Agier (1748–1823) also became fascinated by eschatological studies in the last decade of his life, publishing an analysis of Lacunza's *Venida* in 1818[93] as well as his own work on *Les prophéties concernant Jésus-Christ et l'Église* (1819) and a commentary on *Revelation* (1823). Agier's version of Lacunza's work was used by Lewis Way who was living in Paris in the 1820s and it was probably he who introduced the work to Irving in 1825.[94] The great authority on Lacunza, Alfred-Félix Vaucher, closely

---

89. For the Jansenist fascination with the return of the Jews, see the earlier chapters of Vidal, *La Morte-Raison*.

90. For Lambert, see the articles by M. J. Picot in Michaud, *Biographie Universelle*, 23:51–52; and by M. D. Chenu in Vacant et al., *Dictionnaire*, 8:2470. More precise details are in Plongeron, *Les Réguliers de Paris*, 140–46, 360–61. For a brief taste of Lambert's low view of the Enlightenment, see the quotations in Bradley and Van Kley, *Religion and Politics*, 3. Lambert's outlook must be differentiated from that of the Jansenist reformers discussed by Ward in "Late Jansenism and the Habsburgs," ibid., 154–86.

91. [Lambert], *Avertissement aux fidèles*. My attention has been kindly drawn by Mr. Will Irvine to the interest shown in the Parisian Jansenists by the Irish revolutionary millenarian Thomas Russell in 1802; see Quinn, *Soul on Fire*, 230.

92. This rare book was published in 2 vols. in Paris (1806). I have only belatedly discovered that there is a copy in the Bibliothèque Nationale de France, but that it is not listed under "Lambert, Bernard" because the author is given as "Le P[ère] Lambert." Until very recently therefore I was constrained to use the summary of Lambert's prophetic views in Elliott, *Horae Apocalypticae*, and in Vaucher, *Une célébrité oubliée*, 87–88. However since December 2014 Lambert's text has been available online at books.google.com/books?id=HlPTMVbhfIgC. (vol. 1) and books.google.com/books?id=ti5vbmJg6UQC (vol. 2).

93. [Agier], *Vues sur le second avènement*.

94. Vaucher, *Une célébrité oubliée*, 37, 139n66. For Agier, see the article by Fallot in Michaud,

studied Lambert's *Expositions des prédictions* as well as his supplementary rebuttal of his critics, and carefully identified the similarities and the differences between the work of Lacunza and Lambert. Both interpretations of the prophetic Scriptures are literalist and premillennial but, in one important respect at least, Lambert's must be distinguished from that of Lacunza. While the Jesuit sees Christ's return as one simple event ("tout court") at the beginning of the millennium, Lambert expects the event to be in two stages and foresees an intermediate coming ("un avènement intermédiaire") when Christ first gathers his saints.[95] On the other hand Vaucher argues that although Agier also wrote of an intermediate coming in his earlier commentary on the *Psalms* (1809), he appears to have abandoned the idea after studying Lacunza's work.[96]

The justification for what may appear to be an unwarranted digression into Jansenist eschatology is quite simple. Bearing in mind Darby's earlier Catholic orientation, we may be pretty sure that when he was in Paris (if not before) he became acquainted with the works of Lambert and Agier. It is doubtful whether he had yet made up his mind about a two-stage second coming (as found in his later distinction between Christ's *parousia* and the later *epiphaneia*), but he must have been familiar with the idea before he went to Cambridge and Oxford and therefore before he went to Row in Scotland later in 1830.

Much has been made, in the contemporary eschatological controversy, of Darby's visit to Row and his having heard a prophecy of Margaret Macdonald.[97] It is true that one of her rather incoherent prophecies was circulating in manuscript in the early 1830s and was later published by her widower Robert Norton in 1840.[98] Irving was impressed by the urgency (rather than the teaching) of the prophecy and it may have played a part in the development of the distinctive Irvingite premillennialism that characterized the writings of the *Morning Watch*. There is however no reason to claim that this was the source of Darby's idea of the rapture, as he had already encountered the idea of an intermediate coming in Lambert's work. In 1857 the textual scholar, Samuel Prideaux Tregelles, recalled that "Lambert and Agier were the writers Mr. J. N. Darby studied earnestly before he left the Church of England. I remember his speaking much about them in 1835."[99] For Darby's debt to Lambert there is a fur-

---

Biographie Universelle, 1:222–24; other references in Vaucher, *Une célébrité oubliée*, 145n189.

95. Ibid., 87, 88, 177n460. However Lambert's "avènement intermédiaire" which will precede the last judgment "by several centuries" will be far from a secret event, though it will incorporate the gathering of Christ's saints with the deliverance of the Jewish people (*Expositions des predictions*, 2:26, 42–46, 52–55).

96. Vaucher, *Une célébrité oubliée*, 178n466. In 1819 a reviewer of the Jansenist Abbé Luigi Giudici's *Lettres Italiennes sur l'avènement intermédiaire et le règne de Jésus-Christ* (Lugano, 1816–17), noted that Giudici was following Lambert when he envisaged three comings as opposed to Lacunza who expected only two, *Chronique Religieuse* 2 (1819) 188.

97. For Darby's own account of his visit to Row and his reasons for not being impressed, see Darby, *CW*, 6:284–85.

98. See Oliphant, *Life of Irving*, 2:139; Norton, *Memoirs of Macdonalds*, 171–76.

99. S. P. Tregelles to B. W. Newton, 29 Jan 1857, JRULM, CBA 7181 (7). Tregelles was first

ther piece of circumstantial evidence, which is at least partially corroborative. The French Protestant pastor of Cambrai, Achille Maulvault, wrote an article on Lambert for the *Encyclopédie des Sciences Religieuses* in the late 1870s in which he refers to the Dominican's *Exposition des prédictions*. The article concludes with a curiously unexpected observation: "Ce livre, [sc. *L'exposition*] chose étrange, très en honneur chez les chrétiens darbystes, parait avoir été la source, avec le livre de Lacunza, où M. Darby et les théologiens de son école semblent avoir puisé leurs doctrines particulières."[100]

As Lambert's work was never translated into English, it was perhaps only in France that Darby found it appropriate to recommend his work to his listeners. This in turn may have contributed, in the 1830s and 1840s, to an eschatological perspective among Darby's French followers that was rather different from that of the English-speaking brethren. There was a curiously "millenarian" episode at the end of 1844 when some of the Brethren, near Tence on the border of the Haute-Loire and the Ardèche, were persuaded by the Brethren evangelist Albert Dentan and his wife, that Christ would return on the last day of the year. This and the ensuing excesses were clearly a source of concern to Darby who wrote to warn some French sisters that "we have no need of a dream with respect to matters clearly revealed by God."[101] I am unaware of any comparable incident among English-speaking Brethren.

Conclusions

Before summarizing our conclusions we have to bear in mind that we are navigating between a Scylla and Charybdis of controversy, with a *prima facie* obligation to reject the agenda of both sides. The principal aim of R. A. Huebner and some other

---

associated with the Brethren at Plymouth in 1835. Darby's earlier mention of Lambert and Agier may have prompted Tregelles in September 1850 to visit the Jansenist archbishop of Utrecht who lent him copies of Lambert's and Agier's works; see Tregelles, *Jansenists*, 96–97. Tregelles's Dutch visit is strangely ignored by Clark, *Strangers and Sojourners at Port Royal*.

100. "This book [sc. *L'exposition*], strange to relate, is held in great honor among the Darbyite Christians. It appears to have been the source, together with Lacunza's book, from which Monsieur Darby and the theologians of his school seem to have drawn their distinctive teachings." See the article on Lambert by Maulvault in Lichtenberger, *Encyclopédie*, 7:693. That Lambert was a source for the idea of "the secret rapture of the saints" was recalled in Thomas Croskery's hostile account of the Brethren. The fact that he refers to Père Lambert as "Pierre [sic] Lambert, a Jesuit [sic] Father," suggests an oral tradition rather than his being familiar with Lambert's writings; Croskery *Plymouth Brethrenism*, viii. Croskery (1830–86), a Presbyterian minister from Londonderry, may have been the author of the article "Plymouth Brethrenism" in the *British Quarterly Review* where the same inaccurate attribution is made, 58 (Oct 1873) 409. His earlier *Catechism on the Doctrines of the Plymouth Brethren* had reached its 6th ed. in 1868; on that basis he had been invited to contribute an article on the "Plymouth Brethren" for the *Princeton Quarterly* 1 (1872), 48. It is perhaps worth noting that although Neatby made no mention of Lambert, the earliest historian of the Brethren drew parallels with Jansenism on at least three occasions; Neatby, *History of the Plymouth Brethren*, 173, 216, 267.

101. Darby, *Letters*, 1:76. For the background to these events see three important sources for religious developments in the region all written or edited by Christian Maillebouis, *La dissidence religieuse à Saint-Voy*; *Vie et pensées d'un Darbyste*; and *La Chronique "Deschomets."*

dispensationalist admirers of Darby seems to be to show that Darby's later eschatology and ecclesiology were already established in his mind and can be found in his earliest writings in the late 1820s.[102] At the other end of the polemical spectrum, Dave MacPherson, with the vigorous approval of various opponents of dispensationalism (and of the Scofield Bible), is intent upon discrediting Darby and his hermeneutic. With this object, he proclaims that Darby was a plagiarist who borrowed without acknowledgement from Lacunza, Irving, and more particularly Margaret Macdonald (who in turn is accused of occultism).[103] Both positions effectively demonstrate the danger of over-simplification and the temptation to forget that historical truth is "never pure and rarely simple."

In conclusion therefore we must emphasize that Darby was a highly complex person whose philosophy and understanding of Scripture and theology were continually evolving. Even before his conversion, there are reasons for thinking he may have been attracted both by the sacramental piety of exact churchmanship and by the more romantic and oratorical appeal of the evangelical individualism which characterized younger men like his tutor Joseph Singer and, a little later, Edward Irving. It is worth noting that in 1844 he made no attempt to hide the fact that he had conversed on the subject of ministries and gifts with Irving "at least fourteen years ago" though he insisted that this was "before the system, to which he [Irving] gave his name, was manifested."[104] However, years before he met Irving, Darby had been drawn to eschatological enquiry. Pretribulationist eschatology was undoubtedly a significant element in Irvingite teaching, but this does not necessarily mean that Darby adopted it from them.[105] There was an eclecticism in his early writings that fastened with approval on some points while rejecting others with some virulence. Indeed his reluctance to cite his authorities may have arisen from an awareness that his mind was far from made up. On the other hand, his earlier years of High Church observance following the rejection of his family's rationalist optimism at his conversion and prior to his experience of deliverance in 1827–28 contributed significantly to his spiritual development. It is clearly from these years that we should date his strong opposition to Erastianism and his growing premillennial expectations. The fact that premillennialism was beginning to be more acceptable in evangelical circles may have made it easier for these expectations to be carried over into his own variety of evangelicalism after 1827.

These continuing emphases from the earlier period may help us to appreciate his readiness to learn from Lacunza, and his enthusiasm for the works of Lambert and

---

102. Huebner, *Precious Truths*, 1:v, where he claims that although Darby's "recovery of truth . . . in reality was accomplished by 1835, its foundation was understood in Dec. 1826–Jan. 1827."

103. The fullest exposition of this line is in MacPherson, *Rapture Plot*. I have commented on some of the implications of this book in "Tribulation of Controversy," 91–98.

104. Darby, *CW*, 3:264. I am grateful to Dr. Tim Grass for helping me find this reference.

105. For an excellent discussion of Irvingite pretribulationism and also some very apposite examples of Darby's ongoing undecidedness; see Patterson and Walker, "Our Unspeakable Comfort."

Agier. By the same token, although the experience of 1827–28 was liberating for his soul and strengthened his faith in Scripture, there evidently remained uncertainties in both his ecclesiology and eschatology for some years. We have not dealt with such questions as Darby's belief in "the ruin of the church" and his systematic dispensationalist hermeneutic as he did not fully formulate them until after 1834 when he finally broke with the Establishment but the ambiguities of his personal position between 1827 and 1833 must have contributed to his reluctance for quite a time finally to commit himself on eschatological and related issues.

9

John Synge and the Early Brethren[1]

ONE OF THE NAMES referred to from time to time in connection with the early Brethren is that of John Synge (1788–1845), and yet who he was and the details of his career have always been rather hard to establish. The publication of Edward Stephens's biography of John Millington Synge in 1974 provided some information about the dramatist's grandfather, but even so, the picture is far from complete. The purpose of the present paper is to bring a variety of materials together, in the hope of shedding more light on the aspirations of some of the early Brethren.

The Synge family had been for more than a century, a formidable clerical dynasty in Ireland.[2] John Synge's great grandfather Nicholas Synge (1700–71) was the bishop of Kilfenora, whose father Edward (1659–1741) had been the archbishop of Tuam.[3] Nicholas's son Edward married Sophia Hutchinson and their sixth son Francis Synge (John's father) established the family estates in County Wicklow at Roundwood and Glanmore or Glenmore where he spent a lot of money extending the mansion, which he called Glanmore Castle.

Influence of Pestalozzi

Born in 1788, John Synge was admitted to Trinity College, Dublin, in 1805, but two years later matriculated from Magdalen College, Oxford, where, in 1810, he graduated.[4] Two years later he went on a continental tour spending some time in Spain and Portugal where he was able to watch some of Wellington's exploits in the Peninsular War. In 1814 on his way back from Italy he reached Yverdon in Switzerland and was persuaded with some difficulty to visit Pestalozzi's Institute. Synge was so impressed by Pestalozzi and by the happiness and intelligent interest shown by the children that

---

1. This paper was originally published in the *Journal of CBRF* 28 (1978) 39–59.

2. K. C. Synge, *Family of Synge*; Carpenter, *My Uncle John*.

3. Nicholas Synge had a brother Edward who was also a bishop, and whose recently published letters to his only surviving daughter provide a very human glimpse into the every-day life of some of the Synge family in the eighteenth century. See Legg, *Synge Letters*.

4. *Al. Dub.*, 798; *Al. Oxon.*, 4:1382.

he remained at Yverdon for three months instead of the two hours he had originally intended. He wrote enthusiastic letters to his friend Digges La Touche back in Dublin, explaining Pestalozzi's system.[5]

The educational methods widely practiced at the turn of the nineteenth century were usually authoritarian, often unimaginative and only occasionally successful and then only with a well-motivated child. Synge's original refusal to visit the Institute at Yverdon was because he felt "no small degree of prejudice against the schemes of education from the little he had seen of the mechanical systems practiced at home."[6] Pestalozzi's genius was to see the problem of education from the child's point of view. Abandoning the attitude that the child's mind was a sort of bottle into which as much information and procedural formulae should be poured as was possible in the time available, Pestalozzi believed that there were innate powers of understanding in a child that had to be awakened. He felt that in the innocence of the infant there was still some trace of the divine nature and that it was the responsibility of the teacher to bring this potential to fruition. Indeed he insisted that "intuition is absolutely the foundation of all knowledge."[7]

Obviously Pestalozzi owed a great deal to the thinking of Jean-Jacques Rousseau (in his pioneering educational exposition, *Emile*) and to the ideas of the Romantic Movement more generally; nevertheless, his understanding of the problem was imbued with a spiritual depth, which derived from his own deep Christian faith and compassion. Indeed he applied his child-centered ideas to questions of spiritual understanding as well. In what is probably his most famous work, *How Gertrude Teaches her Children*, Pestalozzi emphasizes the spiritual role of the mother in bringing up her family. In answer to the question, "How does the idea of God develop in my soul?" he answers: "The feelings of love, trust, gratitude, and the readiness to obey must be developed in me before I can apply them to God. I must love men, trust men, thank men, and obey men before I can aspire to love, trust, thank and obey God."[8] And it was precisely in the introduction of the child to such experiences as love, trust and thankfulness that the role of the mother in Pestalozzi's scheme was so crucial.

Child-centered education is a common-place now—in principle at any rate—and if an older generation learnt multiplication at school solely by means of table recitation, our children are more likely to be learning to multiply with apples or counters.[9] Similarly in the spiritual realm, though some evangelical Christians are fearful of a too anthropocentric existentialism, nevertheless they can probably appreciate that it is of

---

5. [Synge], *Biographical Sketch*. Also information from Mrs. Lily M. Stephens of Dublin, the widow of John Synge's great grandson, Edward M. Stephens. For La Touche's enthusiasm for Pestalozzi's methods, see J.D.L[a Touche], "Hints."

6. [Synge], *Biographical Sketch*, v.

7. Silber, *Pestalozzi*, 144.

8. Ibid., 147.

9. When this was written (c. 1970) only one of my teaching colleagues had a calculator!

little use telling a person that God is a loving Father if the person addressed has never known a father who loved him. At the turn of the nineteenth century, child-centered education was something revolutionary calling in question some of the coldly systematic thinking of the enlightenment, and John Synge's enthusiasm was unbounded. On his return home he promptly put his enthusiasm into print by publishing his *Biographical Sketch of the Struggles of Pestalozzi to establish his System of Education, chiefly from his own works, by an Irish Traveller.*

It is clear from this publication that Synge was particularly struck by the happiness and the reduction of infant misery that Pestalozzi's system had made possible. He proceeded to open a school at Roundwood for the villagers and established a printing press to produce manuals and texts for such teaching. A variety of these teaching aids are to be found in the library of Trinity College, Dublin.[10] There can be little doubt that Synge's school was a success. In letters to Pestalozzi, he explains that the children are taught for three or four hours each day in language, arithmetic and geometry; time is also spent reading the Bible. The remainder of the day is occupied with practical work on the land or in the production of footwear or straw hats. Bearing in mind the backwardness of the Irish economy this was fairly revolutionary and it is hardly surprising that Synge reports to Pestalozzi that one teacher who has adopted the new methods has been reprimanded by the governors as the latter are afraid that the children will not be happy with the position of servants if they prove to be cleverer than their masters.[11]

Another advocate of Pestalozzi's methods, Charles Edward Herbert Orpen, writing in the *Christian Examiner*, prefaced an account of his visit to Switzerland in 1817 by saying: "My mind, I confess, was prejudiced in favour of Pestalozzi's plans from what little I had seen of them in my friend Synge's poor school in the County of Wicklow."[12] Where Pestalozzi, largely through lack of money, had often been unsuccessful, Synge's venture seems to have flourished. There is a field near Roundwood where the school formerly stood, and it is still known as "the schoolhouse field."

John Synge was an evangelical churchman, and soon found himself having to defend Pestalozzi from the charge that his principles conflicted with the doctrine of original sin. In 1818 Synge asked Pestalozzi to make it clear that he accepted the doctrine of the fall of man.[13] Pestalozzi was in fact primarily an educational practitioner rather than a theologian, and his statements on such matters never fully satisfied many Evangelicals. Samuel Gobat, for example, himself a child of the Swiss *réveil* of the early nineteenth century and later bishop of Jerusalem, criticized what he considered to

---

10. Trinity College Dublin Library Nos. 22Y 36; 22Y 36 No. 2; Papyrus Case E; Press 9372 No. 5.

11. Synge's letters are in the Zentralbibliothek in Zurich, MSS. Pestalozzi 55a/365. Such anxieties may be compared with those suggested by a correspondent asking whether the Pestalozzi method conflicted with the system of Bell and Lancaster, G.A., "Letter," 231.

12. Orpen, "Pestalozzi," 337.

13. Synge to Pestalozzi, 10 Dec 1818 (Zurich Zentralbibliothek).

be the false foundations of Pestalozzi's system and claimed that Pestalozzi admitted this in his old age.[14] On the other hand one of the greatest admirers of Pestalozzi in England was the educationist J. P. Greaves, whose sister played an important part in the beginnings of the *réveil* in the Canton of Vaud between 1815 and 1822.[15] Both Greaves and Synge refused to accept that Pestalozzi's method was faulty theologically and Synge, in particular, was a staunch Evangelical.[16]

Henry Craik and Hebrew Studies

When in 1818 he married Isabella Hamilton, John Synge took charge of Roundwood, as his father moved to Glanmore Castle. At Roundwood the school continued to flourish, but Synge's activities were clearly not confined to this work. He was in touch with friends like James Digges La Touche and John Vesey Parnell (later Lord Congleton), with whom he would later be "strongly influenced by the teaching of John Nelson Darby."[17] Probably before Synge was in close touch with Darby, he met Anthony Norris Groves who had given up his dental practice in Exeter and in 1826 had begun to attend Trinity College, Dublin for quarterly examinations, with the intention of being ordained and going as a missionary to Baghdad.[18] It was possibly at Groves's suggestion that Synge moved in 1827 to Devon where he rented Buckridge (now spelled Buckeridge) House, near Teignmouth. It was also said that he moved on account of his wife's poor health, but his interest in Groves may well have been a more important factor.[19]

Groves' decision in 1828, to abandon his plans for ordination, and to go to Baghdad almost at once, created problems for two of his associates. The first was the deaf

---

14. Gobat, *Samuel Gobat*, 41.

15. Latham, *Search for a New Eden*, 46–48; Stunt, *From Awakening*, 59, 64–69.

16. J. P. Greaves had a younger brother Richard Greaves, Vicar of Deddington, Oxon (1822–37), who was an enthusiastic evangelical and a friend of both B. W. Newton and John Hill, the vice-principal of St. Edmund Hall. (See above, ch. 6.) Two interesting references to him in Hill's Diary are as follows: "19 July 1823 Mr. Greaves and Mr. Meyers breakfasted with us . . . we found Dr. Mayow of whom we had heard mention made yesterday as having spent three years in Pestalozzi's establishment and having now set up a school of 30 boys at Epsom on that plan. Filled all the time with conversation on the subject of education." "23 Sept. 1823 Mr. [J. P.] Greaves the elder brother of Mr. R. Greaves of Deddington called on his way to Town and brought with him some iron rods to make mathematical figures for John and George and a little book for the nursery. He has been for several years in Switzerland assisting Mr. Pestalozzi and entered very earnestly into the merits of his system." Oxford, Bodleian Library, St. Edmund Hall MS 67, "Diary of John Hill," 4: 4b, 32b. See also Stunt, "Greaves Family," 405–8.

17. Letter to the writer from Mrs. Lily Stephens, 9 Apr 1969.

18. See above, ch. 7.

19. Carpenter, *My Uncle John*, 8. The reference however, is misleading as there was not yet anything that could be called a "gathering of the Brethren" in Devon in 1827. Buckridge House was advertised as being available "to let" in the *Exeter Flying Post*, 29 Mar 1827. I owe this and another reference (in note 41) to Sister Thérèse Boddington of the Convent of Notre Dame, Teignmouth with whom I corresponded in 1979, at which time the Convent's school was located in Buckeridge House.

scholar John Kitto, who had once helped Groves as a dental craftsman and who regarded him as his benefactor and patron.[20] However in April 1829 Kitto heard from Groves that he could take employment "with Mr. Synge, a dear friend of mine, at Teignmouth, for three or six months from the 1st of June next, to help in printing some little works he is carrying on in Greek and Hebrew."[21] In fact, after accepting the offer, Kitto unexpectedly decided to go abroad with Groves. The other of Groves's associates affected by his change of plan was Henry Craik who had been tutoring his children. He too was now offered a post at Buckridge House, as tutor to Synge's children.[22] It appears from Craik's journal that Synge was absent (possibly in Ireland) during June and July 1828 and that Craik may have still been living with Groves, though he was already preparing for his work in the Synge household.[23] Before long, however, he was living at Buckridge and working there.

Synge's object in engaging Craik was not simply to get a tutor for his sons, but also to secure the help of someone with an adequate grasp of classical studies to assist him in the preparation of his educational publications. There are several references in Craik's *Diary* to "Greek Roots for Mr. Synge." The entry for Monday the 10 August 1829, reads: "Morning at Genesis with Mr. Synge. Forenoon, as usual, with my pupils. Spent the afternoon in my study, and had a long and happy solitary walk. Evening engaged with Homer, and Greek Testament translations for Mr. Synge."[24] It appears that Craik's employer was again away in Ireland for a period beginning in December 1829 as the tutor's *Diary* speaks of "removing into my new lodgings" and "walking over to Teignmouth with the proof for the printer."[25]

In fact Craik was an ideal assistant for Synge. Both were enthusiastic in their interest in Hebrew and both were preparing books for students of the language. True to his convictions, Synge's volume followed Pestalozzi's principles and was "intended to enable parents and teachers who consider the original of the word of God the most suitable object of early instruction, to acquire it themselves in the art of teaching."[26] Craik's book was *Principia Hebraica; or an Easy Introduction to the Hebrew Language: exhibiting, in twenty four tables, the interpretation of all the Hebrew and Chaldee words, both primitives and derivatives, contained in the Old Testament Scriptures*. It

---

20. Ryland, *Memoirs of Kitto*, 142–50, 153, 160, 189, 203, 231–32, 236. See also Stunt, *From Awakening*, 120, 128–30, 143. For a fuller account of Kitto's relationship with Groves, see above, ch. 7.

21. Ryland, *Memoirs of Kitto*, 289.

22. Roy Coad suggested that this was only a temporary position, as Synge's main residence was at Glanmore (Coad, *History of the Brethren*, 36). In fact, Glanmore only came to John Synge on his father's death in 1831—an event that he could not have foreseen when he moved to Devon in 1827. Thus Craik's appointment may not have been quite so insecure as it seems in retrospect.

23. Tayler, *Passages from Craik's Diary*, 99–107.

24. Ibid., 109.

25. Ibid., 116.

26. [Synge], *Easy introduction*.

was published in 1831 like Synge's book and printed at Synge's expense on his own printing press.[27]

At the same time, this can hardly have been purely an academic friendship. Both men were sincerely devout and there must have been lengthy discussion between them in spite of the seventeen years' difference in their ages. Craik had been brought up as a Presbyterian but while he was staying at Buckridge he adopted Baptist views and preached at the Shaldon Baptist Church which was probably where he met George Müller in 1829, with whom he was to cooperate for many years to come.[28] It is impossible to imagine that such matters and issues, which were the talking point of so many Christians dissatisfied with the current slumber of both Established and Dissenting Churches, were not debated at length by Synge and his young tutor. Synge was an Anglican but by no means a very traditionally minded one, as would shortly become apparent.

Criticism of the Established Church

In June or July 1831, two or three months after Craik had left Buckridge to become the regular pastor at Shaldon Baptist Chapel, two clergymen from Oxford came on a preaching tour in the West Country. One of them was William Tiptaft, the Vicar of Sutton Courtney, later to secede and become a Strict Baptist, while the other was Henry Bellenden Bulteel, curate of St. Ebbe's, at Oxford, whose University Sermon in February 1831 had rebuked ecclesiastical malpractices in high places, and had dared to ask whether the Church of England was any longer led by the Holy Spirit of God.[29] Bulteel's sermon had been a talking point for some time after[30] as it had concluded with this rousing warning:

> The whole Gentile Church whether Romish or Reformed is under the sentence of "excision" if she continue not in God's goodness. . . . Being shortly about to cut off the whole Gentile Church, God hath now for some few years past been constantly raising up his witnesses to the fact.
>
> God has a twofold purpose in thus acting. One is to gather out his own elect from the midst of the overthrow, the other is to leave those that shall be overthrown without any excuse.[31]

It is clear, just from that brief extract, that Tiptaft was with a man who was very outspoken in his opinions, when he came to preach in the West Country. Bulteel actually was from a distinguished Plymouth family and there was consequently something

---

27. Later published by Bagsters (London, 1864); see Tayler, *Passages from Craik's Diary*, 124.
28. Müller, *Narrative*, 1:45.
29. Bulteel, *Sermon*, 37.
30. Foot, *Gladstone Diaries*, 1:343–46.
31. Bulteel, *Sermon*, 51–52.

a bit shocking when these two men preached for about ten days in Plymouth, drawing crowds to listen to them in the open air to the dismay of scandalized bishop and clergy. Leaving the town they traveled along the South Coast getting a mixed reception from the large numbers who gathered to hear them. Tiptaft in a letter to his sister and brother-in-law Deborah and William Keal described their progress saying that they preached twice at Teignmouth:

> Many of God's dear people showed us great kindness, and those who received us we called Jasons; for they certainly had to bear a cross. Mr. Synge of Buckeridge [sic] House, near Teignmouth, was very kind to us. He stood by us twice in the open air at Teignmouth. We took up our abode with him, and he sent us in his carriage to Totnes, and met us again at Exeter, and stood by us again. May the Lord reward him! He is a man of property, and cousin to your curate.[32]

If Synge was prepared to support the public preaching of vigorous critics of the Establishment like Bulteel and Tiptaft, both of whom expected, not without reason, soon to be in trouble with their bishops, clearly he was far from complacent about the condition of the Church of England. Doubtless, Bulteel told Synge about the current discontent among Evangelicals at Oxford. He probably also gave his host some idea of the deep impression made on several of the younger men of the University by the visits of John Darby. The testimony of this Irish clergyman, whom Synge would have known already, had given fresh meaning to their doubts about the Establishment.[33] In any case, Darby had been invited by Bulteel's young friend, B. W. Newton to visit Plymouth, and Synge may have been in touch with a number of Christians there as well. We know for certain that Synge was well acquainted with a retired naval officer, Captain Percy Hall, who was in Plymouth at this time, and who like Bulteel, Darby and others, was becoming increasingly dissatisfied with his position as a churchman, even though his father had been Dean of Christ Church, Regius Professor of Divinity at Oxford, and eventually the Dean of Durham.[34] It was Percy Hall who sent John Synge a copy of *A Call to the Converted* written by one of the young Oxford Evangelicals, William George Lambert of Corpus Christi College.

Lambert is an obscure figure as far as biographical information is concerned. According to the *Alumni Oxonienses* he was the third son of Edmund Lambert of Slopeston Cottage, Devizes, Wilts. He matriculated at the age of seventeen in February 1822 from Wadham College, and was a scholar at Corpus Christi from 1822–1831, taking his BA in 1826 and MA in 1829. His death occurred in 1866. In addition to this we know that in March 1831, he and B. W. Newton were dining with Dr. John Hill after a meeting of the Society for the Conversion of the Jews at which J. N. Darby had

---

32. Philpot, *Seceders*, 1:168. "Jasons" alludes to the hospitable Thessalonian in Acts 17:5–9.
33. For the malaise at Oxford, see above, ch. 6, and Stunt, *From Awakening*, 183–219, 25–59.
34. Ward, *Victorian Oxford*, 38–39.

been one of the speakers,[35] but by the beginning of 1832 Dr. Hill is lamenting that "Lambert my co-secretary in the Church Missionary Society has left it and the Church of England."[36] It was in July 1831 that Lambert published *A Call to the Converted* in which he advocated secession. If Newton's memory is reliable, "Bishop Sumner (of Winchester then) was Visitor of Corpus; he took proceedings and deprived Lambert of his Fellowship."[37] A conversation with Lambert was one of the main influences on Newton, which led him to secede as well.[38]

John Synge was most interested in Lambert's tract and sympathized with certain of his objectives, namely a fuller experience of the presence of the Holy Spirit among believers, and a visible expression of spiritual unity. Nevertheless, he disagreed strongly with the proposed course of secession and produced a reply to Lambert's tract, which he printed at Teignmouth, presumably on his own press, and which was entitled: *Observations on "A Call to the Converted" as it relates to Members of the Church of England, addressed to Capt. P. Hall, R.N.*

We shall reserve discussion of these two tracts for a later stage, but we may here observe Synge's perspicacity in one interesting aspect. Nothing is known of Lambert's subsequent career apart from the following recollection of his erstwhile friend, B. W. Newton:

> I lost sight of him: he married a lady who was a mystic. Some years afterwards I was at Bath and heard that he was there too. I called on him on a Sunday and found him reading the newspaper. I spoke of something that is in Ephesians etc. "Oh," he said, "do you still believe like that? such as Dr. Hawker and that school? I have got beyond all that."[39]

Whether Lambert's final condition was as unregenerate as Newton implied is open to question, but clearly his later views were very different from those in his tract. In Synge's reply it is therefore somewhat striking to note one of the reasons he puts forward for not seceding:

> Yet one more reason presents itself to my mind for not acting towards the Church as our dear brother would advise, I mean a review of the numbers who have done so, with highly spiritual views, and holding out great prospects of something better, but in the event have either made shipwreck of their faith, or at least failed in the proposed object of a regenerate church . . .[40]

---

35. Diary of Dr. John Hill (see above, n15), 8:36a.

36. Ibid., 9:3b.

37. Newton's reminiscence is in the Fry MS, JRULM, CBA 7049, 279, and is confirmed in the college records.

38. Wyatt MS, 4:118, 11:148. (JRULM, CBA 7059, 7065) For a fuller account of Lambert's Oxford career and secession, in which I have used the Corpus Christi College records, see Stunt, *From Awakening*, 256–58.

39. Fry MS (JRULM, CBA 7049) 279.

40. Synge, *Observations*, 8.

It would be very instructive to know whether Lambert turned to a mystical approach because he found the ideal of a pure church was unattainable.

The Glanmore Estate

The preface to Synge's reply was dated 1 November 1831, and it was probably one of Synge's last concerns before he returned to Ireland, for in the same year his father had died, and in 1832 he took possession of Glanmore Castle.[41] At the time he seems to have returned to Ireland out of duty rather than inclination. Writing to Miss Bridson, the family governess, in December 1831 he gave his reasons: "a demesne of 1600 acres in the midst of a property of 4000 will require attention and labour, and indeed, were I disposed to cast it all behind my back tomorrow, justice to others would oblige me for some time to labour at it."[42] His wife had died in 1830 and on his return to Ireland he married Frances Steele whose sister Emily was two years later to marry his brother Edward.

Glanmore Castle, which was built by John Synge's father, was described in 1837 by Samuel Lewis, the topographer, as "the splendid residence of J. Synge Esq., . . . a handsome and spacious castellated mansion with embattled parapets, above which rises a lofty round tower, flanking the principal façade in the centre of which is a square gateway tower forming the chief entrance."[43] Today [1970] the place is only a shell and the fabric is totally derelict. An enormous monkey-puzzle tree stands close to the house in the chaotic tangle of undergrowth, which prevents the visitor from seeing more than a fraction of the estate. The surroundings, however, are quite fantastic. A nineteenth-century writer described Glanmore Castle very aptly when he referred to it as

> standing on a green platform half-way up the mountain, and hanging over the "Devil's Glen," a deep, long, and rocky gorge, with its precipitous sides lined with trees, between which the river Vartry, rushing from its upper moorlands, flings itself down through a huge cleft rock into a deep, round pool, issuing from which, it traverses the glen in whirl and rapid on its way to the sea, a thing of beauty to the eye, and a song of music to the ear.[44]

John Synge was no less concerned about his tenants and their needs when he moved to Glanmore than when he had been at Roundwood. His great uncle Sir Francis Hutchinson had built a school in 1807 on the Glanmore Estate[45] and naturally

---

41. When Buckeridge House was advertised "to let" in 1832 there was a note that "tenants could be accommodated with part of the furniture of the present tenant," *Exeter Flying Post*, 19 Jul 1832.
42. Carpenter, *My Uncle John*, 9.
43. Lewis, *Topographical Dictionary of Ireland*, 2:144.
44. Brooke, *Recollections*, 33.
45. Letter from Mrs. Lily Stephens to Dr. Kate Silber of Edinburgh, written in 1958.

Synge took great interest in the running of the school. According to Synge's accounts book, the schoolmaster in 1833 was given £20 a year with a house and one acre of land and the grass for one cow. His printing press was re-established near the Castle in the Glen in a building more recently known as the "grandmother's Tea House." Here his printer, Thomas Collins, a deaf-mute taught by another follower of Pestalozzi,[46] produced for use in the local school, wall charts, which were to be held up before the whole class when there was a shortage of books.

It is hard in an age of comparative affluence to imagine either the poverty that existed in Ireland at the time, or the simmering hatred that so often characterized the landlord and tenant relationship. At Glanmore, the Synge family had built a school and a church, but John Synge realized that more would be required than that. The first thing to be done was to find an agent who would be in full sympathy with his own Christian and humanitarian aims. Captain William Graeme Rhind was a retired naval officer who had entered Sidney Sussex College, Cambridge, with the intention of gaining a degree and being ordained. He abandoned this plan and spent some years in active Christian work among the sailors in Plymouth during which time he probably met Synge in Devon. From 1828 to 1832 he was a secretary of the Reformation Society, traveling to various parts of the country. He had been in touch with a number of the Evangelicals we have already mentioned, both at Plymouth and Oxford, which he had visited in 1830.[47] In 1831 together with Nicholas Armstrong he resigned his position with the Society[48] and came to Glanmore at Synge's invitation.

If something was to be done about the tenants' poverty, it was essential that they should be provided with employment. By 1835 Rhind had seventy families occupied with knitting, spinning, and weaving on Synge's estates. On principle Rhind and his family mostly wore clothes made by the Glanmore tenants. In his own words:

> When I tell them my little girl is wearing their home-knit stockings, one can see how happy it makes them. Thus seventy families are clothed by their own industry, and often times I am made their savings bank, until their earnings reach seven or eight shillings, for a little pig, &c. Thus also the shops are aided; and the great wheel goes round easier and better; for although I do not oblige them to take their earnings out in clothing, yet nine tenths prefer it. If they are sick I visit them; and if in need I aid them; and—during the confinement of mothers of families, if my funds admit of it, I give them extra aid—not in money (this, as much as possible, I avoid), but in flannels, baby clothes, &c.[49]

46. For the education of Thomas Collins by Dr. Charles Orpen (1791–1856), see LeFanu, *Life of Dr Orpen*, 12–14, 82–83.

47. For Rhind's earlier life see I[sbell], *Faithful unto Death*. The records of Sidney Sussex College indicate that Rhind only matriculated and took no exams. For Rhind's visit to Oxford, see Hill's Diary 8:2a–b.

48. For the circumstances of Rhind's resignation from the Reformation Society, see Reformation Society, *Fifth Annual Report* (1832), 25–29.

49. I[sbell], *Faithful unto Death*, 41.

In addition to this scheme, which, despite its paternalist overtones, was something quite remarkable in its time, Rhind provided the tenants with medical help. "The kind Christian friend on whose estates I am residing, very handsomely allows me sufficient entirely to support a weekly general dispensary and also one daily call at my own house; to this all are welcome—his own tenants and all around." This included "a great many of 'Nobody's People' as they are emphatically called in this country, being either the tenants of little landlords, almost as poor as themselves, or cabin keepers by the roadside, who are neglected to a proverb; and of whom it may be said no man careth for me. I also vaccinate their children."[50]

Such concern for the physical needs of the poor gave Rhind an opening into their hearts. From Clorah cottage where he lived, at the mouth of the Devil's Glen, he regularly visited Roman Catholics and Protestants alike and his evangelistic work was accepted by people because they knew of his concern for them. When he returned home he would frequently find a long queue of people waiting for medical attention, squatting on the ground outside his house. When someone suggested that such an intrusion was a nuisance, Rhind's reply was characteristic: "I consider it one of the principal ornaments of the place."[51] When the cholera was raging in 1838 Rhind was ready to comfort those dying, even though in doing so he was taking a great risk.[52]

In addition to supporting Rhind in his work Synge was initiating other schemes of development. There was an old slate quarry, which he set out to exploit on a large scale. Welsh slate-cutters were employed. "Metal lines were laid to carry trucks for a mile or more to a small stream by which a watermill was built for dressing slates, flags and gravestones. The loaded trucks ran down by their own weight to an arch under the public road and with little or no assistance through it and down to the mill along the track of the disused Wicklow road." The enterprise was a failure, though Synge used his skilled quarry men to direct other ambitious projects on the estate, including the construction of the Upper Glen path, the River Avenue and a "great flight of 500 rustic steps winding up like a goat track among the trees on the steep side of the Glen." Edward Stephens attributes these schemes to Synge's longing "to make the demesne of Glanmore a place for visitors to admire" and to his hope to make the quarry "profitable."

Another motive is not considered by Stephens but would seem to be quite plausible. Such works provided employment for his tenants about whom he was genuinely concerned. Stephens refers to a "local tradition that in spite of their religious teaching, the Synges were popular with the people in the district." Clearly he was ignorant of Rhind's work and has perhaps completely missed the possibility of a humanitarian mainspring in John Synge's schemes. In fact Synge suffered for his efforts. He borrowed too heavily and although his sons refused to share in his plans he refused to

50. Ibid., 42.
51. Ibid., 43.
52. Ibid., 50–51.

abandon his projects. "In 1845 the inevitable crash came. Judgments were put into execution and the bailiffs were in the house when Synge died."[53] Evidently Synge's building schemes were over-ambitious but to ignore his concern for his tenants and neighbors is to misunderstand the man. A few more resident Irish landlords who took an interest in their tenantry's welfare, as Synge did, could perhaps have reduced some of the misery of nineteenth-century Ireland. But the poor were not the only ones to benefit from his help.

The Powerscourt Conferences

When John Synge was living there, Glanmore Castle became one of the spiritual centers of County Wicklow. "In the Parish of Nun's Cross," wrote Bishop Daly's biographer, "the clergy always assembled [for their monthly clerical meeting] at Glanmore Castle where they were sure to have a large meeting, on an average about forty who were hospitably entertained by Mr. Synge. These meetings were highly prized and felt by all who attended them to be very profitable."[54] Synge, whom the clergy highly esteemed as "an earnest and religious man, and a ripe scholar,"[55] was an influence of importance in the Established Church. The high regard in which he was held by the clergy, is apparent from the following inscription in the church at Nun's Cross:

> This tablet is erected by a few clerical friends of the late John Synge Esq., of Glenmore, a man greatly beloved, of real humility and genuine faith. He truly walked with God, his citizenship in heaven and his affections fixed on things above. Thus affording to all who knew him the surest evidence of being found in his lot amongst the blessed at the coming of the Lord of glory for which he looked and waited daily. 1845.

And yet, as his tract in 1831 had shown, Synge was more than a churchman. In addition to his services to the Established Church, he saw his loyalty as extending to the wider communion of all the children of God. For this reason he was glad to share in the fellowship of the Brethren insofar as they would let him. If their meetings conflicted with his loyalty to the Established Church then he could not join them very frequently, but he was regularly present at their meetings at Powerscourt House, some thirty miles north of Glanmore.

In 1833, Henry Craik, the Hebrew scholar whom John Synge had employed at Buckridge House, received an invitation from Lady Powerscourt, through his former employer, to attend the prophetic conference at Powerscourt together with his fellow pastor George Müller. On Wednesday 18 September they arrived in Dublin, where they were met by Mr. Tims, a Dublin publisher, and on the following day John Synge

---

53. Carpenter, *My Uncle John*, 9–12.
54. Madden, *Memoir Daly*, 148.
55. Brooke, *Recollections*, 33; cf. 34, where Synge is described as a "skilled Hebraist."

arrived and took them to Glanmore Castle. We learn from Craik's Diary some details of life at Synge's home. On Friday, after spending the first part of the day alone, Craik "expounded to the servants," and then spent some further time on his own. From 11 a.m. to 2 p.m., Synge, Hewit, Rhind (who was working on the Glanmore estates), Müller, and Craik engaged in united prayer. They were to have reassembled at three in the afternoon but this was prevented by the arrival of other people on their way to Powerscourt. In the evening Craik addressed the company "with very little power and much discomfort from the fourth Psalm."[56] On Saturday morning, he remained alone until eleven o'clock when again the company gathered for three hours of united prayer after which they dined. From four to seven they were again engaged in prayer "for Ireland, not forgetting Bristol, etc." After tea Craik spent some time with Müller praying for their congregations and families back in Bristol. On Sunday they broke bread from ten to noon and in the afternoon Craik appears to have been on his own again.[57]

One of the visitors who arrived on Friday afternoon was B. W. Newton, whose letter written on Monday morning to his mother has survived:

> I just write a very few lines to say that we arrived in Ireland in safety and well on Friday morning—and are now about 38 miles from Dublin at Glenmore Castle, Mr. John Synge's—our party consisting of J. L. Harris, Miss Trelawny, H. Soltau, my dearest H[annah] and myself. In a half hour's time we set out for Powerscourt. J. N. Darby is now with us and Müller and Craik from Bristol... The entrance of the Devil's Glen, which is in Mr. Synge's ground and is considered one of the most striking spots in Ireland, is just opposite the window at which I am sitting.[58]

That so many leading Brethren should have met at Synge's home before traveling to Powerscourt suggests that they considered him as one of themselves. When, in 1833, Robert Daly withdrew from the chairmanship of the Powerscourt conferences on account of the "anti-church" views expressed by many Brethren, Synge seems to have taken Daly's place and continued as chairman for several years. Stoney's account is emphatic on this point. He refers, if Neatby's history is reliable, to a conference as late as 1838:

> Mr. John Synge was in the chair. He called on each to speak in turn on a given subject. Mr. Darby spoke last, and often for hours, touching on all that had been previously said. Mr. Wigram sat next to him. Captain Hall, Mr. George Curzon, Sir Alexander Campbell, Mr. Bellett, Mr. Thomas Mansell, Mr.

---

56. Tayler, *Passages from Craik's Diary*, 167.
57. Ibid., 168.
58. Letter from B. W. Newton at Glenmore, Wicklow to his mother, 23 Sep 1833, [punctuation supplied] transcribed in Fry MS (JRULM, CBA 7049) 293.

[Thomas] Mahon, Mr. Edward Synge were there. There were clergymen present and Irvingites.[59]

This was long after most Brethren had severed their connections with the Established Church, and yet one who had not done this was respected sufficiently to be their chairman, apparently as late as 1838.

The Problem of Secession

In fact, Synge had made his position very clear as early as 1831 when he replied to Lambert's *Call to the Converted*, and it is to a consideration of these pamphlets that we must now devote some attention.[60] Lambert's tract is perhaps the first English publication to contain all the emphases that later became characteristic of those known as Plymouth Brethren. It reflects for example the preoccupation of the time with the possibility of miracles and tongue speaking, but it takes the matter much further than a simple pentecostalism and deduces certain ecclesiastical implications:

> We are at present, much taken up with considering how far the church hath grounds for expecting the resuscitation of miraculous powers . . . Nothing can be plainer than that the Scripture affords not the least warrant for confining them to one age more than to another, but they are made to depend on faith, and faith only, and that the design and use of them is to glorify Christ risen: but then, brethren, it is equally plain to me that that faith must be embodied in a pure and spiritual church, a church formed and drawn together *solely* by the power of the principles above described, *solely*, that is, by the constraining power of the Spirit. . . . The Spirit of holiness, before he displays to the world a repetition of Pentecostal miracles, will prefer displaying the more astonishing, the more glorious, and the more lovely miracle of stubborn, human wills and lifeless human hearts brought into gracious, sweet and fervent union with the God of heaven and with each other.[61]

The role of the Holy Spirit is of crucial importance in Lambert's thesis because he sees the acceptance of the Holy Spirit's presence as rendering ecclesiastical forms obsolete:

> Greatly, greatly, brethren, have they erred and fallen into the snare of the devil, who have contended hotly and pertinaciously for a form of ecclesiastical government and have put it forward as a distinct question. What hath been the

---

59. Quoted in Neatby, *History of the Plymouth Brethren*, 39. In Bellett, *Interesting Reminiscences*, the same description is printed but with various differences. Clearly the account was circulating in MS for some time and copying resulted in inaccuracies. On the basis of Bengel's textual principle (*proclivi lectioni praestat ardua*), Neatby's version is the more reliable. The only important difference is that *Interesting Reminiscences* gives 183–, instead of 1838.

60. The only copy known to me of Lambert's *Call to the Converted*, is that in the British Library.

61. Lambert, *Call to the Converted*, 10.

> consequence? They have drawn aside attention from what is essential to what is circumstantial, and have begun at the superstructure instead of the basis.[62]

> I consider one system just as worthless as another; in this system, whosoever values the glory of Christ . . . is bound to act on one of two alternatives; either the system must become a spiritual one, or he must renounce the system, and that not without a decided protest against it as a false one. He must give himself to the Lord, Brethren: I have done it myself, as far as it was in my power, and . . . have had clearer, surer, and more abundant experiences of his favour, than I ever had in my life before; and while he is with me, I will not care though the whole world be against me.[63]

Throughout, the writer indicates that, as he understands it, the church must be composed of people who have spiritual experience, and yet he finds such experience a rare commodity:

> What do we know of being filled with the Spirit, of rejoicing with joy unspeakable and full of glory, of the love of God being shed abroad in our hearts by the Holy Ghost, which is given unto us, of being made to sit together in heavenly places in Christ Jesus; of teaching and admonishing one another in psalms and hymns and spiritual songs; of our speech being always with grace, seasoned with salt and ministering grace to the hearers?[64]

Lambert argues that this inexperience derives from the attempt to preserve the right doctrine in ecclesiastical documents instead of in the hearts of the members of a *pure* church:

> For God never designed articles and confessions and canons to be the "pillar and ground of truth": no, he designed the hearts of those in whom "the truth" should dwell, the hearts of whom it should "set free," to be its better shrine, its living receptacle.[65]

Indeed, in a pure church, Lambert maintains, the Spirit of God will direct all worship, and the contemplation of such a church leads the writer into an ecstasy of enthusiasm:

> The Spirit rejoices to display his manifold power in diversity of gifts ministries and operations, dividing to every man severally as he will; if then we belong to any such system, so ordered that it prevents the Spirit thus profusely and variously putting himself forth; if for example, one man only is authorized to pray or otherwise edify the flock, and that perhaps only in a musty, fusty

---

62. Ibid., 13.
63. Ibid., 23.
64. Ibid., 29–30.
65. Ibid., 40–41.

written form, or as much in the flesh, though *not* in such a form, whereas it is the mind of the Spirit that in the assemblies of the Saints (O beautiful and glorious assemblies, in the midst whereof standeth the Lord Jesus and his attentive angels) one should have a psalm, one a doctrine, one a tongue, one a revelation, and one an interpretation, and so all edify each other; if, I say, we are hedged in a system that precludes all this and damnably putteth God's glory under a bushel, let us by all means pray that we may with due dispatch be tumbled out of it.[66]

One suspects that Lambert, of whose spiritual development we know virtually nothing, had been unable to find a "company of believers" with whom he could share his experience of conversion and who might have established him in his faith, but nevertheless his optimism is unwavering:

I will not despair. Even now the Church is rising from the ground on which she hath been lying; even now she stirreth herself up, and is beginning to recognize the high privileges and endowments of which, by the purchase and investiture of her Lord she was once seized; she sees them, I say, and wonders why she hath been so long content to want them. Yea she is altogether as a woman in travail, that laboureth to be delivered. And there are scribes, well instructed unto the kingdom, although in some points suffered still to err, who are giving richer and fuller apprehensions of Christ's person, glory and offices, than have for a long while been rife in the world. Above all a light hath fallen from heaven upon the page of prophecy, and thousands have been called to the hope of the revelation of the day of the Lord.[67]

Lambert's study of prophecy however, is to be no curious speculation for the biblical antiquarian. Rather it will be an aid to the piety and purity of the Church, as it is "a doctrine to cut body and soul asunder . . . to snatch us out of the flesh and elevate us above the world and to sustain us in that elevation."[68] But even as early as 1831 certain hermeneutical tendencies were already beginning to appear which later would become the stock-in-trade of Brethren dispensationalism. Lambert claims that Matthew 14:45–47 implies the existence of a well-ordered and well-governed church (such as "no-one at present can show me") at the "time our Lord comes into the air to receive his saints, a time quite distinct from his coming down to the Jews on earth."[69]

Along with Lambert's ebullient eschatological hopes he displays a characteristic concern about unity and the sin of denominationalism:

What mean these cursed names of division, Churchman, Quaker, Presbyterian? I know they are music in the ears of hell, and carnal man may be

---

66. Ibid., 53–54.
67. Ibid., 58.
68. Ibid., 66.
69. Ibid., 62–63.

indifferent to them; but I know that one who is a disciple of the Lord Jesus should indignantly reject and disclaim any other title than that of "saint."[70]

Surely, the writer continues, the revivified church, which he has been envisaging cannot fail to be united, but how will it be ordered? The answer is so simple that it verges on the naïve, though we know that it was a solution that the Brethren were later to adopt as their own:

> Why are there such scanty notices of church government and church order in the books of the New Testament, whereas those of the Law abound in the most minute and particular directions? Because the fulness of the Spirit's presence made them altogether unnecessary and *because that very omission was designed to be a method of forcing us to trust completely and implicitly in the Spirit's presence and the Spirit's teaching.*[71]

On such a note of confidence *A Call to the Converted* is concluded. It manifests all the optimism of a young man of twenty-six and reflects the hopes of many earnest Christians at that time. It warrants such lengthy quotation partly because there appears to be only three extant copies of the booklet and consequently it seems to be completely unknown, but also because it is remarkable that so many "Brethren" attitudes are to be found so early in a single piece of writing.[72] Even greater interest, however, attaches for our purposes to John Synge's reply, which enshrines both a more generous and more realistic approach to the church of the day, and also a "Brethren" attitude, which has been forgotten in the course of time.

Synge's Reply

Broadly speaking, John Synge approved of Lambert's quest for a fuller experience of the presence of the Holy Spirit, but rejected his proposed course of secession:

> Greatly indeed does my soul bless God for the precious truths it [Lambert's tract] unfolds, in calling the attention of the poor scattered sheep of Christ to look for more *oneness* and more *love*; in pointing out the necessity we have for a Reformation in our believing notions of the promises of the Holy Ghost, and in shewing so forcibly that *that* Reformation must be begun in love and unity among the brethren of the Lord Jesus Christ, if we would look for the full renewal of Pentecostal power . . . I find no one trace among us of our being yet collectively partakers of that blessed Spirit, for where he dwells there will be abounding love to Christ, boldness for Christ, and affectionate unity

70. Ibid., 67–68.

71. Ibid., 69–70.

72. They are in the BL, the Cambridge University Library and the Bodleian. An anonymous abridged version, published in Hereford (1837), is in the JRULM, CBA. The work is not mentioned in either Rowdon, *Origins of the Brethren*, nor in Coad, *History of the Brethren*.

among his members and therefore still farther are we from enjoying any of his outward power and gifts. In all these particulars my heart fully goes along with what our dear brother has set forth, with so much more perspicuity and power than I am capable of doing.[73]

But in spite of this agreement, Synge differs from Lambert over "what he says concerning the necessity of both coming out of the Established Church and testifying against (i.e. abusing) it, as a preliminary step to obtaining that unity and love among the brethren of Christ, in the absence of which and necessity for which I altogether agree with him.... It does appear to me that '*a church so strictly spiritual*' as our friend speaks of, is not so easily attainable, or indeed not attainable at all 'until the spirit be poured upon us from on high, &c.' Is. 32: 15."[74]

The basic ground on which Synge defends the Established Church is that it stands in a similar position:

> to that in which the Temple service stood to the Apostles *after* the day of Pentecost ... Let those that would meet me on the ground that the Established Church stands *higher* than the Temple service, remember that the latter stood on the direct enactment of God, and let those who would place it *lower* because of its corruptions, say, do they desire to speak worse of it than our Lord spoke of the Temple.[75]

Synge implores his readers to remember what a positive blessing the National Establishment

> has been and is to our land, to have throughout it such pipes and conduits for the Word of God to run in, as are our Churches, while they set before the people who attend there so large a portion of that precious *word* in their services, in the course of a year, so much more, be it remembered, than any other denomination of Christians pretends to do; and which the Minister is not at liberty to select according to his own particular doctrines ... Deeply do I deplore that a man no sooner has his eyes open to desire a greater measure of spiritual food, than a National Church is able to supply him with, than he thinks it necessary to turn his back on the Church altogether.[76]

Synge's argument here is based on the claim that the services of the Establishment are sound in form and teaching. He rebukes Lambert for the "levity" of his reference to "musty, fusty written forms." In support of his own position he quotes rather effectively from another tract, which Captain Hall had apparently sent to him:

---

73. Synge, *Observations*, 1, 3.
74. Ibid., 3, 4.
75. Ibid., 4, 5.
76. Ibid., 6, 7.

> It is curious that to these very *"written forms"* the other hostile pamphlet which you sent me, at the same time bears the following honourable testimony: "For a chuch *strictly spiritual*, no form, as all allow, could be more expressive, none more sound."[77]

The quotation was from a tract of which no copy apparently has survived. It was entitled *A Protest against the National Establishment of England* and was written by George V. Wigram, another member of the group of radical evangelicals at Oxford, and one who would later be a leader among the Brethren.

The object of Synge's tract, however, was to do more than merely defend the Establishment which he regarded as "a *store-fold* rather than as a *fattening-fold*."[78] He wants to go some way with Lambert in his suggestions but without seceding, and consequently his enthusiasm is for the prospect of an end to denominational division:

> I do indeed thankfully hail the anticipations [in Lambert's tract] of some closer union in the wisdom and love of our Good Shepherd, through the power of the Holy Ghost, than any we are acquainted with.[79]

But together with this, Synge makes a counterproposal. He suggests that without jettisoning the sound doctrine of the Establishment, people of like spirit

> agreeing on the necessity for some closer fellowship among the children of God than public assemblies admit of . . . invite those, out of *every system*, who feel with them on these points, to assemble as often as circumstances will allow, in some convenient place, forgetting the distinguishing prominences which have kept them asunder; being brought together by the constraining love of Christ, and agreed that whatever unity of opinion may be, unity of spirit *must be* the work of the Spirit and not of the reasoning powers of man.[80]

Synge does not apparently envisage in this tract the breaking of bread taking place, but rather sees this as an occasion for meditation and prayer, the study of the prophetic Scriptures and the investigation of such thorny questions as "how far God's ancient people, the Jews, are interwoven with the hopes of the Church."[81]

In conclusion Synge touches upon the most difficult aspect of his proposition. He believes that such meetings as he has proposed may be arranged "without forsaking the National Church, without denouncing the National Church, or without attending meetings during her appointed hours of prayer."[82] Nevertheless he realizes that men who study together in this way may find themselves constrained to "go by two and

---

77. Ibid., 3.
78. Ibid., 8.
79. Ibid., 9.
80. Ibid., 11.
81. Ibid., 12.
82. Ibid., 13.

two into the villages, and teach and preach Jesus Christ, in the house, or out of the house, as may be convenient."[83] It is precisely here that he sees a difficulty arising, and though he does not mention by name the preachers who had been his guests at Buckridge a few months earlier, the fact that Bulteel's license was withdrawn by the bishop of Oxford after his West Country preaching tour is clearly what Synge has in mind when he imagines the possible consequences:

> A minister for instance, on reading our dear brother's book, may be stirred up to commence such a meeting in his parish, or may see it to be his duty to join one, begun by others; and Canon law may be brought to bear upon him, to the depriving him of his Cure. How earnestly ought we to pray, that instead of denouncing the whole system of the Church, as many have done, when thus assailed for more zeal than carnal superiors will admit of, such a one should have previously counted the cost, and being prepared for such an issue, meet it and receive it in the full spirit of the Apostle's injunction [in 1 Pet 2:20].[84]

How much better, suggests Synge, would the testimony of a minister in this position be if, when suspended from his ministry by the authorities, he "take his seat among the congregation regularly while he continues at other times to teach and to preach Jesus Christ, and to join with the waiting disciples in his neighbourhood who are giving themselves to prayer and the word."[85]

The importance of this pamphlet, which of necessity we have quoted at some length, lies in the fact that its author retained, as we have seen, his connections with the Brethren movement for many years after he wrote it. His pamphlet reflects a point of view, which, though never in the majority, was quite as "primitive" as other early Brethren attitudes. Several points emerge which we must consider.

The fact that neither Synge nor Lambert emphasize the place of the Lord's Supper in their meetings, suggests that Newton's recollections were reliable when he said that Breaking of Bread began at Plymouth rather casually.[86]

Second, Synge's use of the parallel of temple worship with the position of the Established Church, throws light on the development of a more elaborate dispensationalism which later became characteristic among Brethren. If the brother who, like Synge, was reluctant to secede, used the argument that the disciples continued to worship in the temple services, clearly it would be convenient for the separatist to claim that the church was not truly formed until the disciples had cast off all connection with Judaism.[87] That the dispensationalist issue was already developing is ap-

83. Ibid., 14.

84. Ibid., 15.

85. Ibid., 15.

86. Wyatt MS (JRULM, CBA 7059) 4:114; Fry MS (JRULM, CBA 7049) 254. Cf. Stunt, *From Awakening*, 292.

87. It had long been a mystery to the present writer as to why the Scofield Bible had to wait until Acts 15:13 before finding "dispensationally the most important passage in the New Testament." The

parent from the distinction that Lambert makes between the Jewish remnant and the Church, and from the fact that Synge considers the "thorny" question of the relation of the Jews to the Church to be a suitable subject for further Bible study.

Most important however, is the fact that in Synge's pamphlet we have a reasoned apologia for "Brethren" principles *without* secession. Many years ago in the pages of the *Journal of the Christian Brethren Research Fellowship*,[88] a similar thesis was argued by my brother Mr. Philip Stunt and many Brethren were shocked by its apparent novelty. It will not be taken, I trust, as a breach of fraternal piety, if I observe that John Synge's proposals were far more consistent than those of my brother, who suggested that the Anglican pattern of liturgy would make a good basis for Brethren worship. Synge's idea was more logical as it maintained that Brethren worship should be supplementary to the Anglican services, and for that reason it would be generically different. If "extra-establishment" meetings were to take the same liturgical form as Anglican services they would be redundant.

Synge's point of view was not in such a minority as later developments may have led us to think. In 1833 Darby seems to have been fairly sympathetic to Synge's argument as he expresses in a letter (30 Apr 1833) his anxiety about the proposed change at Limerick whereby the Brethren's breaking of bread will coincide with services of the Establishment—thus preventing people from attending both.[89]

On the other hand, as Synge realized, the most difficult issue was for a minister, like Bulteel, whose gift and whose ministry was rejected by the Establishment. Would he have the grace to be subject to unspiritual authorities in the Church? It was easier for Synge who was a layman, and the fact that many Brethren were in or intending to take Holy Orders, may explain the predominance of the separatist spirit.

It is also worth recalling that some separatist Brethren found their position faulty as time went on and grew more open in their approach, drawing nearer to Synge's own ideal. One such was Charles Hargrove who in 1835 had abandoned his clerical position in the Established Church, mainly under Darby's influence, but who later became far more kindly disposed to the Anglican communion. If he had not seceded in the somewhat bitter disillusion of earlier difficulty, one suspects that he would have taken Synge's position. In fact the restraints of ecclesiastical authority upon his ministry[90] had led Hargrove to secede because he was not prepared to submit and, in Synge's words, "take his seat in the congregation regularly" while continuing "at other times to

---

simplest explanation is that before that point, the Editor felt that the early Christians had been far too involved with Jewish worship. In fact this was the sort of dispensationalism that Newton later opposed, complaining, in a letter to Harris, Soltau and Batten in 1845 that people were teaching that "the Pentecostal saints were not in church-standing but were formed for Godly citizenship in the earth," Letter (30 Mar 1845), transcribed in Fry MS (JRULM, CBA 7049) 329. Such a view, of course, was the only answer to Synge's argument in favor of a continuing involvement with the Established Church.

88. Philip H. Stunt, "Towards an Available Mount," *CBRF Journal* 15 (Apr 1967) 30–50.

89. Darby, *Letters*, 1:18.

90. Rowdon, *Origins*, 102.

teach and preach Jesus Christ." By 1846 however, his outlook had changed considerably as the following incident demonstrates.

At one of the earliest meetings of the Evangelical Alliance when its constitution was being discussed, there was considerable surprise among many of the participants who had assumed that Plymouth Brethren would have nothing to do with the project, when Charles Hargrove intervened and announced that not only was he in full sympathy with the Alliance but also that he was a Plymouth Brother:

> I feel just as much in communion with them as ever; but I do not feel so exclusively in communion with the Plymouth Brethren, as not to be just as much in communion with any brother in this room. Furthermore, anything God has given me to minister, I feel as free to minister in another place, as in any building of the Plymouth Brethren. . . . When I heard of this Alliance, my whole heart went out; and when I see the Basis, I see, permit me to say, (I hope I do not offend) that the grand principle of this Alliance is the principle of the Plymouth Brethren.[91]

Hargrove's statement on this occasion is a striking recovery of Synge's original vision, which in many ways did envisage the Brethren as a sort of Evangelical Alliance before that organization had even been thought of.[92] In some ways, Synge's ideal resembles the non-confrontational ecclesiology of the Moravian Brethren who did not secede from the Establishment and whose ideal of *ecclesiolae in ecclesia* was decidedly inclusive. We shall probably never know whether Synge was aware of the parallel.

Conclusion

The life of John Synge is worthy of our consideration for several reasons. First we are reminded that there was from the start a non-secessionist element in Brethren thinking. His ecclesiastical position was well argued and the Brethren movement was impoverished when his point of view disappeared from among them. There is still a good case for arranging services so that they will not clash with those of other Christians. A second point that Synge's career illustrates is that he was far from the socially conservative man of tradition that the early Brethren are often assumed to have been.

---

91. Evangelical Alliance, *Proceedings of the Conference* (1846), 149.

92. In a curious footnote to a pamphlet opposing the Evangelical Alliance, Richard Whateley, the archbishop of Dublin, cast an interesting light on Hargrove's reaction.

"An occurrence which took place in this country [Ireland] a few years before my removal hither [1831], may furnish a useful lesson to those who are disposed to learn from experience.

"In the district of Killaloe, and the adjacent districts, the experiment was tried on a smaller scale, of forming an Alliance substantially of the same character as that now proposed. The results were the originating of a new sect [Kellyites?] (since merged with that of the Plymouth Brethren) and the secession from the church of many of the most influential families in that neighbourhood, who remain Dissenters of some denomination or other, to this day." Whately

Whately, *Thoughts on the Proposed Evangelical Alliance*, 7n.

In his concern for the social welfare of his tenants Synge was setting an example, which was rare in Ireland. Evidently there were among the early Brethren social as well as ecclesiastical radicals.

Synge's interest in new educational ideas was perhaps still more radical as he risked the wrath of critics who said he was threatening the established order of society. Yet his commitment to child-centered education seems to have been deep and genuine. Its extent is still further illustrated in his relationship with his own children. In contrast to so many families, most of Synge's children seem to have accepted rather than rebelled against their father's spiritual attitudes. In the case of his son Francis, Synge's ecclesiastical position seems to have narrowed somewhat. Instead of retaining his father's links with the Establishment, Francis regularly attended the Brethren meeting at Kilfee schoolhouse, but this may have been due to the influence of his wife Editha (née Truell) who, in her second marriage was united with an Exclusive Plymouth Brother. Two other sons of John Synge were evangelists—one in the Aran islands and the other in the Australian bush. The piety of the youngest son, John Hatch Synge, is attested by his own son, the dramatist John Millington Synge, in his accounts of his childhood.[93] All this suggests a good relationship between the two generations. The loyalty of children to a "maverick" father and their maintenance of their parents' values are striking. The indications are that John Synge's conciliatory radicalism in social and ecclesiastical matters was accompanied by domestic love and gentleness.

---

93. For details of Synge's children, see Carpenter, *My Uncle John*, 12–28. There is a useful family tree on pp. xvi–xvii. Since this essay appeared in 1976, Professor McCormack, an acknowledged authority on Irish Protestant culture in the eighteenth and nineteenth centuries, has raised numerous fascinating questions about the Synge family in his two books, *Silence of Barbara Synge* and *Fool of the Family*. Stimulating as these books are, neither of them gives as straightforward an account of the family as the author's masterly piece on John Millington Synge in the *Oxford Dictionary of National Biography*. McCormack is much better informed on the Synge family than on the Plymouth Brethren of whom he is inclined to be dismissive and sometimes scornful.

10

The Soltau Family of London and Plymouth[1]

Biographers and Ancestry

THERE ARE SEVERAL PROBLEMS that confront anyone investigating the life of Henry William Soltau [HWS] (1805–75)—a person whose name is familiar as one of the early Plymouth Brethren and who is often remembered for his books expounding various aspects of The Tabernacle, its furniture and vessels, as well as the priestly garments. Before we consider the problems however, we must identify the various original accounts of his life, which have been used by other writers.

The earliest biographical account was included in the first edition of Henry Pickering's *Chief Men Among the Brethren*[2] and is signed W.S. This was almost certainly the work of his youngest son, William Soltau (1852–1926).[3] A somewhat fuller account (in some respects) is given by Mildred Cable and Francesca French in the opening chapters of their account of HWS's second child, Henrietta Soltau (1843–1934), who was the director of the women's missionary training home of the China Inland Mission.[4] These two accounts are largely complementary and are evidently based on what Henrietta and William heard from their father and mother. A minimal account of HWS was included in the biographical sketch of his eldest son George Soltau,[5] and there is a similarly brief (and creatively different!) account of HWS's early years in the third paragraph of the autobiographical typescript of George's son, Theodore Stanley Soltau (1890–1970s?).[6]

---

1. This was originally part of a larger paper, which also included what is now ch. 18—a study of the careers of Henry Soltau's several children. It was delivered at a conference at St. Briavels, Gloucs, in June 2011, but has not been published. I have often used his initials (HWS) to distinguish him from one of his sons.

2. Pickering, *Chief Men* (1918), 151–55. The second edition (1931) is abbreviated and has a different photograph of Soltau (as an older man), pp. 84–88. In this paper I have used the earlier edition.

3. For William Soltau (1852–1926), see below, ch. 18, [x-ref]nn29–36.

4. Cable and French, *Henrietta Soltau*, 19–30.

5. G. Soltau, *Personal Work*, 9–10. I am indebted and most grateful to Mrs. Elisabeth Wilson, of Tasmania, for details of this volume and other valuable items that I have used in this paper.

6. Manchester, JRULM, CBA, Box 168 (5), "Autobiography of Theodore Stanley Soltau" (typescript copy provided by his granddaughter Eleanor Soltau of Dickson, TN, USA. See below, n16).

The Soltau ancestry is difficult to establish but reference to the International Genealogical Index confirms and supplements the sometimes inaccurate details provided by Burke's *Dictionary of the British Landed Gentry*.[7] HWS's grandfather, George William Soltau (1748–c. 1790), came from Bergedorf-bei-Hamburg (where his father Martin Wilhelm had been the *Burgomeister*), and was naturalized as a British citizen by Act of Parliament in 1777.[8] He was a merchant in the city of London where in 1773 he had married Ann Hodgson in the church of St. Mary Magdalene, Old Fish Street. After his death, his older son, George (1775–1819), carried on the business in partnership with his widowed mother until 1802, when she retired and her place was taken by George's younger brother William (1778–1861).[9] Unlike his younger brother and his sister, Sophia Amelia (born 1777), who appear to have remained in the area of the city of London, the older brother George would later move away.

The Move to Plymouth

Several of George's children were christened in the church of St. Lawrence Pountney, including our subject, the second son, Henry William Soltau [HWS] (born 11 Jul 1805 and christened 1 Jan 1806),[10] but some time after 1808[11] the family moved to Plymouth, a few miles east of Chaddlewood, Plympton, the former home of his wife Elizabeth, née Symons.[12] It was from Plymouth that, as a ten-year-old, HWS was taken out to see Napoleon standing on the H.M.S. Bellerophon in July 1815.[13] George

---

7. Burke, *Genealogical dictionary*, 2:1289.

8. Lower, *Patronymica Britannica*, 323; *Chronological Table*, 1777, c. 20 ("Naturalization of George Soltau"). According to several London directories he was a "merchant" living in the vicinity of Cannon Street from 1779 to 1790 after which only his widow is listed.

9. *London Gazette*, 28 Dec 1802, 11. In a list of subscribing members of the Society for Promoting Christian Knowledge, published in 1811, William Soltau's address is given as St. Helen's Place (member since 1805), and George Soltau's is Suffolk Lane, Cannon Street (member since 1807), see H. Marsh, *National Religion*, 103–4.

10. My enquiries have not been helped by the fact that the Germanic name Soltau regularly challenged the clerks responsible for keeping the parish records. The marriage record of George William in 1773 gives his name as "Solton" and the clerk at St. Lawrence Pountney (or possibly the IGI transcriber) was similarly creative. Henry's older sister is given as Augusta Elizabeth Soltan [sic] and his younger brother and sister as Elizabeth and Frederick Pennington Saltau. Henry William's birthday and baptism were recorded under the name of Sallan. The IGI transcriber consistently refers to the parish as St. Lawrence Pountey [sic.] A similar problem arises in the Census records where almost all the Soltau details are to be found under the name 'Soltan' (or Sottan, Sottar, Soltaw etc).

11. This was the last year in which one of his children was christened in the Church of St. Lawrence Pountney. On the other hand his partnership in London with his brother William was only "dissolved by mutual consent" in June 1810, *London Gazette*, 30 Jun 1810, 9; cf. *Tradesman* 5 (1 Aug 1810) 182.

12. A copy of the marriage settlement between George Soltau of Suffolk Lane, London and Elizabeth Maria Symons of Chaddlewood is held at the Plymouth and West Devon Record Office (81/Y/10/1).

13. Pickering, *Chief Men*, 151.

Soltau's wife came from a respected family in the area and this appears to have given him an entry into Plymouth life, possibly even before he moved there permanently. He was active in business and philanthropy, and was a founder in 1809 of the Plymouth Public Free School where, his grandchildren noted, "the Bible was taught daily, but no child was compelled to attend the Scripture lessons against the wishes of the parents." When the Town Council proposed in 1810 to build a new "Royal Hotel and Assembly Rooms," George Soltau, as a member of the town council unsuccessfully opposed the building of the Theatre Royal (opened in 1813).[14] These rather scarce items of information about his father suggest that HWS was brought up in a home of religious morality though not necessarily confirming the curious claim that when George Soltau died, aged only forty-four, in May 1819, he "seemed to have a vision on his death bed of all his six children safely reaching the heavenly home."[15] The anecdote may be fanciful but at least it *may* be true, which cannot be said of the tale recounted by HWS's grandson, Theodore Stanley, who claimed that on learning that his three sons had joined the Plymouth Brethren, George Soltau "cut them off without a shilling."[16] More than ten years would elapse after George Soltau's death in 1819, before there were any people known as Plymouth Brethren.

Education

A further clue as to the religious outlook of the family is that at the time of his father's death, HWS was attending "Little Bounds," a school in Bidborough, near Tunbridge Wells, run by the Rev. Francis Roach Spragg. Two of his fellow students at this establishment were Samuel and Henry, the younger sons of William Wilberforce, the evangelical abolitionist.[17] Commenting on the inadequacy (as he saw it) of the earlier education of the Wilberforce brothers, Tom Mozley, a genial and often unreliable gossip, reckoned that "the best" of their tutors was a clergyman who "after spending the whole day in his parish, and returning to a late dinner . . . would take them just from nine to ten, when both he and they were good for nothing but bed. A scrambling lesson at any odd hour was the common rule."[18] Before we conclude that Henry

---

14. For details of the Public Free School and the Theatre Royal, see Worth, *History of Plymouth*, 282, 385.

15. Pickering, *Chief Men*, 151.

16. T. S. Soltau, *Autobiography*, 1. The creativity of Theodore's account is further illustrated by his claim that when his twin brother David Livingston Soltau and he, Theodore Stanley Soltau were born in 1890, a postman read (on a postcard) the news of their safe arrival and informed the press that David Livingstone and the explorer Stanley had arrived safely. In fact the explorers had done this more than twenty years earlier.

17. Pickering, *Chief Men*, 151. Soltau recalled that the Wilberforce brothers were his fellow-students. The identity of the school can be found in Newsome, *Parting of Friends*, 40, where the tutor's name is spelt Spragge.

18. Mozley, *Reminiscences*, 1:101–2. References to the Wilberforce connection are liable to be garbled. In a recent account of Henry Soltau that has been repeated elsewhere on the web, John Bjorlie

Soltau's education was defective we should make allowances for Mozley's prejudice against the evangelical clergy. There can be little doubt that William Wilberforce chose Spragg because he was part of the evangelical Establishment. In 1812 Spragg had married a granddaughter of Henry Venn, Eliza Elliott (1786–?), in Holy Trinity Church, Clapham where her uncle, John Venn, was the rector. Spragg, himself had been a Fellow of Queen's College before taking the curacy at Bidborough where he tutored Soltau.[19] Not everyone shared Mozley's opinion of him and some ten years later, when John Henry Newman was asked by Archdeacon Froude for advice about private tutors, he observed that "I have heard a good deal of Mr. Spragg who lives near Chard (Comb[e] St. Nicholas?) as having a great talent in knowing everything that is going on among his pupils."[20] So although there is some doubt as to the quality of the teaching, it is clear that HWS was taught for a time by a respected evangelical schoolmaster. At the end of 1822 he was admitted as a pensioner to Trinity College, Cambridge where he matriculated in the following year and from which he graduated BA in 1827.[21] It is clear that at this stage HWS was a serious minded young man. He studied Hebrew with a view to understanding the Old Testament and while he was at Cambridge "he listened often to Charles Simeon and to other leading evangelicals."[22]

Evangelical Origins

Taken together therefore, there are strong indications that HWS was part of a family that was sympathetic to evangelicalism. His father's earlier subscription to the SPCK, his moral philanthropy, and his choice of Spragg as a tutor, together with Henry's readiness to sit under Simeon's preaching at Holy Trinity, Cambridge,—all these things point in that direction. However, in later years, HWS insisted, that in the preaching he had heard as a young man, "faith in the merits of Christ and doing one's duty" had been inseparably mixed, and this perhaps may serve to remind us how the ministry of a later generation of moderate evangelicals had been liable to lose some of its earlier vitality.[23] It may also illustrate how a listener's needs and interests can dictate what he hears.

---

maintained that "Soltau studied under a private tutor, Samuel Wilberforce . . . the third son . . . of William Wilberforce," http://www.plymouthbrethren.org/article/56; cf. *Uplook* 66.3 (Apr 2000) 19, http://www.uplook.org/images/pdf/2000_03.pdf.

19. For details of Spragg's career (but with no reference to the Bidborough curacy) see *Al. Cantab.*, pt. 2, 5:609. In all probability, the rector of Bidborough had evangelical sympathies as Spragg's successor as curate was his brother-in-law Edward Bishop Elliott; see article on Elliott by A. Pollard in *BDEB*.

20. Kerr and Gornall, *Newman's Letters and Diaries*, 4:285.

21 *Al. Cantab.*, pt. 2, 5:590.

22. Hereafter, unattributed quotations are taken, like this one, from Pickering, *Chief Men* (1918), 151.

23. B. W. Newton, a friend of the Soltau family, once recalled that the doyen of evangelicals at Cambridge, Charles Simeon, "in his old age used to get more orthodox and less of the old Evangelical. Someone reproached him, reminding him of his preaching in the streets and in odd places. He put his

Whatever Henry may have said later, there is evidence that by 1831 some of his family were definitely associated with the evangelicals in Plymouth who would very soon be known as "Plymouth Brethren." According to his son William, Henry's widowed mother was a "woman of great piety." When she made her will, in 1831, she named as her trustees her brother, William Symons, her brother-in-law, William Soltau (of London) and a friend, George Strobe, who were also to be the trustees for her daughters. However, as HWS's younger brother, William Francis, was still under age (having a few months earlier matriculated at Balliol College), his mother nominated three people as guardians to be responsible for the young undergraduate. These were her brother William, her son HWS, and someone whom we may presume to have been a family friend, Benjamin W. Newton. Indeed she specifically required her trustees, in the event of her death, to raise from her estate

> the sum of £300 and to pay the same to Benjamin W. Newton of Exeter College, Oxford, Esq., to be applied or expended by him during the long vacations at Oxford or in such manner as Mr. Newton may think fit in addition to my son William's allowance for the furtherance of my said son's studies.[24]

As we noted in an earlier chapter, Benjamin Newton (1807–99), a native of Plymouth, had grown up among Quakers but had become an Anglican and shortly after his election as a Fellow of Exeter College had experienced an evangelical conversion early in January 1827. Late in 1830 he had come down to Plymouth accompanied by John Nelson Darby with whom he and other local evangelicals, like Percy Francis Hall, engaged in very visible evangelism.[25] Mrs. Soltau would not have named Newton as her younger son's guardian unless she was in substantial sympathy with his activities in the city, so whatever Henry Soltau's later perceptions may have been, the family was broadly sympathetic to evangelicalism. Indeed there is specific evidence of Henry William Soltau's involvement in the earliest activities of the Plymouth Brethren. In a letter of 23 September 1833, written when Newton and other leaders of the newly established assembly at Providence Chapel in Plymouth, traveled to Ireland to attend the Conference at Powerscourt House, he (Newton) stated unequivocally, that "H. Soltau" was a member of the party.[26]

---

hands over his eyes, looked through his fingers and said Oh don't remind me of that!" (JRULM, CBA 7049, Fry MS, 146).

24. A copy of the will and probate from the London, Public Record Office (Prob. 11/1877, indexed under "Soltan") was obtained for me by Ms. Caroline Belam to whom I am indebted for several other discoveries relating to the Soltau family. There is a copy of the will in the Plymouth and West Devon Record Office (81/Y/10/11). In 1851 this younger brother, William Francis Soltau, was living with his wife and children in Plymouth, and is described in the census as "Practising Physician, Graduate of Oxford."

25. See above, chs. 1, 2 and 6; cf. Stunt, *From Awakening*, 289–90.

26. Ibid., 295n60. See also above ch. 9n58.

Conversion and Controversy

However in the early 1830s, Plymouth was not HWS's home, though for family reasons he seems to have visited it from time to time. In January 1831, four years after graduating at Cambridge he was called to the Bar from Lincoln's Inn.[27] From his account of his conversion in 1837 it seems that, prior to that, he was leading something of a double life in the earlier 1830s, moving in circles of piety while he was in Plymouth and leading a more worldly life as a barrister in the metropolis. He was apparently a man of many intellectual and cultural interests and it was to him that his mother bequeathed an "electrical machine air pump and Chymical apparatus," a collection of "shells and fossils" as well as a "case of Butterflies." His son tells us that he was a music lover and "went often to the opera."[28] But when his mother fell ill in 1837 his spiritual need suddenly became apparent to him—all the more so, when he arrived at Plymouth to find that she had died. Soon after this we are told that he was converted through the ministry of Captain Percy Hall, abandoned his practice in London as a barrister and settled with his sisters in Plymouth,[29] where he met with the Brethren.[30]

In 1841 HWS married Lucy Tate Smith, a Yorkshire woman in her late twenties, seven years younger than himself, who on an earlier visit to Plymouth had been attracted to the Brethren assembly. Their early, married life, during which their first six children were born, was overshadowed by the divisions that were emerging in the Plymouth assembly. In March 1845, when Benjamin Newton found himself under strong criticism from Darby, he turned to Soltau for support and as late as December 1846, Soltau was still taking Newton's side and defending him against his critics.[31] In the following year however, when charges of Christological heresy were made, Soltau and others who had previously supported Newton, now, in a highly emotional atmosphere, acknowledged themselves to have been in error and withdrew. Soon after, Soltau began to meet, at least for a time, with Darby and his followers.[32]

---

27. Walker, *Records of Lincoln's Inn*, 4:253.

28. Pickering, *Chief Men*, 151.

29. In the 1841 census he is found living with two of his younger sisters Dorothea and Henrietta in Gasking Street three houses away from the home of B. W. Newton's mother and aunt.

30. In 1840, the Brethren assembly (formerly meeting in Raleigh Street) acquired a larger chapel in Ebrington Street. By then, HWS was a sufficiently respected member of the assembly (or perhaps of sufficient means) to be (with J. L. Harris and B. W. Newton) one of the three joint owners of the property, Tregelles, *Three Letters*, 34n.

31. Rowdon, *Origins of the Brethren*, 236, 249.

32. Tregelles, *Three Letters*, 27–31.

Family Life: Exmouth, Bideford, and Exeter

There can be little doubt that these developments were at least partially the cause of the removal of HWS and his family from Plymouth in 1849 to Littleham, Exmouth[33] where two more of his children were born and then in 1851 to a house in Durrant [Lane] Northam on the outskirts of Bideford where the youngest of the children, William, was born. It was during this time in Bideford that he was "the tutor to the boys in the upper classes" of William Hake's school at Tusculum where one of his students was W. J. Lowe who later testified to the "scriptural instruction" he had received from Soltau.[34] In 1861, by which time HWS was definitely meeting with Open Brethren, the family moved to Exeter where he produced most of the work on the typology of the tabernacle for which he is best remembered.[35] It was in Exeter that HWS secured control of the Cheeke Street Schoolroom for Brethren evangelistic work.[36]

Family life for his nine children was fairly strict and prior to their arrival in Exeter, somewhat isolated. In later years some of the children questioned the rightness of their father in depriving them of the basic education that he had enjoyed and from which, as a well-taught Christian he had benefited.[37] On the other hand it was a close-knit family and though the Brethren identity may not have extended to all of the next generation the evangelistic enthusiasm was vigorously maintained.

One particularly strong link that HWS had with the early Brethren community was his friendship with Richard Hill (1799–1880), a graduate of Exeter College who was the vicar of West Alvington, Kingsbridge, from 1829 to 1835 in which year he seceded from the Establishment.[38] On moving to Plymouth, Hill was associated with the Brethren. His first wife, Frances, appears to have been the mother of his children, as it was only in 1849 that he married Henrietta, the younger sister of HWS,[39] and this was probably when he moved to Littleham, Exmouth, where HWS was his neighbor.[40]

---

33. In the 1851 census he is described as a "Barrister at law not practising" living at Brunswick Terrace, Littleham, on the outskirts of Exmouth with his wife and seven children, his sister Dorothea and five servants, including a Swiss governess.

34. Noel, *History of the Brethren*, 1:123. W. J. Lowe (1838–1927) was at Tusculum before 1858 so the Henry Soltau in question must be HWS rather than his son Henry who was only born in c. 1850.

35. H. W. Soltau, *Holy Vessels*.

36. Beattie, *Brethren*, 48–49, citing the account given by Samuel Blow in his *Reminiscences*.

37. Cable and French, *Henrietta Soltau*, 33–34.

38. His secession was a little later than has previously been supposed. Hill's daughter who was sixteen years old in 1851 was born in West Alvington, and his successor in the parish was appointed in 1835, see *Clergy List for 1841*, 5. This suggests that his secession was in 1835.

39. *Gentleman's Magazine* (May 1849) 536.

40. Although in the census of 1841 he had been identified simply as a person of "Independent means," ten years later, under the heading "Rank, Profession or Occupation," one may perhaps detect a wistful note of disillusion in his census entry: "Was ordained a Clergyman, but having left the Establishment has no longer any Cure of Souls therein." In 1861, by which time he was living outside Bath, he was content to describe himself as "gentleman."

Evangelism

From the time of his conversion, Soltau was passionately involved in evangelism. Together with Joseph Clulow (1797–1848), a retired administrator from Madras,[41] Soltau started the Plymouth "tract depot" in Cornwall Street, which produced and circulated many tracts several of which were written by Soltau, himself.[42] As an evangelist in Devon and sometimes in the open air in London, his work was typical of the outgoing preaching for which some of the Brethren were noted. However, there are good reasons for wondering to what extent the early Brethren in Plymouth were particularly committed to the cause of overseas mission. Preoccupation with the eschatological details of the Savior's return seems to have dimmed, at least for some of them, the clarity of the "great commission." Although A. N. Groves had been associated with Brethren from the outset of the movement, an observer visiting Plymouth, in 1840, commented that many of the Brethren "will not support this good man [Groves] because his spirit is too catholic."[43] This missiological ambivalence is well illustrated by the development of Soltau's fellow worker in the Tract Depot, Joseph Clulow.

Back in Madras, Clulow and his wife, in spite of their Anglican loyalties, had given steady support to John Smith of the London Missionary Society,[44] and, during their final years in India Clulow had warmly responded to the ideal of simplicity with which Anthony Norris Groves had challenged them.[45] When Groves returned to England in 1835 and recruited, in Barnstaple, George Beer and William Bowden for the Indian mission field, Clulow "provided for their passage and offered a yearly contribution of £50."[46] However, sometime in the course of the next year he had second thoughts. Early in 1837, Beer and Bowden learnt that Clulow had adopted "the strange view now gaining wide currency amongst Brethren that it was *not* the respon-

---

41. Clulow was one of several sons of William and Elizabeth Clulow of St. Pancras and Etchingham, Sussex, all of whom died without issue. Joseph Clulow and his wife Emily (née Robertson) appear to have adopted two orphans in India, Isabella and Sarah Frend who, according to the 1841 census, were living with them in Plymouth. For Clulow's career in India, see Dodwell and Miles, *Alphabetical List*, 60–61 and below, chap. 14n61.

42. See his youngest son's account, quoted in the preface to the 2nd ed. of Neatby, *History*, vi–vii. Two of HWS's tracts, *Scarlet Line* and *Serpent of Brass*, had an immense success.

43. Bowes, *Autobiography*, 236. I am grateful to Dr. Tim Grass for drawing my attention to this important source of independent evidence for the criticism and diminishing support from English Brethren to which Groves's widow alluded in chs. 15 and 16 of her *Memoir*.

44. "When first I became acquainted with him [Clulow] more than three years ago he said to me—Mr. Smith whenever you want support for a good cause come to me. I can truly say he has redeemed his pledge—for I never applied to him in vain and during his residence in Madras he has ever been a steady friend of our society though a decided Church man in his sentiment" (London, School of Oriental and African Studies, Council for World Mission Archives, CWM, S. India Tamil, 1834–35, Box 6 Folder 1, Jacket C, Item 16, John Smith to LMS headquarters, 25 Jul 1834).

45. [H. B. Groves], *Memoir*, 285, 297–98.

46. Bromley, *Men Sent from God*, 14. Clulow had served as a judge in Masulipatam and therefore had an interest in establishing a mission in the Telugu field.

sibility of the Church now to promote missions to the heathen, that being the task assigned to another dispensation!"[47] In all probability, Clulow and other Brethren had a significant influence on HWS, in his early involvement in Christian work, and more particularly on his approach to overseas missions, with the result that his evangelistic energies were confined to Devon and London. All the more surprising will it be to discover the crucial part that he played, in the last decade of his life together with his children, in organizing support for foreign missions—and for the China Inland Mission in particular.[48]

47. Ibid., 41.
48. See below, ch. 18.

11

From Wandsworth to British Guiana

The Strong Family Saga[1]

Origins in London and Wandsworth

WHEN MELANCTON [SIC] STRONG (b. 1650) arrived in London in 1685 he was a fugitive from the West Country. Like others from the Somerset village of Nether Stowey, he had become involved in the Monmouth rebellion against the Roman Catholic, King James II. With Judge Jeffreys presiding over the "Bloody Assizes" in Taunton, after the Battle of Sedgemoor, Strong was in great danger and flight to the anonymity of the great metropolis was a wise move. It was only a few years later with the accession of William and Mary in 1689 that he was he able to resume his original identity.[2] The commercial possibilities of the capital, in contrast to the remote and primitive lifestyle of Nether Stowey,[3] were probably self-evident to his son Melancthon (II) Strong (1677–1750), who apparently joined his father in London and was apprenticed to a haberdasher, William Ryfum, in 1694.[4]

Living in the city in the parish of All Hallows the Great, he was married in 1701 to Mary Bampton of a neighboring parish, and Melancthon (II) prospered.[5] Having a sharp eye for business he was one of the entrepreneurs who recognized the possibilities of the Wandle Valley (in what is now Wandsworth in South-West London)

---

1. Some elements in this paper overlap with a more specific essay "Leonard Strong: The Motives and Experiences of Early Missionary Work in British Guiana," published in the *Christian Brethren Review Journal* 34 (1983) 95–105, which, unlike this paper, was written without reference to the letters of Leonard Strong archived by the CMS.

2. Burke, *Landed Gentry of Great Britain*, 2:1333.

3. More than a hundred years later, Nether Stowey could be described as "one of the most retired villages of England," Sydney, "Cradle," 592.

4. I am indebted to Ms. Wendy Hawke, the senior archivist at the London Metropolitan Archives for the following transcription from the "Apprenticeship register of the Haberdashers' Company 1675–1708": "Melanckthorne Stronge son of Melancthorne Stronge of Nether [St?]ronge in the county of Sumersett miller bound to Wm Ryfum Citizen and Haberdr of London for 7 years from the date dated July [25?] 1694," (London Metropolitan Archives, Ms 15860/7, folio 360).

5. Robinson, "Extracts from Registers," 66.

for industrial production within easy reach of the great market of London.[6] In 1727 he took over a gunpowder mill (derelict since the Peace of Utrecht in 1713) and converted it for snuff production.[7] Although his children had all been born in the city, he moved out to Garratt in the parish of Wandsworth sometime in the 1720s, and when his oldest son, Melancthon (III) Strong (1705–57) married Eleanor Sanders, from an old Surrey family, he too settled in Wandsworth where, in the parish church of All Saints, all his children were baptized.[8]

Clearly the Strongs were highly successful in their various enterprises and socially upwardly mobile. In addition to dealing in snuff, Melanchthon (II) was a haberdasher, and his son is described as an "oil-presser and leather dresser."[9] The two older sons of Melanchthon (III) were admitted to Westminster School in 1745,[10] and his oldest surviving son, Thomas Strong (1736–94), some twenty years later married Sophia whose father Robert Alsop, of Great Marlborough Street, was a respected city alderman for forty years as well as having been the lord mayor of London in 1752.

Two centuries earlier, it had been Martin Luther's fellow humanist and collaborator, Philipp Schwartzerdt (1497–1560), who adopted the Greek version of his name and came to be known to posterity by the name Melanchthon. It would be unlikely for a family, in which the eldest son for four generations was given this unusual name, to be anything other than decidedly Protestant. Such convictions in the family seem all the more probable when we recall the Strong family's involvement in the Monmouth rebellion against the Roman Catholic King James II, and we should also note that by relocating in Wandsworth, the family was moving into a decidedly Protestant area. In the same year as the Monmouth Rebellion, the king of France, Louis XIV, had revoked the Edict of Nantes as a result of which large numbers of Huguenots had emigrated. Many of them were involved in the cloth trade and had settled in Wandsworth, which became famous for its Huguenot felt-workers and hatmakers. A haberdasher like Melancthon Strong would have had close links with this community and it is not surprising to find that three generations of Melancthon Strongs were buried in the Huguenot graveyard, at "Mount Nod" in Wandsworth.[11] The last of these was Melancthon (IV) Strong (1732–48) who died in his teens, and it is to the family of his younger brother Thomas (whose wife was the heir of a lord mayor of London) that we now turn.

---

6. "By 1805 the Wandle, only ten miles in length, was said to be the hardest-worked river of its size in the world," Sheppard, *London, 1808–1870*, 161.

7. Gerhold, "Wandsworth's Gunpowder Mills," 181–82. In 1735 Strong claimed to have spent some £2000 on the premises.

8. Squire, *Registers of the parish of Wandsworth*, 170–202.

9. *London Gazette*, 6 Aug 1751, 4; 1 Dec 1761, 6.

10. Barker and Stenning, *Record of old Westminsters*, 2:892.

11. Squire, "Huguenots at Wandsworth," 269.

Ordination and the Move to Brampton Abbotts

We don't know what was Thomas Strong's line of business though his brother Clement Samuel was a wine merchant in St. Pancras, Soper Lane in the City of London. What is clear is that neither of his sons was inclined to follow him in the family business. The older son, Robert Strong (1766–1849) about whom we know rather more, was a sensitive and creative boy who had hated his time at Winchester College.[12] Indeed his family had hoped that he would pursue a career in the church, but at Trinity College, Oxford from which he matriculated at the age of seventeen, he seems to have got into dissipated company. Consequently he felt inadequate for ordination and left Oxford to work for a couple of years in his father's business, where, however, he found the employment "truly distasteful."[13] With encouragement from friends he reverted to his earlier plans, returned to college, resumed his studies, as a gentleman commoner and after graduating, was ordained.[14] His earnestness in matters spiritual is evidenced in his observation that if he had not been accepted for Episcopal ordination he would have "devoted himself to winning souls out of the Establishment."[15]

There can be no question that Robert was bred in a pious, church-going family. Both his sister and he paid tribute to his father's "warm feelings of devotion . . . in public worship," and the influence of "the good example" of his parents and "the religious and sound education" they had bestowed on him.[16] His early ministry as a curate in the parishes of Warlingham, Barnes and then Highgate—all in the London vicinity—was evidently appreciated by his hearers, but his sister, who like him would later be an evangelical, is very clear that at this stage he could not be so identified:

> There were at that period, some few bright and shining lights in the Church of England such as Romaine, Berridge, Grimshawe etc., but his course did not lie among these luminaries . . . To the best of his knowledge then, he set forth the doctrines of the Cross, but he had not received that unction of the Spirit which afterwards led him deeply to search the Scriptures.[17]

---

12. According to the archivist at Winchester College, Robert Strong attended the college as a Commoner from 1777 to 1781, as did his brother Thomas from 1781 to 1784 (e-mail: 20 Dec 2011).

13. Strong, *Gathering*, 41. This volume contains the only known account of Robert Strong's early life, much of it, apparently dictated to his children by his unmarried sister Charlotte. It is a rare volume, and the only copy known to the present writer is the one in his own possession. Its value is considerable but diminished by numerous manifest errors, which seem to have arisen from the ignorance of the person to whom the account was dictated. Thus, the parish of "Clyst St Mary" in Devon is given as "Christ St Mary" (p. 32) and "Edward Bickersteth, the Rector of Watton, Herts" becomes "Rector of Walton, Edward Bickersfeth" (p. 55) and elsewhere "Bickerstatte" (p. 78). Unless otherwise referenced, my account of Robert Strong will be based on this source.

14. He graduated B.C.L. in 1792, *Al. Oxon.*, 4:1367.

15. Strong, *Gathering*, 42.

16. Ibid., 41, 48.

17. Ibid., 46.

Perhaps in these earlier years we should describe him as an exact churchman.

It is curious that although the family's roots were clearly in the London area, both Robert and his younger brother Thomas, who similarly rejected a career in business, settled down as the incumbents of parishes far removed from the capital. Thomas (about whom we know very little) was rector of Clyst St. Mary near Exeter for some forty years, while Robert became rector of Brampton Abbotts in 1799, outside Ross-on-Wye in Herefordshire, where he ministered for the remaining fifty years of his life. It is possible that the death of his father in 1798[18] made Robert readier for such a change, but many of his friends feared that rustic seclusion could put in jeopardy the elegance and refinement, which they so admired in him. Dr. Butler, the bishop of Hereford, who had ordained Robert Strong nine years earlier was a personal friend of his uncle Clement Samuel Strong, and perhaps Robert was attracted by the added challenge that the parish had been without a resident rector for a long time.

Evangelical Developments

The circumstances which led Robert Strong, the churchman to become an evangelical are far from clear, but it was probably some time after 1816 when "the zeal and activity of a neighbouring clergyman[19] in the vicinity of the Forest of Dean attracted and interested him very much," or it may have been in 1817 when he "had a distressing illness, which . . . was a season of deep spiritual trial, struggle and subsequent blessing."[20] Several clergy may have played a part in his coming to adopt evangelical views. The bishop of Gloucester (from 1815–24), the Hon. Henry Ryder is sometimes referred to as the first evangelical bishop, and Henry Berkin (1778–1847), the rector of Trinity Church in the Forest of Dean was similarly inclined.[21] It was Berkin together with the newly arrived Vicar of St. Peter's in Hereford, Henry Gipps,[22] who took the lead in the first meeting of the British and Foreign Bible Society in Ross-on-Wye, at which "Mr. Strong was on the platform but too nervous and diffident to speak, though a resolution was put into his hand."[23] His experience in this transition

18. The year of Thomas Strong's death is often given as 1794 but this is the result of his being confused with another Thomas Strong, an antiquarian of the parish of St. Giles, Cripplegate who, like our Thomas, was born in 1736 and whose obituary is included in the *Gentleman's Magazine* 64 (Dec 1794) 1107. Our Thomas died on the first birthday of his grandson Leonard (see Strong, *Gathering*, 48).

19. The account is confused. The clergyman may have been Matthew Procter, the Vicar of Newland, but the writer may equally be referring to Henry Berkin, of Holy Trinity near Drybrook.

20. Strong, *Gathering*, 53. Commenting on a hortatory letter written in 1809 to his twelve-year-old daughter, Strong's sister wrote, "It is not such a letter as he would have written in after years when he became sensible that we can only with safety stand before our Judge in another righteousness than our own."

21. For Henry Berkin's ministry in the Forest of Dene, see Nicholls, *Personalities of the Forest of Dean*, 130–47.

22. The career of Henry Gipps in Hereford will be discussed at greater length in ch. 13.

23. Strong, *Gathering*, 54.

is reminiscent of an Irish Churchman, who, realizing around this time that he had much in common with the evangelical cause, wondered: "Why not put up my tiny sail and catch some portion of the heavenly breeze which was blowing so strongly in their favour?"[24] Whatever the circumstances, Robert Strong's identification with the evangelical movement was now unmistakable as, from this point on, he regularly chaired local meetings of the Bible Society, the Church Missionary Society, and others like the Irish Scriptural School Society.

Leonard Strong: Sailor and Missionary

In these ventures Robert seems to have enjoyed the sympathy and support of his children. No fewer than three of his sons were ordained in the Anglican ministry. His eldest son, Robert (1796–1856), became the Vicar of Painswick in Gloucestershire and his third son, Clement Dawsonne (1805–1884+) served as his father's curate for some years before moving to Bristol where he would became the rector of All Saints.[25] Robert Strong's second son Leonard (1797–1874) chose to join the navy at the age of fifteen. One of his great grandchildren claimed that Lord Nelson had stayed with the family before the Battle of Copenhagen and that the Admiral had inspired little Leonard to pursue a naval career.[26] This had taken him to America during the War of 1812 and later to the Caribbean and to India, but in 1823 he abandoned the navy and matriculated from Magdalen Hall, Oxford as an undergraduate with a view to ordination. While at Oxford he experienced an evangelical conversion and began to consider the possibility of becoming a missionary in New Zealand—a proposal that delighted his father:

> Like Joseph the husband of Mary, you have been suddenly admonished to arise and take your Saviour's Gospel, if not your Saviour, into New Zealand. Christ's call to you, is like the call He gave to Peter, John and Matthew "Leave all and follow me." May you, my dear Son, be borne up as they were, cheerfully to follow His call . . . No doubt Zebedee had his pangs of heart at losing the society of his children, and so have I in the prospect of being separated and called forth to this service, nay more let us give God thanks.[27]

---

24. Woodward, *Essays*, 457.

25. Clement Dawsonne Strong married Charlotte Symonds, a sister of Dr. Addington Symonds, the father of John Addington Symonds, whose vivid account of his grandmother, Mrs. Sykes, and the "motley crew" of Plymouth Brethren who frequented her home in Bristol, might be considered a forerunner of some of the descriptions in Edmund Gosse's *Father and Son*, which it preceded by more than a decade, Brown, *John Addington Symonds*, 17–19. Cf. P. Grosskurth, *John Addington Symonds*, 13–14.

26. MacManus, *Matron of Guy's*, 1. At the time of the Battle of Copenhagen (2 Apr 1801) Leonard Strong would have been barely four years old!

27. J. L. S. Strong, *Gathering*, 75.

When the season for local CMS meetings in Gloucestershire arrived in May 1824, the former naval officer caused something of a sensation when he recounted how, in India, he "had seen infants, in considerable numbers, thrown by their own mothers into the Ganges, and the alligators contending for them as their prey."[28] He would soon offer his services to the CMS.

In his first interview with the Society's committee in April 1825 Leonard Strong said that he had been a good deal abroad in the Naval Service and that he did not think "a warm climate would agree with him"—an explanation that makes his choice of New Zealand as his field of mission more understandable. As the twenty-eight-year-old naval officer was finding his studies at Oxford rather heavy going, the principal of Magdalen Hall, Dr. Macbride, recommended that Strong complete his studies at home "under the superintendence of his father" to prepare for ordination—a process that was duly completed when he was admitted to priest's orders in May 1826.[29] However, Leonard Strong's plans were becoming more complicated. Some time in early 1826 he became engaged to Frances Sayers Reed whose father, George Reed of New Court, Newent in Gloucestershire, was strongly opposed to the couple going to New Zealand. In fact, Reed had a plantation in British Guiana and his son who was living there wanted someone to instruct his slaves. Parental consent for the marriage would only be forthcoming if the couple's destination were changed to Demerara.[30] As a friend had offered to pay for the construction of a church there, the CMS now bowed to the vested interests involved and agreed to the arrangement, assuming that the bishop of Barbados would license Leonard Strong. Accordingly the couple were married in November 1826 and set sail in the following month.[31]

Evangelical Uncertainty in Britain

The late 1820s in Britain were a time of great uncertainty. After the defeat of Napoleon, as the country began to recover from the post-war economic distress, calls for political and social change were being voiced more strongly. As issues like catholic emancipation and parliamentary reform became more pressing, the religious world was becoming increasingly divided. There were many who felt that the future was full of promise, that the gospel could now be freely proclaimed and that they could expect an outpouring of the Holy Spirit. For such optimists the proliferation of evangelical

28. Quotation from the *Gloucester Herald*, in *Missionary Register* 12 (1824) 169. We know from his father's correspondence (Strong, *Gathering*, 69) that Leonard Strong was in India in 1822, but the practice he described had been made illegal by the Governor Marquis Wellesley twenty years earlier. It is possible that, as with other such practices, the law was not always effective, or that he was describing what others had recounted to him.

29. *Missionary Register* 13 (1825) 598; 14 (1826) 263.

30. For a fuller account of these developments, based on the Minutes of the CMS Committee, see Stunt, "Leonard Strong," 95–97.

31. *Gentleman's Magazine* 96 (Dec 1826) 556; *Missionary Register* 14 (1826) 638.

organizations, in the wake of the newly established Bible and Tract Societies and the Missionary Societies, was a cause for rejoicing and hope. Others were not so sure. With the political uncertainty of the times, there had developed a considerable fascination with the minatory prophetic elements in the Scriptures, and while the optimists felt that their evangelical endeavors would in due course usher in the millennium, there were others who felt that the French Revolution had been but the beginning of a long process of disintegration leading to a falling away in established religion, which would culminate in apostasy leaving only a faithful remnant waiting for Christ's return.

Such matters must have been under discussion in the Strong household before Leonard's departure for Demerara at the end of 1826, and in the following year Robert Strong's growing interest in prophecy led him to examine this aspect of Scripture more closely. One of his conclusions was that the Jews were destined to return to Palestine and in consequence he began regularly to host an annual sermon on behalf of the London Society for the Promotion of Christianity among the Jews. He also now adopted the less optimistic worldview and concluded that Christians could not be expecting the dawn of the millennium but should be waiting for the premillennial advent of Christ.[32] Although Robert Strong was of an irenic temperament and avoided confrontation, this eschatological position meant that he would now find himself, somewhat isolated from the evangelical mainstream. A typical point of principle, on which he felt the need to make a stand, concerned the Bible Society. The fact that there were Unitarians among the supporters and officers of the Society was a source of discomfort to the more radical evangelicals who wanted the society to be professedly Trinitarian, and this was a feeling with which Robert Strong was in sympathy. Likewise he shared their desire to open and close the Society's meetings with prayer. When the committee of the Society rejected these proposals, which would have made the Society less all-embracing, the issue was raised at a stormy annual meeting of the Society in May 1831 when a popular vote endorsed the committee's decision and the rigorist proposal (taking the stricter line) was rejected. It was a development that led Strong, like many of his fellow radicals, a few months later, to subscribe to the Trinitarian Bible Society.[33]

It was also, at about this time, late in 1831 that the events in the Gloucestershire village of Longhope which were described in an earlier chapter, give us evidence of Strong's identification with the premillennial radicals.[34] It will be recalled that at the height of the social unrest of 1831, the vicar of Longhope, Edmund Probyn and his wife (influenced by their supposedly glossolalic children) had planned a pilgrimage to Jerusalem and in so doing had become the laughing-stock of the parish. Not surprisingly it is apparent from Mrs. Probyn's letters that, in the aftermath of the debacle, she

---

32. Strong, *Gathering*, 57–58.

33. For the tensions troubling the Bible Society at this time see Stunt, *From Awakening*, 245–46, 275.

34. See above, ch. 4, "'Trying the Spirits': The Case of the Gloucestershire Clergyman."

and her husband were dejected and embarrassed, though not entirely without friends and sympathizers. In the following month, together with their curate, the Probyns attended one of the Clerical Meetings held each year by Robert Strong at Brampton Abbotts. Her comment concerning their host on this occasion makes clear the rector's feelings in the matter. "The Strongs were most kind. They say they get nearly as much shunned as we do for espousing our cause."[35] Clearly at this stage Robert Strong can be identified as not just an evangelical, but also as a radical premillennialist.

Although some of the correspondence between Robert Strong and his son in British Guiana has survived, it is hard to say whether Leonard would have been as sympathetic to the Probyns as his father was, but as we shall see shortly, he too, was troubled by the direction taken by the Bible Society and he shared his father's premillennial position. Indeed, on the wider ecclesiastical front, it is clear that even before he set out for the Caribbean Leonard Strong was somewhat unsettled in his ecclesiastical position. In a later account, which may be exaggerated but which is surely based on some of his experience at the time of his ordination, Leonard Strong described his doubts:

> My Christian friends were all in the Establishment. We all perceived the falseness of the Catechism and the Baptismal Service, etc., yet I thought there was no other way to get a door for preaching the gospel than by ordination in the Establishment . . . I *was shocked* as the so-called bishop pretended to convey to me the Holy Ghost, and give ME power to remit and retain sins . . . *I knew all that was wrong*, nay, was a *lie*, but thought there was no other way of getting liberty before men to preach the blessed gospel.[36]

But with his arrival in Demerara Leonard Strong found a further, social dimension, to complicate his radical attitudes.

Challenges in British Guiana

The comparatively recent acquisition, in the last years of the eighteenth century, of what would soon become British Guiana, had been an accident of war, and the ecclesiastical arrangements for the country were for some time undecided. With the gradual establishment of the British sugar-cane planters, the presence of the Dutch Reformed Church had begun to dwindle, but as the new landowners were both English and Scots, there were two British Established Churches competing for ecclesiastical territory in the colony, as well as some nonconformist missionaries. None of the Established Churches, Dutch, English or Scots, had taken much interest in the large number of African slaves in the colony, let alone the Amerindians further inland, and the arrangements of the local Anglican Establishment took some time to be settled. In fact for the first part of the nineteenth century, the Anglican clergy in the three

---

35. Juliana Probyn to John James Strutt, 8 Dec 1831 (Terling, Essex, Strutt archives).
36. Strong, *Personal Testimony*, 5.

colonies in Guiana (named after the rivers Demerara, Essequibo and Berbice), were part of the Diocese of London, but the situation soon changed with the consecration of William Coleridge as the first bishop of Barbados in 1824. Just a few months before Leonard Strong set sail, the colonies in Guiana were appended to the see of Barbados out of which, sixteen years later, the diocese of Guiana was created in 1842.[37]

It is clear from the earlier CMS correspondence that the missionary society envisaged at least a part of Strong's ministry as being among the slave population,[38] and this was bound to put him in a potentially awkward position. Less than five years before his arrival there had been a slave rising in Guiana that the authorities had ruthlessly suppressed. In the process an LMS missionary, John Smith, had been accused of complicity and died in prison while awaiting trial. In the course of the debate that followed, the British authorities expressed the opinion that Smith had established "an organized system of influence" and that it was necessary to replace such misguided missionaries with Anglican clergy who would be "more or less under the direct control of the Government, kept so by the advantages which they hold, or expect to derive from it."[39] Of course, when Strong arrived, he could not have realized that in a very few years, the British Parliament, in the wake of the Reform Act, would vote for the abolition of slavery in the colonies, but he must have known that his position would be subject to pressures from a variety of vested interests. It would also be complicated by the fact that, although he was associated with the CMS, he was not technically a missionary but a minister appointed by the bishop of Barbados.[40]

At first, Strong was the rector of the Parish of St. Mary's, which extended for some twenty-seven miles and where, according to one of his early reports, he had a crowded congregation with many candidates for baptism. Having no church as such he held services on the ground floor of his home and in a large building offered by one of the planters.[41] A few months later, in 1827, Charles Carter and John Armstrong, two CMS schoolteachers, arrived, the latter of whom went to work on the Union Plantation in Essequibo, where he soon found that children over seven years old were not allowed to attend his school and that ultimately it was the voice of the planters that counted. It was when Armstrong found that a change in the estate's ownership

---

37. Farrar, *Notes on the history*, 12–14.

38. CMS Minutes 8:483 where there is mention of opportunities "for promoting the spiritual profit of the slave population."

39. Checkland, *Gladstones*, 189.

40. See the testimonial addressed to the bishop, on Leonard Strong's behalf, by his father and Thomas Underwood, the rector of Ross-on-Wye, and countersigned by the bishop of Hereford, 17 Nov 1826 (Photograph in Strong, *Gathering*, 100).

41. Proceedings of the CMS, 28 (1829) 130–31; cf. *Missionary Register* (Feb 1828) 140. The planter was presumably his brother-in-law who was thus fulfilling his earlier promise, but this may refer to the help given by Josias Booker of Broom Hall whom Strong warmly thanked in a letter of 3 May 1827, for providing "a convenient building for preaching the Gospel to the negroes," *Transactions of the Society . . . for the encouragement of arts*, 47 (1829) 190. For Josias Booker's activities in British Guiana, see Hollett, *Passage from India*, 56–61.

resulted in further restrictions on his work, that he began to think about the possibility of going to work among the Amerindians further inland. It appears to have been similar opposition from some planters in St. Mary's parish (where they evidently outnumbered Strong's brother-in-law) that led to Strong being transferred in late 1829 to the neighboring parish of St. Matthew. It had earlier been assumed that St. Mary's was to be an Anglican parish, but it now became a Church of Scotland parish and Strong had to leave. In the words of the bishop forty five years later:

> Mr. Strong was known to be on terms of intimacy with more than one of the members of the London Missionary Society, and he was supposed to lean towards the Emancipation of the labouring class. The flame was speedily kindled, and the agitation against the Church of England was successful.[42]

From the outset of his ministry in Guiana therefore, Strong was clearly troubled by secular influences that he felt were hampering Christian endeavor. As early as January 1828 he was complaining to the CMS that "if they wanted additional help from the Government for the Indian missions in the interior, they had to operate on the Government's terms, that is, preach only to the moral condition of the Indians and leave their material condition as they found it."[43] It is evident that his pessimistic view of the local situation was aggravated by news of political and religious developments in Britain with the result that in one of his letters (dated July 1831) to Dandeson Coates, the secretary of the CMS, Strong suddenly breaks into an extended, almost apocalyptic outburst of eschatological hope mixed with despair:

> I forbear to make any remark on the agitation of all minds in this Colony, I look for revolutions and changes and conflicts, but no regeneration of the world before the coming of the Son of Man to Reign on the Throne of David. I look for the perilous times of the Last days. I behold evil men and seducers waxing worse and worse, deceiving and being deceived. I behold men reprobate concerning the faith, I see them making shipwreck of it, denying faith to be faith, calling doubting, believing.[44] I behold persecutions in a Sister church commencing. I see them casting out the Saints of God[45] and sealing themselves in apostasy, whereas they can retain gamblers, and worldly and covetous and who preach any thing but the gospel to remain within their fold. I behold a fearful amalgamation of Orthodox professors with infidels and a frightful contention in the Churches. Our Bible Society [is] acknowledged by

---

42. Farrar, *Notes*, 156. Strong's own words were a little more direct: "After nearly three years the crafty policy of men succeeded in removing us from the district." L. Strong, *Gospel Reminiscences . . . the Triumph of Grace*, 13.

43. Letter of 30 Jan 1828, quoted in Pinnington, "Factors in the Development," 357.

44. The sentiments here are heavily dependent on 2 Tim 3:1, 13, 8 and 1 Tim 1:19.

45. The Sister Church is the Church of Scotland, which had begun proceedings against Edward Irving and in May 1831 had found McLeod Campbell, Alexander Scott, and Hugh Maclean guilty of heresy.

the majority of its members [to be] not a religious society. I hear them declaiming against an appeal to its sacred truth and declaring the Bible Society to be constituted for the Glory of Man, not for the glory of God.[46] Yea, I behold A Hypocrite Church honouring the Gold above the Altar,[47] And I rejoice to see a little band of the faithful who witness for God, contend for the faith once delivered and cannot bear them that are of the evil one, to be spots in our feasts of charity.[48] And what shall I do with my little flock of sable believers?[49] In the grace of God we will possess our souls in patience, these are the beginning of sorrows, but we will also lift up our heads for our Redemption draweth nigh. We will cry day and night unto him, who will speedily avenge his elect, and pray that when he cometh, in us he may find faith in the earth.[50] Rejoice in the blessing God still pours on the Ch. M. Society. The Lord has a witness yet to send among the nations, an elect yet to gather and I pray that he may pour down upon your Committee his enlightening grace, as well as on all your Missionaries that they may go forth in truth preaching the Gospel of the Kingdom, not only proclaiming a Crucified, risen & [sic] interceding Jesus, on whom to rest their faith! but also a Coming Reigning Jesus upon whom to place their hope, looking for his appearing and Kingdom, to make instal [sic] them as Kings and Priests to reign with him on the earth!![51]

It will be apparent from this and subsequent letters that Strong was very well acquainted with the biblical text and from his quotation we may conclude that Strong's current study of the Scriptures was focusing on the apocalyptic elements in the later Dominical discourses and the Epistle of Jude—a focus that he clearly related to the recent condemnation by the Scottish Assembly of Edward Irving's friends and colleagues as heretics, and the Bible Society meeting to which we referred earlier.

Some Local Allies and Some Progress

On the other hand Strong was not without an ally in the governor's house. Early in 1831, John Armstrong, the CMS catechist, had returned from his reconnaissance expedition into the interior, with an enthusiastic proposal for the establishment of a mission at the junction of the Essequibo and Massaruni Rivers. Strong commended

---

46. The reference is to the annual meeting of the Bible Society in May 1831.

47. The allusion is to Matt 23:17–18 though Strong has conflated the reference to the altar (v. 18) with that of the temple (v. 17).

48. Jude 3, 12.

49. The use of the adjective sable (meaning black or dark brown) is emphasizing the preponderance of Negroes in Strong's chapel.

50. In these two sentences Strong is using the language of Luke 21:19, 28; Matt. 24:8, Luke 18:7–8.

51. Birmingham University; CMS Archives [BU; CMSA] C.W/o81/13 Strong to Dandeson Coates, 25 Jul 1831. A part of this important letter is cited by Pinnington, "Factors in the Development," 365.

the project to the governor, Sir Benjamin D'Urban, who in August granted "unto the said the Rev. Leonard Strong, for and on behalf of the said Church Missionary Society," three hundred roods of land at Bartica Point for the establishment of "a Mission to the free coloured and Indians in that neighbourhood." In due course Sir Benjamin reported the matter to Viscount Goderich, the secretary of state for the colonies, describing the Rev. Mr. Strong as the "Rector of the Parish of St. Michael [sc. Matthew] in this Colony, and an exemplary and invaluable parochial clergyman" who "knew I had very much at heart" the attempt of "establishing the germ of some instruction for the Indians in the districts Mr. Armstrong had been visiting."[52]

In the summer of 1831, mission work began at Bartica Point and a few months later Strong was reporting to the CMS that "Mr. Armstrong has really chosen a fine commodious spot for the Station."[53] Late in 1832, Thomas Youd, another CMS catechist arrived from Liverpool and joined Armstrong in the work. By a prior arrangement, Armstrong returned in the summer of 1833, to England where he remained for more than a year, but some months before Armstrong's departure, Strong reported very favorably on the mission in a long and enthusiastic letter to the governor:

> Mr. Armstrong seized every opportunity of gaining the confidence of the Indians, whom he chiefly employed, and laying before them the simple purpose of his taking up residence among them; "That he came with a message of Mercy, pardon, and invitation, a proclamation of redemption wrought out for Man by the Son of God, himself in human nature; the benefits of which, are now, renovation of Soul and understanding by the spirit of God;—hereafter, the rising in a renovated body to glory, honour, and immortality." He offered to teach their children the doctrines of the Gospel and in all acquirements necessary for raising their condition as useful and civilized members of Society, and declared that solely for their welfare and the glory of God he was ready to live and die among them . . . [Such has been his success that] their native suspicions of all Europeans in their motions concerning them, are dispersing in regard to Mr. Armstrong.—They are acquiring confidence in him, apply to him as a friend, and always are ready to be his crew whenever he may travel, accompanying him to Town, when he has occasion to come down [the river] . . . In addition to this, the desire of Instruction is certainly awakening in the heart of many . . .
>
> May we not then assuredly hope Sir, that since our duty as Christians is plain—the command of our Saviour explicit to go forth and teach all Nations, O may we not hope that if we redouble our efforts, the Lord will deign his blessing and Crown the Missionaries [sic] labours with success in spreading

---

52. "Inclosure 4" with Letter of Sir B. D'Urban to Viscount Goderich, 26 Nov 1832 in British Foreign Office, Unites States Correspondence, 175, 171. Sir Benjamin D'Urban (1777–1849) would very soon be appointed (1833) Governor of Cape Colony where the port of Durban is named after him.

53. *Church Missionary Record* 3 (Feb 1832) 39.

the sweet knowledge of redemption among these neglected Savages, and bringing many of these wanderers to sit down in the Kingdom of God?[54]

Ecclesiastical Issues

The positive and optimistic tone in this letter reveals only a part of Strong's feelings about Armstrong. In fact things were not quite so simple. Armstrong had earlier indicated his hope of being ordained when he returned to England, but when Strong was asked for his opinion in the matter, he felt obliged to express his doubts, as he felt that Armstrong's churchmanship was compromised.

We noted earlier that the ecclesiastical identity of Leonard's father, Robert Strong was difficult to pin down and at this point we encounter a similar problem with his son in Guiana. It is easy to conclude from his association with the CMS that Leonard Strong was an evangelical but it is worth noting that he was also affiliated with the Society for the Propagation of the Gospel, which is often referred to as the "High Church missionary Society."[55] Indeed, in his correspondence Strong's position is somewhat ambiguous. In a letter of August 1830 he expresses the opinion that Armstrong's work will be more effective if he is ordained, describing him as "a man of faith & prayer and *much spiritual understanding* & deadness to the world."[56] However at some stage Armstrong must have expressed a highly critical opinion of the Church of England that would cause Strong to draw back from signing testimonials for him. In early 1833 he again testified to Armstrong's "humble, zealous spirit for this last year," but in October 1834 Strong was unable to forget having heard Armstrong proclaim the Church of England to be

> a harlot and the sister of Babylon the Great, denying the King's supremacy, declaiming against the union of Church and State, deprecating the article on war and a Christian man's oath. These were not Mr. A's secret opinions or doubtful opinions but they were his promulgated opinions interwoven with his character here and of which he was the champion.[57]

---

54. Much of this letter (dated 12 Feb 1833) is included in the official *Correspondence*, 177–78 (cited above in n52), but these quotations are from the fuller text given in Menezes, *Amerindians in Guyana*, 225–26, 228. The investigation of Amerindian history in Guyana by Sister Noel, a much-respected and long-serving scholar of the University of Guyana, has greatly benefited from her systematic use of the CMS archives.

55. Strong is listed as one of the three Anglican clergy in Demerara (six in Guiana) whose maintenance, in 1836, was being assisted by the SPG (Pascoe, *Two hundred years of the S.P.G.*, 1:242n).

56. BU, CMSA, C.W/o81/10 Strong to Dandeson Coates, 18 Aug 1830. Pinnington argues that Strong's desire for Armstrong to be ordained was because he recognized the importance of the sacraments and "the uselessness of . . . the merely exhortatory powers of a catechist" in the face of active opposition from a Romish priest. Pinnington, "Factors in the Development," 365.

57 BU, CMSA, C.W/o81/17a, Strong to Coates 14 Jan 1833; C.W/o81/22 Strong to Coates, 6 Oct 1834. This second letter is mentioned in the account of Armstrong in Rivière, *Absent-Minded*

As if to underline the ambiguity of his own position, Strong adds that he "did not think the worse of him for his opinions." In fact, when Armstrong returned to Guiana in April 1835, relations between Strong and Armstrong deteriorated further, but to understand why we must consider some developments in the previous year.

Another Point of View: Thomas Youd

During Armstrong's absence in England, his younger, fellow worker, Thomas Youd felt the need to relocate the mission a little way away to Bartica Grove, and when in early 1835 the governor enlarged the area of the mission with a further grant of land, Strong established a local committee who would oversee the work of the mission. At this point Strong seems to have begun to warm to Armstrong's fellow catechist. At first, when Youd had arrived in December 1832, Strong had thought he was an immature recruit, of whom "I should think Bunyan would say that he has not gone far on pilgrimage," but some three years later his opinion was more favorable and he reckoned that Youd "has grown much in spirituals."[58] So when Armstrong, newly married, returned from England in 1835, and some tensions developed between him and Youd, the local Committee of the CMS (of which Strong was the chairman) were more sympathetic to Youd than to his predecessor, with whom they now began to find fault.

In an undated report signed by Strong and two others, a CMS deputation that visited Bartica Point (late in 1835) was openly critical of Armstrong. In contrast to earlier approval, they now complained that he had chosen the site of the mission with "an eye for beauty and not for souls" and deplored "a lack of spiritual power and feeling at the station." They criticized the carpenter's shop and blacksmith's forge that Armstrong had built, as well as the kitchen garden that he had planted, citing them as evidence of his preoccupation with secular and worldly cares. On these grounds the committee refused to accede to his request for 110 guilders for planting the land with cassava insisting that "it was not the design of the CMS to supply Indians with provisions," though, as Sister Menezes very fairly observes, Armstrong's simultaneous concern for the secular and spiritual needs of his flock was very much in line with CMS published policy.[59] One suspects however that the position of Leonard Strong and the local committee was diverging somewhat from the CMS evangelicals in London.

Leonard Strong's Developing Ecclesiology

In fact it is clear that Leonard Strong's outlook was rapidly developing a more extreme radical millennialist orientation, and it is perhaps a little ironic that he seems to have

---

Imperialism, 16. The Emeritus Professor of Social Anthropology at Oxford is another distinguished scholar who has effectively made use of the CMS archives for British Guiana.

58. Letters in CMS Archives cited in Rivière, *Absent-Minded Imperialism*, 10, 17.

59. Menezes, *British Policy*, 212–13.

been finding his way to a position much nearer to the one for which he had earlier been critical of Armstrong but which Armstrong now claimed to have abandoned. Exclamatory outbursts not dissimilar to the one we noted earlier, in July 1831, appear more often in Strong's letters of 1835 and 1836, and the hope that he and his readers will be ready "at the Lord's Appearing" is a recurrent theme as is his realization that "the Body of Christ is torn and rent" in "this day of rebuke and blasphemy."[60] There are moments of millennial triumphalism as when he exclaims:

> O Satan thou father of lies and false witness of God, thy day is coming. The Nobleman who has crushed thy power in his Cross and in his opened grave will soon come back having received the Kingdom to take possession. The children of the Kingdom shall rise to reign, the feet of Christ shall stand once more on the Mount of Olives to thy confusion, thou and thy seed shall perish off this earth, the glory of Christ in his risen saints shall be revealed and all flesh shall see it together, then shall the righteous shine forth like the sun in the Kingdom of their Father and the Lord shall reign in Jerusalem on Mount Zion and among his ancients gloriously. Hallelujah![61]

More often, however, the predominant note is one of increasing disillusion with the Establishment. Particularly notable was his indignation in late 1836 at what he considered to be the worldly connections of the Bible Society epitomized by the people to be found in the Georgetown Court House on two successive Wednesdays when the "votaries of worldly pleasure" who had figured at the races and the race ball, were, a week later on the platform holding high office in the newly formed Bible Society.[62] This was what Strong had referred to a few years before as a "fearful amalgamation" of professors and infidels:

> Thus the voice of prayer was stayed, the voice of truth was dumb and the blessed book held forth by false witnesses was made to speak falsely in the lives of those who were elected by members of the Church as heads of the Society and seemed to say to the multitude "Love the World and the things of the World."[63]

We need not be surprised therefore to find in the same letter his uncompromising opinion (expressed in language reminiscent of the earlier remarks of his CMS catechist) that "the Church of Christ truly represents a Babylon, and Christendom in in [*sic*] every country exhibits the character prophetically drawn by Paul in 2nd Tim 3."

---

60. BU, CMSA, C.W.081/24, 20 Jan 1835, L Strong to D. Coates; C.W.081/27, 24 Oct 1835, L Strong to D Coates.

61. BU, CMSA, C.W.081/30, 24 May 1836, L Strong to D. Coates. Strong uses here the phraseology of John 8:44; Zech 14:4; Isa 40:5; Matt 13:43; Isa 24:23.

62. The agent of the Bible Society whose visit so offended Strong was Joseph Wheeler, see Canton, *History*, 2:322.

63. BU, CMSA, C.W.081/31, 18 Nov 1836, L Strong to D. Coates.

In spite of all this, Strong hesitated for two more years. Clearly he found his position in the Establishment hypocritical, but was afraid that secession would cut him off from a ministry that he felt was blessed of God. In the summer of 1837 he returned to England for a few months, and on his own later admission, refrained from speaking frankly with the CMS authorities about the dilemma that he was facing. In a letter of April 1838, when he was back in Demerara, his first concern was with the energetic work of the newly ordained Thomas Youd and how the death of his baby and then of his wife seemed to have been a stimulant to the young man's plans for evangelizing among the Macusie Indians.[64] From that story Strong moved on to describe opportunities for the CMS to establish further schools, but in the middle of this, the ecclesiastical contradictions of his own position once more emerge with the exclamation:

> These are days in which Satan is crying all around us "the temple of the Lord, the temple of the Lord are these!"[65] There is no temple but Jesus in whom we meet God on his mercy seat in the heavens . . . The only temple of God on earth now, is any two or three met in Jesu's name, there God will still dwell in the Spirit, in the broken and contrite heart. O I feel more than ever my own corruptions.[66]

Perhaps Strong's hesitancy and fear that secession would bring his work to an end was aggravated by the untimely death (from fever) in 1837 of his brother-in-law Benjamin Williams whose work, as an assistant pastor in the parish, Strong had greatly valued.

> My brother Williams has finished his course with joy, he counted not his life dear to him. He forsook home [and] country to labour for the Lord at his own cost and now his grave lies before me speaking volumes. May the Lord grant me a double portion of the Spirit that was on him.[67]

Secession

It was only in October 1838 that Strong finally broke the news to the secretary of the CMS. His starting point is the worldliness of the Establishment "mixed up with the

---

64. For Youd's account of his work, written less than two years before his death in 1842, see *Missionary Register* 28 (Dec 1840) 548.

65. Jer 7:4; Matt 18:20; Ps 51:17.

66. BU, CMSA, C.W.081/33, 30 Apr 1838, L Strong to D. Coates.

67. Benjamin Thomas Williams (1800–1837) had studied at Clare Hall, Cambridge, was ordained as a priest in 1830 and married Leonard Strong's sister Emily Margaretta in 1831. He was serving as a curate to Robert Strong in 1832, in Brampton Abbotts, where he baptized his son. By early 1835 he was working with Strong, in the Craig Chapel, Demerara. (See *Al. Cantab.*, 6:484; copies of ordination and baptismal records kindly provided by Mr. Mark Williams of Oklahoma City, a great-great-great grandson; and BU, CMSA, C.W.081/25, 19 May 1835, L Strong to D. Coates.)

pomp and pride of life,⁶⁸ which we are commanded to reject." From there he moves to what he sees as the biblical pattern whereby elders and bishops are identical, and the church should be enjoying a variety of ministries enabled by the manifestations of the Spirit dwelling in each of her members. He laments the evil of the royal headship, which effectively "acknowledges the Church and the World as one."

> Long have I seen this complication of evil & mourned over it in vain, but it is only lately that the Lord shewed me *the sin* of my *remaining* in *connexion* with *that* which my conscience condemned and receiving rank & credit with worldly emoluments from the very establishment I *thought evil*, and on the plea of approval of and conformity with which I alone held my situation as Rector of St Matthews Parish. You may perhaps be astonished at my blindness in remaining so long in connexion with that I so much disapproved but you must know my dear Brother that I am very carnal and nothing blinds one's eyes so much as self-interest.

Regretting that he had not been more frank when visiting England, he explains that he now "perceived that Obedience was the path of blessing, that to obey was better than sacrifice and to hearken than the fat of Rams,⁶⁹ that no service can supersede honesty and that God never can wish us to do evil for the sake of preaching the Gospel. I have therefore resigned the Rectorship of this parish and with it my connexion with the establishment."

> At present my flock cleave to me and we purpose worshipping on together following the Scriptures for rule and *the Scriptures alone*, confident am I that God and the word of his grace are all necessary to build us up and give us an inheritance among the sanctified.⁷⁰

It is hard to say whether the CMS secretary, Dandeson Coates, would at this point have understood from these letters that Strong would, from now on, effectively be associated with the Plymouth Brethren. The assembly in Plymouth was not yet ten years old but only three years previously in 1835 Coates had been warning the Basel Mission authorities to beware of Anthony Norris Groves, whose radical approach to missions in India had made Coates very suspicious of him.⁷¹ On the other hand he may well have failed to identify Strong's position as anything other than an Anglican malcontent. If this was the case, Strong's next sentence might possibly have enlightened him as it contained amidst a torrent of biblical language, two distinctive phrases that would have been recognized by anyone familiar with the writings of the early Brethren:

68. 1 John 2:16.
69. 1 Sam 15:22.
70. Acts 20:32.
71. See above, ch. 7n68.

> We desire to continue in the Apostle's [sic] doctrine and fellowship and in breaking of bread and prayers.⁷² Obeying simply all the commandments of Christ & his Apostles as set forth in the scriptures and so waiting for Jesus from heaven who *hath* delivered us from the wrath to come.⁷³ OPEN COMMUNION *for all who love Jesus* and rest on his blood for pardon, LIBERTY OF MINISTRY for *all whom* God the Holy Ghost *hath gifted* for *prayer* or *exhortation* or teaching. As every man hath received the gift, so let him minister as of the ability, which God giveth.⁷⁴

It is not clear how Strong had encountered the writings of the Brethren but in the mid-1830s, open communion and liberty of ministry had become unmistakable elements in the Brethren's rallying cry.⁷⁵ The kinship of his position to that of the Brethren is still more apparent in his secession pamphlet published in Demerara in 1838.⁷⁶

A source for Strong's familiarity with the Brethren may have been Charles Aveline, who later was an active evangelist with the Brethren in British Guiana. He is described in one account as a midshipman in the navy,⁷⁷ but he appears to have been rather younger than Strong who, five years earlier, had referred to him as "the clerk and catechist of my parish, a man full of faith and the Holy Ghost."⁷⁸ On the other hand, the probability that Aveline seceded at the same time as Strong is suggested by the sympathetic reaction of the local CMS treasurer, William Pollard when he wrote a year later:

---

72. Acts 2:42.

73. 1 Thess 1:10.

74. 1 Pet 4:10–11. BU, CMSA, C.W.081/34, 22 Oct 1838, L Strong to D. Coates. The italics are Strong's, the capitals are mine indicating very typical Brethren emphases.

75. When a journalist gave an account of a Brethren [described as "Darbyite"] conference for prophetic study in Limerick in 1840 he reported that "the principles upon which they profess to meet, are—'open communion,' that is, a willingness to receive all those that they can acknowledge to be real Christians; and 'liberty of ministry,' that is, a willingness to allow all whom they so acknowledge as Christians to speak, if they can speak to the profit of those assembled." Report from the *Limerick Chronicle*, Sep 17, 1840, reproduced in the *Courier* (Hobart, Tasmania), 2 Mar 1841.

76. Strong, *Letter to all the Brethren*. The only copy of this edition known to me is in Strong's file in the CMS archives.

77. H. Case, *On Sea and Land*, 90.

78. BU, CMSA, C.W.081/17, 14 Jan 1833, L Strong to D. Coates. In fact Aveline's family may well have been friends of the Strongs, as his father, James Aveline (1771–1835) was a surgeon in Ross-on-Wye. Charles appears to have arrived in Guiana in 1832 where at least two of his children were born between 1835 and 1837 before his wife returned to England with the children. I have briefly summarized the genealogical evidence for Charles Aveline's family at http://boards.ancestry.com.au/localities.oceania.australia.vic.general/2383.1/mb.ashx.

Messrs Strong and Aveline do not work with us any more, what then? they cease not to serve the same master; Christ is preached, and therein I rejoice, yea, and I will rejoice.[79]

Another possible source for Strong's knowledge of the Plymouth Brethren is John Barlow (c. 1795–1873), an attorney who was for many years the manager of the Taymouth Manor sugar plantation owned by the Bristol merchants, Thomas Daniel and Sons, on the Essequibo river. Barlow had earlier been a member of a Congregational Church in Georgetown, where a missionary from the London Missionary Society, Joseph Ketley was the minister. When, in 1836 the directors of the LMS had formed a local Demerara Mission Committee, Ketley with encouragement from Barlow and other members of his church had insisted on their congregation's independent status and refused to recognize the committee's authority over them.[80] We do not know whether this led Barlow to abandon Congregationalism and it is possible that his association with the Brethren was no earlier than that of Strong, but soon after he too, is identified as "an adherent of the religious principles of the Plymouth Brethren."[81]

Whatever the means of introduction it is clear that almost at once, Strong was associated with the Brethren in England. An English edition of his pamphlet was published in Exeter in 1839[82] in which year, a disenchanted CMS recruit from Switzerland, Johannes Meyer, was wandering the streets of London and chanced on a Brethren meeting where he heard a letter from Strong being read to the congregation. With encouragement from George Wigram he set out for British Guiana where he worked in association with Leonard Strong and Charles Aveline until his death in 1847.[83] Similarly, in the 1840s George Müller began to take an interest in Strong's work in Demerara and in 1843 a Bristol couple, Mr. and Mrs. Barrington sailed with Strong back to Guiana,[84] as did a little later another Bristolian, a hatter named Mordal, who had been one of the earliest members of the Brethren congregation in that town.[85]

---

79. BU, CMSA, C.W.067/2, 21 Sep 1839 W. Pollard to D Coates, cited in Pinnington, "Factors in the Development," 367. William Branch Pollard (1807–79), for whom Strong had the highest regard, had a timber cutting business and was later Auditor-General in the colony; see Pollard, "William Pollard of Devon," 468–72. Pollard's evangelical sympathies are reflected in the names of his eighth child, Edward Bickersteth Pollard (1855–1923).

80. Waddington, *Congregational History*, 472–78. Ketley officiated at Barlow's marriage to Eleanor Gill in August 1836, *West Briton and Cornwall Advertiser*, 4 Nov 1836.

81. Ostertag, "Johannes Meyer," 348. For Barlow's later work with the Brethren, see W. T. Stunt, "History of Assembly Work," 16.

82. Several substantial extracts were given with favorable comment in John Eliot Howard's magazine the *Inquirer* 2 (1839) 282–87.

83. Leonard Strong published *Labours of John Meyer in British Guiana*, which was incorporated into his *Gospel Reminiscences in the West Indies*. For the German accounts, which are more detailed, see Stunt, "Leonard Strong," 105n26.

84. Müller, *Narrative*, 1:517.

85. Tayler, *Passages from the Diary*, 220–21.

Support of this sort must have been an encouragement to Strong, as the years following his secession were not easy. In 1840 his three older daughters were staying with their grandfather in Brampton Abbotts, from where they travelled to Plymouth to attend a school run by Mrs Harriet Eccles, a respected member of the early Brethren assembly in Plymouth.[86] About a year earlier, it seems that Mrs. Strong had given birth to a son, Leonard, who was "sorely affected with yellow fever" in 1839[87] and both he and his mother died soon after. Strong visited England in 1843 and again in 1844, when he married Matilda Dundas of Edinburgh. His younger sister, the widowed Emily Williams appears to have seceded with her brother, and her second husband, John Swainson worked with his brother-in-law in Demerara before moving to the United States.[88] Although Leonard's father never seceded, he appears to have been sympathetic to his son's secessionist apocalypticism. Indeed his words in 1845 when he was almost eighty could have been written by his son:

> These are sifting times, my dear Leonard, times I trust which will through the grace of God embody in one true church and under one title, the spiritual worshippers of our Lord, and instead of that ungodly custom of the present day, saying I am of Paul and I of Apollos, to bind ourselves together under one head Jesus Christ our Lord.[89]

With significant support from a variety of English Brethren, Strong's congregation in Demerara, who had for a while been known as "Strongites,"[90] developed a recognizably "Brethren" identity and continued as such until 1849 or 1850 when Strong and his family returned to England for good, soon after his father's death.

It is hard to say to what extent Robert Strong and his sons could be described as wealthy. Clearly they would have inherited annuities and investments made possible by the family business in Wandsworth, but there are some indications that while living in British Guiana, Leonard Strong managed his finances with some success as he acquired not only some substantial landholdings in Demerara,[91] but also bought some Irish estates including several hundred acres in County Mayo.[92] When he returned to England and settled in Torquay, Leonard Strong became a close friend of Philip Gosse and other Devonian Brethren. His last years were rather quieter and probably rather

---

86. Strong, *Gathering*, 83. For Harriet Eccles, see Rawson, "Barton Hall, Hereford," 54–55; Braga, *All His Benefits*, 26.

87. Strong, *Gathering*, 73.

88. J. T. Swainson (1799–1869) was a brother of the ornithologist William Swainson (1789–1855) and a cousin of the botanist Isaac Swainson (1746–1812); see his obituary in *Witness* 6 (Jan 1870) 26–27.

89. Strong, *Gathering*, 84.

90. Bronkhurst, *Colony of British Guiana*, 429.

91. Robertson, *Four Pillars*, 295–96, 233, 150.

92. This included the Killedan estate, which he gave to his son-in-law James MacManus in 1853, MacManus, *Matron of Guy's*, 5.

more financially settled. In the census of 1851 he described himself as a "Landed Proprietor in the West Indies"—a far cry from the commercial life of his grandfather in Wandsworth. The world around him had likewise changed and seemed to have become rather less tempestuous than it had been fifty years earlier.

12

Elitist Leadership and Congregational Participation among Early Plymouth Brethren[1]

When identifying the "catalyst for disaffection" and the "trigger for individual secessions" from the Establishment in the early nineteenth century, Grayson Carter recently concluded that "theological 'extremism' was probably a more significant irritant than pastoral exasperation."[2] It is nevertheless evident that Episcopal restraints on any ecclesiastical "irregularities" and the dubious spiritual credentials of some of those controlling the appointment of both higher and lower clergy were also significant factors in the discontent of many, who seceded in the 1830s. A quest for freedom from such constraints therefore often accompanied the special doctrinal emphases of those who would sooner or later quit the Establishment. This was particularly true of the seceders commonly known as the Plymouth Brethren whose congregations proliferated in the 1830s and 40s.[3] With clerical ordination abandoned as unscriptural, their meetings came to be noted for spontaneous prayer and exhortation by any member of the congregation, but such an "institutionalizing" of unprogramed participation was liable to attract "free spirits" whose orthodoxy and "manners" could be questionable. The following paper considers the way in which the precise doctrinal convictions and conservative social assumptions of such seceders could come into conflict with and sometimes, at least for a while, keep at bay some of the elements unleashed by their professed desire for ecclesiastical freedom. Of particular interest is the interplay of social and doctrinal motivation.

The social parameters of the early Brethren were interestingly described by one of their former associates. After his secession in 1835, Joseph Philpot's ministry was exercised among the predominantly rural and working class Strict Baptists and he

---

1. This paper was delivered at Liverpool University during the Annual Conference of the Ecclesiastical History Society, summer 2004. It was published in Cooper and Gregory, *Elite and Popular Religion*, 327–36, and is used with the permission of the Society, which retains the copyright of the original essay.

2. Carter, *Anglican Evangelicals*, 45.

3. For accounts of the early Brethren, see Neatby, *History of the Plymouth Brethren*; Rowdon, *Origins*; Coad, *History*; Stunt, *From Awakening*; and Grass, *Gathering to His Name*.

was keenly aware of how different was life among the Brethren. Writing in 1842 he observed three social features of the movement. First, it had:

> *an aristocratic atmosphere*, a kind of Madeira climate which suits the tender lungs of gentility. Gentlemen and ladies dissatisfied with the carnal forms of the establishment can join the Plymouth Brethren without being jostled by "vulgar Dissenters," Baronets and honourables throw a shield of protection over the meaner refugees.

Philpot suggested that parental opposition would be much less if a young lady attended a conventicle where the ministry was given by a titled layman rather than "a poor cobbler or a Calvinistic stocking weaver in a cottage."

Second he noted the effect of the Brethren's "ascetic tendencies":

> Mahogany chairs and tables, as well as carpets, are discarded from their houses; their dress is plain even to [the point of] shabbiness.

A third observation was that:

> *The great liberality shown to poor members* is a strong attraction to that numerous class of professors, who love that religion best which does most to pay their rent, clothe their backs and feed their bellies. Some of them are men of considerable property, and most liberal in the distribution of it. We need not wonder if many of the poorer classes are drawn by such motives.[4]

There was some truth in Philpot's description. Although a generation later the situation would be changed, in the earliest days of the movement, there was a significant sprinkling of sons and grandsons of baronets such as John Parnell,[5] George Wigram,[6] Charles Brenton,[7] and Sir Alexander Cockburn-Campbell.[8] Although the titles of these men's families were almost all of a very recent creation, other Brethren were from a slightly older vintage of nobility. Captain William Wellesley, a cousin of the Duke of Wellington, was a grandson of the Earl of Mornington while Captain Percy Hall's maternal grandfather was the fifth Viscount Torrington. The social standing provided by aristocratic connections of this sort was firmly under-buttressed by a solid phalanx of gentry, which unmistakably identified the early Brethren leaders as predominantly members of the wealthy landed classes.

---

4. Philpot, "Christian Witness," 83.

5. The Parnell baronetcy dated from 1761, but Sir Henry Brooke Parnell was only raised to the peerage in 1841. John Vesey Parnell succeeded as the second Baron Congleton in 1842.

6. George Vicesimus Wigram was the twentieth child of Sir Robert Wigram of Walthamstow. His brother, Robert, succeeded as the second baronet, changing his name to FitzWygram in 1832.

7. Lancelot Charles Lee Brenton succeeded to the baronetcy of his father, Rear-Admiral Sir Jahleel Brenton, in 1844.

8. When Alexander Cockburn succeeded to his maternal grandfather's title in 1824, he was required to add on his grandfather's name, Campbell.

Some of the early Brethren leaders were neither aristocratic nor particularly affluent, but they were well educated and could at least be identified with the professional classes. Thus Benjamin Newton, whose widowed mother was probably dependent upon some financial help from fellow Quakers, could still stipulate, when planning the vacation with his mother, "that the servants should be read to by me morning and evening."[9] Such a paternalistic attitude to the working classes was reflected in Brethren evangelism and in the establishment of their early meetings. The family of Major-General Edward Baynes of Woolbrook Glen, Sidmouth, provides a good example. Shortly after Baynes's death, his widow and daughter, Harriet, were influenced by the teaching of Anthony Norris Groves[10] to engage an evangelist, Christopher Passmore, to preach in his garden in the nearby parish of Colaton Raleigh. The recollections of Passmore's daughter suggest something of the social divide between the circle from whom the Brethren leaders would be drawn and their audience:

> We removed to a village, about four miles from Sidmouth, among a very uncultivated people, and under the influence of a Church minister and his son (who associated with the lower class). There was great persecution.[11]

To avoid the threat of eviction arising from local opposition, Passmore relocated his evangelistic venture to other premises that were owned by Mrs. Baynes. In such ways landed patrons made the spread of the movement more feasible. On the other hand, when such an evangelistic outreach was successful the working class element in the congregation was bound to increase.

The early evolution of the Brethren assembly at Plymouth was a curiously *ad hoc* process by which a chapel that George Wigram had bought to provide a place for expository Bible lectures gradually assumed an ecclesiastical identity with meetings for the Lord's Supper.[12] Divergent teachings and sacramental positions appear to have coexisted and, for a time at least, fraternal love and tolerance seem to have covered a multitude of doctrinal and social differences. With what seems to have been a remarkable degree of social integration, the wealthier members—albeit somewhat paternalistically—made accommodations for the poorer. Many years later, William Kelly described how one of the early teachers, John Darby, went to work in a humbler

---

9. Manchester, JRULM, CBA, 7179 (7), B. W. Newton to Mrs. A. Newton, 23 May 1829. When he resigned his Oxford Fellowship in 1832, Newton had to take pupils for a living, but in later years he was financially comfortable either as a result of a delayed inheritance from his grandfather or following his second marriage.

10. Groves left for Baghdad in 1829 the year of Baynes's death. On his return to England in 1835 he married Harriet Baynes (Stunt, *From Awakening*, 122, 287).

11. Stunt, "Some Very Early Plymouth Brethren," 103; for Harriet Passmore's account and for Passmore's association with Wigram and the earliest Brethren at Plymouth I am indebted to the genealogical researches of Mr. Gordon Faulkner.

12. For this process, see Stunt, *From Awakening*, 291–95.

Plymouth brother's barbershop when the barber was taken ill.[13] A Swiss observer in 1836 was struck by the fact that "the rich meet with the poor without the latter over-reaching themselves," adding that "only the Spirit of God can maintain such a rare balance."[14] The social integration of the community is underlined in a later recollection of Benjamin Newton:

> The Brethren lived a great deal in each other's houses and company. There was no such thing as domestic privacy among the very early Brethren. I always had seven or eight to dinner besides my own household.[15]

Although it is wrong to suggest that in their quest to recover the primitive lifestyle of the apostles the early Brethren practiced the community of goods described in Acts 2:44–45, nevertheless the myth of "communism" was sufficiently established in popular perceptions of the early Brethren for C. M. Davies, an observer in the mid-nineteenth century, to feel the need to deny it.[16]

Participation by the poorer and less well educated in Brethren worship was not unusual—indeed in some assemblies their contributions were liable to predominate. Edward Nangle, had been familiar with several well-educated brethren in Dublin during the very early days of the movement, but when he visited their assembly there he was unimpressed:

> The speakers were all uneducated men of the artisan class; and without a single exception their effort at display in the use of big words, and abortive attempts at oratory, left no room for any feeling but that of thorough disgust.[17]

Another observer commented on how often the manner of such contributions tended to be derived from the example of a more advantaged brother. When Dr. John Epps, a Scotch Baptist, visited the London Brethren, meeting near Cavendish Square in the early 1840s, he noted that:

> Mr. Wigram appeared to be the only one of any striking talent . . . his mode of speech was slow and languid, specialities interesting in him as belonging to him; but when these specialities were assumed by others they became absurd. We could not but notice how, most probably unconsciously, the speakers imitated Mr. Wigram.[18]

---

13. Kelly's account of Darby, written in 1900, is cited in Turner, *John Nelson Darby*, 77.

14. For a fuller extract of Charles de Rodt's letter, including his account of the "restraint and simplicity" of Sir Alexander Campbell's home, see Stunt, *From Awakening*, 302.

15. Manchester, JRULM, CBA 7049, Fry transcript of B. W. Newton, "Recollections," 306.

16. Davies, *Unorthodox London*, 176; the idea lingered on, see *Notes and Queries*, ser. 6, 12 (5 Sep 1885) 188.

17. Nangle, *Recollections of Separatists*, 29; for Nangle's earlier contacts with Brethren, see Seddall, *Edward Nangle*, 44.

18. Epps, *Diary*, 209.

At Plymouth however, although there was a lack of uniformity in some of the assembly's teaching, exception was sometimes taken to contributions from the less "gifted." Newton's recollection of the man in question may be exaggerated but the situation is credible:

> There was a rag-gatherer, a curious figure, blind of one eye and only one-legged . . . He rose in the middle of the chapel, and said he couldn't read—would the man next him [sic] read that chapter about Christ washing the disciples' feet? The man did so and then the rag-gatherer said we ought to do so literally. That, he said, was our duty now . . . [Newton intervened, saying] "It appears to me that what you are saying is not to edification, and I beg you to stop" and happily he did.[19]

That this incident was no isolated case is evident from an independent source. Alfred Harris's parents had Quaker relatives but were members of the Plymouth assembly during the 1840s and 50s and in his reminiscences he described a similar episode. "Peter, a fisherman" was looked upon by the poor and illiterate part of the congregation "as a posterior type of the apostle." His contributions "delighted the illiterate," but embarrassed the educated, "his diction at times being very faulty and his similitudes absurd." When he was asked to stop, he acquiesced, but some left the assembly because of it.[20] Harris also indicated that another brother, William Morris, was excluded not only from ministering but also from the fellowship for his belief in annihilation rather than eternal punishment. Newton, who was responsible for the excommunication, described Morris as "a better preacher than any of us and a most acceptable preacher."[21] Morris established another congregation in Princess Street and "quite a lot of people followed him thither."[22]

Having rejected as unscriptural the traditional practice of ordination, which had resulted in what they pejoratively referred to as "one-man-ministry," the early Brethren laid emphasis on the variety of gifts with which the risen Christ had endowed his Church as taught in Ephesians 4:11 and 1 Corinthians 12:7–12. In later years this meant that Brethren meetings for worship were noted for a somewhat heterogeneous series of contributions but there can be little doubt that in the early days at Plymouth this was not typical.[23] Although ministry was by no means confined to one or two people, there was a presiding elder (at first Benjamin Newton and later James Lampen

---

19. Newton, "Recollections," 261.

20. Harris, "Plymouth Brethren," 94.

21. Newton, "Recollections," (JRULM, CBA 7049, Fry MS, 268).

22. Harris, "Plymouth Brethren," 96. For his heterodox views see Morris, *Question of Ages*. The only extant copy known to me is the 3rd ed. (Plymouth 1887). The 1st (unlocated) ed. was published in or before 1849.

23. See above, ch. 2, "Early Brethren and the Society of Friends," where I suggest that the influx of Quakers to the Brethren in the 1830s following the Beaconite controversy significantly contributed to a less structured congregational worship.

Harris) and it was accepted that he could intervene if he thought the congregation was being subjected to unprofitable ministry. An important witness to this state of affairs was the biblical scholar Samuel Tregelles, who was Newton's cousin by marriage and who from 1835 was regularly associated with the Plymouth Assembly. In a pamphlet written in 1849 when critical opposition to Newton had come to a head, Tregelles insisted (and none of his critics ever contradicted his statement) that intervention by the elders had been the accepted practice. At least once, he claimed, Newton had intervened "to stop ministry which was manifestly improper" in the presence and with the full concurrence of his later critics, J. N. Darby and G. V. Wigram.[24]

In describing the principles of the early Brethren with regard to ministry, both Wigram (in 1844) and Tregelles (in 1849) cited in print the principle that ministry among the Brethren was "stated but not exclusive."[25] In a letter[26] to Newton in 1846 Tregelles gave a fuller explanation of this principle and the letter reveals with whom it originated:

> Edward Foley *used* to call the true thought in connection with ministry "*Stated* ministry but not *exclusive* ministry"; meaning by *stated ministry* the distinct recognition that such and such are *the persons* who at such a place minister, and in fact whose ministry may be expected; while at the same time there was no shut door [sc. excluding other ministry] so that [sc. lest] any whom the Lord might fit for ministry should be prevented from exercising gifts so given.[27]

Ironically although Wigram was later a severe critic of Newton his earlier opinions on ministry (according to Tregelles) were "not at all in accordance with the feelings of those who wished to leave everything without restraint." As a leader of the Brethren assembly at Rawstorne Street in London he had written his tract on ministry, (using Foley's phrase) to oppose these "democratic views of ministry."[28] In another curious episode in the 1830s, Benjamin Newton (who is the sole source of the story) substituted for Wigram in the newly established London assembly and, following his practice

---

24. Tregelles, *Three letters*, 8.

25. Wigram, *On Ministry*, 2–3; an extract from Wigram's tract was cited with approval and the principle was enlarged upon in Tregelles, *Three Letters*, 8–15.

26. S. P. Tregelles (Florence, 13 Apr 1846) to B. W. Newton (Plymouth). I transcribed the letter, which was in the Fry Collection before those papers became part of the Christian Brethren Archive, in the JRULM. The text here is taken from my transcription made in 1962. For the vicissitudes of this ravaged source of primary materials see Stunt, *From Awakening*, 313–14.

27. Tregelles's underlining of the word *used* suggests a change of heart on Foley's part and his subsequent support of Darby and Wigram against Newton. Foley is not mentioned in any Brethren histories but from the Census records and other sources, we may identify him as Captain Edward Foley (1807–94) whose eighth and last child was Frank Wigram Foley (1865–1949). Born in Rochester, Edward Foley presumably left Plymouth in the 1840s and married (1850?) a younger woman; he lived in or near Cheltenham (1852–62), in Switzerland (1864–65), in Bath (1879), and had settled in Tonbridge by 1881; see Debrett's *Peerage*, 929; Foster, *Al. Oxon.*, 1:472; www.thepeerage.com/p1609.htm; and http://www.familysearch.org.

28. Tregelles, *Three Letters*, 12.

in Plymouth, refused to allow an open discussion proposed by a German professor, Friedrich Bialloblotzky who, in consequence, left the meeting in high dudgeon.[29]

There can be little doubt that there were times when Newton somewhat autocratically imposed his will (in the form of approval or disapproval) on the Plymouth congregation and silenced those whom he considered to be lacking in gift or having views at variance with his own. As his views on prophetic subjects did not coincide with those of John Darby we need not be surprised to find the latter taking Newton to task for his authoritarianism in the Plymouth assembly. His account of the situation may well be overstated, but Darby evidently found it easy to pose as the champion of the poorer and less educated elements whose participation appeared to have been muzzled somewhat high-handedly by Newton and his supporters. In a characteristically carelessly written letter of early 1846, Darby criticized Newton's "clericalism":

> Each Sunday was as regularly N.[ewton] and H.[arris] as in the establishment, and everybody knew it: there was no arrangement written—nothing to be proved. A poor man gave out a hymn, no-one would raise it[30] . . . It had been openly taught by N[ewton] and B[orlase?][31] that the Lord did not now use poor uneducated men, as those he chose before his resurrection, but after that such as Paul, Luther and Calvin, Wesley and Whitfield, and myself now. It came to such a point, preventing people speaking in the room, that S[oltau?] called it jockeyship.[32]

When criticized on this point Newton's supporters had apparently replied that even if the intervention to silence the uneducated participant had been hasty it had enjoyed widespread support from the congregation. Darby's scornful portrayal of the scene suggests a further dimension of gender in the conflict, with Newton's authority bolstered by support from the women who were not permitted to take part vocally, but nevertheless appear to have been a force to be reckoned with. Darby continues:

> But what could be proved here? Someone got up too quick, that was all—and perhaps did it in a case where the majority would go with him as to the effect, keeping down some speaker they did not like; and in the particular case the sisters had already tried to silence him by making a noise with their feet.[33]

---

29. Newton, "Recollections" (JRULM, CBA 7049, Fry MS, 262, 301, 304). The episode was unknown to Bialloblotzky's recent biographer; see Railton, *Transnational Evangelicalism*.

30. I.e., no one would lead in the singing. Brethren considered musical accompaniment as unscriptural.

31. Henry Borlase (1806–35) had been a teacher with Newton in the early movement.

32. 20 Jan 1846 to William Kelly, Darby, *Letters*, 1:89.

33. Ibid., 1:89. Two months earlier (12 Nov 1845) Darby had similarly accused Newton of neglecting the poor saying that, of the two ministers, Harris was "the only one who visited, and whom the poor really knew and loved. All the poor, I think I may say, have felt the evil." Ibid., 1:85.

It is an open question whether Darby was really as concerned for the voice of the poor and the uneducated to be heard in the assembly as he claimed or whether the issue was a convenient stick with which to beat Newton whom he clearly saw as a rival. When, a little later, he was able to pin the charge of heresy on Newton rather less was heard of Newton's clericalism and autocratic government. Darby often claimed to love the poor, but his compassion was very paternalistic. He was vocal on such issues as the desirability of keeping the pedestrian (rather than the carriage) gates of the parks open on Sundays, to enable the poor man to enjoy "the one day he has with his family," rather than being concerned with the causes of poverty itself.[34]

With the full development (after 1840) of Darby's ecclesiology by which the church was considered to be irretrievably in ruins, there would be no elders in the assemblies of Exclusive Brethren. In contrast, some of the Open Brethren, tracing their ecclesiastical lineage back to Groves and George Müller, sought to re-create the primitive pattern of the New Testament, and elders were often a feature of their assemblies. Yet Open Brethren would soon be perceived as a working class movement associated with gospel halls and a less sophisticated style of ministry. Fifty years later, the Brethren had lost most of their aristocratic identity and their assemblies had become a happy hunting-ground for socially confident gentlemen with academic inclinations. Self-educated retired officers from the armed services had often replaced the earlier university educated teachers.[35]

Curiously enough when the Brethren movement found its way to Italy, one of its leaders was the aristocratic Count Piero Guicciardini who, as an exile in England had associated with the Open Brethren.[36] The tensions that developed between this Florentine nobleman and his fellow Brethren in Italy call to mind some of those we have considered at Plymouth but Guicciardini was very much an exception. At least one British observer of the development of Protestantism in Italy in the 1850s found that "the strong republican character and tendencies of large masses of the Italian people" were dangerously responsive to "the spiritual socialism of the Plymouthian system."[37] It was a far cry from the "Madeira climate" observed by Philpot in the 1830s. In the long run the popular element appears to have triumphed.

---

34. Darby, "Sabbath," 278.

35. As Edward Groves observed, "A forlorn Brethren's meeting was exactly suited for the development of gift in a retired military officer or civilian. Requiring no support of a material kind from those who formed the assembly, he was free to expound Scripture as he pleased, especially if he undertook to make up the deficiency that constantly happened in the matter of rent and expenses." E. K. Groves, *George Müller*, 375.

36. For the Brethren in Italy see Maselli, *Tra Risveglio e Millennio*; and Stunt, "Via Media," 137–58.

37. Anon., *Religious Liberty in Tuscany in 1851*, 4; cf. Brown, *Italian Campaign*, 103.

13

Radical Evangelicals and Brethren Origins in Hereford

Introduction

WHEN THE GERMAN THEOLOGIAN and historian Ernst Troeltsch defined and elaborated on the difference between an exclusive sect and an inclusive church[1] he was looking at the problem sociologically, but the more one considers the distinction the more one is liable to be drawn into a discussion of psychology and temperament. Quite apart from doctrinal and theological considerations, the sort of person for whom the sectarian community has a particular attraction is liable to be *temperamentally* very different from his inclusive church counterpart. The need to be separate from the majority and to bear witness against their errors has an obvious appeal to the loner who sees himself in a somewhat heroic mold and who has a deep fear of compromise. For such a person, rejection or persecution is not only to be expected but perhaps also welcomed as a proof of the validity of the stance he has adopted. In contrast, the churchman only cursorily questions his allies and co-belligerents about their beliefs and is delighted to learn of the seven thousand who have not bowed the knee to Baal, and probably feels there is no need to ask whether such secret disciples have compromised their faith. Where Bunyan's Pilgrim leaves the City of Destruction and has no intention of returning, the churchman who unexpectedly finds himself engaged in a quest or mission, looks forward to returning home, more in the spirit of Frodo Baggins coming back to the West Farthing where heroes are the exception, not the rule. This temperamental difference can often relate to the nature of the person's conversion experience. A first-generation evangelical Christian, who comes to faith as a mature adult from outside the world of devotion and piety, can easily become a solitary hero with an ongoing quest for purity of principle, while second- or third-generation evangelicals, raised by believing parents, are more inclined to be accommodating and readier to settle for a greater area of grey in their moral and religious thinking.

These generalizations are prompted by a consideration of some ecclesiastical developments in Herefordshire in the early nineteenth century. In October 1802 it was

---

1. Troeltsch, *Social Teaching*, 1:331–43.

noted in the minutes of the Baptist Society, that the bishop of Hereford had recently described his diocese as "the most heathen part of England" and that therefore he welcomed the attempts of Dissenters to provide religious instruction in the county.[2] We cannot say how well informed was the person who penned these minutes nor can we be sure how well the bishop himself understood the state of his diocese. He was in his mid-eighties and only a few months away from death, and we have some reason to question whether spiritual matters came high among his priorities. From his correspondence as preserved in the Surrey Record Office, the bishop in question, John Butler, has been characterized by a distinguished historian of the eighteenth century as a "political hack" whose services were rewarded with, first, the bishopric of Oxford and then that of Hereford. His hatred of the American rebels was such that he once remarked that "mankind cannot suffer by their extirpation," he defended slavery and the slave trade, and one of his principle concerns as a bishop was increasing his income from the lease of Episcopal land.[3] It was perhaps therefore a little ironic that one of the last pronouncements of such a worldly prelate may have been to discredit his own diocese in this way.

On the other hand, it does seem that the evangelical movement, which elsewhere had breathed some life into English ecclesiastical life, made only a minimal impression on rural Herefordshire in the eighteenth and early nineteenth centuries. This was certainly the case with evangelical dissent. The Wesley brothers and George Whitfield hardly spent more than a night in Hereford itself though they preached once or twice further North in Leominster. Significantly, as late as 1831, Samuel Lewis, in his account of Hereford, lists no dissenting chapels or meetinghouses[4] and the Established Church was similarly untouched by the winds of evangelicalism, though we should bear in mind the devoted piety of Robert Strong, whose ministry, just north of Ross-on-Wye, on the southern rim of the county, we considered in an earlier chapter.[5] In reality, Brampton Abbotts, where Strong was rector for so many years, could easily have been mistaken for being a part of the diocese of Gloucester rather than Hereford, and, in any case, it was only in 1817 that he began to be associated with evangelicals.

A Lone Evangelical in Herefordshire: John Randall's Experience

About fifteen miles to the northwest of Hereford was the small parish of Almeley (c. 650 souls) and by chance we have a glimpse here of what was involved when an earnest

---

2. Lovegrove, *Established Church*, 106.

3. P. Langford, *Polite and Commercial People*, 259–60.

4. S. Lewis, *Topographical Dictionary*, 2:364. Methodists in Hereford had apparently been meeting in a room since c. 1809 but their first chapel was only built in 1829—perhaps too late for inclusion in Lewis's work; see Parlby, *Sketch of the Rise of Methodism*. In contrast, in Leominster, Lewis mentions "places of worship for Baptists, the Society of Friends, Moravians and Unitarians" (Lewis, *Topographical Dictionary*, 3:64).

5. See above, ch. 11, "From Wandsworth to British Guiana."

young evangelical Anglican minister began his ministry in that part of England. John Randall had graduated from Trinity College, Cambridge, and was ordained in 1817 when he went to be vicar of Almeley. We know very little about his later career,[6] but in a few letters that he wrote to his fellow evangelical William Phelps, later Archdeacon of Carlisle, we get an idea of some of the problems he faced in his first parish.

It is tempting to conjecture that Randall had read of the Episcopal opinion from which we quoted at the outset. Even before his arrival Randall was prepared for the worst in Herefordshire which he described as "one of the darkest and most ignorant counties in England."

> There is but one clergyman that I can hear of, who preaches the doctrines of the Reformation, about fifteen miles from Almeley and no dissenters near. The parish to which I am ordained is esteemed very respectable as to its inhabitants, and many persons of family attend the church. It is also a healthy and pretty village. There is much, very much to be done, and need for watchfulness, as my [previous] vicar who has been there cannot hear that any one individual is acquainted with vital piety.[7]

Writing a little while after his arrival in 1817 Randall's feelings are mixed:

> I knew I was come to a people "who knew not the Lord," and expected nothing but opposition; but God has hitherto restrained all their hearts, and comparatively little opposition has been raised. The whole of the Sabbath here was almost forgotten and dedicated to business or pleasure. Scarcely any attended church, and the major part of those who did (about forty) were unacquainted with the most common truths of Christianity. I found about five who were evidently under divine influence and who have since, blessed be God, much increased in knowledge, and boldly "professed the faith of Christ crucified."

Working with this small nucleus, Randall apparently felt that he was making some progress with the rest of his parish so that: "All the Sunday bell-ringing and other sports are laid aside and nearly all the parish attend their church, the interior of which, some had not seen for years." He then describes a confrontation with his parishioners over the traditional celebration of a "Church Ale" in the churchyard.[8] Such festive events were liable to devolve into riotous occasions of somewhat abandoned behavior:

> This county abounds with village wakes held on Sunday in the churchyards.
> This was a day I dreaded here, but resolved to do what I could to prevent it in

---

6. From 1826 until his death in 1859. Randall was the Vicar of Lyonshall, Herefordshire (*Al. Cantab.*, pt. 2, 5:242). His move may have been connected with his marriage to Elizabeth Bennett, sister of James Bennett, a silversmith in Salisbury, see Moody, "James Bennett," 185.

7. Hole, *Life of Phelps*, 1:137–38.

8. The Church or parish ale was one of many such occasions (cf. lamb-ales at lamb-shearing, leet-ales when the manorial court or leet was held) but theoretically this one was in honor of the church's patron, who, in Almeley, was the Virgin Mary.

the strength of God. Accordingly I opened the church about the commencement, and performed duty and preached a sermon on the consequences of sin. The church was crowded to excess, and afterwards I went among the crowd and expostulated; upon which they shouted—"We will not keep the feast in the churchyard if *you* do not like it," and all quietly dispersed.[9]

Encouraged by such experiences Randall was ready to innovate in a typically evangelical fashion:

> The people here are, generally speaking, very very low in their morals; but we know that God is able to do great things; and I hope that many may be born of God. I instituted a Sunday School last Sunday under very favourable prospects . . . [Previously] There was never any singing in the church, but some young people have learned, and begin to sing very prettily some simple Berlin tunes.[10] There were two meetings in the neighbourhood, one of which is entirely forsaken and the other never attended by more than ten persons. So you see there are some encouraging things here and *many* which give many a pain.[11]

In a second letter written a year later, after a discussion of the need to avoid card-playing and indeed "to decline visiting in parties where cards are introduced," Randall observes that in spite of the "excessive retirement of a village life" he has been encouraged in his ministry, though clearly the mixed nature of his congregation posed problems for an evangelical who could not regard all his parishioners as Christians.

> For a long time I kept the great privileges of a believer out of sight in my sermons, either from supposing them capable of perversion, or of their being strong meat instead of milk for babes, of which my flock consists, it being only an infant church. Few of them ever got lasting comfort and did not appear to grow. But lately having spoken freely of the privileges of the believer derived from the blood of Christ, a decided alteration has taken place.[12]

Such however was the experience of but one solitary individual and Almeley was but one remote village parish and significantly in these letters Randall was sharing his thoughts with a sympathetic friend outside the county. In and around Hereford

---

9. Hole, *Life of Phelps*, 1:159. Some twenty years later, the Herefordshire wakes were still a problem but opposition to them had become much more widespread. In 1838, with support from the bishop, the dean and archdeacon, as well as from numerous Herefordshire clergy and laymen, a petition from the city of Hereford against "Sunday Wakes" was presented to the House of Commons; see the *Churchman* 2 (Aug 1838) 280–81.

10. For the last forty years of his life, Johann Crüger (1598–1662) had been the cantor of the oldest church in Berlin, the San Nikolai Kirche. Many of the hymn tunes that he composed were included in a collection popularly referred to as Das Berliner Gesangbuch, which went through numerous editions.

11. Hole, *Life of Phelps*, 1:160.

12. Ibid., 1:207.

itself, the evangelical cause had very few protagonists. When John Adams, the sole preacher in the Hereford Methodist circuit, wrote to Jabez Bunting in 1821, his judgment tallied with Randall's overall assessment (and indeed with that of Bishop Butler): "This county (as you know full well) is nearly half a century behind some others in mental, moral and spiritual cultivation. This city imbraces [sic] many teachers but few spiritual ones."[13]

Henry Gipps (1786–1832) in Hereford

However, both the Methodist preacher and the Anglican curate noted a newly arrived evangelical exception in Hereford itself. Adams's (typically Methodist) feelings as expressed to Bunting, were mixed because of the Calvinism of the person in question: "The Establishment can boast of the Rev. H. Gipps, a rich, pious and zealous man of moderate talent, but whose preaching is strongly shaded with the somber hue of Calvinism." In contrast, Randall was decidedly enthusiastic: "There is a burning and a shining light at Hereford; a Senior Wrangler, £3000 a year and great grace. Nearly two hundred souls have received the word."[14] In fact the youthful success and considerable impact that Henry Gipps made on Hereford as curate and later vicar of St. Peter's are worthy of a closer examination than either the Methodist or the Anglican correspondent was prepared to give, and certainly more than we find in the twentieth-century account of his church in Hereford where no mention is made of his work.[15]

Henry Gipps was the second son of George Gipps (1729–1800), a social *parvenu* of Canterbury. George's father had made women's stays at Ashford, Kent and George himself had begun his career first as an apothecary and later as a hop-factor, but his first marriage, although childless, had been financially advantageous. He acquired land in the Canterbury area and later was a partner with a nephew in the bank of Gipps, Simmonds and Gipps. When in 1780 he married his second wife, Sarah Stanton, he was a successful businessman, over fifty years old, and the marriage was solemnized in the fashionable London Church of St. Martin in the Fields. In the same year he began his political career as MP for Canterbury.[16] His second son, Henry, was born in 1786 (by his third wife Elizabeth, née Lawrence),[17] and in 1803, soon after

---

13. Ward, *Early Correspondence of Bunting*, 79.

14. Hole, *Life of Phelps*, 1:208.

15. Evans, *Short History*. In his preface the vicar, Charles Strong, wrote approvingly of the note, by his immediate predecessor, A. J. K. Goss, in which Gipps's successor John Venn is given the entire credit for the establishment of the church's evangelical tradition and Gipps is not mentioned. Equally surprising is the omission of Gipps in Donald Lewis's, *BDEB*—an omission that has led me to give more specific details of the career of this forgotten evangelical than I might have done otherwise.

16. Church, *Emergence of a Community*, www.thanington-pc.gov.uk/history/origins.pdf. I am grateful to Dr. Clive Church for help with some of these biographical details. Cf. Sayers, *Lloyds Bank*, 204.

17. His mother was the daughter of Dr. Thomas Lawrence (*Al. Cantab.*, pt. 2, 3:57). Curiously the

the death of his father, matriculated from St. John's College at Cambridge University. When he took his degree in 1807, he achieved highest honors as Senior Wrangler and first Smith's Prizeman after which he studied law. Having gained his LL.B in 1810 he was then called to the Bar.[18] At this time he was mixing in a fashionable circle of upper-middle-class friends that included the Plumptre family of Fredville, Nonington in Kent, who are mentioned occasionally in the letters of Jane Austen. Henry's name was already associated with Emma Maria Plumptre as early as April 1811, in a playful couplet in one of Jane Austen's letters:

> I am in a Dilemma for want of an Emma
> Escaped from the lips of Henry Gipps.[19]

A year later the couple were married and the following year their first son was born.[20]

Henry's legal work entailed travelling on circuit and in the course of this, he heard a sermon by Gerard Noel, the Vicar of Rainham. Previously Gipps had been "prejudiced . . . against evangelical teaching as fraught with enthusiasm and error," but Noel's sermon led him to search the Scriptures more closely and in 1814 he was converted.[21] His wife appears to have been in full sympathy and indeed it is possible that her brother, John Plumptre may also have had a part in Gipps's conversion though it is equally possible that Gipps's change of heart may have led to Plumptre's adoption of similar views.[22] The following year Gipps was ordained both as a deacon (July) and priest (September) and after three months as a curate of St. Stephen's, Ipswich he took up his appointment in October 1815 as curate of St. Peter's Hereford where nine years later he would be instituted as vicar.[23]

It is clear that this change in Gipps's spiritual outlook was a radical one, involving not only a change in career, but also in his lifestyle. Unlike a man like Randall whose

---

plaque in Henry's honor in St. Peter's Church, Hereford, incorrectly describes him as the second son "of George and Sarah Gipps."

18. *Al. Cantab.*, pt. 2, 3:57.

19. Le Faye, *Jane Austen's Letters*, 186.

20. The marriage was at Nonington, 2 Jun 1812 (IGI). Henry Plumptre Gipps was born at Norton Court, outside Faversham in 1813, Dod, *Parliamentary Companion*, 184.

21. La Trobe, *Burning and Shining Light*, 6. Gerard Noel is identified as the instrument of Gipps's conversion in Beddy, *Journal of a Missionary*, 36.

22. John Pemberton Plumptre (1791–1864), called to the bar 1817; MP for East Kent 1832–52. He was said to have had religious views, which "induced him to think dancing and other social amusements of the same sort, things which ought to be eschewed and avoided by Christian people." He married Catherine Matilda Methuen, of Corsham, to whose family we shall refer later (Le Faye, *Jane Austen's Letters*, 563). Plumptre's evangelical sympathies are evident from his being a member of the Committee of the British and Foreign Bible Society in 1834; see Teignmouth, *Memoir*, 2:589. His daughter Matilda was the first wife of Bishop J. C. Ryle.

23. The months in Ipswich are recorded on the Hereford church plaque (see n17). Henry's second son John Methuen Gipps was born in Ipswich, see *Al. Cantab.*, pt. 2, 3:58.

conversion had occurred when he was a student, Gipps was converted when he was nearer thirty and it involved the upheaval of a career change and significant alterations in lifestyle. In a sermon preached shortly after Gipps's death John La Trobe recalled the dramatic impact of conversion on Gipps and his family: "Seeing that there could be no union between Christ and Belial he renounced the empty vanities and carnal pursuits of the world, and . . . took upon him the cross, in confessing him among his friends and relatives." And in another context the same writer referred to the convert's readiness "in the outset of his religious course, to take up the cross and lay aside deliberately his prospects of worldly distinction, ease and enjoyment."[24] When, some years after his initial appointment, Gipps was instituted as Vicar of St. Peter's in 1825, he himself reminded his parishioners that, having private means, it had not been "for the sake of emolument" that he had come to Hereford, nine years earlier. He went on:

> Nor had I any ties of kindred or connection to draw me among you, inasmuch as I quitted all my relatives and friends and knew not, at my coming, I believe, a single person either in the city or county.[25]

In these matters Gipps is manifestly a first-generation evangelical and clearly fits the heroic mold to which we referred at the outset. His fear of compromise is only too evident. Of course, evangelicals were far from agreed as to what they regarded as legitimate pleasures. The theatre, balls, hunting and card-playing were all disapproved of by some but permitted in moderation by others. But Henry Gipps's conversion was clearly no half-hearted affair. Appropriately described by Randall as a "burning and shining light," Gipps had an unmistakable impact on Hereford. Many years later a contributor to *Notes and Queries* attributed the fact that there was no theatre in Hereford, "the birth-place of Nell Gwyn and David Garrick," to the "influence of the evangelical clergy when the late Rev. Henry Gipps became the incumbent of the united parishes of St Peter and St Owen."[26] Less than two years after his arrival, Gipps had invited Edward Bickersteth to Hereford in March 1817 presumably in connection with the establishment of a local auxiliary of the Church Missionary Society, but Bickersteth also took part in "an immense assembly at the Bible [Society] Meeting"—another distinctive feature of evangelical commitment.[27]

---

24. La Trobe, *Burning and Shining Light*, 7; Gipps, *Sermons*, xviii. It was probably not coincidental that in 1817 (three years after Gipps's conversion) Jane Austen asked of her correspondent Fanny Knight: "Do none of the Plumptres ever come to Balls now?—You have never mentioned them as being at any?—And what do you hear of the Gipps?" (Le Faye, *Jane Austen's Letters*, 332).

25. Gipps's Institution Sermon, 10, is cited in La Trobe's introduction to Gipps, *Sermons*, xx. This social hiatus may well explain the genealogical inaccuracy on his memorial. (See n17.)

26. Alpha, "Drama at Hereford," 141. Mistakenly the writer said that Gipps's responsibility for this "blot in the history of the city of Hereford" dated from his arrival "about thirty years ago" when in fact it had been more than fifty year earlier.

27. Birks, *Memoir of Bickersteth*, 1:318–19. In April 1819 Gipps was chairing the first local anniversary meeting of the CMS in the Shire Hall "in a very impressive manner," *Missionary Register* (1819) 178.

Confrontation

In the following year we find Gipps crossing swords with the local ecclesiastical Establishment. In 1817 John Napleton, an elderly and respected prebendary of Hereford Cathedral, preached (and later published) two sermons[28] —one in favor of baptismal regeneration and the other highly anti-Calvinist in its theology. Gipps may well have felt that the sermons were directed against him and that therefore he was obliged to reply, because, although he "strongly deprecated the use of the term," his doctrinal position was decidedly Calvinistic.[29] Likewise, as the lone evangelical minister in the city, he felt that the issue of baptism was one of critical importance. Undeterred by the Canon's death in the same year he retaliated with a substantial (140 pages) *Treatise on Regeneration*.[30] The effects were noted with interest by a Hereford Unitarian who wrote in 1819 that:

> Mr Gipps has, by his preaching, roused both [clergy and laity] into considerable activity, exciting much opposition on the part of the former, and making a great number of converts among the latter. Very recently a controversy has arisen betwixt the two parties on the nature of baptism and pamphlets have been published on both sides, upon the subject of regeneration.[31]

The writer went on to suggest that these developments could be regarded "as a crisis peculiarly favorable to the introduction of rational [sc. Unitarian] notions of religion" of which Unitarian missionaries could take advantage.

All this had taken place when Gipps was merely the curate of St. Peter's, as he would only become the incumbent in 1825. A young CMS missionary, J. Fawcett Beddy, who had met Gipps in 1824, observed two years later, "It is a rare circumstance to meet with such a servant of the Lord, as the Rev. Henry Gipps, one so enriched and adorned by the grace of God . . . He was one of those highly favoured ones, whose names are cast out as evil, for the Son of man's sake."[32] Beddy's observation is significant, as it makes clear that Gipps was not only unafraid of controversy but inclined to go for confrontation.

We have confirmation of this combative aspect of Gipps's character from the pen of an admirer, his former curate James La Trobe. In his introduction to a posthumous volume of Gipps's sermons, La Trobe didn't mince his words:

> In his appeals, Mr. Gipps has been accused of harshness and perhaps there was occasionally something in his manner severe and repulsive; but it was only in *manner*; and his energy, to those who look below the surface, evidently

---

28. Napleton, *Sermon*; and Napleton, *Universality*.
29. Gipps, *Sermons*, v.
30. H. Gipps, *Treatise on Regeneration*.
31. Letter signed "Bereus," May 11, 1819, in *Monthly Repository of Theology* (1819) 366.
32. Beddy, *Journal of a Missionary*, 36.

proceeded not from severity, but from love. At the same time it must be admitted, that the natural impatience of his temper and fervor of his spirit rendered him better calculated to arouse and awaken than to administer consolation.[33]

The desire to awaken the members of his congregation was of paramount importance for Gipps and not surprisingly we find him responding to Haldane Stewart's insistence on the need to pray for an outpouring of the Holy Spirit. In 1822 he chaired in his home a meeting of eleven clergy who joined with him in a resolution to engage regularly in such prayer and to warn their flocks "against resisting, grieving or quenching" the Holy Spirit.[34] The success of his ministry during a period of less than twenty years was acknowledged in such journals as the *Evangelical Magazine*, which recorded his death, in 1832, by lamenting the "great loss to the cause of religion in the city of Hereford where his ministry had begun to exert a powerful and most beneficial influence."[35]

If however his congregation had markedly grown it was in part because he was prepared to address the issues that concerned them. At a time when millenarian interest was coming into vogue Gipps's attention had been especially drawn to the subject of Christ's second coming, and this had been stimulated "by a spirit of inquiry, which had obtained among his own flock." He therefore resolved to examine

> the Scriptural authorities on which the interpreters of what is termed the Millennarian school rest their views . . . When after due examination he felt himself constrained to pronounce the proofs adduced in defence of [premillennial] opinions, which had so greatly disturbed the minds of his people, insufficient, he set himself like a decided yet tender pastor to root out the evil.[36]

It is unlikely that all his parishioners were happy with his postmillennial conclusions and there are indications, in one of the sermons preached in St. Peters, a few days after Gipps's death, that some of them "while the shepherd yet lived, deserted his fold." To others, who were apparently thinking of doing likewise, the preacher addressed a final exhortation to "be in no hurry to rush to strange pastures."[37] On the other hand Gipps's parishioners had known where they were with him and his forthright and direct way of dealing with them was clearly attractive to many.

On a wider front however his attitude epitomized a confrontational aspect of evangelicalism that some other churchmen found objectionable. In a lengthy article

---

33. Gipps, *Sermons*, xxi. In his commemorative sermon, when one would have expected to hear only positive aspects of the man, La Trobe also referred to Gipps's "nervous irritability of temper which sometimes proved uncomfortable to those connected with him and a stumbling block in his ministry," La Trobe, *Burning and Shining Light*, 22.

34. Stewart, *Memoir of James Haldane Stewart*, 118.

35. *Evangelical Magazine*, n.s., 12 (Feb 1834) 60.

36. Gipps, Sermons, vii–viii. Gipps's conclusions appeared in the last of his books published in his lifetime, *Treatise on "The First resurrection."*

37. Allen, *Gospel Ministry*, 32.

in the *British Critic* a reviewer, of clearly a High Church persuasion indicated that he had considerable reservations about Gipps's Calvinist theology but devoted his most trenchant criticism to the language that Gipps and his editor, James La Trobe, used in controversy. The writer protests against their references to other Anglicans with whom they disagreed as "false ministers," "ungodly ministers," or "blind leaders of the blind who call themselves ministers," and takes exception to their characterizing such ministers' teaching as "unsound discourses" or as food "that is poisonous and diseased." The reviewer went on to argue that the readiness of a man like Gipps "to describe the establishment . . . as almost a mass of rottenness and corruption and the larger portion of its officiating members as 'hirelings' and not 'true shepherds'" was playing into the hands of the dissenters and threatening the very church of which he was a minister.[38]

However Gipps's evangelical position was to remain an uncompromising one even after his death, as a comparatively young man in his mid-forties. In his concern to ensure a continuing evangelical ministry in Hereford he had set up a trust to administer the advowson for the parish of St. Peters and although it is commonly said that Gipps's successor in 1833, John Venn, was appointed by the Simeon Trustees,[39] it is clear from the *Liber Ecclesiasticus* of 1835 that the Patronage of St. Peter with St. Owen was for some time in the hands of "the Trustees of the late Rev. Henry Gipps."[40] In fact before Venn was appointed, the living was offered (unsuccessfully) to William Marsh, formerly of Colchester, whose millenarianism could possibly have been attractive to some of those parishioners whose views had been rebuffed by Gipps in his exposition of prophetic matters.[41]

A New Rector with a Different Style: John Venn

The man who succeeded Gipps, John Venn (1802–1890), was also a successful Cambridge scholar for whom the incumbency of St. Peter's was a first clerical appointment, but in many other respects he was a very different sort of vicar. Unlike Gipps, Venn was a third-generation evangelical. He had grown up in a world where the basic evangelical outlook was normal rather than revolutionary. His grandfather Henry Venn (1724–97) had abandoned the High Church tradition of his upbringing and over the years had evolved his own brand of moderate Calvinist evangelicalism. When the young Charles Simeon had engaged in unconventional preaching outside his church it had been Henry Venn's protests that persuaded Simeon of the need for church order

---

38. *British Critic* 15 (1834) 273–75. At the time, although showing some sympathy for the Tractarians, the *British Critic* was not yet in the editorial hands of John Henry Newman; see Nockles, *Oxford Movement in Context*, 277–78.

39. For example in Arthur Pollard "John Venn," in *BDEB*.

40. *Liber Ecclesiasticus*, table 4, 89.

41. For the offer to "millennial" Marsh, see Marsh, *Life of William Marsh*, 159.

and more dignified conduct. As the rector of Clapham parish church, Henry Venn's son, John (1759–1813), continued the moderate evangelical tradition that would characterize his contributions to the *Christian Observer* and indeed the activities of the so-called Clapham sect. It was typical of his conciliatory and accommodating approach that when there was strong opposition to his proposal that the CMS could use laymen as catechists on the mission field, he withdrew the suggestion. Where others like Augustus Toplady had often vituperatively crossed swords in controversy with Wesleyan Arminians, Venn and Simeon stressed the common ground shared by evangelicals and avoided confrontation. John Venn the younger had been reared in this atmosphere of moderation and it left its mark on him. Noel Annan once drew attention to the Venn family's "sanguine temperament" as well as their "commonsense and cheerfulness,"[42] and these too were important elements that characterized the new Vicar of St. Peter's in Hereford.

In contrast to Gipps, the new vicar avoided confrontation and was noted for the kindliness and sweetness of his temperament.[43] It is true that in 1838, with various other churchmen, he did take up the cudgels against the practice of "Sunday wakes" to which we referred earlier,[44] and in 1844 he engaged in four days of debate or "discussions" as he called them with a Roman Catholic priest in Hereford[45] but his public and measured rejection of these opponents was widely shared and was scarcely a cause of division in the community. It was certainly far from typical of his thirty-seven years of ministry at St. Peter's, where he was better remembered for his philanthropic schemes which ranged from the introduction of a steam mill to the creation of an experimental garden for teaching gardening allotment and small farm work.[46] In Marianne Thornton's famous "Hereford Letter" of 1842, she described the annual parish fête where the vicar was a friend of everyone, "looked excessively happy" and addressed his parishioners, "as only he could, so full of gaiety and of goodness."[47] A few years later, a nonconformist describing Hereford, was insistent that Venn's "evangelical and apostolic labours have endeared him to the largest and most influential congregation in the ancient city" noting that he was "as distinguished for the quiet, unobtrusive virtues of his private life as he is for his pulpit labors."[48] Venn's nephew, Sir Leslie Stephen even claimed that his uncle "had the simplicity of character of a Dr. Primrose" suggesting that his innocence bordered on the naïvety, that characterized the Vicar of Wakefield.[49]

42. Annan, *Leslie Stephen*, 7.

43. Described by his niece, Emelia Russell Gurney, as her "angelical Uncle John" (Gurney, *Letters*, 93).

44. J. Venn, *Sunday wakes*. See above, n9.

45. J. Venn, *Assertions*.

46. Galton and Schuster, *Noteworthy Families*, 73.

47. Forster, *Marianne Thornton*, 174. Cf. Forster's comment that Venn and his sister "managed to combine their peculiarly virulent Evangelicalism with jollification and joy," 171.

48. [Robert Cowtan], *Passages from the Autobiography*, 318.

49. Stephen, *Life of Sir James Fitzjames Stephen*, 38.

Secession

There were bound to be some for whom the change in vicar would prove unacceptable. It is likely, as we noted earlier, that some of Gipps's congregation may have left even before he died, and in all probability the year of uncertainty before Venn's arrival further unsettled the parish, and Venn's amiability and charm could only take him so far. His avoidance of what Simeon had described as "vehement argumentation" was liable to appear as Arminianism to parishioners who were accustomed to Gipps's uncompromising Calvinism. It was later said by some of those, who seceded, that it was this doctrinal issue that was at stake, but more probably, temperament played as important a role as doctrine. The clear-cut and often confrontational ministry of a man like Gipps would always appeal to a minority who were liable to dismiss Venn's mild and unobtrusive qualities as weak or accommodating compromise.

The accounts are far from precise as to the stages in which secession from St. Peter's occurred. In 1837 the wife of a local surgeon, Dr. John Griffiths, visited Plymouth and was sufficiently impressed by what she saw there of the Plymouth Brethren that later in the year Captain Percy Hall was invited to Hereford to conduct some meetings in private houses.[50] In a letter to the *Hereford Journal* in April 1838 it was said that the Brethren "have made a most rapid progress from the time they have been established—about six months..." from which we may conclude that sometime in October 1837 some members of the St. Peters congregation had started meeting regularly as an independent group, which formed the nucleus of the congregation that would soon be gathering in a house in Bridge Street owned by William Yapp.[51] In a pamphlet written in May 1842, John Venn recalled, "It is now four years since some of the Plymouth Brethren as they are generally called first established themselves in our city."[52] With the restraint one could expect from such an engaging character, Venn had avoided a hasty reaction. After all, he was ready to cooperate with other denominations if he could,[53] and for a while, he hoped that his critics "might come to a better mind" and be less confrontational. By the end of 1838 this had become only a remote possibility and in December he preached and published a sermon significantly entitled *A*

---

50. This essay was written some years before the appearance of Michael Schneider's comprehensive account of Percy Hall, "Extravagant side of Brethrenism," which provides more details of this episode (see 32–35).

51. A basic account of the establishment of the Brethren assembly in Hereford is given by Rowdon, *Origins of the Brethren*, 164–67 and [A. Langford], *Account of Brethren*, 3–6. See also Morgan, "William Yapp of Hereford," 293–95. All of these writers have made use of the early typescript account, "Notes of the Early Days of the Work at Hereford," by Charles Brewer, later reprinted as "Early Days in Herefordshire," in Burridge, *Christian Outlook*, 84–93.

52. J. Venn, *Christian Ministry*, 1.

53. Soon after his arrival in Hereford, Venn had risked the disapproval of his Dean by telling him that he was going "to preach for the Moravians with a collection [in favor of the C.M.S]" unless "prohibited positively by him [the Dean]." BU, CMS Archives, Venn MSS c.26, John Venn, Hereford, 9 Dec 1834 to Emelia Venn.

Proselyting [sic] *spirit, the great obstacle to Christian Union*.[54] This may have briefly checked the hemorrhage but the efforts of the seceders continued.

The Griffiths and the Yapps were families of some means and with others they found and furnished a house outside Hereford into which Percy Hall and his wife moved sometime in 1838. Hall published a reply to Venn's sermon and although there is apparently no extant copy, it appears to have been very forthright. In an extract later quoted by Venn, Hall made no concessions to the Anglican minister. Taking his cue from supposed biblical precedents he insisted: "Unconverted men took the place of God's ministry in the Church's earliest days; and the Church was charged to reject them not on the grounds of irregularity but because of their deficiencies or errors."[55] It is not clear whether Hall was thinking of Jewish Rabbis in the very earliest days of the church or Diotrephes, or just unnamed false teachers, his labeling them as "unconverted men" but by implication putting Venn into that category was a decidedly antagonistic move.

By 1842, any hope of reconciliation seemed to be over and Venn could claim that the Brethren "now form a considerable body; and having many individuals amongst them both of wealth and leisure, they are enabled to bring an extensive machinery into operation." He therefore felt that he had to make his position clearer and he delivered a series of lectures on *The Christian Ministry and Church Membership . . . with especial reference to . . . the Plymouth Brethren*.[56] The most thoroughgoing reply to Venn's lectures was the work of the redoubtable Robert Mackenzie Beverley who merits full treatment in his own right and will therefore be the subject of a separate chapter, but in Beverley's approach there was again a confrontational approach that eschewed the possibility of compromise.

The erstwhile members of St. Peter's who seceded in the late 1830s to form the Hereford Brethren assembly were decidedly of that ilk. The account of these people by Charles Brewer makes the point very emphatically:

> One thing marked the conduct and character of each [member]; they made a clean cut from the world and the things of the world. It was a definite, wide separation from all evil, on Scriptural grounds. The house and its furniture, the dress and its fashions, amusements, occupations, business, engagements and customs, were all tested by *the Word*.[57]

It is easy to detect an echo here of the uncompromising stand taken by Hereford's evangelical pioneer Henry Gipps.

---

54. J. Venn, *Proselyting spirit*. A 3rd ed. was published in 1839.

55. Herr Schneider appears to have found a copy, Hall, *To the Christians*. My text is from the citation in Venn, *Christian Ministry*, 102. This is probably the tract referred to as "Hall's Address to the Christians of Hereford," in [A. Langford], *Account*, 4. A further item in the exchange was Garbett's *Reply to Captain Hall's pamphlet*.

56. Venn, *Christian Ministry*, 2.

57. Brewer, "Early Days," 87.

Conclusion

In later years the Brethren may have focused on Gipps's forthright Calvinism and claimed that John Venn was an Arminian, but in practice the folk to whom every aspect of Percy Hall's radical and rigorist message would appeal were "first-generation" evangelicals who had been introduced to vital religion by Henry Gipps, himself, a convert, who had stepped away from fashionable Kent society to begin an evangelical work from scratch in Hereford. Indeed, at the risk of being accused of wild speculation, it is conceivable that, if he had lived, Gipps might have been numbered among the numerous Anglican clergy who in the 1830s seceded and joined the Brethren. We should bear in mind that his pious brother-in-law, John Plumptre, had married a sister of John Andrew Methuen, an evangelical who resigned his position as rector of Corsham in 1832 to be baptized, and met with a group of Brethren in Neston and later Clevedon.[58] Gipps's widow, Emma is recorded as having made a donation to one of the Brethren funds,[59] and, even more striking, their daughter Elizabeth Emily Gipps became the second wife of the Brethren scholar, William Kelly.[60] Clearly we must avoid over-simplification, but in this story temperamental preferences seem to have played an important part. One can certainly argue that the success of the Brethren in Hereford may have lain in their ability to take up the mantle of "heroic separatism" which was characteristic of the first-generation evangelical experience of Henry Gipps and was in danger of being lost when he died and was replaced by the mild and conciliatory John Venn.

---

58. John Andrew Methuen (1794–1869) Christ Church, Oxford, BA 1817, MA 1826, was a younger brother of Paul Methuen, created Baron Methuen in 1838 (*Al. Oxon.*, 3:948). He married Louisa Mary Fuller of Neston Park, who edited for publication the diaries of their deceased daughter, see [L. M. Methuen], *Fountain sealed*. He later moved to Weston-super-Mare where a "small company of believers" was "under his care" and later to Clifton (Pickering, *Chief Men* [1931], 132). It was he (and not his brother Paul, as claimed by Mary Haldane) who visited Robert Burdon-Sanderson at his home in Jesmond, Northumberland and persuaded him to be baptized by immersion in a stretch of water that ran through the grounds (Welford, *Men of Mark*, 3:348; [E. S. Haldane], *Mary Elizabeth Haldane*, 74).

59. [A. Langford], *Account*, 3–4. There is an interesting reference to her (with her name given as Sipps) in a letter written by Elizabeth Barrett (not-yet-Browning) in April 1835: "The widow of Mr Sipps of Hereford, of whom you may have heard, has lately spent a fortnight here. In the course of two years she has lost her sister & her husband—her daughter is dying—and her infant never knew the sight of its father's face. She is a lovely illustration of that lovely contrast of words in Scripture—'much affliction, in joy of the Holy Ghost.'" Kelley, *Brownings' Correspondence*, 3:137.

60. Cross, *Irish Saint and Scholar*, 24, 40n22.

14

Plymouth Brethren and the Armed Services[1]

Early Pacifist Tendencies in South-West England

LIFE ON THE COASTS of Devon and Cornwall had a significantly military dimension during the French Revolutionary and Napoleonic Wars, which overshadowed the childhoods of the earliest Brethren. Some unusual events, like the explosion in 1796 of the frigate *Amphion* in Plymouth harbor, became a part of the local mythology, especially as the captain of the ship, Sir Israel Pellew, unlike the hundreds of the crew who were killed, was blown through a window and landed comparatively unharmed in the rigging of another ship. Benjamin Newton recalled the event in his old age adding: "It was a marvelous escape. I have often seen him. He was a Christian man, a member of Dr Hawker's congregation, and so was his brother Lord Exmouth."[2] For most people living there, the dangers were less spectacular but nonetheless real. Unlike the world wars of the twentieth century these were prolonged periods of conflict. With a brief interlude of fourteen months in 1802–1803, England and France were continuously at war from 1793–1815, and no one living near the coast could ignore the ongoing hostilities.

Inevitably, war games were a part of the children's entertainment. Although he was brought up as a Quaker, B. W. Newton recalled that he joined in enthusiastically:

> When I was a schoolboy at Lostwithiel we fought it all out, Salamanca and so on. One of us was the Duke of Wellington with cocked hat on his charger. I was his aide de camp and got a kick from it [sc. the charger], it was a donkey. We always had great difficulty in getting any boy to be Napoleon. When

---

1. Apart from removing material that appears elsewhere in this volume, this paper is substantially as it originally appeared in Dickson and Marinello, *Culture, Spirituality and the Brethren*. The preparatory work for this paper was all but complete in 2006 before I was able to give close attention to Elisabeth Wilson's excellent articles "Your citizenship is in heaven," and "The eyes of the authorities are upon us," which overlap with this paper in several respects. There is a similarly excellent chapter, "Brethren in Two World Wars," in Tim Grass's, *Gathering to His Name*, 324–41, published in 2006. As my enquiry was pursued independently of the work of both these authors I have thought it best not to provide cross-references.

2. The event is described in the entry for Pellew in the *DNB*. Newton's account is in his recollections (JRULM, CBA 7057, Wyatt MS, 1:354).

we captured him we brought him home in a barrel. Our spears, javelins and swords were terrific!

There was in those days the Press Gang. Your brother might have breakfasted with you and go out to business and never be heard of more! The Warship would land its men with a requisition upon the authorities there to furnish twenty men or so and then the men would pounce on anybody.[3]

As we noted in an earlier chapter, the religious tenets of Quakers forbad any involvement in violence, and consequently the war economy was liable to create special problems, as these beliefs were a very distinctive part of their identity. There can be little doubt therefore that some principled pacifism found its way into the West country life of early Brethren whose assemblies in the 1830s included a fair sprinkling of former Quakers with names like Hingston, Cookworthy, Balkwill, Prideaux, Abbott, Fox, and Tregelles.[4] It was this tradition that appears to have led William Hake, an Anglican associated with several Quakers in the Exeter auxiliary of the Society for the Promotion of Permanent and Universal Peace, to bring to the attention of Norris Groves the problems raised for an Anglican by the thirty-seventh article's endorsement of the lawfulness of "wearing weapons and serving in the wars" at the command of the Magistrate.[5]

On the other hand at least two of the early brethren, Captain W. G. Rhind (1794–1863) and Leonard Strong (1797–1874),[6] had seen active naval service during the Napoleonic Wars and there was a significant aristocratic element in the early movement whose family background was often liable to impose on them what we may call military or naval expectations.[7] Alexander Cockburn (1804–71) is a good case in point. His maternal grandfather, Sir Alexander Campbell had been a distinguished general in India and was created first baronet of Gartsford in 1815. His two sons had died in action—one in the Peninsular Wars and one in India, so by royal patent the

---

3. JRULM, CBA 7049, Fry MS, 47–48. In the same extract, Newton also claimed to have been taken out twice to see Napoleon in the HMS Bellerophon, once with Sir Charles Eastlake who took Napoleon's portrait, though why the Plymouth artist would have been accompanied by a seven-year-old is not clear. Another Plymouth brother, Henry William Soltau, recalled making a similar trip, as a ten-year-old, to see Napoleon (Pickering, *Chief Men*, 151).

4. For Quakers with these names who became Brethren in the early days, see above, ch. 2nn22–23, 30–32, 74–76, 78.

5. See above, ch. 7n22, and Stunt, *From Awakening*, 121; [H. B. Groves], *Memoir*, 41.

6. For Rhind's early years, see I[sbell], "*Faithful unto Death*," 1–20; for Strong, see above, ch. 11n26, and Stunt, "Leonard Strong," 95, 104n2.

7. Such expectations were by no means automatic. Sir Henry Brooke Parnell (later the first Lord Congleton) was embarrassed by his son's fervent Christianity, even before the latter was associated with the Brethren. As a result Sir Henry abandoned the commission he had previously secured for his son, "fearing his Christianity would bring discredit on his military profession," H. Groves, *Lord Congleton*, 11. A reversed expectation operated for Henry Bellenden Bulteel, who was also identified with Brethren for a time. When two of his sons were killed at the attempted assault on Bergen op Zoom (1814), Bulteel's father resolved against a military career for his remaining sons; see my article on Bulteel in *ODNB*.

title passed, on the general's death in 1824, through his daughter to her son on condition that he assumed the name Campbell.[8] Reinforcing the military expectations of his family, Sir Alexander Cockburn-Campbell (as he was now known) married a daughter of General Sir John Malcolm,[9] but his decision to remain a civilian was a significant abandonment of the family tradition. A similar situation may be observed in the case of Charles Brenton whose father's baronetcy was a reward for years of active and courageous naval service.[10] When Brenton inherited the title in 1844, filial piety seems to have obliged him to undertake a revision of his father's biography—a task that his growing pacifism made more complicated. The death of his brother-in-law in the first year of the Crimean War evidently moved him deeply but it was only in the introduction to his re-edition of his father's biography that he made a public declaration of his pacifism.[11] Another instance of family expectations that went awry, occurred in the case of Captain W. H. G. Wellesley, a nephew of the Duke of Wellington, whose naval experiences at the Battle of Navarino in 1827 had played a part in his conversion but who, soon after, resigned his naval commission in the 1830s and was later associated with the Brethren.[12]

It is in this context that we should consider the case of Percy Francis Hall who was descended on his mother's side from the famous naval family of Byng, and the Viscounts Torrington, but who also was a leading figure in the earliest days of the Plymouth assembly. In February 1833, Hall appeared to throw down the pacifist gauntlet in a blaze of principled conviction, when he resigned his naval rank and pension, explaining his reasons in a well-argued pamphlet entitled *Discipleship!*[13] Several points need to be made in connection with Hall's publication. First, in his pamphlet, the pacifist objection is not the first or most important part of the argument, which is far more concerned with the impropriety of a Christian exercising any position of worldly authority or honor. The principle of nonviolence comes lower on the agenda.

---

8. I am indebted to Sir Alexander's Australian descendant Ms. Julia Crawley for clarification in this genealogical puzzle.

9. Malcolm's daughter, Lady Margaret Campbell-Cockburn (c. 1802–41), wrote a hymn of great popularity with Brethren, "Praise ye Jehovah, Praise the Lord most Holy." It is perhaps worth noting that Sir Alexander's second wife, Grace Spence, was from a Yorkshire Quaker family, and was baptized in Wellington in 1837 during the Beaconite controversy, see above, ch. 2n70. Ms Crawley informs me that one of the two witnesses at the wedding was a Wellesley—presumably Captain W. H. G. Wellesley, for whom see below.

10. For Charles Brenton, his father and his uncle see *BDEB*. For Brenton's connections with Brethren see Stunt, *From Awakening*, 209, 259, 296–98.

11. Brenton, *Alas my brother*; Raikes, *Memoir of Sir Jahleel Brenton*. For a discussion of the uncharacteristically patriotic reaction of other Brethren (Philip and Emily Gosse) to the Battle of the Alma, see Brock, "Peace Testimony," 43–44.

12. For Wellesley, see below, ch. 16, "Early Development of Arthur Augustus Rees," nn5–6.

13. Hall, *Discipleship!* (2nd ed., Plymouth 1835). As yet, we have no extant copy of the 1st ed., but Herr Michael Schneider has tracked down the original letter of resignation, which enables us to date the event precisely.

A second point that has only recently come to light is that there had been some indignation in naval circles when Hall, with only limited naval experience was promoted to the rank of Captain in 1827. It was publicly stated at the time that "the most experienced and worn-out officers in Portsmouth are totally at a loss for an excuse for this sudden and unmerited elevation of a person so much their junior" and the influence and patronage of his father the Dean of Durham was suggested as the explanation.[14] Perhaps therefore, we should consider Hall's action more as a renunciation of influence and patronage than an act of principled pacifism. On the other hand we should also note that throughout his life, his fellow Brethren always referred to him as "Captain Hall," though, curiously, in the third edition (1848) of his pamphlet he is described as "Commander Hall," a rank lower than Captain. There is moreover a certain irony in the fact that in 1858 Hall's only child, Emmeline, married George Vincent Fosbery (1832–1907), a Lieutenant-Colonel in the 4th Bengal European Regiment of the Indian Army, who, not only, was awarded the Victoria Cross in 1865 for gallant conduct on the North-West Frontier but also patented the Webley-Fosbery automatic revolver in 1895.[15]

As we observed at the outset, the navy was an integral part of life in Plymouth, so inevitably it was a significant factor in the lives of many who were attracted to the Brethren community that grew so rapidly in that city during the 1830s. Two young ladies provide excellent examples. Charlotte Spicer was the younger daughter of Captain Peter Spicer, of Godwell House, Ugborough (1766–1830), who had earlier served as one of Nelson's Lieutenants on HMS Agamemnon.[16] In 1828 Charlotte had married John Cookworthy, a former Quaker who joined the Plymouth assembly, by whom she had three surviving children before he died in 1835.[17] She continued to attend Brethren meetings in Plymouth as also did her close friend, Frances Bowker. Frances also had a naval pedigree, being the daughter of Captain James Bowker, who had accompanied Sir Francis Pickmore, the governor of Newfoundland, and on the latter's unexpected death in 1818, had assumed responsibilities as the acting governor for the next six months.[18] A staunch Anglican, he appears to have been strongly opposed to his daughter's involvement with the Brethren, but there are few, other than circum-

---

14. For this significant extract from the *Times*, 19 Jul 1827, I am indebted to Captain Paul Benyon's Index to late 18th, 19th and early 20th century naval and naval social history on http://www.pbenyon.plus.com/Naval.html (accessed in early 2006, but this item has now been withdrawn). Curiously there is no mention of Hall's naval connections on his mother's side.

15. *Gentleman's Magazine* (Dec 1858) 629; http://members.tripod.com/~FOSBERY/GVF.html.

16. For Peter Spicer, see Nicolas, *Dispatches and Letters of Lord Nelson*, 2:76, 180, 271, and 336; 5:271n7; Rawlins, *Family Quartet*, 186–87; and "Recollections of a Nonagenarian," 136–38.

17. John was a younger brother of J. C. Cookworthy; see above, ch. 2n28; and Foster, *Revised Genealogical Account*, 18.

18. For Captain Bowker's career, see B. Rigby "Archival Treasures," in *Memorial University of Newfoundland Gazette* (17 Aug 2000), online text formerly but no longer at http://www.mun.ca/marcomm/gazette/2000-2001/August17/arctrs.html. Some of his daughter's correspondence is preserved in Perth, J. S. Battye Library of West Australian History, Private Archives, MN 586/1 Acc.3627A.

stantial, indications that in joining the Brethren these girls were necessarily reacting against their families' naval background. Charlotte would later upset the Brethren by eloping with an Anglican and emigrating to Australia,[19] but Frances Bowker, who moved away from Plymouth to Greenwich when her widowed father was appointed as Captain of the Greenwich naval hospital, continued to have good relations with the wife of Sir Alexander Campbell and other Brethren.

At this point we may conclude that although there was some widespread expression of pacifist principle among some of the very early Brethren, they were declarations of individual conviction rather than a position adopted by the Brethren as a community. Given the significant naval element in the population of the city that hosted their largest assembly, this is hardly surprising. But before we go any further in the development of Brethren attitudes to military service we should acknowledge a mysterious sequel to the earliest Brethren writings on the subject.

In 1841 a young Pomeranian nobleman, Julius Anton von Poseck was called up for military service and was imprisoned on account of his refusal to comply. By way of explanation for his refusal he cited some of the early Brethren's writings on the subject. The authorities apparently accepted his objections as valid and he was released on condition that he went into exile. The story was briefly told by Neatby in his *History*,[20] and J. N. Darby (with whom von Poseck later worked on the text of the German Bible) alludes in a letter of 1854 to his tracts having "been sent to the King [of Prussia], by some circumstances connected with the refusal of military service, by a brother."[21] However von Poseck's recent biographer, August Jung is completely at a loss to explain this episode, as von Poseck was not converted until 1848 in which year W. H. Darby came to Dusseldorf. Jung therefore concludes that the citation of these Brethren works was "utilitarian" rather than based on religious conviction. It is unclear how von Poseck came across the works or where he spent his six years of exile.[22] Nevertheless, it appears that early Brethren writings arguing the case against Christian involvement in the armed services had found their way to Germany in the early 1840s.

---

19. For a brief account of this episode, see the last chapter of Shann, *Cattle Chosen*, online text at http://en.wikisource.org/wiki/Cattle_Chosen/Chapter_9; and Heppingstone and Wilson, "Letters of Charlotte Bussell," 7–9.

20. Neatby, *History*, 256.

21. Darby, *Letters*, 1:234.

22. Jung, *Julius Anton von Poseck*, 28–36. For von Poseck's dramatic conversion experience in 1848 when a stone from the masonry of Cologne cathedral fell and killed a girl standing beside him during the cathedral's 600th anniversary celebrations, see pp.38–39. A convenient English summary of Pastor Jung's findings may be found in his essay, "Julius Anton von Poseck," in Dickson and Grass, *Growth of the Brethren Movement*, 133–44.

Brethren Ideas in India

One of the most important areas in which there was a rapid dissemination of some Brethren ideas was among the military and British civilian population of India and in this respect there can be little doubt that the attractive and winsome personality of Norris Groves was a key factor. But there were some special reasons why India was a peculiarly fertile soil in which to scatter the seeds of Brethrenism. When Groves argued that an ordained ministry was unbiblical, encouraging congregational participation in prayer and exhortation, and proposing that any Christians could break bread together on the Lord's Day, without liturgical restraints, there was an immediate response from many believing army officers and administrators. Their upbringing had previously led them, in all matters ecclesiastical, to turn for direction and leadership to a parish priest or chaplain but in India in the 1830s there was a dearth of such ministers. As Groves made his first reconnaissance of Indian mission stations in 1833–34 he repeatedly laments the lack of workers, and although this is primarily with reference to work among the native population, it was also true of the ordained clergy in general. Even thirty years later, his widow observed, "There are parts of India, where, excepting at a christening or a funeral, a chaplain is not seen."[23]

When John Parnell, the future Lord Congleton, visited the military station at Cannanore in early 1835 a fair number of officers came to break bread with him in his home, including Colonel Stafford, a young adjutant with the 51st Madras Native Infantry who we are told "found in his teaching and principles . . . a simplicity and devotedness, bearing witness to a New Testament Christianity, he had formerly been unacquainted with."[24] A little later, further north, Parnell visited other stations where Groves had already gained the willing ear of men like Captain Chalmers, the superintendent of the Ashtagram Division of the Mysore country and Captain (later General) R. Alexander at Secunderabad in whose house "the Christians of the station were in the habit of meeting once a week, for Scripture reading."[25] A similar experience was that of Colonel Minchin of Masulipatam (Machilipatnam) who had previously "been accustomed to read a sermon in a building used for religious meeting and a good number met every Sunday" but with the arrival of Parnell "my wife and I saw that the

---

23. [H. B. Groves], *Memoir*, 394.

24. H. Groves, *Lord Congleton*, 49. Stafford remained a close and trusted friend of whom Groves could say in 1848 "we have never had a jar among us for so many years," see [H. B. Groves], *Memoir*, 457.

25. Ibid., 52. Capt. Alexander, the Assistant Quartermaster General at Secunderabad, is a shadowy figure though we know that in 1831 he had married Charlotte, the daughter of Lt-Col Josiah Stewart (d. 1839), who, as British Resident at Hyderabad, played an important part in the suppression of thuggee (identified from the Families in British India Society website [FIBIS], www.search.fibis.org; also Kaye, *Administration of the East India Company*, 372n). Alexander may well have been the later campaigner against the opium trade, Major-General Robert Alexander, who published a series of pamphlets including *Rise and Progress of British Opium Smuggling*; see also Gelber, *Opium, Soldiers and Evangelicals*.

early disciples broke bread together every Lord's day and we then for the first time embraced that special privilege."[26] This may perhaps be compared with Captain Bell's experience when he assured Groves in April 1834 that their conversation "had greatly tended to free his mind from difficulties, which had greatly troubled him relative to the establishment and to his own freedom in Christ."[27] For such men of piety, to quote Groves's widow again "it proved no small boon to discover from the Word of God the liberty given to all Christians to edify one another, in public and private: and in obedience to the command of Christ, to remember his death."[28]

Groves's position was however somewhat ambiguous. He repeatedly avowed his scorn for worldly influence and strove to give priority to the interests of the subject natives. He emphasized to British Christians that God had "not sent them here to get the poor people's money, to return to England and spend" but encouraged them to "look on the interests of India as pre-eminent to them." Involvement with the welfare of the continent would mean learning the language of the people instead of retreating into an English-speaking world. There is therefore some irony in the way Groves's own ministry flourished par excellence among the British officers in India.

The Role of Norris Groves

Even before he left England Groves seems to have attracted the friendship of officers in the armed services. In Plymouth one of the naval figures, who, with Captains Percy Hall and William Rhind, regularly addressed the meetings of the evangelical societies,[29] was Captain (later Rear Admiral Sir) James Hillyar (1769–1843), whose wife Mary was a daughter of Nathaniel Taylor, the naval storekeeper on the island of Malta.[30] When Groves was travelling overland to Baghdad one of the members in his party was Mary Hillyar's sister Charlotte Taylor.[31] Another naval officer to whom Groves wrote a lengthy letter describing the first part of his journey to Baghdad, was "my very dear brother and most kind friend," Vice Admiral Richard Harrison Pearson (1765–1838).[32] Another lady in Groves's travelling party, Mrs. Taylor (no relative

26. H. Groves, *Lord Congleton*, 53, but see below, n64.

27. [H. B. Groves], *Memoir*, 296; Captain Bell may be the Major (afterwards General) James Bell mentioned in H. Groves, Lord Congleton, 52. On the other hand he may be the Captain (later Major) Bell mentioned with affection in [H. B. Groves], *Memoir*, 296, 420, 447, 457, 475, 520. Both General Bell and Colonel Bell are listed among the mourners at Lord Congleton's funeral in 1883, H. Groves, Lord Congleton, 134. But see below, n51.

28. [H. B. Groves], *Memoir*, 394.

29. A good example is the annual meeting of the Plymouth auxiliary of the Jews' Society in 1829, *Falmouth Packet and Cornish Herald*, 30 Oct 1829.

30. Marshall, *Royal Naval Biography*, 2:863.

31. See her postscript to a letter from Karl Pfander (in Tabreez, travelling with Groves) to C. G. Blumhardt, 1 Nov 829, Dann, Father of Faith Missions, 107n23.

32. Basel Mission Archives, Gemischte Briefe Series Q–3–4, A. N. Groves to R. Pearson, 14 Oct 1829 [MS Copy]. Pearson's father, Sir Richard Pearson, is remembered for his engagement with John

of Charlotte), was the wife of Major Robert Taylor, the British resident in Baghdad, whose many kindnesses to Groves and his party suggest that he was a friend and not just a good neighbor.[33] It was another friend, Colonel (later General Sir) Arthur Cotton of the Madras Engineers, who had encouraged Groves to come to India in 1833,[34] and repeatedly we find a mutual appreciation developing between this unassuming pacifist and his military acquaintances.[35] Some of them, of course were engineers but many of them were fighting soldiers.

From time to time after some discussion with Groves, one of them would delight him by announcing his intention to "quit that wretched profession of learning to destroy his species."[36] Sometimes too, the missionary effort benefited as when a soldier

---

Paul Jones off Flamborough Head in 1779 (see *DNB*).

33. The name of Major (later Colonel) Robert Taylor is perpetuated in the Taylor Prism (or Cylinder) now in the British Museum on which is inscribed Sennacherib's account of his invasion of Palestine in 701 BC. Like Sir Henry Rawlinson, his successor at Baghdad, Taylor was a formidable scholar and linguist, fluent in Persian and Arabic. He acquired the prism in 1830 in Baghdad (when Groves was there) but that was before Rawlinson's pioneering use of the Behistun inscription to decipher cuneiform, so he may not, at the time, have realized the prism's significance. For details of this scholarly military man see Layard, *Autobiography*, 1:351; cf. Wolff, *Travels and Adventures*, 202; and E. Sollberger, "Mr. Taylor in Chaldaea," 129n3. I am beholden to Professor Alan Millard for the last of these references. It may not be a coincidence that another, somewhat later, scholar of Middle Eastern antiquities, Sir Wallis Budge (who cannot be accused of a bias in favor of evangelical Christianity) makes honorable mention, more than once, in connection with Taylor, of Groves, "the heroic missionary," and his work in Baghdad (Budge, *By Nile and Tigris*, 1:176, 191–92, 210–11). Although Colonel Taylor was not associated with Brethren we may note that the sister of his Armenian wife was the second wife of Lord Congleton who married her in Baghdad. For the extraordinary early life of these Armenian women, see Wolff, *Travels and Adventures*, 208–9. A fascinating parallel with such military pioneers in Middle Eastern archaeology as Taylor and Rawlinson is to be found in the more recent publications of Air Commodore P. J. Wiseman, who served in Iraq as a young man, and of his son Professor Donald Wiseman who served in the RAF with distinction during the 2nd World War and who, like his father, was associated with Brethren (see below, 238).

34. For the career of Sir Arthur Cotton (1803–99), see the article by Peter L. Schmitthenner in *ODNB*, and Lady Hope's account of her father in Hope, *General Sir Arthur Cotton*. Perhaps we should treat with caution this filial biography, as the inventive part played by Lady Hope in the fabrication of the oft-repeated legend of Charles Darwin's deathbed conversion was the cause of great indignation expressed by the Brethren evangelist J. W. C. Fegan, whose letters, questioning Lady Hope's veracity, are available in Moore, *Darwin Legend*, 153–63. The engineering achievements in the Godavari Delta of Cotton and his wife's brother-in-law Lieutenant (later Major-General) Felix Thackeray Haig (both devout Anglicans) were greatly appreciated by the Brethren missionaries Bowden and Beer, whom the engineers invited to evangelize among their laborers, see Bromley, *They were men sent from God*, 78–87.

35. Even unbelieving soldiers were fascinated by Groves. Captain S., "who has no very strong feelings about religion, but came to Bagdad, and feels kindly towards us," took the trouble to write to Groves some years later giving him his opinion of developments in India. [H. B. Groves], *Memoir*, 255.

36. Ibid., 1st ed., 240. It will be apparent from remarks of that sort that Groves (and probably most Brethren who sympathized with him) were pacifists rather than pacificists. Pacificism (the promotion of reforms that would make war less prevalent without waiting for a change in human consciences) was unlikely to figure high in Brethren priorities where "heavenly citizenship" tended to leave little room for political involvement.

called MacCarthy obtained his discharge and joined Groves's little mission based at Chittoor. Groves described him with unfeigned admiration:

> MacCarthy has marvelous strength; he is inured to the climate and can walk forty miles a day without fatigue. He reads and writes Tamil and Telegoo freely and gives up thirty-five rupees a month, a horse and a house, that he may do the work of God. He goes through the Tamil and Telegoo country, in a cart filled with books, tracts and things for sale, preaching the gospel to the natives in their own tongues, as he passes on, and in English to all the soldiers in the military stations.[37]

But far more numerous than those who abandoned the profession were those who continued to serve in the armed forces, and clearly Groves didn't press his pacifist convictions on his military friends. In the case of his young brother-in-law George Baynes, this was partly in deference to his wife's wishes, but the following episode clearly illustrates Groves's respect for individual differences of opinion.

> Before he came, Harriet [Groves's wife] begged I would say nothing to him about the army; and for many reasons I did not; nor did his conversation show the least thought passing in his mind about it. He went with me, and Captain Walker, the aide-de-camp of the Commander in Chief, to Poonamalee, to preach. I chose the Laodicean Church as my subject; his mind became impressed, and he lingered behind us all the way home; and the next day he told Harriet he had made up his mind to quit the army. So strong was his impression that it was not the place of the Christian's *greatest* usefulness, that he would have applied for leave to retire at once, not thinking it right to receive pay, after he had determined to quit; but I persuaded him to let all remain quiet for five or six months, and during that time to write to all who were interested in his welfare, in order to give them at least an opportunity of saying all they had to say. He could also, if he liked, till the expiration of his leave, study the language; and then before he took any irrevocable step, and after he had become acquainted with the work, on which he has proposed entering, go to Bombay and settle all his affairs; for I feel it would take away much from the real moral power of his testimony, if he were to act precipitately, or under the influence of exclusive association with us.[38]

Captain George Walker, who, from Groves's account, accompanied them to Poonamalee, came from a military family and was not only the aide-de-camp of the Commander in Chief but also his nephew. A few months later in May 1837 both Groves and Congleton attended his marriage to Anna the eldest daughter of Daniel Corrie, the recently deceased bishop of Madras for whom Groves had great affection

---

37. Ibid., 392. The first edition of the Memoir contained an errata slip correcting the spelling of his name to Macarthy though the earlier spelling was perpetuated in the second edition. MacCarthy died in 1848 in Madras, ibid., 457.

38. Ibid., 366–67.

and respect.[39] Walker returned to Europe very soon after and it is not clear whether his discharge was connected with his marriage or as a result of his time with Groves.

It is unlikely that Groves was conscious of any parallels that might be drawn between the British imperial presence in India and the Roman occupation of Palestine in the time of Christ. In view of the British Establishment's professed Christianity in contrast to Roman paganism, Groves's verdict (if he had drawn the parallel) would probably have been more severe on his fellow countrymen as it certainly had been in 1834 when he complained of the unfavorable mission situation arising from the drunken behavior of the soldiers in Chuna: "Well may the natives say," he exclaimed, "'Why do you not first improve your own people?'"[40] But Groves persisted in his ministry among the military officers even though, in so doing, he was almost inevitably liable to be identified with the authorities.

We know virtually nothing of the centurion who came to Jesus on account of his servant's sickness except that he was a part of the occupying Roman army and that Jesus marveled at his faith. When in 1845, Captain Thomas Hillman Hull came with his dying wife to stay with Groves, he was coming to a missionary whom he had earlier visited in Baghdad, where Groves had certainly not been identified with the ruling authorities. Hull was not a believer but as a Devonian he had possibly known Groves back in England. Now, when he came to Groves, in India, the dynamics were different. Groves may have been *persona non grata* with some of the religious Establishment but the local judges and many of the officers valued him. Thanks to Groves's ministry, Mrs. Hull died in peace and, contrary to Groves's fears, her widowed husband remained steadfast in the faith that he had discovered at the side of her deathbed.

There was however another part to the story. Unlike the spiritual aspirations of those other God-fearing officers on which Groves had been able to build, Captain Hull's earlier career had been rather more boisterous. From the later Brethren accounts of Captain Hull, one would not have guessed that, some years previous to his marriage, he had twice been before a court martial and on one occasion had been imprisoned for a year when found guilty of manslaughter. This may give a special dimension to Groves's reference to Hull "approaching the mercy-seat where the blood sprinkles the conscience and speaks peace."[41]

The Indian Impact on Brethren in England

When considering the impression that Groves made on some of the Indian army officers, we may begin with the testimony of George Walker, whose marriage we

---

39. H. Groves, *Lord Congleton*, 56. Details of the bride are taken from FIBIS, www.search.fibis.org. For Daniel Corrie, see *ODNB*, and [H. B. Groves], *Memoir*, 294–95, 365.

40. [H. B. Groves], *Memoir*, 308.

41. For Groves's account of Hull see [H. B. Groves], *Memoir*, 406; see also Pickering, *Chief Men*, 55–56. Details of Hull's earlier disciplinary episodes are taken from FIBIS, www.search.fibis.org.

observed earlier and who epitomizes the observant, church-going Anglican officers whose numbers in India had evidently increased in the first decades of the nineteenth century:[42]

> I think the tone of many of us was, in some respects, very austere; we were exercised rather too exclusively, in a *Levitical* way, about clean and unclean things; separation from the world, &c. &c, and hence the value of one [Groves], who, by his life, and conversation, and ministry, showed us more fully our happy liberty to tread the holy courts, and realize the privileges of priests, and the adoption of children in our Father's house . . .
>
> Against all forms of Church assumption, he [Groves] was keenly and unsparingly severe . . . I feel more now than I used years ago, as he did, about the manifestations of catholic union with all Christians; and I feel very happy in being able to attend occasionally their meetings and speak from their platforms. I could not go to the Establishment as I used in India, but, with this exception, I believe the ground we stood on in India is the right one.[43]

Walker's career is difficult to establish but he became unmistakably associated with the Brethren.[44] Returning to his parents' home, which had been in Florence since at least 1820 when his brother Arthur de Noé Walker was born there, George and his younger brother were associated with Count Guicciardini in the 1840s during the formative years of the Count's evangelical experience. Walker then settled in Teignmouth, Devon where he was associated with the Brethren assembly, which had been meeting in Bitton Street since 1832.[45] This explains why Guicciardini spent the winter of 1851 in Teignmouth, which is described by his biographer as "uno dei centri piu fervidi dei 'fratelli,'" and where he worked with Walker on his revision of the Diodati translation of the Italian Bible.[46]

---

42. Cf. Groves in 1834: "Capt Vetch tells me that when he came to India, in 1806, there was but one pious man, a Col. Bronte, between Calcutta and Delhi; and now, I trust, there are some hundreds." [H. B. Groves], *Memoir*, 296.

43. [H. B. Groves], *Memoir*, 515, 516–17 [525, 527].

44. Walker's maternal grandmother had been a friend of the poet, Robert Burns; see Macnaghten, *Burns' Mrs Riddell*, 136–46. His parents were Captain Charles Montague Walker, R.N. (1780–1833), and his wife Anna Maria (née Riddell). They were both buried in the Protestant cemetery in Florence of which the records (http://www.florin.ms/cemetery4.html), together with the IGI, enable us to piece together the details of their children all of whom were christened in Kingston-on-Thames even when the family was resident in Florence. One daughter, Henrietta Gertrude, married Count Antonio Baldelli, whose family gave to the Italian Brethren the property at Poggio Ubertini: see Maselli, *Libertà della Parola*, 112. Alessandra Pecchioli has recently made the Walker family the subject of an excellent Italian essay; see Pecchioli, "Giulia Baldelli" 207–22.

45. Griffiths, *History of Teignmouth*, 53. Discovering in the 1860s that the original trust deed of the Gospel Hall in Bitton Street had been in favor of the Baptists, Walker encouraged the Brethren to vacate the premises and to worship elsewhere, see Walker, *Statement of reasons*. The only copy (known to me) of this and several other pamphlets by Walker, is in the Fondo Guicciardini in the Biblioteca Nazionale Centrale, Florence.

46. Jacini, *Un Riformatore Toscano*, 139.

There were other significant Indian officers who gravitated to the Brethren. We have already mentioned Captain Thomas Hull, who, on his return to England, took a leading part, with his brother William, in the activities of the Exeter Road Room, in Withycombe Raleigh, Exmouth.[47] There was Major James Thomas Molesworth (1795–1872) whose Marathi dictionary is still in use and who was associated with the Brethren by 1837 when he retired from the army.[48] We should also remember Lieutenant James George Deck (1807–1884), the hymn-writer who in 1834 was "packed up for a return to India" and by chance, in Cape Town, encountered Groves returning to England. To Groves's delight the "eyes [of Deck and his wife] are quite turned away from the army and the world, but [they have] decided to devote themselves to the Lord's work."[49] Before emigrating to New Zealand, Deck was a leader among the Brethren in Taunton and Weymouth, where Groves "preached for him" in 1848.[50] Another figure, who is harder to pin down, is Colonel Jasper Higginson Bell (1809–c. 1895) of the Madras Engineers who held various administrative positions in Madras (Master of the Mint, etc.), but whose tracts were produced by Brethren publishers (Yapp and Hawkins; J. F. Shaw) and whose will set up a trust in favor of the Brethren assemblies in Bromley.[51] One final Brethren connection with India is Captain Mark Wood Carmichael-Smyth (1801–72), of the Madras Cavalry, who was a younger brother of the step-father of the novelist, William Makepeace Thackeray. We are told that when Mark became a Plymouth Brother, he "annoyed his family by announcing his determination to give away all his possessions as an encouragement to people generally to share everything in common."[52]

Sometimes of course it was the movements of his regiment that dictated a military man's return from India and therefore retirement was not automatic. His liability to engage in armed combat now became more of a theoretical problem. Newton

---

47. Pickering, *Chief Men*, 55–56.

48. "A solemn word to the saints of God," in the *Christian Witness* 4 (Jan 1837), is attributed to him in two copies endorsed with the names or initials of supposed authors. I am indebted to Dr. Timothy Larson for a reference to him made by Austen Henry Layard in December 1857 in a letter from Poonah: "there is a Major M—— living here, who is a very eccentric man; he has given up the army because it is wicked to be a soldier, eats nothing but vegetables, preaches the Gospel, and is what Lord Somers' friend called a 'Yarmouth bloater' (i.e. Plymouth brother). He never sees any one, but is a man of considerable acquirements, and has lately published a Maharatta dictionary which is considered to be a standard work." Layard, *Autobiography*, 2:214.

49. [H. B. Groves], *Memoir*, 348.

50. Ibid., 461. For Deck, see Peter Lineham's article in the *DNZB* (http://www.teara.govt.nz/en/biographies/1d8/1) and further details below in ch. 16n33.

51. For J. H. Bell, see http://www.antonymaitland.com/emctext/emcprintd.htm, 68–69, and FIBIS, www.search.fibis.org. Bell also circulated an enquiry in 1867 addressed to 45 assemblies asking whether they would receive at the Lord's Table Christians who did not believe in eternal punishment. A copy of his, privately printed, *Abstract of Answers* is in the Fondo Guicciardini in the Biblioteca Nazionale Centrale, Florence. Jasper Higginson Bell was never a General but he may have been the Captain (later Major) Bell mentioned earlier (above n27).

52. Ray, *Buried Life*, 100.

recalled the interesting story of Major Elliott Armstrong who was probably associated with the early Brethren in Plymouth when he first returned from India in the late 1830s.[53] According to Newton, with whom he discussed his predicament, he was "deeply impressed with the wrong position of his being in the Army," but thinking that the bitterness of war was past, he retained his commission and moved with his regiment to Canterbury. In 1838, however, he was made responsible for putting down a rising of Kentish malcontents led by John Nichols Thom who claimed Messianic powers and posed as Sir William Courtenay. In the ensuing "Battle of Bossenden Wood," Armstrong had to give the order to fire on the rebels and then "being mounted, he dashed in among the peasantry."[54] If he thought that this was the last occasion he would be so engaged, he was again mistaken, as in the following year his regiment was sent to South Wales to put down the Chartist rising in Newport. In consequence, Newton observed that he was "twice in great distress of mind at having to draw the sword when he thought that for him all actual fighting was over."[55]

Some of the military men associated with the Brethren were engineers rather than fighting men. The Major Lancey described, in Anna Stoney's recollections, as being associated with the Irish Brethren after 1836,[56] may well have been the Lieutenant William Lancey of the Royal Engineers who in 1835 reluctantly contributed to the Ordnance Survey's *Memoir of Donegal*, protesting his "want of taste and time for such things."[57] However, even if such an officer were not engaged in armed combat his position in Ireland would undoubtedly have involved him in the exercise of authority. This is well demonstrated in Brian Friel's play *Translations* which is imagined in 1833 as a detachment of Royal Engineers (one of whom is "Captain Lancey") begin their work on the British Ordnance Survey in Donegal.[58]

The absence of a clerical system among the Brethren provided plenty of scope for an articulate military man who wanted to participate in ecclesiastical life. Benjamin Newton, who was criticized for his authoritarian tendencies at Plymouth, considered the "do-it-yourself" Indian approach as something of a threat to orderly church life, as he explained:

---

53. Armstrong married Mary Fraser in Madras in Oct 1835, www.search.fibis.org.

54. Account in the Newgate Calendar, http://www.exclassics.com/newgate/ng623.htm.

55. Newton referred to Armstrong as being "sent to Wales to quell the Rebecca riots," which would more correctly refer to the turnpike protests when men, dressed as women, destroyed tollhouses in the 1840s rather than the Chartist rising of 1839, but the disturbances are often conflated as in Newton's recollections (JRULM, CBA 7057, 309).

56. See "Account of Early Days," by Miss A. M. Stoney (1839–1932), transcribed on Mr. Gordon Rainbow's website, My Brethren, www.mybrethren.org/history/framearl.htm. Cf. the reference to William Lancey in [Bellett], *Recollections of J. G. Bellett*, 89.

57. See Day, "Portraying Donegal," www.finnvalley.ie/glenfin/other/statistical/os.html.

58. Friel, *Translations*.

[Joseph Clulow] came to England [from India] and being a Christian person he began ministering here.[59] Most Indian Officers do so. They are so cut off from any ministry out there that, as they feel something should be done, they take a ministerial position. Even unconverted persons have to do so in India when burying the dead, and reading prayers among their soldiers without a chaplain. So coming home they are prepared to engage in Christian work.

And when the Brethren arose, the above was a cause of great dissatisfaction at Plymouth because, *there*, indiscriminate ministry was not allowed, as it was in many places and then these Anglo-Indians were very often mightily offended.[60]

Retired military officers were often articulate, ready to take responsibility, pensioned and therefore had time on their hands to study the Scriptures and other writings that they found profitable. In the second generation of Brethren history this was a significant factor as the wealthier aristocratic element diminished. Edward, the third son of Norris Groves on more than one occasion noted this phenomenon:

A forlorn Brethren's meeting was exactly suited for the development of gift in a retired military officer or civilian. Requiring no support of a material kind from those who formed the assembly, he was free to expound Scripture as he pleased, especially if he undertook to make up the deficiency that constantly happened in the matter of rent and expenses.[61]

Such men sometimes proved to be scholarly and pious, but quite as often it was the trappings of status that gave them the preeminence. In one instance Edward Groves had difficulty in restraining his indignation against one of his father's military acquaintances who, he felt, had proved to be hypocritical and dishonest in certain respects, but who, on returning to England, soon took his place among the Brethren at

---

59. Joseph Clulow is wrongly described by Newton as having been "Governor of Madras." In fact he had lived in Madras where he had been "Acting superintendent of police" in 1831 and later "Acting Treasurer and Secretary to the Government Bank" before his return to England in 1834. Dodwell and Miles, *Alphabetical List of . . . Madras Civil Servants*, 60–61. Cf. [H. B. Groves], *Memoir*, 285, and above, ch. 10n41nn44–45.

60. JRULM, CBA 7049, Fry MS, 353–54. One person, associated with the Indian army, who seems to have accepted Newton's more authoritarian position, was Dr. James Pringle Riach. Originally a surgeon in the Bombay Medical service, Riach was, by 1826, in Persia where he carved his name on the Palace of Darius, see St. John Simpson "Making their mark: Foreign travellers at Persepolis," fig 15, at the website of the International Network of Achaemenid Studies and Researches, http://www.achemenet.com/ressources/enligne/arta/pdf/2005.001-Simpson.pdf. In 1834 the American missionary Justin Perkins found Riach travelling on the Russo-Persian frontier but by 1839 Riach had "retired from Teheran" where he had for a time been the Shah's personal physician (Anderson, *History of the Missions*, 171–72, 188). Some time in the 1840s he joined the Brethren at Plymouth, where he appreciated the ministry of Newton, who in later years was comforted and encouraged by Riach's "friendship and affection." B. W. Newton to Mrs Riach, 7 Feb 1866, JRULM, CBA Box 23 (10). For other details of Riach's earlier career see Dodwell and Miles, *Alphabetical List of Medical Officers*, 136–37.

61. E. K. Groves, *George Müller*, 375. For some of the ecclesiastical context of this phenomenon, see above, ch. 12.

Weston-super-Mare where he found that "military rank, abundance of means, a suave manner, and being one of the earliest of those who broke bread in the simple way of 'Brethren' [were] all the credentials necessary to his immediately becoming a leading man in the meeting."[62]

These retired officers may have provided the Brethren with an articulate and socially dependable leadership, but only occasionally could they be described as the "Chief Men among the Brethren." Indeed bearing in mind that Henry Pickering was inclined to be somewhat in awe of worldly titles of any sort—aristocratic, military or administrative, it is perhaps significant that naval and army officers compose only a small fraction of his biographical collection. In the case of the Earl of Carrick (1835–1901), his conversion occurred some time after his retirement from the army,[63] while Captain Kingscote (1811–93), whose inclusion seems to have rested on his being a friend of the Duke of Cambridge and his having taken part at the funeral of J. N. Darby, is noted as having left the army following his conversion.[64] This was commonly the case among Exclusive Brethren[65] (of whom Kingscote was one) and probably reflects Darby's position though he gave little prominence to the subject in a considerable corpus of writing. In the context of the Franco-Prussian War in 1870 Darby wrote in French to an unknown correspondent that "it is clear to me that a Christian, free to do as he will, could never be a soldier, unless he were at the very bottom of the scale and ignorant of the Christian position." Nevertheless Darby recognized the grey area arising when a sovereign government required military service of its subjects, and like Hall in his early pamphlet, his real objection to Christian involvement in the armed services did not arise from pacifist convictions. Rather it was the patriotic sentiment that he felt was inappropriate in a person whose citizenship was not of this world.[66]

Military Brethren in South-East London

The belief that service in the armed forces was incompatible with Christian belief was certainly not confined to the Exclusive Brethren and the slightly different case of Dr. J. L. Maclean (1830–1906) is of interest as he was one of the first editors of the Open

---

62. E. K. Groves, *George Müller*, 229. There were at least three army officers associated with the assembly at Weston-super-Mare, including General Rice, General Cookson and Colonel Minchin, see Beattie, *Brethren*, 258. For Colonel Minchin's recollection of Lord Congleton's visiting India in 1836, see above, n26.

63. Pickering, *Chief Men*, 147.

64. Ibid., 74.

65. Noel cites the similar experiences of Captain James Barton (1834–1919) and Captain Hatton Turner, both of the Royal Artillery, who, as Exclusive Brethren, also felt obliged to surrender their commissions so as to engage in Christian service, Noel, *History of the Brethren*, 1:139. Barton's resignation came after the Crimean War (see the entry for his son, Sir Sidney Barton in *ODNB*).

66. Darby, *Letters*, 2:110–11. For a balanced discussion of Darby's position, see Brock, "Peace Testimony," 34–36.

Brethren missionary magazine that was later known as *Echoes of Service*. Maclean's father, Sir George Maclean (1795–1861) had been Adjutant-General in the Crimean War for which service he was made a Knight Commander of the Bath in 1856. Maintaining the family's military tradition, his son John Lindsay served in Malta (1847–51) where the Colonel of his regiment took him to a Bible reading, which resulted in his conversion. He continued with his regiment in the West Indies (1851–57) but when testifying to his faith, in an English railway carriage sometime in 1857,[67] he was troubled when a lady questioned the consistency of someone who spread the gospel of peace but also carried a sword. At this point he quit the army and began to study medicine apparently being only a little later introduced to Brethren through Harriett Warren whom he married in January 1863 and whose sister Mary Harris Warren, in May 1860, had married William Yapp (1800/1807?–1874), formerly of Hereford.[68]

Maclean's decision to quit the army was taken in the late 1850s, but we should bear in mind that the way the army was perceived by the nation at large was beginning to change significantly in the mid-nineteenth century. General Sir Henry Havelock (1795–1857), a devout Christian, came to be as well known for his piety as for his military skill and the image was emerging of what Professor Hendrickson has called "a kinder, gentler British army" with the result that the reputation of soldiers at large was improving.[69] There are only two other military figures, included in Pickering's collection, of whom we have not yet made any mention. They are General John Halliday and his son-in-law Major-General Sir Charles Scott, neither of whom appears to have had any qualms about military service, and between them they provide a link between Norris Groves's ministry in India and the twentieth-century Brethren military presence in South-East London with which we shall conclude this paper.

General John Gustavus Halliday (1822–1917) was the very much younger brother of Sir Frederick James Halliday (1806–1901),[70] who was the first lieutenant governor of Bengal. Some time in his early twenties the younger Halliday was converted and valued the ministry of both Groves and his German contemporary, Samuel Hebich, who was also well known for his evangelism among British officers in India. He served for many years as a civil administrator on the Mysore commission, but later reverted to military duty in command of his old regiment, the 12th Madras Native Infantry, in stations in India and Burma until his retirement and return to England in 1876, when he settled in the Lewisham area of South-East London. Sir Charles Scott (1848–1919),

---

67. The event must have been before January 1858 when his regiment was posted to Burma.

68. For most of Maclean's details, see Pickering, *Chief Men*, 172–73, 139. His wife is given as "Harriett Warren of Gloucester-pl., Portman-sq., third daughter of the late Robert Warren," *Gentleman's Magazine* (Mar 1863) 370. Mary Warren was Yapp's second wife. For William Yapp's connection with the Warren family and Dr. Maclean, see Morgan, "William Yapp," 294.

69. Hendrickson, *Making Saints*, 74.

70. See *ODNB* (under F. J. Halliday), and Pickering, *Chief Men*, 208 where his second initial is wrongly given as "S." Colonel (as he was then) J. G. Halliday translated Gundert and Mögling's *Life of Samuel Hebich* into English.

who married Halliday's daughter, was also converted soon after his arrival in India where he served with the Royal Artillery in a variety of campaigns and administrative posts before returning in 1910 to England where he too was an active supporter of the Shrubbery Road Mission in Lewisham, and the Soldiers' Christian Association.

A very few miles northeast of Lewisham is the Royal Military Academy in Woolwich, traditionally the training ground for engineer and artillery officers, and an institution with an ongoing link with evangelical Christianity possibly benefiting from the ministry of John Simons (1735–1836), the rector of St. Paul's Cray, a few miles south of Woolwich.[71] Among the academy's distinguished alumni had been General Gordon, and although Gordon was *not* a Plymouth Brother,[72] he had established evangelical missions for destitute boys down the Thames from Woolwich in Gravesend. These missions had attracted the interest of a thirty-year-old artillery officer Charles Orde-Browne who had recently joined the Brethren in the 1860s. In due course, Orde-Browne with his wife established his own mission in North Woolwich, and then took a leading part in establishing the Open Brethren assembly in Woolwich. Previously Orde-Browne had been mentioned in dispatches for his conduct during the Crimean War and was the author of several authoritative books on armor, ammunition, breech-loading rifles, and field-batteries—subjects on which he lectured in the Academy at Woolwich when he was not engaged in mission work and preaching.[73] Of his several daughters, the youngest, Sybil, married William Dobbie (1879–1964) who had become an active worker with the Brethren during his time at the Woolwich Academy before serving in the 2nd Boer War, Ireland, and in the Marne and Aisne campaigns during the Great War.[74]

Orde-Browne's eldest daughter, Ethel, eventually married another soldier associated with the Brethren, George Wingate (1852–1936), who had been converted in India shortly after being posted to the Indian Staff Corps in 1875.[75] There he had already associated with some Brethren even before he met Orde-Brown in 1878 when he was on leave in London. Ethel Orde-Brown was very much younger than Wingate and they did not marry until 1899, but, on his own, and later with his wife, Wingate combined active armed service with missionary and evangelistic enterprise, and it seems that the authorities accepted the phenomenon. For example, there were no adverse repercussions when Wingate refused to move his troops on a Sunday during the Naga Hills campaign in 1879.

---

71. For Simons's influence on two young artillery officers, Barrington Tristram and Charles Maitland, in 1813 see Hole, *Life of William Whitmarsh Phelps*, 1:123n1.

72. This is a myth invented by Professor Raymond Callahan of the University of Delaware in his article on Orde Wingate in the *ODNB*.

73. For Orde-Browne, see Beattie, *Brethren*, 103–5.

74. For Dobbie see John Keegan's article in *ODNB*.

75. Details of the Wingate family in the next two paragraphs are taken from Royle, *Orde Wingate*, passim.

Slightly younger than George Wingate was Field-Marshall Edmund Allenby (1861–1936) whose reputation as a military man is mixed. Sometimes he is remembered as a hot-tempered martinet, but with affection by others, particularly those who served under his leadership in the Egyptian Expeditionary Force (EEF). Allenby probably benefited from his feud with Haig as it resulted in his removal from the Western front. Unlike George Wingate, whose cultural interests appear to have been limited, Allenby was a man whose diverse enthusiasms included poetry, travel and ornithology. For many Christians however he will always be the evangelical cavalry officer who dismounted before entering Jerusalem on foot in 1917 and who is said to have put his familiarity with Scripture and George Adam Smith's *Historical Geography of the Holy Land* to good tactical use at the battles of Beersheba and Megiddo. Some thirty years earlier Dr. Grattan Guinness (1835–1910) in one of the great historicist expositions of biblical prophecy, had singled out 1917 as a year of crucial importance[76] and Allenby's entry into Jerusalem, in that year, captured many an evangelical imagination. The piety of the Field Marshall is hard to categorize but he appears to have adopted a sort of nondenominational evangelicalism, pretty near to an Open Brethren position. He had grown up in the Anglican Church but when a friend said that he gathered Allenby "had fallen out with the Church of England," the general is said to have retorted, "I never thought it was worth falling out with." Donald McNair, who was an Exclusive Brother but who served under Allenby in the EEF, indicated that he considered Allenby to have been, in effect, an Open Brother.[77]

George Wingate's son Orde (1903–1944) is better known than his father and was hugely influenced by his upbringing among the Brethren, where, in the acerbic words of his sister, he was "reared on a diet of porridge, bread and dripping, and 'the sincere milk of the Word,'"[78] but his career does not really come within the scope of this paper. To his dying day he remained an intensely religious person indelibly marked by his biblical upbringing. His enthusiasm for the Zionist cause, his exploits on behalf of the restoration of Haile Selassie, the "Lion of Judah"—who else would have named his Abyssinian patriot army "Gideon Force"?—his rugged individualism and social contrarianism, all suggest that some of the Brethrenism of his youth was deeply engrained in his way of thinking, but other adjectives that have been used to describe Wingate, like prophetic, Cromwellian, Puritan, and Covenanter also spring to mind and the Brethren cannot claim to have a monopoly in such qualities. Unlike

---

76. "The year 1917 is consequently doubly indicated as a final crisis date, in which the 'seven times' run out, as measured from two opening events, both of which are clearly most critical in connexion with Israel, and whose dates are both absolutely certain and unquestionable." Guinness, *Light for the Last Days*, 222.

77. I am indebted to my esteemed friend Philip McNair both for the account of Allenby's retort concerning the Church of England and his father's opinion of Allenby's ecclesiastical persuasion.

78. Bierman and Smith, *Fire in the Night*, 10. George Wingate appears to have been a severe and repressive father but in later years Orde's sister Sibyl seems to have been more resentful of their gloomy upbringing, than her younger brother was.

his father and grandfather he did not remain within the fellowship of the Brethren, though his upbringing among them left its mark on him for life.

The same cannot however, be said of his uncle, Lieutenant-General Sir William Dobbie whose numerous responsibilities after the first World War ranged from Cairo to Singapore and culminated with his appointment as governor and commander-in-chief of Malta from 1940–42. The man, who later wrote *Active Service with Christ* (1948), was both a professional soldier and a member of the Brethren. Sir John Keegan has more than once quoted in print the words of the Cardinal-archbishop of Malta who said that Dobbie was the only man in whose features he had discerned "the radiance described in the Lives of the Saints."[79] At the height of the bombardment of Malta, Dobbie shared the danger and the shortages suffered by the inhabitants, but every evening after dinner he would lead his household in prayer. In fact, his obituarist in the *Times* noted that his first act on arrival in Malta had been "to issue an order of the day invoking divine aid and protection."[80] More recently there has been criticism of Dobbie, and John Bierman and Colin Smith have argued that Dobbie was replaced in 1942 because of dissatisfaction with such things as his concern for Sunday observance. This, they argue, contributed to two of the supply ships, which succeeded in getting through the blockade, being bombed before they could be properly unloaded—a further deprivation that the Maltese should not have had to endure.[81]

It can be argued that Dobbie epitomized the fact that although many of the early Brethren had been pacifists by conviction, by the twentieth century the situation had changed. At the beginning of the First World War, Henry Pickering's Brethren magazine, the *Witness*, had carried a brief article by Colonel Anthony Oliver Molesworth (1839–1917), entitled "Should Christians Enlist?"[82] The author, who was a nephew of Major J. T. Molesworth, whom we mentioned earlier, treated the question as a matter for individual consciences to decide. As the war proceeded with the introduction of conscription, Pickering shocked many Brethren by abandoning the traditionally neutral ground of the movement and adopting a position in favor of armed service—a position that many felt made it more difficult for Brethren to claim that they were conscientious objectors on religious grounds.

By 1939 when opposition to Nazi Germany seemed to occupy a higher moral ground than mere patriotism, the pacifist position would be even harder to maintain. This was the context in which General Dobbie's pamphlet *Christianity and Military Service* appeared in the later 1930s arguing that in the light of biblical teaching, the

---

79. J. Keegan, "Chindit Myth," *Times Literary Supplement*, 16 Jun 1995, and "Keen on Heroes," *Daily Telegraph*, 5 Oct 2002. He omitted the quotation from his account of Dobbie in the *ODNB*.

80. *Times*, 5 Oct 1964.

81. Bierman and Smith, *Alamein*, 339–40.

82. *Witness* 44 (1914) 155, cited in Dickson, *Brethren in Scotland*, 221. For Molesworth's enthusiastic interest in Napoleon's military strategy, see the brief account of him in 1890, escorting James Wright (Müller's successor at Ashley Down) over the site of the Battle of Marengo in Pierson, *James Wright of Bristol*, 95.

profession of arms is honorable and lawful.[83] It is perhaps also worthy of observation that *The Reason Why*, a very widely circulated booklet by Robert Alexander Laidlaw, a wealthy, Open Brethren businessman from New Zealand, was produced in a special edition for the Army Scripture Readers' and Soldiers' and Airmen's Association, suggesting that Brethren played a significant part in such work among the armed forces.[84]

In contrast we might consider the very curious pilgrimage of the 12th Duke of Bedford (1888–1953) who was briefly attached to the second battalion of the Grenadier Guards but resigned his commission and refused to rejoin his regiment at the outbreak of the First World War—a situation that only added to the bitterness of spirit engendered by his time at Eton, which he had detested. His explanation in 1914 was twofold:

> First . . . quite apart from anything to do with selfish personal inclination, it would be definitely wrong for me, after my known and proved incapacity to do the right thing in a sudden emergency, to take a commission and then, by some blunder on the battlefield, perhaps sacrifice the lives of my men uselessly and needlessly. . . Second . . . in this great time of crisis I ought to go and find some way . . . of serving my fellow men in no matter how humble a capacity.[85]

For the following thirty years, this socially isolated eccentric's pacifist convictions were given increasingly vocal expression in a series of pamphlets and published speeches to the House of Lords[86] with the result that his name was on the list of people who, as a fascist sympathizer, would have been arrested in the event of a German invasion.[87] His conclusion in 1941 that the Church of England was supporting the war led him to sever his ties with the Establishment and join the Brethren.[88] His involvement with the Brethren seems to have been at best a convenience.

---

83. Dobbie, *Christianity and Military Service*. The pamphlet was later reproduced in Dobbie's autobiographical volume, *Active Service with Christ*.

84. Laidlaw, *Reason Why*; cf. Laidlaw, *Story of the Reason Why*. I have been unable to find specific details of Brethren involvement with the Army Scripture Readers Association.

85. Russell, *Silver Plated Spoon*, 30–31.

86. E.g., Russell, *Conscientious Objector*, and *Better Way*.

87. Bob Fenton, "Nobles and Admirals on War 'Suspect List,'" *Daily Telegraph*, 5 Oct 2004.

88. Russell, *Silver Plated Spoon*, 159. In this autobiography his son describes the 12th Duke in manifestly hostile terms: "I don't think [in] all his life he really knew what it was to give affection to anybody, although he demanded it from others. . . . Possessions meant nothing to him. He was only interested in animals and birds and fishing and shooting, religious and social movements, which he picked up and then dropped. He was always waving a banner of some kind, peace or monetary reform or something. He was tremendously sincere about it. The only trouble was that he was convinced that he was always right. He was never wrong about anything, he had never made a mistake in his life, which made him very tiresome to live with." Ibid., 33, 40. Later he describes him as "a lonely and rather desolate man" (188). In contrast Nancy Mitford described the 12th Duke as "pacifist, zoologist and a good man." She also recalled that in his autobiography (which I have not seen) the Duke expressed his special liking for spiders, one of whom had been particularly fond of roast beef and Yorkshire pudding, "English Aristocracy," in Mitford, *Noblesse Oblige*, 56.

Orde-Browne, Dobbie, and the Wingates, were products of the Indian army and its encounter with the Brethren variety of evangelicalism, but just as the British experience in India cannot be treated as a model for all British colonial history or indeed for all British missionary endeavor, so it would be wrong to claim that these men were the authentic voice of Brethren on the subject of service in the armed forces. One of the quintessential qualities of the Brethren approach to truth has been to proclaim its oneness but to encourage a variety of expression. Certainly in the early twentieth century, Brethren assemblies in Southern England contained a wide spectrum of opinion with regard to armed service. The late Roy Coad, who like many others served in the Non-Combatant Corps from 1943 to 1947, has more than once recalled to me that he grew up in a pacifist circle of assemblies in South Hampshire and that his father was inclined to "snort" at a brother being known by his military rank.[89] On the other hand Professor Donald Wiseman's account of his childhood in South-East London recalls a circle of Brethren in which both his maternal grandfather and uncle were officers in the Royal Navy while his father had transferred from the Royal Naval Air Service in 1918 to the newly established RAF in which he served to the end of his life.[90] The link between Brethren and the armed forces is a curiously open ended one. Fortunately, the Lord has assured us that there are many mansions in his house.

---

89. Most recently in personal correspondence, 6 Apr 2007.
90. Wiseman, *Life Above and Below*, 7–9.

Freelance Independents

15

Robert Mackenzie Beverley

A Study in Dissatisfaction

Family Origins

THERE ARE RECORDS OF the Beverley family in the Yorkshire town of Beverley going back to the time of King John.[1] During the reign of Henry VIII one of the family was appointed to inquire into the northern monasteries. Soon after the restoration of Charles II (c. 1663) Major Robert [1] Beverley (1641–86) emigrated to Virginia[2] where his son Robert [2] (1673–1722) was a planter at Beverley Park and wrote a *History of Virginia*. The family remained in contact with their English roots and Robert [2] Beverley and two of his brothers were educated in England. In 1750, Robert [2]'s son, William [1] Beverley (1696–1756) visited England where his son Robert [3] (1740–1800) attended Wakefield Grammar School and later, in 1757 was admitted to Trinity College Cambridge, and in 1761 was called to the Bar.[3] William and his son Robert [3] farmed an estate in Virginia named Blandfield,[4] where William [2] Beverley (1763–1843) was born. The family was loyalist[5] and this may explain why, in spite of the revolutionary war, William [2] was sent back to England to attend Beverley Grammar School and then, like his father, was admitted to Trinity College, Cambridge, in April 1781.

Unlike his several siblings, William [2] remained in Yorkshire where, in April 1792, he eloped[6] with the sixteen-year-old Mary Midgley, whom he married a few

---

1. Burke, *Genealogical Dictionary*, 1:94.
2. For the American ramifications of the family, see McGill, *Beverley Family*.
3. See W. Beverley, "Diary."
4. In Burke's account the estate is named "Blandford."
5. See Calhoon, "Sorrowful Spectator."
6. The elopement to Gretna Green is recorded in the Diary of John Courtney (Apr 5, 1792), but is perplexing, as both the parents of the bride had died before that year and we have no idea of the identity of her guardian. For this and some other details in the next three paragraphs I have drawn on a typescript, "Norwood House," by D. N. Tucker (Beverley, East Riding Archive and Local Studies Service, SL245/9/9).

weeks later in the Church of St. Mary and St. Nicholas, Beverley.[7] Mary, like her older sister Anna-Margaretta (the wife of Lord Grantley), was a daughter and co-heir of Jonathan Midgley (1712–78), a wealthy gentleman of large landed estate who had been mayor of Beverley three times. On the death of his sister-in-law in 1795, William Beverley and his young wife moved into what had been the Midgley home at Norwood House, Beverley, and it was here that he reared his four children.[8] He was a lawyer, mayor of Beverley in 1806–1807, and an alderman as late as 1829.[9] In 1812 and 1818 he stood unsuccessfully as a candidate for Parliament[10] but there is little else about him in the printed sources other than the fact that, because of financial difficulties, he moved to Paris in 1833 where he died in July 1843.[11]

Early Years

William Beverley's only son, Robert Mackenzie Beverley, the subject of this paper, was baptized on 13 May 1798 in the church where his parents had been married.[12] He had two older sisters, one of whom died in infancy, and a third, who was younger than him.[13] His mother died when he was a very small boy and although his father remarried in January 1804,[14] Robert's stepmother, Mary (née Coltman) also died when he was not yet seven years old[15] after which his father appears to have remained single. It was presumably as a boarder that Robert attended Richmond school whose scholarly headmaster, James Tate, formerly a Fellow of Sidney Sussex College, was famed not only for the success of his students at Cambridge—known as "Tate's

---

7. IGI, 1 May 1792.

8. See http://www.midgleywebpages.com/eastyorks.html. The house was sold in 1834. For most of the 20th century it was part of a girls' high school, but has now been developed into offices. For a photograph of the house, see http://www.geograph.org.uk/photo/626411.

9. Oliver, *History and antiquities*, 398.

10. For the voting figures, see Bean, *Parliamentary representation*, 745–46; cf. Oliver, *History and antiquities*, 385.

11. *Gentleman's Magazine* (Sep 1843) 335. The family historian incorrectly gives the date of his death as September 1823 (McGill, *Beverley Family*, 536)—a date that has been repeated on numerous genealogical web sites. For his bankruptcy and move to Paris, see Crowther, *Diary of Robert Sharp*, 193, 405.

12. IGI. The basic biographical information concerning R. M. Beverley is taken from F. Boase, *Modern English Biography*, 4:391–92.

13. His older sister Maria (b. 1795) married Sir Edmund Becket and was the mother of the first baron Grimthorpe. His younger sister, Anna Margretta (1799–1851?), "was of a devotional turn of mind and somewhat eccentric. She resided in a small house adjoining to but separate from that of her father, where she established a small community of pious persons who met in her house for services of prayer and praise" (quoted in the "Tucker typescript"). See also below, n84.

14. *Universal Magazine*, n.s., 1 (Jan 1804) 85.

15. *Gentleman's Magazine* 75 (Mar 1805) 292. Cf. *Monthly Magazine and British Register* 19 (May 1805) 404.

invincibles"—but also for his humane rejection of corporal punishment.[16] This enlightened régime was in stark contrast to life at Eton, which Robert briefly attended as a sixteen-year-old in 1814[17] during the Headmastership of Dr. Keate, whose flogging record was notorious. Beverley later declared that Eton was "unquestionably the worst school in England . . . a more ignorant creature could hardly be found than a first-rate Eton boy."[18] After this brief interlude Beverley apparently returned to Richmond before being admitted to Trinity College, from where he matriculated at Cambridge University in 1816.

For want of specific details, we must beware of making hasty conjectures about Beverley's time at Cambridge. It is true that some fifteen years later and after his evangelical conversion, he wrote a scathing denunciation of what he considered to be the flagrant immorality, prevalent among both the undergraduates and the dons of the university. In response, a number of his critics, who defended the university, sought to discredit Beverley by arguing that his criticisms only reflected the dissolute circle in which he had moved as an undergraduate.[19] In all probability, though again we cannot speak with any certainty, the young man from the North of England with American connections, in the aftermath of the War of 1812, was more likely to have been something of an outsider at Trinity, who would have been an observer rather than a participant. In a comment made many years later, a friend observed that "at Cambridge [Beverley] was repelled by the Port wine Orthodoxy which seems to have been paramount."[20]

The years following his graduation with a law degree from Cambridge in 1821 are something of a mystery.[21] In fact there are only two accounts that include anything about Beverley's activities in the 1820s. One is a brief paragraph in a "Memoir" written many years later, after his death, by Mary Rowntree (née Stickney, 1812–1901), who was born in the city of Beverley and was a Quaker with whom, as an adult, Robert Mackenzie Beverley was well acquainted.[22] The other account is a MS memorandum inserted by Eliot Howard in his copy of one of Beverley's books. Eliot Howard's father, Robert Howard (1801–71), had been a close friend of Beverley in the 1840s and 50s, and Eliot Howard himself (1842–1929) was in touch with Beverley in the last years of

---

16. For Tate and his *Invincibles*, see Wenham, *Letters of James Tate*, x–xvi. For his "aversion to corporeal punishments [and . . .] stripes," see the obituary in the *Eclectic Magazine*, Jan 1844, 141.

17. Stapylton, *Eton School Lists*, 87. Eliot Howard (see below, n23) describes Beverley as "a thoughtful and sensitive boy" who "suffered much from the brutalities of the Eton of his day." According to the "Tucker typescript," Beverley was "expelled" from Eton but there is no record of this in the school lists.

18. Beverley, *Letter . . . Cambridge*, 34–35.

19. For Beverley's *exposée* of Cambridge and the ensuing controversy, see below, 251–52.

20. Eliot Howard's MS Memorandum, see below, n23.

21. For Beverley's LL.B., see *Al. Cantab.*, pt. 2, 1:254.

22. [Rowntree], "Memoir of Beverley," 326–31. For Mary Stickney Rowntree see *Proceedings of the Ackworth Old Scholars' Association* 20 (1901) 89–90.

his life.[23] When writing about Beverley's earlier life, both Mary Rowntree, who was some fifteen years younger than him, and Eliot Howard who was a member of the next generation, must have been almost entirely dependent on what Beverley had told them. Some elements in their accounts however, can be confirmed from independent sources, and where these corroborating details are available I shall make reference to them.

Mary Rowntree describes Robert's father as "an arbitrary and overbearing man, in fact a Tory of the old school," and this may well reflect some antipathy that Robert had for his father. It is true that Beverley Sr. was a Tory but like his son, in 1824, he made a speech in the Beverley town-hall petitioning for the abolition of slavery and as an American, born in Virginia, he had some familiarity with slavery in practice, and, we are told, opposed it strongly, "giving evidence for Wilberforce in the House of Commons."[24] Indeed the dissenting diarist, Robert Sharp, regarded William as a liberal Tory, and listed both him and his son among the "Gentlemen of liberal Opinions," who spoke in 1829, opposing the majority at an anti-catholic meeting at Beverley.[25] On the other hand, bearing in mind that the Beverley household was deprived of a maternal presence when Robert was only seven years old, he may well have found his father overbearing. Two of Robert's friends at Trinity College were sons of a Dorset squire, Sir John Wyldbore Smith (1770–1852). Theirs was a strange family but one into which Robert Beverley apparently was welcomed. Sir John was a hypochondriac who once ruefully reckoned that he "must have taken enough pills in my time to sink a ship," while his wife was so fearful of the outside world that she "used to take her exercise in an upper corridor at an uneasy jog-trot on the stiff springs of a hobby horse with a handle at each end by which two stout varlets propelled and pumped the rider up and down."[26] In spite of such eccentricities it seems that the young Beverley may have felt more at home here than with his father, as, when he published a little novelette (at his own expense), it was "To Lady W. Smith this attempt is dedicated, with every sentiment of regard and affection."[27]

Beverley's later writings are sufficient evidence for his classical expertise and scholarly inclinations, and one is not surprised to learn that, on leaving Cambridge, he traveled abroad for a while. A number of references and citations can be found which are based on Beverley's observations at this time. In the strange anticlerical

---

23. MS memorandum by Eliot Howard inserted in his copy of Beverley, *Posthumous Letters of the Rev. Rabshakeh Gathercoal*, held in the Bodleian Library, Oxford (shelfmark 1304 e 104).

24. W. Beverley et al., *Speeches delivered in the town-hall of Beverley*. William Beverley's support for Wilberforce is also mentioned in the Tucker typescript.

25. Crowther, *Diary of Robert Sharp*, 192–93n24.

26. Grogan, *Reginald Bosworth Smith*, 4–5.

27. [Beverley], *Devotee*. The identity of the author is given by Anne Renier, whose copy is in the Victoria and Albert Archive of Art and Design (861.AA.1285). This is confirmed in the only other copy (known to me) that is bound together with a similar novelette written by Lady Smith's younger son, [William Smith Marriott], *Royal Promise*, in Cambridge University Library, shelf-mark S727 d. 82.

compendium of esoteric knowledge assembled by Godfrey Higgins (1773–1833),[28] attempting to integrate Jewish and Christian traditions with classical and Eastern religions, the writer discusses the dating of the temple of Heliopolis at Baalbek using evidence provided by "an intelligent young friend and traveller."[29] This was very probably Beverley, several of whose other observations on ancient classical monuments (and texts) are cited by Higgins elsewhere.[30]

Anticlericalism, Masonic and Radical Involvement

Godfrey Higgins of Skellow Grange near Doncaster, was, like Robert Beverley, a Yorkshireman, who had studied at Cambridge, a Justice of the Peace, a freemason and a reformer. They both shared a deep distrust of the priesthood and for some years they were evidently good friends. Higgins who admired Beverley's investigation of Egyptian inscriptions, encouraged his friend to publish his work on the zodiac of Dendera but by the time Beverley had read his paper on the subject to the Royal Asiatic Society in 1830[31] the friendship between Higgins and Beverley was finished. In 1829 when Higgins published an apology for the life of Mohammed[32] Beverley's nascent evangelicalism was becoming apparent. In a characteristically caustic reply (a part of which apparently he wrote in Higgins's breakfast room at Skellow Grange) he suggested that the "sausages, black-puddings, excellent ham and delicious port wine," which characterized Higgins's hospitality were inconsistent with his newfound liking for Islam.[33] Hitherto Beverley had found Higgins's anticlericalism much to his taste but now he withdrew from the friendship.

Typical of Beverley's anticlerical outlook was his sporadic involvement with Freemasonry from 1819, when he was initiated and became a member, until 1833 when he was finally expelled from the Constitutional Lodge No 294, "having neglected and refused to pay his amount of quarterages."[34] In fact his Masonic activities

---

28. For Higgins, see *DNB* and De Morgan, *Budget of Paradoxes*, 1:274–77. Morgan knew Higgins personally. For his anticlerical sentiments Higgins was mockingly referred to by one reviewer as a "misohierist," *British Critic* 3 (1828) 421–41.

29. Higgins, *Anacalypsis*, 1:259.

30. For an extract from a letter written by Beverley identifying the God of Genesis with Plato's Vesta, "the soul of the body of the Universe," see ibid., 1:49; cf. Higgins, *Celtic Druids*, where Higgins acknowledges several ways in which Beverley had helped him: "I am indebted to my learned young friend, Mackenzie Beverley" for details of a druidical door at the entrance of a tumulus in Mycenae (226); for help with the Eleusinian mysteries (64, 230); and for a reference to Caesar's account of the Druids in Gaul (304–5).

31. *Asiatic Journal*, n.s., 4 (Jan–Apr 1831) 74.

32. Higgins, *Apology*.

33. Beverley, *Letter to Godfrey Higgins*, cited by Godwin, *Theosophical Enlightenment*. 89. For Higgins's sad sense of abandonment, see Higgins, *Anacalypsis*, 1:681n1.

34. Details of Beverley's Masonic career are based on http://www.scarboroughfreemasonry.org.uk/lodges/Old_Globe200.pdf. There are several letters (1822–32) by Beverley to the Masonic Grand

declined after 1828 but as late as September 1827 he had played a very public role as the Deputy Provincial Grand Master for the North and East Ridings of Yorkshire, when the foundation stone was laid for a new Masonic Hall in Hull. On this occasion he made a brief speech reminding his hearers that

> we are lawful Masons, true to the laws of our country, and professing to fear God who is the Great Architect of all things, to confer benefits on our brethren, and to practice universal benevolence to all mankind. We have amongst us, concealed from the eyes of all men, secrets which may not be revealed, and which no man has discovered. But these secrets are lawful and honourable, and are placed in the custody of Masons, who alone have the keeping of them to the end of time.
>
> Unless our craft were good and our calling honourable, we should not have existed for so many centuries; nor should we have had so many illustrious brothers in our order, ever ready to sanction our proceedings, and contribute to our prosperity.
>
> To-day we are assembled in the face of you all to build a house for masonry, which we pray God may prosper, if it seem good unto him; that it may become a house for great and worthy men to practice beneficent actions, and to promote harmony and brotherly love till the world itself shall end . . . [Beverley then] anointed the foundation stone with oil, and strewed upon it some grains of wheat and salt, and drops of wine, repeating the one hundred and thirty-third Psalm; after which the procession returned in the same order to the Neptune Inn, where about one hundred brethren sat down to an excellent dinner, and the evening was spent with the greatest harmony and brotherly love.[35]

Like his father, the younger Beverley was a magistrate and in 1822 he was commissioned as a deputy Lieutenant for the East Riding of Yorkshire.[36] These were positions to which effectively he was born, and he seems to have taken the responsibilities seriously,[37] but from an early age his political persuasions were unmistakably those of a Whig advocate of parliamentary reform, with a much more radical program than that of a liberal Tory like his father. When in January 1823, the high sheriff of York called a meeting to discuss parliamentary reform, hustings were fitted up in the castle yard and some five thousand people attended the meeting in spite of the time of year.[38] The young Robert Beverley who was not yet twenty-five years old took part in the

---

Secretaries E. Harper and W. H. White in London, Freemasons Hall, Library and Museum of Freemasonry (HC 7/E/6–7, 9, 12–15).

35. Preston, *Illustrations of Masonry* 14th ed., 413–15. This edition was produced by George Oliver, who was present at the occasion in question.

36. *London Gazette*, issue 17902, 8 Mar 1823, 3.

37. Thus in 1825 he was part of a Commission of Enquiry into the running of the Refuge for pauper lunatics at Sculcoates; Bickford, *Private lunatic asylums*, 17.

38. *Edinburgh Annual Register* 16, pt. 3 (1823) 203.

proceedings and in his speech maintained that Jesus Christ had been the "first and best of all Reformers'" and further claimed that if Jesus

> were to appear among us, for the first time in the kingdom of England, and to preach those unpalatable doctrines of radical reform . . . there is very little doubt but that the Gospel, if now produced for the first time within the walls of St. Stephen's [i.e., Parliament], would be voted false, scandalous, and seditious. It should not be forgotten that there never was a greater reformer than Christ—the poor man's friend, the advocate of universal liberty, the enemy and the opposer of aristocratical pride, profligacy, and corruption.[39]

This was sensational stuff and a commentator in the *Yorkshire Observer* felt the need to give young Beverley some cautious advice as "the conversation of our fellow-citizens is so much engrossed by 'Beverley of Beverley' and the arguments he employed to enforce his politics."[40]

In the county of Yorkshire, reformers like Beverley were in the minority but perhaps the most effectively vocal of them all was Sydney Smith, the brilliant rector of Foston-le-Clay, the formidable contributor to the *Edinburgh Review*, and seasoned controversialist. In his MS account of Robert Beverley, Eliot Howard observed that Beverley "was at one time an intimate friend of Sidney [*sic*] Smith," but that later "S.S. ceased from further intercourse." We know that in November 1824, when the diarist Mary Berry and her sister visited Smith at Foston, they met there, "Mr. Vernon one of the innumerable sons of the Archbishop of York[41] and Mr. Beverley, a young Yorkshireman of very good mind and manners." The diarist then adds that Smith commemorated the young men's visit in an imitation of Virgil's sixth Eclogue, beginning:

> Vernon and Beverley, two graceful swains,
> Whom youth made sportive on Fostonian plains
> (This famed for music, and that famed for love),
> Met with their flocks beneath a beechen grove,
> And meeting saw beneath the noonday shade
> Sidneian Smith in drowsy slumbers laid; . . .[42]

The friendship with Smith continued for a while and in late 1825, a few months after Smith had famously found himself in a minority of one, at the Tiger Inn, Beverley, where he put the case *in favor* of Catholic emancipation, we find Robert Beverley

39. By chance Beverley's speech is preserved in a curious anthology of notes, letters, addresses and records published at the time; Milnes, *Warning voice of a hermit abroad*, 71–73.

40. *Yorkshire Observer*, 1 Feb 1823, 109.

41. Charles Vernon Harcourt (1798–1870) was a contemporary of Beverley, and later Prebendary of Carlisle, but a younger brother Egerton Vernon Harcourt (1803–83) was also a frequent guest of Smith, see his account in Reid, *Life and times of Sydney Smith*, 181–82.

42. T. Lewis, *Extracts from . . . Miss Berry*, 3:357–58. Whether this was actually by Smith is questioned by Howard Eliot who notes "a humorous poem on the subject of S.S's home at Foston, published as S.S's own was really from his [Beverley's] pen."

writing to Archdeacon Wrangham (one of Smith's few clerical allies): "I am publishing an enormous edition of Sydney Smith's Beverley Speech."[43] Certainly in the matter of Catholic emancipation, Robert Beverley was a regular advocate of the Catholic Claims. In the same year (1825), when the mayor and corporation of his town once again petitioned in favor of the Protestant ascendancy and against political relief for Roman Catholics, the young Robert Beverley, who was a Capital Burgess, protested in his characteristically sarcastic style:

> This petition is a very old friend: it is kept in a closet and brought forward as a squib against the Pope whenever we very good Protestants presume the Pope wants a squib to keep him in remembrance of our intolerance and persecution . . . let us withdraw our petition and draw in our horns: we are but snails in the state.[44]

The fact that in 1823 this twenty-five-year-old had asked to inspect the charters and records of the corporation[45] and that he seemed to be regularly out of step with the city fathers made him an object of suspicion. Not surprisingly when in 1826 a scurrilous pamphlet appeared, entitled *Horrida Hystrix, Satyricon Castoreanum quod ex schedis manuscriptis deprompsit unus e societate lollardorum*, the young classical scholar was suspected of being the author. The title may be literally translated as "The Prickly porcupine, a 'beaverish' [sc. 'Be(a)verley'] satire which one from the society of Lollards has extracted from manuscript papers," and the Latin text, with its anonymous English introduction, mocked in highly derogatory terms the church's wealth and lack of piety. The fact that the editor claimed to have "discovered" the document "after I had received permission from the right worshipful the Corporation of Beverley, to inspect the ancient records and documents, in the council-chamber of the town,"[46] must have led many to point the finger at Robert Beverley—all the more so, a few years later, when he published, in his own name, similarly biting and venomous attacks on the Established church. In fact, today most libraries attribute *Horrida Hystrix* to Beverley, but it is worth noting that in a letter written to his friend Archdeacon Wrangham, in 1826, Beverley vehemently denied authorship:

> I repeat what I have said with tears in my eyes a thousand times, I know nothing of these matters, which you and others lay to my charge. The Rebellion of the Beasts,[47] the York Festival by *outis*,[48] and the Horrida Hystrix are all

---

43. Smith, *Catholic Claims*. The use of "enormous" to describe the edition may be sarcastic as there are only four pages or it may refer to its folio format, possibly designed for use as a poster. There is an extant friendly letter from Sydney Smith to McKenzie [*sic*] Beverley, dated 23 Oct 1825, concerning voting in Yorkshire. (Oxford, Bodleian, MS Engl. Lett. d.222 f 178.)

44. Beverley, *Catholic Claims*, 4, 19.

45. MacMahon, *Beverley Corporation minute books*, 127.

46. [Beverley?], *Horrida Hystrix*, iii–iv.

47. [Hunt?], *Rebellion of the Beasts*, is usually attributed to Leigh Hunt.

48. Outis, *York Musical Festival*, was a satire on the bombastic style of John Crosse's *Account of*

wicked works sapping thrones and altars and attacking social order in a way that I think most horrid . . . How can you for a moment suppose that I would or could patronize such brimstone writings as these or that I should preserve them for you? No—Far be it from me to buy or have by me these monstrous productions. I leave it to dignitaries of the Church to encourage them. As for myself I throw them into the Hadriatic or the flames.[49]

Beverley's denials may have been truthful but by the early 1830s, his own, acknowledged writings were suspiciously similar.

Beverley's close involvement with radical political reform is well illustrated by his friendship with Major John Cartwright (1740–1824) the founder of the Hampden clubs and advocate of universal suffrage, who was sometimes known as "the Father of Reform." In the last years of Cartwright's life Beverley had corresponded with him and delighted him by using the phrase "*nil desperandum*" with reference to the apparent lack of progress in the cause of popular enfranchisement.[50] When he died in 1826, Cartwright's admirers proposed to erect a monument in his honor, and the committee established for this purpose included the young Robert Beverley alongside other distinguished names like Sir Francis Burdett, Joseph Hume and General Lafayette.[51]

Evangelical Involvement and Anticlerical Polemic

With all these other activities (scholarly, Masonic, judicial, political, and reforming) it is singularly difficult to establish at what point Robert Beverley may be said to have become an evangelical Christian. In 1818 a satirical work *"Cambridge besieged"; or, The rehearsal of a deep tragedy, at the theatre, Barnwell, which is to be performed by serious Christians, at the next meeting of the Bible Society*[52] was published in London. If, as has sometimes been suggested, it was the work of Beverley, it would appear that on leaving Cambridge he didn't regard himself as a follower of the evangelical, Charles Simeon. However, when James Scholefield (1789–1853), who had been one of Simeon's curates, was appointed as the Professor of Greek at Cambridge in November 1825, Beverley could but "rejoice" at the appointment of "a diligent and learned scholar of great quickness of intellect and a very good man," adding that "although the predominant faction dislikes an evangelical person, that gives me additional pleasure."[53]

---

the Grand Musical Festival, and possibly the work of a York newspaper editor, Philip Sydney.

49. MS letter R. M. Beverley to Francis Wrangham, Apr 6 [1826], York Minster Library. One of two letters accompanying a bound volume of three pamphlets, spine labeled "Beverleiana," one of which is *Rebellion of the Beasts*. This labeling suggests that Wrangham did not take Beverley's denials seriously even though, at least in the case of *Rebellion*, they were true.

50. Cartwright, *Life of Major Cartwright*, 2:263.

51. *Examiner*, 4 Jul 1825, 429.

52. [Beverley?], *Cambridge besieged*.

53. Undated [c. Nov 1825] MS letter from R. M. Beverley to F. Wrangham in York Minster Library, see above, n49.

It is interesting to note however that in another letter written in 1826 to Archdeacon Wrangham, who was regarded by many as an evangelical, Beverley makes a characteristically anticlerical allusion to his correspondent's comfortable circumstances, observing "(I speak cautiously) *if* it is requisite to have ecclesiastical wealth, I know no-one who has a better right to it than yourself."[54] Such waspish observations would characterize Beverley's writing long after his evangelical conversion, but there is little doubt that in December 1827 his rather bawdy letter to Sir Francis Wood, in answer to an enquiry about the Venus Callipiges, whose name he translates at one point as "the beautiful bummed Aphrodite," would undoubtedly have shocked many evangelicals.[55] So in the late 1820s it seems that Beverley was *sympathetic* to evangelicals but that he probably did not regard himself as one of them. This is further confirmed by a curious work of poetry that he published in 1827. *Jubal* has a strangely Faustian theme, in which wizards, in league with Lucifer, tempt the subject to seek knowledge greater than is permitted. Job-like, he loses everything but finally defeats the devil and is redeemed. In the poem there is a dualism reminiscent of parts of Blake's work, though much of it is very tedious and littered with what one reviewer described as "incidents outrageously supernatural, and sermonising dialogue of immeasurable and soporific length."[56]

Although it seems that, unlike most evangelicals, Beverley produced no written account of his conversion or the redirection of his convictions and mission that accompanied the event, it is most probable that it occurred some time in 1829. This most prolific of pamphleteers produced nothing between 1827 and 1831 except for his outraged rejection of Higgins's *Apologia for the life and character of Mohammed*—a reaction that suggests that he was abandoning his previously eclectic and speculative approach to the biblical text[57] and was finding in the Scriptures an authority that he had previously not recognized. The year 1829 also saw the passing of Catholic emancipation, which had long been a cause that Beverley had supported, but we should not suppose that his evangelical conversion in any way tempered his capacity for vitriolic and sarcastic mockery. His criticisms of priesthood and clerical wealth would remain for the rest of his life an ongoing feature of his discontent, but in the early 1830s the lifestyle of the Anglican clergy was an accompanying target of his criticism.

---

54. MS letter, 6 Apr [1826] from R. M. Beverley to F. Wrangham, in York Minster Library.

55. MS Letter (14 Dec 1827) from R. M. Beverley to Sir Francis Wood (York, Borthwick Institute, University of York, Halifax A2/22/7). The letter includes one awful pun after another, and throw away lines like: "I doubt not that she presided over the broad-bottomed Administration . . ." He then surmises that this Venus "can have little to do with *the bottomless pit*" but then cautions that such questions have to be decided "by Theologians of a grave & reverend nature, who are apt to probe matters to the bottom." Evangelicals would not have appreciated this scatological (and heavy-handed) wit.

56. *Monthly Review* 6 (Oct 1827) 152.

57. In his evangelical writings Beverley abandons earlier speculative ideas such as the suggestion that the God of Genesis who proposes to "'create man after our own image and likeness' . . . ought in strictness of language to be a male and female God" (see above, n30).

In the tempestuous years leading up to the passing of the Reform Bill in 1832—a measure that fell short of Beverley's own more radical agenda, but one which, for all its moderation, was resolutely opposed by almost all the bishops in the House of Lords—his anticlerical pamphlets had a notorious success all of their own. His *Letter to the Archbishop of York on the present corrupt state of the Church of England*,[58] appears to have gone through sixteen editions in the course of 1831 and provoked at least half a dozen replies from the Establishment, and a second pamphlet in the same year, "On the corruptions of the Church of Christ,"[59] elicited several more. When the Unitarian John Wade, a political and more radical critic, produced a new edition of his encyclopedic critique of the establishment, *The Black Book: Corruption Unmasked*, he referred more than once to Beverley's criticisms of the church but cautioned his readers that Beverley "is evidently an intense evangelical, and, for aught we know, may be a believer in Mr. Irving's new revelation of a 'gift of tongues.'"[60]

When however in the following year, to these blistering attacks on the Establishment, Beverley added a third *exposée*, this time laying bare what he considered to be the scandalous state of affairs in the University of Cambridge, his place was assured in the reference books as an anticlerical controversialist. At the outset, he launched into a relentless criticism of almost every aspect of the university from the "ludicrous ritual of the Senate House" (11) to "the unbroken round of festive debauchery" (12). The Colleges "are nests of licentiousness" (8) where students are "soaking in the stream of dissipation" (14). "The very great expense and very gross debauchery" (14) of undergraduate wine-parties were rendered all the more shocking by Beverley's personal recollection that "thrice in my fresh-man's term was I invited to supper-parties, of which the principal amusement was understood to be the presence of public women, dressed as Undergraduates . . . One of these harlot-festivals was at Caius College, the others were in lodgings."[61] It was, Beverley argued, therefore all the more incongruous that the Fellows of the colleges were required to be celibate, a circumstance which enabled Beverley to refer to the master of a college as the "ruler of the monastery over which he presides" (9). Beverley could thus underline the perceived hypocrisy of the system and roundly proclaim that "Cambridge and Oxford are the only remaining monasteries of England, and they are worse than any that were abolished [sc.in the 16th-century Dissolution.]"[62]

In the course of his work of demolition, Beverley notes that it is not just the moral inadequacy of Cambridge that makes it a pernicious place for the training of

---

58. Beverley, *Letter to the Archbishop of York*.

59. Beverley, *Tombs of the prophets*.

60. [Wade], *Extraordinary Black Book*, 160. Beverley's *Sermon preached at Hull*, was sufficient to demonstrate that he was not a believer in the gift of tongues, as the reviewer in the *Eclectic Review* insisted when he said that "those who have called in question the Writer's orthodoxy, will henceforth have no pretence for their calumnious aspersions," 3rd series, 7 (Jan 1832) 44.

61. Beverley, *Letter . . . Cambridge*, 14n.

62. Beverley, *Letter . . . Cambridge*, iv (preface to 3rd ed.).

the nation's clergy, but that the university's emphasis on the classics to the exclusion of any systematic teaching of divinity is similarly inappropriate for clerical preparation, assuming, as it does, that "a future Bishop should be complete master of Greek tragedies and comedies, that a knowledge of the amours of the gods and goddesses, and of the impurity of the classical writers, is the best groundwork for a parson."[63] Beverley's sarcasm is well exemplified in his suggestion that as Blomfield's elevation to be bishop of London, was at least partly based on his scholarly edition of the tragedies of Aeschylus, then (as of course the Church of England is eternal), "some two thousand years hence . . . the then bishops of Africa or Botany Bay will owe their dignities to successful commentaries on Shakespeare's Hamlet and Othello."[64]

Toward the end of his forty-seven page attack, in which he certainly gives no quarter to his opponents, Beverley's sympathy for the evangelical movement begins to emerge in his praise for the work of the "venerable" Charles Simeon who,

> whilst the University was pouring forth floods of immoral, licentious and mischievous men in all parts of the kingdom, and in every rank of life . . . has fostered the cause of Evangelical Religion in the Church of England, till now it can bear his departure, and not sink down extinguished when his torch shall be burnt out.[65]

On the other hand Beverley ventures to qualify his praise, noting that Simeon "has been deficient in not raising a monitory voice against the boundless wickedness, vices and luxury of his University, which for half a century has been going on in geometrical progression before his eyes" with the result that "what is called the 'Simeonite party' is now manifestly degenerating from its former strictness of piety." This in turn lets Beverley revert to the original target of his attack, namely the Established Church, which, in his opinion, the evangelical party will never be able to redeem. The Simeonites, he continues,

> have also lately become more than ever intolerant and bigoted about their rotten idol, the external government and emoluments of the Establishment; more zealous about trifles and carnal things, which till within a few years they left to the sole embraces of their brethren, the High-Church priests. But this is the general malady of the evangelical party throughout England, and is not confined to the clergy connected with Cambridge. To find an evangelical clergyman, with any sparkling of liberality in him, is as rare as to find a diamond of the first water. Nine-tenths of them are black bigots and opaque conservatives.[66]

63. Beverley, *Letter . . . Cambridge*, 35.

64. Quoted in Burns and Stray, "Greek-Play Bishop," 1024. The authors suggest that Beverley's claim was the origin of an accusation that lingered on throughout the 19th century.

65. Beverley, *Letter . . . Cambridge*, 29.

66. Beverley, *Letter . . . Cambridge*, 30. It is noteworthy that Beverley makes mention here of "the many sermons that I have heard him [Simeon] preach."

In the final analysis however, there can be no question that it is the Established Church, which is the true target of Beverley's attacks. In the words of one reviewer, "the religion of the University" according to Beverley, "is as dry and meagre as the sensuality is gross and succulent."[67] Indeed it can be argued that his demolition of the *raison d'être* of the Anglican Establishment proved to be a formative element in the development of most of his subsequent thinking, much of which would be pervasively and characteristically negative. His earlier anti-clericalism was now channeled into a thoroughgoing critique of the ecclesiastical assumptions and *mores* that were the basis for treating the church as an integral part of the state. In his relentless *Letter to His Grace the Archbishop of York* he adopts a remorselessly primitivist position, and with the first-century church as his ideal, Beverley very entertainingly contrasts the church of the apostles (in which, for a start, there were no Diocesan bishops, no tithes, and no church property) with the nineteenth-century Establishment (characterized by "prebends, large livings, archdeaconries, residentiaries, precentorships, chanceries, sub-deaneries, perpetual curacies, fellowships, masterships, [and] vicarages").

Starting from Augustine's description of a bishop in *De Civitate Dei* (19:19), he outlines the primitive ideal in biblical terms:

> A "Bishop" of the apostolical days was some person of the lower orders, a man of mean birth, but of fair character and upright conduct: he was selected to his office for his piety, constancy, and courage—in short, he was a man whom the early Christians could trust; and whether he was a fisherman, a money-changer, a tent-maker, a day-labourer, a common soldier, or a slave, (for all these were "Bishops,") he was expected to give up every thing in this world, to renounce his family, to travel whithersoever the elders of the Church ordered him, to encounter all the danger and difficulties attending the character of one who was a chief of a forbidden religion; and, in fine, to die for the faith if circumstances called him to martyrdom.

In contrast Beverley gives a sarcastic account of "our Baron-Bishops," for whom the experience nearest to "persecution" is to find oneself landed with one of the poorer dioceses (Llandaff or Bristol). The modern bishop's "wrestlings and struggles with Satan" consist of having to vote in the House of Lords to win ministerial approval and translation to a more remunerative see (like Exeter). But even then, the modern "godly" bishop is not at ease and when the plum dioceses (Winchester or Durham) become vacant:

> Then do all the eagles gather together to the carcase: loud are the screams of the apostolical vultures, and sad the dismay of the first Lord of the Treasury, to know how to satisfy so much pious voracity: at last, after undergoing the threats of a dozen great Lords, each eager for his own client, the Premier makes selection of the hero of this picture, and crowns his hopes with

---

67. Anon., "University of Cambridge," 270.

twenty-five thousand pounds a year, and all the gorgeous dignities of the Durham episcopacy.[68]

At which point Beverley goes on to make great play with the bishop's next concern, namely, to find clerical positions for his younger sons who "are probably the very worst sons of Belial that ever fornicated in the porch of the temple."[69] He grants that in fact this isn't the case for the bishop of Durham, who has no children, nor for the archbishop of York (to whom his pamphlet was addressed and one of whose sons had been his personal friend) but Beverley is not afraid to cite an example based on personal knowledge and, without naming names, gives the appalling case of a bishop's son whose conduct had been so dissolute that

> even he [the son] revolted at the idea of going into the Church, and long resisted the importunities and at last the commands, of his Right Reverend Father on this very infamous plan of aggrandizement. Threats, however, were at last employed, and the profligate was compelled to yield, though he did yield at last with a deep sense of shame and disgust. Circumstances have made me intimately acquainted with this transaction, but when it took place, or where, whether in the north or in the south, whether last year, or twelve years ago, I pray your Grace never to ask of me. I know it, and can vouch for it, and let that be sufficient.[70]

This is but one of several occasions when Beverley takes advantage of personal, anecdotal knowledge gleaned from his having frequented such society at Cambridge and elsewhere during the previous decade.[71] After a while however, the repeated contrast between the primitive simplicity of the first century and the gross (and often immoral) worldliness of his own day becomes somewhat tedious, but in his second work the argument that Beverley makes for disestablishment is a powerful, albeit familiar

---

68. Beverley, *Letter to the Archbishop of York*, 9–11.

69. This is a good example of Beverley's familiarity with Scripture, as he makes no mention of Eli's sons, who "were sons of Belial" and "lay with the women who assembled at the door of the tabernacle of the congregation" (1 Sam 2:12, 22) but is clearly drawing the parallel.

70. Ibid., 11–12. This account probably refers to Marcus Gervais Beresford (1801–85), later archbishop of Armagh. He had been RMB's contemporary at Mr. Tate's School and at Trinity College, Cambridge and, when ordained in 1825, was preferred to the rectory of Kildallon, co. Cavan, in his father's diocese (see *ODNB*). His father George, Le Poer Beresford (1765–1841) was, according to the archbishop of Armagh, William Stuart, writing in 1801, when Beresford Sr. was proposed for the bishopric of Kilmore, "reported to be one of the most profligate men in Europe," (MacDonagh, *Viceroy's post-bag*, 99). For other examples of the irreverent conduct and slovenly laziness associated with this disreputable churchman, see Staveley, "Irish Clerics," 77–78.

71. A similar example is his scornful account of George III's inappropriate conduct when struggling to prevent William Pitt from nominating his old tutor, Bishop Pretyman, as archbishop of Canterbury in 1805. Beverley gives no names or dates for the story but claims his account is based on specific personal knowledge (Beverley, *Tombs of the Prophets*, 38). Beverley's details are substantially confirmed by the account in Charles Elrington's letter to J. W. Croker in Jesse, *Memoirs of King George the Third*, 5:228–29.

one. Indeed, in *The Tombs of the Prophets*, where, at some length, he makes the case against Caesaro-papism and its origins in the fourth century, he claims that "having thus given wealth, privileges, and the power of persecution to the Church, he [Constantine] brought Anti-Christ into the world once more, which had been thrown down at the burning of Jerusalem."[72] In this critique his account of the church as it developed after Constantine effectively becomes a history of the evils of priestcraft working hand in hand with the secular authorities, in which, whenever he has a chance, he draws sacerdotal parallels with Babylon, the Druids, Asiatic Russia and even the Grand Lama in Tibet, while minority groups whether Paulician, Cathar, Albigensian, or Lollard are identified as "humble instruments of preserving the Gospel."[73]

Secession to Congregationalism

Having publicly made the case for the disestablishment of the church, it is hardly surprising to find that by 1834, Beverley had severed his own connections with Anglicanism and was associated with the Congregationalists and was taking an active part in their Ecclesiastical Knowledge Society. His criticisms had been severe and were described, with some reason, by a correspondent in the *Times* as "invidious, envenomed and offensive."[74] It is perhaps therefore a little ironic that at just about the same time another book, *Letters to a Dissenting Minister* was taking aim at the Congregationalists, whom Beverley had joined.[75] The identity of its anonymous author was revealed in the fourth edition to be Michael Augustus Gathercole, who, like Beverley, was a quarrelsome man, similarly distempered and aggressively critical, but who, in contrast to Beverley, had abandoned the dissenters among whom he had been reared, and was now an Anglican priest.[76] Inevitably he alluded in this and subsequent polemics to Beverley who was particularly incensed by the fact that the bishop of London had commended Gathercole's book to his clergy and approved of the author's "sound reasoning," though having reservations about his "sharpness of invective."[77]

Beverley's response to Gathercole's work was the last of his published indictments of the evils of the Establishment but it was a singularly ill-judged and tasteless

---

72. Beverley, *Tombs of the prophets*, 27.

73. Ibid., 31.

74. *Times*, 2 Nov 1833.

75. [Gathercole], L.S.E., *Letters to a Dissenting Minister* The initials L.S.E. are the last letters of the author's names [Michae]L [Augustu]S [Gathercol]E.

76. The most thorough discussion of Gathercole's highly litigious and rather disreputable career is Ged Martin, "Michael Augustus Gathercole (c. 1802–1886): Controversial Anglican Cleric," at http://www.gedmartin.net/index.php/martinalia-mainmenu-3/168-michael-augustus-gathercole-c-1802-1886-controversial-anglican-cleric.

77. [Blomfield], *Charge*, appendix C, 54. In various secondary accounts the word "sharpness" is given as "warmth." Ironically the bishop evoked further dissenting indignation by omitting, without explanation, his comments in a later edition.

piece of work. It took the form of a series of satirical letters, supposedly written by Gathercole's brother and others in his circle. The satire is heavily labored and wildly exaggerated, and Beverley couldn't resist making fun of Gathercole's humbler social origins by respelling his name as "Gathercoal."[78] *The Posthumous Letters of the Rev. Rabshakeh Gathercoal* is probably the nadir of Beverley's published work though a reviewer in the *Baptist Magazine* hailed the anonymous author as "the intrepid friend of freedom and religion."[79] With rather better judgment, a writer in the *Eclectic Review* found the rumor that the work was by Beverley confirmed by internal evidence, questioned whether Gathercole was "worth the powder of this firework," and found Beverley's satire "rather too heavy for jest, or too jocose for earnest."[80] At the end of the day, it seems that Beverley had over-played his hand and had exhausted his arsenal of indignation. Another public notice taken of his work was a brief comment in the *Athenaeum*, where the writer felt that Beverley was probably worse even than Gathercole, that he "assails creeds, liturgies, titles and surplices, with equal rancour and under the pretence of vindicating toleration, manifests a spirit of intolerance, belonging more to the year 1535 than to the year 1835."[81]

Although it is clear that early in the 1830s Beverley had broken with the Established Church, it is more difficult to be precise about his subsequent ecclesiastical identity.[82] The Primitive Methodist William Clowes recounts in his journal a visit to the town of Beverley, sometime in late 1831 when his congregation in Beverley chapel included Robert Beverley who "put a half-sovereign in the collection-box" and with whose younger sister, Clowes took supper after the service.[83] A later historian of Primitive Methodism claimed that "Miss Beverley was, at this period, identified with our cause. She was both gifted and devout, and devoted her time and substance to religious and philanthropic purposes, holding services in her own house and sometimes preaching in our Beverley chapel."[84] At a later stage Robert Beverley went to live more permanently in Scarborough, but it is far from clear where his home was in the 1830s and his presence in the Methodist chapel could have been simply the result of his visiting his sister.

On the other hand, as an advocate for the separation of church and state Beverley was clearly aligning himself with the dissenting movement. Indeed as early as July 1831 Joseph Livesey of Preston (1794–1884) noted that although Beverley had been

78. [Beverley], *Posthumous Letters*; the publishers, Westley and Davis, were a Congregational company.

79. *Baptist Magazine* 27 (Jun 1835) 230.

80. *Eclectic Review* 14 (Aug 1835) 161, 163.

81. *Athenaeum*, 2 May 1835, 337.

82. Even when he was still an Anglican, Beverley had felt free to preach in the Independent chapel in Lairgate, Beverley, "Religious Life," in *History of the County of York East Riding*, vol. 6, *Borough and liberties of Beverley* (1989), 231–50, http://www.british-history.ac.uk/report.aspx?compid=36450.

83. Clowes, *Journals*, 313.

84. Kendall, *Primitive Methodist Church*, 396.

very severe in his criticism of the "vestiary hypocrisy" of the established clergy,[85] he himself was now said to have begun preaching "and to give due weight to his ministrations, he appears in *gown and bands*." In doing this, Livesey argued, Beverley had adopted "an appendage of *clerical pride and avarice*." Let Beverley "read over his own burlesque upon clerical dress, and I think, from his honest zeal, he will be led to *strip his own gown*."[86] Three years later his critic Michael Gathercole claimed that Beverley was associated with the Congregationals and had been "seen in one town actually strutting about the streets in a gown and cassock, and bands and hood, in fine style."[87]

This brings us to Beverley's evident penchant for a somewhat extravagant sartorial style, which seems to have given cause for quite some comment. Quoting Beverley's remarks, John Wade, who was himself a fairly merciless critic of the Establishment, noted "Beverley . . . is such a nice connoisseur in drapery, that we suspect him of being a bit of an exquisite himself."[88] These suspicions were confirmed in the most systematic critique of Beverley's *exposée* of the University of Cambridge, which was made by Adam Sedgwick (1785–1873), the Woodwardian Professor, in a series of letters addressed in 1834 to the *Leeds Mercury*, in the course of which the writer recalled Beverley's own personal vanity:

> For chains and chitterlings [frills], for curls and cosmetics, for rings and ringlets, no man was like him. He was indeed a finished and a fragrant fop a very curious coxcomb.[89]

That there was something about Beverley verging on the effeminate is perhaps confirmed in Mary Rowntree's far from critical "Memoir" in which she recalled that "he looked so youthful on the hustings in the castle yard at York during the county election of 1826 that he was spoken of as 'Miss Beverley with the long flaxen ringlets.'"[90]

In a fascinating essay on "The Dissenting Political Upsurge of 1833–34," Professor David Bebbington has shown how although Beverley was mixing and corresponding with Congregationals and Independents, and even attending the dinner hosted by Thomas Wilson for London independent ministers in autumn 1833, his "firebrand temperament" felt that their caution and hesitancy was very irksome.[91]

---

85 "The same farce in clothing is kept up throughout; at balls, the 'successors of the Apostles' must appear clad in black, or any of the shades of black. Thanks, however, to the ingenuity of tailors and haberdashers, such exquisite tints have of late years been discovered in silk stockings and silk waistcoats, such delicious varieties of light black, raven black, french black, and french whites—the black has been softened into winning lavender-tints, and the white has been so dexterously made to blush a morning blush, that it requires very great ingenuity to discover a layman from a Priest in a brilliant ball-room." Beverley, *Letter to the Archbishop of York*, 26.

86. *Moral Reformer* 1.7 (Jul 1831) 217.

87. Gathercole, *Letter to Charles Lushington*, 74.

88. [Wade], *Extraordinary Black Book*, 160.

89. Clark and Hughes, *Life and Letters of Sedgwick*, 1:411.

90. Rowntree, "Memoir," 326.

91. Bebbington, "Dissenting Political Upsurge," 236.

Having thrown down the gauntlet in no uncertain terms he expected others to do the same, and found the political radicalism of provincial dissent more congenial than the metropolitan ministers who, he claimed, were "pluming themselves on being what they call 'respectable,'" and therefore distancing themselves from him.[92]

Admiration for the Quakers

Whether he was swayed by the protests of critics more radical than himself, or whether, as is more likely, it was his own inexorable logic that was responsible, by the mid 1830s Beverley was moving away from Congregationalism and was frequenting and appreciating the company of several members of the Society of Friends. Indeed in 1836 in a series of published letters addressed to John Angell James (1785–1859), one of the Congregational ministers who had been too cautious for his own "firebrand temperament," Beverley's developing ecclesiology became apparent when he gave the Quakers the credit for having "proclaimed the truth concerning the priesthood" and for "entirely leveling every remnant of distinction between clergy and laity."[93]

On the other hand Beverley had other reasons for liking the Quakers, not least their record in campaigning for social justice. As early as 1824, the young Beverley had taken part in the public demands for the abolition of slavery in the West Indies,[94] and just ten years later he was preaching a sermon at the Independent Chapel, Scarborough, on *Christ victorious* to commemorate the extinction of British colonial slavery.[95] Although in December 1833 he had unsuccessfully written to Joseph Sturge, requesting support from the Society of Friends in his campaign for disestablishment,[96] Beverley still admired Sturge's unremitting efforts to bring slavery to an end.

It is commonly thought that the Emancipation Act of 1833 abolished slavery in the British colonies, and it is often forgotten that in the West Indies a system of apprenticeship allowed slave-owners effectively to retain control of their erstwhile slaves. One of the great campaigners against this state of affairs was Joseph Sturge himself, as a result of whose work, the apprenticeship system was abolished in 1838.[97] It was precisely this sort of radical activism that won the admiration of Robert Beverley rather

---

92. Letter from R. M. Beverley to Joshua Wilson (20 Feb 1834) in Congregational Library MSS cited in Bebbington, "Dissenting Political Upsurge," 236.

93. Beverley, *Letters on the Present State*, 21–22. This was expanded subsequently into his *Heresy of a human priesthood*.

94. W. Beverley et al., *Speeches delivered in the town-hall of Beverley*.

95. Beverley, *Christ victorious*.

96. Tyrrell, *Joseph Sturge*, 68.

97. On the basis of his careful observations, when travelling through the West Indies, Sturge and his companion Thomas Harvey were able to expose the injustice and ineffectiveness of the system; see Sturge and Harvey, *West Indies in 1837*.

than other more familiar heroes.[98] In June 1838 reflecting what has been called the "statumania" of his time, he could write:

> They are going to erect some huge monument to the Conqueror of Waterloo at an immense expense—to commemorate a victory, which has eminently failed in all it's [sic] political intentions—but why not erect some colossal something to Joseph [Sturge]? Let us have him in bronze striding over the rail-road, at the entrance into Birmingham, higher than the Church steeples, & with a broad brim 30 feet in diameter.[99]

For Beverley, the Quaker combination of social activism with their rejection of almost any vestige of an ordained, let alone sacerdotal, priesthood was well nigh irresistible, but his involvement with Friends came at a critical moment in the Society's own development. In the course of the 1830s the growing rift between the Inner Light Quakers and the more evangelical wing of the movement, who emphasized the authority of Scripture, was becoming increasingly apparent.[100] Inevitably, given his respect for the primitive example of biblical Christianity, Beverley's sympathies were with the evangelical Quakers, especially with the Howard family of Tottenham and the Lloyds of Birmingham, to the hospitality of whose domestic life he responded warmly. There were indeed moments when the gentleness of the Quaker lifestyle could be at odds with Beverley's acerbic ruthlessness in debate. It was Rachel, the wife of Samuel Lloyd, who was once pained by some of Beverley's caustic criticism and rebuked him "for sitting in the seat of the scornful."[101] On the other hand the intellectual and scientific interests of the Howards meant that they were kindred spirits for Beverley's naturally inquisitive mind.

Equally inevitably however, Beverley was only too ready to encourage these evangelical Friends when they dared to question traditional Quaker beliefs on biblical grounds. The sacraments of baptism and communion were cases in point. The Quaker tradition sat lightly to these ordinances and claimed that all life should be lived sacramentally. Friends took seriously the many places in the New Testament where the unimportance of external rituals was emphasized (e.g., Gal 5:1–5), while drawing attention to the inconsistency of other Christians in not perpetuating the washing of each others' feet in the way that Christ had enjoined on his disciples (John 13:14). For them spiritual baptism was more important than water baptism and any simple meal could be an occasion for spiritual communion and sustenance. In contrast, the

---

98. In December 1837 we find Beverley delivering an address in Hull on the horrors of the apprenticeship system for the ostensibly free slaves, after which the mayor, another great abolitionist, George Cookman, moved a vote of thanks to Beverley; http://www.hull.ac.uk/mhsc/FarHorizons/Documents/Cookman.pdf.

99. Quoted from a MS in the Sturge papers, in Tyrrell "Bearding the Tories," 32.

100. For further details of these Quaker developments, see above, ch. 2.

101. Lowe, *Farm and its inhabitants*, 68. Beverley was apparently somewhat surprised at Rachel Lloyd's rebuke and later remarked to one of her sons, "Mrs. Lloyd has been giving me such a rap on my knuckles."

Evangelical Friends, who took the New Testament more seriously than any personal revelation of the "Inner Light," were finding that water baptism was an integral part of the Lord's evangelistic commission to his disciples, and that the early Christians observed the Lord's Supper on a regular weekly basis.

In the matter of baptism, the Howard family had taken the lead. To the consternation of his sister Rachel, John Eliot Howard and his wife, Maria, were baptized in August 1836 and resigned from the Society of Friends two months later.[102] Late in 1837 in the last issue of his Quaker magazine the *Yorkshireman*, John's father Luke Howard, the meteorologist, announced that he had decided "that the Friends and I can no more 'walk together' except we were better 'agreed,' [and that he had] submitted to the rite of baptism and communicated with a church of Christ." He had also stopped attending Friends' meetings for worship, and was "accordingly looking to be excluded from membership."[103] It was in the following year (1838) that the Howard family established a Brethren assembly in Tottenham,[104] and in October of the same year, Robert Beverley, who, unlike his Quaker friends *had* been baptized as a child, was baptized by immersion by Henry Bulteel at Oxford. Prior to the baptism, Beverley preached a sermon presenting the reasons for treating the ordinance as an obligation as well as the case against infant baptism. Just one month later his friend Samuel Lloyd, a leading Quaker in Birmingham was also baptized.[105] There is no record of Beverley having formally become a Quaker, but he had followed with interest the process by which Samuel Lloyd was (in his own words) "marvellously extricated" from Quakerism and had then became "the leader of a small Brethren group in Birmingham."[106]

Attraction to the Brethren

It is clear too that Beverley was in full sympathy with his friends in the development of their Brethren identity as can be seen from a long letter written from Birmingham to Robert Howard in July 1838, in which Beverley describes, amongst other things, his efforts to find accommodation for Charles Hargrove, a Brethren minister, who was planning to settle and minister in the area.[107] But, in spite of his involvement

---

102. L. H[oward], *Memoranda of Rachel Howard*, 233. Rachel herself was baptized shortly before her death in 1837.

103. *Yorkshireman* 5.120 (1837) 387. In view of his declaration it was perhaps somewhat ingenuous for Luke Howard, after his disownment in 1837, to publish his *Appeal to the Christian Public*.

104. "Tottenham: Protestant Nonconformity," in *History of the County of Middlesex*, vol. 5, *Hendon, Kingsbury, Great Stanmore, Little Stanmore, Edmonton Enfield, Monken Hadley, South Mimms, Tottenham* (1976), 356–64. http://www.british-history.ac.uk/report.aspx?compid=26995.

105. *Inquirer* 1 (Nov 1838) 351.

106. Lloyd, *Quaker Lloyds*, 263.

107. R. M. Beverley to Robert Howard, 8 Jul [1838], Greater London Record Office, Howard Papers, Acc. 1017/15. For Charles Hargrove's secession to join the Brethren in Ireland in 1835 see Rowdon, *Origins*, 102. For some of his later views, see above, ch. 9n64.

with Brethren, some of Beverley's critics seem to have been unable to keep up with his ecclesiastical evolution. In 1836 Beverley had crossed swords with the respected Congregational Minister, John Angell James of Birmingham in a series of *Letters on the Present State of the Visible Church of Christ*.[108] Commenting, in a review of the book, on Beverley's propensity for controversy, a writer in the *Eclectic Review* described Beverley as a reformer who "might be mistaken for a gladiator"—tendencies that the reviewer found somewhat perverse in one whose "opinions most closely approximate . . . to . . . the views and principles by which the Society of Friends has been most prominently distinguished."[109] Two years later in May 1839 a writer in the same review complained of the destructive intentions of the Plymouth Brethren, drawing attention to the negative criticism that characterized their writings which he contrasted unfavorably with the "friendly suggestions of amelioration" that characterized Beverley's recent pamphlet "although (like a valuable watch dog), his bark is rather too sharp to please our nerves."[110] In fact the reviewer's reluctance to recognize that Beverley was also now effectively a Plymouth Brother may have been a bit of wishful thinking. Responding to this claim, a writer in the *Inquirer* maintained that it was "quite obvious" to any reader of Beverley's *Letters* to John Angell James, that the author "substantially holds those very views" of which the *Eclectic* was so critical. Indeed, in a footnote, the writer in the *Inquirer* drew attention to the "many additions" in the second edition of Beverley's *Letters* which "with the new title of 'The Heresy of a Human Priesthood,' exhibits a still closer approximation of sentiment to the Plymouth Brethren."[111]

Whether an ecclesiastical maverick like Beverley can be thought to have ever become truly a part of the Brethren movement is hard to say. When, in 1842, the Brethren at Hereford were challenged by their former rector John Venn in a pamphlet on *The Christian Ministry and Church Membership*, it was Beverley who took up the cudgels in their defense. In 1840 he had published *An Inquiry into the Scriptural Doctrine of Christian Ministry*,[112] and now he produced what he considered to be a supplement to his earlier work. In *The Church of England examined by Scripture and tradition* he relentlessly set out to demolish Venn's position. True as ever to his anticlerical self, Beverley now insisted that this was not simply a replay of the old "recriminations between the clergymen of the two universities and the clergymen of

---

108. Beverley, *Letters on the Present State*.

109. *Eclectic Review*, n.s., 1 (Jan 1837) 89. He quoted Beverley as saying: "The rule and doctrine of the Quakers are certainly not *perfect*, but it would be difficult to prove that any other sect has approached nearer to perfection; and though there are in other sects to be found some good things which are wanting among the Quakers, yet, on the other hand, they are in possession of valuable truths which have no practical power among other denominations." Beverley, *Letters on the Present State*, 209.

110. *Eclectic Review*, n.s., 5 (May 1839) 571.

111. *Inquirer* 2 (July 1839) 344, see Beverley, *Heresy of a Human Priesthood*.

112. Beverley, *Inquiry into . . . Christian Ministry*. For the situation in Hereford, see above, ch. 13nn50–55.

the dissenting colleges," but rather that he was laying the axe to the root of the tree, making "a deep incision into the very root of *all* clerisy."[113] But, now some ten or more years after his earlier forays into ecclesiastical affairs, he finds that where he had once been a "reformer" to whom quite a number of worthy clergy had turned for encouragement, the situation is significantly changed both for the worse and for the better:

> But let these things pass, as, indeed, all the dreams of those days have passed away. The sober reality of increasing darkness, the disappointment of all grades of reformers, the increase of superstition, and the augmentation of priestcraft, now make it certain that the light of that era was the glare of a meteor, not the dawning of that morning which is to be without any clouds.

When Beverley speaks of the augmentation of priestcraft he is alluding to the Tractarian movement, which he claims has clarified the issue and left the evangelical clergy in an impossible position, and consequently there is now a new ecclesiastical landscape:

> Visitations of sorrow have sobered down the zeal of some, the love of this world has drawn others into apostasy, some have withdrawn into despair, others have retreated into superstition, some have "run greedily into the error of Balaam for reward," and others, comparatively a few it may be, have advanced onwards, *taught* every step of their way by grace, and now understand what it is to be wholly free, in body, soul, and spirit, from all man's innovations in the house of Christ: are released from all sects, liberated from all forms of clerical error, and yet more deeply and sweetly addicted to the service of *that great one*, who, revealing to his elect that his government is through his word and Spirit only, emancipates them from human trappings to make them carry more faithfully his easy yoke and his light burthen.[114]

Clearly, in this last group, Beverley is speaking of the Brethren with whom he has identified. Indeed he even recommends to his readers several Brethren works which together with his own *Inquiry into the Scriptural Doctrine of Christian Ministry* were all published by the Brethren publishing house, in Warwick Square, Paternoster Row. But could the Brethren contain such a "stormy petrel of a man?"[115] The 1840s were turbulent years for the Brethren—years in which their pristine idealism was tarnished by bitter dispute. A controversialist like Beverley was unlikely to be a bystander detached from the strife. For a time he seems to have felt some affinity with Darby's exposition of Scripture, but when Beverley published his own (hostile) analysis of Newton's *Thoughts on the Apocalypse*[116] his criticisms (albeit anonymous) are unmistakably the work of Beverley the liberal Reformer.

113. Beverley, *Church of England examined*, iii.
114. Ibid., v.
115. The phrase is David Bebbington's in "Dissenting Political Upsurge," 236.
116. [Beverley], *Analysis*.

In his critique, Beverley focuses on the centrality of Babylon in Newton's eschatological interpretation, which, he claims, reveals the writer's extreme social conservatism. One cannot help feeling that his analysis of Newton's work is a wildly exaggerated interpretation which serves to demonstrate the huge gulf between Beverley's enlightened liberalism and the ultra-conservative reverence for antiquity that characterized so many of Newton's fellow Brethren. With various references to the universities (reminiscent of his earlier excoriation of his *alma mater*), Beverley suggests that Newton's private feelings "having been first nurtured in the cloisters of Oxford," owe "a good deal . . . to the external impressions of that antique abode of study." In Beverley's opinion Newton's thinking is "deeply imbued with those political ideas which are now scarcely any where to be found, but which used to be too well known in that sorrowful aera [*sic*] when the Stuart dynasty was waging its long war of treachery or violence against the English Constitution. Mr. Newton's feelings about Government are not *Conservative* (according to the modern phrase)—they are the antique ultra-Tory [attitudes] of the closing days of the House of Stuart."[117]

With typical exaggeration, Beverley winds up with a characterization of Newton, which is barely recognizable:

> Wherever there is a constitution, or wherever the plenitude of arbitrary dominion is checked by any safeguard of any popular law or charter—wherever the rights of the people are protected by any legal provision, so as that the people may recognize their *rights* and feel an interest in them, there Mr. Newton sees criminality and corruption, and a provocation of the wrath of God. His favourite pattern of government, is the gorgeous imperial sovereignty of the mighty Nebuchadnezzar, to whom, as to a sort of representative of all Gentile kings, he imagines was intrusted the form, and order, and license of all other governments. To rule like that leviathan of the Chaldean empire with absolute and uncontrolled sway, without any let or hindrance from nobles or people, without any whisper of intervening laws, customs, privileges, immunities, codes, or charters granted to the people, or obtained by the sense of their own need,—this, in Mr. Newton's thoughts, is a holy and divine form of government.[118]

From which point, the critic isolates elements in Newton's thinking, which not only favor royalist absolutism and are scornful of any form of democratic progress but are even disdainful of commercial wealth or prosperity.

Final Isolation

We need not take Beverley's analysis any further, as the purpose of this extract is to demonstrate in what an impossible position he now found himself. By a process of

---

117. Ibid., 18.
118. Ibid., 19.

elimination, his deep antipathy to any form of clerisy had driven him from the Establishment, by way of Congregationalism and then the Quakers to associate with the Brethren, most of whose leaders were, in his perception, part of a social world that was totally opposed to his own liberal ideals. Some of his *quondam* fellow Quakers might be like-minded but they were in a decided minority. Ironically when it came to the great so-called Bethesda division, Beverley found himself defending Newton's orthodoxy and rejecting Darby's arbitrary excommunication of those with whom he disagreed.[119] But for our Yorkshire maverick, this was an ecclesiastical cul-de-sac.

Two decades later when he died in Scarborough in November 1868, Beverley was an isolated figure with no active connection with any particular religious community. Increasingly he had withdrawn into his own world and for these last decades of his life, there are few, other than published, traces of the man. A scholar to the end of his life, he now devoted himself to intellectual and literary pursuits, commenting on the affairs of the day in literary epigrams, and poems, the best known of which is *The Redan*, celebrating the moral heroism of the British army in the Crimea, in a manner reminiscent of the evangelical *Memorials of Captain Hedley Vicars*.[120] Just a year before his death he published an anonymous critique of Darwin's *Origin of Species* in which, controversialist to the end, he "entertained a hope that if there be yet Goliaths in the world, there may be still found some smooth stones of the brook adequate for the formidable duel."[121] But Beverley's world had changed. Financially he had long been in difficulty, supposedly as a result of his father's financial recklessness, and now, he retired to a small house in Scarborough. Like many another impoverished person of his class, he spent time on the continent where his few English sovereigns could eke out a more comfortable lifestyle. There was a final irony in those later years of his life, when, spiritually isolated, this inveterate opponent of "priestcraft" frequently spent his winters in (of all places) Rome itself. Recalling this anomaly Eliot Howard observed: "When living in Rome, although a staunch Protestant, he was, I believe on fairly intimate terms with many of the learned Roman Ecclesiastics, who, however, may not have much relished the lampoons in faultless hexameters, which he launched at Pius IX about the notorious Mortara[122] case and other lapses from strict rectitude."[123] It was a strangely inconclusive and incongruous ending to a turbulent and unsettled life.

---

119. Newton's comment on Beverley is to the point: "He attacked my book on the Apocalypse with great severity and satire. Afterwards when I was assailed on the subject of the Person of the Lord, he defended me most vigorously." Wyatt MS (JRULM, CBA 7060) 6:80.

120. Beverley, *Redan*. In this Beverley was at odds with the pacifism of Sir Lancelot Brenton and other Plymouth Brethren.

121. [Beverley], *Darwinian theory*, iv.

122. The Mortara case in 1859 concerned a Jewish child who was kidnapped from his home in Bologna and taken to Rome, with the authorization of Pope Pius IX, on the grounds that he had been secretly baptized by a servant girl when he was a baby, see Kertzer, *Kidnapping of Edgardo Mortara*.

123. Eliot Howard "Memorandum," see above, n23.

16

Arthur Augustus Rees

The Sailor Who Became the "Pope of the North"[1]

Family and Naval Career

THERE WAS LITTLE PREDICTABLE about the career of Arthur Augustus Rees (1815–1884) who was the seventh child of a landowner in Carmarthen, South Wales. His childhood was unsettled. For reasons that his biographers[2] declined to reveal, his father John lived for some years in France, while his mother Anne (daughter of the American consul in Bristol, Elias Vander Horst), took little interest in her youngest son with the result that "from the age of five to thirteen he was tossed about the country at various schools."[3]

In 1828 when Arthur was thirteen, his father (who had earlier seen service at the battles of Camperdown and Copenhagen) returned from France and obtained for him a position in the Royal Navy as a first-class volunteer. The boy's naval service lasted some five years with a few months break on land in 1831–32 after which he was promoted to the rank of midshipman and served mainly in Portuguese waters. During his earlier period of service (on HMS Wasp) in the aftermath of the Battle of Navarino (1827), Rees's boat was sailing in the eastern Mediterranean and this gave him a chance to see several classical sites including Athens, Thermopylae, Pompeii and Carthage as well as to land in Algiers just after the French had captured it in 1830. There were several moments when his life was in danger—moments perceived by his biographers as occasions when he was spared for "higher service"—but he was not involved in hostile engagements in the way that a slightly older generation of "naval

---

1. This essay was published in *BAHNR* 4 (2006) 22–35, as "Early Development of Arthur Augustus Rees and His Relations with the Brethren."

2. There are three basic sources for Rees's life. The earliest was written during Rees's lifetime, by a Methodist and reflects the author's dislike of the Establishment. Anglican episcopacy is never let off lightly in Everett, *Midshipman* (1867). Everett's work was used by both William Brockie, *Memoirs of Rees* (1884), and, very much more recently by Sydney E. Watson, *Bethesda Free Chapel* (1945). For details of Everett see the article by O. A. Beckerlegge in *BDEB*.

3. Everett, *Midshipman*, 6. The statement is repeated almost *verbatim* by Brockie, *Memoirs of Rees*, 4, and Watson, *Bethesda Free Chapel*, 10. However, his admission papers at Lampeter refer to a school at Hammersmith; see n11.

brethren" had been.⁴ Being a somewhat headstrong lad, Rees found himself more than once on a collision course with his superiors and on several occasions (as one would expect in the British navy of the early nineteenth century) he was subjected to corporal punishment. His being "invalided" out in 1833 was at his own request after just such a confrontation with his commander.

One of the earlier occasions when Rees was the object of naval discipline is of some significance as the man who ordered the lashing would later become a Plymouth Brother. The Honorable William H. G. Wellesley (1806–75) appears to have been in charge of HMS Wasp sometime between 1829 and early 1830⁵ when, on at least one occasion, he ordered Rees to be flogged. Sometime in 1833 or later⁶ Wellesley left the navy from conscientious motives. For a time his "speaking-trumpet of a voice" rendered him something of a celebrity with those who attended the meetings of the evangelical societies at Exeter Hall⁷ but by 1840 he was definitely associated with the Brethren.⁸ Rees, in whose chapel Wellesley later preached on several occasions, recalled that his senior officer's conversion two years before he took charge of HMS Wasp had "originated in the contemplation of the horrors of the battle of Navarino" in October 1827.⁹

Conversion and the "Lampeter Brethren" (1833–41)

Arthur Rees's situation on leaving the navy is far from clear. He had a good singing voice and, having learnt to play the guitar, he spent some time in London on the fringes of the theatrical world and toyed with the idea of a career in entertainment, but he seems to have had no gainful employment during these three years. Equally imprecise are the circumstances attendant on his conversion. There is mention of a

---

4. Both Leonard Strong (1797–1874) and W. G. Rhind (1794–1863) had been in active service during the Napoleonic Wars, Pickering, *Chief Men*, 22–24. See also the following paragraph, for the naval experience of W. H. G. Wellesley.

5. There are fuller details of Rees's early naval career in Everett, *Midshipman*, 7–19, where Wellesley is said to have succeeded Richard Dickenson as commanding officer of the Wasp prior to Brunswick Popham's appointment. In P. Benyon's "Index to Late 18th, 19th, and early 20th century naval and naval social history" (http://www.pbenyon1.plus.com/Extracts/1828/;1829/1830), the Wasp is described as being in the charge of Dickenson (from Aug 1828) presumably until his appointment in May 1830 to be in charge of HMS Talbot. Popham's appointment to the Wasp is given as 31 May 1830. There is no reference to Wellesley being in charge of the Wasp, though there appears to have been an interim period in late 1829 to early 1830 when someone other than Dickenson was in charge.

6. His resignation from the navy cannot have been before his return in HMS Winchester from Jamaica in May 1833 (http://www.pbenyon1.plus.com/Extracts/1833/02.html).

7. Anon., *Random Recollections*, 16–17, cited in J. H. Newman's review of the book in *British Critic* 24 (Jul 1838) 207, 201.

8. See Rowdon, *Origins*, 167, 169, and Pickering, *Chief Men*, 40. For Wellesley's preaching in 1844 in Sheffield, see Stanley, *Way the Lord hath led me*, text available online, http://bibletruthpublishers.com/chapter-2/charles-stanley/incidents-of-gospel-work/c-stanley/la61452.

9. Everett, *Midshipman*, 12.

rebuke from his sister, which led him, for a while, to say the Lord's prayer in his hammock during his second period of service, but more important was the testimony of one of his brothers in 1834 or 1835 to some aspect of prophecy and its fulfillment. This stimulated the nineteen-year-old to study his Bible as a result of which he adopted a more serious approach to life and after further study became a "thorough-going" Christian.[10] Evidence for the single-mindedness of this new convert is to be found in his buying grammars and teaching himself Latin and Greek during the next few months. This must have been a significant factor in his winning the support of some Bristol clergymen who raised funds for him to attend St. David's College, Lampeter where he was admitted as a student on 1 March 1836.[11]

In the same month, another serious young man, four years older than Rees, entered the college, and, together with Rees, was a student there for the next three years preparing for ordination. Henry James Prince (1811–99) is one of the more unusual of the many strange personalities, who enliven the religious history of the nineteenth century.[12] The youngest son of a West Indian plantation owner, Prince was born in Bath and was brought up by his impoverished mother and her lodger, Martha Freeman. After studying medicine at Guy's Hospital he was appointed as medical officer to the General Hospital in Bath but resigned in 1835. A little earlier he had experienced an evangelical conversion and was now intent on ordination. It was with Prince that Arthur Rees was closely associated for the next three years at St. David's College, where they were at the centre of a group of earnest Christian students known as the "Lampeter Brethren." Although the college authorities disapproved of their meetings and their exaggerated piety, this did not prevent Rees from being elected Hannah More scholar in 1837 and Butler scholar in 1838.[13] When he graduated in 1839 or 1840 Rees appears to have spent some time at Prince's home in Bath where he met Prince's sister Ellen (whom he later married) and where he received an invitation to become the curate of the Rev. William Webb, rector of Sunderland to whom he had been recommended by his tutor at Lampeter, Alfred Ollivant (1798–1882), later bishop of Llandaff.

---

10. Brockie, *Memoirs of Rees*, 11, cf. Everett, *Midshipman*, 23–25. Rees's early biographers agree in presenting his conversion as the result of personal study and reflection rather than a response to his brother's challenge. Watson however has Rees trusting Christ in response to his converted brother's testimony and then setting about studying the Scriptures, Watson, *Bethesda Free Chapel*, 14.

11. I am indebted to Professor Nigel Yates, the keeper of archives and manuscripts at the University of Wales, Lampeter for his provision of the archival details of Rees's career at Lampeter.

12. For Prince see my article in *ODNB*, which contains a full bibliography, and the article by Andrew Walls in *BDEB*.

13. For the few known details of the Lampeter Brethren, see Wilson, "Prince and the Lampeter Brethren," 10–20. For a sample of the "exaggerated piety," see Prince, *Letters . . . to his Christian Brethren*.

Ministry and Prohibition in Sunderland and Bath (1841–44)

Rees was ordained by the bishop of Durham in January 1841, but his career as a minister in the Church of England was to be a short one. His total commitment to the evangelical faith seems to have marked him out as bit of an eccentric who would not mince his words and who was not very adept in the worldly skills of diplomacy and tact. It seems that as curate of Sunderland most of his ministry was performed in a daughter church, St. John's Chapel, rather than in the more respectable Parish Church of Holy Trinity. For a while Rees appears to have been given quite a free hand and his congregation grew, as did his popularity. In November 1841 however he was invited to preach at Houghton-le-Spring whose curate had been a fellow mid-shipman with Rees. Here his audience was a little more refined and complaints were made to the bishop about some of his uncompromising language. When asked for a copy of his sermon, Rees had to admit that it had been delivered extempore at which point the bishop forbad him to preach outside his own parish and gave him strict instructions to write his sermons out in full. In spite of these developments he was ordained as a priest in December of 1841 and a further nine months elapsed before his rector's patience was exhausted and Rees was given three months' notice to quit. The local press gave an approvingly sympathetic account of Rees's farewell sermon to a "serious and attentive congregation" of some three thousand people, "spell-bound by the thrilling fervency of his warning and appeal." They also published a cheap edition of the text of the sermon, which characteristically "was commenced and concluded with extempore prayer."[14] Although a local petition was drawn up requesting the bishop to license Rees "to preach in connexion with the Established Church in the Bridge Road Chapel, Monkwearmouth,"[15] the bishop refused and found further fault with Rees for allowing former parishioners to visit him for pastoral help in his lodgings.[16] Early in 1843 Rees, who in the previous year had married Ellen Prince, left Sunderland and returned to Bath to stay with her family.

In Bath Rees was not without friends and after some unsuccessful applications he was invited by Sydney Widdrington, the rector of Walcott St. Swithin, to take responsibility for a chapel in Thomas Street that he (the rector) had recently bought from the Baptists and in September his appointment was announced.[17] Rees predictably took up his duties, as his rector later bore witness, "with zeal and energy . . . specially

---

14. *Sunderland and Durham County Herald*, 9 Dec 1842, 2, column G; see also Rees, *Farewell sermon*.

15. *Sunderland and Durham County Herald*, 13 Jan 1843, 2, column B.

16. Everett, *Midshipman*, 40.

17. *Sunderland and Durham County Herald*, 19 Sep 1843, 5, column C. Watson, *Bethesda Free Chapel*, 21, wrongly refers to *Thames* Street Chapel. A subsequent minister, the Rev. Peter Hall is said to have called the chapel *Saint* Thomas's Chapel even though the name was originally derived from the street, which was named after a shoemaker named Thomas Cottle, see Peach, *Street-lore of Bath*, 141. I am indebted for this reference and other help to Mr. Colin Johnston of the Bath and North East Somerset Record Office.

among the poorer population."[18] However for his appointment to be canonically confirmed and licensed by the bishop, the testimonials, provided by seven Anglican incumbents and countersigned by two bishops, had to be endorsed by the bishop of Durham who adamantly declined to do so. In spite of the protests of both the rector and congregation, Rees was evicted from his ministry without an hour's warning.[19]

Rees later came to believe that he was "born to be a dissenter" but he preferred the label nonconformist because "dissenter implies opposition to doctrines, whereas I was never opposed to the doctrine of the Establishment. Nonconformity imports opposition to discipline, polity and rites."[20] He gave brief but cogent expression to his indignation at the treatment he had received by publishing in Bath a *Solemn protest before the church and nation*[21] but by the middle of March he had returned to Sunderland where he was welcomed by many of his former parishioners who immediately formed the nucleus of a new congregation acknowledging Rees as their pastor. A year later in March 1845, Bethesda Free Chapel, Sunderland was opened and it was here that Rees ministered until his death almost forty years later.

In the words of Harold Rowdon, who perceptively included a miniature account of Rees's career in *The Origins of the Brethren*:

> Rees shed many of his Anglican ideas, and at the close of 1845 sent for George Müller, who had become acquainted with him, to baptize him as a believer. The church, which he gathered never developed into a Brethren assembly, however, since Rees retained an almost autocratic ministerial position as well as a somewhat eccentric style. There remained a close and warm link between Rees and Müller, at least, among the Brethren.[22]

Henry Prince and the Charlinch Revival (1838–42)

At this point however, it is necessary to re-examine the events of 1839–44 that we have considered, but in a wider context and to do this we must go back to Rees's circle of friends when he finished at Lampeter. Henry James Prince was an Anglican but his sympathies lay primarily with evangelical Christianity and there are indications that he was in touch with Brethren. His journal records a visit in August 1835 to Sir C[harles] B[renton] who was connected with the Brethren in Bath.[23] Three years later in July 1838 he attended services at Clifton at which Henry Craik and George Müller

---

18. In a letter dated 13 February 1843, quoted in full in Watson, *Bethesda Free Chapel*, 21–22.
19. *Sunderland and Durham County Herald*, 16 Feb 1844, 5, column A.
20. Watson, *Bethesda Free Chapel*, 19, 23.
21. Rees, *Solemn protest*.
22. Rowdon, *Origins*, 173–74.
23. H. J. Prince, *Prince's Journal*, 14. For Brenton's connection with Bath see Stunt, *From Awakening*, 296–98.

preached to Prince's great satisfaction. He noted in his journal that Müller's "praying was in the style of a *child* addressing his father with reverence and confidence; his appearance solemn and impressive; his manner of preaching very mild and persuasive. Our spirits clave to him."[24] A little earlier than Rees, Prince had been ordained in 1839. In June 1840 he became curate of Charlinch, near Bridgewater, Somerset, where the rector, Samuel Starky, was permanently absent on account of ill health. Prince labored for a year on his own in this rural parish with very little sign of his ministry having any impact on its bucolic population. However, in the summer of 1841, when Rees in Sunderland had just begun to make an impression on his urban flock, things changed for Prince. By a curious chance, his rector, who believed he was near to death, was given and read a copy of a sermon by Prince and after reading it made a full recovery.[25] He hastened back to Charlinch to find that his curate was beginning to make an impression on the parish.

Prince's account of his success in Charlinch makes clear that he used a variety of far from conventional evangelistic activities.[26] Weekly prayer meetings became the order of the day, women sobbed and cried out, children collapsed under conviction of sin. When Prince tried to separate the parishioners whom he believed to be "truly converted," from the traditional churchgoers he upset some of the local gentry and in May 1842 the bishop dismissed him from his curacy.[27] Probably with help from Starky's good social connections[28] Prince obtained another remote curacy at Stoke-by-Clare in Suffolk but by November 1842 the bishop of Ely had also prohibited him from preaching.

Adventist Expectations, Rejection and the Brethren

At this juncture we should glance briefly at an even wider framework for these unusual events. In the United States the followers of William Miller had proclaimed 1842–43 as the year of Christ's return. Miller's impact on British society was much less dramatic but the letters of the Adventist Robert Winter (1817–1909) indicate that there was fertile ground for the Millerite seed of millennial preaching.[29] It was only

24. H. J. Prince, *Prince's Journal*, 352.

25. This part of the story is dependent on the much later account given by Starky to Hepworth Dixon, see Dixon, *Spiritual Wives*, 240. There is no surviving sermon of Prince published in 1841. However Starky may have seen an earlier edition of Prince, *Strength in Jesus* (1842), or Prince, *How you may know* (1842).

26. Prince, *Charlinch revival*, 7–13.

27. See Schwieso, "Founding of the Agapemone," 114.

28. His maternal grandfather was Sir Andrew Baynton-Rolt, 2nd Bt, whose wife was a daughter of the 6th Earl of Coventry.

29. See Robert Winter's letters from England dated May and Nov 1843 published in the *Midnight Cry* for 1843 and 1844, quoted in ch. 10 of Nichol, *Midnight Cry*, which can be consulted online at www.maranathamedia.com.au. There are other reasons to believe that millennial expectations were

in 1844 with the "great disappointment" that the popular response began to wane.[30] It is in this context that we should consider Prince's unusually wild revivalism. He now moved back nearer to his previous area of ministry. While Starky went to work in Weymouth, Prince began preaching in Adullam Chapel, Brighton. Now, however he was an independent evangelist proclaiming that his rejection by the Established Church was not only proof of its apostasy but a further sign of the imminent return of Christ. The parallel with the experiences of Arthur Rees in Sunderland and Bath is immediately apparent, as both of them had been turned out of the Establishment. The more critical of Prince's biographers however draw attention to another less attractive aspect of his conduct. Whereas Rees had recently married Prince's impecunious sister, Prince's somewhat unexpected first marriage in 1838, when he was a student at Lampeter, to his mother's considerably older (and wealthier) lodger, Martha Freeman, had been financially more advantageous. When she died in April 1842 and, barely three months later, Prince married Julia Starky, the sister of his well-connected former rector, there was, hardly surprisingly, some adverse comment.[31] In the days before the Married Women's Property Act (1882), a wife's assets were automatically at the disposal of her husband. To the more cynical observer therefore, Prince seemed to have realized that, without a position in the Church of England, he would need some other source of financial support.[32]

Nevertheless, by early 1843, many evangelical Christians in the West Country were aware that there were two enthusiastic evangelists, recently cast off by the Establishment, Arthur Rees and Henry Prince, both of whom had been in touch with Brethren and indeed were regarded favorably by them. One Brethren evangelist in particular, James George Deck (1807–1884),[33] a leading member of the Brethren

---

high at this time. It is possible that J. N. Darby may have expected the Second Coming to occur in 1842, see Coad, *History of the Brethren*, 118. For other exaggerated adventist expectations among Plymouth Brethren in France on the last day of 1844, see Gribben and Stunt, *Prisoners of Hope*, 66.

30. The progress of the Millerites in England is well covered in Billington, "Millerite Adventists in Great Britain," in Numbers and Butler, *Disappointed*, 59–77.

31. Typically hostile is the account of Prince's marriages in Mander, *Reverend Prince*, 53, 67. Mander unfairly and inaccurately writes of Julia Starky: "She was no beauty, would not see fifty again and had little to offer, apart from an annuity." In fact according to the *International Genealogical Index* she was born in 1813 and at 29 was only two years younger than Prince.

32. Significantly, one of the factors that, a few years later, completely ruined Prince's reputation with the world at large, was the revelation in the Courts, of the dubious way in which he had arranged for the Nottidge sisters (spinster heiresses) to marry three of his followers. The case of Nottidge v Ripley and Another (1849) and some of its sad, albeit slightly comic, attendant circumstances are conveniently summarized in Scull, *Social Order / Mental Disorder*, 282–83. Cf. Schwieso, "Religious Fanaticism," 159–74.

33. For Deck, see Peter Lineham's article in the *Dictionary of New Zealand Biography* (http://www.dnzb.govt.nz/dnzb). However, *pace* Lineham, the early chronology of Deck's life poses some problems. According to DNZB, Deck returns to India in 1830, "resign[s] his commission in 1835 and after his return to England he was rebaptized." Certainly his rebaptism was after July 1835 when his son J. F. Deck was baptized as an infant in the church of Deck's father-in-law at Hatherleigh, Devon. Prior to that however, Deck seems to have been involved with the Brethren in Plymouth having taken

assembly in Weymouth was probably hoping that both Rees and Prince would throw in their lot with them.[34]

Unfortunately, Prince was rapidly moving in a different direction. For a time he kept his peculiar views to himself or shared them privately with Arthur Rees, but Prince's views may well have been a factor in Rees's decision to move back to Sunderland away from the area where his brother-in-law was operating. By 1844 it was apparent that not only was Prince claiming to be Elijah and calling Starky and himself "the two witnesses" of Revelation 11, but he was also referring to himself as "the Holy Ghost personified" and "the Holy Ghost (in measure) manifested in the flesh." The high hopes Deck and his fellow Brethren had entertained of Prince and the extent of his horrified disappointment will be apparent from some passages in a tract he published in 1845:

> Men, whom many of us loved and esteemed as brethren and true servants of the Lord Jesus Christ, are now *openly* preaching in this and other places, new and unheard-of doctrines . . . God is my witness how often, with other brethren, I have remembered them in my prayers . . . I have letter upon letter by me, of different brethren, who have loved and honored him [Prince] with the deepest Christian affection. In June last [1845] when he and Mr. Starkey [*sic*] came into the neighbourhood of Taunton, I went with two other brethren, both of known and tried Christian standing and experience, to hear their preaching at the opening of the church at Charlinch: we desired, in dependance [*sic*] upon God, to *prove* for ourselves, whether their work was of God or not. The Lord knows how gladly we would have given the right hand of fellowship to our brethren, if we could have recognized their testimony to have been of God: and how deeply we were grieved to be compelled to judge it otherwise.[35]

Peter Embley's observation was highly relevant when he observed that "unlike some Brethren, Deck was never a prolific pamphleteer, and it seems most unlikely that he would have ventured into print unless at the very least some of the Brethren

---

a vocally paedobaptist position against Groves in 1829 ([H. B. Groves], *Memoir*, 231), and against B. W. Newton in early 1832 at Plymouth. ("Newton's Recollections" in JRULM, CBA 7057, 315; 7059, 116–17; 7049, 310). Both incidents occurred in England. The chronology is further complicated by Norris Groves's encounter in Cape Town in October 1834 with Lt. Deck "packed up for a return to India" with his eyes "quite turned away from the army," Groves, *Memoir*, 348. Deck seems to have spent much more time in England or on board ship to and from, rather than in India!

34. See P. L. Embley, "Origins and Early Development of the Plymouth Brethren," (PhD diss., Cambridge, 1966, in University Library, Cambridge; now available online at http://www.bruederbewegung.de/pdf/embley.pdf), 148–49. There is some truth (if not the whole truth) in Embley's point that "to a large extent the Plymouth Brethren movement grew by absorbing disaffected Christians from other denominations" (148).

35. Deck, *Word of Warning*, 5–6. The tract contains transcripts of several letters that Prince had written to Rees and which the latter had made available to Deck. In this respect it is a more substantial pamphlet than Arthur Rees's own twelve page tract, Rees, *Rise and progress of the heresy*.

at Weymouth were in danger of associating themselves with Prince."[36] Indeed, Newton in his recollections refers to friends among Brethren who "had deeply valued his [Prince's] ministry" and for whom his later deviation was "a bitter trial."[37]

Arthur Rees and the Brethren: The Aftermath

Prince's scandalous later life and the establishment of the Agapemone at Spaxton need not detain us apart from their effect on Brethren historians and Arthur Rees's biographers.[38] The unsavory details of Prince's subsequent career were an embarrassment and therefore any association with him was to be downplayed or if possible eliminated. Everett's account of Rees manages to make absolutely no allusion to Prince at any point, while Brockie's *Memoirs* make a solitary reference to him but studiously conceal the fact that Rees's wife was Prince's sister. In contrast, Watson gives the name of Rees's wife but makes no mention of her brother—let alone providing information about him.[39]

The subsequent ministry of Arthur Rees may be characterized as zealously evangelical, orthodox, but independent. Everett claims that when he seceded, Rees "became acquainted with several leaders of the Plymouth Brethren and was strongly urged to join their body."[40] His authoritarian insistence on being "*the* minister" of his chapel made such a possibility very remote, but he made no secret of his friendship and appreciation of many members of the Brethren. We mentioned earlier in this paper his continuing links with Captain W. H. G. Wellesley—a friendship all the more remarkable as Wellesley sided with the Exclusive wing of the Brethren. In another interesting connection we should note that it was at the home of Henry Bewley, a leading brother in Dublin, that Rees met D. L. Moody as a result of which his chapel was one of the first to host Moody's English mission in 1873—it being Rees who coined the phrase, with reference to Sankey, "singing the gospel." It is in fact from Sankey that we learn of the autocratic reputation that Rees had in the region, reflected in his local nickname the "Pope of the North."[41]

In two *Friendly Letters* Rees engaged the Brethren on certain issues on which he took a different path from them, namely *Worship* and *Ministry*. In the second letter he described how at a Brethren conference in Freemasons' Hall he had challenged them as to "whether those Christians who met without open ministry, met in the name of Jesus. After a pause a brother had stepped forward and replied, 'No; let us never give

---

36. Embley, *Dissertation*, 255n264. For Prince's success in Weymouth, see Schwieso, "This Frightful and Blasphemous Sect," 15–16.

37. "Newton's Recollections" (JRULM, CBA 7061, 20; cf. CBA 7057, 355).

38. There are several accounts, which, with a liberal sprinkling of imagined detail, dwell on the more lurid parts of Prince's later career. My account in *ODNB* is confined to established facts.

39. Brockie, *Memoirs of Rees*, 12; Watson, *Bethesda Free Chapel*, 18.

40. Everett, *Midshipman*, 109.

41. See Sankey, *My Life*, 49–50. For Bewley, see Neatby, *History*, 150 n2.

up our principle on that point.'" Rees then claimed that although this answer seemed to meet with silent acquiescence from the assembled gathering, several brethren including John Eliot Howard had later assured him of their dissent from that point of view.[42] In a later comment, the first historian of the Brethren observed that if, among the "Open Brethren," those who shared the dissenting view of Howard were in fact the majority, he could not help thinking that "the majority sometimes allows itself to be 'talked down.'"[43] Perhaps there would have been a place for Rees among the Brethren if those with truly open principles had given more vocal expression to them.

There are other aspects of Arthur Augustus Rees's career that we have had to leave on one side. His fifteen years of mutually appreciative correspondence with Spurgeon,[44] his vigorous espousal of millennial views and his readiness to relate these to the rise and fall of Napoleon III,[45] and the way his published opposition to the participation of women in the 1859 Revival[46] stung Catherine Booth into writing one of the great feminist pamphlets of the nineteenth century[47]—these are all facets of Rees's lively and unique career that are worthy of investigation. Our purpose has been confined to establishing the context of his early development and his emergence as a somewhat autocratic alternative to the ways of the Brethren on whom at one stage his career had impinged so closely.

---

42. Rees, *Second Friendly Letter*, 4.

43. Neatby, *History*, 202, where the episode is said to have occurred in 1869.

44. Spurgeon's side of the correspondence can be followed at http://www.godrules.net/library/spurgeon/NEW2spurgeon19.htm.

45. For example, Rees, *Moral of the war*.

46. Rees, *Reasons for not co-operating in the alleged "Sunderland revivals."*

47. Booth, *Female Teaching* (1861), but extant copies of the pamphlet are rare, see Walker, "Chaste and Fervid Eloquence," 300n10.

17

George Henry Stoddart

An Ecclesiastical "Rolling Stone"[1]

THERE IS AN INTRIGUING document in a "scrapbook of personal documents relating to the life of J. N. Darby" preserved in the Sibthorp collection of the Christian Brethren Archive, in Manchester.[2] It is an undated proposal for a translation of the New Testament, which was envisaged in the following brief notes, copied exactly as written:

> Taking the present one as the basis—only eliding positive errors & introducing undeniable improvements.
>
> The work severally to be got ready D.V. in 6 4 months.—& revised jointly in 4 [sc. and] printed [sc.in] other 6 4 months.—
>
> To be printed with numbers of verses at the side—and a few amendments in the division of verses & chapters.

A second explanatory note adds the following:

> The whole to be revised by *general Committee of all* with the addition of [Percy Francis] Hall, [Alexander] Campbell, [James Thomas] Molesworth, [John] Moseley, [Richard] Hill, [Joseph] Clulow—& six more, Jackson Smith, [Henry] Craik —[Henry Bellenden] Bulteel.

The rest of the page assigns the different books of the New Testament to different scholars. Nearly all the names are familiar ones associated with the early Plymouth Brethren. The only additions in my transcriptions from this document are in [square brackets] where for the sake of clarity I have inserted the person's first name where it is known, and some explanatory notes.

- Mat., Mark, Luke: [Henry William] Soltau & Stoddart

1. This appeared originally in the *Brethren Historical Review* 10 (2014) 10–20.

2. The document is listed in the JRULM, CBA as "JND/1/1/16." I have taken the text from the photographic reproduction of the "scrapbook of personal documents relating to the life of J. N. Darby," newly accessible online at http://enriqueta.man.ac.uk/luna/servlet/media/book/showBook/nonconform~91~1~393282~126877. For the availability online of this fascinating collection of materials we are deeply indebted to the archivist Mr. Graham Johnson, who has also given me permission to transcribe the text.

- John Gospel & Epistles: [John Gifford] Bellett, [Charles Frear] Hargrove & Dublin [sc. Brethren]
- Acts: [George Vicesimus] Wigram & [Lancelot Charles Lee] Brenton
- Romans: [Benjamin Wills] Newton
- Corinthians: The Writer in the *Witness* [In some annotated copies of *The Christian Witness*, vol. 4 (1837), the article entitled "Some considerations on the two epistles to the Corinthians" is attributed to William Henry Darby.]
- Gal., Ephes., Coloss: [James Lampen] Harris.
- Philipp. & Thessalonians: [Thomas] Mahon
- Timothy and Titus: [Lancelot Charles Lee] Brenton & [William] Morshead
- Hebrews: Fitzgerald & [Thomas] Maunsell.
- Peter and Jude: [Samuel Prideaux] Tregelles.
- Revelations [*sic*]: [John Nelson] Darby and [Benjamin Wills] Newton.
- & all help each

From internal evidence, the document appears to date from the late 1830s or early 1840s and is of particular interest in that it assigns the book of Revelation jointly to Darby and Newton whose interpretations of the last book of the Bible differed significantly. Perhaps we are not surprised to find that the plan did not come to fruition!

The names of two of the Brethren, to whom a specific book was assigned, are not readily associated with the movement and their identification is all the more difficult, as no first names are included. Fitzgerald was such a common name in Protestant Irish society that we may never know the identity of the man to whom joint responsibility for the Letter to the Hebrews was assigned, other than that he was probably the "Mr. Fitzgerald" mentioned in connection with the Clifton conference of 1838.[3] The other unfamiliar name is Stoddart, who was assigned joint responsibility, with Henry William Soltau, for the synoptic gospels. It is with this person that the following article is concerned.

The name can ultimately be identified with some certainty as George Henry Stoddart [GHS] (c. 1801–76). Born at the turn of the nineteenth century into a military family from Ipswich, GHS matriculated from the Queen's College, Oxford and graduated BA in 1824.[4] Unlike his more famous, albeit unfortunate, younger brother

---

3. Stunt, "Early Account of the Brethren," 6. The name Fitzgerald is also to be found in some copies of the *Christian Witness* whose owners endorsed their copies with the names of the (otherwise anonymous) authors.

4. *Al. Oxon.*, 4:1357.

Colonel Charles Stoddart,[5] GHS did not follow in the family's military footsteps, but was ordained by the bishop of Norwich in 1825.[6]

His ecclesiastical career is hard to establish and the appointments with which his name can be identified were hardly ones of great importance and they do not seem to have been of long duration. In 1829 he had married his cousin Charlotte Stoddart[7] and for some years appears to have been living on the outskirts of South East London, where his first three children were baptized in the Church of St. Mary Magdalene, Woolwich, Kent.[8] We have no information about any ecclesiastical living to which Stoddart may have been appointed at this time, but he was not inactive because in 1833 he produced an 85 page abstract of essays published by other writers on "Church Reform," summarizing their opinions and proposals, with "additional remarks" of his own on the subject.[9] Two years later, a further publication of his appeared on the Psalms though, again, he made no claim to originality of thought and stressed his dependence on earlier writers.[10] Sometime in 1835 he moved to Ramsgate, where he appears to have been earning a living by taking six to eight private pupils in his family. In all probability, he sat under the ministry of his neighbor in Effingham Place, George William Lewis (c. 1796–1858), another Anglican priest who also took pupils and was curate of the Ramsgate Chapel of Ease.[11]

In 1836, George Henry Stoddart published a brief pamphlet in which he gave his reasons for seceding from the Established Church.[12] His decision was not without consequence and later in the year we find the following announcement in the *Patriot*, a dissenting newspaper:

> THE Rev. G. H. STODDART, A.M., late of Queen's College, Oxford, who has for some years received from six to eight Private Pupils into his family, has, by his recent secession from the Established Church, several VACANCIES, which he would be glad to fill by other Pupils, sons of Dissenters, or liberal

---

5. Charles Stoddart's imprisonment and execution as a spy by order of the emir of Bokhara in 1842 would cause a major sensation (see below). Another brother in the army was Captain John Alfred Stoddart who died in Madras, 22 Mar 1840, *Gentleman's Magazine* 168 (Oct 1840) 445.

6. Ordained as a deacon, 17 Oct 1824, and as a priest, 19 Jun 1825; *Clergy of the Church of England Database* (http://theclergydatabase.org.uk).

7. *New Monthly Magazine and Literary Journal* (Sep 1829) 410. She was the daughter of his uncle, John Stoddart, the celebrated blind Headmaster of Northampton Grammar School; see Serjeantson, *History of the Church of St. Peter*, 134.

8. The dates of birth and christenings are recorded in the IGI. The first child Richard George (born 1831) appears to have died at an early age, as he is not recorded with the other children in the census of 1841.

9. Stoddart, *Evidence of the necessity of church reform*.

10. Stoddart, *Imagery ... of the Book of Psalms*.

11. See G. W. Lewis, *Sermons*, xxvi, where Stoddart is listed as a subscriber. For Lewis's career see, *Al. Cantab.*, pt. 2, 4:161.

12. Stoddart, *Reasons for my seceding*. I have not seen this pamphlet, which is apparently only held by the British Library and the University Library of Cambridge.

Churchmen, who may wish Gospel instruction to be made a prominent feature in the education of their children.[13]

In the paragraph which followed the announcement, the first "references" given by Stoddart, as people to whom inquiries could be made, are the names of two respected congregational ministers, Henry Townley (1784–1861) of Hackney and George Clayton (1783–1862) of Walworth. This gives us, perhaps, some indication of Stoddart's new ecclesiastical direction (especially as his secessionary pamphlet had been produced by a publisher with congregational connections), but he may well have also been reconsidering his position in the matter of baptism. It is only circumstantial evidence but neither his son George, born in Woolwich in 1836, nor a brother John, born in Plymouth three years later, were baptized until 1852 by which time their father seems to have been reconciled to the Establishment.

The fact that GHS was living in Plymouth when his fifth son was born in 1839, but had moved away by 1841 to Sheffield where, in the Census of that year, his employment is given as "2nd Master of Wesleyan Preparatory school," suggests that it was in 1839 that the proposal was made (in the document described at the outset of this article) for him to work with Henry Soltau on the synoptic gospels. If the basis for this conclusion seems slightly tenuous, there is another significant piece of evidence. It was not customary for the editor of the Brethren magazine, the *Christian Witness* to give the names of its contributors, but there are some extant copies in which the owners have attributed articles to their supposed authors. In two of these the name of Stoddart has been written against an article, in two parts, entitled "Specific Meanings of some of the words in the New Testament," and the article appeared in the issues for January and April 1839.[14] For Stoddart to have been a contributor to the *Christian Witness* and for his name to have been included as a participant in the proposed edition of the New Testament, together with so many respected Brethren scholars, suggests that he was held in high esteem by the Brethren during his brief stay in Plymouth.

One can only speculate how long Stoddart was *persona grata* with the Brethren. In the 1840s he moved to Brighton and then became a private tutor at Eton, as well as getting involved with such organizations as the Poor Man's Guardian Society,[15] the United [Irish] Relief Association,[16] and the Church Reform Society of which he was the secretary.[17] A few years later it was finally established that his brother,

---

13. *Patriot* 5 (Aug 3, 1836) no. 250.

14. [Stoddart], "Specific Meanings," 63–69; 180–83. One of the endorsed copies was in the collection of the late Mr. Edwin Cross. The other was (when I consulted it, some forty years ago), in the Offices of the Editors of *Echoes of Service* and had been owned by one of the editors, W. R. Lewis. Its attributions were made by Charles E. Franck whose wife's mother was a cousin of H. W. Soltau and "a great personal friend of J. L. Harris," the editor of the *Christian Witness*, who is said to have given her the names of the authors.

15. *Poor Man's Guardian* 1 (6 Nov 1847) 16.

16. *Spectator*, 27 Mar 1847, 295.

17. *Newspaper*, 7 Jun 1851, 182; Alison, *Our Future Policy*, 84.

Charles Stoddart, had been executed by order of the emir in Bokhara in 1842, and there was considerable public outrage when the whole sorry story was described in a book by Captain John Grover.[18] A noisy patriotic meeting was convened in Exeter Hall in 1845, at which GHS was unwise enough to be critical of Grover's very patriotic account.[19] His intervention on this occasion provoked the indignation of a writer in the *New Quarterly Review* whose reference to him is of particular significance for our purposes, when he described him as:

> the pseudo-Clergyman, the Plymouth Brother, the insulter of Captain Grover, the Rev. G. H. Stoddart.[20]

Such epithets suggest that GHS was already something of a loose cannon, whose ecclesiastical moorings would never be very firmly attached. In 1856 the London *Observer* announced his appointment to the "Classical Professorship and Chaplaincy of the Cavalry College" in Roehampton Surrey,[21] but as the foundation stone of this college (later known as the Richmond Cavalry College) was not laid until the following year, the appointment seems to have been more of a proposition than a reality, and sadly we may conjecture that with the death of his wife in 1859 his already somewhat protean identity began to go to pieces. We find him as the chaplain to the Abingdon Workhouse in 1860[22] but this was only for a short period as by 1861 he is recorded as living in the Camden Town area of North London where three years later in 1864 he married Sarah Tincknell.[23]

Perhaps he felt this was a new start especially as in the same year his *History of the Prayer Book* was published.[24] There is also mention in 1868 of his being appointed to another chaplaincy at the Eastry Union workhouse, near Sandwich, Kent,[25] but by the end of the year he had "resigned and left."[26] In fact the evanescent character of Stoddart's endeavors becomes more apparent in the following year when, not for the first time, his bankruptcy is declared in the *London Gazette*.[27] The announce-

18. Grover, *Bokhara Victims*.

19. He reaffirmed his criticisms in a letter from 131 High Street, Eton (8 May 1845), to the editor of the *Norfolk and Norwich Chronicle*, which was included as an appendix in the 2nd ed. of Grover's *Bokhara Victims*, 352–58.

20. *New Quarterly Review* 6 (Oct 1846) 270.

21. *Observer*, 29 Dec 1856.

22. *Accounts and Papers of the House of Commons . . . 1861*, 55 (1861), "Chaplains in Workhouses," 3.

23. She was forty years younger than Stoddart and the daughter of a farming family in Somerset.

24. Stoddart, *History of the Prayer Book*.

25. Canterbury Cathedral Archives, Diocese of Canterbury, Chaplains' Licences DCb/F/F/Ea/2 1868.

26. Ibid., DCb/F/F/Ea/4 1869.

27. *London Gazette*, 5 Jan 1869, issue 23456, 84. I cannot pretend to understand the mysteries of mid-nineteenth-century bankruptcy procedure, but as early as July 16, 1847 a petition to the Bankruptcy courts in the name of the Reverend George Henry Stoddart, "an insolvent debtor" had been

ment gives us some idea of the increasingly peripatetic lifestyle that GHS had lately been obliged to adopt as it lists (in reverse chronological order) his various recent addresses—three in the Sandwich area of Kent, two around Brighton in Sussex, one in Camden Town, London, and one in Somerset, presumably at the time of his second marriage. One suspects that the numerous changes of residence were because he had been trying to avoid creditors. In the early 1870s three more children were born, but in 1876, their father died in Brighton.

****

It would be palpably false to suggest that this was a typical Brethren story as, for every GHS among them, there were hundreds of single-minded Brethren of painstaking endurance who could never be described as anything resembling an ecclesiastical will-o'-the-wisp. If some of their endeavors appeared to be short lived, the reality was often long lasting, albeit perhaps only spectacular for a short while. On the other hand the Brethren movement did sometimes attract freelance characters, who were inclined to march to their own drum. Evangelists, particularly in the Open wing of the Brethren, like Russell Hurditch[28] (1839–1918) and Henry Varley[29] (1835–1912) epitomize the unpredictability of the movement's identity, bucking the trend and defying oversimplified generalizations.[30] In some cases it seems that their youthful spectacular individuality resulted in premature burn-out. The news-making early careers of men like Henry Bulteel[31] (1800–66) and Sir Charles Brenton[32] (1807–62), which seemed to mark them out as radicals firebrands destined to be Brethren, apparently exhausted them before their time, resulting in an aftermath of hesitant and retiring tranquility.

The mavericks like GHS are harder to document because the Brethren preferred to forget about them or disown them, treating them perhaps as the seed that "fell on stony ground" having "no root in themselves and so endure but for a time." This brings us to another interesting example in the case of Trelawney William Saunders (1821–1910),[33] who as a very young man, with a special interest in biblical geography was associated with the Brethren in Plymouth where he almost certainly was in contact with Stoddart. As a teenager he traveled from Plymouth to London in 1839 as an "outside passenger" on the stagecoach, and nearly froze to death, crossing Salisbury

---

heard in London (*London Gazette*, issue 20754, p. 2636) and fifteen years later, Stoddart had again been "adjudged bankrupt," *London Gazette*, 7 Mar 1862, issue 22605, 1341.

28. Coad, *History of the Brethren*, 178–79; Grass, *Gathering to His Name*, 141–42.

29. See the article by Donald Lewis and Timothy Stunt in *ODNB*.

30. I would include in this category the recently discovered, Thomas George Bell (1811–71), see Stunt, "Early Account of the Brethren," 6–8.

31. See my article in *ODNB*.

32. See Stunt, *From Awakening*, 209, 259, 296–98.

33. The only account of Saunders, known to me is Bolton's obituary in the *Geographical Journal* 36 (Sep 1910) 363–66.

Plain in a snowstorm, but safely arrived in the capital to work in the Bible House of Samuel Bagster and Sons.

As with Stoddart our assessment of Trelawney Saunders is liable to be circumstantial and therefore conjectural, but the spiritual and intellectually inquisitive energy that, early in his life, had attracted him to the Brethren in Plymouth was soon to find other outlets of expression, first in establishing a stationer's business near Charing Cross, publishing books and maps, then in advocating emigration to Australia and campaigning for a colonial settlement on the Gulf of Carpentaria (Port Flinders). Saunders enthusiasm was likewise engaged in producing a weather map of the British Isles, in serving as librarian and map curator for the Royal Geographical Society and even in promoting an abortive plan for a "Western University" in South Wales. All this was in the course of some ten years before settling down to the serious cartographical work for which he will always be remembered, producing, in his day, the most up to date maps of London, Palestine, Sinai, Babylonia and India.

Saunders's previous connection with the Brethren in Plymouth may explain why one of his first publications was by Stoddart himself. When in the late 1840s, Stoddart was riding off in all directions and getting involved in (amongst other things) Irish affairs and the United Relief Association, he addressed a letter to Lord John Russell, entitled *The true cure for Ireland, the development of her industry*—a pamphlet published by Trelawney Saunders of 6 Charing Cross.[34] Saunders and Stoddart were people who had more to offer than the Brethren could cope with, and they could both be said to have had rather too many irons in the fire for them to be contained by the Brethren. In this respect they were not alone. A brief consideration of some parallel cases may put them in context.

In the case of Francis Newman (1805–97), the restless pilgrim in due course gave a blow-by-blow account of the vagaries of his intellectual and spiritual journey[35] but more often in such cases the picaresque details have to be gleaned from obscure announcements and allusions made by others. The strange career of Robert Mackenzie Beverley (1798–1868), whom we considered in an earlier chapter, is a classic example where, hitherto there has been no single account of his religious trajectory and the biographer has to assemble the story from sundry scraps of evidence.[36] A Whig political campaigner from Yorkshire who excoriated the Established Church into which he was born, Beverley charged his alma mater, the University of Cambridge, with being a hotbed of gross immorality. He soon became a Congregational minister, from there shuffling his way into the world of the Quakers, with some of whom he moved

---

34. Stoddart, *True cure for Ireland*. The only extant book published by Saunders before 1847 dating from 1842, is Anon., *Select Hymns for Christian Emigrants*.

35. F. W. Newman, *Phases of faith; cf.* my article in *ODNB*.

36. See above, ch. 15. Prior to this the only printed account of him was in Boase, *Modern English Biography*, 4:391–92, and an irenic obituary written more than thirty years after his death: [Rowntree], "Memoir of Beverley, 326–31.

on to join the Brethren—but only for a time. In the last years of his life Beverley was an isolated figure having no active connection with any particular religious community, living in Rome, a minority of one, criticizing anyone and everyone for the inadequacy of their faith. The move by way of Congregationalism and the Quakers to a time with the Brethren, and the ultimate isolation bring the parallel with Stoddart to mind.

The rolling stone, which gathers no moss, is a phenomenon with which we are all familiar. It was only to be expected that such independent and enquiring characters would for a while be attracted by the aspirations of the early Brethren with their liturgical freedom and professed fear of systematic doctrinal creeds. Sometimes strong-minded and original scholars like John Darby[37] and William Kelly[38] made the Brethren their permanent home. In Benjamin Newton's case his youthful Christological speculations contributed to his later separation from them,[39] while Francis Newman's relentless quest for intellectual honesty eventually isolated him from not only the Brethren but from all but a handful of people calling themselves Christians. His words written to Edwin A. Abbott in 1892, when he was nearly ninety years old, are a suitable commentary on that long and elusive quest:

> While I cannot be a Christian if weighed in any historical balance yet my moral and spiritual sentiment is unchanged since I joyfully surrendered myself to God in 1819.[40]

In the case of George Henry Stoddart (and for a while perhaps with Trelawney Saunders) we have a rolling stone, who lingered briefly among Brethren but whose nomadic transience meant that he had "no continuing city" with the result that he seems to have remained only a sojourner and pilgrim to the end.

---

37. Stunt, "Darby: The Scholarly Enigma."
38. Cross, *Irish Saint*.
39. For Newton's speculative Christology, see Burnham, *Story of Conflict*, 188–200.
40. Cited by Stunt, "Francis William Newman" (*ODNB*).

18

The Soltau Family and Christian Missions[1]

Hudson Taylor, the Brethren and Henry William Soltau

TO UNDERSTAND THE WAY in which the missionary cause suddenly became the principal focus of Henry William Soltau [HWS] during the last decade of his life, we have to look at the earlier experiences of one of the great nineteenth-century mission pioneers. In his formative years, long before the founding of the China Inland Mission, Hudson Taylor had come into contact with a variety of people associated with the Brethren both in the North of England and in London. Even before Taylor went to China, William Neatby in Barnsley, Andrew Jukes in Hull and William Collingwood of Liverpool together with John and Robert Howard of the Brook Street assembly in Tottenham had been important influences in the development of his thinking, and while he was in China during the 1850s, men like William Berger and George Müller had taken his work to their hearts. Other Brethren who were interested in Taylor's activity included Philip Gosse, whom he had known in Hackney, and Henry Bewley of Dublin.

So when he was back in London in July 1865, it was understandable that on an impulse he decided one Sunday to attend the Brethren assembly in Welbeck Street.[2] This was the occasion of his meeting with Lord and Lady Radstock and subsequently their son-in-law Sir Thomas Beauchamp. It also seems to have been the moment when he first came into contact with HWS with whose family, in Exeter, he connected in the following year.[3]

Making use of the archives of the Overseas Missionary Fellowship, the late James Broomhall gave a fascinating account of that visit of Hudson Taylor to the West Country in April 1866. One of Broomhall's sources is an account left by HWS's second daughter, Henrietta (1843–1934), who described how her father came back from

---

1. This was originally part of a larger essay, the first part of which is to be found above in chapter 10. The independent thinking of Soltau's children can only be described as *sui generis* and provides us with an instructive postscript from a later generation. They are more than qualified to conclude this last section of "Free-lance Independents."

2. Taylor, *Hudson Taylor and the C.I.M*, 35. The assembly had moved from Orchard Street to Welbeck Street in 1860, H. Groves, *Memoir of Congleton*, 91.

3. Taylor, *Hudson Taylor and the CIM*, 61.

Teignmouth where he had been listening to Hudson Taylor in the home of Leonard Strong. "The first thing he said was 'I have seen a missionary from China . . . Go to Mr. Cole and secure the Athenaeum for him tonight and ask him to get out bills as quickly as possible to fill the hall!' We three sisters went off and told everyone we could . . . and when the evening came the hall was crowded . . . My sister Agnes and I hardly slept that night and in the morning she said to me, 'If only I was not going to be married next month, I should go to China, but you must go, and Richard [Harris Hill, her fiancé] and I will help to support you.' The next day I offered to go, with my parents' support."[4]

In retrospect it can be seen as a key moment in the life of the Soltau family. Of the three sisters who were HWS's "trusted lieutenants in open air evangelism,"[5] the eldest, Lucy died in 1873. When, two years later, HWS himself died, his widow moved to Tottenham, and Henrietta, who had devotedly looked after her parents, was now free at the age of thirty-two to follow an independent career which we shall consider shortly. But even before the death of HWS the family's center of gravity had been moving to the London area and into the orbit of the China Inland Mission.

The Soltau Family Returns to London

When in 1866, Agnes Soltau married Richard Harris Hill [c. 1837–1909],[6] she was marrying a newly qualified civil engineer who would later establish his reputation in the field of architecture where his designs for such charitable institutions as the Mildmay Mission Hospital and the Scandinavian Seamen's Temperance Home, were noted for their plainness of style.[7] More important for our purposes is the fact that he would soon design the headquarters of the China Inland Mission, at Newington Green, on whose Council of Referees he was an honorary secretary from 1872. It was Hill, who (presumably at a well attended meeting), whispered to Geraldine, Hudson Taylor's daughter-in-law and biographer, that the great majority of the CIM's earliest supporters, like himself, were either Plymouth Brethren or practically so, but nevertheless, as Alvyn Austin observes, "in her thirty books the word 'Brethren' never passed Mrs. Taylor's pen."[8]

---

4. Broomhall, *Hudson Taylor . . . Survivors' Pact*, 141–42.

5. Cable, *Henrietta Soltau*, 61.

6. For Hill's family, see above, ch. 10nn38–40.

7. Hill had been elected as an Associate of the Institute of Civil engineers in 1865 and became a member of the Royal institute of British Architects in 1892; Institution of Civil Engineers, *Charter*, 57; R.I.B.A, *Kalendar*, 76. Pevsner, *Buildings of England*, 563, where RHH is described as "the hospital specialist," and "a specialist in such institutions, very plain," 673.

8. Austin, *China's Millions*, 94. A glance at the CIM magazine, *China's Millions*, as late as 1876 confirms Hill's statement. The 24 referees included the following Brethren (or Brethren fellow-travelers): Thomas Barnardo, Henry Bewley, Robert Chapman, William Collingwood, John Elliot Howard, John Morley, George Müller, Lord Radstock, J. Denham Smith, Henry Varley, and Colonel Woodfall.

There is good reason for not expanding unduly on the remarkable story of Agnes's older sister, Henrietta, as, unlike any of her siblings, she is the subject of a biography, and she has even been included in the *Oxford Dictionary of National Biography*.[9] After her father's death she established a home for missionaries' children first at Tottenham and then at Hastings[10] where she also founded a YWCA. When Hudson Taylor established the Ladies' Council of the CIM, Henrietta served as the secretary, and in 1889 she brought into being a women's missionary training home in Islington. In the course of the next thirty years, many hundreds of recruits lived under her supervision and, of those who were deemed suitable for service, more than five hundred joined the CIM. In 1897–98, in her early fifties, she spent more than a year in China informing herself of the circumstances of missionary life, so that she could continue her work for twenty more years before retirement. It was a career that led Broomhall to describe her as "one of the most outstanding women in the China Inland Mission."[11] Piecing together the careers of her brothers is more difficult.

George Soltau (1847–1909): Evangelist

Even before Agnes moved to London with her husband, one of her brothers George Soltau had obtained a clerkship in 1865 in the Office of Works and Public Buildings and by 1871 was living in Goswell Street, Holborn, helping in his free time with the Cow Cross City Mission.[12] In 1874, having married Grace Tapson, the daughter of a respected London physician, he abandoned the civil service and joined forces with Thomas Barnardo, so that in 1875 he and his wife became the first governor and lady superintendent of the thirteen cottages that comprised Dr. Barnardo's Village Home for Orphan and Destitute Girls in Barkingside, Ilford.[13] After seven years in this work, George became an itinerant evangelist in the United Kingdom. In 1883 he published

---

The Council of Management included Theodore Howard, Richard Harris Hill, and George Soltau, while the Honorary Auditors were the firm of Theodore Jones.

9. For the biography, see Cable, *Henrietta Soltau*; the *ODNB* article is by Harold Rowdon.

10. Henrietta's ongoing connection with Open Brethren is apparent, in the 1881 Census, which records the presence in her home at Hastings of three of the children of William Macdonald (1839–1911). In close touch with the Brethren at Loughborough Hall, Lambeth, Macdonald, a solicitor's clerk, was a close friend of my great-grandfather Francis and his brother Alfred Stunt, who supported him when he went as a missionary to Penang in 1866. Family tradition recalls that Macdonald's passage to Penang was paid for (at least in part) by the sale of some of the wedding presents of Alfred (married 1863) and Francis (married 1865).

11. Broomhall, *Hudson Taylor . . . Survivors' Pact*, 142.

12. G. Soltau, *Personal Work . . . with Biographical Sketch*, 11; George's account of the ragged-school work of the Cow Cross Mission appeared in the *Christian*, 23 Nov 1871. Mrs. Elisabeth Wilson has kindly drawn my attention to numerous subsequent reports of George Soltau's work appearing in *The Christian* between 1872 and 1894.

13. See the accounts in Anon., "East End Juvenile Mission," 444–46; and Barnardo, *Memoirs*, 130. By 1907 there were more than sixty cottages.

an address that he had given "to the Christian Workers who had undertaken to instruct and converse with inquirers in connection with the meetings of Mr. Moody and Mr. Sankey,"[14] and in 1884, at the suggestion of Annie Macpherson, went to Canada and then the United States where he worked for five months in cooperation with Moody.[15] On his return to England, he was invited by Mrs. Henry Reed, in 1886 to become the pastor of the Christian Mission Church, established by her late husband, in Launceston, Tasmania. There, George Soltau and his wife served for seven years and were involved in the establishment of the Australian council of the CIM in 1890.[16] After visiting his brother in South India, and some two years of mission work in New Zealand he moved back to North London in 1898 where he was living in 1901 before moving to the USA where he taught in a Bible school in New York, pastored Churches in Iowa and then Chicago before moving to California where he died in 1909, after which his widow returned to England.[17]

George's time in Australia may have been connected to the earlier move there of his sister Charlotte Soltau (c.1851–1916) who in 1880 had married an Irish doctor William Warren (1852–1915) in Melbourne where, with her husband, she opened a Training Home for missionaries in the 1890s on undenominational lines.[18]

Henry Soltau (1850–1911): Medical Missionary

Henry Soltau the second son of HWS, followed a rather different course from George but he too exemplifies the passionate but independent commitment that characterized his father.[19] As a young man of twenty-one he was appointed to be the clerk to the Plymouth school board in the year of its foundation[20] but in the following year,

14. G. Soltau, *Enquiry Room* as advertised in *Footsteps of Truth* (Jan 1884) 53.

15. G. Soltau, *Personal Work . . . with Biographical Sketch*, 16–17. Cf. the retrospective account in a New Zealand newspaper, which refers to his "commanding pulpit presence and a strong voice which he uses at times to advantage in a vigorous manner," *Mataura Ensign* 17 (11 Jun 1895) 5; http://paperspast.natlib.govt.nz/cgi-bin/paperspast?a=d&d=ME18950611.2.2.

16. Taylor, *Hudson Taylor and CIM*, 489, 490n. An Australian website, honoring Tasmanian women, names Grace Soltau as the "first president of the Tasmanian Woman's Christian Temperance Union, and describes her husband as a Christian Brethren Missionary. However, my esteemed friend Elisabeth Wilson has very kindly drawn my attention to an account of George Soltau by a later Brethren writer who claimed that Soltau had abandoned his earlier Brethren position as their distinctive teachings restricted his access to a wider ecclesiastical audience (Ferguson, *Reminiscences*, 26). In the 1901 census, Soltau described himself as a "congregational minister."

17. G. Soltau, *Personal Work . . . with Biographical Sketch*, 24–29; further details of George's time in the United States are provided in T. S. Soltau, *Autobiography* (Manchester, JRULM, CBA).

18. *India's Women* 14 (1894) 206. For biographical details of William Warren, see http://home.people.net.au/~ousie/dr_william_warren.htm.

19. Apart from his own writings in magazines like *China's Millions* the only account of Henry Soltau's life, known to me, is an obituary in the *British Medical Journal* (7 Oct 1911) 865.

20. See http://www.plymouthdata.info/Schools-Board-Plymouth.htm. Although it is often said that HWS's association with the Brethren led to his being cut off from members of his family, it is

1872, he moved to London where he was an honorary secretary of the CIM until 1875 when he set out as a missionary for Burma.[21] In September, with a Scotsman J. W. Stevenson, he left Rangoon in British Burma for Mandalay the capital of "Burma Proper" where they obtained permission from the king to settle in Bhamó.[22] It was from there, five years later, in November 1880 that Soltau and Stevenson set out on a historic trek to Shanghai, being the first Europeans to cross China from Burma.[23]

From Shanghai in 1881 he returned to Britain, where he "pursued a course of medical study" in Edinburgh[24] and married the daughter of a Free Church Minister, Jessie Barbara McIntyre with whom in late 1883 he was returning to Burma by way of Calcutta.[25] By January 1884 he was back with Stevenson in Bhamó, but in December hostilities broke out which led to the third Anglo-Burmese War in 1885–87 as a result of which Burma came entirely under British control.[26] Henry's health suffered and in 1886 he was invalided home with his wife and infant daughter, Lucy Marianne (born 1885), settling in Scotland where he completed his medical studies and where his son Henry (1887–1971) was born.[27] In 1892 he went out to South India as a medical missionary and in 1895 was one of the main speakers at the Ootacamund holiness convention[28] when he was invited to lay the foundation stone of Union Church (where C. T. Studd would become the pastor a few years later), but again his health gave way and he returned to England in 1896. From then until his death in 1911 he devoted himself to medical mission work among the poor of London in connection with the

---

worth noting that when he was "Clerk of the Plymouth School Board," HWS's son Henry was residing, at the time of the 1871 census, in the home of his cousin, George Soltau Symons, in Plympton St. Mary.

21. H. Soltau, "From Glasgow to Burmah."

22. H. Soltau, "From Rangoon to Bhamó."

23. Soltau read his account of the journey to the Royal Scottish Geographical Society in Edinburgh in 1888; see H. Soltau, "Across China."

24. In October 1882 he passed the final exams in Edinburgh and was admitted L.R.C.P., L.R.C.S., Edinburgh and L.F.P.S., Glasgow, *Lancet* 3 (Nov 1882) 895.

25. *China's Millions* 102 (Dec 1883) 172. Her father, Rev. Malcolm McIntyre (1819–1903) was the Free Church minister of Monikie, Forfar, for more than fifty years. Jessie's brother David McIntyre succeeded Andrew Bonar as minister of Finnieston, Glasgow and married Bonar's daughter Jane. He was the principal of the Bible Training Institute, Glasgow from 1913–1938. I am grateful to Mr. Gordon Shepherd, of the Open University, for help in identifying Jessie Barbara's family.

26. See H. Soltau, "[Extracts] from the Diary of Mr. Henry Soltau." Nearly ten years earlier Henry had expressed the opinion: "Were the English to take possession of the whole country, I am not at all certain that it would be a moral gain to the natives, though it might be a commercial gain to them," quoted in Anon., "Burma, Opium and the Trade Route to Yunnan," 295. A "Memorandum on Burmah," (1885) by Henry Soltau is among the papers of Sir Richard Temple in the Private Papers of the Oriental and India Office Collections of the British Library (Mss Eur F86/246).

27. Henry Kenneth Victor Soltau Jr. also pursued a career in medicine. He was educated at Monkton Combe School and at St. Bartholomew's Hospital, joining the Royal Army Medical Corps in 1914, and serving in France and Salonica, *British Medical Journal*, 2 Jan 1971, 54. His sister Lucy Marianne attended Oak Hill (boarding) School in Hampstead and later graduated from Westfield College in 1907. Her later married name was Cuthbert.

28. Wilson-Carmichael, *Walker of Tinnevelly*, 174.

London Medical Mission of Endell Street, St. Giles of which he was the superintendent for a time. In 1904 he was appointed the secretary and superintendent of the Medical Missionary Association and also lectured on "diseases of India" at Livingstone College, Leyton.[29] That he retained his connections with the Brethren is evident from his being one of the speakers at the graveside of Robert Cleaver Chapman in 1902.[30]

William Soltau: A French Connection

The youngest son of HWS was William Soltau (1852–1926) and, like his father and brothers, he was a loyal supporter of Hudson Taylor. When his brother left for Burma in 1875, William took over his secretarial role for the China Inland Mission and his interest in his brother's work is reflected in an interesting article that he wrote for Russell Hurditch's *Footsteps of Truth* describing the earlier work of the American missionary Justus Vinton in Burma.[31] However his later career was significantly shaped by his marriage in 1886.

His wife Louise Monod (1858–1918) came from one of the great Anglo-French evangelical families.[32] She was the eldest surviving child of Gustave Monod (1831–1904) and of his English wife Charlotte (née Brown, 1835–1918). Louise's grandfather Frédéric Monod (1794–1863), who also had an English wife, Suzanne (née Smedley), had been, with his brother Adolphe (1802–56), a key figure in the early nineteenth-century evangelical *réveil*.[33] With in-laws of that distinction, William's marriage thrust him into the considerable evangelical activity of the Protestant world in Paris.

In the aftermath of the Franco-Prussian War and the abortive Commune of 1871, an English congregational minister, Robert Whittaker McAll (1821–93) had established what he called a "Mission to the working men of France," later referred to as the "Evangelistic Mission in France known as the McAll Mission," or "La Mission Populaire Évangélique de France."[34] From the outset members of the Monod family and other French Protestants like the hymn-writer Ruben Saillens gave active support to the work, which was very interdenominational.[35] Under its auspices, Lord Radstock

---

29. Johnson, "Colonial Mission and Imperial Tropical Medicine," 556.

30. Bennet, *Robert Cleaver Chapman*, 113.

31. W. Soltau, "People prepared for the Lord."

32. The evangelical significance of the Monod dynasty has been seriously neglected by church historians. Some convenient genealogical details can be found (together with a lot of abusive slurs) in a disgraceful account of the family by the xenophobic, antisemitic, rightwing politician, Charles Maurras in a series of scurrilous articles in *L'Action Française* (1899–1900) later reprinted in Maurras, *Au signe de Flore*, 155–246. For a more sympathetic and constructive approach (but with less detail), see Osen, *Prophet and Peacemaker*.

33. For the francophone *réveil* associated with Geneva and its impact on the Monod brothers see Stewart, *Restoring the Reformation*, 116–18, 128.

34. McAll, *Robert Whitaker McAll*, 135–41.

35. "Ecclesiastically it ranges from High Church folk—and many evangelicals—to Congregationalists, with the two species of Baptists, Wesleyans, Presbyterians of several distinct species, the

conducted meetings in Paris in 1883, and the Mission was a work ideally suited to the youngest Soltau brother who, even in the year before his marriage, accosted a stranger "sauntering along the great boulevard" in Paris and took him to hear Theodore Monod, with the result that the stranger, who turned out to be a French landed proprietor, was in due course converted.[36] William Soltau and his French wife soon became an integral part of the McAll Mission. In 1887 the "business office" of the mission was said to be "in the hands of Madame Soltau" and by 1889 her husband, William, was described as the Mission's "Finance Secretary."[37] One particular part of the mission work with which he was involved was the acquisition of a boat (at first on the Seine, but later on other inland waterways) from which the Mission engaged in evangelism.

With the death of Robert McAll in 1893, Soltau took an even greater part in the work and we find him (together with McAll's widow) giving an account of the Mission at the Jubilee meetings of the Evangelical Alliance in 1896.[38] A few years later he is writing to the *Christian* with an account of a new venture in the city of Amiens.[39] By the time that the Great War broke out, William and his wife were living in England, but their involvement with the Mission continued, so that the *American McAll Record* was reporting in 1916 that "among the children of the Mission who are now at the front are ... Roger H. Soltau, the elder son of M. William Soltau, Secretary of the English Committee, who is attached to the Friends' Ambulance unit. His brother, Wilfrid G. Soltau, is in training in the Princess Patricia Canadian Light Infantry."[40]

Daughters and Grandchildren: The Gribble Family

For HWS to have begotten three sons and a daughter whose lives were devoted to full time mission work was notable, but it is perhaps worth noting that the torch was also passed on from them to later generations. Of George's children, Mabel served with the China Inland Mission, Eleanor pursued a medical career and worked in India with the Scottish Presbyterian mission and Theodore served as a Presbyterian Missionary in Korea from 1914 to 1937. More recently, of Theodore's children, George served as a missionary for thirty years in Japan and Eleanor Anne was a medical missionary in Jordan for some forty-five years.

Reformed and Free Churches of France and Switzerland, and the Brethren." Ibid., 177.

36. McAll et al., *Cry*, 46–50.

37. Ibid., 145; Ashton, *Christian Traveller*, 1.

38. Evangelical alliance, *Jubilee*, 186–88. This article contains a portrait of William Soltau. In the same volume there is a picture of his brother Henry (p. 139). These are the only portraits known to me of either of them.

39. The letter was reproduced in *Record of Christian Work* 20 (1901) 450.

40. *American McAll Record* 34 (Jan 1916) 2. Roger Henry Soltau (1887–1953), a respected scholar and author, was, for some twenty years, professor of political science at the American University of Beirout. His *Pascal: The Man and the Message* was reprinted as recently as 1970.

However, to return to the children of HWS... Of the two other daughters, Elizabeth Maria lived with her mother until the latter's death, but in the 1901 census is described as the honorary lady superintendent of the hostel at Morley House, George Street, Hanover Square, which was the headquarters of the YWCA. Within a few years, however, her blindness rendered her totally dependent upon her older sister Henrietta, until her death in 1928.[41]

The story of HWS's other daughter Mary Amelia is interestingly different. Like her sister Agnes she married a civil engineer. Theodore Graham Gribble (1851–1947) was the son of the Rev. Charles Besley Gribble (1807–78)[42] an evangelical Anglican who worked with the London City Mission, in the St. Paul's Church for Seamen, Whitechapel, where Theodore was born. The success of Mary Amelia's husband as a civil engineer is partly reflected in his textbook on surveying which went through five editions between 1890 and 1908, but also by the considerable responsibilities that were entrusted to him. As a young man he had been the resident engineer on the Norwich branch of the Eastern and Midlands Railway and then on a section of the Canadian Pacific Railway, on the north shore of Lake Superior. From 1886 to 1890 he was the chief engineer to the Hawaiian Railways and Tramways[43] and later on, to the elevated railway of Chicago.[44] In all probability the children stayed with their grandmother or went to boarding school, but evidently Mary Amelia accompanied her husband to Hawaii. The couple took an interest in the Hawaiian Mission Children's Society[45] but some idea of their social lifestyle may be glimpsed from the following announcement in a Hawaiian newspaper in 1889:

> We are requested to state to the friends and acquaintances of Mr. and Mrs. T. G. Gribble, that, owing to the illness of the former they are advised to leave Honolulu for England by the City of Pekin, and therefore they fear that it will be impossible to pay their farewell calls as they had hoped to.[46]

There are reasons for thinking that the Gribbles regarded themselves as "Brethren" but one suspects that some Brethren would have considered Theodore's professional interests a trifle worldly. During his time in America he contributed extensively to the American *Engineering Magazine* on aspects of transport possibilities in North

---

41. Cable, *Henrietta Soltau*, 233, where she is referred to as Elsie.

42. For further details of C. B. Gribble (who later was chaplain to the British Embassy in Constantinople and Canon of Gibraltar), see http://www.stgite.org.uk/media/gribble.html. He was born in Barnstaple and was probably distantly related to the Robert Gribble, who was associated with Brethren in the West Country (Rowdon, *Origins*, 147).

43. Kuykendall, *Hawaiian Kingdom*, 3:95–96.

44. For fuller details of Gribble's professional career, see the obituary in *Journal of the Institute of Civil Engineers* 28 [7] (1947) 280–81. In 1901 in private practice he carried out surveys for the development of water-power in Java and Sumatra where he was later responsible for hydroelectric installations.

45. Hawaiian Mission Children's society, *37th Annual Report* 10, 68.

46. *Honolulu Daily Bulletin*, 5 Oct 1889.

America and even on political issues like the advisability of the American annexation of Hawaii.[47] Many years later the spiritual side to Theodore Gribble found expression in a booklet *The Glory of Christ in the Everlasting Covenant: A message to Jew and Gentile*,[48] but when, as a younger man, in the 1890s he returned to England and told his children something about the wonders of the United States, it may have failed to ring true with the professed otherworldliness of the family's Brethren identity. Their youngest child was Harry Wagstaff Gribble (1890–1981) and his second name was that of the American millionaire, an associate of the Rockefellers, whose daughter had married Theodore Gribble's brother—another indication of the social circles in which the family were wont to move.

Looking back Harry Gribble, who later made his name as a successful playwright-director in the United States, recalled that his father's "description of the country, and especially of New York City's sky line, fascinated me." In the only account of his early life, the dilemma facing him is apparent:

> Always a rebel against tradition, young Gribble first asserted himself when he refused to become a missionary for the Plymouth Brethren, as other Gribbles had done, and announced his conversion to Episcopalianism. Shortly afterward he was confirmed by the Bishop of London in Westminster Abbey.[49]

In all probability when the writer referred to members of the Gribble family being Plymouth Brethren missionaries, he should really have written Soltau instead of Gribble. One suspects that all those maternal uncles evangelizing on four continents—not to mention his aunt Henrietta, were just too much for Harry, whose own inherited creative energy instead found expression in his dramatic productions on the New York stage.

The Social Context of Nineteenth-Century Missions

To understand the phenomenon of the Soltau family saga, it is essential that we recognize the social context in which it occurred. The rising fortunes of the Soltau's in London and Plymouth at the turn of the nineteenth century had enabled them to invest in annuities, which would have given HWS and his siblings an independent income. If he or his brother chose to be a barrister or a physician it was not out of necessity and HWS's abandonment of his legal career at the time of his conversion was not an enormous sacrifice financially. It seems clear that his invested income was properly managed and was passed down to his children who were in a financial position to pursue their altruistic and missionary concerns. To those of us who would (however reluctantly) consider ourselves as some sort of "middle class citizens," the

---

47. Gribble, "American Annexation of Hawaii," 898–905.
48. Gribble, *Glory of Christ* (1937).
49. Anon., *Current Biography*, 250.

changed meaning of this label is apparent when we discover, in the nineteenth and early twentieth-century census records, that the Soltau families almost invariably had at least one domestic servant and often also a cook, resident in their households. The same is true for most of the first- and second-generation leading Brethren known to us. When Richard Hill (Agnes Soltau's father-in-law) resigned his living as Vicar of West Alvington, he evidently had an unearned income to fall back on, because in 1851 he had three servants and a governess for his children. Likewise his son in 1871 (recently married to Agnes) had two servants, though their only child was less than a year old.[50]

In the column of the census headed "Rank, Profession or occupation," more often than not, Brethren are described as an "Annuitant," being of "Independent" means or, in the case of a widow like Harriet Groves in 1871, having a "Jointure." It is true that Anthony Norris Groves had suggested in his pamphlet *Christian Devotedness* that Christians should be unreservedly dependant on God rather than on their savings and investments, but this does not appear to have been taken as the normal course of action by most Brethren. Beer and Bowden, the West Country missionaries, who followed Groves to India, were men of lower social status with the result that when Joseph Clulow decided to stop supporting them they were indeed cast upon the mercies of God, but we shouldn't assume their case to have been a typical one in the mid-nineteenth century. The administration of an organization, like the China Inland Mission was often in the hands of people of independent means, who didn't need to claim their expenses. Henry Soltau, whose medical work in India and amongst the London poor can scarcely have been remunerative, was able to send his daughter to a boarding school in Hampstead and his son to Monkton Combe.

Perhaps one of the most remarkable features of the Brethren and their vibrant missionary tradition is that when their social identity was changing in the later nineteenth century, they responded to the challenge with remarkable powers of adaptation. With a diminished foothold in the ranks of the aristocracy and gentry they were soon tapping into the wealth of the successful professional and managerial classes. A typical example would be the massive financial and personal support for mission work made by a man like Huntington Stone, and his sister, Mrs. Flockhart Jones—support made possible by their father's successful management of the Peek Frean biscuit company. That sort of beneficence gave the benefactor a voice in the way the funds were spent—a dynamic of control, which must be distinguished from the previous situation of the self-directing gentleman or lady evangelist. This earlier role was epitomized by Henry William Soltau, and, more especially, by his children, who were free to do and go just as they believed the Lord was directing them—some of the last of the freelance independents.

---

50. In 1881, the elderly bachelor John Nelson Darby had a valet and two other domestic servants.

Bibliography

[Agier, Pierre Jean]. *Vues sur le second avènement de J.-C., ou Analyse de l'ouvrage de Lacunza sur cette importante matière*. Paris: Eberhart, 1818.
Alexander, Robert. *The Rise and Progress of British Opium Smuggling, and Its Effects upon India, China, and the Commerce of Great Britain: Four Letters Addressed to the Right Honourable Earl of Shaftesbury*. London: Seeley, Jackson and Halliday, 1856.
Alison, A[lexander]. *Our Future Policy: Second Address to the Electors*. London: Ridgway, 1852.
Allen, Humphrey. *The Gospel Ministry; a Sermon preached in St Peter's Church, Hereford on Sunday Morning December 30, 1832, occasioned by the death of the Rev. Henry Gipps, LLB., late rector of St Peter's and Rector of the united parish of St Owen in that city*. London: Nisbet, 1833.
Allen, William. *Life of William Allen with selections from his correspondence*. 3 vols. London: Gilpin, 1846.
Alpha. "The Drama at Hereford." *Notes and Queries*, 4th series, l (15 February 1868) 141–42.
Alumni Dublinenses [*Al. Dub.*]. See Burtchaell, G. D., and T. U. Sadleir.
Alumni Oxonienses [*Al. Oxon.*]. See Foster, Joseph.
Alumni Cantabrigienses [*Al. Cantab.*]. See Venn, J. A.
Ambrose of Milan. *De Officiis* [*Ministrorum*]. Vol. 1, *Introduction, Text and Translation*. Edited by Ivor J. Davidson. Oxford Early Christian Studies. Oxford: Oxford University Press, 2001.
The American McAll Association. *The American McAll Record*. Periodical. Philadelphia: The Association, 1883–1933.
American National Biography [*ANB*]. See Garraty, A., and Mark C. Carnes.
Anderson, Rufus. *History of the Missions of the American Board of Commissioners for Foreign Missions to the Oriental Churches*. 2 vols. Boston: Congregational, 1873.
Andrews, John S. "Brethren Hymnology." *Evangelical Quarterly* 28 (1956) 208–29.
Annan, Noel Gilroy. *Leslie Stephen, His Thought and Character in Relation to His Time*. Cambridge: Harvard University Press, 1952.
Anon. "Brief Notice of *Fisher's Drawing Room Scrap Book*." *Eclectic Review*, n.s., 24 (1848) 765–66.
———. *A Brief Record of the last days of Robert Howard*. N.p.: privately printed, 1871.
———. *Brook St. Chapel, N.17, opened June 1839: A little history, our present stand*. London: Brook Street Chapel, 1963.
———. "Burma, Opium and the Trade Route to Yunnan." *Friend of China: The organ of the Anglo-Oriental Society for the suppression of the Opium Trade* 10 (1876) 290–98.

———. *Current Biography Yearbook: Who's News and Why, 1945*. New York: Wilson, 1971.

———. "East End Juvenile Mission." *Sunday at Home* 15 (1878) 444–46.

———. "The Evils of Separatism." *Church of England Magazine* 7 (1839) 176.

———. "Francis Fox of Plymouth, 1765–1812." *Journal of the Friends Historical Society* 17.2 (1920) 46.

———. *Guide to Kendal, with a short description of the ancient halls and pleasant walks in the vicinity*. Kendal, UK: Robson, 1883.

———. "John Thomas of Bristol and the Kennet and Avon Canal." *Journal of the Friends Historical Society* 17 (1920) 29–32.

———. *A Letter from a Friend in America to Luke Howard of Tottenham, near London, in which the character of our late friend, Job Scott is vindicated and defended . . .* N.p.: 1826.

———. "Memoir of R. de Rodt." *Calcutta Christian Observer*, October 1843, 561–84.

———. "Nineteenth Century Apprentice Became Scholar and Theologian: Thomas Byrth of Plymouth Dock." *Devon and Cornwall Notes and Queries* (1958) 270–73.

———. *Open Communion with Liberty of Ministry the only practicable ground for real union amongst Christians. By an Ex-member of the Society of Friends*. 4th ed. London: Central Tract Depot, 1840.

———. "The Plymouth Brethren." *Congregational Magazine*, n.s., 6 (1842) 698–707.

———. "Plymouth Brethrenism." *British Quarterly Review* 58 (1873) 378–413.

———. *Random Recollections of Exeter Hall in 1834–1837, by one of the Protestant Party*. London: Nisbet, 1838.

———. *Religious Liberty in Tuscany in 1851: Documents relative to the trial and incarceration of Count Guicciardini and others exiled from Tuscany by decree 17 May 1851*. London: Nisbet, [1852].

———. *Select Hymns for Christian Emigrants to sing or repeat on the voyage. By an intending emigrant*. London: Trelawney Saunders, [1842].

———. "The University of Cambridge." *Tait's Edinburgh Magazine* 4.21 (1833) 265–75.

———. "The University of Dublin." *Quarterly Journal of Education* 6 (July 1833) 5–27; 201–37.

Armistead, Wilson, ed. *Journal of George Fox being an historical account of the Life, Travels, Sufferings . . .* 7th ed. 2 vols. London: Cash, 1852.

Armstrong, N[icholas]. *Cain, Balaam and Core, types of the apostate church: A Sermon preached at St Saviour's church, Southwark, on behalf of the British Reformation Society, on Sunday afternoon, October 23, 1831*. London: Harding, [1831].

Ash, Edward. "The Beacon Controversy and the Yearly Meeting Committee of 1835–37." *The Friend*, September 1870, 207–11, and November 1870, 256–67.

Ashton, R[obert] S[tone], ed. *The Christian Traveller's Continental Handbook*. 4th ed. London: Elliot Stock, 1889.

Asiatic Journal and Monthly Miscellany.

The Athenaeum.

Austin, Alvyn. *China's Millions: The China Inland Mission and Late Qing Society, 1832–1905*. Grand Rapids: Eerdmans, 2007.

Ball, Richard. *Dissuasive Considerations more particularly in reference to joining the Established Church, addressed to the Society of Friends . . .* London: Hamilton, Adams, 1837.

———. *Holy Scripture, the Test of Truth: An Appeal to its paramount authority against certain passages in Dr. Hancock's "Defence". . . .* London: Hamilton, Adams, 1835.

———. *Principles and their Results*. Introduction by J. E. Howard. London: Nisbet, 1851.

Barfoot, Peter, and John Wilkes, eds. *The Universal British Directory of Trade, Commerce, and Manufacture comprehending Lists of the Inhabitants* . . . 5 vols. London: Champante and Whitrow, 1790–98.

Barker, George Fisher Russell, and Alan Herbert Stenning, eds. *The record of old Westminsters: A biographical list of all those who are known to have been educated at Westminster school from the earliest times to 1927.* 2 vols. London: Chiswick, 1928.

Barnardo, Mrs. [Syrie Louise Elmsie], and James Marchant. *Memoirs of the late Dr. Barnardo.* London: Hodder and Stoughton, 1907.

[Barry, D. T., ed.] *Church Missionary Society Register of Missionaries and Native Clergy Part 1 from 1804 to 1894.* [London]: CMS, [1896].

Baxter, Robert. *Narrative of the Facts characterising the Spiritual Manifestations in members of Mr. Irving's congregation, and other individuals, in England and Scotland, and formerly in the writer himself.* London: Nisbet, 1833.

Baylee, Joseph. *The Institutions of the Church of England are of Divine Authority . . . An answer to a tract entitled "Are the Institutions of the Church of England human or divine?"* 3rd ed. Dublin: Curry, 1838.

Bean, William Wardell. *The parliamentary representation of the six northern counties of England: Cumberland, Durham, Lancashire, Northumberland, Westmoreland, and Yorkshire, and their cities and boroughs . . . [1603–1886].* Pt. 1. Hull: Barnwell, 1890.

Beattie, David J. *Brethren: The Story of a Great Recovery.* Kilmarnock: Ritchie, 1940.

Bebbington, David W. "The Dissenting Political Upsurge of 1833–34." In *Modern Christianity and Cultural Aspirations*, edited by David W. Bebbington and Timothy Larsen, 224–45. London: Sheffield Academic, 2003.

Beddy, J. Fawcett. *Journal of a Missionary returning from India.* London: Macintosh, 1872.

[Bell, J. H.] *Abstract of Answers to the Appeal, dated May 1867.* N.p., [1867].

Bellett, John Gifford, et al. *Interesting Reminiscences of the Early History of "Brethren."* In a letter by J.G.B[ellett] to James McAllister, with a series of post-scripts by other Brethren. N.p.: n.d.

[Bellett, L. M.] *Recollections of the Late J. G. Bellett by his daughter.* London: Rouse, 1895.

Ben-Ezra, Juan Josafat. See Lacunza y Diaz, Manuel de.

Bennet, W[illiam] H[enry]. *Robert Cleaver Chapman of Barnstaple.* Introduction by James Wright. Glasgow: Pickering & Inglis, 1902.

[Beverley, Robert Mackenzie]. *Analysis, by a student of prophecy of "Thoughts on the Apocalypse," by B. W. Newton.* London: Longman, Brown, Green & Longmans, 1845.

———. *"Cambridge besieged"; or, The rehearsal of a deep tragedy, at the theatre, Barnwell, which is to be performed by serious Christians, at the next meeting of the Bible Society, written by a Saint, a Member of the University of Cambridge.* London: Barnard and Farley, 1818.

———. *Catholic Claims and the anti-Catholic Petitioners.* Selby: Booth, 1825.

———. *Christ victorious: A sermon preached at the Independent Chapel, Scarborough, to commemorate the extinction of British colonial slavery, on Thursday evening, July 31st, 1834.* Beverley: Johnson, [1834].

———. *The Church of England examined by Scripture and tradition: In an answer to lectures by John Venn on the Christian ministry.* London: Groombridge, 1842.

———. *The Darwinian theory of the transmutation of species: Examined by a graduate of the University of Cambridge.* London: Nisbet, 1867.

———. *The Devotee: A Tale.* Cambridge: Hodson, 1823.

———. *The heresy of a human priesthood, traced in letters on the present state of the visible church of Christ, addressed to John Angell James, Minister of the Gospel in Birmingham.* London: Simpkin, Marshall & Dinnis, 1839.

———. *Horrida Hystrix, Satyricon Castoreanum quod ex schedis manuscriptis deprompsit unus e societate lollardorum.* Hull: Wilson, 1826.

———. *An Inquiry into the Scriptural Doctrine of Christian Ministry.* London: Groombridge, [1841].

———. *A letter to Godfrey Higgins, Esq. in answer to his "Apology for the life and character of Mohammed."* Beverley: Turner, 1829.

———. *A letter to His Grace the Archbishop of York on the present corrupt state of the Church of England.* Beverley: Johnson, 1831.

———. *A letter to H.R.H. the Duke of Gloucester, chancellor, on the present corrupt state of the University of Cambridge.* 3rd ed. London: Dinnis; Simpkin & Marshall, 1833.

———. *Letters on the Present State of the Visible Church of Christ, addressed to John Angell James.* London: Dinnis, 1836.

———. *The Posthumous Letters of the Reverend Rabshakeh Gathercoal, late Vicar of Tuddington, now first published, with explanatory notes, and dedicated to the Lord Bishop of London.* London: Westley and Davis, 1835.

———. *The Redan, a poem.* 2nd ed. London: Hamilton, Adams, 1856.

———. *Sermon preached at Hull on the 13th November, MDCCCXXXI, on the Unknown Tongues.* London: Westley and Davis, 1831.

———. *The tombs of the prophets, a lay sermon on the corruptions of the Church of Christ.* Beverley: Johnson, 1831.

Beverley, William. "Diary of William Beverley of 'Blandfield' during a visit to England 1750." *Virginia Magazine of History and Biography* 36 (1928) 27–35, 161–69.

[Beverley, William, J. Coltman, and R. M. Beverley]. *Speeches delivered in the town-hall of Beverley at a . . . meeting . . . for the purpose of petitioning Parliament to abolish slavery in the West Indies, February 26th, 1824.* Beverley: Turner, 1824.

Bible Society. *Twenty-eighth Report of the Bible Society.* London: 1832.

Bickford, James Arscott Raleigh, and M. E. Bickford. *The Private Lunatic Asylums of the East Riding.* Beverley: East Yorkshire Local History Society, 1976.

Bierman, John, and Colin Smith. *Alamein: War without Hate; The Desert Campaign of 1940–43.* London: Viking, 2002.

———. *Fire in the Night: Wingate of Burma, Ethiopia and Zion.* London: Macmillan, 1999.

Birks, T[homas] R[awson]. *Memoir of the Rev. Edward Bickersteth, late rector of Watton, Herts.* 3rd ed. 2 vols. London: Seeleys, 1852.

Blackwell Dictionary of Evangelical Biography [BDEB]. See Lewis, Donald M.

[Blomfield], C[harles] J[ames], Bishop of London. *A Charge delivered to the Clergy of the Diocese of London at the Visitation in July 1834.* London: Fellowes, 1834.

Blow, Samuel. *Reminiscences of Thirty Years' Gospel Work and Revival Times.* Kilmarnock: Ritchie, ca. 1885.

Boase, C[harles] W[illiam]. *The Elijah Ministry (with "Supplementary Narrative").* Edinburgh: Grant, 1868.

Boase, Frederic. *Modern English Biography . . .* 6 vols. Truro: Netherton and Worth, 1908.

Boase, George Clement, and William Prideaux Courtney. *Bibliotheca Cornubiensis: A catalogue of the writings of Cornishmen and of works relating to the county of Cornwall.* 3 vols. London: Longmans, Green, Reader & Dyer, 1874–1882.

Bogue, David. *Discourses on the Millennium*. London: Hamilton, 1818.
Bolton, John. "Obituary: Trelawney William Saunders." *Geographical Journal* 36.3 (1910) 363–66.
Booth, Catherine M[umford]. *Female Teaching; or, The Rev. A. A. Rees versus Mrs. Palmer, Being a Reply to a Pamphlet by the Above Gentleman on the Sunderland Revival*. London: Stevenson, [1861].
Borthwick, John Douglas. *History and Biographical Gazetteer [sic] of Montreal to the year 1892*. Montreal: Lovell, 1892.
Bouterwek, Karl Wilhelm. *Leben und Wirken Rudolf's von Rodt VDM, weil. Missionars der Londoner Missionsgesellschaft in Indien*. Elberfeld: Friderichs, 1852.
Bowes, John. *The Autobiography or History of the Life of John Bowes*. Glasgow: Gallie, 1872.
Boys, Thomas. *The Christian Dispensation Miraculous*. Republished from *The Jewish Expositor*. 2nd ed. London: Seeley, 1832.
Bradley, James E., and Dale K. Van Kley, eds. *Religion and Politics in Enlightenment Europe*. Notre Dame: University of Notre Dame, 2001.
Braga, Stuart. *All His Benefits: The Young and Deck Families in Australia*. Australia: priv. printed, 2013. [ISBN 9780959726138.]
Braithwaite, Joseph Bevan, ed. *Memoirs of Anna Braithwaite: Being a sketch of her early life and ministry and extracts from her private memoranda, 1830–59*. London: Headley, 1905.
———. *Memoirs of Joseph John Gurney with selections from his Journal and Correspondence*. 2nd ed. 2 vols. Norwich: Fletcher and Alexander, 1855.
Braithwaite, Robert. *The Life and Letters of Rev. William Pennefather*. London: Shaw, 1878.
Brecht, Martin. "The Relationship between Established Protestant Church and Free Church: Hermann Gundert and Britain." In *Protestant Evangelicalism: Britain, Ireland, Germany and America, c. 1750–c. 1950; Essays in Honour of W. R. Ward*, edited by Keith Robbins, 135–51. Oxford: Blackwell, 1990.
Brenton, [Lancelot] Charles [Lee]. *Alas my brother, I Kings xiii.30: A letter to the friends of Harry George Chester, late Lieut.-Col. of the 23rd Royal Welsh Fusiliers, who fell at the Battle of Alma, Sept 20, 1854*. London: Longman, [1854].
———. See Raikes, Henry. *Memoir. . . reedited by Brenton*.
———. *A Sermon on Revelations [sic] XIV. 13: Tending to shew the absurdity and impiety of the promiscuous use of the church burial service, preached in the parish church of Stadhampton, Oxon. On Sunday, December 11, 1831*. Oxford: Baxter, 1831.
———. *A Sermon on Revelation . . .* 2nd ed. Ryde: Partridge and Oakey, 1849.
Brethren Archivists and Historians Network Review [BAHNR], later *Brethren Historical Review* [BHR].
Brethren Historical Review [BHR], previously *Brethren Archivists and Historians Network Review* [BAHNR].
B[rewer], C[harles]. "Early Days in Herefordshire." In *The Christian Outlook: A compendium of papers on various aspects of Christian Life and Doctrine*, edited by J. H. Burridge, 84–93. Glasgow: Pickering and Inglis, [1899].
Briggs, Asa. *The Age of Improvement 1783–1867*. 2nd imprint with corrections. London: Longman, 1960.
Brightwell, Cecilia Lucy. *Memorials of the Life of Amelia Opie, selected and arranged from her Letters, Diaries and other Manuscripts*. Norwich: Fletcher and Alexander, 1854.
Brissot, J[acques]-P[ierre]. *Nouveau voyage dans les États-Unis de l'Amérique septentrionale, fait en 1788*. 2 vols. Paris: Buisson, 1791.

British Critic, Quarterly Theological Review and Ecclesiastical Record.

British Foreign Office. *United States. No. 1 (1896). Correspondence respecting the question of the Boundary of British Guiana.* London: H.M.Stationery Office, 1896.

The British Medical Journal.

Brock, Michael. *The Great Reform Act.* London: Hutchinson, 1973.

Brock, Peter. "The Peace Testimony of the Early Plymouth Brethren." *Church History* 53 (1984) 30–45.

Brockie, William. *Memoirs of Arthur Augustus Rees: Minister of the Gospel at Sunderland.* London: Simpkin, Marshall, 1884.

Bromley, E[ustace] B. *They were men sent from God: A Centennial Record (1836–1936) of Gospel Work in India amongst Telegus in the Godavari Delta and neighbouring parts.* Bangalore: Scripture Literature, 1937.

Bronkhurst, H. V. P. *The Colony of British Guiana and its labouring population.* London: Woolmer, 1883.

Brooke, Richard Sinclair. *Recollections of the Irish Church.* London: Macmillan, 1877.

Broomhall, A[lfred] J[ames]. *Hudson Taylor and China's Open Century.* Book 4, *Survivor's Pact.* London: Hodder and Stoughton, 1984.

Brown, Horatio [Robert] F[orbes]. *John Addington Symonds: A Biography compiled from his papers and Correspondence.* London: Nimmo, 1895.

Brown, James Wood. *An Italian Campaign or the Evangelical movement in Italy, 1845–87, from the letters of R. W. Stewart of Leghorn.* London: Hodder and Stoughton, 1890.

Brown, Judith M., and Robert Eric Frykenberg, eds. *Christians, Cultural Interactions and India's Religious Traditions.* Grand Rapids: Eerdmans, 2002.

Browning, Robert, and Elizabeth Browning. See Kelley, Philip.

Budge, E[rnest] A[lfred] Wallis. *By Nile and Tigris: A Narrative of Journeys in Egypt and Mesopotamia on behalf of the British Museum between the years 1886 and 1913.* 2 vols. London: Murray, 1920.

Bulteel, H[enry] B[ellenden]. *A Sermon on I Corinthians 2:12 preached before the University of Oxford, at St Mary's on Sunday, Feb. 6, 1831.* Oxford: Baxter, 1831.

Burgh, William. *The Apocalypse Unfulfilled; or, An Exposition of the Book of Revelation.* 2nd ed. Dublin: Tims, 1833.

———. *Lectures on the Second Advent of Our Lord Jesus Christ and connected events: With an introduction on the use of unfulfilled prophecy.* Dublin: Tims, 1832.

Burgon, John William. *Lives of Twelve Good Men.* 3rd ed. 2 vols. London: Murray, 1889.

Burke, [John] Bernard. *A genealogical and heraldic dictionary of the landed gentry of Great Britain and Ireland.* 5th ed. 2 vols. London: Harrison, Pall Mall, 1871.

Burnham, Jonathan D. *A Story of Conflict: The Controversial Relationship between Benjamin Wills Newton and John Nelson Darby.* Carlisle: Paternoster, 2004.

Burns, Arthur, and Christopher Stray. "The Greek-Play Bishop: Polemic, Prosopography, and Nineteenth-Century Prelates." *Historical Journal* 54.4 (2011) 1013–38.

Burtchaell, George Dames, and Thomas Ulick Sadleir, eds. *Alumni Dublinenses: A Register of the Students, Graduates, Professors and Provosts of Trinity College in the University of Dublin.* London: Williams and Norgate, 1924.

Buxton, Charles ed. *Memoirs of Sir Thomas Fowell Buxton, Baronet, with selections from his correspondence.* Philadelphia: Longstreth, 1849.

Cable, Mildred, and Francesca French. *A Woman Who Laughed: Henrietta Soltau who laughed at Impossibilities and cried: "It shall be done."* London: CIM, 1934.

Calhoon, Robert M. "'A Sorrowful Spectator of These Tumultuous Times': Robert Beverley Describes the Coming of the Revolution." *Virginia Magazine of History and Biography* 73 (1965) 41–55.

Callahan, James Patrick. *Primitivist Piety: The Ecclesiology of the Early Plymouth Brethren.* Lanham, MD: Scarecrow, 1990.

Canton, William. *A History of the British and Foreign Bible Society.* 5 vols. London: Murray, 1904.

Cardale, John Bate. "On the Extraordinary Manifestations in Port-Glasgow." *Morning Watch* 2 (1830) 869–72.

Carpenter, Andrew, ed. *My Uncle John: Edward Stephens's Life of J. M. Synge.* London: Oxford University Press, 1974.

Carron, Theodore William. *The Christian Testimony through the Ages.* Worthing: Lindisfarne, 1956.

Carter, Grayson. *Anglican Evangelicals: Protestant Secessions from the Via Media, c. 1800–1850.* Oxford: Oxford University Press, 2001.

Cartwright, F[rances] D[orothy], ed. *The Life and Correspondence of Major Cartwright.* 2 vols. London: Colburn, 1826.

Case, Henry W. *On Sea and Land, on Creek and River: Being an Account of Experiences in the Visitation of Assemblies of Christians in the West Indies and British Guiana.* London: Morgan and Scott, 1910.

Catalogue of the Library of the Late J. N. Darby, Esq. N.p., 1889.

Chadwick, Owen. *The Victorian Church.* 3rd ed. Part 1. London: Black, 1966.

Chantin, Jean-Pierre. *Les Amis de l'Œuvre de la Vérité: Jansenisme, miracles et fin du monde au XIXe siècle.* Lyon: Presses Universitaires de Lyon, 1998.

Chapman-Huston, Desmond, and Ernest C. Cripps. *Through a City Archway: The Story of Allen and Hanbury's, 1715–1954.* London: Murray, 1954.

Checkland, S. G. *The Gladstones: A Family Biography 1764–1851.* Cambridge: Cambridge University Press, 1971.

China's Millions.

The Christian.

The Christian's Monthly Magazine and Universal Review. London: Simpkin, Marshall.

Christian Witness.

Chronique Religieuse. Paris, 1819–21.

Chronological Table of the Private and Personal Acts of the Parliaments of Great Britain, 1777 (17 Geo. 3) c. 20: "Naturalization of George Soltau, Gerhard Berck, Henry Hammelburg and Gunter Kroger." http://www.legislation.gov.uk/changes/chron-tables/private/18.

Church, Clive H. *The Emergence of a Community: An Introduction to the Origins and Development of the "Thanington High Lanes" Area outside Canterbury.* 30 July 2005. www.thanington-pc.gov.uk/history/origins.pdf.

Church Missionary Record, detailing the Proceedings of the Church Missionary Society.

The Church of England Zenana Missionary Society. *India's Women: The Magazine of the Church of England Zenana Missionary Society.*

The Churchman, a magazine in defence of the Church and Constitution.

Cicero, Marcus Tullius. *De Officiis.* With an English translation by Walter Miller. Loeb Classical Library. London: Heinemann, 1913.

Clark, John Willis, and Thomas McKenny Hughes. *Life and Letters of the Reverend Adam Sedgwick.* 2 vols. Cambridge: Cambridge University Press, 1890.

Clark, Ruth. *Strangers and Sojourners at Port Royal: Being an Account of the Connections between the British Isles and the Jansenists of France and Holland*. Cambridge: Cambridge University Press, 1932.

The Clergy List for 1841. London: Cox, 1841.

Clergy of the Church of England Database. http://theclergydatabase.org.uk.

Clowes, William. *The Journals of William Clowes, a Primitive Methodist Preacher*. London: Hallam and Holiday, 1844.

Coad, F. Roy. *A History of the Brethren Movement*. Exeter: Paternoster, 1968.

Coate, Mary. *Cornwall in the Great Civil War and Interregnum, 1642–1660: A Social and Political Study*. Oxford: Clarendon, 1933.

Cohn, Norman. *The Pursuit of the Millennium: Revolutionary Millenarians and Mystical Anarchists of the Middle Ages*. 3rd ed. London: Temple Smith, 1970.

Coleridge, Ernest Hartley, ed. *Letters of Samuel Taylor Coleridge*. 2 vols. London: Heinemann, 1895.

Collard, Edgar Andrew. *Oldest McGill*. Toronto: Macmillan, 1946.

Cornwall, E. E. *Songs of Pilgrimage and Glory: Notes on the Hymns of Certain Hymn Writers*. London: Central Bible Truth, 1932.

The Courier. Hobart, Tasmania.

[Cowtan, Robert] R. Fitz-Roy Stanley, ed. *Passages from the Autobiography of a "Man of Kent" together with a few rough pen-and-ink sketches . . . , 1817–1865*. London: Whittingham and Wilkins, 1866.

Cox, G. V. *Recollections of Oxford*. 2nd ed. London: Macmillan, 1870.

Craik, Henry. *Principia Hebraica; or, An Easy Introduction to the Hebrew Language: Exhibiting, in twenty four tables, the interpretation of all the Hebrew and Chaldee words . . . in the Old Testament Scriptures*. London: Bagsters, 1864.

Crewdson, Isaac. *A Beacon to the Society of Friends*. London: Hamilton, Adams, 1835.

[Crewdson, Sarah, et al.] *A Short Memorial of William Dillworth Crewdson, who entered, into rest, Dec. 2 1878, from Memoranda written by his wife & other friends*. Kendal: Robson, 1879.

Cripps, Ernest C. *Plough Court: The Story of a Notable Pharmacy, 1715–1927*. London: Allen and Hanbury, 1927.

Croskery, Thomas. *A Catechism on the Doctrines of the Plymouth Brethren*. 6th ed. London: Nisbet, 1868.

———. *Plymouth Brethrenism: A Refutation of its Principles and Doctrines*. London: Mullan, 1879.

Cross, Edwin N. *The Irish Saint and Scholar: A Biography of William Kelly*. London: Chapter Two, 2004.

Crosse, John. *Account of the Grand Musical Festival held in September 1823 in the Cathedral Church of York . . .* York: Wolstenholme, 1825.

Crossley, Alan, and C. R. Elrington, eds. *A History of the County of Oxford*. Vol. 4, *The City of Oxford*. Victoria History of the Counties of England. Oxford: Oxford University Press, 1979.

Crowther, Janice E., and Peter A. Crowther, eds. *The Diary of Robert Sharp of South Cave: Life in a Yorkshire Village 1812–1837*. Oxford: Oxford University Press, 1997.

Cuff, Teddy, and James Brooks. *An Outline History of Stanford in the Vale*. Faringdon: Portwell, 1996. http://www.stanford-in-the-vale.co.uk/history_schoollib.shtml.

Daily Telegraph.

Daly, Robert, ed. *Letters and Papers of the late Theodosia A. Viscountess Powerscourt.* 5th ed. London: Seeley, Burnside and Seeley, 1845.

Dann, Robert Bernard. *Father of Faith Missions: The Life and Times of Anthony Norris Groves.* Milton Keynes: Authentic, 2004.

Darby, John Nelson. *The Collected Writings of J. N. Darby* [CW]. Edited by William Kelly. 34 vols. Kingston-on-Thames: Stowe Hill Bible and Tract, n.d.

———. *Letters of J.N.D[arby].* 3 vols. Kingston-on-Thames: Stowe Hill Bible and Tract, n.d.

———. *Notes and Comments on Scripture, from the notebooks of J. N. Darby.* 7 vols. London: James Carter, [1883].

———. *Notes and Jottings from various meetings.* Lancing: Kingston Bible Trust, [1978].

———. "On the presence and action of the Holy Ghost in the Church." [Valence, 1844]. In *Darby's CW* 3:207–313.

———. "Reflections upon the Prophetic Inquiry and the Views advanced in it." [Dublin, 1829]. In *Darby's CW*, 2:1–31.

———. "Remarks on Light and Conscience" [Plymouth: Rowe, 1837, reprinted from the *Christian Witness*, October 1836]. In *Darby's CW*, 3:57–72.

———. "The Sabbath or, Is the Law Dead, or Am I?" In *Darby's CW*, 10:270–303.

Darlington, William. *Memorials of John Bartram and Humphry Marshall with notices of their botanical contemporaries.* Philadelphia: Lindsay & Blakiston, 1849.

Davenport, Rowland A. *Albury Apostles, the Story of the Body Known as the Catholic Apostolic Church.* 2nd ed. London: Neillgo, 1974.

Davies, C. Maurice. *Unorthodox London; or, Phases of Religious Life in the Metropolis.* London: Tinsley, 1873.

Day, Angélique. "Portraying Donegal: The Ordnance Survey Memoirs." *Donegal Annual* 51 (1999) 77–92.

Debrett, [John]. *Peerage, Baronetage, Knightage and Companionage.* London: 1902.

Deck, James G. *A Word of Warning to all who love the Lord Jesus: The Heresy of Mr. Prince with extracts from his letters.* London: Simpkin and Marshall, 1845.

De Morgan, Augustus. *A Budget of Paradoxes.* 2nd ed. Edited by David Eugene Smith. Chicago: Open Court, 1915.

Devon and Cornwall Notes and Queries.

Dickson, Neil T. R. *Brethren in Scotland 1838–2000: A Social Study of an Evangelical Movement.* Carlisle: Paternoster, 2002.

Dickson, Neil T. R., and Tim Grass, eds. *The Growth of the Brethren Movement: National and International Experiences; Essays in Honour of Harold H. Rowdon.* Milton Keynes: Paternoster, 2006.

Dickson, Neil T. R., and T. J. Marinello, eds. *Culture, Spirituality and the Brethren.* Troon: BAHN, 2014.

Dictionary of American Biography. See Johnson, Allen, and Dumas Malone.

Dictionary of National Biography [*DNB*]. See Stephen, Leslie, and Sidney Lee, eds.

Dictionary of New Zealand Biography [*DNZB*]. See Oliver, W. H., and Claudia Orange, eds.

Dixon, William Hepworth. *Spiritual Wives.* 2 vols. 2nd ed. London: Hurst and Blackett, 1868.

Dobbie, William [George Sheddon]. *Active Service with Christ.* London: Marshall, Morgan and Scott, 1948.

———. *Christianity and Military Service.* London: Officers Christian Union, 1936.

Dod, Charles R. *Parliamentary Companion.* Twentieth year. 2nd ed. New Parliament. London: Whittaker, 1852.

Dodwell, Edward, and James Samuel Miles. *Alphabetical List of the Hon East India Company's Madras Civil Servants, 1780–1839*. London: printed Woking, for EIC, 1839.

———. *Alphabetical List of the Medical Officers of the Indian Army, 1764–1838*. London: printed Woking, for EIC, 1839.

Douglass, Jane Dempsey. "Calvin in Ecumenical Context." In *The Cambridge Companion to John Calvin*, edited by Donald K. McKim, 305–16. Cambridge: Cambridge University Press, 2004.

Drummond, Andrew Landale. *Edward Irving and his Circle, including some consideration of the "Tongues" movement in the light of modern psychology*. London: Clarke, [1934].

Drummond, Andrew Landale, and James Bulloch. *The Scottish Church, 1688–1843*. Edinburgh: Saint Andrew, 1973.

[Drummond, Henry]. *The Spirit in Mr. Baxter tried by Scripture*. London: Douglas, 1833.

D[unkin], A[lfred] J[ohn], ed. *Monumenta Anglicana: Coggeshall, Stanford in the Vale, Dartford*. Dartford: priv. printed, 1852.

———. *A Report of the proceedings of the British Archaeological Association, at the fifth general meeting, holden in Worcester . . . August 1848*. London: priv. printed, 1851.

Dunkin, John. *The History and Antiquities of Dartford with Topographical Notices of the Neighbourhood*. London: Smith, 1844.

Eadie, J. *Life of John Kitto, DD, FSA*, Edinburgh: Oliphant, 1858.

Early Days. Journal of the Royal Western Australian Historical Society.

Eclectic Magazine. New York: Leavett, Trow.

Eclectic Review.

Edinburgh Annual Register.

Edwards, G. T. "Charles Stokes Dudley." *Bible Society Monthly Reporter* (1892) 152–54, 167–69.

Ehret, Joseph. "Der Rückzug der Basler Mission aus Russland." *Basler Zeitschrift* 53 (1954) 159–204.

Elliott, Edward Bishop. *Horae Apocalypticae; or, A Commentary on the Apocalypse, Critical and Historical*. 4th ed. 4 vols. London: Seeley, Burnside and Seeley, 1851. 5th ed., 1862.

The Engineering Magazine.

Enright, Flan. "Edward Synge, The Dysert Proselytiser." *The Other Clare* 6 (1982) 8.

Epps, John. *Diary of the late John Epps, MD*. Edited by Mrs. [E.] Epps. London: Kent, [1875].

Evangelical Alliance. *The Evangelical Alliance: Proceedings of the Conference held at Freemasons' Hall, London from Aug. 19th to Sept. 2nd 1846*. London: 1847.

———. *Jubilee of the Evangelical alliance: Proceedings of the 10th international conference held in London, June–July 1896*. London: Shaw, 1897.

Evangelical Magazine [EM].

Evans, Charles. *A Short History of St. Peter's Church, Hereford*. Gloucester: British Publishing, 1967 [1952].

Everett, James. *The Midshipman and the Minister: The Quarter-deck and the Pulpit*. London: Hamilton, Adams, 1867.

The Examiner.

Exeter Flying Post.

Exeter Pocket Journal (1827).

Falmouth Packet and Cornish Herald.

Farrar, Thomas, ed. *Notes on the history of the church in Guiana*. Berbice, British Guiana: Macdonald, 1892.

Farrell, Stephen. "Dublin University." In *The History of Parliament: The House of Commons 1820-1832*, edited by D. R. Fisher. Cambridge: Cambridge University Press, 2009. http://www.historyofparliamentonline.org/volume/1820-1832/constituencies/dublin-university.

Ferguson, Franklin. *Reminiscences of Christian Experience and Service in New Zealand from Very Early Days*. [Palmerston North: self published, ca. 1941.]

Feuille de la Commission des Églises Associées pour l'Évangélisation. Vol. 1, 1836-1837. Geneva: M.-E. Carey, 1837.

First, Ruth, and Ann Scott. *Olive Schreiner: A Biography*. London: Deutsch, 1980.

Fitzpatrick, John C., ed. *The Writings of George Washington from the Original Manuscript Sources*. Online at the Electronic Text Center of the Library of the University of Virginia, http://etext.lib.virginia.edu/washington/fitzpatrick.

Foot, M. R. D., ed. *The Gladstone Diaries*. 2 vols. [1825-39.] Oxford: Clarendon, 1968.

Footsteps of Truth.

Forster, Edward Morgan. *Marianne Thornton: A Domestic Biography 1797-1887*. New York: Harcourt, Brace, 1956.

Foster, Joseph. *Alumni Oxonienses [Al. Oxon.]: The Members of the University of Oxford, 1715-1886*. 4 vols. London: Foster, 1887.

———. *A Pedigree of Forsters and Fosters of the North of England and of some of the families connected with them*. London: priv. printed, 1871.

———. *The Pedigree of Wilson of High Wray and Kendal, and the families connected with them*. London: priv. printed, 1871.

———. *A revised genealogical account of the various families descended from Francis Fox of St Germans, Cornwall . . .* London: priv. printed, 1872.

Fox, D. C., ed. *The Wellington Hymn Book: A selection of Psalms and Hymns, adapted for public, social and private use*. London: Simpkin, Marshall, 1857.

Fox, Hubert C. *Quaker Homespun: Life of Thomas Fox of Wellington, Serge Maker and Banker, 1747-1821*. London: Allen and Unwin, 1958.

[Fox, Samuel Middleton]. *Two Homes, by a grandson*. Plymouth: Brendon, 1925.

Friel, Brian. *Translations*. London: French, 1981.

The Friend of China. The organ of the Anglo-Oriental Society for the suppression of the Opium Trade.

Fromow, George H. *Teachers of the Faith and the Future: B. W. Newton and Dr. S. P. Tregelles*. London: Sovereign Grace Advent Testimony, n.d.

Froom, LeRoy Edwin. *The Prophetic Faith of Our Fathers: The Historical Development of Prophetic Interpretation*. 4 vols. Washington, DC: Review and Herald, 1950-54.

Frykenberg, Robert Eric, ed. *Christians and Missionaries in India: Cross-Cultural Communication since 1500*. Grand Rapids: Eerdmans, 2003.

———. "The Impact of Conversion and Social Reform upon Society in South India during the Late Company Period." In *Indian Society and the Beginnings of Modernization, c. 1830-1850*, edited by C. H. Philips and Mary Doreen Wainwright, 187-243. London: School of Oriental and African Studies, 1976.

Furneaux, Robin. *William Wilberforce*. London: Hamilton, 1974.

G., A. Letter to the editor. *Christian Observer* 18 (1819) 231.

Galton, Francis, and Edgar Schuster. *Noteworthy Families (Modern Science): An Index to Kinships in near degrees between persons whose achievements are honourable and have been publicly recorded*. London: Murray, 1906.

Garbett, Charles. *Reply to Captain Hall's pamphlet entitled "An Address to the Christians," &c.* Hereford: Vale, 1839.

Garnett, Jane, and Colin Matthew, eds. *Revival and Religion since 1700: Essays for John Walsh.* London: Hambledon, 1993.

Garraty, A., and Mark C. Carnes, eds. *American National Biography [ANB].* 24 vols. New York: Oxford University Press, 1999.

Gash, Norman. *Aristocracy and People, Britain 1815-65.* London: Arnold, 1979.

Gathercole, M[ichael] A[ugustus]. *A Letter to Charles Lushington, Esquire, M.P., in Reply to a Remonstrance addressed by him to the Bishop of London on account of his Lordship's having recommended in his late charge to the clergy of his diocese the letters to a dissenting minister signed L.S.E.* London: Whittaker, 1835.

[———]. *L.S.E. Letters to a Dissenting Minister of the Congregational Independent Denomination: Containing remarks on the principles of that sect: and the author's reasons for leaving it and conforming to the Church of England.* London: Groombridge, 1834.

Gelber, Harry Gregor. *Opium, Soldiers and Evangelicals: England's 1840-1842 War with China, and afterwards.* Basingstoke: Palgrave, Macmillan, 2004.

Gentleman's Magazine.

The Geographical Journal.

Gerhold, Dorian. "Wandsworth's Gunpowder Mills 1656-1713." *Surrey Archaeological Collections: Relating to the History and Antiquities of the County* 82 (2002) 171-83.

Gilley, Sheridan. "Edward Irving: Prophet of the Millennium." In *Revival and Religion since 1700: Essays for John Walsh*, edited by Jane Garnett and Colin Matthew, 95-110. London: Hambledon, 1993.

Gipps, Henry. *Sermons and Sketches of Sermons by the late Rev. Henry Gipps, LLB, vicar of St Peter's and Rector of the united parish of St Owen in the city of Hereford.* Revised, with introductory remarks by J. A. La Trobe. London: Seeley and Burnside, 1833.

———. *A Treatise on Regeneration.* London: Hatchard, 1818.

———. *A Treatise on "The first resurrection" and "The thousand years" foretold in the twentieth chapter of the Book of Revelations.* London: Nisbet, 1831.

Giudici, Luigi (L'abate). *Lettres Italiennes sur l'avènement intermédiaire et le règne de Jésus-Christ.* Lugano, 1816-17.

Gladstone, William Ewart. "The Evangelical Movement: Its parentage, progress and issue." In *Gleanings of Past Years*, 7:201-41. 7 vols. London: Murray, 1875-79.

———. *Diaries.* See Foot, M. R. D.

Gobat, Samuel. *Samuel Gobat Bishop of Jerusalem: A Biographical Sketch drawn chiefly from his own journals.* London, Nisbet, 1884.

Godwin, Joscelyn. *The Theosophical Enlightenment.* Albany: State University of New York Press, 1994.

Good, Donald G. "Elisha Bates and Social Reform." *Quaker History* 58 (1969) 81-92.

———. "Elisha Bates and the Beaconite controversy." *Quaker History* 73 (1984) 34-47.

The Gospel Standard.

Grass, Tim. *Gathering to His Name: The Story of Open Brethren in Britain and Ireland.* Milton Keynes: Paternoster, 2006.

———. "The Restoration of a Congregation of Baptists: Baptists and Irvingism in Oxfordshire." *Baptist Quarterly* 37 (1998) 283-97.

———. "'The Taming of the Prophets': Bringing Prophecy under Control in the Catholic Apostolic Church." *Journal of the European Pentecostal Theological Association* 16 (1996) 58–70.

———, ed. *Witness in Many Lands: Leadership and Outreach among the Brethren*. Troon: BAHN, 2013.

Graves, Algernon. *The Royal Academy of Arts: A Complete Dictionary of contributors and their work from its foundation in 1769 to 1904*. 8 vols. London: Graves and Bell, 1905–1906.

Graves, Richard. "Essay on the character of the Apostles and Evangelists" [1798]. In *The Whole works of Richard Graves, DD . . . now first collected with a Memoir of his life and writings by his son* [R. H. Graves]. 4 vols. 1:ccxvii–ccxxxvi, 1–223. Dublin: Curry, 1840.

Gribben, Crawford, and Timothy C. F. Stunt, eds. *Prisoners of Hope? Aspects of Evangelical Millennialism in Britain and Ireland, 1800–1880*. Carlisle: Paternoster, 2004.

Gribble, T[heodore] Graham. "American Annexation of Hawaii." *Engineering Magazine* 4 (1893) 898–905.

———. *The Glory of Christ in the Everlasting Covenant: A Message to Jew and Gentile*. London: Marshall, Morgan & Scott, 1937.

Griffiths, G[ordon] D[ouglas], and E[dith] G[race] C[halmers] Griffiths. *History of Teignmouth*. Teignmouth: Brunswick, 1973.

[Grogan, Ellinor Flora Bosworth Smith]. *Reginald Bosworth Smith: A Memoir. By his daughter Lady Grogan*. London: Nisbet, 1909.

Grosskurth, Phyllis. *John Addington Symonds: A Biography*. London: Longman, 1964.

Grover, John. *The Bokhara Victims*. 2nd ed. London: Chapman and Hall, 1845.

Groves, Anthony Norris. *Christian Devotedness*. 2nd ed. London: Hatchard, 1826.

———. *Christian Devotedness*. 3rd ed. London: Nisbet, 1829.

———. *Extraits du Journal de M. Groves, missionnaire à Bagdad*. Neuchâtel: Michaud, 1834. [Copy in Zürich Zentralbibliothek.]

———. *Journals*. See Scott, Alexander John.

———. "Letter from Madras, 28 September 1836." *Feuille de la Commission des Églises Associées pour l'Évangélisation* 1.10 (1837) 261–64.

———. "Letter from Milford Haven, c. 20 March 1836." *Feuille de la Commission des Églises Associées pour l'Évangélisation* 1.5 (1836) 121–22.

———. *On the Nature of Christian Influence*. Bombay: American Mission, 1833.

———. "Undated letter [late 1836?] to Auguste Rochat." *Feuille de la Commission des Églises Associées pour l'Évangélisation* 1.12 (1837) 299–301.

Groves, Edward K[ennaway]. *George Müller and His Successors*. Bristol: priv. printed, 1906.

[Groves, Harriet Baynes]. *Memoir of the Late Anthony Norris Groves containing extracts from his Letters and Journals*. Compiled by his widow. 2nd ed. London: Nisbet, 1857.

Groves, Henry. *Faithful Hanie; or, Disinterested Service: Memoirs of a Ninevite Servant*. London: Nisbet, 1866.

———. *Not of the World: Memoir of Lord Congleton*. London: Shaw, 1884.

[Grubb, Edward.] "Pictures of the Past: II Friends in Ireland." *British Friend* 11 (1902) 311–14.

Grubb, Mollie. "Abraham Shackleton and the Irish Separation of 1797–1803." *Journal of the Friends Historical Society* 56 (1993) 262–71.

Guinness, Henry Grattan. *Light for the Last Days: A study historic and prophetic*. 2nd ed. London: Hodder and Stoughton, 1888.

Gundert, Hermann. *Calwer Tagebuch 1859–1893*. Stuttgart: Frenz, 1986.

———. *Herrmann [sic] Moegling: A Biography*. Edited by Albrecht Frenz. Translated by C. Steinweg and E. Steinweg-Fleckner. Kottayam, Kerala, India: D.C. Books, 1997.

———. *Schriften und Berichte aus Malabar mit Meditationen und Studien*. Stuttgart: Frenz, 1983.

———. *Tagebuch aus Malabar 1837–1859*. Stuttgart: Frenz 1983.

[Gundert, Hermann, and H. Mögling]. *The life of Samuel Hebich: By two of his fellow-labourers*. Translated by J. G. Halliday. London: Seeley, Jackson & Halliday, 1876.

[Gurney, Ellen Mary, ed.] *Letters of Emelia Russell Gurney*. Edited by her niece. London: Nisbet, 1902.

Gurney, Joseph John. *Observations on the religious peculiarities of the Society of Friends*. London: Arch, 1824.

[Haldane, Elizabeth Sanderson]. *Mary Elizabeth Haldane: A Record of a hundred years 1825–1925*. Edited by her daughter. London: Hodder and Stoughton, 1925.

Halévy, Elie. "The Triumph of Reform." In *History of the English People in the 19th Century*. Vol. 3 of 6. London: Benn, 1961 [1927.]

Hall, Percy Francis. *Discipleship! or, Reasons for resigning his naval rank and pay*. 2nd ed. Plymouth: Rowe, 1835.

———. *To the Christians who heard or may have read Mr. Venn's sermon preached at Hereford, December 9th 1838*. Leominster: Chilcott, [1839].

Hamm, Thomas D. *The Transformation of American Quakerism: Orthodox Friends 1800–1907*. Bloomington: Indiana University Press, 1988.

Hancock, John. *Reasons for withdrawing from Society with the People called Quakers . . . and Serious Considerations on Revelation, the Scriptures, Religion, Morality and Superstition . . .* Belfast: Smyth, 1802.

Hancock, Thomas. *A Defence of the Doctrines of Immediate Revelation and Universal and Saving Light in reply to some remarks contained in a work, entitled "A Beacon to the Society of Friends."* 2nd ed. Liverpool: Hodgson, 1835.

Hankin, Christiana C., ed. *Life of Mary Anne SchimmelPenninck*. 2nd ed. London: Longman, 1858.

Hare, Augustus J. C. *The Gurneys of Earlham*. 2 vols. London: Allen, 1895.

Hargrove, Charles. *Reasons for retiring from the Established Church*. Dublin: Tims, 1836.

Harris, A[lfred] N[ewton]. "The Plymouth Brethren, Reminiscences of over Fifty Years Ago, November 1911." *BHR* 5 (2009) 88–101.

Harris, James Lampen. *A Letter to the Christians meeting in Mr Hingston's Loft, Kingsbridge, Nov. 6 1847*. London: Campbell, 1847.

Harrison, J[ohn] F[letcher] C[lews.] *The Second Coming: Popular Millenarianism 1780–1850*. London: Routledge & Kegan Paul, 1979.

Hawaiian Mission Children's Society. *37th Annual Report of the Society*. Honolulu: Press Publishing, 1889.

[Hawkins, Abraham]. *Kingsbridge and Salcombe, with the intermediate Estuary, historically and topographically depicted*. Kingsbridge: Southwood, 1819.

Hendrickson, Kenneth E. *Making Saints: Religion and the Public Image of the British Army 1809–1885*. Madison, NJ: Fairleigh Dickinson University Press, 1998.

Heppingstone, Ian D[avid], and H. Margaret Wilson. "'Mrs John': The Letters of Charlotte Bussell of Cattle Chosen." *Early Days* 3 (Pt. 4, 1972) 7–28; 7 (Pt. 5, 1973) 41–77.

Hicks, Elias. *Journal of the Life and Religious Labours of Elias Hicks: Written by Himself*. 5th ed. New York: Hopper, 1832.

Higgins, Godfrey. *Anacalypsis, an attempt to draw aside the veil of the Saitic Isis; or, An inquiry into the origin of languages, nations, and religions.* 2 vols. London: Longman, Rees, Orme, Brown and Longman, 1836.

———. *An apology for the life and character of the celebrated prophet of Arabia called Mohamed, or the Illustrious.* London: Rowland Hunter 1829.

———. *The Celtic Druids; or, An attempt to shew that the Druids were the priests of Oriental colonies . . . and the builders of Stonehenge, of Carnac, and of other Cyclopean works in Asia and Europe.* London: Rowland Hunter, 1829.

Hole, Charles. *The Life of the Reverend and Venerable William Whitmarsh Phelps, M.A., Late Archdeacon and Canon of Carlisle.* 2 vols. London: Hatchards, 1871.

Hollett, Dave. *Passage from India to El Dorado: Guyana and the Great Migration.* Cranbury, NJ: Associated University Presses, 1999.

Honolulu Daily Bulletin.

Hope, Elizabeth. *General Sir Arthur Cotton: His Life and Work by his daughter, Lady Hope with some Famine Prevention studies by William Digby.* London: Hodder and Stoughton, 1900.

House of Commons. *Accounts and Papers 1861.* Vol. 22, *Poor; Poor (Ireland); Vaccination: Session 5 February–6 August 1861.* [London]: [HM Stationery Office], 1861.

Howard, Elizabeth F. *Downstream: Records of Several Generations.* London: Friends Home Service, 1955.

Howard, John Eliot. *A Caution against the Darbyites, with a word to the Authors of Two recent Pamphlets, and the Testimony of Lord Congleton.* London: Stevenson, 1866. [An expansion of Howard's introduction to Richard Ball, *Principles and their results.*]

Howard, Luke. *An appeal to the Christian Public against a sentence of disownment passed upon a member of the Society of Friends for absenting himself from their silent meetings and submitting to the ordinances of Christ.* London: Thomas Ward, 1838.

[———]. *A Brief Apology for Quakerism inscribed to the Edinburgh Reviewers.* London: Darton and Harvey, 1808.

———. *A Letter from Luke Howard of Tottenham, near London, to a Friend in America containing observations upon a treatise written by Job Scott, entitled Salvation by Christ, &c.* N.p., 1825.

———. *Memoranda of Rachel Howard.* London: Simpkin and Marshall, 1839.

———. *On the Modifications of Clouds and on the principles of their production, suspension, and destruction.* London: Taylor, 1803.

Howard, Robert. *Church Principles.* New ed. London: Hawkins, 1878.

Hudson, D. Dennis. *Protestant Origins in India: Tamil Evangelical Christians, 1706–1835.* Grand Rapids: Eerdmans, 2000.

Huebner, R. A. *Precious Truths Revived and Defended through J. N. Darby.* 3 vols. Morganville, NJ: Present Truth, 1991–95.

[Hunt, Leigh]. *The Rebellion of the Beasts; or, The ass is dead: long live the ass. By a late fellow of St. John's College.* London: Hunt, 1825.

Hunt, Stephen, ed. *Christian Millenarianism: From the Early Church to Waco.* London: Hurst, 2001.

India's Women. The Magazine of the Church of England Zenana Missionary Society.

The Inquirer. London: Central Tract Depot, 1838–40.

Institution of Civil Engineers. *Charter, Bye-Laws and Regulations and List of Members of the Institution of Civil Engineers.* London: Institution of Civil Engineers, 1879.

International Genealogical Index [IGI].

Irving, Edward. "Facts Connected with Recent Manifestations of Spiritual Gifts." *Fraser's Magazine* 4 (1832) 754–61; 5 (1832) 198–205, 316–20.

———. *For Missionaries after the Apostolical School: A Series of Orations in four parts.* London: Hamilton, Adams, 1825.

I[sbell], J. B. *Faithful unto Death: A Memoir of William Graeme Rhind.* London: Yapp, 1863.

Jacini, Stefano. *Un Riformatore Toscano dell'epoca del Risorgimento: Il Conte Guicciardini (1808–1886).* Florence: Sansoni, 1940.

Jackson, Samuel Macauley, et al., eds. *The New Schaff-Herzog Encyclopedia of Religious Knowledge.* 12 vols. New York: Funk and Wagnalls, 1908–12.

Jefferson, Thomas. *Letters of Thomas Jefferson.* http://founders.archives.gov/documents/Jefferson/01-18-02-0068.

[Jeffrey, Francis]. "Review of *A Portraiture of Quakerism* by Thomas Clarkson." *Edinburgh Review* 10 (1807) 85–102.

Jensen, Merrill, ed. *The Documentary History of the Ratification of the Constitution.* Vol. 2, *Ratification of the Constitution by the States, Pennsylvania.* Madison: State Historical Society of Wisconsin, 1976.

Jesse, John Heneage. *Memoirs of King George the Third, His Life and Reign.* 5 vols. Boston: Page, 1902.

Johnson, Allen, and Dumas Malone, eds. *Dictionary of American Biography.* 22 vols. New York: Scribner, 1928–1958.

Johnson, Ryan. "Colonial Mission and Imperial Tropical Medicine: Livingstone College, London, 1893–1914." *Social History of Medicine* 23.3 (2010) 549–66.

Jones, Tod E., ed. *Letters of Francis William Newman, Chiefly on Religion: The Braithwaite Correspondence, 1868–1897.* Online at the Philosophy Documentation Center 2009, http://secure.pdcnet.org/lettersfwn/free.

Journal des Missions Évangéliques. Paris, 1834.

Journal of Ecclesiastical History [JEH].

Journal of the Christian Brethren Research Fellowship [JCBRF], later *BAHN Review*, and *BHR*.

Journal of the Institute of Civil Engineers.

Jowett, William. *Christian Researches in the Mediterranean, from MDCCCXV to MDCCCXX in Furtherance of the Objects of the Church Missionary Society.* 3rd ed. London: Seeley, 1824.

Julian, John, ed. *A Dictionary of Hymnology setting forth the origin and history of Christian hymns of all ages and nations.* 2nd ed. London: Murray, 1907.

Jung, August. *Julius Anton von Poseck: Ein Gründervater der Brüderbewegung.* Wuppertal: Brockhaus, 2002.

———. "Julius Anton von Poseck (1816–1898) and Brethren Origins in Germany." In *The Growth of the Brethren Movement: National and International Experiences*, edited by Neil T. R. Dickson and Tim Grass, 133–44. Carlisle: Paternoster, 2006.

Kaye, John William. *The Administration of the East India Company: A History of Indian Progress.* 2nd ed. London: Bentley, 1853.

Keegan, John. "Chindit Myth." *Times Literary Supplement*, 16 June 1995.

———. "Keen on Heroes." *Daily Telegraph*, 5 October 2002.

Kelley, Philip, and Ronald Hudson. *The Brownings' correspondence.* Vol. 3, January 1832–December 1837. Winfield, KS: Wedgestone, 1985.

Kelly, William, ed. *The Collected Writings of J. N. Darby* [*C.W.*]. Kingston-on-Thames: Stowe Hill Bible and Tract, n.d.

Kendall, Holliday Bickerstaff. *The Origin and History of the Primitive Methodist Church.* London: Robert Bryant, [1900].

Kennedy, Thomas C. "The Condition of Friends." In *British Quakerism, 1860-1920: The Transformation of a Religious Community*, 12-46. Oxford: Oxford University Press, 2001.

Ker, Ian, and Thomas Gornall, eds. *The Letters and Diaries of John Henry Newman*. 4 vols. Oxford: Clarendon, 1978-80.

Kertzer, David I. *The Kidnapping of Edgardo Mortara*. London: Picador, 1997.

Kienzle, Beverly Mayne, and Pamela J. Walker, eds. *Women Preachers and Prophets through Two Millennia of Christianity*. Berkeley: University of California Press, 1998.

Kirkwood, J. H., and C. H. Lloyd, eds. *John Eliot Howard, Fellow of the Royal Society 1807-1883: A Budget of Papers on His Life and Work*. Oxford: Lloyd, 1995.

Kitto, John. *The Lost Senses: Deafness and Blindness*. New York: Carter, 1852.

Kuykendall, Ralph S[impson]. *The Hawaiian Kingdom 1874-1893: The Kalakaua Dynasty*. Vol. 3 of *The Hawaiian Kingdom*. Honolulu: University of Hawaii Press, 1967.

[Lacunza y Diaz, Manuel de] Juan Josafat Ben Ezra [pseud.]. *The Coming of Messiah in Glory and Majesty*. Translated with a preliminary discourse by Edward Irving. 2 vols. London: Seeley, 1827.

Laidlaw, Robert A[lexander.] *The Reason Why*. London: Army Scripture Readers' and Soldiers' and Airmen's Christian Association, n.d.

———. *The Story of the Reason Why*. London: Pickering and Inglis, 1969.

Lake, Kirsopp, ed. *The Apostolic Fathers*. Loeb Classical Library. 2 vols. London: Heinemann, 1917-19.

[Lambert, Bernard]. *Avertissement aux fidèles, sur les signes qui annoncent que tout se dispose pour le retour d'Israël et l'exécution des menaces faites aux gentils apostats*. Paris: Le Clere, 1793.

[———]. *Expositions des Prédictions et des Promesses faites à l'Église pour les derniers temps de la Gentilité; par le P[ère] Lambert*. 2 vols. Paris: Ange Clo / Le Clere, 1806.

Lambert, W[illiam] G[eorge.] *A Call to the Converted*. Oxford: Wheeler, 1831.

The Lancet.

Lang, George H. *Anthony Norris Groves: Saint and Pioneer; A Combined Study of a Man of God and of the Original Principles and Practices of the Brethren with Applications to Present Conditions*. London: Paternoster, 1949.

[Langford, Alfred]. *An Account of Brethren in Hereford*. Hereford: Hereford Times, 1958.

Langford, Paul. *A Polite and Commercial People: England 1727-1783*. Oxford: Clarendon, 1988.

Larson, Timothy, ed. *Biographical Dictionary of Evangelicals*. Leicester: InterVarsity, 2003.

Latham, Jackie E. M. *Search for a New Eden, James Pierrepont Greaves (1777-1842): The Sacred Socialist and His Followers*. Madison: Fairleigh Dickinson University Press, 1999.

L[a Touche], J. D. "Hints on the New System of Education in Ireland." *Christian Observer* 16 (1817) 701-9.

La Trobe, John Antes. *A Burning and Shining Light: A Sermon preached in the parish church of St Peters, Hereford on Sunday evening December 30, 1832 . . .* London: Seeley, 1833.

Layard, Austen Henry. *Autobiography and letters from his childhood until his appointment as H.M. Ambassador at Madrid*. Edited by William N. Bruce. 2 vols. London: Murray, 1903.

Leadbeater, Mary, ed. *Memoirs and Letters of Richard and Elizabeth Shackleton, Late of Ballitore, Ireland.* London: Gilpin, 1849.
LeFanu, E. L. *Life of Dr Orpen.* London: Westerton, 1860.
Le Faye, Deirdre, ed. *Jane Austen's Letters.* 3rd ed. Oxford: Oxford University Press, 1997.
Legg, Marie-Louise, ed. *The Synge Letters: Bishop Edward Synge to His Daughter Alicia: Roscommon to Dublin.* Dublin: Lilliput, 1996.
Leslie, James Blennerhassett, and W. J. R. Wallace, eds. *Clergy of Dublin and Glendalough: Biographical Succession Lists.* Belfast: Ulster Historical Foundation, 2001.
Lewis, Donald M., ed. *Blackwell Dictionary of Evangelical Biography 1730–1860* [BDEB]. 2 vols. Oxford: Blackwell, 1995.
Lewis, George William. *Sermons delivered in the Chapel of Ease, Ramsgate.* London: Hatchard, 1836.
Lewis, Samuel. *A Topographical Dictionary of England.* 4 vols. London: Lewis, 1831.
———. *A Topographical Dictionary of Ireland.* 2 vols. London: Lewis, 1837.
Lewis, Theresa, ed. *Extracts from the journals and correspondence of Miss Berry, from the year 1783 to 1852.* 3 vols. London: Longmans, Green, 1865.
Liber Ecclesiasticus. An authentic statement of the revenues of the Established Church, compiled from the report of the Commissioners appointed "to inquire into the revenues and patronage of the Established Church in England and Wales," presented to Parliament . . . June 22 1835. London: Hamilton, Adams, 1835.
Lichtenberger, F., ed. *Encyclopédie des Sciences Religieuses.* 13 vols. Paris: Sandoz et Fischbacher, 1877–1882.
Liebau, Heike. "Country Priests, Catechists, and Schoolmasters as Cultural, Religious, and Social Middlemen in the Context of the Tranquebar Mission." In *Christians and Missionaries in India: Cross-Cultural Communication since 1500,* edited by Robert Eric Frykenberg, 70–92. Grand Rapids: Eerdmans, 2003.
Lilly, W[illiam] S[amuel]. "Cardinal Newman." *Fortnightly Review,* n.s., 151 (1879) 1–23.
Lloyd, Humphrey. *The Quaker Lloyds in the Industrial Revolution.* London: Hutchinson, 1975.
Lloyd, J. J. "A Link That Failed." *Journal of the History of Earth Sciences Society* 5 (1986) 106–13.
[Lloyd, Samuel]. *Descendants of Samuel Lloyd, born 1768, married Rachel Braithwaite 1791.* N.p., 1914.
———. *The Lloyds of Birmingham with some account of the founding of Lloyd's Bank.* 3rd ed. Birmingham: Cornish, 1909.
London Gazette.
Lovegrove, Deryck W. *Established Church, Sectarian People: Itinerancy and the Transformation of English Dissent, 1780–1830.* Cambridge: Cambridge University Press, 1988.
Lowe, Rachel J. *Farm and its Inhabitants with some account of the Lloyds of Dolobran.* [London]: Chiswick, 1883.
Lower, Mark Antony. *Patronymica Britannica: A Dictionary of the Family Names of the United Kingdom.* London: Smith, 1860.
Lowth, Robert. *Isaiah: A new translation; with a preliminary dissertation, and notes critical, philological, and explanatory.* 3rd ed. London: Cadell, 1795.
Lowth, William. "Commentary on the Prophets." In *A Commentary upon the Old and New Testaments.* Vol. 4 of 6. Edited by Symon Patrick et al. London: Bagster, 1809.

MacDonagh, Michael. *The viceroy's post-bag: Correspondence, hitherto unpublished, of the Earl of Hardwicke, first lord lieutenant of Ireland, after the union*. London: Murray, 1904.

MacLean, John. "History of the Manors of Dene Magna and Abenhall and their Lords." *Transactions of the Bristol and Gloucestershire Archaeological Society* 6 (1881–82) 123–209.

Macleod, Norman. *The Earnest Student; being Memorials of John Mackintosh*. 9th ed. Edinburgh: Constable, 1858.

MacMahon, Kenneth A., ed. *Beverley Corporation minute books (1707–1835)*. Yorkshire Archaeological Society Record 122. London: Brown, 1958.

MacManus, Emily E. P. *Matron of Guy's*. London: Melrose, 1956.

Macnaghten, Angus. *Burns' Mrs Riddell: A Biography*. Peterhead, Scotland: Volturna, 1975.

MacPherson, Dave. *The Rapture Plot*. Simpsonville, SC: Millennium III, 1995.

Madden, Mrs. Hamilton. *Memoir of the late Right Rev. Robert Daly, Lord Bishop of Cashel*. London: Nisbet, 1875.

Maillebouis, Christian. *La Chronique "Deschomets" de Mazelgirard, près de Tence, en Velay*. Le Chambon sur Lignon: Histoire de la Montagne, 1992.

———. *La dissidence religieuse à Saint-Voy, canton de Tence: "Les Momiers" 1820–1845*. Le Chambon sur Lignon: Histoire de la Montagne, 1990.

———. *Vie et pensées d'un Darbyste: A. Dentan, 1805–1873*. Le Chambon sur Lignon: Histoire de la Montagne, 1991.

Mander, Charles. *The Reverend Prince and His Abode of Love*. Wakefield: EP, 1976.

[Marriott, William Smith]. *The Royal Promise: A Tale*. Cambridge: Hodson, 1824.

[Marsh, Catherine]. *The Life of the Rev. William Marsh, DD*. By his daughter. London: Nisbet, 1868.

Marsh, Herbert. *The national religion the foundation of national education . . . To which is annexed an account of the Society for Promoting Christian knowledge*. 2nd ed. London: Rivington, 1811.

Marshall, John. *Royal Naval Biography or Memoirs of the Services . . . with copious addenda*. 4 vols. London: Longman, Rees, Orme, Brown and Green, 1823–35.

Martin, Ged. "Michael Augustus Gathercole (c. 1802–1886): Controversial Anglican Cleric." http://www.gedmartin.net/index.php/martinalia-mainmenu-3/168-michael-augustus-gathercole-c-1802-1886-controversial-anglican-cleric.

Maselli, Domenico. *Libertà della Parola: Storia delle chiese cristiane dei Fratelli 1886–1946*. Turin: Claudiana, 1978.

———. *Tra Risveglio e Millennio, Storia delle Chiese Cristiane dei Fratelli 1836–1886*. Turin: Claudiana, 1974.

Mataura Ensign.

Matthew, H. Colin G., and Brian Harrison, eds. *Oxford Dictionary of National Biography [ODNB]*. 61 vols. Oxford: Oxford University Press, 2004.

Maurras, Charles. *Au signe de Flore: la fondation de l'Action française, 1898–1900*. Paris: Les Oeuvres Représentatives, 1931.

McAll, Robert Whittaker, et al. *A Cry from the land of Calvin and Voltaire: A sequel to "The white fields of France"; Records of the McAll Mission*. Introduction by Horatius Bonar. London: Hodder and Stoughton, 1887.

———. *Robert Whittaker McAll, founder of the McAll Mission, Paris: A fragment by himself, a souvenir by his wife*. New York: Revell, 1896.

McCormack, W. G. *Fool of the Family: A Life of J. M. Synge*. London: Weidenfeld and Nicolson, 2000.

———. *The Silence of Barbara Synge*. Manchester: Manchester University Press, 2003.

McDowell, R. B., and D. A. Webb. "Trinity College in 1830." *Hermathena* 75 (1950) 1–23; 76 (1950) 1–24.

McGill, John. *The Beverley Family in Virginia: Descendants of Major Robert Beverley (1641–1687) and Allied Families*. Columbia, SC: Bryan, 1956.

McManners, John. *Church and Society in 18th Century France*. 2 vols. Oxford: Clarendon, 1998.

McNeile, Hugh. "The Nature and Design of Miracles, a sermon preached at St Clement Danes, 6 Dec.1831." *Preacher* 3 (1831) 225–45.

Menezes, Mary Noel. *The Amerindians in Guyana, 1803–73: A Documentary History*. London: Cass, 1979.

———. *British Policy towards the Amerindians in British Guiana, 1803–1873*. Oxford: Clarendon, 1977.

Methodist Quarterly Review.

[Methuen, Louisa Mary]. *"The Fountain sealed": A memoir of Mary M.C. Methuen. By her mother*. Bath: Binns and Goodwin, 1857.

[Meyer, Louisa Clara] Mrs. F. B. Meyer. *The author of the Peep of Day, being the life story of Mrs. Mortimer*. London: Religious Tract Society, 1901.

Michaud, Louis Gabriel, ed. *Biographie Universelle, Ancienne et Moderne*. 82 vols. Paris: Michaud, 1843.

Middleton, R[obert] D[udley]. *Newman at Oxford: His Religious Development*. Oxford: Oxford University Press, 1950.

Miller, Edward. *The History and Doctrines of Irvingism, or of the so-called Catholic and Apostolic Church*. 2 vols. London: Paul, 1878.

Miller, Jon. *The Social Control of Religious Zeal: A Study of Organizational Contradictions*. New Brunswick, NJ: Rutgers University Press, 1994.

Milnes, Richard [of Horbury]. *The warning voice of a hermit abroad, who has been compelled to write in his justification, and he hopes for the good of mankind, under the protecting hand of divine providence* . . . Wakefield: Waller, 1825.

Mingins, Rosemary. *The Beacon Controversy and challenges to British Quaker Tradition in the early nineteenth century: Some responses to the Evangelical Revival by Friends in Manchester and Kendal*. Lampeter, UK: Mellen, 2004.

Missionary Register.

Mitchell, J[ohn] Murray. *Memoir of the Rev. Robert Nesbit*. London: Nisbet, 1858.

Mitford, Nancy. "The English Aristocracy." In *Noblesse Oblige: An Enquiry into the Identifiable Characteristics of the English Aristocracy*, edited by Nancy Mitford, 39–62. London: Hamilton, 1956.

M'Neile. See McNeile.

Molesworth, A[nthony] O[liver]. "Should Christians Enlist?" *Witness* 44 (1914) 155.

Moncreiff, G. R., ed. *Remains of Thomas Byrth, Rector of Wallasey, with a memoir of his life*. London: Hatchard, 1851.

The Monmouthshire Merlin.

Monthly Magazine and British Register.

The Monthly Repository of Theology and General Literature.

The Monthly Review. London: Hurst, Chance, 1827.

Moody, Robert. "James Bennett of Salisbury, (1797–1859) Jeweller and Newspaper Proprietor." *Wiltshire Archaeological & Natural History Magazine* 94 (2001) 182–94.

Moore, James. *The Darwin Legend*. Grand Rapids: Baker, 1994.

The Moral Reformer and Protester against the Vices, Abuses and Corruptions of the Age. Edited by J. Livesey.

Morgan, F[rederick] C[harles]. "William Yapp of Hereford." *Notes and Queries*, July 1977, 293–95.

The Morning Watch [MW].

Morris, William. *The Question of Ages: What is man? Outlines of testimony in relation to life, death and immortality*. 3rd ed. Plymouth: Trythall, 1887.

Mozley, T[homas]. *Reminiscences chiefly of Oriel College and the Oxford Movement*. 2 vols. London: Longmans, Green, 1882.

Müller, George. *A Narrative of Some of the Lord's Dealings with George Müller written by himself*. 8th ed. 2 vols. London: Nisbet, 1881.

Murray, Iain H. *The Puritan Hope: Revival and the Interpretation of Prophecy*. Edinburgh: Banner of Truth, 1971.

Nangle, Edward. *Recollections of Separatists, a plea for the Reformed Church of England*. Dublin: Herbert, 1867.

Napleton, John. *A sermon [on John 3:5] on Regeneration and Conversion*. Hereford: Wright, 1817.

———. *The universality of the gospel call to salvation: A sermon*. Hereford: Wright, 1818.

Neatby, W. Blair. *A History of the Plymouth Brethren*. 2nd ed. London: Hodder and Stoughton, 1902.

Nebeker, Gary L. "John Nelson Darby and Trinity College, Dublin: A Study in Eschatological Contrasts." *Fides et Historia* 34 (2002) 87–108.

Neill, Stephen. *A History of Christianity in India 1707–1858*. Cambridge: Cambridge University Press, 1985.

Newhouse, Neville H. "The Irish Separation of 1800—A Lesson for 1971." *Friends Quarterly* 17 (1971) 123–29, 169–80.

———. "John Hancock Junior, 1762–1823." *Journal of the Royal Society of Antiquaries of Ireland* 101 (1971) 41–52.

Newman, Francis William. *Phases of Faith or Passages from the History of my Creed*. London: Manwaring, 1850.

Newman, John Henry. *Letters and Diaries*. See Ker, Ian, and Thomas Gornall.

——— "Suggestions respectfully offered to individual resident clergymen of the University in behalf of the Church Missionary Society." In *The Via Media of the Anglican Church: illustrated in lectures, letters, and tracts written between 1830 and 1841*. 2 vols. 2:3–10. London: Basil Montagu Pickering, 1877.

New Monthly Magazine and Literary Journal.

The New Quarterly Review; or, Home, Foreign and Colonial Journal.

Newsome, David. "Justification and Sanctification: Newman and the Evangelicals." *Journal of Theological Studies* [JTS] 15 (1964) 32–53.

———. *The Parting of Friends*. London: Murray, 1966.

The Newspaper.

[Newton, Benjamin Wills]. *Answers to questions on the propriety of leaving the Church of England*. Signed B.W.N. London: Wertheimer, 1841.

———. *A Remonstrance to the Society of Friends*. London: Nisbet, 1835.

———. *A Vindication of "A Remonstrance to the Society of Friends."* London: Nisbet, 1836.

Nichol, Francis D[avid.] *The Midnight Cry: A Defense of the Character and conduct of William Miller and the Millerites, who mistakenly believed that the second Coming of Christ would take place in the year 1844.* Washington, DC: Review and Herald, 1945. Available online at www.maranathamedia.com.au.

Nicholls, Henry George. *The personalities of the Forest of Dean; being a relation of its successive officials, gentry, and commonality, drawn from numerous sources, but chiefly from unpublished data and local information, forming an appendix to "An historical and descriptive account of the Forest of Dean."* London: Murray, 1863.

Nicholson, Cornelius. *The Annals of Kendal being a historical and descriptive account of Kendal and the neighbourhood with Biographical sketches of many eminent personages connected with the town.* 2nd ed. London: Whitaker, 1861.

Nicolas, Nicholas Harris, ed. *Dispatches and Letters of Vice Admiral Lord Viscount Nelson.* 6 vols. London: Colburn, 1845.

Nockles, Peter [Benedict.] "Church or Protestant Sect? The Church of Ireland, High Churchmanship, and the Oxford Movement, 1822–1869." *Historical Journal* 41 (1998) 457–93.

———. *The Oxford Movement in Context: Anglican High Churchmanship 1760–1857.* Cambridge: Cambridge University Press, 1997 [1994.]

Noel, B[aptist] W[riothesley.] *Remarks on the Revival of Miraculous Powers in the Church.* London: Nisbet, 1831.

Noel, Napoleon. *The History of the Brethren.* 2 vols. Denver: Knapp, 1936.

Norton, Robert. *Memoirs of James and George Macdonald of Port Glasgow.* London: Shaw, 1840.

———. *Neglected and controverted Scripture Truths; with an Historical Review of Miraculous Manifestations in the Church of Christ; and an Account of their late Revival in the West of Scotland.* London: Shaw, 1839.

———. *The Restoration of the Apostles and Prophets in the Catholic Apostolic Church.* London: Bosworth & Harrison, [1861].

Norway, Arthur H. *History of the post-office packet service between the years 1793–1815.* London: Macmillan, 1895.

Notes and Queries.

Numbers, Ronald L., and Jonathan M. Butler, eds. *The Disappointed: Millerism and Millenarianism in the Nineteenth Century.* Knoxville: University of Tennessee Press, 1993.

Observer.

Oliphant, Mrs. M[argaret] O. W. *The Life of Edward Irving, Minister of the National Scotch Church, London: Illustrated by his journals and Correspondence.* 2 vols. London: Hurst and Blackett, 1862.

Oliver, George. *The history and antiquities of the town and minster of Beverley, in the county of York, from the most early period.* Beverley: Turner, 1829.

Oliver, W. H., and Claudia Stone, eds. *Dictionary of New Zealand Biography* [*DNZB*]. 5 vols. Wellington: Allen and Unwin, 1990–2000.

Orpen, Charles Edward Herbert. "Pestalozzi and His Plans." *Christian Examiner and Church of Ireland Magazine* 7 (1828) 335–41, 413–22.

Osen, James L. *Prophet and Peacemaker: The Life of Adolphe Monod.* Lanham, MD: University Press of America, 1984.

Ostertag, A. "Johannes Meyer." *Evangelisches Missions-magazin* (1859) 429–59, 521–52.

Outis, [Philip Sydney]. *The York Musical Festival, a Dialogue*. London: Bohn, 1825.

Oxford Dictionary of National Biography [ODNB]. See Matthews, H. C. G.

Paine, Thomas. "Worship and Church Bells: A letter to Camille Jordan" [1797]. In *The Writings of Thomas Paine*, edited by Moncure Daniel Conway, 4:247–57. 4 vols. New York: Putnam, 1894–96.

Parlby, William. *Sketch of the Rise of Methodism in the County and City of Hereford: A historical souvenir to mark the centenary of the Wesleyan Methodist Church, Bridge Street Hereford, 1829–1929*. Hereford: Adams, 1930.

Pascoe, Charles Frederick. *Two hundred years of the S.P.G.: An historical account of the Society for the propagation of the gospel in foreign parts, 1701–1900*. London: SPG, 1901.

The Patriot.

Patterson, Mark, and Andrew Walker. "'Our Unspeakable Comfort': Irving, Albury and the Origins of the Pretribulation Rapture." *Fides et Historia* 31 (1999) 66–81. More recently in *Christian Millenarianism: From the Early Church to Waco*, edited by Stephen Hunt, 98–115. London: Hurst, 2001.

Peach, R[obert] E[dward] M[yhill]. *Street-lore of Bath: A record of changes in the highways and byways of the city*. London: Simpkin, Marshall, 1893.

Pecchioli, Alessandra. "Giulia Baldelli: Una prima breve panoramica delle famiglie Walker, Baldelli e Tommasi." In *La Chiesa "degli italiani": All'origine dell'Evangelismo Risvegliato in Italia*, 207–22. Rome: GBU, 2010.

[Penney, Norman]. "Notes on the Life of Emma Marshall." *Journal of the Friends Historical Society* 17 (1920) 114–17.

———. "Treffry, of Devon and Cornwall." *Journal of the Friends Historical Society* 19 (1922) 37–41.

Penstone, John Jewell. *A Caution to the readers of "A Caution against the Darbyites," together with a few words on "The Close of twenty-eight years association with J.N.D."* London: Morrish, 1867.

———. *The dustless tomb. (Fragmentary remarks made at the burial of a beloved one, whose remains, in Arno Vale, await the resurrection)*. London: priv. printed, 1888.

———. "Forged Assignats." *Notes and Queries*, series 2, 6.137 (1858) 134–35.

———. *Inductive theories of baptism, considered, chiefly in their injury to the present testimony of God*. Stanford-in-the-Vale: priv. printed, 1872.

[———]. *Notes on passing events (1862–1871)*. Signed "P." Reprinted with a few additions. Manchester: Darling, 1871.

———. *Occasional reflections: Chiefly suggested by reading recent bitter and ministerial attacks upon the Brethren*. London: Morrish, 1870.

———. "Pictures of Raffaelle in England, and in what collections?" *Notes and Queries*, series 2, 2.33 (1856) 130.

———. *Songs of Salvation and Records of Christian Life*. Illustrated with etchings on steel by the author. Oxford: Shrimpton, 1876.

———. *To brethren in Christ, May 1, 1879*. Stanford-in-the-Vale: Penstone, 1879.

———. *Village teachings concerning the Lord Jesus*. London: Morrish, 1874.

———. "Was Addison a plagiarist?" *Notes and Queries*, series 2, 2.29 (1856) 49.

Peterson, Indira Viswanathan. "'Bethlehem Kuravañci' of Vedanayaka Sastri of Tanjore: The Cultural Discourses of an Early-Nineteenth Century Tamil Christian Poem." In

Christians, Cultural Interactions and India's Religious Traditions, edited by Judith M. Brown and Robert Eric Frykenberg, 9–36. Grand Rapids: Eerdmans, 2002.

Pevsner, Nikolaus. *Buildings of England, London 5: East*. Revised by Bridget Cherry and Charles O'Brien. New Haven: Yale University Press, 2005.

Philips, C[yril] H[enry], and Mary Doreen Wainwright, eds. *Indian Society and the Beginnings of Modernization, c. 1830–1850*. London: School of Oriental and African Studies, 1976.

Phillipps, Thomas, ed. "Supplement to the Pedigree of Probyn and Spicer" (1866). In *Genealogia, a collection of pedigrees*. Middle Hill: priv. printed, 1840–71.

Philpot, J[oseph] C[harles]. "The Christian Witness." *Gospel Standard* 8 (1842) 77–84.

———. *Memoir of the late William Tiptaft, with a selection from his letters*. 2nd ed. London: Gadsby, 1867.

Philpot, J. H., ed. *The Seceders (1829–1869): The Story of a Spiritual Awakening as told in the Letters of Joseph Charles Philpot and William Tiptaft*. 2 vols. 2nd impr. London: Farncombe, 1931–32.

Pickering, Henry, ed. *Chief Men among the Brethren*. London: Pickering and Inglis, 1918. 2nd ed., 1931.

Pierson, Arthur T. *James Wright of Bristol, a Memorial of a Fragrant Life*. London: Nisbet, 1906.

Pietrocòla-Rossetti, T. *La religione di stato*. Turin: Stamperia di compositori-tipografi, 1861.

Piggin, Stuart, and John Roxborogh. *The St. Andrews Seven: The Finest Flowering of Missionary Zeal in Scottish History*. Edinburgh: Banner of Truth, 1985.

Pinnington, John. "Factors in the Development of the Catholic Movement in the Anglican Church in British Guiana." *Historical Magazine of the Protestant Episcopal Church* 38 (1968) 355–69.

[Pitts, John]. *The Character of a Primitive Bishop in a letter to a non-juror*. By a presbyter of the Church of England. London: Bragge, 1709.

Plongeron, Bernard. *Les Réguliers de Paris devant le serment constitutionnel: Sens et conséquences d'une option 1789–1801*. Paris: Vrin, 1964.

Pollard, W. B. "William Pollard of Devon and the West Indies and Some of His Descendants." *Journal of the Barbados Museum and Historical Society* 25 (1958) 54–74. Reprinted in *Genealogies of Barbados Families*, compiled by James C. Brandow, 455–477. Baltimore: Genealogical Pub., 1983.

Poor Man's Guardian.

Powell, Avril A. *Muslims and Missionaries in Pre-Mutiny India*. London: Routledge Curzon, 1993.

Preston, William. *Illustrations of Masonry*. 14th ed. Edited with additions by George Oliver. London: Whittaker, Treacher, 1829.

P[rideaux], F[anny] A[sh]. *In Memoriam F[rederick] P[rideaux]*. N.p., 1891.

Prideaux, Frederick. *Handbook of Precedents in Conveyancing*. [1st ed.] London: Wildy and Sons, 1852.

———. *Handbook of Precedents in Conveyancing* [a.k.a. *Prideaux's Precedents*]. 25th ed. London: Sweet and Maxwell, 1985.

Prince, H[enry] J[ames]. *Br[other] Prince's Journal, an account of the destruction of the works of the Devil in the Human Soul by the Lord Jesus Christ*. London: Hall, Virtue, 1859.

———. *The Charlinch revival; or, An account of the remarkable work of grace which has lately taken place at Charlinch, in Somersetshire*. London: Nisbet, 1842.

———. *How you may know whether you do, or do not, believe on Jesus Christ*. Bath: Noyes, 1842.

———. *Letters addressed by H. J. Prince to his Christian Brethren at St. David's College, Lampeter*. 2nd ed. Llandovery: Rees, 1841.

———. *Strength in Jesus*. Bath: Noyes, 1842.

Proceedings of the Ackworth Old Scholars' Association.

Proceedings of the Church Missionary Society for Africa and the East [CMS].

Proceedings of the Dorset Natural History and Archaeological Society.

Proceedings of the Somersetshire Archaeological and Natural History Society.

Punshon, John. *Portrait in Grey: A Short History of the Quakers*. London: Quaker Home Service, 1984.

Pym, Horace N., ed. *Memories of Old Friends, being extracts from the Journals and Letters of Caroline Fox of Penjerrick, Cornwall, from 1835 to 1871*. 2nd ed. London: Smith, Elder, 1882.

Quarrell, W. H. "Penstone." *Notes and Queries* 187 (1944) 58.

Quinn, James. *Soul on Fire: A Life of Thomas Russell, 1767–1803*. Dublin: Irish Academic, 2002.

Raikes, Henry. *Memoir of the life and services of Vice-Admiral Sir Jahleel Brenton. Reedited by his son [Sir Charles Brenton]*. London: Longman, 1855.

Railton, Nicholas M. *Transnational Evangelicalism: The Case of Friedrich Bialloblotzky (1799–1869)*. Göttingen: Vandenhoeck & Ruprecht, 2002.

Raistrick, Arthur. *Quakers in Science and Industry: Being an Account of the Quaker Contributions to Science and Industry during the 17th and 18th Centuries*. London: Bannisdale, 1950.

[Rathbone, William]. *A narrative of events, that have lately taken place in Ireland among the society called Quakers with corresponding documents and occasional observations*. London: Johnson, 1804.

Rawlins, Cosmo W[indham] H[ooper]. *Family Quartet*. Yeovil: priv. printed, 1962.

———. "The Recollections of a Nonagenarian: Charlotte Bussell (1808–1899)." *Devon and Cornwall Notes and Queries* 5 (1952–53) 133–39.

Rawson, David. "Barton Hall, Hereford: a History." *BHR* 7 (2011) 43–67.

Ray, Gordon N[orton]. *The Buried Life: A Study of the Relation between Thackeray's Fiction and His Personal History*. Oxford: Oxford University Press, 1952.

The Record.

Record of Christian Work. E. Northfield, MA.

Rees, Arthur A[ugustus]. *Farewell sermon of the Rev. Arthur A. Rees: Curate of Sunderland, delivered on Sunday evening, December 4, 1842, in St. John's Chapel, Sunderland*. Sunderland: Vint and Carr, [1842].

———. *The moral of the war, (the humiliation of France, and the dethronement of the never-crowned Napoleon): A lecture delivered in Bethesda Free Chapel, Sunderland, on Thursday, September 5 1870*. Sunderland: Williams, 1870.

———. *Reasons for not co-operating in the alleged "Sunderland revivals"* . . . Sunderland: Hills, 1859.

———. *The rise and progress of the heresy of the Rev. H. J. Prince*. London: Simpkin and Marshall, [1846].

———. *A Second Friendly Letter to the Christians called "Brethren" on the subject of Worship and Ministry*. London: Passmore and Alabaster, [1869].

———. *Solemn protest before the church and nation of the Rev. Arthur A. Rees, late minister of Thomas Street Episcopal Chapel, Bath, against his virtual ejection from the ministry of the Church of England*. [Bath]: Noyes, 1844.

Reformation Society. *Fifth Annual Report of the British Society for promoting the religious principles of the Reformation*. London: Reformation Society, 1832.

Reid, Stuart J[ohnson]. *The life and times of Sydney Smith: based on family documents and the recollections of personal friends*. London: Sampson Low, Marston, Searle, and Rivington, 1884.

Reid, William. *Plymouth Brethrenism unveiled and refuted*. Edinburgh: Oliphant, 1875.

Reiling, J[annes]. *Hermas and Christian Prophecy: A Study of the Eleventh Mandate*. Supplements to *Novum Testamentum*. Leiden: Brill, 1973.

Religious Tract Society. *31st Annual Report*. London: RTS, 1830.

Reynolds, J. S. *The Evangelicals at Oxford, 1735-1871: A Record of an Unchronicled Movement*. Oxford: Blackwell, 1953.

Rhenius, C. J[ohann]. *Memoir of the Rev. C. T. E. Rhenius, comprising Extracts from his Journal and Correspondence, with Details of Missionary Proceedings in South India*. By his son. London: Nisbet, 1841.

R.I.B.A [Royal Institute of British Architects]. *Kalendar 1903-1904*. London: R.I.B.A, 1904.

Rideout, Adelaide. *The Treffry Family*. Chichester: Phillimore, 1984.

Rigby, B. "Archival Treasures." *Memorial University of Newfoundland Gazette*, August 17, 2000. Text consulted online, but no longer available, at http://www.mun.ca/marcomm/gazette/2000-2001/August17/arctrs.html. See also Newfoundland, Colonial Office records, at http://www2.swgc.mun.ca/nfld_history/CO194/CO19but 4-61.htm.

Rivière, Peter. *Absent-Minded Imperialism: Britain and the Expansion of Empire in Nineteenth-Century Brazil*. London: Tauris, 1995.

Robbins, William. *The Newman Brothers: An Essay in Comparative Intellectual Biography*. London: Heinemann, 1966.

Roberts, M. J. D. "Reshaping the Gift Relationship: The London Mendicity Society and the Suppression of Begging in England, 1818-1869." *International Review of Social History* 36 (1991) 201-31.

Robertson, Kenneth Joyce. *The Four Pillars: A Genealogical journey*. Self-published, Bloomington, IN: XLibris, 2010.

Robinson, Charles J. "Extracts from Registers of All Hallows the Great." In *Miscellanea Genealogica et Heraldica*, 4 vols., edited by Joseph Jackson Howard, n.s., 4 (1884) 66. London: Hamilton, Adams, 1874-84.

Rodt, Rodolphe de. "R. de Rodt's letters (May 1833-July 1835.)" *Calcutta Christian Advocate* 5 (1843) 220-379.

Rosman, Doreen M. *Evangelicals and Culture*. London: Croom Helm, 1984.

Rowdon, Harold Hamlyn. *The Origins of the Brethren 1825-50*. London: Pickering and Inglis, 1967.

Rowe, J. Brooking. "The Rev. Samuel Rowe, M.A., Vicar of Crediton, 1835-53." *Report and Transactions of the Devonshire Association for the advancement of science, literature and art* 14 (1882) 395-401.

Rowntree, Mary Stickney. "Memoir of Robert Mackenzie Beverley." *Transactions of the Congregational Historical Society* 2 (1905-1906) 326-31.

Royle, Trevor. *Orde Wingate: Irregular Soldier*. London: Phoenix, Orion, 1995.

Russell, George W. E. *A Short History of the Evangelical Movement*. London: Mowbray, 1915.

Russell, John Robert [13th Duke of Bedford]. *A Silver Plated Spoon.* London: Cassell, 1959.

Russell, Hastings William Sackville [12th Duke of Bedford]. *The Conscientious Objector: Speech Delivered to the House of Lords.* Glasgow: Strickland, 1943.

———. *The Better Way: Written for Those Who Hate War but See No Alternative.* Glasgow: Strickland, 1944.

Ryland, J. E., ed. *Memoirs of Dr. John Kitto, D.D., F.S.A.* Edinburgh: Oliphant, 1856.

Sandeen, Ernest R. *The Roots of Fundamentalism: British and American Millenarianism 1800–1930.* Chicago: University of Chicago Press, 1970.

Sankey, Ira D[avid]. *My Life and the Story of the Gospel Hymns and of Sacred Songs and Solos.* Introduction by Theodore L. Cuyler. Philadelphia: Ziegler, 1906.

Savić, Svenka. *How Twins Learn to Talk: A Study of the Speech Development of Twins from 1–3.* London: Academic, 1980.

Sayers, Richard Sidney. *Lloyds Bank in the History of English Banking.* Oxford: Clarendon, 1957.

Schlienz, C[hristoph] F[riedrich]. *The Pilgrim Missionary Institution of St Chrischona.* Introduction by Dr Kitto. London: Shaw, 1850.

Schneider, Michael. "'The Extravagant Side of Brethrenism': The Life of Percy Francis Hall (1801–84)." In *Witness in Many Lands: Leadership and Outreach among the Brethren,* edited by Tim Grass, 17–44. Troon: BAHN, 2013.

Schwieso, Joshua J[ohn]. "The Founding of the Agapemone at Spaxton, 1845–46." *Proceedings of the Somersetshire Archaeological and Natural History Society* 135 (1991) 113–21.

———. "'Religious Fanaticism' and Wrongful Confinement in Victorian England: The Affair of Louisa Nottidge." *Social History of Medicine* 9 (1996) 159–74.

———. "'This Frightful and Blasphemous Sect': Apocalyptic Millenarians in Victorian Dorset." *Proceedings of the Dorset Natural History and Archaeological Society* 114 (1992) 13–18.

[Scott, Alexander John], ed. *Journal of a Residence at Bagdad during the years 1830 and 1831, by Mr. Anthony N. Groves, Missionary.* London: Nisbet, 1832.

———. *Journal of Mr. Anthony N. Groves, Missionary, during a Journey from London to Bagdad through Russia, Georgia and Persia . . .* London: Nisbet, 1831.

Scott, Douglas F. S., ed. *Luke Howard (1772–1864): His Correspondence with Goethe and His Continental Journey of 1816.* York: Sessions, 1976.

Scottish Geographical Magazine.

Scull, Andrew T., ed. *Madhouses, Mad-Doctors and Madmen: The Social History of Psychiatry in the Victorian Era.* Philadelphia: University of Pennsylvania Press, 1981.

———. *Social Order/Mental Disorder: Anglo-American Psychiatry in Historical Perspective.* Berkeley: University of California Press, 1989.

Seebohm, Benjamin, ed. *Memoirs of the Life and Gospel Labours of Stephen Grellet.* 2 vols. London: Bennett, 1840.

Seddall, Henry. *Edward Nangle, the Apostle of Achill: A memoir and a history.* London: Hatchards, 1884.

Sedgwick, Adam. *Four Letters to the Editors of the Leeds Mercury in reply to R. M. Beverley, Esq.* Cambridge: Pitt Press, by John Smith, 1836.

Selleck, A. D. *Plymouth Friends: A Quaker History.* Pts. 1 and 2. Reprinted from the *Transactions of the Devonshire Association* 99 (1970–71). Plymouth, n.d.

Serjeantson, R[obert] M[eyricke]. *A history of the Church of St. Peter, Northampton, together with the Chapels of Kingsthorpe and Upton.* Northampton: Wm. Mark, 1904.

Singh, Brijraj. *The First Protestant Missionary to India: Bartholomaeus Ziegenbalg*. Oxford: Oxford University Press, 2000.

Shadwell, Charles Lancelot, ed. *Registrum Orielense, an account of the members of Oriel College, Oxford*. 2 vols. London: Frowde, 1893, 1902.

Shann, E[dward] O[wen] G[ildin]. *Cattle Chosen: The Story of the First Group Settlement in Western Australia 1829-1841*. London: Oxford University Press, 1926. Text at http://en.wikisource.org/wiki/Cattle_Chosen/Chapter_9.

Sheppard, Francis Henry Wollaston. *London, 1808-1870: The Infernal Wen*. Berkeley: University of California Press, 1971.

Sheva. "Reflections on the late meetings in May." *Evangelical Magazine* 28 (1820) 277-80.

Silber, Kate. *Pestalozzi: The Man and His Work*. London: Routledge and Paul, 1965.

Slater, Arthur Walter, ed. "Autobiographical Memoir of Joseph Jewell, 1763-1846." *Camden Miscellany* 22 (1964) 113-78.

Smith, George. *The Life of Alexander Duff*. 4th ed. London: Hodder and Stoughton, 1904.

———. *The Life of William Carey: Shoemaker and Missionary*. London: Murray, 1885.

[Smith, Sydney]. "Indian Missions." *Edinburgh Review* 12 (1808) 151-81.

Smith, Sydney. "Catholic Claims: Substance of a speech at a Meeting of the Clergy of the Archdeaconry of the East-Riding of Yorkshire, held at Beverley, in that Riding, on Monday, April 11, 1825, for the purpose of petitioning Parliament." In *The Works of the Rev. Sydney Smith*, 3:82-92. Philadelphia: Carey and Hart, 1844.

Smyrl, Steven C. *Dictionary of Dublin Dissent: Dublin's Protestant Dissenting Meeting Houses 1660-1920*. Dublin: Farmar, 2009.

Social History of Medicine.

Sollberger, E. "Mr. Taylor in Chaldaea." *Anatolian Studies* 22 (1972) 129-39.

Soltau, George. *The Enquiry Room: Hints for dealing with the Anxious*. London: Morgan & Scott, 1883.

———. *Personal Work for Christ, and Some Experiences, with a biographical sketch by his wife*. Edited by E. A. Helps. London: Roberts, [1911].

Soltau, Henry. "Across China: From Bhamó to Shanghai." *Scottish Geographical Magazine* 4 (1888) 83-98.

———. "[Extracts] from the Diary of Mr. Henry Soltau [during the outbreak of hostilities in Bhamó in December 1884]." *China's Millions* (April 1885) 48-49.

———. "From Glasgow to Burmah: Notes from the Diary of Mr. Henry Soltau." *China's Millions* 1 (1875) 9-10, 20-22, 34-35, 47-48.

———. "From Rangoon to Bhamó: Extracts from the Journal of Mr. Henry Soltau." *China's Millions* 1 (1876) 152-53, 194-95, 221-22.

Soltau, Henry William. *An Exposition of the tabernacle, the priestly garments and the priesthood*. London: Morgan & Chase, 1864.

———. *The Holy Vessels and Furniture of the Tabernacle of Israel*. London: Bagster, 1851.

Soltau, Roger Henry. *Pascal: The Man and the Message*. Westport, CT: Greenwood, 1970.

Soltau, William. "'A People prepared for the Lord': A Sketch of Mission Work among the Karens in Lower Burmah." *Footsteps of Truth* 2 (1884) 634-40.

The Spectator.

Spini, Giorgio. *Risorgimento e Protestanti*. Naples: Edizioni scientifiche italiane, 1956.

Squire, John Traviss. "The Huguenots at Wandsworth in the county of Surrey and their burial ground at Mount Nod." *Proceedings of the Huguenot Society of London* 1 (1885-86) 229-42, 261-93.

———. *The registers of the parish of Wandsworth in the County of Surrey, 1603–1787.* Lymington: King, 1889.

Staehlin, Ernst. *Die Christentumsgesellschaft in der Zeit von der Erweckung bis zur Gegenwart: Texte aus Briefen. Protokollen und Publikationen.* Basel: Reinhardt, 1974.

Stanley, Arthur Penrhyn. *Life and Correspondence of Thomas Arnold.* 2 vols. London: Fellowes, 1844.

Stanley, Charles. *The Way the Lord hath led me; or, Incidents of Gospel work.* London: Morrish, [1889].

Stapylton, H[enry] E[dward] C[hetwynd]. *The Eton School Lists from 1791 to 1850 (every third year after 1793) with notes.* 2nd ed. London: Williams, 1864.

Staveley, Robert. "Irish Clerics." *Temple Bar, a monthly magazine for Town and Country Readers* 125 (1902) 74–87.

Stephen, Leslie. *The Life of Sir James Fitzjames Stephen, a Judge of the High Court of Justice.* By his brother. London: Smith, Elder, 1895.

Stephen, Leslie, and Sidney Lee, eds. *Dictionary of National Biography [DNB].* 23 vols. London: Smith, Elder, 1885–1900.

Stewart, David Dale. *Memoir of the Life of the Rev. James Haldane Stewart.* By his son. London: Hatchard, 1857.

Stewart, Kenneth J. *Restoring the Reformation: British Evangelicalism and the Francophone "Réveil," 1816–1849.* Milton Keynes: Paternoster, 2006.

Stock, Eugene. *History of the Church Missionary Society, its environment, its men and its work.* 3 vols. London: CMS, 1899.

Stoddart, George H[enry]. *Evidence of the necessity of church reform compiled from the publications of Lord Henley* [et al.] . . . *with additional remarks by the Rev. George H. Stoddart.* London: Dalton, 1833.

———. *The History of the Prayer Book: The Derivation of most of its formularies from previous Liturgies . . .* London: Longman, Green, Longman, Roberts and Green, 1864.

———. *The imagery and poetical ornaments of the Book of Psalms; its prophetic language, and apocalyptic character . . .* London: Parker, 1835.

———. *Reasons for my seceding from the established church.* London: Westley and Davis, 1836.

[———]. "Specific Meanings of some of the words in the New Testament." *Christian Witness* 6 (1839) 63–69, 180–83.

———. *The true cure for Ireland, the development of her industry: being a letter addressed to the Rt. Hon'ble Lord John Russell, M.P.* London: Saunders, 1847.

Story, Robert Herbert. *Memoir of the Life of the Rev Robert Story.* Cambridge: Macmillan, 1862.

Strachan, C[harles] Gordon. *The Pentecostal Theology of Edward Irving.* London: Darton, Longman and Todd, 1973.

Strong, J. Leonard S., ed. *The Gathering of the Clan.* Medina, OH: [Pro Arts], 1979.

Strong, Leonard. *Gospel Reminiscences in the West Indies: A brief and simple record of the Lord's gracious work among the Indians of British Guiana, by his servant John Meyer during four years and a half.* London: Bateman, 1850.

———. *Gospel Reminiscences in the West Indies: The Triumph of Grace.* London: Bateman, n.d.

———. *A Letter to all the Brethren in Christ, declaratory of those serious convictions that have led to separation from the Established Church of England and Ireland*. Demerary [sic]: 1838.

———. *A Personal Testimony to the Truthfulness of C. H. Spurgeon's witness concerning the evangelical clergy and the errors of the Prayer Book*. London: Passmore and Alabaster, 1864.

Strutt, Charles R. *The Strutt Family of Terling, 1650–1873*. London: Mitchell, Hughes & Clarke, 1939.

Stunt, Timothy C. F. "Anthony Norris Groves in an International Context: A Re-assessment of His Early Development." In *The Growth of the Brethren Movement: National and International Experiences*, edited by Neil T. R. Dickson and Tim Grass, 223–40. Milton Keynes: Paternoster, 2006.

———. A Brethren Rolling Stone: George Henry Stoddart (c.1801–76.)" *BHR* 10 (2014) 10–20.

———. "An Early Account of the Brethren in 1838 with Some Explanation of Its [the early account's] Origins and Context." *BHR* 8 (2012) 1–9.

———. *Early Brethren and the Society of Friends*. Pinner: CBRF, 1970.

———. "The Early Development of Arthur Augustus Rees and His Relations with the Brethren." *BAHNR* 4.1 (2006) 22–35.

———. "Elitist Leadership and Congregational Participation among Early Plymouth Brethren." In *Elite and Popular Religion*, edited by Kate Cooper and Jeremy Gregory, 327–36. SCH 42. Woodbridge, UK: Boydell and Brewer, 2006.

———. "Evangelical Cross-Currents in the Church of Ireland, 1820–33." In *The Churches, Ireland and the Irish*, edited by W. J. Sheils and Diana Wood, 215–21. SCH 25. Oxford: Blackwell, 1989.

———. "Francis William Newman." *ODNB*.

———. *From Awakening to Secession: Radical Evangelicals in Switzerland and Britain 1815–35*. Edinburgh: T. & T. Clark, 2000.

———. "The Greaves Family: Some Clarifications." *Notes and Queries* 28 (1981) 405–8.

———. "Irvingite Pentecostalism and the Early Brethren." *Journal of CBRF* 10 (1965) 40–48.

———. "John Henry Newman and the Evangelicals." *Journal of Ecclesiastical History* 21 (1970) 65–74.

———. "John Jewell Penstone (1817–1902): His Family and the Brethren." *BHR* 5 (2008) 25–39.

———. "John Nelson Darby: The Scholarly Enigma." *BAHNR* 2.2 (2003) 70–74.

———. "John Synge and the Early Brethren." *Journal of CBRF* 28 (1976) 39–62.

———. "Leonard Strong: The Motives and Experiences of Early Missionary Work in British Guiana." *Christian Brethren Review Journal* 34 (1983) 95–105.

———. "The Plymouth Family of A. N. Harris." *BHR* 6 (2010) 34–36.

———. "Some Unpublished Letters of S. P. Tregelles relating to the Codex Sinaiticus." *Evangelical Quarterly* 48 (1976) 15–26.

———. "Some Very Early Plymouth Brethren." *BHR* 5 (2009) 102–5.

———. "The Tribulation of Controversy: A Review Article." *BAHNR* 2.2 (2003) 91–98.

———. "Trinity College, John Darby and the Powerscourt Milieu." In *Beyond the End: The Future of Millennial Studies*, edited by Joshua Searle and Kenneth Newport, 47–74. Sheffield: Sheffield Phoenix, 2012.

———. "'Trying the Spirits': The Case of the Gloucestershire Clergyman (1831)." *JEH* 39 (1988) 95–105.

———. "'Trying the Spirits': Irvingite Signs and the Test of Doctrine." In *Signs, Wonders and Miracles: Representations of Divine Power in the Life of the Church*, edited by Kate Cooper and Jeremy Gregory, 400–409. SCH 41. Woodbridge, UK: Boydel, 2005.

———. "The *Via Media* of Guicciardini's Closest Collaborator, Teodorico Pietrocola Rossetti." In *Piero Guicciardini 1808–1886: Un Riformatore Religioso nell'Europa dell'Ottocento*, edited by Lorenza Giorgi e Massimo Rubboli, 137–58. Atti del Convegno di Studi, Firenze, 11–12 April 1986. Florence: Olschki, 1988.

Stunt, W. T. "History of Assembly Work in British Guiana." *Echoes Quarterly Review* 8 (1956) 14–18.

Sturge, Joseph, and Thomas Harvey. *The West Indies in 1837: Being the journal of a visit to Antigua, Monserrat, Dominica, St. Lucia, Barbados, and Jamaica* . . . London: Hamilton, Adams, 1838.

Summers, W. H. *Memories of Jordans and the Chalfonts and the Early Friends in the Chiltern Hundreds*. London: Headley, 1895.

The Sunday at Home.

Sunderland and Durham County Herald.

Swift, David E. *Joseph John Gurney: Banker, Reformer and Quaker*. Middletown, CT: Wesleyan University Press, 1962.

Sydney, William Connor. "The Cradle of the Lake Poets." *Gentleman's Magazine* 275 (1893) 590–605.

[Synge, John]. *A Biographical Sketch of the struggles of Pestalozzi to establish his system of education, compiled and translated chiefly from his own works by an Irish Traveller*. Dublin: William Folds, 1815.

[———]. *An easy introduction to the Hebrew language on the principles of Pestalozzi, By Parens*. Pt. 1, *A teacher's assistant*; pt. 2, *A short Hebrew grammar*; pt. 3, *The Hebrew roots*. London: Seeley and Burnside, 1831.

———. *Observations on "A Call to the Converted" as it relates to Members of the Church of England, addressed to Capt. P. Hall, R.N.* Teignmouth: Barnett, 1831. Another edition, London: Seeley, 1831.

Synge, K[atherine] C[harlotte]. *The Family of Synge or Sing*. London: priv. printed, 1937.

Tayler, W. Elfe, ed. *Passages from the Diary and Letters of Henry Craik of Bristol*. London: Shaw, 1866.

Taylor, [Frederick] Howard and [Mary] Geraldine. *Hudson Taylor and the China Inland Mission: The Growth of a Work of God*. London: Morgan and Scott, 1918.

———. *Hudson Taylor in Early Years: The Growth of a Soul*. London: CIM, 1911.

Teignmouth, Lord. *Memoir of the Life and Correspondence of John Lord Teignmouth*. London: Hatchard, 1843.

[Thomas, Anna Braithwaite]. "The Beaconite Controversy." *Bulletin of Friends Historical Society* (Philadelphia) 4.2 (1912) 70–81.

———. *J. Bevan Braithwaite: A Friend of the 19th century by his children*. London: Hodder and Stoughton, 1909.

[Thompson, Thomas]. *A letter to I[saac] Crewdson on his recent publication "The Beacon" signed "Thomas Thompson."* Liverpool: Hodgson, 1835.

———. *A Letter to the Author of a Work entitled "A Beacon to the Society of Friends," with a reply by I[saac] Braithwaite*. London: Hamilton, Adams, 1835.

Thornton, Thomas, ed. *Notes of Cases in the Ecclesiastical and Maritime Courts.* London: Blenkarn, 1843.

The Times [London].

Times Literary Supplement.

The Tradesman or Commercial Magazine.

Transactions of the Congregational Historical Society.

Transactions of the Society instituted at London for the encouragement of arts, manufactures, and commerce.

[Treffry, Joseph]. *Strictures on a late publication entitled "A Remonstrance to the Society of Friends."* London: Arch, 1836.

Treffry, Roger. *Dissertation on Smut Balls amongst Wheat and other Grain.* Plymouth: Clarence, 1793.

Tregelles, S[amuel] P[rideaux]. *The Jansenists: Their Rise, Persecution by the Jesuits, and Existing Remnant: A Chapter in Church History.* London: Bagster, 1851.

———. *Three Letters to the author of "A Retrospect of Events that have taken place amongst the Brethren."* 2nd ed. London: Houlston, 1894.

Trevor, Meriol. *The Pillar of the Cloud.* London: Doubleday, 1962.

Troeltsch, Ernst. *The Social Teaching of the Christian Churches.* Translated by Olive Wyon. 2 vols. Chicago: University of Chicago Press, 1981.

Trott, Michael. *The Life of Richard Waldo Sibthorp: Evangelical, Catholic and Ritual Revivalism in the Nineteenth-Century Church.* Brighton: Sussex Academic, 2005.

Turner, W. G. *John Nelson Darby.* 2nd ed. London: Hammond, 1944.

Tyrrell, Alex. "Bearding the Tories: The Commemoration of the Scottish Political Martyrs of 1793-94." In *Contested Sites: Commemoration, Memorial and Popular Politics in Nineteenth-century Britain*, edited by Paul A. Pickering and Alex Tyrrell, 25–56. Aldershot: Ashgate, 2004.

———. *Joseph Sturge and the Moral Radical Party in early Victorian Britain.* London: Helm, 1987.

Universal Magazine.

Vacant, Alfred, et al., eds. *Dictionnaire de Théologie Catholique.* 15 vols. Paris: Letouzey et Ané, 1923–72.

Vaucher, Alfred–Felix. *Une célébrité oubliée: Le P. Manuel de Lacunza y Diaz (1731–1801).* Collonges-sous-Salève: Fides, 1941.

Venn, J. A. *Alumni Cantabrigienses [Al. Cantab.]: A Biographical List of all known students, graduates and holders of office at the University of Cambridge from the earliest times to 1900.* 2 pts., 10 vols. Cambridge: Cambridge University Press, 1922–54.

Venn, John. *Assertions of a Roman Catholic priest examined and exposed; or, The correspondence between the Rev. John Venn, M.A., Vicar of St Peter's . . . and the Rev. James Waterworth, Roman Catholic Priest, of Newark . . . [in the Hereford Journal and the Hereford Times, November 23, 1844–April 9, 1845].* Hereford: Anthony, 1845.

———. *The Christian Ministry and Church-Membership: According to Scripture and the Church of England; With a more especial reference to the views of . . . the Plymouth Brethren.* London: Hatchard, 1842.

———. *A proselyting [sic] spirit the great obstacle to Christian Union.* Sermon preached December 9, 1838. London: Seeley, 1838.

———. *Sunday wakes: A Sermon preached against Sunday wakes at the Parish Church of Sellack in the County of Hereford on Sunday May 6, 1838.* London: Seeley, 1838.

Vickers, Vikki J. *"My Pen and My Soul have ever gone together": Thomas Paine and the American Revolution.* New York: Routledge, 2006.

Vidal, Daniel. *La Morte-Raison: Isaac la juive, convulsionnaire janséniste de Lyon 1791-1841.* Grenoble: Millon, 1994.

Vipont, Elfrida [Elfrida Vipont Foulds]. *The Story of Quakerism 1652-1952.* London: Bannisdale, 1954.

Waddington, John. *Congregational History 1800-1850, with special reference to the Rise, Growth, and Influence of institutions, Representative Men, and the Inner life of the Churches.* London: Longmans, Green, 1878.

[Wade, John]. *The Extraordinary Black Book: An exposition of abuses in church and state, Courts of Law, Representation, Municipal and Corporate Bodies; with a précis of the House of Commons, past, present, and to come . . .* London: Effingham Wilson, 1832.

Wake, William. *The Genuine Epistles of the Apostolic Fathers.* London: Ric. Sare, 1693.

[Wakefield, Edward]. *A few brief remarks on the Scriptural Evidence in favour of the observance of water baptism and the Lord's Supper . . .* Kendal: Hudson and Nicholson, 1836.

Walker, George James. *Statement of reasons for leaving the Chapel in Bitton Street.* Plymouth: Brendon, [1866]. The only copy (known to me) of this (and many other pamphlets by Walker) is in the Fondo Guicciardini in the Biblioteca Nazionale Centrale, Florence.

Walker, James Douglas, ed. *Records of the Honorable Society of Lincoln's Inn: The Black Books.* Vol. 4, *1776-1845.* London: Lincoln's Inn, 1902.

Walker, Pamela J. "A Chaste and Fervid Eloquence: Catherine Booth and the Ministry of Women in the Salvation Army." In *Women Preachers and Prophets through Two Millennia of Christianity,* edited by Beverly Mayne Kienzle and Pamela J. Walker, 288-302. Berkeley: University of California Press, 1998.

Ward, W[ilfrid] R[eginald], ed. *The Early Correspondence of Jabez Bunting, 1820-29.* London: Royal Historical Society, 1972.

———. "Late Jansenism and the Habsburgs." In *Religion and Politics in Enlightenment Europe,* edited by James E. Bradley and Dale K. Van Kley, 154-86. Notre Dame: University of Notre Dame Press, 2001.

———. *Victorian Oxford.* London: Cass, 1965.

Ward, W[ilfrid] R[eginald], and R. P. Heitzenrater, eds. *Works of John Wesley.* Vol. 21, *Journals and Diaries.* Nashville: Abingdon, 1992.

Wardlaw, Ralph. *Friendly Letters to the Society of Friends on some of their distinguishing principles.* Glasgow: Fullarton, 1836.

Watson, Sydney E. *Bethesda Free Chapel [Sunderland] Centenary 1845-1945.* [Sunderland]: The Chapel, 1945.

Weaver, Frederick William, and Charles Herbert Mayo, eds. *Notes and Queries for Somerset and Dorset.* Sherborne: Sawtell, 1897.

Welford, Richard. *Men of Mark 'twixt Tyne and Tweed.* 3 vols. London: Scott, 1895.

Wenger, Leslie. "The Baptist Church in Eynsham." *Eynsham Record* 13 (1996) 9-15.

Wenham, L. P., ed. *Letters of James Tate.* Yorkshire Archaeological Society Record 128. Wakefield: Yorks, 1966.

Weremchuk, Max S. *John Nelson Darby: A Biography.* Neptune, NJ: Loiseaux, 1992.

The West Briton and Cornwall Advertiser.

Whately, Richard. *Thoughts on the Proposed Evangelical Alliance, in a letter to a clergyman.* 2nd ed. London: Fellowes, 1846.

Whitfield, Frederick. *The Plymouth Brethren: A Letter to Rev. Osmond Dobree, B.A., Guernsey, containing Strictures on Mr. William Kelly's Pamphlet Entitled "God's Principle of Unity."* London: Shaw, 1863. [As yet unlocated.]

[Wigram, George Vicesimus]. *On Ministry in the Word.* London: Central Tract Depot, [1844].

———. *A Protest against the National Establishment of England.* [As yet unlocated.]

Wilbur, Henry W. *The Life and Labors of Elias Hicks.* Philadelphia: Friends General Conference, 1910.

Williams, John, ed. *The Works of the Rev Robert. Hawker, D.D., late vicar of Charles, Plymouth: With a memoir of his life and writings.* 10 vols. London: Palmer, 1831.

Wilson, Daniel. *The character of the Good Man as a Christian Minister: A sermon occasioned by the death of the Rev. Basil Woodd . . . to which are subjoined notes on the controversy between the Professor of Divinity at Oxford and the Rev. Mr. Bulteel.* 3rd ed. London: Stevens, 1831.

Wilson, Elisabeth. "'The Eyes of the Authorities Are upon Us': The Brethren and World War I." *BAHNR* 3.1 (2004) 2–17.

———. "'Your Citizenship Is in Heaven': Brethren Attitudes to Authority and Government." *BAHNR* 2.2 (2003) 75–90.

Wilson, Owain W. "Prince and the Lampeter Brethren." *Trivium* 5 (1970) 10–20.

Wiseman, Donald John. *Life Above and Below: Memoirs.* N.p.: priv. published, 2003.

The Witness [magazine].

Wolff, Joseph. *Travels and Adventures of Joseph Wolff.* London: Saunders, Otley, 1861.

Woodward, Henry. *Essays, Thoughts and reflections, and Letters, with a Memoir by his Son Thomas Woodward.* London: Macmillan, 1864.

Worth, Richard Nicholls. *History of Plymouth from the Earliest Period to the Present Time.* Plymouth: Brendon, 1890.

The Yorkshireman: A Religious and Literary Journal by a Friend.

Yorkshire Observer.

Zentner, Carola. *Twins.* Newton Abbott: David & Charles, 1975.

Archives Consulted

Aberystwyth, National Library of Wales, Mysevin MSS

NLW, Ms. 13232 (**Mysevin MS 12**), S. P. Tregelles to Aneurin Owen-Pugh, Jul, Sep 1833.

Alnwick, Northumberland Archives, Drummond Papers

C/1/200, 201, A. N. Groves to H. Drummond, 2 undated letters [c. Feb–Jun 1829].

C/9/8–44, Edward Irving to Henry Drummond, 14 Sep 1832–11 Nov 1834.

Basel, Switzerland, Mission Archives [BMA]

Gemischte Briefe [GB] Q-3-4
F. Cunningham to C. G. Blumhardt, May 1821.
A. N. Groves to R. Pearson, 14 Oct 1829 [MS copy].

Personalfaszikell series Q-13 BV235
A. N. Groves to Blumhardt, 22 Jun 1834.
A. N. Groves to W. Büchelen, 30 Nov 1835 and 22 Mar '36.

CMS correspondence series QK-3, 1D
D. Coates to C. G. Blumhardt, 12 Mar 1835.

Basel, Staats-Archiv

Pr. Arch. 653.v.11, A. N. Groves to C. F. Spittler, 7 Apr 1835; Dec '35.

Beverley, East Riding Archive and Local Studies Service

SL245/9/9, "Norwood House," a typescript by D. N. Tucker.

Birmingham, Birmingham Oratory

F. W. Newman file 2

Birmingham, University Library, CMS Archives [BU; CMSA]

CMS Minutes viii. 483
C.W/o81/1–34, Letters from L. Strong to D. Coates 1827–1838.
G/Ac/3, John Hill to Josiah Pratt, 20 Feb and 11 Mar 1830.
G/C/1, A. N. Groves to E. H. Bickersteth (25 March 1825).
Venn MSS c.26, John Venn, Hereford to Emelia Venn, 9 Dec 1834.

Cambridge, Sidney Sussex College, Admission Records

Cambridge, University Library, BFBS Archives

A. N. Groves, Five Letters to BFBS, 5 June '29; 28 Aug. '30; 18 Sept. '31; 2 May and 20 Oct. '32.
Embley, Peter L., "The Origins and Early Development of the Plymouth Brethren," PhD dissertation, Cambridge University, 1966 available online at http://www.bruederbewegung.de/pdf/embley.pdf (consulted 27/6/06).

Canterbury, Cathedral Archives, Diocese of Canterbury

Chaplains' Licences DCb/F/F/Ea/2 1868; Ea/4 1869.

Dublin, Trinity College Archives

MS 6189, env. 1., Mrs L. S. La Touche Truell to John Synge, 27 Oct. '31.
TCD MUN/V/23/4, Trinity Admissions Register.

Dublin, Trinity College Library

Synge materials, Nos. 22Y 36; 22Y 36 No. 2;
   Papyrus Case E; Press 9372 No. 5.

Dublin, Representative Church Body Library

J. B. Leslie, ed., "Biographical Succession Lists."

Archives Consulted

Edinburgh, New College Archives

CHA 4.60.5, 7, R. Nesbit to T. Chalmers 17 Feb and 13 Mar 1826.

Exeter, Cathedral Archives

ED 11/85 ii. 23-4, "Bishop Phillpott's Visitation Journal."

Lampeter, Archives and Manuscripts at the University of Wales

Records relating to A. A. Rees [kindness of Professor Nigel Yates].

London, British Library

Oriental and India Office Collections, Private Papers: Sir Richard Temple Mss Eur F86/246, Henry Soltau, "Memorandum on Burmah" (1885).
BL Shelves, C.61. c.8., S. T. Coleridge's copy of Irving's *Missionary Sermon*.

London, Dr William's Library, Congregational Library

R. M. Beverley to Joshua Wilson, 20 Feb 1834, cited in Bebbington.

London, Freemasons Hall, Library and Museum of Freemasonry

HC 7/ E/ 6-7, 9, 12-15, R. M. Beverley, letters (1822–32) to E. Harper and W. H. White.

London, Greater London Record Office

Howard Papers, Acc. 1017/15, R. M. Beverley to Robert Howard, 8 July [1838].

London, India Office Records

L/PS/9 [**Persia 1831**] 46 p. 497., R. Taylor's Despatch, 17 June 1831.

London, London Metropolitan Archives, Clerkenwell

LMA, Ms 15860/7, folio 360., "Apprenticeship register of the Haberdashers' Co. 1675–1708."

London, Public Record Office

Prob. 11/1877, Soltau will and probate.

London, School of Oriental and African Studies

Council for World Mission Archives A2 [14] 1:3
"Journal of Richard Knill" 1 (23 June–4 July 1829) 252–55.
CWM S. India Tamil, 1834-5, Box 6 Folder 1, Jacket C, Item 16)
John Smith to LMS headquarters, 25 July 1834.

Manchester, John Rylands University Library

Christian Brethren Archive [JRULM, CBA]
Box 168 (5), "Autobiography of Theodore Stanley Soltau," typescript copy provided by his granddaughter Eleanor Soltau of Dickson, TN, USA.
    CBA 7049, Newton's recollections, Fry MS Book.
    CBA 7057, Newton's recollections, Wyatt MS Book 1.
    CBA 7059-61, Wyatt MS Books 5–7.
    CBA 7064
    CBA 7179 (1, 3, 5, 7), Letters from B. W. Newton to Mrs [Anna] Newton, 23 Apr '27; 3 Sep '27; 30 Dec '27; 23 May 1829.
    CBA 7181 (7), S. P. Tregelles to B. W. Newton 29 Jan 1857.
Box 23 [10], Newton to Cookworthy, June 1837.
Box 23 [10], B. W. Newton to Mrs Riach, 7 Feb 1866.
Darby Sibthorp Collection, Box 157
CBA MS 5540 Capt Rock to J N Darby, 2 Feb 1829.

Nottingham University, Dept of MSS and Special Collections

Bentinck Papers, Pw Jf 791-2, 1834,
Joseph Clulow to Lord William Bentinck, with copy of Groves's proposal for using the Tigris.

Oxford, Bodleian Library

Dep CMJ, Minutes of the General Committee of the LSPCJ 13 (1829).
Engl. Lett. d.222 f 178, Sydney Smith to McKenzie Beverley, 23 Oct 1825, concerning voting in Yorkshire.
Shelfmark 1304 e 104, MS memorandum by Eliot Howard and original letters inserted in R. M. Beverley, *The Posthumous Letters of the Rev. Rabshakeh Gathercoal, late Vicar of Tuddington, now first published, with explanatory*

notes, and dedicated to the Lord Bishop of London, 2nd ed., (London [Westley and Davis] 1837).

St Edmund Hall MS 67/7, 67/8, Diary of John Hill, 29 Oct 1829; 25 Oct 1830.

Perth, Australia, J. S. Battye Library of West Australian History

Private Archives, MN 586/1 Acc.3627A
Correspondence of Frances Bowker.

Plymouth, Plymouth and West Devon Record Office

81/Y/10/1, Copy of marriage settlement between George Soltau of Suffolk Lane, London, and Elizabeth Maria Symons of Chaddlewood.

81/Y/10/11, Copy of Soltau will.

MS 105/109, Marriage certificate of George Fox and Rachel Collier Hingston, at Plymouth Quaker Meeting House, 4 August 1819.

Acc.61, H. Prideaux, "Tis sixty years since," typescript c. 1870.

Sydney, NSW, Australia, State Library of New South Wales

Sir Joseph Banks Archive, Series 72.191.

William Vaughan to J. Banks, 16 July 1794, with extract from letter by Samuel Vaughan.

Terling, Essex, Strutt Archives

Juliana Probyn to John James Strutt, 12–15 Nov; 8 Dec 1831; 30 May 1835.
Edward Irving to Edmund Probyn, 10 Nov 1831.
Isabella Irving to Mr and Mrs Probyn, 25 Nov 1831.
Henry Drummond to J. J. Strutt, 10 Nov 1831.

Winchester, Hampshire Record Office

York, Borthwick Institute, University of York

Halifax A2/22/7, R. M. Beverley to Sir Francis Wood, Dec 14, 1827.

York, Minster Library

MS letter R. M. Beverley to Francis Wrangham, April 6 [1826], in a bound volume of three pamphlets (spine labeled "Beverleiana"), one of which is *The Rebellion of the Beasts*, by Leigh Hunt[?].

Zurich, Zentralbibliothek, MSS. Pestalozzi 55a1 365

Letters of John Synge to Pestalozzi.

Unpublished Theses, Dissertations

Cartmell, John. "Friends and Brethren in Kendal: A Critical Analysis of the Brethren Church in Kendal from the Quaker Meeting between 1835 and 1858." Dissertation, Glasgow, 1999.

Lively, Robert Lee, Jr. "The Catholic Apostolic Church and the Church of Latter-Day Saints: A Comparative Study of Two Minority Millenarian Groups in 19th Century England." DPhil diss., Oxford, 1977.

Livesay, D. A. "Children of Uncertain Fortune: Mixed Race Migration from the West Indies to Britain, 1750–1820." (PhD diss., University of Michigan, 2010.

Willmer, H. "Evangelicalism 1785–1835." Hulsean Prize essay, 1962, Cambridge.

Index

A

Abbott, Edwin A., 282
Abbott, Hannah. See Newton, Hannah (née Abbott)
Abbott, John, of Kendal, l39
Abbott, Sarah (née Wilson), 39
Account of the Grand Musical Festival (Crosse), 248–249n48
Act of Parliament (1777), 167
Active Service with Christ (Dobbie), 236
Adair, Rob, Quaker, 30
Adams, John, Methodist preacher, 208
Adventists, 270–271
Age of Reason, The (Paine), 16n39
Agier, Pierre-Jean, Jansenist, 138, 139, 142
Alderson, See Opie, Amelia (néeAlderson)
Alderson, Dr., James, 14
Alexander, Captain R., 223
Alexander, Charlotte (née Stewart), 223n25
Alexander, Major-General Robert, 223n25
Alexander, Michael, Bishop of Jerusalem, 109
Allen, William, Quaker, 7-11.
  emphasis on Scripture, 16
  evangelical sympathies, 15, 28, 31, 33
  opposition to capital punishment, poverty, ignorance, cruelty, 8–9
  pharmaceutical business, 7, 10, 59n1
  protest of Slave Trade and slavery, 7, 9
  references to God, 8n4
  rejection of social injustice, 8–9
  role in Mendicity Society, 106n19
  spiritual life of, 9–10
  view of Buxton's defense of Quakers, 14n34
  view of French Revolution, 7-8
Allenby, Field Marshall Edmund, 235
Alsop, Robert, Lord Mayor of London, 176
Alsop, Sophia, See Strong, Sophia.
Alumni Oxonienes, 149

Ambrose, Saint. 122n14
America, 33, 45, 270
American McAll Record, 289
Amien, Peace of, 8
Amphion, HMS, explosion of, 218
Anglo-Burmese War, 287
Annan, Noel, 214
Antichrist, 135n76
anticlericalism, 245–255
anti-Erastian voice, 96, 98, 131
antinomianism, 96, 126
Antoine, Nicolas, Protestant convert and crypto-Jew, 3
apocalypse. See eschatology; Second Coming of Christ
Apocrypha, 84, 87
Apologia for the life and character of Mohammed (Higgins), 250
Apologia pro Vita Sua (J. H. Newman), 130
Apostasy of the Successive Dispensation, The (Darby?), 54
Apostles,
  calling of in Catholic Apostolic Church, 69,78
  conduct in early church, 127
Appeal to the Christian Public (Howard), 260n103
archbishop of Canterbury, 127n45
armed services
  Brethren in India, 223–224
  Groves's role in Brethren attitude, 224–227
  pacifism of Plymouth Brethren in South-West England, 218–222
  Quaker stand on, 8, 9, 219
Arminianism, 106, 126, 128, 215, 217
Armstrong, John, school-teacher in British Guiana 183, 185–189
Armstrong, Major Elliott, Indian Army Officer, 230
Armstrong, Mary (née Fraser), 230n53

333

Armstrong, Nicholas, Irvingite preacher and Apostle, 76–77, 85n22, 96, 152
Arnold, Thomas, Headmaster of Rugby school, 78
Athenaeum (Plymouth Institution), 22, 256
Austen, Jane, novelist, 209, 210n24
Austin, Alvyn, 284
Aveline, Charles, business man in British Guiana, 192–193
Aveline, James, 192n78
Awakening to Secession, From (Stunt), 1, 3

B

Baldelli, Count Antonio, Tuscan Plymouth Brother, 228n44
Baldelli, Henrietta Gertrude (née Walker), 228n44
Balkwill, John, Plymouth Brother, Kingsbridge, Devon, 37
Balkwill, Richard, 37
Ball, Caroline. See Caroline Howard, née Ball)
Ball, Fanny. See Fanny Prideaux (née Ball)
Ball, John, St John's College, Oxford, 94
Ball, Mary, (née Mary Beck Ash), 49
Ball, Richard, Plymouth Brother, of Taunton and Bristol, 34, 48, 49, 51
Bampton, Mary, 175
Banks, Miss (governess to Juliana Probyn), 72–73, 75
Banks, Sir Joseph, 123
baptism
    Frank Newman's stand on, 99
    of Brethren, 48–49
    Brethren's stand on, 63
    crisis in Herefordshire over, 211
    Quaker stand on, 9, 34, 259–260
    separatist controversy over, 19
Baptist Magazine, 256
Barclay, John, Quaker, 14
Barclay, Mr., Irvingite, 85n22
Barclay, Robert, early Quaker, 12, 15, 34
Barlow, Eleanor (née Gill), 193
Barlow, John, manager of sugar plantation in British Guiana, 193
Barnardo, Thomas, 284n8, 285
Barrett [Browning], Elizabeth, poetess, 217n59
Barrington, Mr. and Mrs. (missionaries to British Guiana), 193
Barton, Captain James, 232n65
Basel Mission Institute, 103, 112–117
Bates, Elisha, Evangelical American Quaker, 33

Batten, James Ebenezer, (1803 - ?) Plymouth draper, Plymouth Brother, 162–163n87
Baxter, Robert, solicitor and critic of Irvingism, 70, 73, 87
Baylee, Joseph, Irish Quaker and Anglican, 18–20
Baynes, Ann Frances (née Cator), mother of Harriet Baynes, 106n16
Baynes, George, 226
Baynes, Harriet, See Harriet Groves (née Baynes), 105–107, 115, 198, 223, 224, 292
Baynes, Major-General Edward, 106, 198
Baynes, William Craig, 106n16
Baynton-Rolt, Sir Andrew, 270n28
Beacon to the Society of Friends, A (I. Crewdson), 34, 43
Beaconite controversy, 29, 33–34, 40, 43, 57, 200n23
Beattie, David, 40, 47
Beauchamp, Sir Thomas, 283
Bebbington, David, 257
Becket, Maria (née Beverley), 242n13
Becket, Sir Edmund, 242n13
Beddy, J. Fawcett, former CMS missionary, 211
Beer, George, missionary in the Godavari Delta, India, 173, 225n34, 292
Belam, Caroline, 170n24
Bell, Captain James, 224
Bell, Colonel Jasper Higginson, 229
Bell, Thomas George, 280n30
Bellett, Elizabeth (née Denny), 48n72
Bellett, George, 48n72, 128
Bellett, John Gifford
    account of Grove's visit to Dublin, 20
    account of Powerscourt conferences, 156n59
    association with Plymouth Brethren, 104
    on Darby's accident, 131n59
    family of, 48n72
    at Powerscourt Conferences, 155
    inaccurate chronology of early Brethren movement, 135n78
    proposal for translation of New Testament, 276
    relationship with Darby, 128
Bennett, Elizabeth, married John Randall, 206n6
Bennett, James, 206n6
Bentham, Jeremy, 124
Bentinck, Lord William, Governor-general of Bengal and India, 114n55
Benyon, Captain Paul, 221n14
Beresford, George Le Poer, Bishop of Kilmore, 254n70
Beresford, Marcus Gervais, Archbishop of Armagh 254n70

INDEX

Berger, William, Chemical Manufacturer and Plymouth Brother, 283
Berkeley, George, Philosopher and Bishop of Cloyne, 126
Berkin, Henry, rector of Trinity Church in the Forest of Dean, 178
Berry, Mary, 247
Bethesda Division, 50, 56–57, 264
Bevan, John Gurney, business partner of William Allen, 7
Bevan, Silvanus, Quaker, founder of Old Plough Court pharmacy, 59n3
Beverley, Mackenzie, 245n30
Beverley, Major Robert [1], 241
Beverley, Maria, 242n13
Beverley, Mary (née Coltman), stepmother of R.M. Beverley, 242
Beverley, Mary (née Midgley), wife of William Beverley [2], 241–242
Beverley, Robert [2], 241
Beverley, Robert [3], 241
Beverley, Robert Mackenzie, Chapter 15, 241-264
    admiration of Quakers, 258–260
    admiration of Samuel Lloyd, Sr., 40
    anticlericalism, Masonic and radical involvement, 245–248
    attraction to the Brethren, 260–263
    education of, 242–245
    evangelical involvement and anticlerical polemic, 249–255, 261–262, 282
    family origins, 241–242
    final isolation of, 263–264, 281–282
    reply to Venn's Christian Ministry and Church Membership, 216
    secession to Congregationalism, 255–258, 281
Beverley, William [1], 241
Beverley, William [2], 241–242, 244
Bewley, Henry, Quaker and Plymouth Brother, 56n117, 273, 283, 284n8
Bialloblotzky, Friedrich, 202
Bible Society, 91–92, 179, 181, 182, 189, 210
Bickersteth, Edward, Secretary of the CMS, 108, 109, 110, 210
Bierman, John, 236
Biographical Sketch of the Struggles of Pestalozzi to establish his System of Education (Synge), 145
Birkbeck, Susannah, See Wakefield, Susannah.
Bisse, Henry, Fellow of Worcester College, Oxford, 97, 100
Bjorlie, John, 168–169n18
Black Book, The (Wade), 251
Bloody Assizes, 175

Bloxam, John Rouse, Fellow of Magdalen, Oxford, 95
Blumhardt, Christian Gottfried, (Director of Basel Institute), 103, 115, 116–117
Boddington, Sister Thérèse, 146n19
Bonar, Andrew, 287n25
Bonar, Jane, See Jane McIntyre, 287n25
Booker, Josias, 183n41
Booth, Catherine, wife of William Booth, Salvation Army, 274
Borlase, Henry, Plymouth Brother, editor of the *Christian Witness*, 202
Bowden, William, missionary in the Godavari Delta, India 173, 225n34, 292
Bowes, John, 117
Bowker, Captain James, 221–222
Bowker, Frances, 221–222
Boys, Thomas, 84, 87
Braithwaite, Anna, of Kendal, wife of Isaac Braithwaite of Kendal, 34n15, 45–46
Braithwaite, Deborah. See Deborah Crewdson,
Braithwaite, George, 35
Braithwaite, Isaac, of Manchester; author of *A Beacon to the Society of Friends,* 34n15,
Braithwaite, Isaac, of Kendal, husband of Anna Braithwaite, 35 Braithwaite, John Bevan, son of Isaac and Anna Braithwaite, 51
Braithwaite, Rachel, see Rachel Lloyd, 35, 259
Braithwaite, Robert, Jr., convert to Roman Catholicism, 34n15
Braithwaite, Robert, Sr., Vicar of Chipping Camden, 34
Braithwaite family, 35, 43
Bramston, John, Dean of Winchester, 99
Brenton, Sir Lancelot Charles Lee, baronet
    aftermath of early career of, 197n7, 280
    association with Brethren, 101n58
    condemnation of Establishment, 99
    Henry Prince's visit, 269–270
    Hill's influence on, 97
    Pacifism, 220, 264n120
    proposal for translation of New Testament, 276
    remarks about Catholic Emancipation, 97n33
    socioeconomic status of, 197, 220
Brenton, Sir Jahleel, 197n7, 220
Brethren
    Beverley's attraction to, 260–263
    development of Darby's views, 54–56
    developments in North of England, 38–47
    developments in South of England, 48–52
    division among, 60, 262
    emergence of, 20, 32
    evangelicals among, 41–44, 117

Brethren (continued)
  government within, 53–54, 56–57
  in Herefordshire, 215–216
  identity change in later nineteenth century, 292
  missionary cause, 283–284
  origins of, 59–60, 204–217
  as peculiar people, 1–2
  Penstone and, 59–65
  Prince and Rees and, 271
  Quaker converts, 36–58, 56–57, 57
  Quaker cultural influences on, 52–53
  Quaker ecclesiastical and theological influence on, 53–57
  Rees and, 273–274
  secession to Church of England, 155
  secession issue, 156–159
  support and later disapproval of Groves, 105
  Synge's connection with, 162
  See also specific person associated with Brethren
Brethren: The Story of a Great Recovery (Beattie), 40
Brewer, Charles, 216
Bridson, Miss (Synge family governess), 151
Brief Inquiry into the Prospect of the Church of Christ in connexion with the Second Advent (Noel), 121
Brief Remarks on... water baptism (Wakefield), 47n64
Brissot, Jacques Pierre, leading Girondist in the French Revolution 10
Bristol riots (1831), 76
British and Foreign Bible Society, 114, 178
British Guiana, 182–185
British Parliament
  abolition of slavery, 183
  Catholic Emancipation, 69, 76, 97, 180, 247–248, 250
  Married Women's Property Act (1882), 271
  reform, 69, 76, 180, 183, 246–247, 251
Broad Clyst, 104
Brockie, William, 273
Bronte, Colonel, Indian Army Officer, 228n42
Broomhall, James, 283, 285
Brothers, Richard, millennisl enthusiast, 121n7
Brown, Charlotte, See Charlotte Soltau, 288
Brown, David, 85n22
Budge, Sir Wallis, Egyptologist, 225n33
Bulteel, Henry Bellenden
  aftermath of early career of, 280
  association with Brethren, 101
  association with Irvingites, 101
  baptism of Beverley, 260
  at Church Missionary Society meeting, 92
  condemnation of Establishment, 99
  conversion to Irvingites and Brethren, 99
  criticism of Established Church, 148–149
  evangelical conversion of, 27
  influence of, 96–97
  opposition to, 30, 93, 94, 97
  preaching visit to Plymouth and South Coast, 149
  proposal for New Testament translation, 275
  proposal to oust J. H. Newman, 101
  radical evangelism of, 97
  reversed military expectation, 219n7
  view of manifestations of the Holy Spirit, 82, 87
  withdrawal of his license, 162, 163
Bulwer-Lytton, Rosina, Lady Lytton, 61
Bunting, Jabez, 208
Burdett, Sir Francis, 249
Burdon-Sanderson, Robert, 217n58
Burgh, William, expositor of prophecy, 135n76
Burlamaqui, Jean-Jacques, 127
Burns, Robert, 228n44
Butler, John. (bishop of Hereford), 178, 205, 208
Buxton, Anna (née Hanbury), 14n33
Buxton, Hannah (née Gurney), 12, 14n33
Buxton, Thomas Fowell, 14
Byrth, John, 20–21, 22–23
Byrth, Mary (née Hobling), 20
Byrth, Thomas, Quaker and Anglican, 20–21, 24, 26–27

C

Cable, Mildred, 166
Caird, Mary (née Campbell), 78, 81–82, 85n22
Caird, William, Irvingite, 85n22
Call to the Converted, A (Lambert), 149, 150, 156–159
Calvinism, 94–95, 106n17, 126, 128, 208, 211–212, 217
"*Cambridge besieged*" (Beverley?), 249
Cambridge University, 251–253, 281
Campbell, Mary, See Mary Caird
Campbell, McLeod, 83, 184n45
Campbell, Sir Alexander, General in India, maternal grandfather of Sir Alexander Cockburn-Campbell, 219–220
Campbell-Cockburn, Sir Alexander, 155, 197n8, 199n14, 219–220n9
Campbell-Cockburn, Lady Margaret (née Malcolm), 220n9
capital punishment, 8–9

INDEX

Cardale, John B., Irvingite Apostle, 79, 81, 83, 85n22
Cardale, Miss Emily, J.B. Cardale's sister, 85, 86, 87
Carey, William, pioneer Baptist missionary in India, 120
Carmichael-Smyth, Captain Mark Wood, 229
Carrick, Earl of, 232
Carron, Theodore William, 136
Carter, Charles, CMS schoolteacher in British Guiana, 183
Carter, Grayson, 196
Cartmell, John, 47n64
Cartwright, Major John, "the Father of Reform", 249
Catechism on the Doctrines of the Plymouth Brethren (Croskery), 140n100
Catholic Apostolic Church
 call of apostles, 69, 78
 charismatic era of, 78
 Irving and, 108
 origins of, 69-72, 81-82
 See also Irivingites
Catholic Emancipation
 Irvingite opposition to, 69, 76
 passing of, 250
 Peel's opposition to, 97
 religious division over, 180
 Sydney Smith's and Beverley's views of, 247-248
Cator, Ann Frances, mother of A.N. Groves's 2nd wife, 106n16
Chadwick, Owen, 101n58
Chalmers, Frederick Skene Courtenay, Captain in Indian army, later ordained in England 223
Chalmers, Thomas, "Scotland's greatest 19th century churchman", 81n6
Chalon, Alfred Edward, 61
Chapman, Robert, of Barnstaple, 32, 284n8, 288
Character of a Primitive Bishop in a letter to a non-juror, The (Pitts?), 128-129
Charge (archiepiscopal) of 1826 (Magee), 132
charismatic movement
 authentication of miracles, 84-88
 debate over doctrine concerning, 82-84
 Groves's view of, 108
 Irvingites and, 69-79
 manifestations, 81-82
 See also Gloucestershire clergyman case
Charlinch Revival, 270
Chief Men Among the Brethren (Pickering), 60, 63, 166
child-centered education, 144-146, 165

China Inland Mission (CIM)
 Brethren promotion of, 49, 51
 Soltau family and, 166, 174, 284, 284-285n8, 288, 289, 292
 Taylor's work with, 283-285
 Theodore Howard as home director of, 51
Chinese Evangelization Society, 49
cholera epidemic, 37, 69, 76, 153
Christian, The (William Soltau's letter to), 289
Christian and Brotherly Advices given forth from time to time by the Yearly Meetings [of Quakers] *in London*, 17
Christian Devotedness (Groves), 105, 108, 110-111, 292
Christian Examiner, 145
Christian Ministry and Church Membership, The (Venn), 216, 261
Christian Observer, 82, 214
Christian Researches (Jowett), 109
Christian Witness, 54, 278
Christianity, 1-2.
 See also Brethren; Established Church; Irvingites; Plymouth Brethren; Quakers
Christianity and Military Service (Dobbie), 236
Christology
 of Hicks, 33
 of Irvingites, 83-84, 87, 88
 of Newton, 282
 Quaker division over, 43
Church, Dr. Clive, 208n16
church bells, 15-16
Church Missionary Society (CMS)
 attitude toward Armstrong, 188
 Bickersteth's involvement with, 210
 crisis of 1829-30, 91-95, 100-101
 Groves's connection with, 104, 108-112
 Groves's membership, 104
 Henry Gipps as chairman of auxiliary meeting, 210n27
 Leonard Strong's work with, 180, 183-**192**
 missionary recruits, 102-103
 requirements for missionaries, 104-105, 108-109
 Robert Strong's work with, 179
Church Missionary Society College, 113n47
Church of England, 187. See also Established Church
Church of England examined by Scripture and tradition, The (Beverley), 261
Church of Scotland, 184n44, 185
Churchill, Edith, 61n13
churchmanship. See also exact churchmanship; staunch churchmanship; strict churchmanship

337

Index

Cicero, 122
Clapham sect, 214
Clayton, George, Congregational minister, 278
clothing
    of Brethren, 52
    of Quakers, 2, 50n88
Clowes, William, Primitive Methodist, 256
Clulow, Joseph, 114n55, 173–174, 231, 275, 292
Clulow family, 173n41
CMS, See Church Missionary Society (CMS)
Coad, Roy, 59n1, 147n22, 237
Coates, Dandeson, Secretary of CMS,110n32, 116n68, 183, 191
Cockburn-Campbell, Grace (née Spence), 48, 220n9
Cockburn-Campbell, Sir Alexander, 48n70, 197, 219–220, 275
Coleridge, Samuel Taylor, 25n84, 80, 88
Coleridge, William, First Bishop of Barbados, 183
Collingwood, Frances (née Collingwood), 13
Collingwood, Samuel, 12–14
Collingwood, William, 13n28, 283, 284n8
Collins, Thomas, 152
Coltman, Mary. See Beverley, Mary (née Coltman)
Commune (Paris) of 1871, 288
communion. See Lord's Supper
confessional authenticity, 84–86.
    See also Trying the spirits
Congregational Magazine, 47–48, 49
Congregationalism, 255–258
conscription, 236
Considerations addressed to the Archbishop of Dublin (Darby), 131
Constantine, Emperor, 255
Conybeare, John (1692-1755) Bishop of Bristol, 127
Cookman, George, slavery abolitionist, 259n98
Cookson, General, 232n62
Cookworthy, Charlotte (née Spicer), 221–222
Cookworthy, John, Quaker and Plymouth Brother, 37, 221
Cookworthy, Joseph, Quaker and Plymouth Brother, 37
Cookworthy, William, Pioneer of porcelain manufacture, 21, 37
Cope, Richard, Congregational minister, 21
Corbauld, Edward, 62
Corrie, Anna, See Walker, Anna (née Corrie)
Corrie, Daniel, Bishop of Madras, 226
"On the corruption of the Church of Christ" (Beverley), 251

Cottle, Thomas, 268n17
Cotton, Sir Arthur, of the Madras Engineers, 104, 111–112n41, 225n34
Courtney, Septimus, 30
Cox, G. V., 13
Craik, Henry
    baptizes Mary and Richard Ball, 49
    Bethesda Question, 50, 53
    at Powerscourt Conferences, 154
    Presbyterian background of, 32
    proposal for New Testament translation, 275
    relationship with Muller, 148
    services at Clifton, 269–270
    visit to Glanmore Castle, 154–155
    work with John Synge, 147–148
Crawley, Julia, 48n70, 220n8
Crewdson, Deborah (née Braithwaite), 35
Crewdson, Isaac, of Manchester, author of *A Beacon to the Society of Friends,* 34, 38, 40, 43
Crewdson, Maria, See Howard, Maria (née Crewdson) Crewdson, Rachel, See Fox, Rachel (née Crewdson), 51
Crewdson, Sarah (née Fox)
    Childhood "sister" of Hannah Newton (née Abbott) 39
    Hannah Newton's view of, 46
    association with Brethren, 43
    on Quaker origins of Brethren, 31
    relationship with William Pennefather, 41, 42–43, 46, 52
    marriage of, 39, 41
Crewdson, Sarah. See Sarah Fox (née Crewdson) daughter of W.D. Crewdson, snr., 35, 48–49
Crewdson, William Dillworth, Jr., 39, 40–41, 43, 45, 46–47, 52
Crewdson, William Dillworth, Sr., 35, 40–41, Crewdson family, 35, 40–41, 43
Croker, J. W., 254n71
Cronin, Edward, 20, 104
Croskery, Thomas, 140n100
Cross, Edwin, 278n14
Crosse, John, 248–249n48
Cruger, Johann, hymn tune composer, 207n10
Cunningham, Francis, Rector of Pakefield, 14, 14n32
Cunningham, John, Vicar of Harrow, caricatured by Frances Trollope, 14n32
Cunningham, Richenda (née Gurney), 12, 14n32
Curzon, George, 155
Cuthbert, Lucy Marianne (née Soltau), 287n27

338

D

Daly, Robert, Bishop of Cashel 127, 130, 136–137, 155
Dann, Robert Bernard, 103n6-7
Darby, Ann (née Vaughan), mother of J.N. Darby, 123
Darby, Christopher, 124
Darby, Sir Henry D'Esterre, Admiral, Uncle of J N Darby 123n18
Darby, John Nelson
   acceptance of his ideas, 56–57, 60, 63
   affinity of R.M. Beverley with, 262
   complexity of, 141–142
   concern about secession, 163
   conversion of, 121–122, 128–131, 130n53, 131n57, 141
   criticism of Benjamin Newton, 171, 202–203
   deliverance of, 134
   development of his views, 54–58
   early time in France, 136-140
   early work in Plymouth, 30-31, 135n79, 149
   ecclesiology of, 135, 141, 203
   education and Trinity College, 124–129
   eschatology of, 121–122, 125, 131–133, 135,139–142, 270–271n29
   evangelical involvement, 135–136, 170
   family of, 122–124
   influence of, 97, 99, 119, 146
   influences on, 121–122, 124–128
   leader of Exclusive Brethren, 107
   library of, 134n72
   lifestyle of, 198–199
   maintenance of church order, 201
   ministry of, 41–43, 44
   Müller's criticism of, 64
   portraits of, 59n1, 62, 64–65
   at Powerscourt Conferences, 155
   proposal for translation of New Testament, 275, 276
   relationship with Groves, 104
   "Remarks on Light and Conscience," 43n52
   speech at Society for the Conversion of the Jews, 149–150
   spiritual renewal of, 121
   visit to Cambridge, 135-136
   visit to Glanmore Castle, 155
   visits to Oxford 99, 135, 149–150
   work with F.P.Monod in Paris, 136
   work with von Poseck, 222
   years of uncertainty, 129–134
Darby, John Sr., 122–123
Darby, Susannah, See Pennefather Susannah (née Darby) sister of J.N. Darby, 124, 131
Darby, William Henry, 129–130n52
Darwin, Charles, 225n34, 264
Darwin, Dr. Erasmus, 9n8, 15
Das Berliner Gesangbuch, 207n10
Davies, C. M., 199
Davis (Baptist minister of Tottenham), 48
Davy, Humphrey, 7
De Officiis (On Duty) Cicero, 122
Deck, J. F., 271n33
Deck, Lieutenant James George, 229, 271–272
Decline and Fall of the Roman Empire, The, (Gibbon), 127
Defence of the doctrines of Immediate Revelation, A (Hancock), 34
Deism, 15–16
Denny, Elizabeth, 48n72
Denny, Sir Edward, 48n72, 62
denominationalism, 158–159
Dentan, Albert, 140
deprivation theory, 69n3caik
Dickenson, Richard, 266n5
Dictionary of National Biography, 61
Dictionary of the British Landed Gentry, 167
Discipleship! (Hall), 220–221
dispensationalism
   of B. W. Newton, 162–163n87
   of Darby, 119, 134
   of Plymouth Brethren, 162–163
"Dissenting Political Upsurge of 1833-1834, The"(Bebbington), 257
Dixon, Hepworth, 270n25
Dobbie, Lieutenant-General Sir William, 234, 236, 237
Dobbie, Sybil (née Orde-Brown), 234
Dorman, William Henry (Congregational convert to Plymouth Brethren), 32
Dornford, Rev. Joseph (fellow of Oriel College), 92
Doyle, Elizabeth, 17
Drummond, Henry
   Albury conferences on prophecy, 98
   meetings for prophetic study in home of, 120
   on Baxter's account of Probyn prophecies, 70
   on Baxter's critique of Irvingites, 87n29
   on Cardale's prophecy, 87
   on Fancourt's account of her healing, 81n6
   meeting with Groves, 114
   opposition to Irving, 79
   on reading of Probyn's letter, 85n22
Dubois, Julie, 115
Dudley, Charles Stokes, 18
Dudley, George, 18
Dudley, Mary, 18
Duff, Alexander, 111n37

Index

Duff, Alexander Groves, 111n37
Dundas, Matilda, See Matilda Strong (née Dundas), 194
Dunkin, Alfred John, 61
D'Urban, Sir Benjamin, Governor of British Guiana, later of Cape Colony, 186
Dustless tomb (Penstone), 60n7
Dutch Church in Dublin, 18–19
Dyer, John, 48
Dymond, George, 107
Dymond, Jonathan, 107n22
Dymond family, 38

E

Eastlake, Sir Charles, 219n3
Eccles, Harriet, 194
Ecclesiastical Knowledge Society, 255
ecclesiology
    of Beverley, 258
    of Darby, 135, 141, 203
    evangelical preoccupation with, 96
    of Groves, 223
    Lambert's tract on, 156–159
    of Quakers, 53–57
    of Leonard Strong, 187–191
    Youd in British Guiana and, 188
Echoes of Service, 233
Eclectic Review, 62, 256, 261
Edict of Nantes, 176
Edinburgh Review, 10, 82, 119
educational practices, 144–146
Edwards, Edward, Rector of Lynne, 13
Egan, Dr., 20
elders, 53–54, 56–57
Elliot, Eliza, 169
Elliott, Edward Bishop, 169
Elrington, Charles, 254n71
Elrington, Thomas, Provost of Trinity College Dublin, Bishop of Leighlin and Ferns, 126
Emancipation (slavery) Act (1833), 258
Embley, Peter L., 272
Emile (Rousseau), 144
Enamoured Days (painting by J. J. Penstone), 62
Encyclopédie des Sciences Religieuses, 140
Engineering Magazine (U.S.), 290
England
    Christianity in early nineteenth century, 1–2, 291–292
    developments among Quakers in North, 38–48
    developments among Quakers in South, 48–52
    evangelical uncertainty in, 180–182
    Indian impact on Brethren, 227–232
    Napoleonic Wars, 119, 123, 127, 180, 218–222
    pacifism of Plymouth Brethren in South-West, 218–222
    political turmoil, 69, 76, 78
    Quakers in, 7–16, 25–35, 38–58
England (continued)
    See also; British Parliament; Church Missionary Society (CMS); Established Church; Irvingites; Plymouth Brethren; Quakers
Enlightenment, 10, 119, 124, 126–127
Epps, Dr. John, 199
Erastianism, 96, 97, 137, 141
Erskine, Thomas, 78, 133–134
eschatology
    Brethren's preoccupation with, 117, 173
    of Darby, 131–133, 135, 139–142
    Darby's influence on, 119
    of Gipps, 212
    of Irvingites, 141
    of Jansenists, 137–139
    of Père Lambert, 158–159
    outlook in evangelical world, 119–122
    perspectives in 1820s, 120–122, 181
    of Robert Strong, 181–182
    of Leonard Strong, 184–185, 189
Established Church
    Armstrong's description of, 76
    Beverley's attack on, 248–256
    in British Guiana, 182–183
    Bulteel's criticism of, 148–149
    in Herefordshire, 205
    Lambert's call for secession from, 150
    Rees and, 268–269
    rejection of Henry Prince, 270–271
    Synge's criticism of, 148–151
    Synge's work with, 154
    See also secession from Established Church
Evangelical Alliance, 164
Evangelical Magazine, 82, 120, 121, 212
evangelical piety, 126–127, 127
Evangelical Quakers, 43, 53, 258–259
evangelicals
    George Soltau, 285–286
    among Brethren, 41–44, 43–44, 117
    among Irvingites, 71
    among Quakers, 15–16, 27–31, 28, 32–35, 38–39, 40, 45, 62

call for secession from Established Church, 149, 150, 156–164
discontent at Oxford, 149
divisions among, 96
eschatological outlook, 119–122, 181
Fellows and Graduates of Trinity College, 127–128
Gipps as, 208–213
Hatchard, John, in Plymouth 30
Luke Howard's association with, 10–11
influence on Henry William Soltau, 169–170
legitimate pleasures for, 210
Passmore, Christopher, 198
Roman Catholic distancing from, 130
secession from Established Church, 96, 99
Venn, John, as, 213–214
See also China Inland Mission (CIM); Church Missionary Society (CMS); London Missionary Society;
Everett, James, 273
exact churchmanship
Robert Strong and, 178
Darby and, 128, 130, 141
effect on Bellett brothers, 128
Groves and, 106
Trinity College and, 125–126
Exclusive Brethren, 107, 203, 232
Exeter Mendicity Society, 106
exorcism of Probyn children, 70, 72, 73n21, 74, 75, 77–78, 85
Expositions des prédictions (Lambert), 138–139, 140
Eynard, Charles, 132

F

false prophets, 86n25
Fancourt, Eliza, 81, 84
Fancourt, Rev. Thomas, 81, 82
Faulkner, Gordon, 198n11
Fegan, J. W. C., 225n34
Fell, Margaret, 62–63
Female Teaching (Booth), 274
Fisher's Drawing Room Scrap Book, 62
Fitzgerald, Mr., 276
FitzWygram, Robert, 197n6
Foley, Captain Edward, 201
Foley, Frank Wigram, 201n27
Fool of the Family (McCormack), 165n93
foot washing, 200, 259
Footsteps of Truth (Hurditch), 288
On the Formation of Churches (Darby), 55
Fortnightly Review, 91–92, 95

Fosbery, Emmeline (née Hall), 221
Fosbery, Lieutenant-Colonel George Vincent, 221
Fox, Alfred, of Falmouth, 35
Fox, Benjamin, of Plymouth, husband of Sarah Treffry, 24
Fox, Caroline, Quaker Diarist, 70, 73–75
Fox, Charles, of Wellington, husband of Sarah Crewdson, 48
Fox, Francis, Plymouth chemist, father of Sarah Crewdson, 39
Fox, George, founder of Quakers, 8, 11, 23n71, 33, 62–63
Fox, Henrietta Maria, 51
Fox, Henry, 51
Fox, Margaret (née Fell), wife of George Fox, 62
Fox, Rachel Collier (née Hingston), married in Plymouth, 23n71
Fox, Rachel (née Crewdson), 51
Fox, Sarah Maria (née Howard), 51
Fox, Sarah (née Crewdson) daughter of W.D. Crewdson, snr., married Charles Fox of Wellington, 35, 48–49
Fox, Sarah (née Lloyd), wife of Alfred Fox, 35
Fox, Sarah (née Treffry), wife of Benjamin Fox, 24
Fox, Thomas, 51
Fox family, 35, 48-9, 51
France
Darby's time in, 136–140
French Revolution, 7–8, 119, 127, 137, 181, 218
Napoleonic Wars, 25–26, 31, 119, 123, 127, 180, 218–222
William Soltau's ministry in, 288–289
Franck, Charles E., 278n14
Franklin, Benjamin, 124
Fraser, Mary, 230n53
Freedom of the Gospel (Erskine), 133
Freelance Independents.
See Beverley, Robert Mackenzie; Rees, Arthur Augustus;
Soltau family; Stoddard, George Henry
Freeman, Martha, 267, 271
Freemasonry, 245–249
Freethinkers, 15–16
French, Francesca, 166
French Revolution, 7–8, 119, 127, 137, 181, 218
Frere, J. H., 120–121
Friel, Brian, 230
Friendly Letters (Rees), 273
Friendly Letters to the Society of Friends (Haldane), 43n52
Froom, LeRoy Edwin, 121n7

Froude, Robert, Archdeacon of Totnes, 169
Fry, Elizabeth (née Gurney), Quaker Reformer, 9, 12
Fuller, Lousia Mary, 217n58

G

Galton, Lucy, 15
Galton, Mary Anne, See SchimmelPenninck, Mary Anne (née Galton), 9n8,15
Galton, Samuel, 9n8, 15
Gathercole, Michael Augustus, 255–256, 257
Geldart, Thomas, 34
general redemption doctrine, 83–84, 87
George III (king of England), 254n71
German missionary recruits, 102–103, 112–113
Gibbon, Edward, 127
Gill, Eleanor, 193n80
Gipps, Elizabeth Emily, 217
Gipps, Elizabeth (née Lawrence), mother of Henry Gipps, 208
Gipps, Emma Maria (née Plumptre), 209, 217
Gipps, George, father of Henry Gipps, 208
Gipps, Henry, Vicar of St Peter's, Hereford, 178, 208–212, 215, 216–217
Gipps, Henry Plumptre, 209n20
Gipps, Sarah (née Stanton), 208
Giudici, Abbé Luigi, 139n96
Glanmore Estate, 143, 146, 147n22, 151–154
Gleaner in the Missionary Field, The (Ball), 49
Glory of Christ in the Everlasting Covenant, The (Gribble), 291
glossolalia
    approach to determining authenticity, 84–88
    in Irving's congregation, 82
    Irving's investigation of, 2, 69–70
    outside Irving's congregation, 81–82
    of Probyn children, 72–73, 181–182
    in Western Scotland, 78
Gloucestershire clergyman case, 69–79, 85, 86, 181–182
Gnosticism, 130n53
Gobat, Samuel, Bishop of Jerusalem, 105, 112, 145–146
Goderich, Viscount, 186
Godwin, Francis, 14
Gordon, Charles George, General, Governor of Sudan, 234
Goss, A. J. K., 208n15
Gosse, Philip, 194, 283
Gould, Matilda Harman, See Penstone, Matilda Harman (née Gould) 60
Grantley, Anna-Margaretta (née Midgley), 242

Grass, Dr. Tim, 117n76, 173n43
Graves, Richard, Professor of Divinity, Trinity College, Dublin, 126, 127
Great Separation (of Quakers in America), 33
Greaves, Joseph P., mystic and educator, 115, 146
Greaves, Richard, Vicar of Deddington, 98n35, 146n16
Grellet, Stephen, Quaker evangelist, 33
Gribble, Harry Wagstaff, 291
Gribble, Mary Amelia (née Soltau), 290
Gribble, Theodore Graham, 290
Gribble family, 290–291
Griffiths, Dr. John, of Hereford, 215–216
Gros, Ferdinand, 115
Grover, Captain John, 279
Groves, Anthony (father of Anthony Norris Groves), 103–104n7
Groves, Anthony Norris
    Basel connection, 112–117
    biography of, 103–105
    connection with Church Missionary Society, 104, 108–112, 114
    connection with Plymouth Brethren, 107, 173, 191
    ecclesiology of, 223
    as hero of the faith, 3
    historiography concerning, 105–108
    influence of, 146, 198, 223–224
    ministry among military, 224–229, 233
    mission to India, 104–105, 113–114, 173, 223–224
    mission to Persia, 78, 104, 108–109, 146–147, 198n10
    nonsectarianism of, 117–118
    opposition to ministry of, 271n33
    position on military service, 219, 224–227
    proposal for trade route to India, 114
    Quaker connection, 106–107
    Quaker influence on, 38
    reestablishment of New Testament patterns, 203
    relationship with Kitto, 22, 106
    socioeconomic status of, 292
    visit to Dublin, 20
Groves, Edward, 203n35, 231
Groves, Frank, 105n14
Groves, Harriet (née Baynes), Second wife and biographer of A N Groves, 105–107, 115, 223, 224, 292
Groves, Henry, 105n14
Groves, Lydia, 103–104n7, 112n44
Groves, Mary, Sister of A.N. Groves, 113n47
Groves, Mary Bethia (née Thompson), First wife of A N. Groves, 104

Guicciardini, Count Piero, 203, 228
Guinness, Dr. Grattan, 235
Gundert, Hermann, 115, 116
Gundert, Julie (née Dubois), 115
Gurney, Catherine, wife of John Gurney, 12
Gurney, Elizabeth, See Elizabeth Fry (née Gurney) 9, 12
Gurney, Emelia Russell, 214n43
Gurney, Hannah, 12, 14n33
Gurney, John, 11–12
Gurney, Joseph John
    Beaconite controversy and, 34
    call for recognition of Scripture as authority, 33, 34
    education of, 12–13
    emphasis on Scripture, 16
    evangelical sympathies, 13–14, 15, 28, 31
    influence on Amelia Opie, 15
Gurney, Richenda, 12, 14n32
Gurney Family, 11-14

H

Haffner, Charlotte (née Whittle), 54n106
Haffner, Thomas Pittman, 54
Haig, Lieutenant Felix Thackeray, 225n34, 235
Haile Selassie, 235
Hake, William, 106–107, 110, 172, 219
Haldane, Mary, 217n58
Haldane, Robert, 43n52
Hall, Captain Percy Francis
    ancestry of, 197
    conversion of Henry William Soltau, 171
    early leader of Plymouth Brethren, 30–31, 224
    evangelistic activities of, 45, 170
    at Powerscourt Conferences, 155
    preaching in Herefordshire, 215, 216
    proposal for New Testament translation, 275
    secession from Established Church, 149
    tract sent to Synge, 160
    view of military service, 220–221
Hall, Emmeline, 221
Hall, Miss, Irvingite prophetess, 85n22
Hall, Rev. Peter, 268n17
Halliday, General John Gustavus, 233
Halliday, Sir Frederick James, 233
Hallowell, Benjamin, 123
Hamilton, Isabella, wife of John Synge146
Hancock, John, II, Irish Quaker, 17–18
Hancock, Thomas, 34
Harcourt, Charles Vernon, (son of Archbishop of York), 247n41

Harcourt, Egerton Vernon, (son of Archbishop of York), 247n41
Hargrove, Charles, Early Plymouth Brother, 20n52, 49, 163–164, 276
Harris, Alfred Newton, 15n38, 200
Harris, James Lampen
    Accused of clericalism of, 202
    Editor of the *Christian Witness,* 278n14
    as elder of Plymouth Brethren, 53–54, 200
    at Glanmore Castle and Powerscourt conferences, 155
    letter from Newton on dispensationalism, 162–163n87
    letter to Kingsbridge assembly, 37
    proposal for translation of New Testament, 276
Harvey, Thomas, 258n97
Hatchard, John, Vicar of St Andrew's, Plymouth, 22, 30
Havelock, General Sir Henry, 233
Hawke, Wendy, 175n4
Hawker, Robert, 27, 28, 30
healings, 69–70, 78, 81–82
Hebich, Samuel, 115, 233
Hendrickson, Professor, 233
Hereford Brethren, 215–216
Hereford Journal, 215
"Hereford Letter" (Thornton), 214
Herefordshire
    Gipps's ministry in, 208–213, 217
    Randall's experience in, 205–208
    secession from Established Church, 215–216
    spiritual condition of residents, 204–205
    Venn's ministry in, 213–217
"Heresy of a Human Priesthood" (Beverley), 261
Hewit, 155
Hicks, Elias, 33
Hicksite controversy, 45
Higgins, Godfrey, 245, 250
High Calvinism, 96
Hill, Agnes (née Soltau), 284
Hill, Dr. John, vice-principal of St Edmund Hall, Oxford
    account of CMS subscribers meeting, 100
    despair at secession from Establishment, 99, 150
    division among evangelicals and, 96
    meeting for establishing Church Missionary Association in Oxford, 98
    on meeting of Church Missionary Society meeting, 100–101
    ministry of, 97
    opposition to Newman's proposal to CMS, 93–95

Hill, Dr. John (continued)
    Probyns' non-arrival, 72
    proposal of Newman as secretary of CMS, 92
    relationship with Lambert, 149-150
    relationship with Richard Greaves, 146n16
    view of miracles, 87
Hill, Frances, 172
Hill, Richard, 172, 275, 292
Hill, Richard Harris, 284, 284-285n8
Hillyar, Captain James, 224
Hillyar, Mary (née Taylor), 224
Hingston, Catherine Phillips (née Tregelles), 37
Hingston, Charles, 37
Hingston, Louisa Jane (née Parker), 37
Hingston, Rachel Collier, 23n71
Hingston family, 37
History (Neatby), 222
History of the Prayer Book (Stoddard), 279
History of Virginia (Beverley), 241
Hobling, Mary, 20
Hodgson, Ann, Wife of G.W. Soltau, 167
Holy Scripture, the test of Truth (Ball), 34
Holy Spirit
    Brethren and, 53-54, 200-201
    charismatic movement, 77-79
    Darby's later position, 55
    evangelical expectations, 180
    Irvingites' prayer for outpouring, 69-70, 81
    Lambert's view of, 156-159
    Leonard Strong's position on, 191
    manifestations of, 81-82
    Quaker disagreement over role of, 17
    Quaker emphasis on role of, 10, 33, 43, 53, 259
    See also glossolalia; healings; Inner Light doctrine; prophecy
Honeychurch, Amy, 25, 39
Honeychurch, Jane (née Treffry), 24-25, 39
Honeychurch, Joseph, 24-25, 39
Honeychurch, Mary, 25, 30, 35, 39
hopes of the Church of God, The (Darby), 54-55
Horrida Hystrix, Satyricon Castoreanum quod ex schedis manuscriptis deprompsit unus e societate lollardorum (Beverley?), 248
How Gertrude Teaches her Children (Pestalozzi), 144
Howard, Caroline (née Ball), 51
Howard, Eliot, 243, 244, 247, 264
Howard, Henrietta Maria (née Fox), 51
Howard, John Eliot
    association with Brethren, 49-50
    baptism of, 260
    conversion to Brethren, 40
    as editor of *Inquirer*, 48, 63
    family of, 51-52
    influence on Hudson Taylor, 283
    married to Maria Crewdson, 35
    relationship with J. J. Penstone, 60
    scientific interests, 53
    support of China Inland Missions, 284n8
    view of worship, 274
Howard, Luke
    break from Quakers, 260
    evangelical sympathies, 10, 31
    family of, 49-50
    pharmaceutical business, 7, 10, 49, 59n1
    piety of, 10-11
    Quaker affiliation, 50
Howard, Maria (née Crewdson), 35, 50, 260
Howard, Rachel (née Lloyd)
    baptism of, 50n87, 260n102
    marriage of, 35, 40, 49-50
Howard, Robert
    association with Brethren, 49-50
    family connections, 51
    influence on Hudson Taylor, 283
    lifestyle of, 52
    marriage of, 35, 40
    relationship with Beverley, 243, 260
Howard, Maria (née Crewdson), 35, 50, 260
Howard, Theodore, 51, 284-285n8
Howard family, 35, 48-52, 259, 260
Huebner, R. A., 140-141
Hughes, Maria, 82
Huguenots, 176
Hull, Captain Thomas Hillman, 227, 229
Hull, William, 229
Hume, David, 122n15
Hume, Joseph, 249
Hurditch, Russell, 280, 288
Hutchinson, Sir Francis, 151-152
Hutchinson, Sophia, 143

I

impressment, 219
India
    Groves's missionary work in, 104-105, 113-114, 173, 223-224
    impact on Brethren in England, 227-232
    infanticide in, 180
    massacre of Europeans, 119-120
    prohibition of missionary work lifted, 103
    spread of Brethren ideas in, 223-227
infant baptism, 260
Inglis, Sir Robert, 97

Inner Light doctrine of Quakers, 10, 33, 43, 53, 258-259
Inquirer (Howard, ed.), 45, 48, 50, 261
Inquiry into the Scriptural Doctrine of Christian Ministry, An (Beverley), 261, 262
International Genealogical Index, 167
Ireland
    Darby's time in, 41-42, 124-134
    Groves in, 103-104
    Pennefather, William in Dublin, 41-43
    Powerscourt Conferences, 42, 64-65, 154-156, 170
    Quaker malcontents and uncertainty in, 16-20
    Synge family in, 143, 151–156
    Synge's school in, 145–146
Irish Scriptural School Society, 179
Irvine, Will, 138n91
Irving, Edward
    account of Gloucestershire clergyman case, 73
    Albury conferences on prophecy, 98
    challenge from Coleridge, 80
    Christology of, 83–84, 87, 88
    Church of Scotland's proceedings against, 184n45, 185
    concern about confessional authenticity, 85
    criticism of, 78–79, 80
    Darby and, 121, 133–134, 141
    disdain for reform, 76, 77
    enthusiasm for German missionaries, 113n46
    expulsion from Regent Square church, 69
    histrionic tendencies and eccentricities of, 120
    introduction to work of Agier and Lacunza, 138
    manifestations of the Spirit and, 81
    question of genuineness of glossolalia, 2
    relationship with Groves, 108
    sermon to London Missionary Society, 102
    trying of spirits of Probyn children's prophesy, 75
    view of Margaret Macdonald's prophecy, 139
Irvingites
    case of the Gloucestershire Clergyman, 69–79
    Catholic Apostolic Church, 69–72, 78, 81–82, 108
    confessional authenticity, 84–86
    debate over doctrine and manifestations, 81–84
    influence on Darby, 54
    at Powerscourt Conferences, 155
    premillennialism of, 139
Irwin, Henry, 42n50
Italy, Brethren movement in, 203

J

Jacobins, 138
James, John Angell, 258, 261
James II (king of England), 175, 176
Jansenists, 137–138
Jarratt, William, 48n72, 97
Jefferson, Thomas, 123n25
Jeffrey, Francis, 10
Jeffreys, George, Judge, 175
Jenkins, Paul, 103n5
Jewell, Ann, 59
Jewell, Joseph, 10, 59
Jewish Expositor, 84
Jewish return to Palestine, 134, 137–138, 181
Johannine test of spirits, 84–86
Johnston, Colin, 268n17
Jones, Mrs. Flockhart, 292
Jones, Theodore, 284–285n8
Jourdan, Camille, 15
Journal des Missions Évangéliques, 115
Journal of a Residence (Groves), 107, 115
Journal of the Christian Brethren Research Fellowship, 59n1, 163
Journals of Caroline Fox (C. Fox), 70
Jowett, William, 109
Jowitt family, 51
Jubal (Beverley), 250
Jukes, Andrew, 283
Jung, August, 222
justification by faith,
    Crewdson on, 34
    Established Church and, 126
    John Eliot and Maria Howard embrace doctrine, 50
    Luther's teaching on, 125n35
    Quakers and, 27, 43, 48

K

Kaye, John, Bishop of Bristol, 23n72
Keal, Deborah (née Tiptaft), 149
Keal, William, 149
Kearney, Henry, Graduate of Trinity College, Dublin, 128
Keate, Dr. John (headmaster of Eton), 243
Keegan, Sir John, 236
Kelly, Elizabeth Emily (née Gipps), 217

Kelly, William, Brethren expositor of scripture, 38, 198–199, 217
Kellyites, 164n92
Kendal Quakers, 43–48, 52
Ketley, Joseph, Congregational Minister in British Guiana, 193
Kilham, Sarah, 107n23
Kingscote, Captain Robert F., 232
Kitto, John
    Basel connection, 112–113
    relationship with Groves, 22, 106, 108, 116, 147
    work for CMS, 112
Knight, Dr. James, 126
Knight, Fanny, Correspondent of Jane Austen, 210n24
Knill, Richard, LMS worker in St Petersburg, 116
Kyle, Samuel, Provost of Trinity College, Dublin; Bishop of Cork, 126

L

"La Petite Église," 137
La Touche, James Digges, 144, 146
La Trobe, John, 210, 211, 212n33
La Venida del Mesias en gloria y magestad (Lacunza), 133, 138
Labadie, Jean de, 3
laborers' revolt (1831), 76
Labours of John Meyer in British Guiana (Strong), 193
Lacunza, Manuel, 133, 138, 141
Ladies' Council for CIM, 285
Lafayette, Marie-Joseph, Marquis de, 249
Laidlaw, Robert Alexander, 237
Lambert, Père Bernard, Dominican exponent of prophecy, 138-141
Lambert, Edmund, 149
Lambert, William George
    Call to the Converted advocates secession, 149, 150, 156–159,
    in circle around John Hill, 97
    condemnation of Establishment, 99
    separation from Church Mission Society and Church of England, 150–151
    Synge's response to *Call to the Converted*, 159–164
    tract on secession, 149, 150, 156–159
    Lampen, Robert, 106, 112n42
Lampeter Brethren, 267
Lancey, Major, 230
Langley, William Hawkes, Perpetual Curate of Wheatley, 94

Larson, Dr. Timothy, 229n48
Lawrence, Elizabeth, See Gipps, Elizabeth née Lawrence, 208
Lawrence, Thomas, 208n17
Layard, Austen Henry, archaeologist, 229n48
Leeds Mercury, 257
Les prophéties concernant Jésus-Christ et l'Église (Agier), 138
Letter to the Archbishop of York (Beverley), 251, 257n85
Letter to the Author of "The Beacon" (Thompson), 34
Letters on the Present State of the Visible Church of Christ (Beverley), 261
Letters to a Dissenting Minister (Gathercole), 255–256
Lewis, George William, 277
Lewis, Samuel, 151, 205
Lewis, W. R., 278n14
Life and Letters of William Pennefather, The, 41–42
Lilly, William Samuel, 91–93, 101
Lively, Robert Lee, Jr., 79n49
Livesey, Joseph, of Preston, 256–257
Lloyd, Deborah, See Stacey, Deborah (née Lloyd), sister of Rachel Howard (née Lloyd), 51
Lloyd, Mary (née Honeychurch), wife of Samuel Lloyd, jnr 25, 30, 35, 39
Lloyd, Rachel. See Howard, Rachel (née Lloyd), 35, 40, 49–50, 260n102
Lloyd, Rachel (née Braithwaite), 35, 259
Lloyd, Sampson, 40
Lloyd, Samuel, Jr.
    family of, 50
    interest in Brethren, 45
    marriage of, 25, 30, 35, 39
Lloyd, Samuel, Sr., 39–40, 45, 50, 260
Lloyd, Sarah. See Crewdson, Sarah Fox (née Lloyd), 39
Lloyd family, 35, 39–40, 259
Locke, John, 126, 127
London, military Brethren in South-East, 232–238
London Gazette, 279–280
London Missionary Society, 182–183, 193
London Society for Promoting Christianity among the Jews, 113n47, 114, 181
Lord's Supper
    among Brethren, 162, 198
    Brethren's position on, 63
    Darby's earlier attitude, 55
    Groves's separation from Church Missionary Society over, 110
    Quaker position on, 9, 34, 259–260

Index

Louis XIV (king of France), 176
Louis XVIII (king of France), 8
Love Is Strong as Death (painting by J. J. Penstone), 61n13
Lowe, W. J., 172
Lowth, Robert, Bishop of London, 133n67
Lowth, William, 133
Luther, Martin, 3

M

Macbride, Dr. John David, Principal of Magdalen Hall, Oxford, 92, 94
Macdonald, James, 81, 85
Macdonald, Margaret, 81, 139, 141
Macdonald, William, Brethren missionary in Penang, 285n10
Macdonald brothers, 81, 83, 85
Maclean, Dr. John Lindsay, 232-233
Maclean, Harriett (née Warren), 233
Maclean, Sir George, 233
MacManus, James, son-in-law of Leonard Strong, 194n92
Macpherson, Annie, evangelist, 286
MacPherson, Dave, 133n70, 141
Magee, William, Archbishop of Dublin, 126, 132
Mahon, Thomas, 155, 276
Malcolm, Lady Margaret, 220n9
Malcolm. General Sir John, 220
Manchester Quakers, 43-45
Mander, Charles, 271n31
Mansell, Thomas, 155
marriage regulations of Quakers, 17
Married Women's Property Act (1882), 271
Marriott, John, 104
Marsh, William, Rector of St Peter's, Colchester, 96, 97
Marshall, J. W., 47n64
Martin, Hannah, See Geldart Hannah (née Martin) 34
Martin, Richard, Fellow of Exeter College, Oxford, 94
Maturin, Henry, Fellow of Trinity College, Dublin, 127
Maulvault, Achille, 140
Maunsell, Thomas, 276
Mayer, Lewis, exponent of prophecy, 121n7
Mayers, Walter, Curate of Over Worton, Oxon, 98
Mayow, Dr.Charles, proponent of Pestalozzi's educational methods, 146n16
McAll, Robert Whittaker, 288, 289

McBride, Dr. Samuel, 137n85
McCarthy, Indian army evangelist, 225-226
McCormack, Professor W.G., 165n93
McIntyre, David, 287n25
McIntyre, Jane, (née Bonar), daughter of Andrew Bonar, 287n25
McIntyre, Jessie Barbara, 287
McIntyre, Rev. Malcolm, 287n25
McNair, Donald, 235
McNair, Dr Philip, 235n77
McNeile, Hugh, Curate of Albury, Curate of St Jude's, Liverpool, 81, 88, 96, 97-98
Mede, Joseph, 120
Memoir (Groves), 105-107
Memoir of Donegal, 230
Memoirs of Arthur Augustus Rees (Brockie), 273
Menezes, Sister, 188
Merlin (Monmouthshire newspaper), 73-74, 75
Methuen, Catherine Matilda, See Plumptre, Catherine Matilda (née Methuen) sister-in-law of Henry Gipps, 209n22, 217.
Methuen, John Andrew, 217
Methuen family, 217n58
Meyer, Johannes, Swiss missionary in British Guiana, 193
Meyers, Mr., 146n16
Midgley, Anna Margaretta, See Lady Grantley (née Midgley), sister-in-law of William Beverley, 242
Midgley, Jonathan, 242
Midgley, Mary, 241-242
military service. See armed services
Millard, Alan, 225n33
millennial attitudes
    evangelicals today and, 119
    expectation of Second Coming of Christ, 270-271n29
    Gloucestershire clergyman case and, 75-77
    in Herefordshire, 212
    of Irvingites, 69-70, 74
    perspectives in 1820s, 120-122, 181
    of Leonard Strong, 188-190
    See also eschatology; postmillennialism; premillennialism; Second Coming of Christ
Miller, Jon, 102
Miller, William, adventist preacher, 270-271
Millerites, 270-271
Minchin, Colonel, 223, 232n62
On Ministry in the Word (Wigram), 55-56
miracles
    Brethren and, 200-201
    confessional authenticity, 84-86
    debate over doctrine and, 82-84

miracles (continued)
   eclectic approach to determining authenticity, 86–88
   Lambert's tract on, 156–159
   manifestations of, 81–82
   scornful approach to, 80
   See also glossolalia; healings
missionary movement, 102. See also Evangelicals
Missionary Register, 114
Missionary Societies, 181
Moberly, George, Fellow of Balliol College, Oxford, 94
Molesworth, Colonel Anthony Oliver, 236
Molesworth, Major James Thomas, 229, 236, 275
Monmouth rebellion, 175, 176
Monod, Adolphe, 288
Monod, Charlotte (née Brown), 288
Monod, Fréderick P., 136, 137, 288
Monod, Gustave, 288
Monod, Louise, See Soltau, Louise, (née Monod), 288, 289
Monod, Suzanne (née Smedley), 288
Monod, Theodore, 289
Montazet, Malvin de, 138
Montefiore, Dr., 114n55
Monumenta Anglicana (Dunkin), 61
Moody, D. L., 273, 286
Moravian Brethren, 164
Mordal, Mr. (missionary to British Guiana), 193
Morley, John, 284n8
Morning Watch, 70, 82, 84, 139
Morris, William, 200
Morshead, William, 276
Mortara case, 264n122
Moseley, John, 275
Mozley, Tom, Fellow of Oriel College, Oxford, 97, 100, 101, 168–169
Müller, George
   Bethesda Question, 50
   Craik's relationship with, 148
   interest in Hudson Taylor's work, 283
   interest in Leonard Strong, 193
   interview between Darby and, 64
   as leader of Open Brethren, 107
   marriage of, 113n47
   as pastor of Bethesda chapel, 53
   Henry Prince's admiration of, 269–270
   reestablishment of New Testament patterns, 203
   reports of Groves's work, 113
   support of China Inland Missions, 284n8
   support of Groves, 105
   visit to Glanmore Castle and Powerscourt Conference, 154–155

Müller, Mary (née Groves), 113n47

N

Nahum, Peter, 61n13
Nangle, Edward, 199
Napier, David, 60n7
Napleton, John, 211
Napoleon Bonaparte, 8, 26, 137, 167, 180, 219n3
Napoleon III, 274
Napoleonic Wars (1793-1815), 25–26, 31, 119, 123, 127, 180, 218–222
Narrative of Events that have lately take place in Ireland among the Society called Quakers, A, 17
Natural Law (Burlamaqui), 127
Natural Religion (Conybeare), 127
Neatby, William Blair, 50, 57, 156n59, 222, 283
Nebeker, Gary, 125n35
Nelson, Lord, 123n18, 179
Nesbit, Robert, Missionary, 106n17, 111
"Neutrality" (J. J. Penstone), 64
New Quarterly Review, 279
Newman, Cardinal. See Newman, John Henry
Newman, Francis (Frank) 281
   on appropriation of promises to Israel, 134n75
   association with Brethren, 101
   comments on Darby, 131n58, 132, 134n72
   correspondence with Robert Braithwaite, Jr., 34n15
   Darby's influence on, 97
   isolation of, 282
   rebuttal of Lilly's account of J. H. Newman, 91–93, 95
   relationship with B.W. Newton, 97
   role in J. H. Newman's expulsion from secretaryship of Oxford CMS, 94, 100–101
   as tutor to Pennefather's children, 42n51
   view of Establishment, 99
   view of sacraments and infant baptism, 99
Newman, John Henry
   Apologia pro Vita Sua, 130
   association with evangelicals, 96–98
   disagreement with Evangelicals in CMS, 91–95, 98, 99–101
   as editor of *British Critic*, 213n38
   expulsion from Secretaryship of Oxford CMS, 95, 100–101
   view of Spragg, 169
   view of Tucker's account of India, 116n68

Index

Newton, Anna (née Treffry), mother of B W Newton, 24, 25–26, 26n88, 28–29
Newton, Benjamin Wills (father), 24
Newton, Benjamin Wills (son)
- on Armstrong's return from India, 229–230
- ascetic attitude of, 46–47
- association with Plymouth Brethren, 36, 101
- baptism of Richard Ball, 49
- Beverley's criticism of, 262–263
- birth certificate of, 24
- Christology of, 282
- comments on Simeon, 169n23
- connection to Northern England, 39
- conversion of, 27–28, 96-97, 170
- criticism of, 201, 202–203
- Darby's criticism of, 133n67, 171
- disappointment over Henry Prince, 273
- dispensationalism, opposition to, 162–163n87
- education and criticism of Quakers, 23, 25–31
- excommunication of Morris, 200
- final ecclesiastical identity of, 52
- influence on Quakers, 36, 43-46, 51
- invitation to Darby to visit Plymouth, 149
- as joint owner of Plymouth Brethren meeting house, 171n30
- on Lambert's later spiritual state, 150
- maintenance of church order, 201–202
- ousting of Newman as secretary of Oxford CMS, 92, 100
- as presiding elder of Plymouth Brethren, 53–54, 200
- proposal for translation of New Testament, 276
- recollections concerning John Darby's contracts during Napoleonic Wars, 123n18
- recollections of Napoleonic Wars, 218
- recollections of Probyn family, 72n17, 73n21
- relationship with Greaves, 146n16
- relationship with Joseph Cookworthy, 37n28
- relationship with Lambert, 149
- relationship with Lloyds, 39–40
- secession from Church of England, 150
- separation from Brethren, 282
- on social integration of Plymouth Brethren, 199, 200
- socioeconomic status of, 198
- students of, 37
- as trustee for William Francis Soltau, 170
- view of Establishment, 99
- view of impulsive guidance, 53
- view of retired Indian army officers, 230–231
- view of J. H. Newman as examiner, 98
- visit to Glanmore Castle, 155

Newton, Hannah (née Abbott), wife of B.W. Newton
- on Crewdsons and Sizergh Hall, 46–47
- description of Plymouth Brethren, 31
- letter about Benjamin's health, 44
- marriage of, 27n96, 36
- relationship to other Quaker families, 39
- relationship with Anna Braithwaite, 45
- visit to Glanmore Castle, 155
- on Edward Wakefield, 47

Newton, John, 29–30
Newton, Valance, 103–104n7
Nisbet, James, 108
Noel, Gerard, 121, 209
Noel, Rev. Baptist, 83, 87, 88
Noel, Sister, 187n54
nonresistance
- of Plymouth Brethren, 218–238
- of Quakers, 8, 9, 26, 219

Norton, Margaret (née Macdonald), 81, 139, 141
Norton, Robert, 81, 139
Norway, Captain John, 26
Notes and Queries, 60, 62
Nottidge v Ripley and Another, 271n32

O

oaths, 9, 11–12
Observations on "A Call to the Converted" as it relates to Members of the Church of England (Synge), 150
Observer (London), 279
Ochino, Bernardino, Vicar-General of the Capuchins, 3
Olivier, François, 137
Ollivant, Alfred, Bishop of Llandaff, 267
Omicron Letters (Newton), 29
Open Brethren
- Chief Men among 136n83
- ecclesiology of, 203
- establishment in Woolwich, 234
- members, 13n28, 172, 203, 237, 285n10
- Quaker influence on, 56
- Rees and, 274
- rift between Exclusive Brethren and, 107–108, 172
- unpredictability of identity, 280

Opie, Amelia (née Alderson), 14–15
Opie, John, 14
Orde-Brown, Charles, 234, 237
Orde-Brown, Ethel, 234

Orde-Brown, Sybil, 234
Origin of Species (Darwin), 264
original sin, Pestalozzi's ambivalent attitude to, 145
Origins of the Brethren (Rowdon), 269
Orpen, Charles Edward Herbert, 145
Outis, 248n48
Owen, Rev. Henry John, Incumbent of Park St Chapel, Chelsea, 82
Owen, Robert, 9
Oxford Dictionary of National Biography, 285

P

pacificism, 225n36
pacifism
    of Plymouth Brethren, 218–238
    of Quakers, 8, 26, 219
Paget, Elizabeth (Bessie), 38, 104, 106–107
Paget family, 38
Paine, Thomas, 15–16
Paley, Archdeacon, 8n4
Parker, Admiral Sir William, 37
Parker, Louisa Jane, See Hingston, Louisa Jane (née Parker), 37
parliamentary reform, 69, 76, 180, 246–247
Parnell, John Vesey, 2nd Baron Congleton, 104, 146, 197, 197n5, 223–224
Parnell, Sir Henry Brooke, 1st Baron Congleton, 197n5, 219n7
Pascal (Roger Henry Soltau), 289n40
Passmore, Christopher, 198
Patriot, 50, 277
Paul, Saint, 3
Pearson, Sir Richard, 224n32
Pearson, Vice Admiral Richard Harrison, 115, 224
Peccability of Christ according to Irving, 83–84
peculiar people, 1–3, 11
Peel, Julia, Countess of Jersey, 62
Peel, Sir Robert, 97
Pellew, Sir Israel, 218
Penn, William, 34
Pennefather, Edward, brother-in-law of J.N. Darby, 124, 130
Pennefather, Susannah (née Darby), 124, 131
Pennefather, William, Vicar of Chipping Camden, 41–43, 46, 52, 53
Penstone, Ann (née Jewell), 59
Penstone, Edward, 59n1, 60, 61, 62
Penstone, Elizabeth Messer (née Wright), 60, 63
Penstone, John, 59
Penstone, John Jewell, 50, 59–65

Penstone, Matilda Harman (née Gould), Wife of John Jewell Penstone, 60
Penstone, William, 60, 62
Penstone family, 60
Pentecostal gifts. See charismatic movement; glossolalia; healings; miracles
Perceval, Spencer, Irvingite Apostle, 76
Perkins, Justin, 231n60
Persia, 78, 104, 108–109, 146–147, 198n10
Pestalozzi, Johann Heinrich, educational pioneer, 143–146, 146n16
Pestalozzi's Institute, 143–145
Petition to the House of Commons for Protection (Magee), 132
Pfander, Karl Gottlieb, Missionary, 104, 113, 115
Phelps, William, Archdeacon of Carlisle, 206
Philpot, Joseph Charles
    association with J. H. Newman, 98, 101
    Church Missionary Society and, 94, 100
    evangelical conversion of, 97
    observation of "Madeira climate" among Brethren 203
    opposition to ministry of, 97, 100
    Strict Baptist affiliation, 101
    view of Establishment, 99
    view of Plymouth Brethren, 196–197, 203
Pickering, Henry, 232, 236
Pickmore, Sir Francis, 221
Pinnington, John, 187n56
Pitt, William, 254n71
Pitts, John, 128–129
Pius IX (pope), 264n122
plague epidemic (Baghdad), 114n55
    A N Harris's experience, 15n38, 200
    Breaking of Bread in, 162, 198,
    Bulteel in, 148-149 Plumptre, Catherine Matilda (née Methuen), 209n22
Plumptre, Emma Maria, 209, 217
Plumptre, John Pemberton, 209, 217
Plumptre family, 209
Plymouth
    Byrth family in, 20-21, 23
    Sarah Crewdson's letters from, 31, 39
    Darby's time in, 30-31, 135n79, 149
    Harriet Eccles's school in, 194
    Evangelicals in, 30
    A N Groves in, 104
    Missionary attitudes, 117, 173
    Naval presence in 218, 221, 224
    B.W.Newton and family in 24-29, 30, 36, 53, 200-202, 230-31
Plymouth Athenaeum, 22
Quakers in, 36-37, 39, 42-43, 218,
W.G Rhind in, 152

Samuel Rowe's bookshop in, 21
Soltau family in, 167-168, 170-171, 173, 286
Stoddart in, 278, 280
Roger Treffry in, 23-24
S.P. Tregelles in 36, 139n99, 201,
Plymouth Brethren
    Breaking of Bread among, 162
    dispensationalism of, 162
    division among, 107, 171
    elitist leadership and congregational participation among, 196-203
    emergence of, 30-31, 36-41, 198-199
    Evangelical Alliance and, 164
    evangelicals among, 101, 117, 173-174
    expectation of Second Coming of Christ, 270-271n29
    Indian impact on, 227-232
    influence on Henry William Soltau, 169-170
    leadership within, 53-54
    military Brethren in South-East London, 232-238
    principles of, 192n75, 201
    Quaker converts, 36-58
    secession issue, 156-159, 196
    spread of ideas in India, 223-224
    Leonard Strong's association with, 191-193
    support of CIM, 284
    view of armed services, 218-238
    See also Darby, John Nelson; Hall, Captain Percy Francis; Newton, Benjamin Wills; Soltau, Henry William; and other specific Brethren
"Plymouth Brethrenism" (Croskery?), 140n100
Plymouth Institution (Athenaeum), 22, 256
Plymouth Literary Magazine, 21
Plymouth Public Free School, 168
Plymouth Tract Depot, 173
political turmoil, 69, 76, 78
Pollard, Edward Bickersteth, 193
Pollard, William Branch, 192-193
Poor, Daniel, 111-112n41
Poots, Andrew, 134n75, 136n84
Pope, Richard Thomas Pembroke, 18-20
Popham, Brunswick, 266n5
Poseck, Julius Anton von, 222
possession by spirits, 70-79
Posthumous Letters of the Rev. Rabshakeh Gathercoal, The (Beverley), 256
postmillennialism, 136, 212
Powerscourt, Lady, 64-65, 136, 137n85, 154
Powerscourt Conferences, 42, 64-65, 154-156, 170
Pratt, Rev. Josiah, General Secretary of CMS, 94, 100

predestination, 28, 34
premillennialism
    of Brethren, 117
    Darby's view of, 125, 135, 136, 139-140, 141
    of Gipps, 212
    of Groves, 111n41
    of Irvingites, 139
    of Jansenists, 139
    of Robert Strong, 181-182
    of Leonard Strong, 182
    Trinity College, Dublin and, 125
Pretyman, George, Bishop of Lincoln, 254n71
Price, Anna, 36
Price, Peter, Quaker of Neath Abbey Iron works, 36
Prideaux, Humphrey, Dean of Norwich,133
Prideaux, Fanny Ash (née Ball), 37
Prideaux, Frederick, 37
Prideaux, John, 22
Prideaux, Sarah Anna, 37, 39n35
Prideaux, Sarah Elizabeth Ball (née Hingston), Wife of Walter Prideaux, 37
Prideaux, Walter, of Wadebridge and Plymouth, 37
Priestly, Joseph, 15, 25, 124
Prince, Ellen, a.k.a. Eleanor, See Rees, Ellen (née Prince) Sister of Henry Prince, wife of A.A. Rees, 267, 268
Prince, Henry James, 267, 269-270, 271-273
Prince, Julia (née Starky), 2nd wife of Henry Prince, 271
Prince, Martha (née Freeman), 1st wife of Henry Prince, 271
Principia Hebraica (Craik), 147-148
Principles and their Results (Ball), 49
Probyn, Edmund, 70, 71-76, 77, 85, 181-182
Probyn, Julian, 72, 73-74, 75, 85, 86
Probyn, Juliana (daughter), 72-74, 85-86
Probyn, Juliana (née Webb), wife of Edmund Probyn, 71-75, 77-78, 181-182
Proctor, Matthew, 178n19
Prophecy,
    evangelicals' study of, 96
    See glossolalia
proposal for translation of New Testament, 275-276
Proselyting spirit, the great obstacle to Christian Union, A (Venn), 215-216
Protest against the National Establishment of England, A (Wigram), 161
Proto-Plymouth Brethren, Oxford, 91-101
Pusey, Philip, 61

INDEX

Q

Quakers
   affluence of, 8, 10, 11–15
   associations with unbelievers, 9, 10, 12–13
   authority within, 16–17, 33–34, 53, 259
   Beaconite controversy, 34–35, 40, 43, 259
   beliefs of, 8, 9–10, 15n38, 16, 17, 33–34, 53–54
   Beverley's admiration of, 258–260
   Clothing, 2, 9, 12, 14, 15, 37n26, 50n88, 52
   conversion to Brethren, 36–58, 56–57, 57, 200n23
   influences on Brethren, 52–53, 53-57
   development of Plymouth Brethren and, 30–31, 32
   developments in South of England, 48–52
   developments in the North of England, 38–47
   division among, 29, 31, 32–35, 40, 43, 45, 57, 220n23
   evangelicals among, 15–16, 27–34, 38–39, 40, 43, 45, 62
   families and intermarriage, 35, 51–52
   founding of, 11
   Freethinkers and, 15–16
   government within, 57
   Hicksite controversy, 45
   influence on Groves, 106–107
   malcontents in Ireland, 16–20
   B.W. Newton's criticism of, 25–31
   as peculiar people, 2, 11
   Penstone and, 59–65
   piety of, 7–11
   uncertainty in Ireland and Devon, 20–25
   See also Allen, William; Howard, Luke
Quarrell, W. H., 62

R

Radical Evangelicals, 91–101, 204–217
Radstock, Lord and Lady, 283, 284n8, 288
Randall, Elizabeth (née Bennett), 206n6
Randall, John, 205–208, 210
rapture. See Second Coming of Christ
rationalism, 10, 22, 124
Rawlinson, Sir Henry, 225n33
"Reading the word of God A.D. 1838" (etching by J. J. Penstone), 64
Reason Why, The (Laidlaw), 237
Reasons for retiring from the Established Church (Hargrove), 49
Rebellion of the Beasts, 249n49
Recollections (Cox), 13
Record, 83
Redan, The (Beverley), 264n120
Reed, Mrs. Henry, 286
Rees, Ann (née Vander Horst), 265
Rees, Arthur Augustus
   Brethren and, 273–274
   conversion and "Lampeter Brethren," 266–267
   family and naval career, 265–266
   later ministry 273-274
   ministry and prohibition in Sunderland and Bath, 267–268
   relationship with Prince, 269–273
Rees, Ellen (née Prince), 267
Reflections on the Ruined Condition of the Church (Darby), 55
Reform Bill (England, 1831-32), 76, 183, 251
Religious Tract Society, 41n45
"Remarks on Light and Conscience" (Darby), 43n52
Remarks on the State of the Church (Darby), 55
Remonstrance to the Society of Friends, A (Newton), 29–30, 43–44
Reynolds, John, 96
Rhenius, Karl Gottlieb Ewald, 104–105, 113, 116
Rhind, Captain William Graeme, 152–153, 155, 219, 224, 266n4
Riach, Dr. James Pringle, 231n60
Rice, General, 232, 232n62
Rickards, Samuel, Fellow of Oriel College, Oxford, 93
Riddell, Anna Maria, See Walker, Anna Maria (née Riddell), mother of George Walker, 228n44
Robertson, Emily, See Clulow, Emily (née Robertson),173n41
Rodt, Rodolphe de, 115
Rogers, Elizabeth (née Doyle), 17
Rogers, John (J. J. Gurney's tutor), 12, 13
Rogers, John (Irish Quaker malcontent), 17
Romantic Movement, 127, 144
Rossetti, Teodorico Pietrocola, 53
Rousseau, Jean-Jacques, 144
Rowdon, Harold, 269
Rowe, Samuel, 21–22
Rowntree, Mary (née Stickney), friend of R.M. Beverley, 243, 244, 257
Royal Military Academy, 234
Ruin of the Church, doctrine of J.N.Darby, 54–56
Russell, Charles Taze, 64
Russell, Hastings William Sackville, 12th Duke of Bedford, 237
Russell, Lord John, 281

Russell, Thomas, 138n91
Ryder, Henry, Bishop of Gloucester, 178
Ryfum, William, 175
Ryle, John Charles, Bishop of Liverpool, 209m22
Ryle, Matilda (née Plumptre), 209n22

S

sacramental rationalism in Trinity College, Dublin, 126, 128
sacraments
    Frank Newman's position on, 99
    Brethren's position on, 63
    Quaker view of, 9, 43
    See also baptism; Lord's Supper
Salter, Thomas, 110n35
sanctification, 11, 27, 126
Sanders, Eleanor, See Strong, Eleanor, (née Sanders),176
Sankey, Ira David, 273, 286
Saunders, Trelawney William, cartographer, 280–281
Saxon Bride, The (painting by J. J. Penstone), 61
Schaff-Herzog Encyclopedia, 136
Schaffter, Paul Pacifique, Swiss missionary, 112
SchimmelPenninck, Mary Anne (née Galton), 9n8, 15
Schlienz, Christoph, Principal of St Chrischona, Basel113n45
Schneider, Michael, 220n13
Scholefield, James, Curate of Charles Simeon, 249
Schwartzerdt, Philipp, a.k.a Melanchthon, 176
Scott, Alexander, assistant minister of Irving, 83, 108, 184n45
Scott, Job, 10
Scott, Major-General Sir Charles, 233-234
Scriptural views on the subject of elders (Darby), 56, 57
Scripture, Quaker view of, 16–17, 33–34, 43
Scripture references
    1 Samuel 2:12, 22, 254n69
    1 Samuel 15:22, 191n69
    Song of Solomon 8:6, 61n13
    Isaiah 32, 134
    Isaiah 32:15, 160
    Isaiah 51:1, 1
    Ezekiel 38, 133n67
    Amos 7:14, 12n19
    Matthew 14:45-47, 158
    Matthew 23:17-18, 185n47
    Matthew 24:8, 185n50
    Luke 18:7-8, 185n50
    Luke 21:19, 28, 185n50
    John 13:14, 259
    Acts 2:42, 192n72
    Acts 2:44-45, 199
    Acts 15:13, 162n87
    Acts 20:32, 191n70
    Romans 7, 129n52
    Romans 8, 131
    1 Corinthians 12:3, 84
    1 Corinthians 12:7-12, 200
    Galatians 5:1-5, 259
    Ephesians 4:11, 200
    1 Thessalonians 1:10, 192n72
    1 Timothy 1:19, 184n44
    2 Timothy 3, 189
    2 Timothy 3:1, 13, 8, 184n44
    2 Timothy 4:13, 134n72
    Hebrews 10, 129n52
    Hebrews 12:26, 132
    1 Peter 2:9, 1
    1 Peter 2:20, 162
    1 Peter 4:10-11, 192n72
    1 John 2:16, 191n68
    1 John 4:1-2, 84
    Jude 3, 12, 185n48
    Revelation 11, 272
secession from Established Church
    of Beverley, 255–258
    of Brethren, 1, 32
    of evangelicals, 96, 99
    in Herefordshire, 215–216
    of Richard Hill, 172
    Lambert's tract calling for, 149, 150, 156–159
    by Newton, 150
    by Richard Pope, 18–20
    by Stoddard, 277
    by Leonard Strong, 190–194
    Synge's response to Lambert, 150, 156–159, 159–164
    by Tiptaft, 148
    Wigram's tract calling for, 99, 161
secession from Quakers, 16–20, 26, 27–28, 36–58
Second Coming of Christ
    Leonard Strong's view of, 184–185, 189
    Brethren's preoccupation with, 117, 173
    Darby's interest in, 131–132, 139–140
    Gipps interest in, 212
    Gloucestershire clergyman case and, 74–77
    Lacunza and Père Lambert's views of, 139
    W.G. Lambert's view of, 158–159
    Millerites' date for, 270
    perspectives in 1820s, 181
    pre- and post-millennial views, 120–122
    Probyn's view of, 76

Index

Second Coming of Christ (continued)
    See also eschatology; millennial attitudes; postmillennialism; premillennialism
Sedgwick, Adam, 257
"*Servant's Path in a Day of Rejection, The*" (J. J. Penstone), 63–64
Servetus, Michael, 3
Shackleton, Abraham, 17
Sharp, Robert, 244
Shelburne, William Petty, 2nd Earl of, 124
Shepherd, Gordon, 287n25
Shepherd of Hermas, The, 86n25, 87
Shillitoe, Thomas, 14
"Should Christians Enlist?" (Molesworth), 236
Shute, Nevil, 26n88
Sibthorp, Richard W., Fellow of Magdalen College, Oxford, 93 94, 95, 99
Silence of Barbara Synge (McCormack), 165n93
Simeon, Charles
    Avoidance of controversy, 214
    Beverley's attitude to, 249, 252
    Darby's meeting with, 136
    Later conservatism, 169n23
    Opposition to "violent argumentation", 215
    H W Soltau listens to 169
    as traditional evangelical, 96
    trustees, 213
    Henry Venn's exhortation to, 213–214
Simons, John, 234
Singer, Joseph Henderson, Fellow and tutor of Trinity College, Dublin, 127–128, 135, 141
slavery, abolition of, 7, 9, 183, 244, 258–259
Slazenger, Gwen, 64n30
Smedley, Suzanne, See Monod, Suzanne, (née Smedley), wife of Frédéric Monod, 288
Smith, Colin, 236
Smith, J. Denham, 284n8
Smith, Jackson, 275
Smith, John, LMS Missionary,173, 183
Smith, Lucy Tate, See Soltau, Lucy Tate (née Smith), wife of H.W. Soltau, 171
Smith, Sir John Wyldbore, 244
Smith, Sydney, 119, 247–248
Society for the Investigation of Prophecy, 120
Society for the Propagation of the Gospel, 187
Society of Friends. See Quakers
Solemn protest before the church and nation (Rees), 269
Soltau, Agnes, 284
Soltau, Ann (née Hodgson), 167
Soltau, Charlotte, See Warren, Charlotte (née Soltau) daughter of H W Soltau, 286
Soltau, Charlotte (née Brown), wife of Gustave Monod, mother of Louise Monod, 288
Soltau, David Livingston, 168n16
Soltau, Dorothea, 171n29
Soltau, Elizabeth Maria (daughter of HWS), superintendant of YWCA, 290
Soltau, Elizabeth Maria (née Symons), 167–168, 170, 171
Soltau, Elizabeth (sister of HWS), 167n10
Soltau, Frederick Pennington, 167n10
Soltau, George, 284–285n8, 285–286
Soltau, George (father of HWS), 167–168
Soltau, George (son of HWS), 166
Soltau, George William, 167
Soltau, Grace (née Tapson), 285, 286n16
Soltau, Henrietta, See Hill, Henrietta (née Soltau) Sister of H W Soltau, 171n29
Soltau, Henrietta, daughter of H W Soltau, director of CIM women's training home166, 283–284, 285, 290
Soltau, Henry, 2nd son of H W Soltau, medical missionary, 286-288
Soltau, Henry Kenneth Victor, Jr., 287, 292
Soltau, Henry William, early Plymouth Brother, biographical accounts of, 166
    conversion and controversy, 171, 286n20
    education of, 168–169
    evangelistic activities of, 173–174
    family life, 172
    Hudson Taylor's visit 283-284
    as joint owner of Plymouth Brethren meetinghouse, 171n30
    missionary cause, 283–284
    move to Plymouth, 167–168
    Newton's letter to HWS concerning early church, 162–163n87
    at Powerscourt Conferences, 170
    proposal for translation of New Testament, 275, 278
    socioeconomic status of, 291
    visit to Glanmore Castle, 155
Soltau, Jessie Barbara (née McIntyre), wife of Henry Soltau, 287
Soltau, Louise (née Monod), Wife of William Soltau, 288, 289
Soltau, Lucy, eldest daughter of H W Sotau, 284
Soltau, Lucy Marianne, daughter of Henry Soltau, 287
Soltau, Lucy Tate (née Smith), wife of H W Soltau, 171
Soltau, Martin Wilhelm, 167
Soltau, Mary Amelia, See Gribble, Mary Amelia (née Soltau), daughter of H W Soltau, 290

Soltau, Roger Henry, Professor, 289n40
Soltau, Sophia Amelia, Aunt of H W Soltau, 167
Soltau, Theodore Stanley, son of George Soltau, 166, 168, 289
Soltau, William Francis, 170
Soltau, William (son of H W Soltau), 166, 170, 171,172, 288–289
Soltau, William (uncle of H W Soltau), 167, 170
Soltau family, 167n10, 289
    biographers and ancestry, 166–167n10
    Christian missions and, 283–292
    conversion and controversy, 171
    descendants, 289-90
    education of, 168–169
    errors in parish records, 167n10
    evangelical origins, 169–170
    evangelism of, 173–174
    life in Exmouth, Bideford and Exeter, 172
    move to Plymouth, 167–168
    return to London, 284–285
    socioeconomic status of, 291–292
Songs of Salvation and Records of Christian Life (J. J. Penstone, illustrator), 64
Southcote, Joanna, 121n7
Southwood, Richard, bookseller, 21n63
speaking in tongues. See glossolalia
"Specific Meanings of some of the words in the New Testament" (Stoddard), 278
Spence, Grace, 48, 220n9
Spicer, Captain Peter, 221
Spicer, Charlotte, See Cookworthy, Charlotte (né221
Spicer, John William Good, husband of Juliana Probyn, 77n39
Spragg, Eliza (née Elliott), 169
Spragg, Rev. Francis Roach, Curate of Bidborough, Kent, 168–169
Spurgeon, Charles Haddon, 274
Stacey, Mary, 51, 53
Stafford, Colonel, 223
Stanley, Brian, 120n4
Stanton, Sarah, See Gipps, Mary (née Stanton), 2nd wife of George Gipps, 208
Starky, Julia, See Prince, Julia (née Starky), 271
Starky, Samuel, 270, 271
staunch churchmanship, 125
Steele, Emily, See Synge, Emily (née Steele) wife of Edward Synge, 151
Steele, Frances, See Synge, Frances (née Steele) 2nd wife of John Synge, 151
Steele, Mrs. (Lady Powerscourt's sister), 137n85
Stephen, Sir Leslie, 214
Stephens, Edward, 143, 153

Stephens, Rev. William, Parson of Levens, near Kendal, 41
Stevenson, J. W., 287
Stewart, Charlotte, See Alexander, Charlotte (née Stewart) 223n25
Stewart, J. Haldane, 98
Stewart, Lt-Col Josiah, 223n25
Stickney, Mary, See Rowntree, Mary, (née Stickney), Friend of R M Beverley, 243, 244, 257
Stock, Eugene, 116n68
Stoddart, Captain John Alfred, brother of G H Stoddart, 277n5
Stoddart, Charlotte (née Stoddart), cousin and 1st wife of G H Stoddart 277
Stoddart, Colonel Charles, brother of G H Stoddart 277, 279
Stoddart, George Henry, 275–280, 281, 282
Stoddart, George son of G H Stoddart, 278
Stoddart, John, Headmaster, 277n7
Stoddart, John, son of G H Stoddart, 278
Stoddart, Richard George, son of G H Stoddart 277n8
Stoddart, Sarah (née Tincknell), 2nd wife of G H Stoddart, 279
Stokes, Whitley, Walkerite, 126–127
Stone, Huntington, 292
Stoney, Anna, 230
Stopford, Joseph, Fellow of Trinity College, Dublin,126–127
strict churchmanship, 110
Strictures (Treffry), 44n55
Strobe, George, 170
Strong, Charles, 208n15
Strong, Charlotte (née Symonds), 177n13, 179n25
Strong, Clement Dawsonne, 179
Strong, Clement Samuel, 177, 178
Strong, Eleanor (née Sanders), 176
Strong, Emily, See Williams, Emily, (née Strong)194
Strong, Leonard
    allies and some progress in British Guiana, 185–187
    association with Plymouth Brethren, 191–193
    ecclesiology of, 182, 187–191
    eschatology of, 189
    evangelical conversion of, 179
    last years of, 194–195
    missionary in British Guiana, 179–190
    ordination 182
    as sailor, 179, 219, 266n4
    secession from Established Church, 190–195

Index

Strong, Leonard (early death of son), 194
Strong, Mary (née Bampton), 175
Strong, Matilda (née Dundas), 2nd wife of Leonard Strong, 194
Strong, Melancthon I, 175
Strong, Melancthon II, 175-176
Strong, Melancthon III, 176
Strong, Melancthon IV, 176
Strong, Robert, father of Leonard Strong
   ecclesiastical point of view, 187-188
   eschatology of, 181-182
   evangelical developments, 178-179, 205
   interest in prophecy, 181
   ordination of, 177-178
   piety of, 205
   support of Probyns, 78n43
   sympathy with Leonard's views, 194
Strong, Robert, brother of Leonard Strong, Vicar of Painswick, 179
Strong, Sophia (née Alsop), 176
Strong, Thomas, Father of Robert Strong, 176, 177, 178
Strong family, 175-176
Strutt, Guy, 72n14
Strutt, John James, 71-72, 77
Stuart, William, 254n70
Studd, C. T., 287
Stunt, Alfred, 285n10
Stunt, Francis, 285n10
Stunt, Philip, 163
Sturge, Joseph, Quaker, 258-259
Sumner, Charles, Bishop of Winchester, 150
Sunday wakes, 208, 214
Swainson, Emily Williams (née Strong), 194
Swainson, Isaac, 194n88
Swainson, John, 194
Swainson, William, 194n88
Swarthmoor Hall, 62
Swiss missionary recruits, 102-103, 112-117
Sydney, Philip, 248-249n48
Sykes, Mrs. (grandmother of J. A. Symonds), 179n25
Symonds, Charlotte, See Strong, Charlotte, (née Symonds) wife of Clement Dawsonne Strong, 179n25
Symonds, Dr. Addington, 179n25
Symonds, John Addington, 179n25
Symons, Elizabeth Maria, See Soltau, Elizabeth Maria, (née Symons) Wife of George Soltau,167-168, 170, 171
Symons, Rev. Benjamin Parsons, Warden of Wadhan College, Oxford, 92
Symons, William, 170
Synge, Editha (née Truell), 165

Synge, Edward (brother of Nicholas), 143n3
Synge, Edward archbishop of Tuam (father of Nicholas), 143
Synge, Edward (John's brother), 151, 155
Synge, Edward (son of Nicholas) grandfather of John Synge, 135, 143
Synge, Edward, cousin of John Synge, "maverick Protestant landlord" in County Clare, 135n77
Synge, Emily (née Steele), 2nd wife of John Synge, 151
Synge, Frances (née Steele), 151
Synge, Francis, father of John Synge, 143, 165
Synge, George, brother of Francis Synge,135n77
Synge, Isabell (née Hamilton), 1st wife of John Synge, 146
Synge, John
   criticism of Established Church, 148-151
   education of, 143
   family of, 135n77, 143, 146
   at Glanmore Estate, 151-156, 165
   Kitto's employment option, 112, 147
   legacy of, 164-165
   letter from Mrs. Truell, 70-71
   Pestalozzi's influence on, 143-146, 165
   Powerscourt Conferences, 154-156
   relationship with Craik and Müller, 154-155
   response to W.G.Lambert's tract, 150, 156, 159-164
   work with Craik, 147-148
Synge, John Hatch, son of John Synge, 165
Synge, John Millington, grandson of John Synge, playwright, 143, 165
Synge, Nicholas, Bishop of Kilfenora, 143
Synge, Sophia (née Hutchinson) mother of Francis Synge,143

T

Tamil pastors, 113
Taplin, Edward Oliver, 79, 82, 85n22, 86, 87
Tapson, Grace, See Soltau, Grace, (née Soltau) wife of George Soltau, 285, 286n16
Tate, James, Headmaster of Richmond School, 242
Taylor, Charlotte, 224
Taylor, Geraldine, daughter-in-law and biographer of Hudson Taylor, 284
Taylor, Hudson, 49, 51, 52, 283-284
Taylor, Major Robert, diplomat and scholar, British Resident in Baghdad, 225n33
Taylor, Mary, See Mary Hillyar (née Taylor), 224
Taylor, Mrs. Robert, 224-225

Index

Taylor, Nathaniel, 224
Taylor Prism (Cylinder), 225n33
Thackeray, William Makepeace, 229
Thom, John Nichols, a.k.a. Sir William Courtenay, Messianic revolutionary, 230
Thomas, Hannah (Hanie), 104n12
Thomas, John, 30
Thompson, Dr. James, 85n22, 104
Thompson, Mary Bethia, See Groves, Mary Bethia (née Thompson), 1st wife of A N Groves, 104
Thompson, Thomas, Quaker of Liverpool, 34
Thornton, Marianne, 214
Thoughts on the Apocalypse (Newton), 262
Tillotson, John, Archbishop of Canterbury, 133
Times, 76, 91n2, 119n2, 221n14, 236, 255
Tims, Richard M., (Dublin publisher), 154
Tincknell, Sarah, See Stoddart, Sarah (née Tincknell), 2nd wife of G H Stoddart, 279
Tiptaft, Deborah, See Keal, Deborah, (née Keal), 149
Tiptaft, William, 97, 99, 101n58, 148-149
tithe payment, 8
Todd, James Henthorn, Fellow of Trinity College, Dublin, 128n50
Tombs of the Prophets, The (Beverley), 255
Toplady, Augustus, 214
Toulmin, Amy Jane, 25, 29, 36, 39
Toulmin, Amy (née Honeychurch), 25, 39
Toulmin, John Butler, 25, 39
Toulmin, Joshua, 25
Townley, Henry, Congregational minister, 110, 278
Tract Society, 181
Tractarian movement, 98, 262
Trad, Mokayel, 105
Translations (Friel), 22, 230
Treatise on Regeneration (Gipps), 211
Treffry, Anna, See Newton, Anna (née Treffry) 24, 25-26, 28-29
Treffry, Jane, See Honeychurch, Jane (née Treffry), sister of Roger Treffry, 24-25, 39
Treffry, Joseph, Son of Roger Treffry, 24, 28n99, 29-30, 44n55
Treffry, Mary (née Veale), Wife of Roger Treffry, 23
Treffry, Richard, Son of Roger Treffry, 24
Treffry, Robert, Son of Roger Treffry, 24
Treffry, Roger, 23-24
Treffry, Samuel, Son of Roger Treffry, 24
Treffry, Sarah, See Fox, Sarah (née Treffry), 24
Treffry family, 24-25, 35
Tregelles, Catherine Phillips, 37
Tregelles, John, 36n22
Tregelles, Samuel Prideaux
    on congregational participation among Plymouth Brethren, 201
    on Darby's study of eschatology, 139
    on Darby's view of Brethren, 55
    early years and conversion to Brethren, 36-37
    final ecclesiastical identity of, 52
    marriage of, 37, 39n35
    portraits of, 64-65
    on principles of Plymouth Brethren, 201
    proposal for translation of New Testament, 276
    view of impulsive guidance, 53
    view of Whitfield, 38
    visits Jansenist archbishop in Utrecht, 139-140n99
Tregelles, Sarah Anna (née Prideaux), 37, 39n35
Trelawny, Eleanor, 155
Trench, Frederick FitzJohn, 136n81
Trench, Frederick FitzWilliam, 135, 136
Trench, George Frederick, 136n81
Trench, John Alfred, 136n81
Trench, Richard Chenevix, 136n81
Triggs, Arthur, 30
Trinitarian Bible Society, 181
Trinity Chapel, 29, 30
Trinity College, Dublin, 104, 124-129, 130
Troeltsch, Ernst, 204
Trotter, William, (Methodist convert to Brethren), 32
Trower, Walter John, Bishop of Gibraltar, 99
true cure for Ireland, the development of her industry, The (Stoddard), 281
Truell, Editha, 165
Truell, Mrs. L. S. La Touche, 70-71, 72-73, 77
Truell, Robert Holt, 71
trying the spirits
    confessional authenticity, 84-86
    eclectic approach, 86-88
    of Irvingite prophets, 77, 79
    of Probyn children's prophecy, 70, 75, 77, 78, 85
Tucker, John, 116n68
Tudor, John, 85n22
Turner, Captain Hatton, 232n65
12th Duke of Bedford, See Russell, Hastings William Sackville, 237
Tyndale, Thomas George, Rector of Holton, Oxon, 94

U

Unitarianism
    Mary Galton's view of, 15
    John Wade's critique of Establishment, 251
    view of Henry Gipps Treatise on regeneration, 211
    Hicks's Christology and, 33
    F W Newman's eventual position, 101
    support of Bible Society, 181
    of Vaughan family, 124
universal pardon, 83–84, 87

V

Vallack, Benjamin, 30
Vander Horst, Ann, 265
Vander Horst, Elias, 265
Varley, Henry, freelance Brethren evangelist, 280, 284n8
Vaucher, Alfred-Félix, 133, 138–139
Vaughan, Ann, See Darby, Ann (née Vaughan), daughter of Samuel Vaughan, mother of J N Darby 123
Vaughan, Benjamin, son of Samuel Vaughan, friend of Lord Shelburne 124
Vaughan, John, son of Samuel Vaughan, wine merchant and librarian 124
Vaughan, Samuel, businessman in Jamaica and Maine, 123
Vaughan, Samuel, Jr., son of Samuel Vaughan, 123
Vaughan, William, son of Samuel Vaughan, London merchant, 123
Veale, Mary, See Treffry, Mary (née Veale) 23
Venn, Henry, 169, 213–214
Venn, John, Rector of Holy Trinity, Clapham 169,
Venn, John, Rector of St Peter's, Hereford, 208n15, 213–217, 261
Vernon [Harcourt], Charles, (son of Archbishop of York), 247n41
Vernon [Harcourt], Egerton, (son of Archbishop of York), 247n41
Vetch, Captain, 228n42
Via Media, (J.H. Newman) 93
Vicar of Wrexhill, The (Mrs Frances Trollope), 14n32
Vicar of Wrexhill, Mrs Frances Trollope's caricature of John Cunningham, 14n32
Village teaching concerning the Lord Jesus (J. J. Penstone), 63
Vindication (Newton), 44n55
Vinton, Justus, Missionary in Burma, 288

W

Wade, John, Critic of the Establishment, 251, 257
Wadge, John, 28
Wakefield, Edward William, 44, 47, 51
Wakefield, John, 47n64
Wakefield, Rachel Crewdson (née Fox), 51
Wakefield, Susannah (née Birkbeck), 47n64
Walker, Anna Maria (née Riddell), 228n44
Walker, Anna (née Corrie), wife of George Walker, 226
Walker, Arthur de Noé, Son of Charles Walker, 228
Walker, Captain Charles Montague, R. N., 228n44
Walker, Captain George, Son of Charles Walker, friend of Count Guicciardini, 226–228
Walker, Henrietta Gertrude, See Baldelli, Henrietta Gertrude (née Walker) daughter of Charles Walker 228n44
Walker, John, Fellow of Trinity College, Dublin and seceder, 126–127
Ward, Maisie, 98n40
Wardlaw, Dr. Ralph, 43n52
Warren, Charlotte (née Soltau), daughter of H W Soltau, wife of William Warren, 286
Warren, Harriett, See Maclean, Harriett, (née Warren), wife of Dr John Lindsay Maclean, 233
Warren, Mary Harris, See Yapp, Mary Harris (née Warren), 233
Warren, William, 286
Washington, George, 123
Watson, Sydney E., 273
Way, Lewis, 120–121, 138
Webb, Juliana, See Probyn, Juliana, (née Webb), 71–75, 77–78, 181–182
Webb, Philip, 71n13
Webb, Rev. William, Rector of Sunderland, 267
Wellesley, Captain William H. G., 197, 220, 220n9, 266, 273
Wellesley, Richard Colley, 1st Marquess, Governor General of India, 180
Wellington assembly, 48–49
Wellington Hymn Book, 49
Weremchuck, Max, 123n19, 125n31, 132n63
Wesley, Charles, 205
Wesley, John, 125–126, 205
Whateley, Richard, Archbishop of Dublin, 164n92
Wheeler, Joseph, agent of Bible Society in British Guiana, 189n62
Whitfield, Edward Elihu, 136
Whitfield, Frederick W., 38, 52

Whitfield, George, 205
Whittle, Charlotte, See Haffner, Charlotte (née Whittle) 54n106
Wigram, George Vicesimus, 55–56, 97, 100, 101
    condemnation of Establishment, 99, 161
    criticism of Newton, 201
    encouragement of John Meyer as missionary, 193
    family of, 197n6
    as leader of Brethren in Plymouth, 30–31
    on ministry among Plymouth Brethren, 201
    at Powerscourt Conferences, 155
    proposal for translation of New Testament, 276
    socioeconomic status of, 197
    style of speaking, 199
Wigram, Sir Robert, father of G V Wigram, 197n6
Wigram, Sir Robert, 2nd baronet, later FitzWygram, 197n6
Wilberforce, Henry, 168
Wilberforce, Robert, 94
Wilberforce, Samuel, Bishop of Oxford, 168
Wilberforce, William, 76, 168-169, 244
Wilbur, John, American Quaker, 14
Wilkinson, John, Evangelical Quaker, 33
Williams, Benjamin Thomas, Brother-in-law of Leonard Strong, 190
Williams, Emily (née Strong), Sister of Leonard Strong, 194
Williams, Mark, 190n67
Williamson, Barbara, 59n1
Wilson, Daniel, Bishop of Calcutta, 96, 99
Wilson, Elisabeth, 166n5, 285n12
Wilson, Elizabeth, Kendal Quaker, 51
Wilson, Isaac, Kendal Quaker, 39
Wilson, Sarah, See Abbott, Sarah (née Wilson) 39
Wilson, Thomas, 257

Wingate, Ethel (née Orde-Brown), 234
Wingate, George, 234, 235, 237
Wingate, Orde, 235–236, 237
Wingate, Sibyl, 235n78
Winter, Robert, Adventist, 270
Wiseman, Professor Donald, 237
Witness, 236
Wolfe, Robert Barbour, 75, 77, 77–78, 85
Wolfe, Robert Cope, 73n21, 74, 75
Wolff, Joseph, 78, 98, 105, 108–109, 114
Wollstonecroft, Mary, 14
women in ministry, 34
Wood, Sir Francis, 250
Woodfall, Colonel, 284n8
Woodhouse, Francis, Irvingite apostle79
Woodward, Henry, 130
Woollcombe, Henry, 22
Works (Graves), 127
World War I, 236, 237, 289
World War II, 225, 236
Wrangham, Archdeacon, 248, 249n49, 250
Wright, Elizabeth Messer, See Penstone, Elizabeth Messer, (née Wright) 60, 63
Wright, James Ireland, Sr., 49
Wright, James, Jr., 49, 60
Wright, Mary, 49
Wright, Rachel, 49
Wyatt, F. W., 24n82

Y

Yapp, Mary Harris (née Warren), 233
Yapp, William, 215–216, 233
Yates, Professor Nigel, 267n11
Yorkshireman, 260
Youd, Thomas, 186, 188, 190
YWCA, 285

www.ingramcontent.com/pod-product-compliance
Lightning Source LLC
Chambersburg PA
CBHW080407300426
44113CB00015B/2426